HISTORY OF

United States Naval Operations

IN WORLD WAR II

★

VOLUME TWELVE

Leyte

June 1944–*January* 1945

Rear Admiral Clifford A. F. Sprague USN

"Taffy 3" in the Battle off Samar

HISTORY OF UNITED STATES NAVAL OPERATIONS IN WORLD WAR II

VOLUME XII

Leyte

June 1944–*January* 1945

BY SAMUEL ELIOT MORISON

WITH AN INTRODUCTION BY
Thomas J. Cutler

NAVAL INSTITUTE PRESS
Annapolis, Maryland

This book was brought to publication with the generous assistance of Marguerite and Gerry Lenfest.

Naval Institute Press
291 Wood Road
Annapolis, MD 21402

First Naval Institute Press paperback edition published 2011

Library of Congress Cataloging-in-Publication Data
Morison, Samuel Eliot, 1887–1976.
History of United States naval operations in World War II / Samuel Eliot Morison.
v. cm.
Originally published: Boston : Little, Brown, 1947–62.
Includes bibliographical references and index.
Contents: v. 1. The Battle of the Atlantic, 1939–1943 — v. 2. Operations in North African waters, October 1942–June 1943 — v. 3. The Rising Sun in the Pacific, 1931–April 1942 — v. 4. Coral Sea, Midway and Submarine Actions, May 1942–August 1942 — v. 5. The Struggle for Guadalcanal, August 1942–February 1943 — v. 6. Breaking the Bismarcks Barrier, 22 July 1942–1 May 1944 — v. 7. Aleutians, Gilberts and Marshalls, June 1942–April 1944 — v. 8. New Guinea and the Marianas, March 1944–August 1944 — v. 9. Sicily-Salerno-Anzio, January 1943–June 1944 — v. 10 The Atlantic Battle Won, May 1943–May 1945 — v. 11 The Invasion of France and Germany, 1944–1945 — v. 12 Leyte, June 1944–January 1945.
ISBN 978-1-59114-547-9 (v. 1 : alk. paper) — ISBN 978-1-59114-548-6 (v. 2 : alk. paper) — ISBN 978-1-59114-549-3 (v. 3 : alk. paper) — ISBN 978-1-59114-550-9 (v. 4 : alk. paper) — ISBN 978-1-59114-551-6 (v. 5 : alk. paper) — ISBN 978-1-59114-552-3 (v. 6 : alk. paper) — ISBN 978-1-59114-553-0 (v. 7 : alk. paper) — ISBN 978-1-59114-554-7 (v. 8 : alk. paper) — ISBN 978-1-59114-575-2 (v. 9 : alk. paper) — ISBN 978-1-59114-576-9 (v. 10 : alk. paper) — ISBN 978-1-59114-577-6 (v. 11 : alk. paper) — ISBN 978-1-59114-535-6 (v. 12 : alk. paper) 1. World War, 1939-1945—Naval operations, American. I. Title.
D773.M6 2010
940.54'5973—dc22 2009052288

Printed in the United States of America on acid-free paper

19 18 17 16 15 14 13 12 11 9 8 7 6 5 4 3 2 1

First printing

To

The Memory of

CLIFTON ALBERT FREDERICK SPRAGUE

1896–1955

Vice Admiral, United States Navy

Preface

THIS volume covers the Battle for Leyte Gulf, greatest naval battle of all time; amphibious and aircraft carrier operations up to and including the landings on Leyte; seven weeks of almost continuous fighting on land, sea and in the air until Leyte was secured; and contemporary submarine operations in the western Pacific.

Preparations for this volume began at the time of the operation itself. The late Lieutenant Commander Henry Salomon Jr. USNR of my small staff sailed up to Leyte in Vice Admiral Wilkinson's flagship, received first impressions of the landings and the battle, interviewed many participants, and shortly after the war visited Tokyo in search of Japanese material. I spent most of the winter of 1945–1946 at the Naval War College, Newport, working up a preliminary draft. In 1950, with Mr. Roger Pineau of my staff, I visited Japan and discussed the battle with leading Japanese participants. I resumed work on this volume in 1956 with the aid of Rear Admiral Bern Anderson USN (Ret.) who, as a staff officer of Seventh Amphibious Force, was familiar with Seventh Fleet operations and who has been my very able chief assistant in recent years.

Rear Admiral Richard W. Bates USN (Ret.) afforded me immeasurable assistance in the final preparation. He and his staff have been working on an exhaustive and detailed study of the Battle for Leyte Gulf, which I have cited as the *War College Analysis.* His collection of translated Japanese action reports and memoirs, and his own conclusions, were generously placed at my disposal. At the time I went to press his research had gone through the Battle of Surigao Strait only. For the Battles off Samar and Cape Engaño all basic research has been done by Admiral Anderson and myself.

Mr. Donald R. Martin, who has been with me for fifteen years, having joined my staff as its first member a few months after this historical project began, prepared the task organizations and did important pieces of research. He and Miss Antha E. Card typed the early drafts and he shared the final ones with Yeoman 2nd Class Edward Ledford. Dr. K. Jack Bauer, former Marine Corps historian, who relieved Mr. Pineau in 1957, has put in much time and effort on this volume. Captain Toshikazu Ohmae, formerly chief of staff to Admiral Ozawa, has been generous in answering queries. Mr. Clarke H. Kawakami and Mrs. Lily Y. Tanaka made most of the translations of Japanese documents. And I am most grateful to two old friends and former shipmates, Rear Admirals John B. Heffernan and Ernest M. Eller, successive Directors of Naval History, and to Captain F. Kent Loomis, their exec.; to Miss Loretta MacCrindle, head of the Historical Records Branch of the Division of Naval History, and Mr. John F. di Napoli, Librarian of the War College. Three successive Presidents of the United States Naval War College at Newport, R.I., the late Vice Admiral Lynde D. McCormick, Rear Admiral Thomas H. Robbins, and Vice Admiral Stuart H. Ingersoll, have given this work their countenance and support, and Mr. John Lawton has had oversight of the maps. Captain E. John Long USNR (Ret.) provided many of the illustrations. Lieutenant J. Pennington Straus USNR sent me the original message on the Battle of Surigao Strait, and Commander C. C. Cunningham lent me the characteristic photograph of Rear Admiral Clifton Sprague from which the frontispiece is produced.

My beloved wife, Priscilla Barton Morison, accompanied me to Japan in 1950 and has given me constant encouragement and constructive criticism.

Printed works used throughout this volume, without frequent citation, are the following: —

M. Hamlin Cannon *Leyte: The Return to the Philippines (1954)*, in the *U.S. Army in World War II* series.

Wesley F. Craven & James L. Cate *The Pacific: Matterhorn to Nagasaki* (1953), Vol. V in *Army Air Forces in World War II* series.

James A. Field *The Japanese at Leyte Gulf* (1947). The author participated in the Battle off Samar and later served on Admiral Ofstie's staff interrogating Japanese naval officers. The results of this questioning were printed by the Navy as *U. S. Strategic Bombing Survey Naval Analysis Division Interrogations of Japanese Officials* (2 vols., 1946).

General MacArthur's Staff *Historical Report of Operations in the Southwest Pacific Area* (Tokyo, 1951) is the famous MacArthur History, of which only three copies were printed (and don't ask me where I saw one, I can't tell!). Volume I is the story from the General's point of view. Volume II on Japanese operations, written by their generals and admirals, is the best history of this campaign from the Japanese point of view. The *Historical Report* is supplemented by a volume prepared by General Headquarters Southwest Pacific Area shortly after the war called *The Philippines Campaign 1944–45*.

Two important reference books are JANAC (Joint Army-Navy Assessment Committee) *Japanese Naval and Merchant Shipping Losses During World War II by All Causes* (Navy Dept. 1947) and Military History Section Special Staff General HQ Far Eastern Command *The Imperial Japanese Navy in World War II* (*1952*).

All times used in this volume are Zone Item (Z minus 9), unless otherwise stated; and the dates are East Longitude dates.

In accordance with military security, all American messages that were originally coded are paraphrased.

This volume is dedicated to the memory of Vice Admiral Clifton A. F. Sprague, who as Rear Admiral in command of "Taffy 3" took the rap in the Battle off Samar on 25 October 1944. Born in Boston 1896, he graduated from the Roxbury Latin School where his "conscientious spirit in studies and athletics won admiration from all," according to his class report. He then entered the Naval Academy and graduated well up in the Class of 1918. After the usual young ensign's duty, in gunboat *Wheeling* in World War I, he helped fit out battleship *Tennessee* and served in her, then qualified as a naval aviator. After commanding a squadron of patrol planes and a two-year duty at N.O.B. Hampton Roads, where he designed an arresting gear for carrier flight decks, which has saved many an aviator's life, he helped fit out carrier *Yorktown* and became her air officer in 1937. During the Pearl Harbor attack he won distinction as commanding officer of seaplane tender *Tangier*, which was the first naval vessel to open fire on the Japanese planes. He helped fit out the second carrier *Wasp* and served as her C.O. in the Battle of the Philippine Sea. In August 1944 he was promoted rear admiral and placed in command of the escort carrier unit which particularly distinguished itself in the Battle off Samar. In the Iwo Jima and Okinawa campaigns, he commanded escort carrier divisions. He was C.O. of carrier *Shangri-La* in the Bikini tests. From August 1946 he had charge of Naval Air basic training at Corpus Christi. His last sea command was Comcardiv 6 *(Kearsarge,* flag) in 1948, and for the remaining three years of his active naval career he was Commander Alaskan Sea Frontier. He died at San Diego 11 April 1955.

Admiral Sprague was the sort of officer who is known as "all Navy," dedicated to his profession, thorough and conscientious. Among the pilots who flew from the carriers that he commanded he was noted for his constant thought for their safety. Modest and retiring by nature, he used to give his senior, Rear Admiral Thomas Sprague, all the credit for stopping Kurita off Samar; but "Tommy" Sprague, with equal generosity, ascribes the victory to his junior. The "ultimate of desperate circumstances" in which their escort carriers were involved off Samar, and the cool, skillful and courageous manner in which they were extricated, are the subject of Chapters XII and XIII of this Volume.

Samuel E. Morison

Lat. 42°21′25″ N
Long. 71°04′21″ W
1 April 1958

Contents

List of Illustrations

(All photographs not otherwise described are Official United States Navy)

List of Maps and Charts

Abbreviations

Officers' ranks and bluejackets' rating are those contemporaneous with the event. Officers and men named will be presumed to be of the United States Navy unless it is otherwise stated; officers of the Naval Reserve are designated USNR. Other service abbreviations are USA, United States Army; USCG, United States Coast Guard; USCGR, Reserve of same; USMC, United States Marine Corps; USMCR, Reserve of same; RAN, Royal Australian Navy; RN, Royal Navy; IJN, Imperial Japanese Navy. See Preface for abbreviations of books in footnotes.

A.A.F. — United States Army Air Force
AK — Cargo Ship; AKA Attack Cargo Ship
AP — Transport; APA — Attack Transport
APD — Fast Destroyer Transport
A/S — Antisubmarine
B.C.S. — British Chiefs of Staff
BLT — Battalion Landing Team
Bu — Bureau; Buord — Bureau of Ordnance; Bupers — Bureau of Naval Personnel
C.A.P. — Combat Air Patrol
C.I.C. — Combat Information Center
Cincpac — Commander in Chief, Pacific Fleet (Admiral Nimitz)
Com — Commander; Comdesron — Commander Destroyer Squadron, etc.
Cominch — Commander in Chief, United States Fleet (Admiral King)
C.N.O. — Chief of Naval Operations
C.O. — Commanding Officer
CTF — Commander Task Force; CTG — Commander Task Group
CVE — Escort Carrier
DD — Destroyer; DE — Destroyer Escort
H.M.A.S. — His Majesty's Australian Ship; H.M.S. — His Majesty's Ship
H.Q. — Headquarters
J.C.S. — Joint Chiefs of Staff
LC — Landing craft; LCI — Landing craft, Infantry; LCM — Landing craft, mechanized; LCT — Landing craft, tank; LCVP — Landing craft, Vehicles and Personnel

LSD — Landing ship, dock; LSM — Landing ship, medium; LST — Landing ship, tank; LVT — Landing vehicle tracked (generally called Amphtrac or Buffalo); (A), (G), (L), (M) and (R) added to above types mean armored. gunboat, large, mortar and rocket
N.O.B.— Naval Operating Base
O.T.C. — Officer in Tactical Command
PC — Patrol craft; PCE — Patrol craft, escort
PT — Motor torpedo boat
RCT — Regimental Combat Team
TBS — Talk Between Ships, voice radio
TF — Task Force; TG — Task Group; TU — Task Unit
SC — Submarine chaser
UDT — Underwater Demolition Team
USSBS — United States Strategic Bombing Survey
U.S.C.G.C. — United States Coast Guard Cutter
WDC — Washington Document Center document
YMS — Motor minesweeper; YP — Patrol vessel

Aircraft Designations (numeral in parentheses indicates number of engines)

United States

B-17 — Flying Fortress, Army (4) heavy bomber; B-24 — Liberator, Army (4) heavy bomber; B-23 — Mitchell, Army (2) medium bomber; B-26 — Marauder, Army (2) medium bomber; B-29— Superfortress, Army (4) heavy bomber
C-47 — Skytrain, Army (2) transport
F4F — Wildcat; F4U — Corsair; F6F — Hellcat; Navy (1) fighters
OS2U — Kingfisher, Navy (1) scout-observation float plane
P-38 — Lightning, Army (2); P-39 — Airacobra; P-40 — Warhawk; P-47— Thunderbolt; P-61 — Black Widow, Army (2) fighters
PBM-3 — Mariner, Navy (2) patrol bomber (flying boat)
PBY — Catalina (2) seaplane; PBY-5A— amphibian Catalina; PB4Y —Navy Liberator bomber (4)
PV-1 — Ventura, Navy (2) medium bomber
SB2C — Helldiver; SBD — Dauntless; Navy (1) dive-bombers
SOC — Seagull, Navy (1) scout-observation float plane
TBF, TBM — Avenger, Navy (1) torpedo-bombers

Japanese

Betty — Mitsubishi Zero-1, Navy (2) high-level or torpedo-bomber
Fran—Nakajima P1Y, Navy (2) land all-purpose bomber
Hamp — Mitsubishi Zero-2, Navy (1) fighter
Irving — Nakajima JIN, Navy (2) night fighter
Jake — Navy (1) float plane
Jill — Nakajima B6N, Navy (1) torpedo-bomber
Judy — Aichi D4Y, Navy (1) dive-bomber
Kate — Nakajima 97-2, Navy (1) torpedo-bomber
Oscar — Nakajima Army (1) fighter
Val — Aichi 99, Navy (1) dive-bomber
Zeke — Mitsubishi Zero-3, Navy (1) fighter

Introduction

THE once well-known military correspondent of the *New York Times*, Hansen W. Baldwin, described Samuel Eliot Morison as "a modern Thucydides."[1] This is no minor accolade, for students of history and of strategy have long understood the importance of that ancient Greek's powerful *History of the Peloponnesian War*. Indeed, for many decades the Naval War College has relied upon that great work as a seminal case study in the art of strategic thinking. In many ways, Morison was much like Thucydides, in that both were contemporaries of the events they wrote about and each provided a comprehensive and sweeping history of a great war, yet embellished it with their writing talents and seasoned it with their insight.

Volume 12, *Leyte: June 1944–January 1945*, of Morison's *History of United States Naval Operations in World War II* series is certainly no exception. The Morison touch is as evident in *Leyte* as in all his other volumes. The color is exemplified in this passage:

> Thus, when Mississippi discharged her twelve 14-inch guns at Yamashiro . . . she was not only giving that battleship the *coup de grace*, but firing a funeral salute to a finished era of naval warfare. One can imagine the ghosts of all great admirals from Raleigh to Jellicoe standing at attention as Battle Line went into oblivion, along with the Greek phalanx, the Spanish wall of pikemen, the English longbow, and the row-galley tactics of the Salamis and Lepanto.[2]

And Morison's characteristic willingness to adjudicate and commemorate great events is evident, as when he describes the battle off Samar as "forever memorable, forever glorious."[3]

[1] James D. Hornfischer, "Revisiting Samuel Eliot Morison's Landmark History," *Smithsonian* (February 2011): 77.

[2] Samuel Eliot Morison, *Leyte: June 1944–January 1945* (Annapolis, MD: Naval Institute Press, 2011), 241.

[3] Morison, 338.

By many different measures, the battle that took place in October 1944 as a result of the American landings on the Philippine island of Leyte was one of the greatest in naval history. Many have proclaimed it *the* greatest naval battle in history, and there is much to support that contention. Involving every facet of naval warfare (air, surface, submarine, and amphibious), it was fought by more ships than any other engagement, spanned more than 100,000 square miles, and included nearly 200,000 men. Every naval weapon was brought to bear, and dozens of ships were lost. Yet, even though virtually all Americans have heard of Pearl Harbor and of D-day, relatively few have heard of Leyte Gulf.

The reason for this anonymity is primarily a matter of timing. By late 1944, unlike the harrowing early months of the war, Americans had come to expect successes and victories. And although Leyte was marred by mistakes and near misses that could have ended in disaster, it ultimately was a resounding victory that marked the end of the Japanese navy as a viable fighting force. Had it ended in an American defeat, it would likely have been more memorable. Further, Leyte was one slice of meat in a Dagwood sandwich that included layers of gargantuan events such as the Normandy landings, the slaughter at Iwo Jima, the rain of kamikazes at Okinawa, and the great cataclysms of Hiroshima and Nagasaki.

Yet, despite its relative obscurity, the Battle of Leyte Gulf is an essential chapter in the American story. It is an array of facts necessary to the integrity of the tale, yet it is much more. The battle demonstrates both our capabilities and our shortcomings in an edifying manner and is riddled with moments of jaw-dropping courage and sacrifice that make the term "awe-inspiring" seem inadequate.

Morison corralled and organized the facts with the expertise of a skilled historian, while capturing the human drama in a manner that rivals the essence of Greek tragedy. His early chapters set the scene by weaving complex events into a thematic whole as illustrated by such titles as "After the Marianas, What?" "Admiral Halsey and the Strategic Shift," and "Ulithi and Its Neighbors." The plot thickens with chapters like "Clipping the Cat's Whiskers" and "Moves on the Naval

Chessboard," and the climax — spanning hundreds of pages of gripping battle drama — captures the human contradictions of warfare, providing a stage for what is worst and what is best about mankind.

Because President Roosevelt and Secretary of the Navy Frank Knox officially sanctioned Morison's history, one might expect it to be a whitewashed account. Yet, to Morison's credit — as well as to the Navy's — this is largely a warts-and-dimples rendering of events. No account, no matter how large and ambitious, could be expected to cover every moment, nor to embrace every contentious issue, and this work has been fairly criticized for some thin coverage in places and for instances of parochial vision. Yet, this is a nitpicker's view when the work is taken as a whole.

Take, for example, what most historians would agree is the most contentious issue of the entire Leyte campaign, the debacle that allowed Kurita's still-potent (despite the earlier hammering from Halsey) Center Force to surprise the "Taffies" off Samar. This tragic event resulted in losses of ships and men that would have been avoided had not the "fog of war" descended upon key American commanders at critical moments. The debate over who should have done what and when has been resurrected many times over the years since — from polemics to reasoned analyses — and yet, despite much scrutiny (and some manipulation) of the facts at hand, none has ever significantly altered Morison's straightforward and unflinching assessment.

Beginning with "Admiral Halsey's erroneous estimate that the Japanese Center Force had been too badly damaged to be a serious menace was the primary event in a chain of wrong assumptions,"[4] Morison then dispassionately but effectively distributes responsibility among the various participants. He points out erroneous conclusions born of wishful thinking, reasonably attributing the errors to faulty reckoning rather than malice or personal shortcoming. Ultimately Morison concludes that "the reason why Kurita was able to sortie from San Bernardino Strait and steam toward Leyte Gulf for about seven hours, completely undetected, was a series of faulty assumptions on the

[4] Ibid., 289.

part of his enemies."[5] Of course, these faulty assumptions could not have taken root and flourished had the command structure at Leyte not been so egregiously constructed. Specifically, despite two U.S. fleets operating in the same area in support of the same operation, their respective chains of command led all the way back to Washington, D.C., before one finds a common commander — something Morison does not address directly but is nonetheless implicit in his assessment. Critical evaluation such as this is not the work of a propagandist. Today's Navy could learn much from this example.

There is evidence that Halsey and Morison were not without some mutual personal animosity, which might make Morison's criticism suspect. Indeed, in private correspondence, Halsey referred to Morison as a "son of a bitch" and threatened to take him on publicly (which he refrained from doing on the advice of friends). And in a later lecture, Morison described Halsey's actions as "blundering" at Leyte Gulf.[6] Yet, Morison refrained from such language in the account (volume 12) that he left for posterity, and his assessment comes across as appropriate and reasonable, especially when compared with many other evaluations (for example, *Life* magazine's 1947 critique of Halsey bore the inflammatory title "Bull's Run").

Some critics find Morison's assessment too lenient, arguing that Halsey's actions were so flawed that he should have been punished, including being relieved of command. My own account, published on the fiftieth anniversary of these events, spread the blame among several of the participants, as did Morison. My account was harshest on Halsey, asserting that he should have divided his forces, contending that as commander of the most powerful fleet ever assembled to that time, he could well afford to have gone after Ozawa's Northern Force *and* left behind a potent enough force to protect the Seventh Fleet.[7] But my account also explained I was making the assessment "from the comfort of a desk chair . . . surrounded by books and documents with a

[5] Ibid., 293.

[6] Evan Thomas, *Sea of Thunder: Four Commanders and the Last Great Naval Campaign 1941–1945* (New York: Simon & Schuster, 2006), 345–49.

[7] Thomas J. Cutler, *The Battle of Leyte Gulf: 23–26 October 1944* (New York: HarperCollins, 1994), 287–96.

hundred times the information available to those on-site commanders, [perusing] them at my leisure, pressured only by a publisher's deadline . . . [writing] on a machine that dutifully erases my errors, and [sipping] coffee as I write." More important, my account noted that "most of all, no one must live or die by what I do here."[8] Morison's conclusions — although without a similarly overt caveat — followed the same basic guidelines, offering constructive criticism without passing judgment and without rendering a punitive sentence, as some other people are wont to do.

Another topic that has given birth to much debate is why Vice Admiral Takeo Kurita, commander of the powerful Japanese Center Force, broke off his attack on Taffy 3 despite having that grossly inferior American force on the ropes. Kurita was mostly silent on the subject for the remainder of his life (he died in 1977), only occasionally giving hints or (sometimes contradictory) explanations. Morison — working without those hints and explanations — concluded that "partly from what he knew, but still more from what he imagined, Kurita reached the conclusion that his prospects in Leyte Gulf were both thin and grim, and that he had better save the rest of his fleet, possibly to fight another day."[9] To reach that assessment, Morison explains that Kurita believed that the ships he was pursuing were making much better speed than they actually were, and, based upon reports from his staff, that he had encountered a more formidable force than it actually was. Morison also includes a possible fatigue factor by pointing out that Kurita had been forced to "swim for his life on the 23rd, and had taken a beating from Third Fleet on the 24th." Also, he allows for the influence of a message that told Kurita of a bigger force to the north that might warrant his attention more than the one he had engaged (Taffy 3).

Morison reasonably attributes the misjudgment of the Americans' speed to a Japanese lack of radar capability that was compounded by the Americans' effective use of smoke screens, which impeded the efforts of the Japanese optical range finders.[10]

[8] Ibid., xvi.
[9] Morison, 300.
[10] Ibid., 296–300.

The misidentification of the American ships is also very plausible. One must bear in mind that, despite the ferocious combat that had taken place between these two navies for nearly three years at this point, they rarely saw one another. Many of the engagements were over-the-horizon battles fought by aircraft, many others were through the lens of a periscope, and the surface-to-surface engagements were largely fought at night. So it is little wonder that Kurita's staff did not know what they were seeing when the ships of Taffy 3 loomed up in their binoculars. Any sailor can affirm the difficulty of accurate identification of ships at sea under the best of conditions, and the smoke screens probably compounded the problem. Clearly, preconception contributed as well — Kurita and his staff were, after all, unaware that Halsey had taken the whole Third Fleet northward and were most likely expecting to encounter some or all of Halsey's powerful forces. Morison writes that Kurita's "staff evaluated [Taffy 3] as part of Halsey's Third Fleet — Sprague's CVEs were either *Independence* class CVLs or *Ranger* class CVs; the *Fletcher* class destroyers were all *Baltimore* class heavy cruisers (their profiles are somewhat alike); a *Pennsylvania* class battlewagon was reported to be lurking among the carriers; and when Taffy 2 [further to the south] was sighted from *Yamato*'s lofty masthead it was reported as another fast carrier group."[11]

Morison's mention of the fatigue factor is interesting because in 1954 Kurita lent credence to this hypothesis, saying in a rare interview that "my mind was extremely fatigued" and that his decision to withdraw "probably should be called a 'judgment of exhaustion.'" But in 1970, he retracted this statement, asserting that "in a war, you don't get tired. If you make a mistake in decision-making because you did not sleep three or four days, then you are not qualified to be the commander of a fleet. I did not make mistakes." To explain his earlier conflicting contention, he claimed that the journalist who had interviewed him in 1954 "made me say it that way," although it is not clear *how* the journalist accomplished that.[12]

[11] Ibid., 298.
[12] Thomas, 351–52.

Regarding the message telling Kurita that "an enemy task force lay only 113 miles north of Suluan Island," Morison describes it as "mysterious" and in his footnote attributes it to Kurita's after-action report but notes that it does not appear in *Yamato*'s message file.[13] It now appears that this message was a figment of Kurita's imagination. Morison obviously did not know this at the time but apparently suspected it.

My own account, written thirty-five years after Morison's, concurred with him on the misidentification factor and was even more forgiving than he was when it came to the mysterious message.[14] My account failed to identify the message as most likely bogus, as others have subsequently done (notably Evan Thomas, who devotes an entire chapter to the subject in his *Sea of Thunder*).[15]

Unlike Morison's volume, my account did address the proverbial "elephant in the room" by discussing the possibility of a loss of nerve, but concluded that while "Kurita's war record is not one of notable intellectual brilliance . . . there is not the slightest hint of cowardice to mar his performance in the several years of combat he endured before Leyte Gulf." Instead, my account concluded that "exhaustion is a far more plausible explanation for Kurita's actions." Despite Kurita's waffling on the subject, human limitations are a more compelling explanation than the superhuman expectations that Kurita later claimed — the latter something we are reminded of even today, when military commanders use such terms as "110 percent" and "24/7."[16]

Of course, no serious accounting for the reasons that Kurita turned away can omit the most important of them all. Morison concludes that Kurita's retirement from the scene was "due, in the last analysis, to the indomitable spirit of the Spragues' escort carriers, with their screen and aircraft. It was they that stopped the most powerful surface fleet which Japan had sent to sea since the Battle of Midway."[17] My own

[13]Morison, 299.
[14]Cutler, 286–87.
[15]Thomas, 307–24 and 352.
[16]Cutler, 286–87.
[17]Morison, 312.

account likened the battle to Alfred Lord Tennyson's *Charge of the Light Brigade* because, coincidentally, Taffy 3's charge occurred on the anniversary of the Battle of Balaclava (the subject of Tennyson's epic poem) but, more important, for the awe that both battles evoke.[18] Nothing in the long and impressive history of the U.S. Navy surpasses that astonishing charge in terms of raw courage and sacrifice.

Comparing Morison's ultimate explanation for Kurita's withdrawal to Evan Thomas' conclusion in his well-received *Sea of Thunder: Four Commanders and the Last Great Naval Campaign 1941–1945*, published in 2006, one finds a definite similarity. As noted earlier, Morison points out that "Kurita reached the conclusion that his prospects in Leyte Gulf were both thin and grim, and that he had better save the rest of his fleet, possibly to fight another day,"[19] while Thomas writes that "in the end, Kurita had not been willing to sacrifice his men in a futile gesture of nobility."[20]

So, again, Morison deserves high marks for creating an early account that has remained viable despite the limitations he was saddled with by writing when he did. It is a remarkable achievement due largely to Morison's proficiency as a historian, presenting as much narrative and analysis as the existing record would allow, while avoiding the temptation to stray into the minefield of over-speculation.

The story of the Battle of Leyte Gulf has been told many times since Morison penned this epic account. Some of these are dramatic and beautifully written — James Hornfischer's *Last Stand of the Tin Can Sailors* comes easily to mind — and others are more scholarly and analytic — H. P. Wilmott's *The Battle of Leyte Gulf: The Last Fleet Action* and Milan Vego's *Battle for Leyte, 1944: Allied and Japanese Plans, Preparations, and Execution* are two examples. Some accounts are timeless, such as C. Vann Woodward's *The Battle for Leyte Gulf: The Incredible Story of World War II's Largest Naval Battle* (originally published in 1947 but resurrected in 2007), and others are more vicariously "deckplate" in their viewpoints (as seen through the eyes of participants), such as David Sears'

[18] Cutler, 219–48.
[19] Morison, 300.
[20] Thomas, 355.

The Last Epic Naval Battle: Voices from Leyte Gulf and Hornfischer's account mentioned above.

One might wonder if the books about Leyte Gulf that have followed in Morison's wake have rendered his no longer relevant. To be sure, declassification of some sources, the successful further mining of documents by ardent researchers, revisionist thinking, and evolving attitudes have all served to expand upon Morison's narrative, offering corrections and other improvements. But a good story can be told countless times (witness the plethora of Lincoln biographies) without lessening the value of the earliest attempts.

In the final analysis, no single book can claim to have replaced Morison's iconic version. Some books supplement Morison's, of course. Others extrapolate, to be sure. But none obviate! Perhaps the most obvious measure is that no serious author begins to write on this subject without first reading Morison's account. Like Thucydides, Morison brings to his pages an inimitable authenticity that only a contemporary who had witnessed some of these events could hope to achieve. This is by no means a memoir, yet there is a veracity — a virtual *flavor* — that can be within the reach only of someone who lived through these times, who knew the feel of a steel deck beneath his feet, who saw this war reflected in the eyes of its recent participants as well as in the pages of the countless documents he surveyed.

Just as many successful treatises on the Peloponnesian War, including at least five new books in the last decade alone, have not diminished Thucydides' original, so Morison's seminal work remains on its pedestal as an essential component of the history and the historiography of the momentous events portrayed, analyzed, and ultimately preserved for posterity.

Baldwin had it right.

Thomas J. Cutler

PART I

Strategy and Preliminaries

CHAPTER I

After the Marianas, What?[1]

June–September 1944

1. *Divergent Roads to Tokyo*

BETWEEN April and August 1944, events in the Pacific moved at breathless pace. General MacArthur's Southwest Pacific Forces, mostly American but with Australian Naval and Aviation Engineer increments, made the landings that secured Hollandia in Dutch New Guinea on 22 April, established a new forward base and airdrome, and, in a series of well conceived and smartly executed moves, took Wakde, Biak, Noemfoor and Sansapor. This meant an advance of a thousand miles in less than four months, and carried the General to the Vogelkop, head of the New Guinea Bird. There we left him, in Volume VIII, gazing impatiently northwestward toward the Philippines, which he was determined to liberate at no distant date. In the Central Pacific, under Admiral Nimitz's overall command, Admiral Spruance administered a stinging defeat to the Japanese Fleet in the Battle of the Philippine Sea, and by August Amphibious Forces Pacific Fleet had possession of the Marianas. But we were still a long way from Japan – some 1200 miles by the shortest route for the B–29s from Saipan. So studded with Allied victories were the spring and sum-

[1] Records of the Joint Chiefs of Staff and manuscript "History of the J.C.S." by Lt. Grace P. Hayes USNR. Of the printed books, the most useful are King & Whitehill *Fleet Admiral King*, Ehrman *Grand Strategy* V (chap. xii on British discussions of Pacific and Far Eastern strategy), Cannon *Leyte*, Robert R. Smith *The Approach to the Philippines* and Maurice Matloff *Strategic Planning for Coalition Warfare 1943–44*, read in manuscript. *The Philippines Campaign 1944–45* (see my Preface) gives a good summary of General MacArthur's thoughts and of his successive "Reno" plans.

mer of 1944 as to create an unwarranted expectation that the European War would be over by Christmas, when the Pacific War could be pressed to a prompt conclusion. General Montgomery was quoted in *Time* of 28 August as saying "The end of the war is in sight"; and that was so much the prevailing view that Admiral Wilkinson felt obliged to write home from Pearl Harbor, "Don't kid yourself that the end is in sight out here; we're still nibbling at the edges and the predominant Japanese Army has not really yet been hurt."

The strategists were unable to keep up with events, and the planners had no rest. Occupation of the Palau Islands by Central Pacific Forces was on the cards for 15 September and General MacArthur had made the target date for Mindanao 15 November; but in August it was still undecided what routes would be chosen for the final offensive against Japan, which islands would be occupied en route, and which would be bypassed.

The guiding concept for Pacific strategy, as laid down by the Combined Chiefs of Staff at Cairo on 3 December 1943, was "obtaining bases from which the unconditional surrender of Japan can be forced." But what bases? The uncertainty as to the next move after the Marianas may be seen in the Joint Chiefs of Staff directive to Admiral Nimitz and General MacArthur of 12 March 1944: "The J.C.S. have decided that the most feasible approach to Formosa, Luzon and China is by way of the Marianas, the Carolines, Palau and Mindanao." [2]

At that time the J.C.S. regarded Formosa, Luzon, and some place on the Chinese coast as alternate bases from which the final assault on Japan should be made. But they had not resolved the essential conflict between the MacArthur and the King-Nimitz concepts. The General still believed in what he called the "New Guinea-Mindanao Axis" approach, liberating the Philippine Islands from south to north before attacking Japan itself. Admiral King, and (less emphatically) Admiral Nimitz, believed in a two-pronged approach to Japan from the new bases they were confident of

[2] Volume VIII of this History pp. 7, 9. Summary, not direct quote.

acquiring shortly in the Marianas. The right prong would be an aërial ascent by B–29 bombers "up the ladder of the Bonins," and the left one would capture Formosa and a base on the coast of China. General MacArthur's rôle in this Navy plan would be to liberate Mindanao and set up air bases whence the Far Eastern Air Forces could pound down Japanese air power on Luzon, after which he would help the Pacific Fleet to capture Formosa. The protagonists of the Navy plan argued that "battering our way through the Philippines," as Admiral King put it, would be a long and costly process; that possession of Formosa would "put the cork in the bottle" of enemy sea communications, choking off all Japanese traffic in and out of the South China Sea, and would enable Allied naval forces and the B–29s to strangle Japan by surface, air and submarine blockade. They argued that this bold, direct strategy would bring the defeat of Japan much nearer, and that bypassing the Philippines would work no real hardship on our loyal allies in the Archipelago; might even liberate them earlier than a series of operations for their special benefit.

The Japanese, naturally, did not wait for us to make up our minds. They made two moves which had a considerable effect on Allied strategy. Toward the end of February 1944 they sailed the major part of their Fleet from the Inland Sea of Japan to Lingga Roads, off Singapore. The real reason for this shift of base was to be near the source of fuel oil; but to the British it looked like a threat to India. It spoiled the British plan to deploy a part of the Royal Navy in the Central or the Southwest Pacific, where it would have been a welcome reinforcement to "MacArthur's Navy," the United States Seventh Fleet.

The second Japanese move came at the end of May 1944, when their Army began a southward advance from Hankow along the axis of the railroad to Hanoi, Indochina. Hengyang, the important junction to Canton, fell on 8 August, and by that time the XIV United States Army Air Force had been forced to retire from forward airfields in China. On 10 November the Japanese captured Kweilin and Linchow, together with their airfields; by the end of

1944 they had cut Chiang Kai-shek off from all China east of the railway. This ruled out Allied prospects of landing on friendly Chinese shores, and made it almost inevitable that the Marianas-Formosa-China plan would be scrapped. In addition, it precipitated a political-diplomatic crisis at Chungking, in which Chiang and Generals Stilwell, Chennault and Patrick Hurley were principal actors, and which ended in leaving both Chiang and the American air forces in China out on a limb.

When the Joint Chiefs of Staff visited London, shortly after Normandy D-day in June 1944 – in case Eisenhower should suffer a setback and a quick C.C.S. decision be necessary – they discussed Pacific and Far Eastern strategy with the British Chiefs of Staff. There was a general agreement to do the unexpected when fighting Japan; but what did Japan expect, and what form should the unexpected take? The only thing that came out of these discussions, and that, obviously, as a result of the Japanese southward thrust from Hankow, was a suggestion thrown out by the J.C.S. on 13 June in the form of a query to Admiral Nimitz and General MacArthur: what did they think of bypassing not only the Philippines but Formosa, in favor of a direct attack on Kyushu, southernmost of the main Japanese islands? In reply it appeared that both C. in C.'s preferred the strategy already agreed upon, and MacArthur was outraged by the presumption of the J.C.S. He answered this suggestion with an eloquent plea for honoring his (and America's) word to the Filipinos, to liberate them from Japanese tyranny at the earliest possible moment. He observed that logistical considerations ruled out any speed-up in the existing timetable. He warned the J.C.S. of the consequences of leaving the Archipelago, with its loyal population of 16,000,000 people, to "wither on the vine" until Japan was defeated. Not only would that inflict unpredictable hardships on the Filipinos; it would cause all Asia to lose faith in American honor. General Marshall, who was loath to get the Army involved in costly land campaigns on the road to Japan, answered (24 June) that the possibility of bypassing the Philippines should at least be investigated, and that personal and political considerations should not be allowed to override the main objective of defeating Japan.[3] On the constructive side, MacArthur submitted a plan called "Reno V," dated 15 June 1944, which proposed the following timetable: –

Invade Mindanao at Sarangani 25 October 1944, and quickly establish air bases, to provide cover for an attack on Leyte 15 November. Having secured Leyte, Central Pacific forces would land at Aparri on the north coast of Luzon 15 January 1945; Southwest Pacific forces on the Bicol Peninsula, and on Mindoro in February. Then, in concert with the Pacific Fleet, make an "end run" northabout, through Balingtang Channel, to Lingayen Gulf 1 April 1945, land six divisions and advance on Manila.

Admiral King drafted a sharp reply to this proposal, which he described as a projection of the General's "desires and visions" rather than a practical plan for the defeat of Japan. It was indeed questionable strategy, which even General Kenney criticized for weakness in air support. Nevertheless, there occurred a deadlock in the J.C.S. between the MacArthur concept and a new Cincpac plan for the Marianas-Formosa-China strategy, called Granite II. The latter approach to Japan was still favored by Admirals King and Nimitz, despite the Japanese advances in South China which were rapidly sealing off the coast.

At this juncture President Roosevelt intervened. In the course of an inspection tour of the Pacific that he had planned for July, he decided to summon General MacArthur to Honolulu to discuss the next moves directly with himself, and Admiral Nimitz. Neither General Marshall nor Admiral King, who was then in the Pacific, were invited; their views were already known to the President. He was accompanied only by Admiral William D. Leahy, chief of staff to the C. in C., Rear Admiral Wilson Brown, and Major General Edwin M. ("Pa") Watson.

As Mr. Roosevelt had just consented to stand for a fourth term, and was nominated on 20 July when he was passing through Cali-

[3] The gist of MacArthur's dispatch and of Marshall's reply is in Courtney Whitney *MacArthur, His Rendezvous with History* (1956).

fornia, political implications were read into this journey. The real reason for it, apart from the President's natural curiosity to see Hawaii and visit the armed forces in forward areas, was to exchange ideas with the senior Army and Navy commanders in the Pacific, and if possible reach an agreement. He was particularly eager to have General MacArthur's views at first hand; and MacArthur had previously asked to be allowed to come to Washington to present them, if bypassing the Philippines was being seriously considered.[4]

The presidential party, after witnessing amphibious exercises by the 5th Marine Division at Oceanside, California, embarked at San Diego in heavy cruiser *Baltimore* (Captain Walter L. Calhoun) on 21 July. Two days later, Commander Hawaiian Sea Frontier reported a possible Japanese task force due north of Hawaii and only 220 miles distant. This report caused a brief flurry at Pearl Harbor before it was evaluated as an imaginary sighting of lights on the sea by a search plane at dusk. But it caused no deviation from *Baltimore's* course.

At Pearl Harbor the forthcoming visit was top secret. Every officer in the know, when questioned about it, vigorously denied the rumor; but word got around among the enlisted men, so that in the early afternoon of July 26, when *Baltimore* passed Diamond Head, a sizable crowd of soldiers and sailors had assembled at the Navy Yard. There, 26 flag and general officers in whites had assembled to pay their respect to the President. Off Fort Kamehameha the cruiser slowed down to permit Admiral Nimitz, Lieutenant

[4] Rear Adm. Wilson Brown "Log of the President's Inspection Trip to the Pacific," and his ms. memoirs, and Fleet Admiral Leahy *I Was There* (1950) give the best accounts of the conference. The General, in his reply to the J.C.S. message of 13 June 1944 to consider bypassing the Philippines, said, "If serious consideration is being given" to attacking Formosa or Japan directly, "I request that I be accorded the opportunity of personally proceeding to Washington to present fully my views." Whitney *MacArthur* p. 122. As the President was then about to leave Washington for California and Hawaii, the obvious place for him to meet MacArthur was Oahu. General Whitney further states (p. 126), "I have never heard MacArthur associate himself with the viewpoint that it [the conference] was more political than strategical," denying the charges in Frazier Hunt *The Untold Story of General MacArthur* (1954) and Rexford Tugwell *The Democratic Roosevelt* (1957).

General Robert C. Richardson USA and other notables to board her from a tug. She then stood up the channel, flying the presidential flag at the main, while every ship in the harbor manned rails. After Captain Calhoun had laid *Baltimore* alongside pier 22–B, so gently that she wouldn't have crushed an eggshell, the landing stage was rolled up and Vice Admiral Charles H. ("Soc") McMorris, Cincpac-Cincpoa chief of staff, who was in charge of the contingent in whites, ordered a "Right Face!" It was so long since the admirals had done close order drill that two of them turned left, which provoked a delighted cheer from the crew of *Baltimore*. However, that was soon corrected and "Soc" marched his formation on board, to the tune of such pipings, ruffles and flourishes as had not been heard in Pearl Harbor for years. They were presented to the President in the flag cabin, and all except Admiral Nimitz departed.

Mr. Roosevelt then asked to see General MacArthur. The General's plane from Brisbane had landed just as *Baltimore* was entering the harbor and he had gone to General Richardson's quarters at Fort Shafter. Within a few minutes of the President's request, cheers, police whistles and the noise of a motorcycle escort were heard in the direction of Honolulu. Presently an Army car showing the four stars of a general came tearing down to the dock and stopped opposite the gangway. To the surprise and admiration of all beholders, out stepped General MacArthur, clad in the familiar khaki trousers, brown leather air force jacket and Philippines' field marshal's cap. He mounted the gangway briskly amid a chorus of boatswain's pipes, smartly saluted the quarterdeck and disappeared within to report to the President.

After the usual greetings, F.D.R. turned to a chart of the Pacific on a bulkhead, pointed to Mindanao, and said: –

"Douglas, where do we go from here?"

"Leyte, Mr. President, and then Luzon!" [5]

They might as well have made it a top-level decision then and

[5] This is as the President told it to the writer later the same year; but I think that his memory was slightly at fault, and that the dramatic scene took place later, at the beginning of the discussions at Waikiki.

there, since that is what we did – and, in addition, bypassed Mindanao. But there had to be plenty of discussion first, in which the General had an opportunity to repeat to the President the eloquent plea he had earlier made to the J.C.S. for keeping our word with the Filipinos.

This important discussion took place between the President, the General and the Admiral at the residence of the late Chris R. Holmes on Kalaukau Avenue, Waikiki.

The debate centered on the question, should or should not the Philippines, or at least Luzon, be bypassed? Nimitz's primary consideration was to sever Japanese lines of communication southward. He was inclined to believe, though not convinced, that taking Formosa was the way to do it. MacArthur ably and eloquently presented his case: that both national honor and sound strategy required the liberation of the Philippines before we went further. Only these two talked; the President and the others listened. All were converted; "and from hindsight," wrote Admiral Nimitz some seven years later, "I think that decision was correct." [6] They further agreed "that the Philippines should be recovered with ground and air power then available in the Western Pacific" (no need to wait until the defeat of Germany), "and that Japan could be forced to accept our terms of surrender by the use of sea and air power without an invasion of the Japanese homeland." Rear Admiral Wilson Brown stated that in no conference attended by him did the speakers stick so close to the subject or make such clear, concise and candid expressions of opinion. Actually no firm decision was made – that was for the J.C.S. – but an agreement was reached on major strategy. When General MacArthur took his leave after lunch on 27 July, he assured the President that he need have no concern about differences of opinion between Admiral Nimitz and himself. "We see eye to eye, Mr. President," he said; "we understand each other perfectly." [7]

[6] Letter of Admiral Nimitz to the writer, 10 Feb. 1951.

[7] From a source close to General MacArthur I have it that, upon departing by plane from Oahu, he told an aide who accompanied him, "We've sold it!" That is, convinced the President and the Admiral. *Time* magazine for 21 August

After inspecting military establishments on Oahu and visiting the wounded from Saipan in the new hospital at Aiea, the President sailed in *Baltimore* for Adak on the evening of 29 July 1944.

The J.C.S. do not seem to have been particularly impressed by this top-level accord, since they continued to argue the question "Luzon, Formosa, or what?" for months thereafter. At their meeting on 1 September 1944 Rear Admiral Forrest Sherman, Admiral Nimitz's chief planner, presented the problem. He remarked that it was high time a decision was reached; even a bad one would be better than none. Central Pacific armed forces had had no directive for anything beyond the Palaus, which was coming up in two weeks! Admiral King still opposed liberating Luzon, predicting that it would slow up the war for mere sentimental reasons. But General Marshall now supported MacArthur's concept. The factor of national honor appealed to him, as did the argument that Luzon would be far easier to capture than Formosa. Nevertheless, the only agreement then reached by the J.C.S. was to direct General MacArthur to occupy Leyte on 20 December 1944, six weeks after the target date for Mindanao. Admiral King insisted that we should capture Formosa before the Japanese had time to reinforce it; but Marshall always brought up the query, "Where would we go from Formosa?"

A timetable of operations up to 1 March 1945, worked up by J.C.S. planners with General MacArthur's representatives, was presented at the OCTAGON Combined Chiefs of Staff Conference with the President and Prime Minister, which opened at Quebec on 11 September 1944. Although this timetable [8] was mostly scrambled within a week, it still has interest: –

15 September, Southwest Pacific forces occupy Morotai; Central Pacific forces occupy Peleliu 5 October; occupy Yap, with Ulithi to follow.

1944 states that the President at a press conference said that United States fighting forces would return to the Philippines under General MacArthur; but according to the best evidence, F.D.R. never said this; it was merely the inference of a smart reporter.

[8] Included herein are operations for which directives had already been issued.

15 October, Southwest Pacific forces occupy Salebaboe Island; 15 November, land at Sarangani Bay, Mindanao; 20 December, at Leyte.

Southwest Pacific and Central Pacific forces then combine to occupy either (1) Luzon to secure Manila by 20 February, or (2) Formosa and Amoy on the China coast by 1 March 1945.[9]

2. *Admiral Halsey and the Strategic Shift*

By the summer of 1944 the Pacific Fleet command, but not the ships themselves, had been divided into two "teams." These were Fifth Fleet under Vice Admiral Raymond A. Spruance, and Third Fleet under Admiral William F. Halsey. While one Admiral's "team" – that is, his staff – was at sea, the other stayed ashore to plan the next operation. This arrangement may be compared to a change of quarterback in a football game, while the line and the rest of the backfield stay in; the line in this case being the fire support ships and the backfield, Fast Carrier Forces Pacific Fleet. This latter force, whether it was designated TF 38 or TF 58, was commanded by Vice Admiral Marc A. Mitscher; but in the operations covered by this volume, when Halsey was in overall command, he often assumed the tactical command as well.

At this time TF 38, Fast Carrier Forces, were divided into the following task groups, which were subject to change: –

TG 38.1 Vice Admiral John S. McCain, in WASP: Two fleet carriers, two light carriers, three heavy cruisers and 15 destroyers.

TG 38.2 Rear Admiral G. F. Bogan, in BUNKER HILL: Three fleet carriers, two light carriers, two battleships, four light cruisers, 18 destroyers.

TG 38.3 Rear Admiral Frederick C. Sherman, in ESSEX: Two fleet carriers, two light carriers, four battleships, four light cruisers, 14 destroyers.

[9] J.C.S. to MacArthur and Nimitz 9 Sept. 1944.

TG 38.4 Rear Admiral Ralph E. Davison, in FRANKLIN: Two fleet carriers, two light carriers, two cruisers, 11 destroyers.

Since every fleet carrier's air group included about 40 fighter planes, 35 dive bombers and 18 torpedo bombers, and every light carrier took to sea some 23 fighters and 10 torpedo bombers, it will be appreciated that Fast Carrier Forces Pacific Fleet carried a terrific punch.

Preliminary to the operations outlined in the OCTAGON timetable, Admiral Halsey led TF 38 out from Eniwetok, on 28 August 1944, to bomb Yap, the Palaus and Mindanao, and to make a one-group diversionary strike on the Bonin Islands. The object was to destroy Japanese air forces, which might challenge the forthcoming landings on Morotai and Peleliu, and to deceive the enemy as to our next target. The Palaus were bombed on 6–8 September; Mindanao airdromes near Sarangani Bay on 9–10 September. These strikes were not even opposed by the enemy. This lack of opposition caused Halsey to cancel later strikes scheduled for Mindanao, and to shift to the Visayas on the 12th. Here he found the same situation. With the mountains of Samar in sight from flight decks, 2400 sorties were flown in two days; about 200 enemy planes shot down or destroyed on the ground, many ships sunk, and numerous installations destroyed. It seemed to Halsey and his staff that the Japanese air forces were about finished; and at noon September 13 he made a highly important suggestion. In a dispatch to Nimitz, who passed it on to King and MacArthur, he recommended that the Palau, Yap, Morotai and Mindanao landings be canceled as unnecessary, and that troops which were to be used at these targets, as well as TF 38, be made available to General MacArthur for an immediate seizure of Leyte.

A radical change in the timetable, indeed! Halsey had always wished to accelerate the Pacific war; here was a Heaven-sent opportunity. Yet, ironically enough, his brilliant strategic suggestion was based on a partly incorrect premise. The Japanese air forces were not as weak as he assumed; they were being held back, in readiness for the major landings that Imperial General Headquarters expected shortly. Another factor was the weather. Leyte Valley has such unstable soil as to be unsuitable for airfield development during the rainy monsoon season, which is at its worst in the last three months of the year. Colonel William J. Ely USA of Sixth Army Engineers pointed this out to General MacArthur's staff, warning them against "undertaking an overambitious program" impossible of completion in the time allotted, and thus delaying future operations.[10] The colonel was right, but the risk was accepted. Owing to weather and soil difficulties on Leyte itself the fast carriers had to remain in support long after the human factor demanded their retirement, and the Mindoro, Lingayen and Okinawa operations had to be postponed. On the other hand, the countervailing advantages of the speed-up were immense. It kept the Japanese Army off balance and caught the Japanese Navy with untrained air groups.

General MacArthur on 13 September was on board *Nashville* en route to Morotai, maintaining radio silence; but his chief of staff, Lieutenant General R. K. Sutherland at Hollandia, immediately fell in step with Halsey, knowing that MacArthur would approve. Cautious and deliberate in his movements during the lean years, the General had planned the liberation of the Philippines in a series of airfield steppingstones, so that his troops would always be within reach of land-based air support. But the fast carrier forces had effected a tactical revolution, the significance of which the General had grasped. So there was no longer any need to develop airfields in the Southern Philippines before invading Leyte or Luzon; the Navy could furnish all air support that the Army wanted until it acquired new airfields at the target island. Southwest Pacific Command had planned to land 30,000 troops on Mindanao 15 November. But why not bypass Mindanao and lift them directly to Leyte? And if the XXIV Army Corps, earmarked to be landed at Yap by Rear Admiral Wilkinson's III 'Phib, could be

[10] Cannon *Leyte* pp. 35–6; *Engineers of SW Pacific* VI, *Airfield and Base Development* (1951) pp. 286–7.

diverted to Leyte, you had an invasion force worth thinking about. So, General Sutherland, in MacArthur's name, informed the J.C.S. and Cincpac on 14 September that if Halsey's recommendations were adopted, General MacArthur would invade Leyte 20 October – a step-up of two months in the target date. Admiral Nimitz agreed, except that he felt that the Palaus operation should go through as planned, in order to secure an air base and anchorage.

Fortunately the OCTAGON Conference of the Combined Chiefs of Staff with the President, the "P.M." and Premier Mackenzie King of Canada was then in session at Quebec. Word of the Halsey-Nimitz-MacArthur agreement arrived on the evening of 15 September when the J.C.S. were being entertained at dinner by Canadian officers. The Joint Chiefs interrupted their meal for a brief consultation. "Having the utmost confidence in General MacArthur, Admiral Nimitz and Admiral Halsey," wrote General Marshall, "it was not a difficult decision to make. Within 90 minutes after the signal had been received in Quebec, General MacArthur and Admiral Nimitz had received their instructions to execute the Leyte operation." Target date was 20 October, skipping the three intermediate landings (Yap, the Talauds and Mindanao) previously approved. "General MacArthur's acknowledgement of his new instructions reached me while en route from the dinner to my quarters." [11]

After another exchange of dispatches between Quebec, Washington, Hollandia and Pearl Harbor, directives to General MacArthur and Admiral Nimitz were issued in the following tenor: –

1. Admiral Wilkinson's YAP ATTACK FORCE, the XXIV Army Corps, then loading or at sea, to be assigned to General MacArthur to land at LEYTE 20 October.
2. All shipping used in the Palaus operation, after unloading, to be sent to Southwest Pacific ports to help VII 'Phib lift General Krueger's Sixth Army to LEYTE.

[11] *Biennial Reports of Chief of Staff U.S. Army to Secretary of War* pp. 227–8.

3. All Fire Support Ships and Escort Carriers used in the Palaus operation to be assigned temporarily to Admiral Kinkaid, Commander Seventh Fleet, to help cover LEYTE.
4. ULITHI to be seized promptly, as an advanced fleet base.

This radical shift of plan was not easy to perform. A series of planning conferences by topflight commanders was held at the newly constructed headquarters on the banks of Lake Sentani, a beautiful body of water in the Cyclops Mountains above Hollandia, New Guinea. Admiral Kinkaid, General Krueger and important members of Southwest Pacific staff were already there, on 15 September. General MacArthur returned in *Nashville* to Hollandia on the 17th. Rear Admiral Barbey arrived about the same time. "Ping" Wilkinson, after spending five days directing the Palaus landings, arrived Hollandia 20 September, bringing Commodore Paulus P. Powell and several members of his planning staff. Rear Admiral "Mick" Carney, Admiral Halsey's chief of staff, flew in for a three-day conference to coördinate Third Fleet operations with those of the Seventh Fleet.

Wilkinson's transports lifting XXIV Corps were already combat-loaded for Yap, where beach conditions were very different from those at Leyte; but it was too late to redistribute the troops and change types of landing craft. *Mount Olympus*, the III 'Phib flagship, sailed to Manus, where Wilkinson's task force waited until it was time to leave for Leyte. The problem of troop-lift for Krueger's Sixth Army was solved by using the transports already available to VII 'Phib, together with those that took the 1st Marine and 81st Divisions to Peleliu, Angaur and Ulithi. There was just enough time to get these vessels back to Hollandia and replenish.

In short, the concept of the Leyte operation (code name KING II) [12] was bold, original and far-reaching. It employed practically all American military forces that were not engaged in fight-

[12] Code names for operations were much less used in the Pacific than in the European theater, where TORCH, OVERLORD, HUSKY, etc. are as well known as the actual objectives. KING II is largely forgotten in favor of the simple "Leyte operation."

ing Germany, or in garrison duty in outposts like the Aleutian and Marshall Islands. No Australian troops were used; they relieved United States troops in rear areas and prepared for operations in the Netherlands East Indies; but several vessels of the Royal Australian Navy took part, and one of the Royal Navy: H.M.S. *Ariadne*.

The OCTAGON Conference at Quebec dissolved 16 September without making any further decisions about Pacific strategy. Discussion of the Luzon *vs* Formosa question continued in the J.C.S. and among the top commanders concerned.[13]

At a conference in San Francisco during the last week of September, General Millard F. Harmon, commanding Army Air Forces in Central Pacific, and General Simon Bolivar Buckner, commanding Tenth Army, presented strong arguments against attempting to capture Formosa, or even a part of it. Admiral Nimitz was convinced, as Admiral Spruance had been several months earlier, that Formosa would not be worth the probable cost in time and casualties. The line of reasoning went somewhat as follows: If the Leyte objective was attained without too much delay, the III and VII Amphibious Forces would be capable of putting over a second major landing before the end of 1944. Formosa would require an assault force of at least nine divisions, which, in view of the Army's commitments in Europe, could not even be collected before the middle of 1945. And Okinawa lay too deep in enemy territory to be assaulted before Japanese air strength had been further reduced. Consequently, an assault on Luzon would be the most profitable employment for the two amphibious forces after Leyte. And, as Formosa would be too strong for a direct attack, even in mid-1945, the best solution early in the new year would be (1) to take Iwo Jima, as a rung in the "ladder up the Bonins" to Japan, and (2) to take Okinawa, as a suitable base from which to launch the final invasions of the Japanese home islands.

Admiral Nimitz presented this estimate of the situation to the

[13] The OCTAGON Conference also made the important decision that a task force of the Royal Navy would serve in the Pacific after the defeat of Germany; this will be discussed in Volume XIV.

Joint Chiefs of Staff, which on 3 October 1944 issued a directive to him and to General MacArthur as follows: –

> General MacArthur will liberate Luzon, starting 20 December, and establish bases there to support later operations. Admiral Nimitz will provide fleet cover and support, occupy one or more positions in the Bonin-Volcano Island group 20 January 1945, and invade the Ryukyus, target date 1 March 1945.

The General had finally won his point. Leyte and then Luzon it was to be; liberation of the Philippines had priority. Landings on the China coast were ruled out – partly by the strength of the guardian island, Formosa, partly because of the weakness of the Chinese Nationalist forces, and the enmity between Chiang Kai-shek and General Stilwell. The two rival roads to Tokyo were already converging on Leyte, where they formed the superhighway which led to the surrender of Japan less than eleven months after the OCTAGON Conference, and a little more than three months after the defeat of Germany.

CHAPTER II

Morotai[1]

September–November 1944

1. *The Island and the Landings, 15 September*

THE OCCUPATION of Morotai Island off Halmahera, whether we regard it as the last of the New Guinea campaign or the first in that of the Philippines, deserves attention before we go on to the Palaus.

General MacArthur pitched on Morotai as a result of a conference between his planners and those of Admiral Nimitz at Pearl Harbor in July 1944. He had earlier intended to make Mindanao in two hops from the Vogelkop of New Guinea, first to Halmahera and then to Sarangani Bay. But not enough amphibious shipping would be available, owing to the drain of Operation OVERLORD in Europe,[2] nor could Admiral Nimitz spare Fast Carrier Forces to cover the 350-mile jump from Halmahera to Mindanao. So the plan was changed to provide an intermediate stop at Salebaboe Island in the Talauds and the first target was changed from Halmahera to Morotai on the principle of "hitting 'em where they ain't." [3]

Halmahera, generally called Jilolo before the twentieth century, straddles the Equator at longitude 128° E. It is the largest of the Molucca or Spice Islands, discovered by the Portuguese in 1512

[1] Commander Alamo Force (Lt. Gen. Walter Krueger) "Report of Morotai Operation"; CTF 77 (Rear Adm. D. E. Barbey) Action Report 8 Nov. 1944. Office of Chief Engineer Army Forces Pacific *Engineers of the Southwest Pacific* I, VI (Washington 1947) and "Amphibious Engineers Operations" IV, W. F. Heavy *Down Ramp* (1947).

[2] See Volume XI 56 for the deployment of U.S. and British landing and beaching craft at this period.

[3] See Volume VI 226–7.

and visited by Sebastian del Cano, ranking survivor of the Magellan expedition, in 1521. Two tiny islands, Ternate and Tidore, off the western coast of Halmahera, were centers of a fabulously wealthy spice trade under the Portuguese. Under Dutch rule for three centuries, Halmahera was a good example of "salutary neglect," Ed-

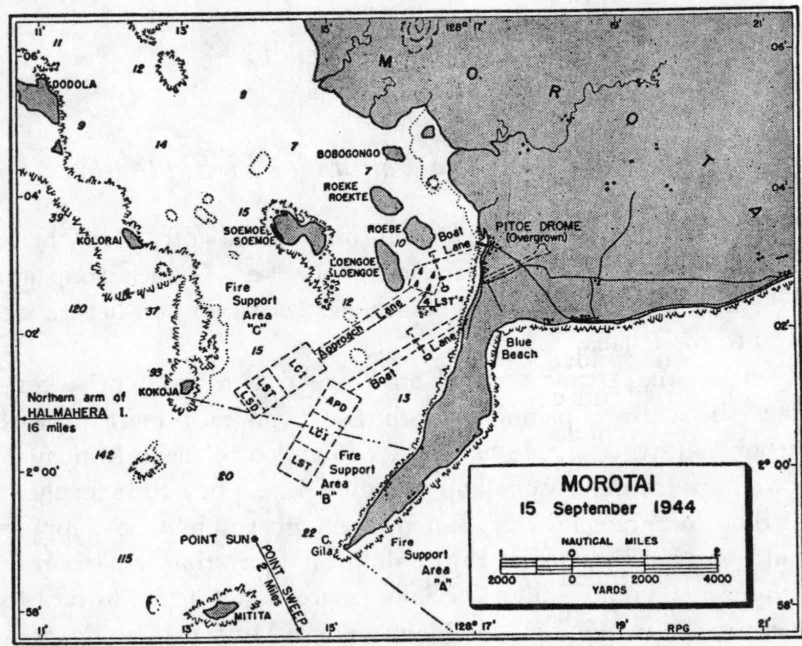

mund Burke's prescription for an inoffensive colonial policy. Before 1942 this was a tranquil, half-forgotten backwater of the Pacific. The Japanese, however, regarded Halmahera as a link between the Philippines, the Celebes and New Guinea in their "Greater East Asia Co-Prosperity Sphere." They occupied the island in 1942, by 1944 had built or were building eight or nine airfields, and had assembled a garrison of some 37,000 troops. Obviously the capture of an island so strongly held, with excellent natural defenses, would not be worth the cost. That is why Morotai was substituted.

Morotai or "Morty," lying ten miles from Cape Djodjefa, the northern promontory of Halmahera, is 44 miles long on a north-south axis and 25 miles wide. A mountainous, jungle-covered island, its one military attraction is a tiny coastal plain on Gila Peninsula, the southernmost point. There, near a village called Pitoe, the Japanese had begun work on an airstrip. They never finished it, probably finding the terrain too boggy, and not more than 500 troops were left on the island. But at Galela and Waisile on Kau Bay, Halmahera, the one 30 and the other 50 miles from Pitoe, the enemy had strong garrisons and enough barges to be a menace to Morotai if they could get there. About 28,000 combat troops under Major General Charles P. Hall of XI Corps were assigned to assault Morotai, together with 12,200 service troops to develop it as an airdrome. The nucleus of this force was the 31st Infantry Division (Major General John C. Persons) which had lately been engaged in mopping up the Wakde-Sarmi sector of New Guinea. Rear Admiral Daniel E. Barbey,[4] commanding VII 'Phib, handled the naval part. Joint planners decided to make the landings on beaches designated Red and White, on each side of the Pitoe airstrip. Rear Admiral William M. Fechteler[5] commanded the Red attack group and Barbey took on the White group. The approaches to these beaches were foul and intricate, but the anchorage was good and the roadstead protected. Rear Admiral R. S. ("Count") Berkey,[6] in *Phoenix*, commanded the support group, consisting of three U.S. light cruisers, two Australian heavies (commanded by Commodore John A. Collins RAN), eight U.S. and two Australian destroyers.

[4] Brief biography in Volume VI 131*n* with portrait.

[5] Brief biography in Volume VIII 64*n* and portrait at p. 48. He was C.N.O. during the Korean War and to Aug. 1953 when appointed C. in C. Allied Forces Southern Europe; retired July 1956.

[6] Russell S. Berkey, b. Indiana 1893, Annapolis '16. Served in *New York* during World War I; flag sec. to Com. Destroyer Force Atlantic Fleet 1920–24; assistant commandant of midshipmen, Naval Academy; flag lieut. to Combatdiv 4, 1923–25; gunnery officer *Concord* 1926–27; flag sec. C. in C. U.S. Fleet 1927–32; C.O. *Panay* and *Smith Thompson* 1933–36; port director N.O.B. Norfolk 1936–38; senior course Naval War College; Com Mobile Target Div. 1, 1939–40; C.O. *Lassen* 1941; Ass't. Com. N.O.B. Iceland 1942; C.O. *Santa Fe* 1943 in Aleutians and Gilberts opns.; Comcrudiv 50 and Rear Admiral 1943; Com Cruisers Seventh Fleet 1943 and through Philippines and Borneo campaigns. After the war served in office of C.N.O.; commanded New York Naval Base, Naval Forces Far East and Seventh Task Fleet 1948–49, with rank of Vice Admiral. Chief of Information Navy Dept. and retired 1950. See also Volume VIII, index.

Air support furnished by three separate commands was more than ample. Six escort carriers, under Rear Admiral Thomas L. Sprague, were to rendezvous with Admiral Barbey's Attack Force two days before the landing to provide antisubmarine and combat air patrol; V Army Air Force, based at Biak and Noemfoor, was alerted to keep enemy airfields in Halmahera pounded down and patrol the air between Geelvink Bay, New Guinea, and Morotai; and Vice Admiral John S. McCain's fast carrier task group was contributed by Admiral Nimitz to operate 50 miles north of Morotai on D-day and the next, to strike enemy airfields on the Celebes. Although this setup appears complicated, it was very well coördinated. One of the destroyers had a fighter-director team on board, and Commander Support Aircraft was with Admiral Barbey in flagship *Wasatch* until General Hall established his command post ashore.

The chief difficulty, from the Navy's point of view, was the intricate landing and transportation schedule necessary to assemble, lift and land 19,960 troops on D-day, to be followed by as many more in the next 16 days. This was not unprecedented – more had been landed at Hollandia – but most of the troops were spread all along New Guinea from Wakde to Finschhafen.

Admiral Barbey led off with Beach White group from Aitape on 10 September, and off shore joined Fechteler's Beach Red group, which sortied from Wakde. The troop lift comprised the amphibious command ship, 2 Australian attack transports, 5 APD, 45 LST, 24 LCI, 20 LCT and 1 LSD. They were screened and covered by 24 destroyers, 4 frigates, 11 LCI gun or rocket craft, 6 PC, 2 tugs and 4 coastal minesweepers.

The attack force took the shortest route to its objective: about 1034 miles from Hollandia and 854 from Biak, well within sight of enemy-held points on New Guinea. The cruisers, destroyers and escort carriers joined off the Vogelkop on 13 September. Apparently they reached Morotai undetected by the enemy – an indication of his aërial weakness in the Moluccas and Celebes.

D-day, September 15, broke fair with a partial overcast. At 0510 Admiral Berkey's cruisers, including *Nashville* with General Mac-

Arthur embarked, pulled out to bombard the Japanese strongpoint on Galela, across the Strait. An hour's shooting provoked no reply. The cruisers then recrossed the Strait to Cape Gila, where Admiral Barbey and General Hall boarded *Nashville* to report to General MacArthur. Thereafter the cruisers steamed about southward of Morotai, ready to provide gunfire support, which was never required.

The main convoy halted at 0620, five miles short of the gap between Cape Gila and Mitita Island, through which it had to pass. LSTs towing LCTs cast off towlines and all vessels, rolling gently in a long ground swell, formed up in single column, led by the small minesweepers. No mines were found. The "parade" started at 0630 and continued for two hours, while the Australian Navy contingent and two destroyers bombarded landing beaches and other points on the Gila Peninsula, from the eastward. There was momentary unpleasantness when destroyer *Fletcher*, then 300 to 400 yards off the west side of the peninsula, reported that Australian shell fragments were falling near her. This impression was caused by shells detonating in the tops of heavy tropical hardwood trees close to the shore.[7]

The landings were unopposed. On Beach Red the leading assault waves, coming ashore in LVTs (amphtracs) which had been brought up in LSTs, landed exactly on H-hour, 0830. Three more LVT waves followed. Then came two waves of LCI. The troops carried by these "Elsie Items" had to wade ashore in water armpit-deep over a very uneven bottom. Aërial photographs, the only information on these out-of-the-way beaches, had revealed neither the gradient nor the character of the bottom, which turned out to be a very sticky mud interspersed with coral heads. Almost three-quarters of the vehicles launched from LCTs drowned out or bogged down and had to be towed ashore by bulldozers which were landed later over a pontoon causeway. Captain Richard M. Scruggs, the LST flotilla commander, did not get his ships un-

[7] CTG 77.2 (Rear Adm. Berkey), endorsement to Commo. John Collins RAN Action Report of 18 Sept. 1944.

loaded until next day, when two LCTs were coupled together and filled with sandbags to form a solid causeway.

At Admiral Barbey's Beach White conditions were similar. The assault waves landed from craft carried on the davits of five destroyer-transports. Troops had to wade ashore through water shoulder-high. The LCM and LCT grounded as much as 80 yards off shore; an LST could get no nearer the beach than 100 yards. But they found a better beach some 1500 yards southerly, and by the end of D-day, 6000 troops and 7200 tons of supplies and equipment were ashore there. Another good beaching point was found across the Gila Peninsula, where, on Blue Beach, 12 LST unloaded 500 troops each, and many vehicles, on 16 September.

Shortly after noon D-day General Persons established his command post ashore, without having heard a shot fired; so far only two Japanese had been found on the island. A pathetically feeble banzai attack the first night ashore was promptly liquidated. Shore operations resolved themselves into minor patrol actions against small parties of Japanese, at a cost of 31 killed or missing and 85 wounded. By 4 October the total number of enemy killed and captured was 117. An estimated 200 had been liquidated by the PT boats when trying to escape to Halmahera by barge, and the rest of the garrison, less than 200 in number, took to the mountains. There they were let be; no attempt was made by the Army to overrun the entire island. A perimeter two and a half by three and a half miles was sufficient for protection of the airdrome. In addition radar search warning stations were established on the coast and outlying islands. The Japanese put on a few two-plane raids from Halmahera which accomplished nothing.

Liberty ships began to arrive on 16 September carrying the equipment needed to build the air base. Before the end of the month 73 LST loads and 19 Liberty ship loads were landed there. Docks were constructed to help the unloading and the construction went rapidly forward by United States Army Engineers and two airfield construction squadrons of the Royal Australian Air Force.

Here occurred the first disappointment in the operation. It had been hoped that planes of the V A.A.F. could be based on the reactivated Japanese strip, but that proved to be hopelessly boggy and heavy rains delayed the construction of a new one near Wawama. Not until 4 October could the Army fighters move in, and the escort carriers, which had been closing the gap between the expected and the real, move out. Medium bombers began operating from Wawama against Mindanao shortly after; and on 19 October (A minus 1 day for Leyte) Navy Fairwing 17 arrived with Venturas and Liberators.

Morotai played an important rôle in the great operation coming up, because it was the only Allied air base from which short-range fighters and light or medium bombers could be staged up to Leyte, and the only base from which long-range aircraft could reconnoiter north and west of Leyte. The V A.A.F. used it as a springboard, fleeting up 162 aircraft ready to go in as soon as the airstrip was ready. By A-day, 20 October, the Morotai fields were so crowded with aircraft poised for transfer to Leyte that there was no room for land-based Liberators. This want was well filled by 20 Navy Catalinas based on tenders *Tangier*, *Orca* and *San Pablo* in the roadstead.[8]

In November, when the V A.A.F. moved up to Leyte, it was relieved here by the XIII A.A.F. The airfield facilities were not finished until the latter part of that month. By that time the center of our war effort had moved well north, but the planes based on Morotai were usefully employed in bombing Mindanao, the Visayas and the Netherlands East Indies. And the Australian I Army Corps used Morotai to mount operations for the invasion of Borneo, beginning in April 1945.[9]

2. *Rescue, Retaliation and Patrol*

Fairly early in the occupation there took place near Morotai a notable air-sea rescue, and a submarine attack which ended tragically.

[8] *War College Analysis* I 40. [9] *Engineers in Southwest Pacific* I 197.

Ensign Harold A. Thompson USNR, flying a Hellcat from escort carrier *Santee*, was making a strafing run on Japanese barges at Waisile in Kau Bay, Halmahera, on 16 September, when he was shot down by antiaircraft fire. Thompson, wounded in the left hand, splashed about 300 yards off shore. A PBY "Dumbo" rescue plane [10] dropped a life raft, which he boarded and in which he drifted to a pier that offered him some protection from enemy fire, while his fellow pilots kept the Japanese gun positions busy by strafing. In so doing two Hellcats were shot down, one pilot was lost and a second rescued by Dumbo. Thompson, in the meantime, paddled with his one good hand to a Japanese barge anchored in the bay and moored his raft to its chain cable.

Captain Bowling was summoned on board *Wasatch* by Admiral Barbey to work out an emergency air-sea rescue with him and with Admiral Sprague. In accordance with their plan, Lieutenant Arthur M. Preston USNR in *PT-489*, accompanied by *PT-363*, by fighter cover and smoke-equipped Avengers from *Sangamon* and the other escort carriers, left the Morotai roadstead for Waisile Bay. At the narrows by Lolabata Point, coastal gunfire was so heavy that the PTs retired until their attendant planes could work over the coastal batteries. They tried again at 1600 to run through, and succeeded by dint of a smoker plane which, honoring a radio request from Lieutenant Preston, dropped a complete smoke container between the PTs and the nearest battery, while the shots from other Japanese guns were dodged by evasive maneuvers at flank speed. By 1730 the two boats had reached Ensign Thompson, whose position had been marked by a smoke pot. He was picked up by *PT-363* (Lieutenant Alfred Tatro USNR), just in time, as the Japanese on the barge to which he had tied up were coming to life and were about to weigh anchor. *PT-489* in the meantime hovered about and the planes hung another smoke curtain between them and the shore, which fairly bristled with enemy guns. Boats

[10] For the birth and early exploits of "Dumbo" see Volume V p. 332. For this incident, CTF 77 (Rear Adm. T. L. Sprague) and *Santee* Action Reports, MTBron 33 War Diary for Sept. 1944, oral information from Cdr. Stanley E. Hindman and other participants; track chart in *Sangamon* Report of 30 Sept. 1944.

and planes then retired full speed from the bay, pursued by gunfire, but none were hit. More than 50 aircraft were involved in the rescue, which "sure was a wonderful show to watch," remarked Ensign Thompson, object of all this effort, when he was back on board *Santee*.

On 3 October 1944, the day before the escort carriers were to depart for another assignment, they were attacked by Japanese submarine *RO–41*, one of five which were sent south to Morotai and the Palaus in September. A task unit commanded by Rear Admiral Clifton A. F. Sprague, composed of escort carriers *Fanshaw Bay* and *Midway* [11] and four destroyer escorts, was maneuvering some 38 miles east of the northern part of Morotai. Immediately after the forenoon watch destroyer escort *Shelton* (Lieutenant Commander Lewis G. Salomon USNR) of the screen was torpedoed aft. The explosion killed 2 officers and 11 men and wounded 22. *Richard M. Rowell* (Lieutenant Commander Harry A. Barnard) drove off the submarine with a few depth charges before it could do further damage and took off the crew of the sinking *Shelton*, which later capsized under tow.

It happened, most unfortunately, that U.S.S. *Seawolf*, a seasoned veteran of the Pacific submarine fleet, was steaming north, about 20 miles distant, at the time of this Japanese attack. Commanded by Lieutenant Commander A. L. Bontier, she was carrying passengers and stores to the Filipino guerrillas on Samar. A "submarine safety lane" had been set up north of Morotai, and Commander Seventh Fleet, informed of its existence and limits, had passed the word to Admiral Sprague, but the plane pilots were not properly briefed. *Seawolf* was never heard from after exchanging recognition signals with *Narwhal* in the safety zone at 0756 October 3. A few miles away, and three and a half hours later, an Avenger from escort carrier *Midway* sighted a submarine in the safety zone and, assuming it to be the one that torpedoed *Shelton*, dropped two bombs. *Rowell*, on receiving the aviator's report, hastened to the position indicated by a dye-marker, made sound contact on a submarine at

[11] Renamed *St. Lo*.

1310, and delivered a series of attacks. The C.O. knew that he was in the submarine safety zone, but he had not been informed of the 0756 exchange of signals; and as the latest daily submarine position report in his possession mentioned no friendly boat within 70 miles, he assumed that he was attacking a Japanese submarine. After *Rowell's* second attack *Seawolf*, for it is now certain that it was she, attempted to send a recognition signal by her sound gear. Unfortunately "the stuttering transmission bore no resemblance to the proper recognition signal," and the skipper of *Rowell* considered it an attempt to jam his own sonar. He persisted in his attacks, and after the sixth, *Seawolf* sank with all hands.[12]

The tragic fate of *Seawolf* caused Seventh Fleet to order a prompt dissemination of friendly submarine position reports. After that no accident of this kind occurred.

Morotai made a perfect motor torpedo boat base. Captain S. S. Bowling, commanding Seventh Fleet PTs, arrived 16 September in tender *Oyster Bay*, together with tender *Mobjack* and boats of Squadrons 9, 10, 18 and 33. A detachment of the 116th Seabees built them an advanced base on an islet off Beach Red. As Japanese barge activity on Halmahera declined, the tenders and the boats were gradually withdrawn, until, in February 1945, only Squadrons 18 and 11 (which had relieved 10) were left.

Up to the end of the war these PTs made nightly patrols which protected Morotai from raids by the Japanese garrisons on Halmahera and Eastern Celebes. Two boats were lost in October by grounding on reefs. On 25 November *PT-363* (Lieutenant Frank K. Mitchell USNR), when patrolling in company with *PT-362*, was holed by machine-gun fire from the shore and had to be abandoned, after Lieutenant Mitchell had been mortally wounded; Lieutenant (jg) William K. Paynter USNR of *PT-362* made a gallant rescue of the survivors.

In patrolling, the boats worked in concert with Army observation planes, which spotted targets for them up the rivers and

[12] Roscoe *Submarine Operations* pp. 417-18; Admiral Lockwood *Sink 'Em All* pp. 223-4. *RO-41* returned safely to Japan, but was sunk by U.S.S. *Hudson* 4 Apr. 1945.

dropped smoke bombs as indication. They also carried Australian, Dutch and native scouts to the Talaud and other islands and picked them up when their missions were accomplished. Other activities were "barnstorming tours" of the west coast of Halmahera and adjacent islands to destroy Japanese storehouses at Tidore, Batjan, Moti and elsewhere.

But the PT payoff came in response to a distress signal from the Sultan of Ternate, whose ancestors had been lords of the spice trade. He was being badly used by the Japanese, and "wanted out." And out he came, in two PTs, complete with court and harem. This was in May of 1945; the Sultan had only a short wait before returning to "his own, his native land."

CHAPTER III

The Palaus and Ulithi[1]

September–November 1944

1. *Preliminaries*

THE PALAU ISLANDS are generally considered the westernmost of the Caroline groups, though far distant from the rest. Babelthuap, largest of the Palaus, lies 240 miles west of Yap and 470 miles east of Mindanao. Discovered by Villalobos in 1543, these islands were annexed though never developed by Spain. At the breakup of Spain's Pacific empire in 1899 they were sold to Germany, and in 1919 taken over by Japan as spoils of World War I.

The Palaus were even less known in the Western World than the Moluccas. There was a momentary interest in them in 1783 when the East India Company's ship *Antelope*, Captain Wilson, was wrecked on Koror, where he was well received by the local potentate, for whose canoe navy he furnished musketry fire support. This so overawed the King of Peleliu that he surrendered that highly defensible island without a fight. The King of Koror then sent his son, Prince Lee Boo, with Captain Wilson to England to be educated; the lad soon died from the rigors of the English

[1] Com. Third Fleet Report on Seizure of Southern Palaus 12 Nov.; Action Reports of CTF 31 (Vice Adm. Wilkinson) 11 Nov.; CTF 32 (Rear Adm. Fort) 16 Oct.; CTG 32.2 (Rear Adm. Oldendorf) 26 Sept.; CTG 32.3 (Rear Adm. Blandy) 1 Oct. 1944. Report of Maj. Gen. Julian C. Smith USMC 12 Oct. 1944. Message file and letters of Vice Adm. Wilkinson; George McMillan *The Old Breed, A History of the 1st Marine Division* (1949) and Maj. F. O. Hough USMC *The Assault on Peleliu* (1950) in the Marine Corps series. The name Palau is the German equivalent of the Spanish *Islas Palaos*, which is derived from the native name for the group.

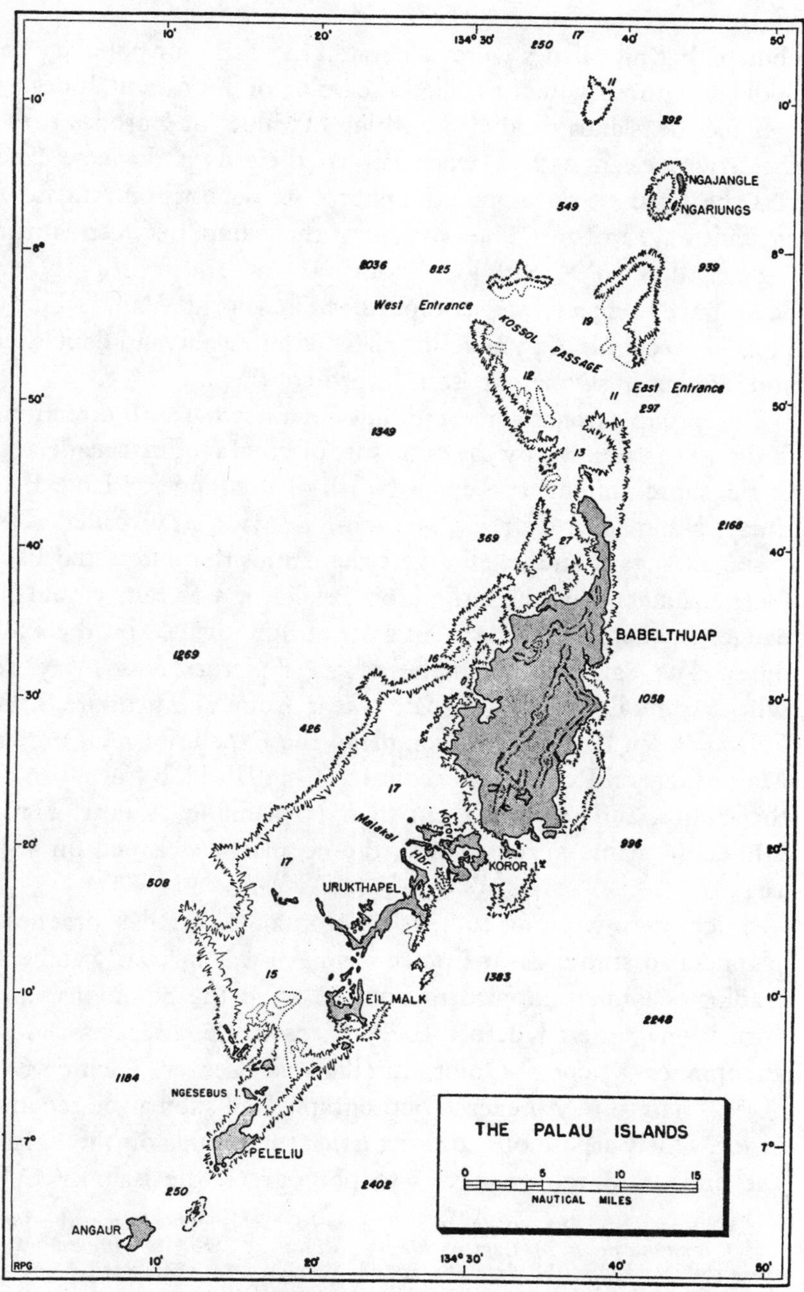

THE PALAU ISLANDS
NAUTICAL MILES
0
5
10
15
BABELTHUAP
KOROR
URUKTHAPEL
EIL MALK
NGESEBUS I.
PELELIU
ANGAUR
NGAJANGLE
NGARIUNGS
West Entrance
East Entrance
KOSSOL PASSAGE
Malakal Hbr.
Koror
RPG
134° 30'
10'
20'
40'
50'
8°
7°

climate, but his virtues were celebrated in a series of popular chapbooks like those which extolled the valor of John Paul Jones.[2]

Since the islands produced nothing of value for European trade, the Micronesian natives were left to their own devices, except that the Japanese developed the phosphate deposits on Angaur for agricultural fertilizer. The position of the group, between latitudes 6°50′ and 8°10′N and longitudes 133°08′ and 134°45′E, suddenly gave them a strategic importance in World War II. This the Japanese recognized by building airfields on Peleliu and Babelthuap, and moving in strong garrisons to protect them.

The group extends some 110 miles in a north–south direction. It is almost surrounded by the same sort of coral reef that made access to the shore difficult at Saipan. North of the biggest island, Babelthuap, hemmed in by reefs, is a ten-mile wide strait called Kossol Passage. Angaur and Peleliu were the islands that interested Pacific Fleet planners. For the airfield on Peleliu, it was felt, would be a danger in enemy hands, yet an asset in our advance on the Philippines. The Palaus were in the strategic picture from May 1944 when Admiral Nimitz designated Rear Admiral Theodore S. Wilkinson (Com III 'Phib) to command the Expeditionary Force and Major General Roy S. Geiger USMC (Com III 'Phib Corps) to head the troops, and ordered them to start planning at Pearl Harbor. Under the name STALEMATE II, the op plan was issued on 7 July 1944.

Since there were no tourists' photographs of Palau beaches for planners to study, as in France – no Australian coastwatchers or trading-schooner skippers to consult, as in the Solomons; no information gathered before the war, as in the Marianas and the Philippines – Jicpoa (Joint Intelligence Center Pacific Ocean Areas) had to rely on aërial photographs and submarine reconnaissance. One purpose of the fast carrier force raids on the Palaus at the end of March 1944 was to photograph the islands.[3] Special

[2] George Keate *An Account of the Pelew Islands*, composed from the *Journals and Communications of Captain Henry Wilson . . . who in August 1783 was there shipwrecked in the Antelope*, 4th ed., London 1789; chap. xxvii is on "Anecdotes of Lee Boo."

[3] See Volume VIII pp. 29–33.

photographic missions were flown in July and August. But the 1:20,000-scale maps compiled from those aërial photos were defective, owing to cloud cover, heavy jungle growth and clever Japanese camouflage which concealed the important features of Peleliu and gave the general impression that this rugged island was low and flat.[4]

This was not corrected by the reconnaissance of Peleliu and Angaur by eleven UDT "frogmen" under Lieutenant C. E. Kirkpatrick, because they were interested only in the beaches. Departing Midway Island 15 July in submarine *Burrfish*, Lieutenant Commander W. B. Perkins, this team arrived off Peleliu on the 27th and cruised about the Palaus, taking photographs for over two weeks. On the night of 13 August, in the dark of the moon, Kirkpatrick's party went ashore in two rubber boats, landed on one of the beaches subsequently used in the assault, and observed its characteristics. After delivering data and photographs to submarine *Balao* for quick delivery at Pearl Harbor, *Burrfish* reconnoitered Yap; four men of the UDT who went ashore there never returned.[5]

Admiral Halsey, as we have seen, proposed on 13 September to bypass the Palaus, but Admiral Nimitz did not accept this suggestion. He felt that Peleliu and Kossol Passage were needed as staging points for Leyte, and Wilkinson's expedition was already at sea and within two days of the objective when Halsey's proposition was put to him. From hindsight it seems probable that STALEMATE II should have been countermanded. It was useful, but hardly worth the expenditure of 1950 American lives.

D-day for Peleliu, as for Morotai, was 15 September. The plan, in general, was a pre-assault naval bombardment on the 13th and 14th, minesweeping of the channel between Peleliu and Angaur, and in the entrance to Kossol Passage (which we liberally mined in March), and clearing approaches by underwater demolition

[4] Marine Corps Monograph *Peleliu* p. 15; information from Col. Spencer S. Berger USMC.

[5] Information from Lt.(jg) M. R. Massie, second officer of the UDT group, in Sept. 1944.

teams. On D-day the veteran 1st Marine Division (Major General Rupertus), mounted at its so-called rest area in the Russell Islands, was to land in three regimental combat teams abreast in LVTs, on five beaches opposite the Japanese airfield. The 81st Division U.S. Army (Major General Mueller), known as the "Wildcats" and originally a National Guard outfit from the Carolinas and Georgia, was held in floating reserve under command of Rear Admiral W. H. P. Blandy.

Peleliu was honored by the participation of a large number of flag and general officers. Vice Admiral Wilkinson and Major Generals Julian Smith and Rupertus were on board Rear Admiral Fort's amphibious command ship *Mount McKinley*. General Geiger was on board *Mount Olympus*, to which Wilkinson shifted at Eniwetok. Rear Admiral Blandy and General Mueller were in *Fremont*. Rear Admiral Jesse B. Oldendorf in *Louisville* commanded a formidable fire support group of five battleships, five heavy cruisers, three light cruisers and fourteen destroyers; and they had two more flag officers, Rear Admirals Ainsworth and Kingman, embarked. Rear Admiral Ralph Ofstie commanded between seven and eleven escort carriers to provide combat air and antisubmarine patrol, and Rear Admiral William D. Sample had a carrier division under him. Admiral Halsey dropped in on Peleliu 17 September; in the entire chain of command, only Admiral Nimitz stayed away.

Starting at 0530 September 12, when they arrived at Peleliu, the big ships steamed back and forth, bombarding pre-selected targets and areas. After two hours they checked fire, and escort carrier aircraft took over for the next two hours. This pattern was maintained for three days of preliminary bombardment. At 1050 the APDs closed the reef and landed two UDT units, veterans of Saipan and Guam, in rubber boats, supporting them with 40-mm fire on beach defenses. Aircraft helped to divert the attention of the Japanese from the UDTs, who completed their mission.

Next day the "frogmen" worked on the reef off the landing beaches, clearing out boulders, coral heads and mined wooden obstacles, and chipping away at the coral to make tracks over the reef for LVTs and berths for LSTs to beach.

One unit of minesweepers peeled off to sweep Kossol Passage, and others swept around Peleliu and Angaur. Japanese mines were simple compared with those used by the Germans off Normandy, but one of them sank minecraft *Perry* on the 13th, with the loss of seven men. Destroyer *Wadleigh* was damaged and *YMS-19* sunk by mines in Kossol Passage on 16 and 19 September.

Naval bombardment blew off most of the scrubby jungle growth on the ridge behind the airstrip and beaches, revealing numerous caves; but few gave them a thought. Admiral Oldendorf was so pleased with the results of his three-day bombardment that on the evening of 14 September, over voice radio to Admiral Fort, he made a very unfortunate remark: "We have run out of targets." And General Rupertus rashly predicted to news correspondents that Peleliu would be secured with four days.

The Japanese defenders had different notions. The Army Section of Imperial General Headquarters had been giving special attention to defense against amphibious assault. The old tactics of meeting the enemy on the beach had failed, everywhere. But at Biak the garrison, probably acting on an extempore hunch by its commander, had holed up, which greatly prolonged resistance in that island; [6] and very likely this gave the top brains at Tokyo an idea. At any rate, in July 1944 they worked out a new set of tactics to meet amphibious assaults: (1) preparation of a main line of resistance at a sufficient distance from the beach to escape naval bombardment; (2) organizing defensive positions deep in the rear; (3) placing substantial forces in reserve to mount counterattacks at opportune moments; (4) delaying the enemy only temporarily at the beach.[7]

About 5000 Japanese naval troops had been in the Palaus since early in the war. In May 1944 these were reinforced by the 14th Infantry Division, Lieutenant General Sadae Inoue, whose head-

[6] See Volume VIII chap. viii.

[7] MacArthur *Historical Report* II p. 297.

quarters were at Koror on Babelthuap. He took no part in the fight for Peleliu, which was sustained by the 2nd Infantry Regiment, Colonel Kunio Nakagawa, numbering 5300 fighting men and about as many more supply and construction troops. On 3 September General Inoue was warned that the Yanks were coming, but he did not alert his command until the 11th. Nakagawa had the honor of being the first to use these new tactics, which were to be applied spectacularly by General Kuribayashi at Iwo Jima. Although beach obstacles were laid out and pillboxes constructed to command the beaches with machine-gun fire, the emphasis was placed on interior lines of defense. The natural caves in the jagged limestone ridges north of the airfield were developed into an interconnected series of underground strongpoints which were so strongly protected by coral sand and concrete as to be almost impervious to aërial bombing or naval bombardment. One shudders to think what would have happened if Hitler had built anything like this along his Atlantic Wall three months earlier.

There was nothing wrong in American planning for Peleliu except something exceedingly wrong – a woefully inadequate knowledge of the terrain. Admiral Wilkinson, who graduated first in the class of 1909,[8] "had the memory of an encyclopedia," according to his chief of staff, "and his rapidity and capacity for solving difficult problems rivaled that of the newly created calculating machines." [9] But he was unable to plan for a problem that had not even been posed.

2. *D-day at Peleliu, 15 September*

D-day opened fair with light airs ruffling a calm sea, and few clouds. Owing to the fringing coral reef the assault waves were boated in tracked LVTs which were carried to the transport area in LSTs and supported by LVT(A)s, amphtrac tanks. Referring to the chart, Colonel Lewis B. ("Chesty") Puller was to land the

[8] See frontispiece Volume VI for portrait and p. 282 for brief biography.

[9] Rear Adm. Paulus P. Powell USN (Ret.) to the writer, 25 Feb. 1952.

1st Regimental Combat Team on the two northernmost beaches, White 1 and 2, and move into the Umurbrogol Ridge north of the airfield; Colonel Harold D. Harris was to land the 5th RCT on Beaches Orange 1 and 2 and cross the island; and Colonel Her-

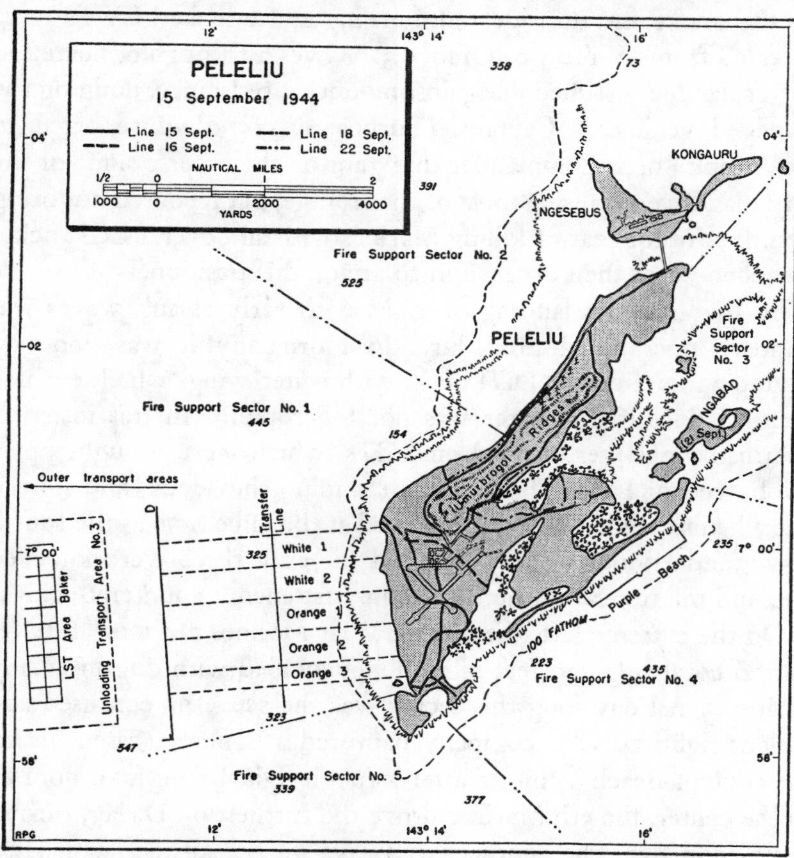

man H. Haneken, landing his 7th RCT in column of battalions on Beach Orange 3, was to clean up on the southern end of the island.

While assault waves were forming up, the bombardment group delivered a final shoot, followed by aërial bombing and strafing and flights of rockets, the pattern that had become standard for Pacific amphibious operations at Saipan. The initial wave, boated in LVT(A)s, hit the beaches at 0832, two minutes late. Gunfire, quickly mounting in volume, greeted them from the high ground, from cleverly concealed concrete casements on the left of Beach White 1, and from a battery which enfiladed the entire line of beaches from a tiny, unnamed island south of Beach Orange 3. As the smoke and dust cleared, burning and wrecked LVTs were revealed from White 1 to Orange 3. Waves 2 through 6, boated in LVTs, landed on schedule against mounting resistance, dodging the damaged vehicles.[10] Captain Thurber of *Honolulu* reported to the Attack Force Commander that guns on the reverse slope of the tiny island were causing most of the trouble, but he dared not bring it under fire for fear of killing Marines with an "over." LCI rocket launchers were then ordered in to attack this position.

By this time the landing of tanks with early assault waves was standard operational procedure. In Normandy it was done by equipping dual-drive (DD) tanks with water-wings which enabled them to float if the water was not too rough.[11] In this instance, Sherman tanks were loaded on LCTs, which were brought up in the bowels of LSDs, three to each landing ship dock, and floated out when needed. These tanks landed at the same time as the fourth wave; and although every one was hit only three were knocked out, and the rest saved the day at the first enemy counterattack.

On the extreme left, the 3rd BLT 1st Marines ran into an unreported coral ridge 30 feet high, honeycombed with dug-in enemy positions. All day long this sector was the scene of confused and violent fighting. One company captured a concrete casement on the edge of Beach White 1 after a tough fight lasting two hours.[12] In the center, the 5th Marines drove the furthest on D-day, throwing a loop over the southern runways on the airfield which extended nearly to the east coast of the island. Units on the right flank made slight progress against a well-coördinated system of defense.

[10] Only 26 LVT were actually destroyed on D-day, but 60 LVT and dukws were either destroyed or damaged during the operation. Hough p. 37.

[11] See Volume XI p. 98.

[12] Vividly described by Capt. George P. Hunt USMC, the company commander, in *Coral Comes High* (1946).

At 1650 the Japanese counterattacked the Marines' salient with 13 light tanks, infantry clinging to them at every possible place. They rolled forward with open throttles, recalling a cavalry charge in a "western." This was just what the Marines wanted. Sherman tanks, pack howitzers, antitank guns, bazookas and even a dive-bomber from overhead opened up on the hapless "tankettes," some of which managed to penetrate the Marines' lines for 150 yards. All were eventually destroyed, and the foot soldiers following them were killed or routed. Nevertheless, by nightfall the anticipated phase line had been only half attained, and the Marines had sustained heavy losses for a D-day assault.[13]

Naval gunfire support, by now an essential feature of amphibious assaults, was very little used on D-day at Peleliu because of the confused nature of the fighting. Cruisers *Louisville*, *Portland* and *Indianapolis* were idle most of the day. But Admiral Ofstie's eleven escort carriers flew 382 sorties on D-day in support of the troops, besides making interdiction strikes on the airfield at Babelthuap and bombing enemy ships in Malakol and Koror harbors. No Japanese aircraft appeared in opposition.

The first eight assault boat waves, dispatched as planned, were followed by twenty waves which waited at the transfer line off the reef, and were sent ashore on call as needed. This prevented the usual confusion and congestion when reinforcements and supplies, sent in on a fixed schedule, pile up at the water's edge. Everything seems to have worked smoothly except the landing from *Leedstown* of the 2nd BLT, 7th Marines, a part of the divisional reserve, whose experiences are thus related in the war diary of the battalion commander, Colonel Spencer S. Berger: –

Late in the afternoon of D-day this BLT was ordered to embark in any boats available and proceed to the transfer line at Orange Beach for transfer to amphibious vehicles for landing. But, upon its arrival at the transfer line, no control officer knew anything about landing this unit. After being batted about from one control vessel to another, the Colonel attempted to report to Commanding

[13] Hough p. 406 states 210 killed, 901 wounded; and these casualties are official.

General 1st Marine Division by radio, but the radio operator on the divisional network announced he was securing, and promptly went off the air. Efforts to raise the Division over other circuits were unsuccessful and it was decided to attempt to get over the reef in the boats they were in, as a message had come from shore that the reserve was urgently needed. An unsuccessful attempt to clear the reef was made at dusk. The boats drew too much water and the enemy called down intensive mortar fire on them as they were withdrawing. Orders were now received to return to *Leedstown.* Many boats had no compasses, and none of the boat officers had received compass courses for a return trip. After a long search, it was ascertained that all transports had retired to an outer area, miles off shore, whither the boats proceeded. When they at last located *Leedstown* around midnight, the captain of the ship at first refused to let the men come on board, saying that his orders were to land them, and that's what they should do. Eventually Colonel Berger was allowed on board and used ship's radio to contact 1st Division and clarify his orders to return on board and land at first light. The rest of the night was spent in trying to round up boats which were unable to find *Leedstown,* and these included more than half the reserve. They spent the whole night at sea and were finally landed around 0800 the following morning.[14]

The night of 15–16 September was a hideous one for the Marines ashore, as small parties of Japanese infiltrated frequently. Cruiser *Honolulu* and three destroyers remained in the fire support area all night to provide illumination with star shell, but all other ships retired out of range of the suspected – but largely nonexistent – coastal batteries.

3. *The Island Conquered, 16 September–25 November*

For the next three days, 16–18 September, the fighting continued briskly, under the direction of General Rupertus, who established

[14] War Diary BLT 2-7, 1st Marine Div.

his command post ashore at 0913 September 16. The Marines expanded and consolidated their positions. Concrete blockhouses untouched by naval gunfire were taken from the rear. One of these, however, was successfully crumbled by the 14-inch guns of *Pennsylvania*[15] on the 17th, and all inside were killed. This blockhouse being eliminated, the Marines rushed to their first foothold on the Umurbrogol Ridge.

An atmosphere of optimism still obtained among the attackers. On 17 September, Admiral Wilkinson believed that the 81st Division, held in reserve, would not be needed, and sent it in to assault Angaur. Unloading, by this time, had become well organized, with cranes on pontoon barges at the reef edge; and by the 21st the Seabees had a pontoon causeway running from deep water to Beach Orange 3, right over the reef. On shore, the Marines made daily gains; and by 22 September – as may be seen by the line on our chart – they had secured a perimeter extending from coast to coast across the narrowest part of the island. But that narrowest part included the sinister Umurbrogol Ridge.

The strategic objectives of the Peleliu operation, it may be said, were completed in the first week, at a cost of 3946 casualties to the 1st Marine Division. In the same period, 24,424 tons of assault cargo had been unloaded.[16] Emergency landings of carrier-based planes on the airfield wrested from the enemy were made as early as the 18th, and on the same day Piper-Cubs and other light spotting planes began using the field. By 1 October the entire Marine Air Group 11 was based there, and within a week a 6000-foot bomber strip was completed.

In the meantime, the shortage of fresh water on the island was becoming critical, not only for the men ashore but for the sailors. Water tanker *Ponaganset* arrived on 23 September and relieved the situation. By that time nine wells had been sunk within our lines, eventually supplying 2000 gallons per day.

[15] Not *Mississippi*, as stated in Hough *Peleliu* pp. 79–80; she was then loading ammunition.

[16] Hough p. 103; Rear Adm. Fort Action Report p. 7.

The Japanese garrison on Peleliu was not reinforced during operation STALEMATE II, except for a mere 500 troops who trickled in by barge from Babelthuap. American air and sea superiority completely cut off the estimated 25,000 troops under General Inoue in the big island, until the general surrender in 1945. Kossol Passage was sufficiently mineswept to be safe by 24 September, and three days later 66 Allied ships and craft were anchored there. Tankers and repair ships serviced a fast carrier group there on the 28th.

On the other hand, there was nothing that air and sea power could do about the Umurbrogol Ridge. The Japanese, with the aid of professional miners, had excavated a system of interlocking caves in the soft coral that was almost impregnable. The area measured only about 500 by 1000 yards, but the enemy labyrinth was too deeply buried for naval bombardment and air bombing to reach. Nor could the ridge be ignored. Several of the cave entrances overlooked the airfield only a few hundred yards away, and the Japanese were well provided with weapons and ammunition as well as food. They had to be rooted out or sealed off. The Marines – and a regiment of the 81st Division which was sent over from Angaur to help on 23 September – had to fight in the sun when the thermometer was 115° F in the shade. After a bloody battle they might win a cave mouth only to find that it was deserted, or capture a summit and smell rice and fish being cooked by three or four layers of Japanese resting comfortably underneath them, ready to sally forth in a counterattack. The biggest cave – which the troops encountered on 27 September – contained more than a thousand Japanese. The only weapon that could cope with them was a new long-range flame-thrower, first mounted on LVTs and later on Sherman tanks, which threw a wicked tongue of fire that could penetrate 40 or 50 feet and even lick around a corner. Attrition by this means gradually reduced the enemy to about 30 soldiers who occupied an inner cave, and, as late as December 1944, killed a number of foolish GIs who wandered in looking for souvenirs.

On 12 October the "assault phase" was announced by III Amphibious Corps to be "at an end," a phrase that occasioned almost as much sarcastic comment as Admiral Oldendorf's "no more targets." [17] Six weeks more of bitter fighting lay ahead. The 1st Marine Division, whose commanding general had predicted the operation would be over in four days, was relieved on 15 October by two fresh regimental combat teams of the 81st Division, U.S. Army. Two days later a Marine battalion, which had been detained a few days as reserve, had to engage a force of Japanese which infiltrated its medical area, and lost a company commander. On the night of 24–25 November, 45 Japanese were killed in the last organized resistance, and the garrison commander, Colonel Nakagawa, with his adviser, Major General Murai, committed suicide.[18] The "Wildcats" then moved in on the ridge from all sides, and at 1100 the colonel of the 323rd Regiment reported to his general that the Peleliu operation was over. For all practical purposes, it was; the only pocket of resistance left was that of the 30 Japanese holed up in an inner cave. Nineteen of them were killed by setting off several explosive charges simultaneously, but it was not until 1 February 1945 that the last five Japanese dug their way out and surrendered.

4. *Angaur, 16 September–23 October* [19]

Angaur, southernmost of the Palaus, lying six miles southwest of Peleliu, was the really profitable part of this island group for the Japanese. Although only two and a half miles long, and flat, it contained valuable deposits of phosphate for agricultural fertilizer.

[17] The date was chosen because it marked the transfer of command over the forces at Peleliu from Rear Adm. Fort and Gen. Rupertus to Vice Adm. J. H. Hoover, Commanding Central Pacific Forward Area, Rear Adm. J. W. Reeves, Commanding Western Carolines sub area, and Brig. Gen. H. D. Campbell USMC, the island commander.

[18] Hough *Peleliu* p. 177 and p. 200 for the curious reasons for Murai's presence there.

[19] Same sources as for footnote 1 to this Chapter, plus CTG 32.2 (Rear Adm. Blandy) Action Report 1 Oct. 1944, and Com. 81st Division (Maj. Gen. P. J. Mueller) Operation Report "Capture of Angaur Island."

This was mined by the strip system, and hauled from the producing areas by narrow-gauge railways (to which our soldiers gave names of American trunk lines) to a plant on the west shore of the island, near a village called Saipan. The American planners for Operation STALEMATE II wanted Angaur for a very different purpose: the establishment of a bomber strip. The 81st Division was given the mission; but as insurance against their being wanted to capture Peleliu, they were left in floating reserve, under the command of Rear Admiral W. H. P. Blandy, instead of being sent in on D-day. On the afternoon of 16 September (Peleliu's D-day plus 1), Admiral Fort and General Geiger, with the approval of Admiral Wilkinson, decided that the Marines could handle the bigger island without assistance, and the "Wildcats" were committed. Later, as we have seen, they had to send one of their regimental combat teams over to Peleliu to help the Marines.

Angaur was defended by only one battalion of Japanese troops, numbering about 1600 men, commanded by Major Goto. They were subjected to a prolonged pounding, five days of it before the landings, by battleships *Pennsylvania* and *Tennessee*, four light cruisers and five destroyers. Both fast carrier and escort carrier aircraft contributed a substantial tonnage of bombs. Minecraft swept the approaches and UDT 10 reconnoitered and cleared obstacles from the selected beaches, Blue on the southeast and Red on the northeast coast of the island.

The landings by the 321st RCT on Beach Blue, at 0830, and of the 322nd RCT on Beach Red, at 0834, were unopposed, and by 0857 all assault waves were ashore. The beaches were good enough – LSTs could beach dry-ramp – but behind the beaches the troops ran into a thick, matted rain-forest jungle so dense as to constitute an impenetrable barrier. Beach congestion became so bad that unloading from the transports had to be held up. And there were few calls for naval gunfire.

This was first combat experience for the "Wildcats" and, like other green troops, they passed an unhappy first night in the jungle, shooting at shadows. Toward dawn the shadows materialized as counterattacks which caused one regiment to retire about 50 yards. With the help of escort carrier planes, and with gunfire from an "Elsie Item" gunboat, all counterattacks were repulsed. From that point on, the Japanese were kept off balance and at 1034 September 20 General Mueller reported organized re-

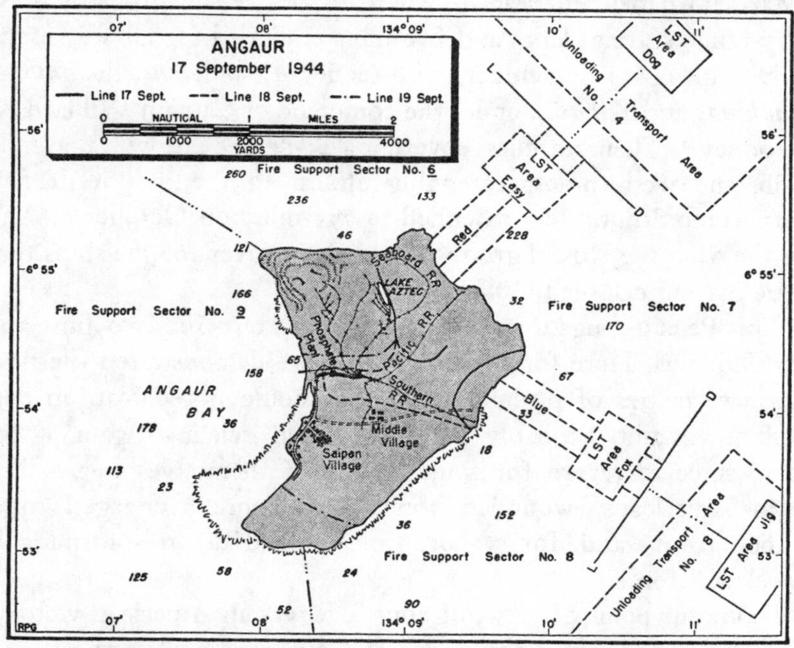

sistance to be at an end and the island secured. He could well afford to send his 321st RCT to Peleliu on the 23rd.

Actually, the greater number of Major Goto's troops had retreated to Ramuldo Hill on the northwest corner of the island, where they produced a miniature edition of the Umurbrogol caves on Peleliu. The job of rooting them out was entrusted to RCT 322, which went about it methodically and had overrun the hill on 23 October. Of Major Goto's battalion, about 1500 were killed and 45 taken prisoner, at a cost to the 81st Division of 237 killed and 907 wounded.[20] But the process of reducing this pocket of resistance

20 R. R. Smith p. 530.

did not hinder the construction of an airfield by Army Engineers. The first transport plane landed on Angaur 15 October, two 6000-foot runways were completed two days later, and 13 Liberators began operating thence on the 21st.

Kossol Passage, some 60 miles north of Angaur, became a PBM (Mariner) patrol and search plane base. Three squadrons of these long-range search planes and five units equipped for air-sea rescue arrived on 16–17 September, with tenders *Chandeleur*, *Pocomoke*, *Mackinac* and *Yakutat*, under the command of Captain Williard K. Goodney.[21] Their searches, covering a 45-degree arc with 600-mile radii, the westernmost extending almost to the mouth of San Bernardino Strait, were extended to 775 miles on October 8. And on the 21st, the Kossol group provided air cover for the ships that were towing crippled *Canberra* to Ulithi.

This Peleliu-Angaur operation set the pattern for Iwo Jima and for Okinawa. Here for the first time were demonstrated the new Japanese tactics of prolonging, if they could not defeat, an amphibious assault. Probably they considered Peleliu-Angaur a victory, since in return for some 13,600 of themselves they killed 1950 Americans, wounded about 8500 more,[22] engaged some 42,000 troops and, for a short time, pinned down a formidable naval task force.

From our point of view, of course, it was an American victory, since the islands were conquered and put to use as staging points for ships and aircraft during the rest of the war. Kossol Passage afforded an anchorage, not tenable in foul weather, for ships seeking replenishment from service force vessels, or awaiting their turn to unload at Peleliu, where there was no shelter. The Kossol roadstead was extensively used (some 60 vessels were anchored there 27 September), and although within range of Japanese guns

[21] *War College Analysis* I 42–4, 55–6, 499–500 and Diagram B. This was a part of TG 30.5 (activated 2 Oct.) under Commodore Dixwell Ketcham, which included the reconnaissance and rescue squadrons and tenders at Saipan, Tinian and Ulithi.

[22] Smith pp. 573, 577 and Hough p. 183. Broken down as follows: 1st Marine Division 1250 killed, 5275 wounded; 81st Division 542 killed, 2736 wounded; Navy 158 killed, 505 wounded.

on Babelthuap, it was never molested. General Inoue probably did not wish to provoke a bombardment.

It would take more arguments than this writer can muster to prove that operation STALEMATE II was necessary, or that the advantages were worth the cost. Admiral Halsey had the right idea; they should have been bypassed when the great strategic step-up was decided upon. The most valuable contribution to victory of this costly operation was to prepare the Army and the Marine Corps for what they would experience at Okinawa.

5. *Ulithi and Its Neighbors* [23]

On 16 September 1944, Vice Admiral Wilkinson, in *Mount McKinley*, off Peleliu, received an order from Admiral Halsey to "seize Ulithi as early as practicable . . . with resources at hand." [24] Halsey arrived off Peleliu next day in battleship *New Jersey*. On the 21st he ordered executed the plan to occupy Ulithi with the 323rd RCT of the 81st Division, provided that it would not be needed in the Palaus. As optimism still prevailed about a speedy submission of Peleliu, the 323rd was readily spared, and Rear Admiral Blandy's task group was withdrawn from Angaur to cover and support it.

The occupation of Ulithi was retained in the STALEMATE II plan, after the dropping of Yap, because the Fleet needed an advance base for operations against the Philippines, with a sheltered anchorage and possibilities for recreation. Eniwetok had filled the bill during the Marianas operation, but that atoll was now too far to the rear. Ulithi, with almost as extensive a lagoon and more solid land in the surrounding ring of islets, has a symmetrical position with respect to other islands which the Navy had taken or intended to take. It

[23] CTF 31 (Vice Adm. Wilkinson) Report on STALEMATE II 11 Nov. 1944; CTG 32.2 (Rear Adm. Blandy) Action Report for Ulithi 1 Oct. 1944; W. M. Sult USNR War Diary of Ulithi; Lt. J. L. Vollbrecht USNR "The Ulithi Encyclopedia," a 28-page pamphlet "Published at Ulithi 10 March 1945"; Lt. Tilden Euster USNR "A History of Ulithi," a report written for this History in 1948.

[24] Wilkinson Report p. 8.

lies halfway on the direct route from Guam to Peleliu (about 360 miles from each), 830 miles from the Admiralties and 900 from Leyte. A 1200-mile radius from Ulithi cuts Okinawa and Lingayen Gulf, and passes close to Formosa. Pearl Harbor is about 3660 miles distant. This atoll became the hub of naval operations in the Western Pacific after September 1944.

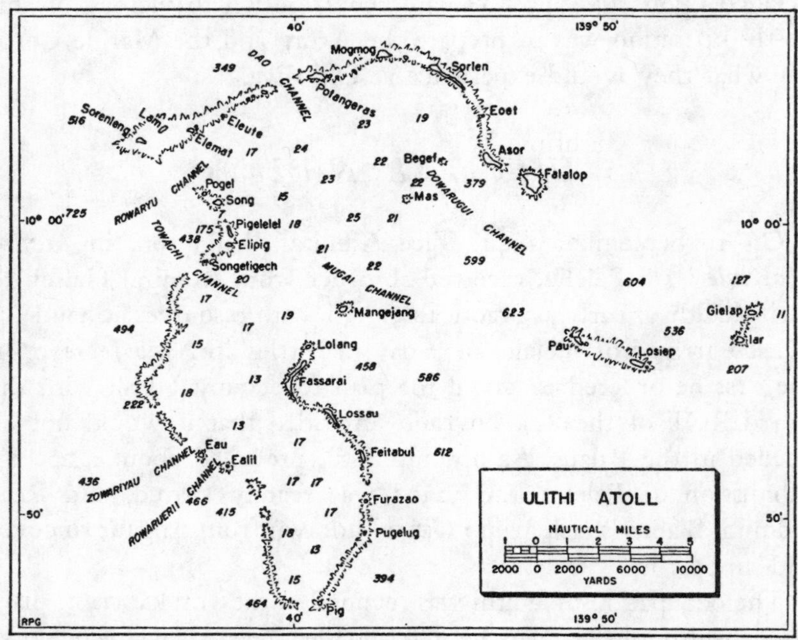

Ulithi, discovered by the Portuguese navigator Diego da Rocha in 1526, remained undisturbed by Europeans until 1731, when Spanish priests who attempted to start a mission were driven off by the Micronesians. These people were a sturdy lot; they developed a strong tribal organization and a remarkable architecture which featured great communal houses built out of driftwood logs, with high-peaked roofs covered with pandanus thatch. The Japanese established a radio and weather station on one of the islets early in the war, and made a limited use of the lagoon as a fleet anchorage and seaplane base, but their engineers estimated that no islet was big enough for an airstrip. Fast carrier forces of the United States Pacific Fleet bombed the installations thrice in 1944, between the end of March and early September. During the last strike the atoll was practically deserted, since the Japanese high command, believing that it would be of no use to friend or foe, had evacuated the garrison and most of the adult able-bodied natives to Yap. A few of them managed to escape from Yap by canoe, and when the Americans landed, there were present the "King" of Ulithi, Ueg by name, and a few score friendly Micronesians.

Colonel Arthur P. Watson's regiment drew the easy assignment of occupying Ulithi on 23 September 1944. The landing was unopposed and unloading was completed in two days' time. Vice Admiral Hoover, Commander Forward Areas Western Pacific, assumed the responsibility for developing Ulithi as an advanced fleet base. Survey ship *Sumner*, Lieutenant Commander Irving Johnson USNR,[25] at once began sounding and buoying the lagoon. A few days later a battalion of Seabees arrived, with Commodore O. O. Kessing as Atoll Commander, and construction started immediately. Falalop Islet, on the northern side of the main channel, was selected for the air base, as it was possible to contruct a 1200-yard airstrip there. Asor Islet, next to Falalop on the west, became the seat of the advanced fleet base. A boat pool and a 100-bed hospital were established on Sorlen, and helmet-shaped Mogmog became one of the most important fleet recreation centers in the Pacific. This island supported a native village, with some remarkable examples of the cathedral-like native architecture, but King Ueg was amenable to the suggestion that his subjects remove to Fassarai for the duration. "Radio Ulithi" was in operation 13 October. Commodore Dixwell Ketcham of Third Fleet Air and Reconnaissance Command arrived in tender *Hamlin*, with a squadron of Mariners, on the 17th. Colonel Watson's troops were relieved by a few hundred garrison troops next day. Since early October the lagoon had been used by the fast carriers and their screen. The

[25] Master of the famous around-the-world ocean cruiser, brigantine *Yankee*. He did an outstanding job of sounding and surveying the atolls of Micronesia.

airstrip on Falalop was operative 26 October and Marine air transportation flights were inaugurated next day.

"Scrappy" Kessing was one of the best-known characters in the Navy. He had literally escaped from hospital to take part in the Pacific War, and as Commander at Tulagi had "stayed with flagons" countless heroes going or returning from runs up the Slot, a hospitable service that he resumed at Ulithi. Under his genial command the atoll became a haven of rest and recreation for the Fleet and for expeditionary forces. As many as 20,000 men were entertained on Mogmog one record day. All was not peaceful, however, in this pretty lagoon. The Japanese before evacuating had mined at least six of the dozen or more passes. *YMS-385* was sunk by a mine explosion when sweeping Zowariyau Channel on 1 October, with a loss of 9 killed and 14 injured. The typhoon of 3 October caused *LCT-1052* to sink off Asor, and two others to be beached, and destroyed 14 LCM and 65 LCVP. Net tender *Viburnum* struck a mine in Dao Channel 28 October, with the loss of one life.

Japanese submarine *RO-46* reconnoitered the atoll on 7 October and reported one carrier (*Bunker Hill*), several cruisers, ten destroyers and 13 transports present. If the boat had arrived a day earlier it would have seen something more interesting, as two complete carrier groups (TG 38.2 and TG 38.3) departed for their strikes on Formosa on the 6th.[26]

After the lagoon had been surveyed by *Sumner*, it was judged capable of accommodating over 700 naval vessels; and at one time – in mid-March 1945, just before the Okinawa operation – 617 sail were actually anchored there. When Ulithi was first occupied, however, the southern part of the lagoon was unknown water. As insurance, in case it turned out to be foul ground, another lagoon was sought for overflow and the choice rested on Ngulu, halfway between Ulithi and the Palaus and 40 miles from Yap.

A Japanese chart captured at Saipan showed that the Ngulu lagoon was capable of accommodating about 300 ships, but it had

[26] *War College Analysis* I 215.

been mined by the Japanese and had to be swept. That operation was performed between 15 and 23 October 1944 by Captain R. W. Clark in destroyer-minesweeper *Montgomery* with five YMS, supported by survey ship *Bowditch*.[27] A native of Ngulu picked up at Ulithi piloted them through the mines protecting the channel. The enemy radio and weather stations were shot out by gunfire, and 70 moored contact mines were swept up; but not before *Montgomery* had swung on one of them when at anchor. It blew her after engine room, killing her engineer officer and six men, and she had to be towed to Pearl Harbor for repairs. Following the sweep, the atoll was occupied by a company of infantry from the Ulithi garrison, supported by destroyer *Ellet*. These troops disposed of the few Japanese on the atoll, operators of the radio station. On 18 November, after the survey of Ulithi lagoon had been completed, Admiral Halsey decided to abandon Ngulu.

Although Ulithi lies only 60 miles from Yap, which was strongly held by the Japanese, no hostile action developed against it until 20 November 1944. Early that morning fleet oiler *Mississinewa*, fully loaded (among other items) with over 400,000 gallons of aviation gas, was torpedoed and sunk at her berth in the lagoon with a loss of 50 officers and men. Rescue and hunter-killer operations started immediately, under the direction of Commodore Carter. Twenty minutes earlier, destroyer *Case* (Lieutenant Commander R. S. Willey) rammed and sank a midget submarine just outside the entrance to Mugai Channel,[28] and another was depth-charged by planes of Marine Air Group 45 the same day. These midgets were forerunners of a new type of "human torpedo" called by the Japanese *Kaiten*, meaning "the turn towards Heaven." A *Kaiten* was carried on the deck of a conventional submarine which launched it fairly close to the intended victim; a special device ejected the operator about 150 feet from the target. Submarine

[27] *LCI(G)-472* Action Report.

[28] Comdesdiv 100 and Comcortdiv 61 Action Reports; Rear Adm. W. R. Carter *Beans, Bullets and Black Oil* (1952) pp. 261–2. Outstanding in rescue work was Lt(jg) B. C. Zamucen USNR, pilot of an SOC from cruiser *Santa Fe*. He taxied in and out of the areas of burning oil, trailing a knotted line to which floating survivors held, to be hauled out of danger.

I–36 had launched one outside Mugai Channel, and *I–47* at 0430 launched four more, one of which got the tanker. Both submarines returned safely to Kure.[29]

About 50 miles ESE of Ulithi is the small island of Fais, about a mile and a half long and three quarters of a mile wide. It is not a coral atoll but a miniature Nauru, with limestone cliffs 60 feet high and a flat interior from which phosphate rock was extracted. The Germans had established a processing plant and loading station on a small rocky point that juts out from the northwest shore of the island, and the Japanese South Seas Development Company continued the business. They also had a weather and radio station on Fais, and were suspected (without reason) of having used it for refueling submarines. After July 1944 they wound up their phosphate operations and, anticipating an American attack, removed all personnel, leaving only a corporal's guard to operate the radio station.

As a reconnaissance on 3 December 1944, by Commander J. W. Buxton of Commodore Kessing's staff, observed no sign of human life on Fais, two other attempts were made, on 20 and 27 December. A native of the island then resident at Ulithi went along and talked to his friends ashore through a bull-horn. He managed to call a number of natives out of the bush, who came on board and informed Commander Buxton that 17 armed Japanese were on the island. "Scrappy" Kessing wanted to move in at once with 50 Seabees; but Rear Admiral J. W. Reeves, Jr., Commander Western Carolines, feeling not too certain of the natives' arithmetic, organized a small amphibious operation to do the job. Accordingly, Fais was taken possession of on 1 January 1945 by Lieutenant Commander J. F. McFadden, commanding what was locally known as "the Ulithi Navy," consisting of *LCI–725*, *LCI–77*, *LCI–81* and *LST–225* and destroyer escort *Seid*. Brigadier General Marcus B. Bell USA commanded the "occupation force," 238 officers and men

[29] Mochitsuka Hashimoto *Sunk, The Story of the Japanese Submarine Fleet 1942–45*, translated by Cdr. E. H. M. Colegrave RN (London 1954) pp. 125–27.

and 5 tanks of the Wildcat Division, which were lifted from Peleliu. Landing was made without opposition on the southern coast of the island 1 January 1945, and two days were spent in an unsuccessful search for the enemy, hiding in thick underbrush. On the third day a close patrol flushed eight members of the redoubtable Special Naval Landing Force from a cave near the western extremity of the island. The Japanese killed three and wounded three more "Wildcats" with one burst of machine-gun fire, then retired to the cave, and were finally blasted out by tanks and either killed or taken prisoner. The American flag was hoisted over Fais on 4 January.

Shortly after, General Bell turned over the island government with appropriate ceremonies to Mahoru, the native chief, withdrew his troops, and sent in a few Marines as liaison with the 170 to 200 natives. These were friendly, well governed and self-sufficient, having profited by the rich soil of their little island. Much valuable Japanese radio and other equipment was salvaged and put to good use by the Seabees and Marines on Ulithi.[30]

With Yap and Woleai still in enemy possession, Ulithi could not escape occasional nuisance attacks. On 12 January 1945, a human torpedo intended for ammunition ship *Mazama* exploded – fortunately about 40 yards short of its target. On the 22nd, a hunter-killer team of destroyer escorts *Conklin*, *Raby* and *Corbesier* sank submarine *I-48* that had been sighted off Ulithi and attacked unsuccessfully by a patrol plane. Other and more serious intrusions took place when the Pacific Fleet was assembling to attack Okinawa. Ulithi lagoon, by reason of its size, depth and strategic situation, became not only a useful but an indispensable fleet anchorage, replenishment, repair and service base during the last six months of the war.

In November of 1944 the VII Amphibious Force was called upon to seize the Mapia group of three small islands surrounded by a

[30] Brig. Gen. M. B. Bell USA Report on Fais Operation 12 Jan. 1945; Ulithi War Diary; conversations with Cdr. Buxton at Ulithi in March 1945 and his Report on the Reconnaissance, 3 Dec. 1944.

reef, lying about 130 miles NW of Biak and 360 miles ESE of Morotai, and the similar group of Asia Islands lying about 190 miles west of the Mapias and 180 miles SE of Morotai. The object was to install weather stations and Loran – long range radio aid to navigation. Admiral Barbey entrusted this mission to Captain Lord Ashbourne RN in H.M. cruiser-minelayer *Ariadne*, with 12 LSM, four LCI and four LCI(G). Destroyers *Caldwell* and *Shaw* and DE *Willmarth* were the support group. A regiment of the 31st Division was embarked at Morotai 13 November and landed on Pegun Island of the Mapia group two days later. The Japanese had evacuated to another island, to which the American troops moved after a destroyer bombardment, and cleaned out a force of about 200 at a cost of 17 killed and 30 wounded. H.M.S. *Ariadne* then returned to Morotai, embarked a company of infantry with service troops on 18 November, and landed them on the Asia group next day. There was no opposition, and all combatant troops from both island groups were soon returned to Morotai.[31]

It is time that we leave these small and pleasant atolls and get on with the main business of the Third and Seventh Fleets: the liberation of Leyte.

[31] Captain Lord Ashbourne RN Report of 27 November 1944.

CHAPTER IV

Plans and Commands for Leyte

September–October 1944

1. *American Command Structure and Plan*

IN VIEW of the magnitude of the Leyte operation, the overall plan was fairly simple; but the command set-up was complicated.

Four "top" commands, which had no common superior under the J.C.S. and the President, were involved: —

I. GENERAL DOUGLAS MACARTHUR, Supreme Commander Southwest Pacific Area since 1942, commanded all ground forces, some air forces and Seventh Fleet.

II. ADMIRAL CHESTER W. NIMITZ, Commander in Chief Pacific Fleet and Pacific Ocean Areas, from whom stemmed Admiral Halsey's Third Fleet and the VII Army Air Force.

III. GENERAL H. H. ARNOLD commanded the XX Army Air Force – the B–29s, through his deputy, Major General Curtis E. LeMay.

IV. GENERAL J. W. STILWELL of the China-Burma-India command, from whom stemmed the XIV Army Air Force.

Under MacArthur

Vice Admiral Thomas C. Kinkaid, Commander Seventh Fleet since the previous November,[1] now designated Commander Central

[1] For brief early biog., see Volume V 88*n*. Since the Battle of Midway he had been Com North Pacific Force Jan.–Oct., and Com Seventh Fleet Nov. 1943.

Philippines Attack Force; and Lieutenant General Walter Krueger, Commanding General Sixth Army since January 1943, now Commander Expeditionary Force.

Under Admiral Kinkaid

Two attack forces: the NORTHERN, to land at Tacloban; and the SOUTHERN, to land at Dulag – both on the western shore of Leyte Gulf.

NORTHERN ATTACK FORCE was under Rear Admiral D. E. Barbey, who had directed several amphibious operations in the Southwest Pacific; the ground forces were X Corps (Major General Franklin C. Sibert).

SOUTHERN ATTACK FORCE, switched to Leyte from Yap, remained under Vice Admiral Theodore Stark Wilkinson, also a veteran of many amphibious assaults. The troops of this force consisted of the newly formed XXIV Corps (Major General J. R. Hodge). Earlier in the Pacific war, General Hodge had commanded the 24th Division at Guadalcanal. In reserve for both forces were the 32nd and 77th Infantry Divisions (Major Generals W. H. Gill and A. D. Bruce).

General Krueger received General MacArthur's "Warning Instructions," which embodied the top-flight decisions made at Quebec, on the very same day, 15 September. On the 21st he received MacArthur's Operations Instruction Number 70, a directive which consolidated all previous instructions into one integrated plan. In this directive, the tasks assigned to Admiral Kinkaid's naval force by General MacArthur were stated as follows: –

1. To transport and establish landing forces ashore in the Leyte Gulf-Surigao Strait area, as arranged with the Commanding General, Sixth U.S. Army.
2. To support the operation by: –

Promoted Admiral Apr. 1945, he directed many activities in Far Eastern waters at the end of the war, became Com Eastern Sea Frontier Jan. 1946, and retired 1950.

(*a*) Providing air protection for convoys and direct air support for the landing and subsequent operations, including anti-submarine patrol of the Gulf and combat air patrol over the amphibious ships and craft, from his escort carriers;

(*b*) Lifting reinforcements and supplies to Leyte in naval assault shipping;

(*c*) Preventing Japanese reinforcement by sea of its Leyte garrison;

(*d*) Opening Surigao Strait for Allied use, and sending Naval Forces into "Visayan waters" to support current and future operations;

(*e*) Providing submarine reconnaissance, lifeguard service and escort-of-convoy.[2]

Now let us turn to the duties of II, the Nimitz-Halsey command.

After a consultation in Hollandia between Rear Admiral Forrest Sherman (Admiral Nimitz's plans officer) and Major General S. J. Chamberlin (General MacArthur's operations officer), and by agreement (since Admiral Halsey was not under General MacArthur), Third Fleet, which consisted for the most part of Vice Admiral Mitscher's fast carrier forces (TF 38), undertook, toward the end of September: –

To cover and support the Leyte Operation by: –

(*a*) Striking Okinawa, Formosa and Northern Leyte on 10–13 October;

(*b*) Striking Bicol peninsula, Leyte, Cebu and Negros, and supporting the landings on Leyte, on 16–20 October;

(*c*) Operating in "strategic support" of the Leyte Operation, by destroying enemy naval and air forces threatening the Philippines area, on and after 21 October.[3]

So much for the agreement; as translated into actual orders from Admiral Nimitz (his Operation Plan 8–44 of 27 September),

[2] CTF 77 (Vice Adm. Kinkaid) "Report of Operation for Capture of Leyte."

[3] Com Third Fleet (Adm. Halsey) Op Order 21–44 (dispatch of 3 Oct.); *War College Analysis* I 15–16.

Halsey's general duty was to "cover and support" Southwest Pacific Forces "in order to assist in the seizure and occupation of all objectives in the Central Philippines," and to "destroy enemy naval and air forces in or threatening the Philippines Area." In addition, section 3x of the operation plan contained this pregnant order:—

"In case opportunity for destruction of major portion of the enemy fleet is offered or can be created, *such destruction becomes the primary task.*"

This clause, which, as we shall see, became "the tail that wagged the dog," added a new and overriding duty, that of destroying the enemy fleet.[4] And that Halsey regarded this as his primary task is clear from a clause in the "mission paragraph" of his own operation order:—

> If opportunity exists or can be created to destroy major portion of enemy fleet this becomes primary task.[5]

The story of how the "destroy enemy fleet" clause got into the orders and plans is interesting. Admiral Nimitz's op plan for the Marianas contained no such clause; Admiral Spruance was instructed only to "support" the amphibious forces. In every amphibious operation the covering force has the duty to engage any enemy fleet that may challenge the landings, and normally the top naval commander has a battle plan drawn up for that eventuality.[6] But he is not supposed to go out and seek battle while the amphibious forces require his protection. The Japanese Navy had challenged our amphibious operations in the Solomons and the Marianas. In June 1944 Admiral Spruance put his battle plan into effect and went out to seek the enemy; but, not making contact, turned back to perform his primary duty of covering the amphibious

[4] It should, however, be said that in Cincpac-Cincpoa's Plan GRANITE II, the Outline Campaign Plan for 1944 dated 15 Jan., it is stated: "The conduct of operations will be designed to: (a) destroy the Japanese Fleet at an early date," followed by attrition of enemy air forces, attacks on enemy shipping, air attacks on Japan, and keeping China in the war.

[5] Com Third Fleet Operation Order 21–44 of 3 Oct.

[6] It was so in the Gilberts and Marshall Islands operation, in the carrier air strike on the Palaus of Mar. 1944 (Volume VIII 28–9) and at the Marianas.

operation at Saipan. Later, in staff and informal discussions at Pearl Harbor, Spruance was strongly criticized by some of his colleagues, especially by the naval aviation flag officers, both for turning east when he did, and for not pursuing the enemy fleet after he had destroyed its air groups.[7] That, no doubt, is what Halsey would have done; and now Halsey saw to it that there should be no doubt about his authority to do just that if he found the opportunity off Leyte, or could create it.

There is a philosophy of strategy behind the differing concepts that ruled Halsey and Spruance respectively. "Destruction of the enemy's fleet" had become a sort of fetish in the British and American Navies, following the Nelson and the supposed Mahan tradition, just as "destruction of the enemy's army" had become the fetish of the land strategists, following Clausewitz taken out of context or misunderstood. On the other hand, one of the leading British writers on naval strategy, Sir Julian Corbett, wrote in 1911 that "the paramount function of a covering force in an amphibious operation is to prevent interference with the . . . landing, support and supply of the Army." [8] On that principle the covering and support forces of the United States Pacific Fleet had hitherto been acting. This concept stems from the principle that destruction of enemy forces is not an end in itself, but merely one possible means to victory. It follows that the main and overriding objective of a naval force supporting or covering an amphibious operation is to support and cover, unless it is expressly ordered to do something different.

If Spruance had gone roaring out after the enemy fleet in June, and, by a mistaken course, had given it the opportunity to break up the assault on Saipan, his name would have become infamous. Halsey's determination not to repeat what he regarded as Spruance's undue caution and lack of offensive spirit, led to the most controversial episode in the Battle for Leyte Gulf.

In effect, Admiral Halsey had an overriding objective assigned

[7] Volume VIII 313–16.

[8] *Some Principles of Maritime Strategy* (London 1918) p. 261.

to him by Nimitz apart from and independent of General MacArthur's, which was the prompt liberation of Leyte. Halsey was the sole judge of his primary duty at any critical juncture. Nothing in his orders or in Nimitz's operation plan required him to obtain the General's concurrence in any action he chose to initiate, or even to advise him as to a change of plan.[9] To give divergent duties to two such strong and aggressive characters as Halsey and MacArthur, and expect them always to coöperate, was to invite trouble. And the only reason it did not create a great deal of trouble was that the General kept his hands off the Navy, and allowed his naval commander, Admiral Kinkaid, to determine his own relations with Third Fleet and Admiral Halsey.

The air situation was highly confused, since *six* distinct air commands were involved. Only two were under General MacArthur – General Kenney's land-based Air Forces Southwest Pacific and the escort carriers of Seventh Fleet. Two stemmed from Admiral Nimitz: the fast carriers of Third Fleet and VII Army Air Force (Major General Willis H. Hale USA) based largely in the Marianas, a part of the Forward Areas Central Pacific Command (Vice Admiral John H. Hoover), who was also under Nimitz. The other two were independent of either: XIV Army Air Force (Major General Claire L. Chennault), based on Chinese airfields and belonging to the China-Burma-India Theater (General Joseph W. Stilwell), and XX Bomber Command (Major General Curtis E. LeMay), which took orders directly from the Joint Chiefs of Staff.

We have seen the vital importance of deceptive measures in the European war, to obtain tactical surprise.[10] In the Pacific, owing largely to the overwhelming strength of Allied forces, surprise, though desirable, was not essential. That was fortunate, because the two Allied attempts to deceive the enemy as to the target were completely ineffective. The first was a bombardment of tiny Marcus Island on 9 October, which was supposed to suggest that we were coming "up the ladder of the Bonins." The second and more elab-

[9] *War College Analysis* I 17–18.
[10] Volume XI 74–5.

orate was a British naval attack on the Nicobar Islands in the Indian Ocean. Admiral King asked the Royal Navy to lay this on in the hope that it would mislead the Japanese into expecting the main Allied attack in Malaya or Indonesia, and that it would pin down the major part of their fleet near Singapore. The British Eastern Fleet under Admiral Sir James Somerville RN, recently augmented by two fleet carriers and H.M. battleship *Howe*, carried out a series of aërial and surface bombardments on the Car Nicobar and Nancowry Islands between 17 and 21 October. These made no impression whatsoever on the Japanese; Kurita's fleet, the very day after the last attack, sortied from Lingga Roads to execute the SHO-GO plan.

2. *The Allied Objective*

General MacArthur was returning to the Philippines by an historic route. On 16 March 1521, Ferdinand Magellan entered Leyte Gulf by the channel between Homonhon and Calicoan Islands. Sailing through Surigao Strait, the fleet came to an anchor off the little island of Limasawa near Panaon. It was there that Magellan's Malay servant Henriquez, whom he had picked up at Malacca on a previous voyage, was able to make himself understood by the Moros. At Limasawa westward-advancing Christianity first met eastward-advancing Islam; so it was fitting that in the same waters and on the same shores, almost four and a quarter centuries later, the Navies representing the Western and Eastern hemispheres should grapple.

Magellan sailed on through the Camotes Sea, became entangled in local politics and lost his life on Mactan; it was Sebastian del Cano in *Vittoria* who completed the first voyage around the world. Twenty-two years later, the Visayan chief of Leyte received Ruy Lopez de Villalobos "with special consideration and appreciation." Miguel Lopez de Legaspi, the founder of Manila, spent much time on Leyte in the 1560s, when the inhabitants were converted to Christianity. By 1735 the Province of Leyte, including Samar,

LEYTE
OCTOBER—DECEMBER
1944
Main Roads
Secondary Roads
0 10 20
Naut. Miles
125°00'
30'
11°00'
10°00'
SAMAR SEA
Maripipi I.
BILIRAN
Rabin Pt.
Carigara Bay
Babatngon
La Paz
San Juanico Strait
SAMAR
San Isidro
Pinamopoan
Carigara
Barugo
Limon
Villaba
Kananga
Jaro
Tacloban
San Pedro Bay
Palo
Tanauan
Mt. Mamban
Dolores
Palompon
Ormoc
Ipil
Burauen
Dulag
LEYTE GULF
Rizal
Damulaan
Tarragona
Caridad
Homonhon I.
CAMOTES ISLANDS
Ponson I.
Abuyog
Pacijan I.
Poro I.
Baybay
LEYTE
CAMOTES SEA
Hindang
CANIGAO CHANNEL
EAST CANIGAO CHANNEL
Sogod Bay
Surigao Strait
DINAGAT
PANAON
Lapinin I.
Limasawa I.
BOHOL
MINDANAO SEA
MINDANAO
JAC

had a population of over 55,000. Piratical attacks by the Moros kept numbers down until well into the nineteenth century. After 1900, when the rich Leyte Valley began to develop under American rule, there came a phenomenal increase in population. By 1939, there were 915,853 individuals in the 2,785 square miles of Leyte Island. Placid, kind, tolerant of foreigners, predominantly Catholic in religion and speaking two Visayan dialects, the Leyte people depend almost entirely on agriculture for their livelihood.

Leyte in shape may be compared with a very roughhewn Winged Victory of Samothrace, her left wing clipped off and her left shoulder separated from Samar by the narrow San Juanico Strait. Below her waist, marked by the girdling Abuyog-Baybay road, is a rough mountainous country covering the lady's hips and legs, which stand on Surigao Strait. Her right wing is the mountainous San Isidro peninsula, on the Camotes Sea. Between that peninsula and the 4000-foot central massif is the Ormoc Valley, of some military significance. But the most important part of Leyte, which on the map looks like a wide scarf hung over Victory's left shoulder, is the thickly populated Leyte Valley, heavily cultivated with rice, corn and other foodstuffs, and fringed by coconut plantations. This is a valley only where a line of hills separates it from San Juanico Strait; properly it is a coastal plain, ten to twenty miles wide, extending from Carigara Bay on the north to San Pedro Bay, and then down along Leyte Gulf to Dulag, with a narrow strip running farther south to Abuyog.

Leyte Valley was our primary objective. On its gulf side are the best landing beaches that Americans had encountered in the Pacific. It was wanted by General MacArthur to establish a great air and logistics base as a springboard for Luzon. In that respect it proved a disappointment, for it is much too boggy. In the monsoon season roads become impassable for heavy vehicles, and outside the roads in many parts there are rice paddies, impassable for anything but ducks. It was unfortunate for American troops that they had to fight during the rainy season in the soggiest section of the Philippines, and tough on the Fleet to have to operate in the typhoon belt. But that was the price we had to pay for acceleration. The drier west coasts of the Philippine Islands were inaccessible until the narrow sea approaches were secured.

An important phase of the preparations was the warm contact that had been maintained since 1943 between General MacArthur's command and the Philippine guerrillas.[11] Commander Charles ("Chick") Parsons USNR, who had been a resident of Manila before the war, managed to stay there for some time under the Japanese occupation as honorary consul of Panama, although Panama had also declared war on Japan. In 1942 he was evacuated and reached New York, where he resumed active duty in the Navy, and was sent to General MacArthur, who made him his staff officer for relations with the guerrillas. In that capacity he made several trips by submarine to various parts of the Archipelago to deliver medical and military supplies, and to coördinate guerrilla activities with General MacArthur's plans. He also set up for the Navy a series of coastwatcher stations, whose value was demonstrated by the accurate reports of Japanese fleet movements that they sent in before the Battle of the Philippine Sea. In April 1943 he made contact on Leyte with Colonel Ruperto K. Kangleon, one of the ablest guerrilla leaders, who subsequently became Secretary of National Defense to the Philippine Republic, and Senator.

Submarines *Nautilus* (Commander G. A. Sharp) and *Narwhal* (Lieutenant Commander Jack C. Titus), altered for transport purposes, made repeated missions to the Archipelago in 1944 with arms, supplies and messages for the loyal Filipinos, and other submarines did so occasionally. The story of their adventures goes far to explain both General MacArthur's concern for a prompt "return," and the wholehearted coöperation that he received in the Philippines.

Commander Parsons's last trip to Leyte before A-day was made

[11] Cdr. Charles Parsons USNR, ms. account of submarines' special missions to Philippines 1 Feb. 1943–23 Jan. 1945, compiled immediately after the war; letters from Cdr. Parsons, 1957–58; Travis Ingham *Rendezvous by Submarine* (N.Y. 1945 and Manila 1956). See also Volumes VI 85 and VIII 21–2. These submarines delivered about 330 people to and evacuated 472 from the Philippines, and landed some 1325 tons of supplies.

in a "Black Cat" PBY from Morotai. In company with Colonel Frank Rouelle USA, he landed 10 October on a beach south of Tacloban. Even before reaching Colonel Kangleon at guerrilla headquarters in southwestern Leyte, he spread the word among the civilian population on the east coast of the island that there was to be a big bombardment, so that they had better evacuate. That they did, except from the provincial capital Tacloban, where the Japanese garrison refused to let the people depart. As a result (since Tacloban was spared), not one Filipino lost his life in the pre-landing bombardment. Parsons found that Colonel Kangleon's troops were already deployed in the best manner to knock off the Japanese as they retreated from the beaches, and on the night of 19–20 October he began sending messages by runners to alert all guerrilla commands. He also furnished valuable intelligence to the invasion forces. From his radio messages they learned of the absence of underwater obstacles from the landing beaches, of strongpoints on Catmon and other hills, of mines in northen Surigao Strait, and that Leyte south of the Abuyog–Baybay road was free of Japanese.

The size of this operation can best be appreciated by comparing it with the military situation in the Philippines in 1941. United States Army Forces in the Far East, then commanded by Lieutenant General (and Field Marshal) Douglas MacArthur, had a total strength on 20 December 1941 of 120,500 officers and men, much the greater part being Filipinos. Three years later some 145,000 American troops were scheduled to land on Leyte during the first five days, with over 55,000 more to come.

3. *Japanese Plans and Military Situation* [12]

After the American capture of Saipan the Tojo Cabinet fell. A few days later Admiral Toyoda, Commander in Chief Combined

[12] *War College Analysis* I chap. iii; General MacArthur *Historical Report on Allied Operations in Southwest Pacific*, Vol. II on the Japanese side, chap. x "Philippine Defense Plans" by Major Toshiro Magari.

Fleet, called on the new Navy Minister, Admiral Yonai. In Toyoda's words: –

"Can we hold out till the end of the year?" he asked. I replied simply, "It will probably be extremely difficult to do so." [18]

This was equivalent to an American's asking "Is the war already lost?" and a reply, "It is, and you had better hurry up and make peace."

The Japanese were not surprised by the American invasion of the Philippines, nor were they unprepared. Their only uncertainty, down to mid-October, was the exact island which would first be attacked. They never discounted the strategic importance of the Archipelago. After MacArthur had taken Hollandia in April 1944, and Saipan had fallen to Nimitz's forces in July, it was clear that Japan must fall back on an inner chain of defense extending from the Kuriles and the Japanese home islands, through the Ryukyus, Formosa and the Philippines to the Netherlands East Indies. In this chain the Philippines were the key links. Continued possession of them would allow Japan to draw upon her satellites to the southward and to protect her convoys running through the Formosa Channel and the South China Sea. Loss of them would cut her off from all outside resources except those in China.

Imperial General Headquarters as early as March 1944 guessed that the two prongs of the American Pacific offensive, from the Southwest and the Central Pacific, would converge on the Philippines, and then push north via the Ryukyus. It is interesting that the Joint Chiefs' decision to do this, reached after much travail, had already been anticipated by smart strategic thinkers at Tokyo. The capture of Hollandia and of Saipan confirmed this Japanese estimate; and in August Imperial General Headquarters decided that top priority in preparation for a "general decisive battle" along the inner defense line must be assigned to the Philippines. I.G.H. anticipated the preliminary moves against Palau and Morotai in mid-September, but did not expect the major assault before mid-

[18] *The End of the Imperial Navy* (Tokyo, 1950) pp. 149–54.

November. That, too, was a good guess at our original target date for the Leyte landings.

For the Japanese, the Philippines were a source of abaca and of certain minerals; but their main value, apart from their strategic situation, was for basing troops and staging ships. In the hope of obtaining more coöperation from the Filipinos, Japan recognized with appropriate ceremonies, in October 1943, the independence of the puppet government that it had set up under Laurel. But Laurel was unable either to appease the guerrillas or to obtain more production. Imperial General Headquarters sadly realized in March 1944 that "even after their independence, there remains among all classes in the Philippines a strong undercurrent of pro-American sentiment . . . something steadfast, which cannot be destroyed. . . . Guerrilla activities are gradually increasing." [14]

The Philippines were in the zone of the Japanese Southern Army, which we could have called an army group. Field Marshal Terauchi, the commander, transferred his headquarters to Manila in May 1944. At that time the Fourteenth Army, that part of the Southern Army immediately responsible for Philippine defense, comprised only four independent mixed brigades and the 16th Infantry Division, which had been fighting Chinese and Americans since 1937. Terauchi estimated that fifteen more divisions would be required for effective defense of the Archipelago; but he had slight hope of getting them. The Fourteenth Army commander, from 5 October 1944, was General Tomoyuki Yamashita, the conqueror of Singapore. He boasted to President Laurel that he would soon demand MacArthur's surrender in the same words he once used to General Percival at Singapore: "All I want to know from you is, *Yes* or *No*." Less than a year later, it was Yamashita who surrendered to Major General W. H. Gill at Baguio. Before the Japanese were forced out of Leyte, six divisions (the 1st, 8th, 16th, 28th, 30th, and 102nd) had been committed to its defense, but only the 16th (Major General Makino) was present on 20 October.

Although the Japanese were prepared to give "general decisive

[14] MacArthur *Historical Report* II 288.

battle" – a constantly recurring phrase in their reports and directives – on whatever island the Allies chose, they were mainly concerned with holding Luzon. That island was more important to them than all the rest of the archipelago. Even if they were forced to relinquish Mindanao and the Visayas (which included Leyte and Samar), retention of Luzon would enable them to maintain communication with their conquests in Malaya and Indonesia.

Japanese command structure for air forces was even more peculiar than ours. The Navy had a series of "Base Air Forces" – land-based air wings covering certain areas – and the Army had overlapping "Air Armies" which might or might not come temporarily under joint command; each stemmed from the top command of its respective arm. The most important units in the Leyte operation were: –

Sixth Base Air Force, commanded by Vice Admiral Fukudome, which covered Southern Kyushu, the Ryukyus and Formosa. Sixth Base Air Force, including its army components, had 737 planes (223 of them fighters) available 10 October, and during that and the next four days flew in 688 more, including 172 from the Navy's carriers. Fukudome had also organized an élite flying group, under Captain Shuzo Kuno, called the "T Attack Force" – T standing for Typhoon. Stationed in Kyushu, they were supposed to be intensively trained; but half their number were army pilots, with only two to six months' training in oversea flying, and their performance was a bitter disappointment to the Admiral.

Fifth Base Air Force, Vice Admiral Teraoka, and Fourth Air Army, Lieutenant General Tominaga, covered the Philippines, with headquarters at Manila. Both suffered heavily in the American carrier strikes of September, and from malaria or dengue fever attacking senior officers. Fifth Base Air Force had only 203 aircraft (115 of them fighters) available on 10 October; Fourth Air Army at about the same date had available 237 aircraft, 83 of them fighters. Vice Admiral Onishi relieved Teraoka 20 October.

Formerly the Japanese Army Air Force had refused to lend a hand in naval operations, but after the fall of Saipan it had a change of heart and now coöperated fully. Army and Navy agreed, on 24 July 1944, as to air coördination when the "general decisive battle" was joined. Admiral Fukudome would command all air power in Formosa and the Ryukyus; whilst in the Philippines, Admiral Teraoka would have tactical command when the primary emphasis was on operations over the ocean, and General Tominaga take over when emphasis shifted to land operations. These two officers agreed that Navy planes should make the long-range patrols and searches, and both Army and Navy planes share the short-range flights.

In Japanese plans for Philippine defense, aircraft were not to attack the enemy until he was about to land, when they would concentrate against amphibious shipping and the attack force. Admiral Toyoda rescinded this, to his subsequent regret, when the fast carrier forces appeared off Formosa.

The enemy had plenty of airfields: 11 naval air stations (some with as many as five runways), 15 army airfields and 2 seaplane bases on Formosa; 19 airfields, including our old Nichols and Clark fields, with a capacity of over a thousand planes, on Luzon; 5 to 8 airstrips including 2 near the American target on Leyte; and 20 more on Negros, Cebu and Mindanao.[15]

The Imperial Japanese Navy was as ready as it could be under the circumstances for "general decisive battle." Postponing details until Part III, when the battle is actually joined, we may here observe that Admiral Toyoda, C. in C. Combined Fleet, had headquarters near Tokyo; that the principal surface forces, under Admiral Kurita, returned to Lingga Roads after the Battle of the Philippine Sea in order to be near their fuel supply; whilst carrier forces, under Admiral Ozawa, remained in the Inland Sea of Japan in order to train new air groups. If the American attack had been

[15] *War College Analysis* I 210–13, 221–37; Vice Adm. S. Fukudome "Strategic Aspects of Battle off Formosa" U.S. Nav. Inst. *Proceedings* LXXVIII (1952) 1285–95.

delayed until November the carriers too would have been sent south.

The overall plan for "general decisive battle," drawn up by Imperial General Headquarters, was called SHO-GO, meaning simply

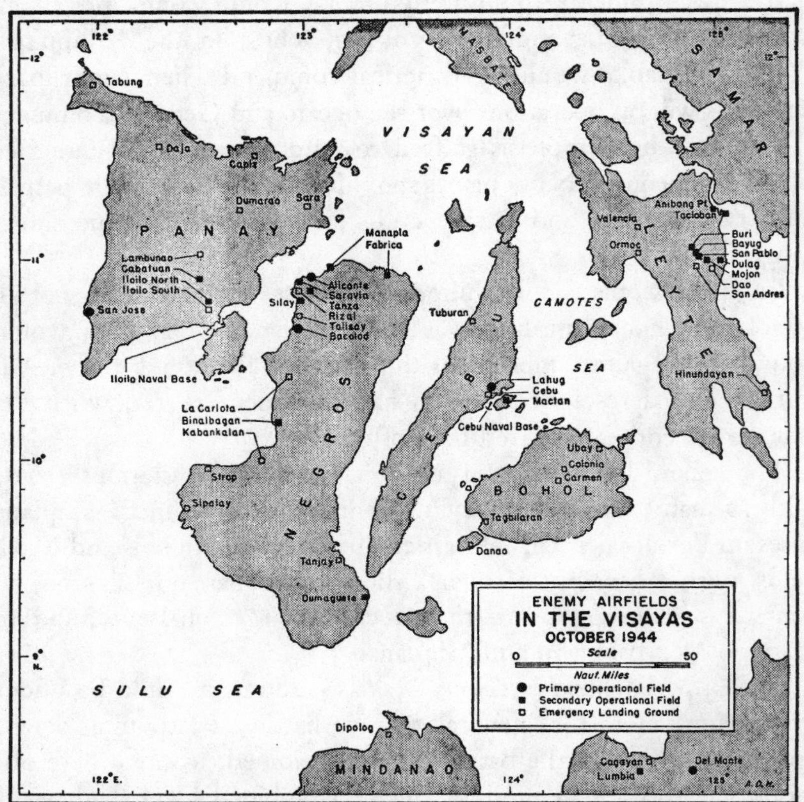

"Victory Operation." Since Intelligence could not be certain where the landings would take place, four separate SHO plans were drawn up, between 24 July and 1 August, to deal with possible landings in Philippines, Formosa-Ryukyus, Honshu-Kyushu and Hokkaido-Kuriles, respectively. I.G.H. awaited certain indications of the Allied target before choosing which SHO should go into effect; but everyone was betting on the Philippines.

Although Allied forces, when the battle started, congratulated themselves that they had "caught the Japs flat-footed," the contrary was true. The Japanese high command obtained very little advance intelligence from reconnaissance, but a good deal from other sources and by inference. One important bit came from Moscow, on 6 October. The Japanese ambassador there learned from the Soviet Foreign Office early in October that, through a diplomatic "leak," they had heard that the United States XIV and XX Army Air Forces, based in China, would make attacks designed to isolate the Philippines.[16] That an Allied diplomat's tongue should have been loosed at a Russian vodka party is understandable; but why did the "People's Commissariat for Foreign Affairs" impart this indiscretion to their ally's enemy, the Japanese? It seems probable that official Russia did not exactly approve American efforts to win victory promptly, and hoped that the Pacific war would drag along until such time as the Soviets found it con-enient to come in.

The Allied attack came a little sooner than the Japanese expected, d much earlier than they wished. On 7 October Admiral Toyoda ited Manila for a conference with top Army and Navy comnders. At that time he anticipated that any day Third Fleet ht launch a massive carrier-plane attack on Okinawa, Formosa or the Philippines as a prelude to invasion. He knew that a heavy concentration of transports had been seen in Hollandia and Wakde. Apparently his planes and submarines had failed to reconnoiter Manus; and, as we have seen, they arrived a day too late at Ulithi. The latest directive of the Navy section of Imperial General Headquarters predicted that the landing would take place somewhere in the Philippines during the last ten days of October, and guessed that the target would be Leyte.[17]

By contrast, Allied intelligence of Japanese movements and intentions was spotty and defective.[18] Admirals Nimitz and Halsey

[16] *War College Analysis* I 217, 241.

[17] *War College Analysis* I 214–18.

[18] Air Evaluation Board Southwest Pacific Area, *Leyte Campaign, Philippines, 1944*, a folio volume issued in 1945, pp. 14, 199; *War College Analysis* I 22 and 23 and III Plate II.

issued no early predictions, but from the latter's operation order to "seek out and destroy" the Japanese Fleet it is clear that he entertained the possibility that it would come out to fight; and, being Halsey, he hoped very much that it would. Southwest Pacific Intelligence, which had the main responsibility for discovering enemy intentions (since the Philippines were in General MacArthur's bailiwick), went almost completely wrong. "The objective is relatively undefended – the Japanese will not offer strong resistance to the operation," predicted General Kenney, Commander Allied Air Forces Southwest Pacific, on 24 September 1944, and on 4 October he thought that a fleet action was "less likely than ever." Inaccurate estimates even increased with the approach of A-day, as D-day for Leyte was designated. On 19 October (A minus 1), Admiral Halsey suggested to MacArthur that the Japanese Fleet would be deployed into small dispersed groups to make "Tokyo Express" runs on Leyte.[19]

On A-day itself, General MacArthur's headquarters issued a broadsheet headed "Enemy Capabilities of Naval Reaction to Allied Landings on the Philippines," in which it was confidently stated that an approach of the Japanese Fleet through Surigao or San Bernardino Straits would be "impractical because of navigational hazards and the lack of maneuvering space." On A-day plus 1, the Southwest Pacific Intelligence Summary announced that there was "no apparent intent" of the Japanese Navy "to interfere with our Leyte landings." And Admiral Kinkaid, from his flagship in Leyte Gulf during the small hours of 23 October, sent out a dispatch stating that he regarded the approach of Japanese warships to Coron Bay as the beginning of "Tokyo Express" runs, and that there was a possibility of enemy carrier planes operating from west of Palawan. Halsey and Kinkaid guessed right on the "Tokyo Express" business, because that is the way the Japanese reinforced their Leyte garrison, through Ormoc; and their estimate that the

[19] Cardiv 24 message file; "Tokyo Express" referred to the night runs "up the Slot" that the Japanese Navy put on during the Guadalcanal campaign; see Volume V, index.

Japanese had no intention of committing the major part of their fleet to battle, while completely wrong, did no harm.

As General MacArthur's Air Evaluation Board frankly concluded after the war, "Enemy intentions rather than capabilities were predominant." The situation was the reverse of that in operation OVERLORD (the Normandy Invasion), where the Allied plan was based on an exact knowledge of enemy capabilities.

Although the Japanese high command guessed fairly accurately what the Allies were about to do, and made all possible preparations to meet them, they *could not be sure* of the exact time or target. That was fatal, because the uncertainty prevented them from starting SHO-GO until it was too late to attack the Allied landings in their "naked" phase, when the troops were being boated ashore and the Gulf was full of vulnerable shipping. Admiral Toyoda dared not even alert his forces until our warships were actually seen entering Leyte Gulf. Thus the main landings on 20 October met only local opposition, and four more days elapsed before the Japanese Navy reached waters where it could challenge the Third and Seventh Fleets, United States Navy.

CHAPTER V

Leyte Logistics[1]

1. *Third Fleet*

LOGISTICS, the art of furnishing an army, fleet or air force in action with the ammunition, provisions, supplies and reinforcements that it needs, was particularly important in operations like those in the Pacific that were projected over such vast distances.

Logistics for the Leyte, Mindoro and Lingayen operations were divided, though not sharply, between Third and Seventh Fleets. The Army and a part of Seventh Fleet were taken care of through the normal logistics channels of the Southwest Pacific, coming up through Australia and the Admiralties, Mitscher's Fast Carrier Groups, Wilkinson's Southern Attack Force, which had originally been destined for Yap, and all vessels of the Pacific Fleet temporarily placed under Admiral Kinkaid's command obtained their sustenance through Service Force Pacific Fleet, of which Vice Admiral William L. ("Uncle Bill") Calhoun was commander, until relieved in March 1945 by Vice Admiral W. W. ("Poco") Smith.

Between 6 October 1944 and 26 January 1945 Fast Carrier Forces Pacific Fleet were at sea for thirteen weeks out of sixteen. This unprecedented stretch of fighting activity would have been impossible without a very high quality of logistic support.

[1] This chapter continues the story told in Volume VIII ch. xviii. Important sources are Rear Adm. W. R. Carter *Beans, Bullets and Black Oil* (1952) chs. xix–xxii, and Cincpac Monthly Analysis for Oct. 1944 pp. 28–32. Rear Adm. Henry E. Eccles USN (Ret), and other officers here mentioned have supplied me with much additional information.

Fuel for ships, vehicles and planes was the first problem. Petroleum products reached forward bases in commercial tankers from the West Coast, the Netherlands West Indies, and the nine-million-barrel oil storage at Pearl Harbor. When Eniwetok was abandoned as advanced fleet anchorage in favor of Ulithi on 1 October 1944, 1400 miles in each direction were added to the voyage of each merchant tanker, and their turn-around slowed down accordingly. So, when Commodore Worrall R. ("Nick") Carter in *Prairie* shifted his Mobile Service Base (Service Squadron 10) from Eniwetok to Ulithi during the first two weeks of October, he brought along six to eight obsolete tankers of 60,000 to 100,000 barrels capacity each, to act as a "floating tank farm." This was more satisfactory than building tanks ashore at Ulithi, which would not long be wanted; the "floating tank farm" could be shifted, and actually did move up to Leyte in mid-May 1945. Guam and Saipan, on the other hand, were regarded as permanent bases which the Navy intended to keep and develop; tank storage was therefore provided on both islands with a capacity of about 430,000 and 100,000 barrels respectively. The Philippines operation put an undue strain on fuel oil and aviation gas (avgas) consumption, but, thanks to these needs being anticipated, the Fleet never ran short.

The vital link between bases and the Fleet was filled by a unique product of this war, the At Sea Logistics Service Group, commanded by Captain J. T. Acuff when operating under Third Fleet, and by Captain E. E. Paré when operating under Fifth Fleet.[2] This was almost a fleet in itself, comprising 34 fleet oilers, 11 escort carriers, 19 destroyers, 26 destroyer escorts and a number of seagoing tugs. These were divided into ten or twelve task units in order to fuel the Fleet in echelons. From nine to twelve tankers

[2] For its exact composition, see Appendix. The ships remained the same, drawn from Service Squadron 8, of which Commodore A. H. Gray was commander. By this device, tactical and logistic planning were integrated at the top command levels and at the staff working levels, and an understanding of the concepts of the commander was attained. It is an interesting commentary on World War II promotion policies in the Navy that the command of At Sea Logistics Group was not considered worthy of flag rank, although an aviation rear admiral had to be temporarily removed from command of the escort carriers in order to permit them to operate under the command of a captain from the Service Force!

were kept in one fueling group, operating within easy distance of Task Force 38 and steaming from one rendezvous to another. About every three or four days a task unit of three oilers, suitably escorted, would join this fueling group to relieve those that were almost empty; these in turn transferred the remainder of their oil to other tankers that were partly full, retiring to Ulithi to procure a new load from merchant tankers. Each unit was accompanied by an escort carrier which brought up, from aircraft pools at Eniwetok, Guam and Manus, replacement planes and pilots for the fast carriers of Third Fleet and for the escort carriers of Seventh Fleet. Eight more escort carriers provided combat air patrol and antisubmarine patrol for the oiler groups. One or two fleet tugs operated with the fueling group in readiness to be sent forward, if required, to pass a towline to a damaged combat ship.

The ranging kind of carrier operation that Admirals Halsey and Spruance employed required a flexible, almost day-to-day operation plan, so it was impossible to work out fueling schedules beforehand, as had been done in the more simple schedules with the Third Fleet staff at sea. Admiral Halsey usually fixed a rendezvous by dispatch. The fueling areas were always set if possible at the extreme limit of enemy land-based air, and the Japanese never managed to discover one of these rendezvous.

From 2 September 1944, when the Palaus operation began, through the first phase of the Philippine liberation, which ended 23 January 1945, fleet tankers of the At Sea Logistics Service Group delivered to the Fast Carrier Forces at sea about $8\frac{1}{4}$ million barrels of fuel oil and $14\frac{1}{4}$ million gallons of aviation gasoline. Over half – $4\frac{1}{2}$ million barrels of fuel oil, $7\frac{1}{4}$ million gallons of gas – was dispensed before the end of October, 1944.[3] The 34 oilers of this group constituted the principal liaison between forward bases and the fleet at sea; consequently they had to double as freighters and tenders for everything that the carriers needed. They delivered thousands of drums of lubricating oil in 14 different grades, compressed gases, bottled oxygen for aviators, food for issue to de-

[3] Cincpac Monthly Analysis for Oct. 1944 p. 31.

stroyers and destroyer escorts, spare belly tanks for planes, personnel replacements, mail and emergency freight.

The initial replenishment of the fast carrier groups before the Leyte operation was hampered by a typhoon, the edge of which hit Ulithi on 3 October, three days before they were scheduled to sail, and required three days to pass over. So heavy a sea made up in the big lagoon that lighters could not operate nor provision vessels come alongside.[4] Many ships had to sail with their storerooms only half filled; one carrier, two cruisers and some destroyers received no provisions whatever before their scheduled departure, which they had to postpone for twenty-four hours in order to get food on board. Nobody in the fleet went hungry; but owing to this contretemps and the insufficient number of reefer (refrigerated provision) ships in the Pacific, fresh and frozen provisions could not be delivered in the quantities to which sailors, especially the naval aviators, were accustomed. Menus became somewhat supercharged with Spam and beans.

Service Force Pacific Fleet replenished dry provisions for the entire Third Fleet, including the combat ships temporarily assigned to Admiral Kinkaid. As yet no means had been devised for the transfer of food at sea, except by sending out limited packages in the oilers; but that would come before the war was over.

Aviation spare parts were furnished by Aviation Stores Issue Ships *Fortune*, *Supply* and *Grummium*, anchored at Ulithi. They issued the parts to tankers and replacement escort carriers, which delivered them to the Fleet.

The Navy did not have nearly enough ammunition supply vessels (AE) to carry bombs and bullets over great distances to an expeditionary force and two fleets. A dozen or more Victory ships under merchant marine command were converted as auxiliary ammunition supply vessels (AKE). Six of the Navy AE and several AKE were assigned to Third Fleet; one AE and four Victories to

[4] During this typhoon of 3–5 Oct. at Ulithi, *LCT–1052* sank; all hands except the C.O., Ens. A. E. Smith USNR, were rescued by a motor launch from provision storeship *Aldebaran*.

Seventh Fleet. Altogether, these vessels carried from American West Coast ports to Kossol Passage, the usual anchorage for ships to replenish, 60,000 short tons of ammunition. About 30,000 tons of initial supply was issued to Third Fleet before the Palaus operation began, and 20,000 tons for ground forces were carried in four freighters. This added up to 110,000 tons ammunition delivered to the Fleet ashore or in Philippine waters before 1 December 1944. At that time a second ammunition echelon reached forward bases, and a third echelon arrived early in the New Year. The fast carriers used about 10,000 tons of ammunition, mostly aviation bombs, in September and October. After that the average monthly expenditure decreased to 3500 tons, owing to lack of targets and decrease in proportion of bombers to fighters. More than enough ammunition was provided for the Navy in the Leyte and Lingayen operations; the surplus was used to build up a "backlog" in advanced bases for later use at Okinawa.

Whilst most of the converted AKE did very well, there were several instances of lack of coöperation, the most notorious of which happened to Captain Roland Smoot of Desron 56, in Leyte Gulf, after the landings and before his squadron participated in the Battle of Surigao Strait. On 23 October – A-day plus 3 – the squadron attempted to replenish from two AKE. The service obtained from one of them "was nothing short of disgraceful. With a serious enemy threat developing, with all ships greatly depleted, and with time a very potent factor, the commanding officer of this ship put every obstacle he could possibly think of in the way of replenishment operations. He was the most disagreeable, uncoöperative individual it has ever been my misfortune to run up against. He refused to work through the noon hour. Ships would arrive alongside on schedule and his hatches would still be battened down. He refused to handle lines. This would add from one to two hours to each day's operations. His disreputable crew would sit around and pass disparaging remarks to the already overworked and tired enlisted men." (One of their repeated remarks which Captain Smoot well remembered was "Suckers! Suckers! I get twenty bucks a day, whadda youse guys get?") The master "sat up on his bridge in his undershirt and cursed and yelled at our officers and men." [5]

Now, for the first time, a system was devised for sending ammunition forward from bases left far behind as the Navy moved west and north. Little by little, almost every kind of bullet, bomb and explosive was fleeted up from the Marshalls, the Marianas and the South Pacific to Ulithi and Kossol Passage. In early October, after the Third Fleet had replenished at Ulithi and departed for Leyte, all ammunition ships less that half full were discharged into magazines afloat or ashore at Ulithi or Manus and dispatched to the West Coast for more. Kossol Passage proved an unsuitable roadstead for handling ammunition, as indeed it was for most purposes. Heavy swells, and want of shore storage and of stevedores, made transfer difficult and at times impossible, and the fact that the Japanese forces still held Babelthuap Island meant that danger from floating mines was constant. *Boulder Victory* hit a mine there on 20 December 1944 and No. 3 hold was flooded. By the turn of the year all ammunition ships were sent direct to Leyte Gulf. Transfer of ammunition in the open sea was not attempted in this operation.

The use of aircraft rockets greatly increased during the carrier strikes at the turn of the year. Napalm (gasoline jelly) incendiary bombs were used for the first time in Pacific carrier operations in September 1944.

Replacement planes for fast and escort carriers were constantly being brought up from rear areas in specially assigned CVEs. In one replacement group, escort carrier *Anzio* (Captain G. C. Montgomery) and *Lawrence C. Taylor* (Commander Ralph Cullinan) were providing antisubmarine patrol on 18 November, about 300 miles east of Samar, when they made contact on *I–26*, and sank it in an attack that was well coördinated between the carrier planes' bombs and the DE's hedgehog.

[5] Comdesron 56 Action Report 3 Nov. 1944, with endorsements by Adms. Wilkinson, Oldendorf and Kinkaid; conversation with Rear Adm. Smoot in Jan. 1952.

When Service Squadron 10 moved up to Ulithi, Service Squadron 12, known as the "harbor stretchers," continued working on major harbor improvements at Guam and Saipan. Service Squadron 2, which included all the repair, salvage and hospital ships of the Pacific Fleet, sent units to Ulithi, Manus, the Marianas and up to Leyte Gulf.[6] These ships kept the LSTs and smaller craft operating, and effected temporary battle-damage repairs on such ships as *Honolulu*, *Ross* and *A. W. Grant*, which enabled them to reach Guam or Manus where a floating dry dock, big enough to take a battleship, had been towed in sections and put together.

Many temporary repair jobs were done to carriers and other ships at Ulithi, but there the main activity was replenishment. When a fast carrier task group came in for a few days, almost everyone in Servron 10 had to work around the clock, while sailors in from the sea took their turns enjoying a brief rest and limited supplies of beer at the ex-royal residence on Mogmog. The very numerous ships, few of which carried any boats topside, created a boat problem which was never solved. Our British allies, who imagined that the Pacific Fleet was swamped with landing craft while they were being starved, would have been surprised to see the expedients to which the Ulithi boat pool had to resort, merely to take men ashore and get them back on board.

2. *Seventh Fleet*[7]

Service Force Seventh Fleet, commanded by Rear Admiral R. O. Glover,[8] was a small organization compared with "Uncle Bill"

[6] Commo. A. G. Quynn, Admiral Calhoun's chief of staff, was more immediately concerned with Squadron 2.

[7] CTF 77 (Adm. Kinkaid) Operation Plan 13–44, Annex E; Logistics Planning Officer Seventh Fleet (Lt. Cdr. R. C. Voils USNR) special report on logistics.

[8] Robert O. Glover, b. Norfolk, Va. 1894, Annapolis '15. Served in *Michigan* until 1917 and in several destroyers successively in World War I. Taught engineering at Annapolis and other naval schools. In *Maryland* 1923–26; flag sec. to Rear Adm. F. H. Clark 1929; engineer officer of *Houston* and C.O. *Pope* 1932–5. After various shore duties became C.O. of *Massachusetts* 1942–3; asst. director logistic plans div. office of C.N.O. 1943–4, when became Com. Service Force Seventh Fleet. Hydrographer at office of C.N.O. 1946; retired 1948.

Calhoun's, because Seventh Fleet, before the Leyte operation, was composed largely of submarines, amphibious craft and motor torpedo boats. Consequently, this Service Force was ill equipped to provide logistic support when Seventh Fleet was suddenly bloated by dozens of warships, from battleships down to patrol craft, lent by the Pacific Fleet. Logistics have to be planned many months in advance of an operation, and when the Leyte schedule was radically advanced in mid-September, everything was thrown off balance. The task was only accomplished by improvisation, stretching supply lines to the breaking point, and the utmost energy and devotion on the part of Admiral Glover's officers and men.

When the logistics support base for Third Fleet was transferred to Ulithi, that of Seventh Fleet remained at Manus. Admiral Barbey's Northern Attack Force had to receive its initial supply out of the Manus depot, which reduced the reserve stock counted upon for later phases of the operation. Shifting the fast carrier groups' base from Seeadler Harbor (as originally planned) to Ulithi had a disorganizing effect upon the logistic situation at Manus, because merchant ships destined for that place, carrying integral cargoes for the Naval Supply Depot to issue to both fleets, were now diverted to Ulithi and partially unloaded there. And the tactical situation long remained in such a state of flux that it was impossible to predict with any degree of accuracy the proportion of supplies required at Ulithi and Manus.

Seventh Fleet had always drawn on Australia as its principal source for provisions, but Australia was unable to produce the enormous quantities now required. It was necessary to augment the supply of fresh and frozen provisions from the United States. Every third load obtained by the three Seventh Fleet reefers, *Mizar*, *Calamares* and *Octans,* was procured from the West Coast of America; the other two were loaded in Australia. These three reefers took care of the initial supply of Northern Attack Force transports and amphibious craft, and there was always one standing by off Manus to replenish the larger units of the Seventh Fleet when their provisions became depleted. Pacific Fleet reefers attempted to take care of all combatant ships lent to the Seventh Fleet, but were not always able to do so. LSTs and smaller vessels at Leyte Gulf were supplied from the larger ships. Plenty of dry provisions reached the sailors in Philippine waters, but the supply of fresh meat, eggs and vegetables had to be spread thin. The escort carriers, for instance, could obtain less than one third the amount of fresh provisions normally supplied.

Fuel oil, gasoline and lubricants for Seventh Fleet came largely from Aruba in the West Indies and the West Coast of the United States. A beginning was made of obtaining black oil from the Persian Gulf, which meant a voyage covering only 90 degrees of longitude, as against 150 degrees for the Panama–Pacific transit. Commercial tankers carried petroleum products to Australia, Manus and Hollandia, where the shore and floating storage facilities that we have described were used to capacity in order to facilitate a quick turn-around of the fast fleet oilers. Of these, equipped for fueling at sea, the Seventh Fleet possessed only three – *Salamonie*, *Chepachet* and *Winooski* – before the operation began.[9] Commodore "Gus" Gray of Service Squadron 8 lent three more – *Saranac*, *Ashtabula* and *Suamico* – to make another fueling unit, together with *Kishwaukee* for aviation gasoline. The last-named followed the escort carriers about as best she could; the rest operated between Kossol Passage and Leyte Gulf.

When the movement to Leyte began, three oilers preceded the combat ships to a point about 150 miles west of the Palaus to fuel under way all minecraft, fire support ships and units of the Dinagat Attack Group as they passed. They then rendezvoused with Admiral Wilkinson's LST groups of the Southern Attack Force and acted as their milch cows the rest of the voyage to Leyte Gulf. Thereafter, they ran a shuttle service between Kossol Passage (where a commercial tanker was always held in readiness for replenishment) and a convenient point for fire support ships

[9] All other tankers in Seventh Fleet, because of age or equipment, were only capable of serving as harbor fuelers.

wanting fuel, about 100 miles east of Leyte Gulf. A reserve of half a million barrels of black oil was kept afloat at Manus for replenishing this and the borrowed fueling units. And the bombardment and fire support ships were able to obtain about one quarter of their fuel requirements from Pacific Fleet oilers of Service Squadron 8.

Ammunition for Seventh Fleet was shipped directly from the United States in converted Victory ships to magazines in Australia, Manus and Hollandia. Thence it was sent up to forward areas in similar vessels, or in one of the two Australian ammunition ships – H.M.A.S. *Poyang* and *Yunnan* – which belonged to the Fleet. *Mazama,* lent by the Pacific Fleet, and three AKE from the same source (*Durham, Iran* and *Bluefield Victories*) were promptly moved up to Kossol Passage. *Durham V*. and *Mazama* arrived in Leyte Gulf in time to replenish Admiral Oldendorf's force before and after the Battle of Surigao Straits; and, when depleted, were replaced by others from Kossol. Although this meant at least three handlings of ammunition before it could be issued to the Fleet, including one in an exposed open roadstead, no other method was possible with the ships and facilities on hand. By the turn of the year, more AKE were available and an expeditious method was devised for replenishing units at Lingayen Gulf.

For a considerable time after the landings at Leyte, a system of resupply echelons was operated by Service Force Seventh Fleet. From a pool of five ammunition ships, three cargo ships for dry provisions, two AKs for general issue ships' stores, three fleet oilers, two Australian Navy oilers, four auxiliary oilers and a number of gasoline and diesel tankers, an echelon was selected to be included in each regular follow-up convoy. These departed Hollandia, Manus or Biak every six days for Leyte Gulf. Although the Japanese Navy had instructions to seek out and destroy all supply units, the only damage done to any Seventh Fleet Service Force ship during the entire operation was through one hit by a torpedo bomber on oiler *Ashtabula* (Lieutenant Commander W. Barnett USNR) when under way off Samar on the evening of 24 October. The explosion opened a hole 24 by 34 feet on her port side and flooded a pumproom. She listed 12 degrees, but the damage control crew promptly transferred fuel to tanks on the undamaged side, and within 25 minutes she was making ten knots. Rejoining her temporary task unit she spent the night under way, but sustained two more air attacks shortly after dawn. One, of three planes, was thwarted by evasive maneuvers and a smoke screen; the second, by a single plane, was disposed of by *Ashtabula's* antiaircraft gunners. On the 26th she was able to fuel a cruiser and a destroyer and transfer 128,598 gallons of aviation gasoline to her sister ship *Salamonie*. That day she drove off two more aircraft attacks. After *Suamico* had relieved her of over 200,000 more gallons of avgas, *Ashtabula* transferred the task unit commander (Captain J. D. Beard) to *Saranac* and proceeded to Kossol Passage, where the rest of her cargo was salvaged before she returned to base for repairs.[10]

Another supply problem, drinking water, was well handled by the Seventh Fleet. It had always been difficult in amphibious operations to supply fresh water to the beaching and other small craft that had no distilling apparatus. So far, the large vessels had given of their plenty to the small; but in an operation employing an enormous number of small waterless ships, the charity of the great could not be depended upon. Accordingly, in the summer of 1944, the Navy converted several fleet oilers into water tankers, each of which could carry 100,000 barrels (4,000,000 gallons) of fresh water. *Severn*, the first, arrived Leyte 24 October, while *Ponaganset*, which had rendered a similar service at Peleliu, lay in Kossol Passage issuing fresh water there. She serviced 125 vessels in October and 206 in November.

It is curious that, with many modern antiseptics available, these ships experienced as much trouble with water going foul as did the old sailing vessels with their wooden casks and interminable voyages. A naval surgeon and staff had to be shipped in each water tanker to make frequent tests; yet, despite their efforts, bacteria

[10] Carter *Beans, Bullets and Black Oil* pp. 239–40.

found steel tanks and tropical heat so congenial that many thousands of gallons of fresh water gone wrong had to be emptied into the ocean.

By these means, in spite of initial difficulties due to want of ships, derangement of logistics schedules, a fluid tactical situation and the limited supplies available in Australia, the energy and intelligence of Service Force Seventh Fleet overcame most of its difficulties.

CHAPTER VI

Formosa Air Battle

10–20 October 1944

1. *Carrier Strikes on Okinawa and Formosa 10–14 October*[1]

TYPHOONS were the bane of the Pacific Fleet in 1944–1945, but the one that gave Ulithi a whirl on October 3–4 did not hold up Admiral Halsey and half of Task Force 38 was not there. Vice Admiral McCain's Group 1, which had replenished at Seeadler Harbor, sortied thence on 4 October. Rear Admiral Davison's Group 4, which had left the same harbor in the Admiralties on 24 September, was now operating west of the Palaus to cover the Peleliu operation, and broke off on 5 October. Rear Admiral Bogan's Group 2 with Admiral Halsey in *New Jersey*, and Rear Admiral Frederick Sherman's Group 3 with Vice Admiral Mitscher in *Lexington*, sortied from Ulithi during the afternoon of 6 October, right on the tail of the typhoon. Its center, fortunately, lay far to the north, but it left a trail of high easterly winds and heavy seas in the Western Pacific.

Shortly before dark 7 October, about 375 miles west of the Marianas in clearing weather and high crested seas of the deepest ultramarine, the entire carrier task force made rendezvous. The age of steam has afforded no marine spectacle comparable to a meet-

[1] *War College Analysis* I 91–158, 244–451; Com Third Fleet (Admiral Halsey) Report of Operations Preliminary to Support of Leyte-Samar 28 Nov. 1944; CTF 38 (Vice Adm. Mitscher) and TG commanders' Action Reports; Vice Adm. Fukudome's article in U.S. Nav. Inst. *Proceedings* LXXVIII (1952) 1285–95.

ing of Fast Carrier Forces Pacific Fleet. Now that the seaman's eye has become accustomed to the great "flattops" and has learned what they can do to win command of the sea, they have become as beautiful to him as a ship of the line to his bell-bottomed forbears. They and the new battleships with their graceful sheer, tossing spray masthead-high and leaving a boiling wake, evoked poetic similes, such as Thomas Gray's

> . . . coursers of ethereal race
> With necks in thunder clothed and long resounding pace.

For nothing except a thoroughbred horse is comparable to a fine ship.

From the rendezvous, TF 38 with its fueling group of nine fleet oilers proceeded to lat. 19° N, long. 139° E, where the entire day 8 October was spent fueling. The weather was still unfavorable, with heavy confused seas and large swells as a result of the typhoon. Oilers' decks were awash and seamanship was given a severe test, which the fleet met.

In an effort to deceive the enemy as to Third Fleet intentions, and to suggest that the main Allied attack was to be directed "up the ladder of the Bonins," a task group commanded by Rear Admiral Allan E. ("Hoke") Smith, consisting of heavy cruisers *Chester*, *Pensacola* and *Salt Lake City* and six destroyers, struck Marcus Island on 9 October "with great fanfare." [2] By taking advantage of a heavy weather front, they approached undetected, and the fanfare took the shape of smoke puffs dispersed over the horizon, floats with dummy radar targets and assorted pyrotechnics. The bombardment, spread out between dawn and dust, was supposed to make the enemy expect a landing on Marcus, but he seems in no way to have been impressed.

Although the complete composition of Task Force 38 is given in an appendix, a brief summary at this point may be useful to the reader: —

[2] Com Third Fleet Report on Seizure of Palau, Ulithi . . . Morotai, 14 Nov. 1944.

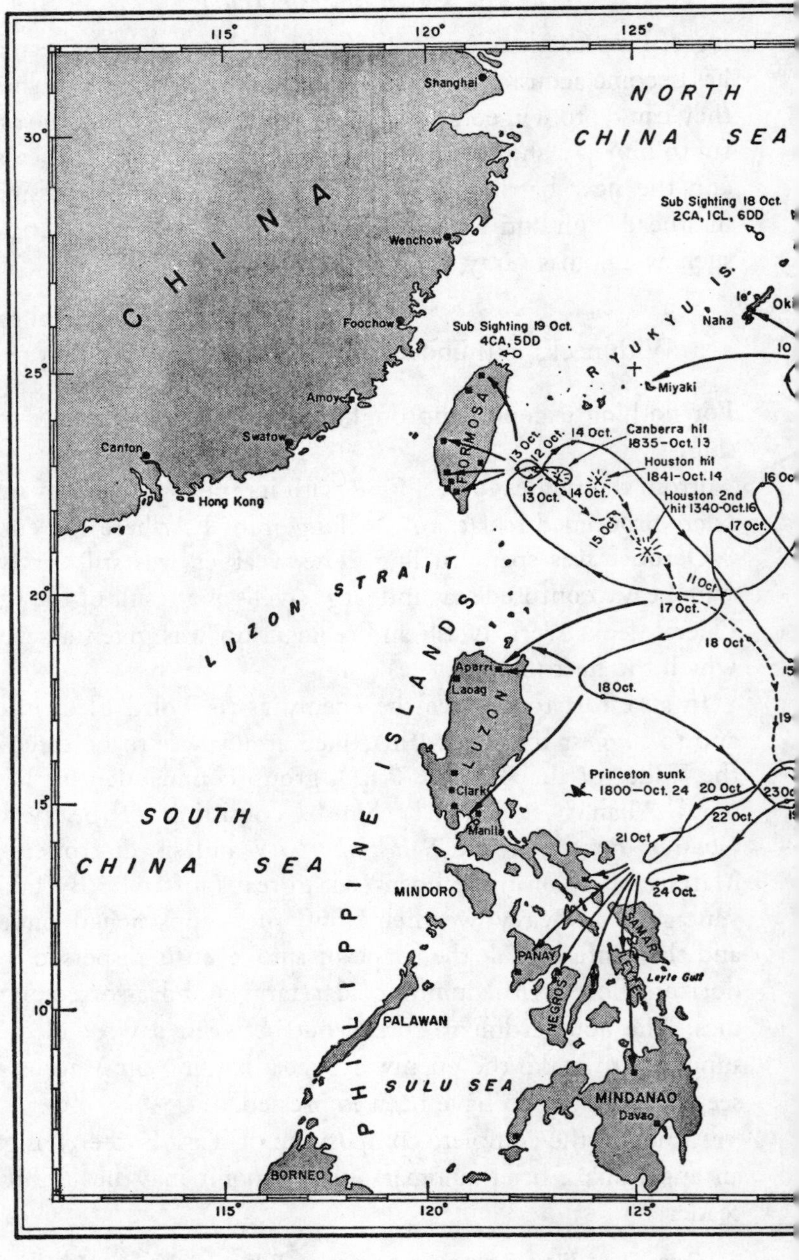

115°
120°
125°
NORTH
CHINA SEA
Shanghai
30°
Sub Sighting 18 Oct.
2CA, 1CL, 6DD
Wenchow
CHINA
RYUKYU IS.
Naha
Foochow
Sub Sighting 19 Oct.
4CA, 5DD
25°
Miyaki
Amoy
FORMOSA
Swatow
Canton
Canberra hit
1835-Oct. 13
Houston hit
1841-Oct. 14
Houston 2nd
hit 1340-Oct. 16
Hong Kong
13 Oct.
12 Oct.
14 Oct.
15 Oct.
16 Oct.
17 Oct.
LUZON STRAIT
20°
11 Oct.
18 Oct.
Aparri
Laoag
LUZON
PHILIPPINE ISLANDS
Princeton sunk
1800-Oct. 24
20 Oct.
22 Oct.
21 Oct.
24 Oct.
Clark
Manila
15°
SOUTH
CHINA SEA
MINDORO
SAMAR
PANAY
LEYTE
Leyte Gulf
NEGROS
10°
PALAWAN
SULU SEA
MINDANAO
Davao
BORNEO

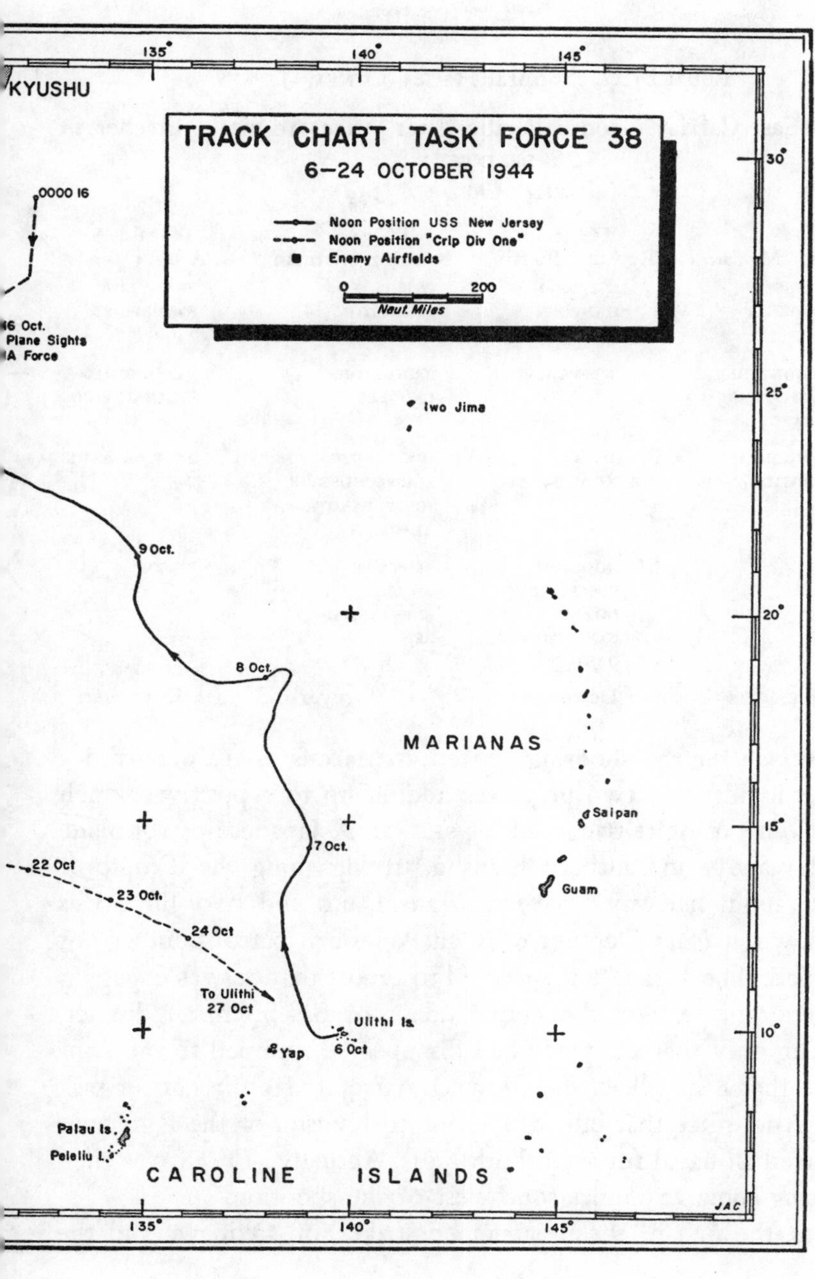
TRACK CHART TASK FORCE 38
6–24 OCTOBER 1944
Noon Position USS New Jersey
Noon Position "Crip Div One"
Enemy Airfields
0
200
Neut. Miles
KYUSHU
0000 16
16 Oct.
Plane Sights
A Force
Iwo Jima
9 Oct.
8 Oct.
MARIANAS
Saipan
7 Oct.
Guam
22 Oct
23 Oct.
24 Oct
To Ulithi
27 Oct
Ulithi Is.
6 Oct
Yap
Palau Is.
Peleliu I.
CAROLINE ISLANDS
135°
140°
145°
30°
25°
20°
15°
10°
JAC

Third Fleet, Admiral Halsey in NEW JERSEY

TF 38 Fast Carrier Groups Pacific Fleet, Vice Admiral Mitscher in LEXINGTON

(*As of 14 October 1944*)

	TG 38.1 V. Adm. McCain	TG 38.2 R. Adm. Bogan	TG 38.3 R. Adm. Sherman	TG 38.4 R. Adm. Davison
CV	WASP HORNET	INTREPID HANCOCK BUNKER HILL	ESSEX LEXINGTON	FRANKLIN ENTERPRISE
CVL	MONTEREY COWPENS CABOT	INDEPENDENCE	PRINCETON LANGLEY	SAN JACINTO BELLEAU WOOD
CA	WICHITA BOSTON CANBERRA			CA NEW ORLEANS
BB		IOWA NEW JERSEY	WASHINGTON MASSACHUSETTS SOUTH DAKOTA ALABAMA	
CL		HOUSTON VINCENNES MIAMI SAN DIEGO OAKLAND	SANTA FE MOBILE BIRMINGHAM RENO	BILOXI
	15 Destroyers	17 Destroyers	14 Destroyers	12 Destroyers

Shortly after the shooting started at Marcus, there occurred a curious incident of two negatives adding up to a positive, which almost but not quite triggered off SHO-GO. A Japanese patrol plane out of Kanoya in southern Kyushu,[8] flying along the Tropic of Cancer about halfway between Okina Daito and Iwo Jima, was shot down at 0845 October 9 by an American patrol bomber out of Tinian. The Japanese pilot failed to report that he was engaging an enemy plane, and the commandant of Sasebo naval district, knowing only that the plane had disappeared, jumped to the conclusion that it had been shot down by aircraft from a carrier task force. And, since that boded no good to Kyushu or the Ryukyus, he alerted all naval forces in both areas. Actually, TF 38 was then operating some 225 miles southwest of the shooting.

Thus, the first of the prearranged strikes, on Okinawa and the

[8] Lat. 23°45′N, long. 137°30′E. *War College Analysis* I 43, 92, 243.

smaller Ryukyus, on 10 October, was no surprise to the enemy, but that did not help him much. TF 38 flew 1396 sorties between dawn and dusk on the 10th. The destruction of shipping (a submarine tender, 12 torpedo boats, 2 midget submarines, 4 cargo ships, and a number of auxiliary sampans) was more extensive than our pilots reported; and although the enemy never disclosed the number of aircraft destroyed, it was probably not far short of the 111 claimed. The cost to us was 21 aircraft, 5 pilots and 4 crewmen. Lifeguard submarine *Sterlet*, stationed off Okinawa, recovered 6 of those who had splashed. With the exception of carrier *Hornet* and the submarines, no United States ship had been so close to the Japanese homeland during the war, or penetrated the inner line of defenses. Our nearest base, Saipan, lay over 1200 miles from the target; we were sticking our necks into a bag of enemy air power represented by the airfields that lay in a great, inverted U from Iwo Jima through Kyushu, Korea, East China, Formosa and Luzon. The Ryukyus, moreover, were formidable air bases in themselves. Task Force 38 found their harbors glutted with war shipping and the airfields well supplied with combat planes.

Admiral Toyoda, C. in C. Combined Fleet, got the news of the Okinawa strike in Formosa. At his Hyoshi headquarters his chief of staff, Rear Admiral Kusaka, rightly guessing that this meant the beginning of something important, took it upon himself at 0925 October 10 to alert the Japanese Navy's base air forces for SHO–1 (Leyte) and SHO–2 (Formosa). At 0930 he ordered Vice Admiral Fukudome, commanding Sixth Base Air Force, "to attack and destroy the enemy." And at 1019 Kusaka, in Toyoda's name, issued an order of immense importance for the immediate future, directing that carriers *Zuikaku*, *Zuiho*, *Chitose*, *Chiyoda*, and the half-converted battleship carriers *Ise* and *Hyuga*, stand by to transfer all their operational planes to land bases. Admiral Toyoda, caught at Formosa, now knew that air preliminaries to the "general decisive battle" had started, and decided to direct them from his temporary headquarters.[4] Vice Admiral Mikawa at Manila gave

[4] *War College Analysis* I 243–9.

him an accurate estimate to the effect that the next air attack would be on Formosa.

To defend Formosa, Admiral Fukudome depended on the approximately 230 fighter planes operational on the island; and to counterattack the carrier force, on his élite "T" Force based in Kyushu.

Before hitting Formosa, however, TF 38 had planned a strike on Aparri airfield, on the north coast of Luzon. The carriers fueled from twelve oilers in the morning, and at 1240 October 11, the McCain and Davison groups commenced launching from a distance of 323 miles. This strike of 61 planes, 22 of them armed with rockets, was unopposed. It destroyed about 15 planes on the ground and we lost 7 planes, all but one operational. During the day C.A.P. shot down three enemy planes, one within 25 miles of the task force. These were the first attacks on TF 38 in accordance with Admiral Toyoda's orders. "I should have struck Formosa first," admitted Admiral Halsey,[5] for the Aparri strike accomplished nothing worth while, yet gave Formosa another day's grace.

During the afternoon three Service Squadron escort carriers transferred 61 replacement planes, 3 pilots and 11 crewmen to TF 38. Refueling was completed at 1748. During the night of 11–12 October the task force steered about NNW at 24 knots toward the launching position for Formosa, where Admirals Halsey and Mitscher planned to deliver their most lethal punch.

Next day, 12 October, began the big business – the three-day effort to knock out Japanese air strength on Formosa, and to deny it to the enemy as a staging base toward Leyte. TF 38 arrived at its dawn launching position, 50 to 90 miles east of Formosa before dawn, expecting at that time an enemy attack (since it was evident that they had been shadowed); but none developed. At 0544, an hour before sunrise, the first strike, a fighter sweep to gain command of the air over Formosa and the Pescadores, was launched. Flying weather throughout these three days (as also on the two

[5] *War College Analysis* I 130; *Admiral Halsey's Story* (1947) p. 205.

previous days) was good to excellent; enough wind to make launching and recovery easy, good visibility and enough cloud coverage to help the pilots.

No fewer than 1378 sorties were flown 12 October from all four carrier groups on Formosan airfields and shipping. Admiral Bogan's group took the north end of the island, Admiral Sherman's the center, Admiral McCain's the south and Admiral Davison's the Takao area. Their day's grace did the Japanese no good. Admiral Fukudome describes how the aërial combat began immediately over his command post, how when planes began dropping he assumed that they were the attackers, clapped his hands and shouted "Well done! Tremendous success!" – and how a second look showed that the falling stars were Japanese. "Our fighters," he wrote, "were nothing but so many eggs thrown at the stone wall of the indomitable enemy formation." There was also "terrific damage" to the Japanese ground installations, including the complete destruction of Fukudome's headquarters. One third of the Admiral's fighter strength, including many of the leaders, was destroyed by the first American strike that day. Only about 60 fighters were operational when the second wave came over and none left the ground to intercept the third.[6] Nevertheless, American losses were heavy – 48 planes. The carriers were snooped throughout the day, and at 1900 Japanese Bettys armed with torpedoes began a series of raids and harassing operations, which went on until midnight. These were of the "T" Force. Fukudome admitted losing 42 planes in these raids, which accomplished nothing.[7] Some were shot down by the C.A.P. maintained by *Cabot* and *Independence;* others by antiaircraft fire from Admiral Bogan's group.

At dawn 13 October TF 38 arrived at its launching position about 70 miles bearing 110° (E by S) from Seikoo Roadstead, Formosa. Launching began at 0614, half an hour before sunrise. The pattern of strikes was similar to that on the first day, but only

[6] U.S. Nav. Inst. *Proceedings* LXXVIII 1292–3.
[7] *War College Analysis* I 105.

974 sorties were flown, all before noon. The pilots found several airfields whose existence had not been previously known; in the area assigned to TG 38.3 there were at least 15 instead of the 4 indicated in the operation plan. During the evening twilight, when she was recovering planes, carrier *Franklin* of Admiral Davison's TG 38.4 was attacked by four low-flying Bettys, undetected by radar. One was shot down by antiaircraft fire with the assistance of Lieutenant A. J. Pope, flying a fighter already in the landing circle; a second was shot down by the screen; a third, after dropping its torpedo, hedge-hopped *Franklin's* bow, and was then shot down; Captain Shoemaker by ringing up full speed astern just missed the torpedo. The fourth enemy pilot, after dropping a torpedo which passed under *Franklin's* fantail, and catching fire, crashed the carrier's flight deck, slid horribly across it, burst into flames, and lurched overboard.

Little damage was inflicted.[8] But in Admiral McCain's TG 38.1 heavy cruiser *Canberra* took a bad torpedo hit. As a consequence of this, and the efforts to save her, which we shall relate shortly, a small third day's assault on Formosa was set up for 14 October. This was limited to one strike of 146 fighters, of which 17 were lost, and 100 bombers, of which 6 were lost. Lack of naval air strength was compensated by the XX Bomber Command, Army Air Force, which sent 109 B–29s from China to bomb the Takao area. Also, at dawn on the 14th, Admiral Davison's TG 38.4 flew a series of small fighter strikes on the Aparri and Laoag fields in northern Luzon. These destroyed a few enemy planes on the ground.[9]

The results of this three-day Formosa air battle were over 500 enemy planes destroyed,[10] some twoscore freighters and small

[8] *Franklin* Report of Action with Japanese Aircraft 13 Oct. 1944.

[9] *War College Analysis* I 115–17.

[10] CTF 38 claimed 655, including those shot down near the task force; the Japanese admitted 492, including an estimated "100 Army aircraft of all types." Since the Japanese were always reluctant to admit losses, even to themselves, and since American pilots were optimistic in claims, the probability is that total enemy losses were somewhere between 550 and 600. *War College Analysis* I 122.

craft sunk, and many others damaged; and an enormous destruction of ammunition dumps, hangars, barracks, shops and industrial plants.

2. *Cripdiv 1 and Concluding Strikes,*[11] *13–20 October*

In this "knock-down, drag-out fight between carrier-based air and shore-based air," as Admiral Halsey described the three days' battle, the Japanese made exaggerated claims of damage inflicted by their land-based planes. They never sank a ship, but TF 38 did not get off scot-free. At dusk of the second day, Friday 13 October, the new heavy cruiser *Canberra* in Admiral McCain's task group was hit by an aërial torpedo and badly crippled. The following evening, light cruiser *Houston* took a torpedo hit and on the 16th she got another. The story of towing these two severely damaged ships out of enemy waters – *Canberra* when hit lay 90 miles from the coast of Formosa and *Houston* only 80 miles south of the Sakishima Gunto – is one of the notable salvage exploits of the war.

Admiral Mitscher's planes were still being recovered at 1835, after sundown, when a group of eight enemy torpedo-bombers flew in low out of the sunset, not heralded by radar. Six were shot down by antiaircraft fire but one torpedoed *Canberra* between her two firerooms below the armor belt, blowing a huge, jagged hole and killing 23 men instantly.[12] Flames flashed masthead-high, and as both engine rooms and after firerooms were flooded, she coasted to a dead stop. About 4500 tons of water rushed in before a damage control party managed to isolate the compartments. There seemed to be no possible way to get the ship home under her own power.

Although the normal procedure would have been to scuttle the crippled cruiser, Admiral Halsey made the bold decision to tow

[11] Rear Adm. T. B. Inglis, former C.O. of *Birmingham*, gave me valuable information in 1946. The operations of this group are covered in *War College Analysis* I 110–13, 130–1, 146–8, 199, 201, II 34–5, 43–5, 190–1, 305, 312.

[12] Position at the time: lat. 22°40′N, long. 123°35′E.

her clear and to cover that operation with more air attacks.[13] That is why the Formosa strike of 14 October, not in the original plan, was laid on.

At 1845, ten minutes after *Canberra* was torpedoed, *Wichita* received the word from Admiral McCain, "stand by to take under tow." The following account of rigging the tow [14] may be skipped by readers impatient to resume the story of the battle, but is commended to mariners as proof that the United States Navy, while growing wings and sprouting radar, had not neglected old-fashioned marlinspike seamanship.

Under the direction of *Wichita's* damage control officer, Lieutenant Commander Richard Edwards USNR, and Chief Boatswain's Mate Edwin Oberbroeckling, rigging "went as smoothly as a daytime drill" and was accomplished in darkness in twenty minutes. *Wichita* was provided with a 150-fathom, 1⅛-inch plow-steel towing wire complete with manila mooring lines and messenger, snubbing gear, chafing gear, and lizard of 4½-inch manila. The bitter end of the tow wire led from a reel and was stopped off along her topsides at deck level, to the towing chock aft, and through that to the link, secured by a pelican stopper shackled to the towing padeye. First, the balance of the wire towline was stripped from the reel and faked down on starboard side of turret 3, bights being stopped to the nearest bitts. To the outboard end of this towing hawser was bent a 120-fathom 7-inch manila mooring line; to the end of that, a 50-fathom 4½-inch manila line; and to the end of that, a 30-fathom 3-inch manila and a 20-fathom 21-thread line that were already spliced together to serve as the messenger. All manila lines were faked down on deck athwartship.

At 1928, when *Wichita* closed the leeward side of *Canberra* to pass the tow, the stricken cruiser was wallowing in the trough of a heavy ground swell which imparted a corkscrew motion to both

[13] *War College Analysis* I 112.

[14] Taken almost word for word from Comcrudiv 6 Action Report for Operation of TU 30.3.2, 15–16 Oct. 1944, Enclosure A by Lt. Cdr. Edwards.

ships, and there was a gusty 22-knot wind on the starboard beam. *Canberra* shot over her own line, which was promptly bent onto *Wichita's* heaving lines and messenger. She then hauled on board the manila part of the towline when only one bight of it, together with the entire wire hawser, remained on *Wichita's* deck. Inopportunely the two ships kissed in a heavy roll, then yawed violently apart, so that the standing part of the 4½-inch manila line jerked away from *Wichita's* crew, pinned three men to the deck or to vent cowls (breaking their bones), then slacked, threw a half-hitch around a fire hydrant and parted; the high-pressure hydrant came away at the deck, letting a geyser of water shoot high into the air. Amid all this confusion, the men heaved a handline to *Canberra*, recovered the manila lizard and bent it to the tow wire. The hawser was then passed without further difficulty. There was some delay in securing it on board *Canberra* owing to its thimble being too small for her chain shackle bolt; and for a time it looked as if the old adage "For want of a nail . . ." would be illustrated. While this juggling was going on, the bight of the wire was kept clear of *Wichita's* screws by the lizard. *Canberra* eventually produced a shackle that fitted, secured the wire hawser to her anchor chain, and at 2112 reported she was ready to be towed.

Wichita moved slowly ahead, paying out towline. The stopper was duly slipped, releasing the snubbing chain; stops were cut, and the wire led fair through the after quarter chock, where it was puddened or keckled with sheet lead and copper to prevent chafe. At 2154 *Wichita* took up strain on the tow wire, and *Canberra* reported she was making headway. Speed was gradually built up, course very cautiously changed from WNW to SE, on which both ships were steadied shortly after midnight. By two bells in the midwatch 14 October, the cruisers were making 3.8 knots.[15] Although this was still not enough to clear enemy land-based plane radius by dusk, it put an undue strain on the wire; as *Canberra's*

[15] Towing threw out the dead-reckoning tracer and speed was measured by an old-fashioned chip log of the type used by Francis Drake and John Paul Jones. *Wichita* turned up revolutions to make speed of 7 knots in order to obtain 3.8 knots through the water for tow.

bow lifted and dipped in the long swells, the hawser alternately tautened and slacked until there was danger of its parting. *Canberra* accordingly veered 70 fathoms of chain from her hawsepipe. That improved the catenary, and *Wichita* was able to make good four knots on course 133°.

In the meantime, fleet tug *Munsee* (Lieutenant Commander J. F. Pingley) had been signaled for, and came tearing over from where she was standing by at sea with the fleet oiler group (TG 30.8) which she and *Pawnee*, providentially, had been ordered to join on the 8th. At 0643 October 15, wind and sea much abated, *Munsee* passed her tow wire to *Canberra*, who hauled her chain in on deck, unshackled *Wichita's* wire, and eased it out, aided by *Wichita's* men, who had spliced a 5-inch manila line onto the link in the towing gear. All hands laid onto this line and "ran away with it" along the deck in old man o' war fashion. Thus no fouling occurred, and by 0700 *Wichita* was clear of the tow and ready to proceed, while *Munsee* took care of *Canberra*.

While this tow steamed slowly southeasterly, Admiral McCain's carrier group, to which *Canberra* belonged, operated well to the north in order to intercept any attempt to attack the slow-moving Cripdiv from that direction. On the morning of the 14th three of the TF 38 carrier groups sent fighter sweeps against the Formosan airfields. The enemy did not take these Parthian shots lying down. At dusk he sent in a heavy air attack, consisting of 11 to 16 torpedo-carrying Frans, against Admiral McCain's Group, one of whose light cruisers, *Houston*, caught it.[16] An aërial torpedo struck her starboard side amidships at 1845 October 14 and damaged her severely – worse than *Canberra* the previous day. Her engineering spaces were completely flooded, all power was lost, the ship appeared to be breaking up and destroyers closed to take off the crew. Her C.O., Captain W. W. Behrens, confused by con-

[16] This raid was first detected 30 miles from TG 38.1. Destroyer *Woodworth*, stationed 12 miles east of the force, gave the first warning and helped break up the attack by shooting down three. Four others were subsequently shot down by antiaircraft fire.

flicting reports from damage control parties, advised Admiral McCain at 1933 that he was planning to abandon ship; he did not then think that there was any use trying to save her.[17] At 2020, before all the crew had been taken off, Captain Behrens changed his mind, ordered abandonment discontinued and signaled that he wanted a tow. Admiral McCain ordered Rear Admiral Wiltse, in heavy cruiser *Boston* (Captain E. E. Herrmann), to undertake this delicate operation.

Admiral Halsey now faced another dilemma. Should he attempt to save both crippled cruisers, at the expense of strikes scheduled for Luzon and the Visayas on 16 October? For, if he were to keep them afloat, his carrier group would have to stand by to protect them. By quick staff work it was decided that protecting the cripples could be done without hampering the most important strikes, those on Leyte, Cebu and Negros.

A moderating wind and sea made the process of passing the towline from *Boston* to *Houston* less troublesome than in the case of *Wichita* and *Canberra*, but there were some new complications. *Boston* was rigged for passing the towline from her starboard quarter but found she could not keep station off the port (lee) side of the deeply settled *Houston*. Consequently, she had to take a new station to windward of the cripple and re-rig the line on her port quarter. The night was so black that when *Boston's* stern was finally brought to *Houston's* stem, "nothing of *Houston* could be seen from *Boston's* bridge, and conning had to be based on telephoned reports from the fantail." [18] After the hawser was secured at 2320, great difficulty was experienced in bringing *Houston* around from her dead-in-the-water heading of W b. N, through the eye of the southwest wind, to the desired course of about SE b. S; but the turn was finally completed by six bells in the midwatch, 15 October, and the tow proceeded at a speed of five to six knots on course 150°. As the line appeared to be too short to

[17] Position of *Houston* at 2000 Oct. 14, was lat. 22°33'N, long. 124°04'E, about 150 miles, 104°, from southern Formosa.

[18] *Boston* Action Report 14–24 Oct., 25 Oct. 1944, Enclosure A to her Action Report for 2–27 Oct.

give the proper catenary, *Houston* bent on her anchor chain and paid it out to the extent of 120 fathom.

Cruisers *Santa Fe*, *Birmingham* and *Mobile*, under command of Rear Admiral Laurance T. DuBose, accompanied by eight destroyers, was set up as Task Force 30.3, better known as "Cripdiv 1," to tow the two cruisers. At the same time (1635 October 15) Admiral Halsey detached light carriers *Cowpens* and *Cabot* with *Wichita*, *Mobile* and four destroyers, as a covering unit. Fleet tug *Pawnee* (Lieutenant H. C. Cramer USNR) arrived between 1021 and 1036, 16 October, and with some difficulty took over the tow of *Houston*. In so doing the cruiser drifted down on the tug, and fouled her starboard anchor on *Pawnee's* bulwarks, which were torn off for about six feet.

The two pairs, *Munsee* towing *Canberra* and *Pawnee* towing *Houston*, steamed abreast one mile apart, screened by Admiral DuBose's task group, while the light carriers operated in support about 15 to 20 miles away. This peculiar disposition presented some nice problems in relative ship movements. The tow could make only 3½ knots, while the cruisers and destroyers zigzagged violently at 12 knots in order to maintain their relative positions yet not expose themselves to submarine attack. When an air attack developed or threatened, as was the case most of the time, the screen steamed at 15 knots in a tight circle around the tow.

There were no more strikes on Formosa, after 14 October. Admiral Davison's Task Group 4 hit Luzon on the 15th and 16th, but TGs 38.2 and 38.3 milled around in the hope that Toyoda would commit his surface fleet and give them some new targets. But that did not happen. During these three days the fighting swung away from Formosa toward the crippled ships. TF 38, instead of knocking down planes on or over the big island, was on the receiving end, beating off air counterattacks by interception and antiaircraft fire as it slowly retired southeasterly.

Admiral Toyoda, on the basis of Japanese aviators' reports, sent Admiral Fukudome a message on the afternoon of 14 October to the effect that Third Fleet was retiring in defeat, and ordering him to annihilate the "remnants" next day. But at 0800 October 15 he received the report on an intact carrier force, bearing 66° distant 240 miles from Manila. This was Admiral Davison's TG 38.4, then making a shattering attack on the Manila airfields, its planes shooting down or driving off the 50 to 60 interceptors that rose to meet it.[19] Fukudome dispatched a small fighter and light bomber strike which came in on this group at about 1046. *Franklin* was not at general quarters at the time. A staff signalman sighted three Judys orbiting directly overhead, the word was passed and antiaircraft gunners opened up. Two were shot down while in their dives. The third was hit by 40-mm when about 200 yards on the port side and forced to splash, but its bomb hit a corner of the deck-edge elevator and exploded, killing three and wounding 12 officers and men. The material damage was slight.

At 1400 a second group of 90 Army and Navy planes took off from Clark Field, Luzon, to attack Davison's task group. The interesting thing about this strike is that Rear Admiral Masafumi Arima tagged along, piloting a Judy, to make the first sacrificial attack. He got the reputation in the Japanese Navy of having "lit the torch" of the Kamikazes by crashing a carrier; but actually his plane and about 19 others were shot down by Davison's C.A.P. and the rest returned ingloriously to base; not one got near enough the ships to attack.[20]

Fukudome also sent three unsuccessful strikes against Cripdiv 1 on the 15th. The first, from Shinchiku, failed to find the cripples. The second, from Okinawa, ran afoul of Admiral McCain's TG 38.1 and got badly mauled. The third, dispatched from Formosa in the afternoon, returned to base when the flight commander's plane developed engine trouble.[21]

Speed of advance seemed excruciatingly slow to the members of Cripdiv 1. When would they ever get outside enemy air range?

[19] *War College Analysis* I 375, 385, 135.

[20] *War College Analysis* I 407–9; *Inter. Jap. Off.* I 60; *Franklin* was hit by a Kamikaze on 30 Oct. 1944 and in March 1945 was almost destroyed in a bombing attack.

[21] Same I 402.

A reconnaissance plane sighted them at 0920 October 16. An attack group of 99 carrier-type planes, half fighters and half bombers, took off from Kyushu to finish them off. This strike was canceled – presumably by Admiral Toyoda – and why, nobody has been able to explain.[22] But in the afternoon the good angel who had hitherto taken care of Cripdiv 1 nodded. A big flight of 107 aircraft, which took off from Formosa about 1000, reached the group at 1315, when it was still crawling across the entrance to Luzon Strait. More than half the number was intercepted by fighters from *Cabot* and *Cowpens*, which shot down an estimated 41 planes (the Japanese admitted loss of 27),[23] but three managed to penetrate the screen. *Houston's* five-inch mounts were inoperative through power failure when a Fran pressed an attack on her through the fire of several ships astern. Sailors boiled up from below to man the nearest 20-mm or 40-mm gun, opening fire on manual control. The plane, when 3000 yards astern and about 75 feet above the water, released a well-aimed torpedo. It struck square on the cruiser's stern, blowing the hangar hatch 150 feet into the air like a stove lid, and knocking about 20 men overboard. The plane then paralleled *Houston* about 200 yards away, and was shot down. Several minutes later, a Kate made for *Santa Fe*, which not only evaded the torpedo but shot the plane in two so close to her bow that the ship passed through a circle of flame like a trained animal in a circus.

Immediately after this second hit on *Houston*, fleet tug *Pawnee* sent her a visual signal that deserves a place among the Navy's historic phrases: –

WE'LL STAND BY YOU!

Stand by she did; there was no slack in the towline at any time. *Santa Fe* closed and Admiral DuBose roared through the bull-horn to *Houston's* bridge, "Is your case hopeless?" Captain Behrens replied, "Not hopeless, grave." He requested the removal of about

22 *War College Analysis* I 434.
23 Same II 147.

300 men who were not necessary to work the ship when under tow. This was handled in a seamanlike manner by the destroyers, without loss or injury. The second torpedo explosion had ruined the hangar and burst so many bulkheads that *Houston* had over 6300 tons of salt water on board. No ship had ever been so flooded and survived. Her damage control parties did a splendid job, restoring enough power to keep leaks under control. Eventually, all but 200 of her crew were taken off. The destroyers and cruisers became expert in the art of breeches-buoy and suspended stretcher, and expended all their heavy manila line – a critical matter before Manila was liberated and a fresh supply obtained.

From the enthusiastic reports put forth by Radio Tokyo, it seemed that the Japanese were under the delusion that Cripdiv 1 represented the last remnants afloat of Task Force 38. Admiral Halsey attempted to profit by this hallucination. He stationed Admiral Sherman's TG 38.3 between the cripples and Japan, hoping that *Houston* and *Canberra* would act as bait to the Japanese Fleet, and withdrew two other carrier groups to the eastward, in a position to spring a trap. Thus Cripdiv 1 acquired another nickname: "Baitdiv 1."

This was the occasion for an exchange of pleasantries: –

> HALSEY to DUBOSE: Don't worry!
> DUBOSE to HALSEY: Not worrying, just wondering and waiting.
> CAPTAIN INGLIS of *Birmingham* to DUBOSE: Now I know how a worm on a fishhook must feel.

The ruse almost worked. Vice Admiral Shima's Second Striking Force, consisting of heavy cruisers *Nachi* and *Ashigara*, a light cruiser and a destroyer division, sortied from the Inland Sea and cautiously approached the scene of battle, in the hope of knocking off crippled carriers. On the morning of 16 October, when refueling his screen from the cruisers east of Okinawa, Shima was attacked by two planes from carrier *Bunker Hill*. He drove them off; but within half an hour, evidently estimating that there were more "remnants" of TF 38 than met the eye, he reversed course to retire. And that afternoon, he received a dispatch from Admiral Fukudome advising him that "more than six carriers" were still operating east of Formosa.[24] Thus Second Striking Force was saved to play an inglorious part in the Battle of Surigao Strait.

As Baitdiv 1 edged out of reach of enemy planes, the supporting cruisers and destroyers were detached. On 18 October, when it had reached the latitude of Cape Engaño, fleet oilers *Pecos* and *Kennebago* fueled the tugs alongside while the tow continued. This delicate operation was completed successfully in a heavy groundswell, at a speed of 4.3 knots.[25]

Salvage vessel *Current* came out and put some of her experts on board the two cripples, and the two gallant tugs were relieved by others. PBMs from Ulithi gave continual coverage. After a few more changes in the composition of the protecting vessels, Cripdiv 1 entered the sheltered waters of Ulithi Lagoon at noon October 27. *Houston* and *Canberra* proceeded to Manus for temporary repairs, thence to Pearl Harbor and East Coast yards for a complete overhaul.

3. *Results of Formosa Air Battle*

The results of these heavy counterattacks on the carrier groups east and southeast of Formosa between 12 and 16 October were spectacularly slight. Task Force 38, in defending itself, engaged nearly a thousand enemy aircraft. Approximately 43 per cent of them were met and dealt with beyond or near the force. With the possible exception of the Battle of the Philippine Sea, this was the heaviest series of air attacks ever launched by the Japanese against American naval forces; and these, be it noted, were made exclusively by land-based planes which, according to many so-called experts at the start of the war, were supposed to be fatal to floating carriers. That the Fast Carrier Force could beat off such determined attacks without loss of a ship gave additional proof that its

[24] *War College Analysis* I 424–26.
[25] Airmailgram Com Third Fleet to Cominch 23 Oct.

defensive strength, already evidenced in June, was more than ample for its protection.

Carrier operations were ably supported by B–29s of XX Army Air Force, controlled operationally by the Joint Chiefs of Staff through General H. H. Arnold USA, Commanding General Army Air Forces.[26] The XX Air Force was subdivided into the 20th and 21st Bomber Commands, the former in October 1944 operating from bases in China. With conditions in China almost intolerable from a logistics point of view, the early days of the 20th Bomber Command were a nightmare. One B–29 holds as much gasoline as a railroad tank car, but in China, gas had to be brought in "by the bucket." With this short fuel supply a limiting factor, three strikes on Formosa in support of Third Fleet was the limit of 20th Bomber Command's operations for the month. But the Joint Chiefs of Staff insisted on further attacks on Formosa in order to prevent the reinforcement of Japanese air power in the Philippines. Accordingly, on 14, 16 and 17 October, the 20th made 232 plane sorties against shipping, aircraft assembly plants and airfields on Formosa, dropping 1290 tons of bombs.[27] The Okayama aircraft assembly plant alone received 650 tons of bombs on 14 October, almost as much as Task Force 38 spread over the island in its two heaviest days' strikes. On 16 October 29 P–51s and 21 P–40s of General Chennault's XIV Army Air Force, whose biggest bombers were B–24s and B–25s, operating from Liuchow, China, struck shipping and waterfront installations in the Hong Kong area.[28] This, too, was to prevent reinforcements reaching the Philippines.

By 17 October – A-day minus 3 for Leyte – the battle over and around Formosa was over. Admiral Halsey, still doubtful of the Japanese Navy's will to challenge, prepared to send his carrier groups alternately to Ulithi for rest and replenishment, in preparation for support of General MacArthur and the Leyte landings. Cripdiv 1, now out of danger, was still creeping toward Ulithi

[26] Craven & Cate V 137–39.

[27] Some of these were dropped on alternate enemy targets on the China Coast. *War College Analysis* I 49–50.

[28] Com Third Fleet War Diary for October 1944; *War College Analysis* I 47.

at a speed that an old-time China trader would have considered slow. The cost to the Navy in aircraft during these six days, 11 to 16 October, though far less than that of the enemy, was still great: 76 planes in combat and 13 operationally, with 64 pilots and crewmen, who, in addition to the sailors killed in the damaged ships, gave their lives to prepare the liberation of the Philippines.

On 17 October Admiral Halsey began his planned direct support of the landings on Leyte. This phase of Fast Carrier Force activities lasted until 24 October, when the enemy fleet became its primary target. Owing in part to our heavy strikes on Formosa, but also to a deliberate policy of saving planes until our amphibious forces were sighted, Japanese air activity subsided after 18 October. For five days there was an ominous quiet in the air. This interval was being improved by the enemy to stage in fresh planes, and on the 24th the Japanese air forces once more spread their wings.

Admiral Davison's Group 4, after fueling on 16 October, resumed striking Luzon on the 17th and continued for two days more. Admiral McCain's Group 1, after fueling on 16 October, joined Bogan's and Sherman's groups on 17 October in an unsuccessful search for the Japanese Fleet, elements of which had been reported as coming out to clean up "remnants." Sherman's Group 3 fueled on the 18th and then stood by to the eastward of Luzon. Planes from *Wasp*, *Hornet*, *Franklin* and *Enterprise* struck the big airfields north and east of Manila Bay during the morning and afternoon of the 18th and, in addition, attacked shipping in the Bay. In the meantime, carriers *Intrepid*, *Hancock* and *Bunker Hill* of Bogan's group launched strikes against airfield installations and shipping at Laoag, Aparri and Camiguin Island in Northern Luzon. On the 19th Bogan's group fueled while McCain's *Wasp* and *Hornet* again struck airfields in the Manila area, and *Franklin* and *Belleau Wood* of Davison's group sent a fighter sweep against aircraft around Manila and then flew strikes against shipping in Manila Bay.[29]

[29] Comairpac Air Analysis, Carrier Operations in Support of the Leyte Campaign, 17–31 Oct. 1944, 4 Feb. 1945.

During this important third week of October, Lieutenant General George C. Kenney's Far Eastern Air Forces, based on Morotai, Biak and New Guinea fields, turned on the heat against enemy airfields in Mindanao. As many as 59 heavy bombers led the strikes on two occasions, and fighters were over the area daily. In order to prevent Japanese planes being staged in from the Netherlands East Indies, that area came in for a great deal of attention. Daily strikes were flown against Halmahera, Ambon, Ceram, Geelvink Bay and the Vogelkop. On A-day 20 October, Army Air Forces made nearly 300 plane sorties. Other targets for moderate strikes by Far Eastern Air Force were the oil centers of Balikpapan in Borneo and Makassar in the Celebes. Flores, Timor, Tanimbar and the Aroe Islands in the Arafura Sea; Palawan, Cebu and Negros in the Philippines. The Northern Solomons mixed air command, based at Torokina in Bougainville and Emirau in the St. Matthias Group, took care of isolated enemy garrisons in Truk and the Caroline Islands, flying over 1100 sorties of fighter planes and medium bombers during October. Farther east, Central Pacific air forces made certain that no enemy air power survived in the bypassed Marshalls. Even in the far north, our land-based planes were hitting the Kuriles.[80]

Thus, during the week prior to the assault on Leyte, Southwest Pacific land-based planes hammered away at the enemy's southern flank in the Netherlands East Indies and Mindanao; Halsey's carrier-based planes hit the northern flank; the China-based B–29s and XIV Army Air Force pounded the northwestern approaches; Army, Navy and Marine Corps planes in South and Central Pacific saw to it that we had no interference from the Marshall and Caroline Islands, and diversionary attacks were made on the Kurile Islands. The Philippines were now completely encircled by Allied air power, but not by Allied sea power. There had to be a great naval battle and more besides before the many straits and seas of the Archipelago were secure.

[80] Task Force 94, consisting of light cruisers *Richmond* and *Trenton* with nine destroyers of Desron 57, made two offensive sweeps of the northern Kuriles, 16–19 and 22–29 Oct., but encountered no enemy vessels.

A-day for the liberation of the Philippines, 20 October 1944, had arrived. Bogan's and Sherman's carrier groups rendezvoused at latitude 15°30′ N, longitude 128°00′ E, well east of Cape San Ildefonso, Luzon, in order to intercept any naval forces that might try to interrupt the Leyte landings, while McCain's and Davison's groups stood by off Leyte to augment the escort carriers' direct support, and to launch strikes on airfields in Cebu, Negros, Panay and northern Mindanao.

Japanese aircraft losses in the week beginning 10 October were catastrophic.[31] Nor was that the whole story. Rear Admiral Matsuda, a carrier flag officer, later remarked that this week divided the naval air war into two periods. Before it, the Japanese "had a satisfactory number of instructors and also a considerable amount of fuel; after that loss, gasoline and instructors ran short and got worse and worse by degrees. . . . Also, the mechanics and engineers who kept planes in operation were left on islands. As islands fell, pilots came home; but maintenance men did not, and gradually skilled mechanics ran short. . . . And of course the skilled men producing planes got lower and lower in standards so that the output of planes was inferior." [32] But aircraft losses while the factories that make them are intact – as they still were in Japan – are not irreparable, and the Japanese air forces made a spectacular comeback later in the year.

Furthermore, the Japanese government had not yet activated the special air attack corps known as the Kamikaze.

No such counsel of desperation was entertained by the enemy in mid-October. He felt that he could accept aircraft losses owing to the mighty victory over Third Fleet. The Navy section of Imperial General Headquarters, accepting aircraft pilots' reports of sinkings at their face value, issued an official communiqué on 16 October to the effect that the United States Navy had been diminished by 11 carriers, 2 battleships, 3 cruisers and one destroyer or light cruiser. In addition, they claimed that 8 carriers, 2 battleships,

[31] See Chapter IX, below, for estimates.
[32] USSBS Interrogation No. 345 (Navy No. 69) 12 Nov. 1945.

4 cruisers, one destroyer or light cruiser and 13 unidentified ships had been damaged, and at least a dozen more set afire.[33] Japanese officers who were asked about these fantastic claims, after the war, grinned sheepishly and said that of course they didn't believe the half of it; but the nation certainly did. It was "swept by a sudden wave of exhilaration which dispelled overnight the growing pessimism over the unfavorable trend of the war." The Emperor issued a special rescript; mass celebrations of the "Glorious Victory of Taiwan" were held throughout Japan, and at all headquarters of armed forces in the Philippines. The Army even assumed that there would be no American invasion. Army section of Imperial General Headquarters, believing its own propaganda, had started planning a "radical modification of Operation SHO-GO" when the vanguard of American invasion forces for Leyte was sighted off Suluan on 17 October.[34]

Shortly after noon that day, Admiral Halsey made the most effective possible reply to these Japanese claims in a message to Admiral Nimitz, which Cincpac promptly released, on the 19th, to the joy of the American public:

> ADMIRAL NIMITZ HAS RECEIVED FROM ADMIRAL HALSEY THE COMFORTING ASSURANCE THAT HE IS NOW RETIRING TOWARD THE ENEMY FOLLOWING THE SALVAGE OF ALL THE THIRD FLEET SHIPS RECENTLY REPORTED SUNK BY RADIO TOKYO.[35]

[33] *War College Analysis* I 418.
[34] MacArthur *Historical Report* II 335–6.
[35] *Navy Dept. Communiqués 301 to 600* p. 250. A version of the original is in *Admiral Halsey's Story* pp. 207–8.

PART II

The Amphibious Phase

CHAPTER VII

Preliminaries[1]

7–20 October 1944

1. *Rehearsals, Staging and Passage*

EARLY in October, General MacArthur's military and naval forces began to concentrate at Manus and at various places along the coast of New Guinea. Over seven hundred ships were to make up the Central Philippines Attack Force; fewer than those that took part in the invasion of Normandy in June, but mounting a heavier striking power.[2] If we add the 18 fleet carriers, 6 battleships, 17 cruisers and 64 destroyers of Third Fleet,[3] this was the most powerful naval force ever assembled. But new records were being hung up by the Pacific Fleet every few months, and the one for Leyte would be equaled at Lingayen Gulf in January 1945 and surpassed off Okinawa in April.

Before this immense expeditionary force set sail, it was desirable that as many groups and units as possible rehearse. Major General J. R. Hodge's XXIV Corps of the Southern Attack Force had a proper rehearsal with Rear Admiral Wilkinson's III 'Phib on the island of Maui, whose inhabitants were given a preview of every amphibious performance of the Pacific Fleet after Tarawa. The scene of Hodge's actual performance was changed from the coral reefs of Yap to the sand beaches of Leyte; yet this was all to the

[1] Action Reports of Admirals Kinkaid, Barbey, Wilkinson, Oldendorf, T. L. Sprague and subordinate commanders concerned.

[2] The 738 ships in Seventh Fleet for this operation comprised 157 combatant ships, 420 amphibious types, 84 patrol, minesweeping and hydrographic types and 73 service types. Cincpac Monthly Analysis for Oct. 1944.

[3] Including Rear Adm. A. E. Smith's Crudiv 10.

good because the teamwork was not affected and the change of objective was like substituting a new and weaker opponent in a football game.

Major General F. C. Sibert's X Corps, ground troops for the Northern Attack Force, did not fare so well, being the victims of a tight shipping schedule forced upon Rear Admiral Barbey's VII 'Phib by the acceleration of the Pacific campaign. The distance from Hollandia to Leyte is 1250 miles, and some X Corps units were picked up 600 miles further away. As the LSTs used for part of the troop-lift were capable only of a nine-knot speed, initial ship movements had to start on 4 October. This was only 18 days after the decision had been made to step up the landing date, and only 16 days before A-day.[4] In the meantime, all VII 'Phib shipping was engaged in the Morotai operation and its resupply. The last of these vessels returned to Hollandia 6 October, two days after the shipping movement for Leyte had to begin. "By careful arrangement of the shipping schedule," wrote Admiral Barbey, "enough time was obtained between operations to fuel and take on stores, but little else. This has been the customary experience of the VII Amphibious Force which has carried out fourteen assault landings and their resupply in the previous twelve months."[5]

Nevertheless, the two divisions of X Corps managed to squeeze in a rehearsal of sorts. The 1st Cavalry Division used the Admiralty Islands which it had helped to capture earlier in the year; the small Panaon and Dinagat landing forces rehearsed at Tanahmerah Bay, New Guinea, on 10 October; and the 24th Infantry Division held a practice landing on beaches about six miles east of Hollandia on the 12th.

As the ships lay at anchor in Seeadler Harbor and Humboldt Bay, baking in the tropical sun, a casual observer might wonder why there were so few signs of activity. These harbor scenes were peaceful enough except for LCVPs and motor whaleboats darting

[4] Owing to the publicity over the Normandy operation, which fixed D-day in the public's mind as 6 June 1944, General MacArthur designated 20 October as A-day.

[5] CTF 78 (Rear Adm. Barbey) "Report on the Leyte Operation," 14 Nov. 1944.

about. Signalmen sweated it out topside as they tried to keep up with the huge volume of traffic. Below decks, staff officers and yeomen tapped out the latest amendments and corrections to the operation plan and provision details struck below their last supplies. The troops originally destined for Yap, on board ship since 27 August, would have concurred in the opinion of Justice Holmes, "War is an organized bore." They were tired of sitting around and reading, and found no pleasure in writing letters since military censorship forbade their saying where they were, or indeed anything interesting. Men of the Northern Group were better off in this respect, since they had been in New Guinea for some time and had been allowed to say so. But to compensate for this, soldiers and sailors in the Southern Group, who had just come in from Maui, could write about the terrors of crossing the Line; or, if they were already "shellbacks," describe their enjoyment as members of King Neptune's Royal Police Force over paddling "pollywogs" and making the green young ensigns shine their shoes.

Fleet post offices ashore were scenes of febrile activity. Sailors swarmed through these improvised buildings in the dust and heat, dragging heavy mailbags. Most of the letters delivered on board ship were a month or more old. Once in a while more recent mail arrived in small amounts, and the lucky recipients had to read selections aloud to their friends. Plenty of officer messenger mail came on board, but that always meant more work for somebody; when it stopped coming, look for the payoff!

Every so often the men enjoyed a liberty ashore. This met nobody's idea of a "terrific" time (the current adjective in 1944); but one could play a little baseball, swim in tepid water and drink a few cans of beer – which, if one arrived early, might still be cool. The officers fared no better as they pushed their way through a sweating crowd, six deep, to the bar at the Manus officers' club, decorated with ships' life preservers.[6] The so-called "officers'

[6] Commodore Boak had constructed this on the model of the famous Espiritu Santo Officers' Club, which I believe still holds the record for the "longest bar in the Pacific."

club" at Hollandia consisted of a cluster of Army tents on platforms which had been laid on the pilings of a native village evacuated by the Dutch. It was on the edge of a coral reef and accessible only by boat.

No one was sorry when the ships began to get under way. No one expected to cherish happy memories of Manus or Hollandia; yet, however unpleasant may be one's immediate recollections, something satisfactory sticks. Come now, you who were at Seeadler, New Guinea or Leyte; do you not feel a certain glow of pride that you were "there"? Men have always felt that way about wars they have been through, since ancient Rome, when Virgil had Æneas say, as he spun his yarn of Troy to Dido: *Quaeque ipse miserrima vidi, quorum pars magna fui* – "These most lamentable events I witnessed, and a great part of them I was."

On 10 October the northward movement started, all aiming for a position called "Point Fin" off the entrance to Leyte Gulf (lat. 10°28′30″ N, long. 125°56′20″ E), 1250 miles from Hollandia, through which all units of the Expeditionary Force must pass. This table shows where each group was mounted, and its estimated time of arrival at Point Fin: –

	Departed	*Date*	*E.T.A., Point Fin*
Minesweeping and Hydrographic Group [7]	Manus	10 Oct.	0600, 17 Oct.
Dinagat Attack Group	Hollandia	12 Oct.	0616, 17 Oct.
Bombardment and Fire Support Group (including 12 CVEs)	Manus	12 Oct.	1000, 17 Oct.
Southern LST Group	Manus	11 Oct.	2300, 19 Oct.
Northern Transport Group [8]	Hollandia	12 Oct.	0000, 20 Oct.
Northern LST Group (including Close Covering Group)	Hollandia	13 Oct.	0030, 20 Oct.
Southern Transport Group	Manus	14 Oct.	0315, 20 Oct.
Fleet Flagship Group	Hollandia	15 Oct.	0340, 20 Oct.

The ocean passage was marked by constant alertness for air or submarine attacks that never materialized. Until nearing the Philippines the weather stayed clear but a following wind made the heat

[7] Together with a few units of the Bombardment and Fire Support Group, to support the sweepers.

[8] Excepting the San Ricardo transports which departed Manus.

intense. Some of the more enterprising men tossed a medicine ball in an effort to work off the starch which they consumed at every meal. All hands knew they were growing soft, but with the rigid watch schedules that must be maintained in enemy waters, only a few sailors felt like spending idle moments keeping fit.

The Formosa Air Battle was raging as the amphibious forces plodded along. The extravagant claims broadcast by the Japanese through every known means of radio communication, and of which the only grain of truth was the torpedoing of *Houston* and *Canberra*, reached the enlisted men through the popular "Tokyo Rose" and occasioned an unprecedented amount of "scuttlebutt." But one of the best laughs of the war came from Admiral Halsey's message to Admiral Nimitz that he was "retiring toward the enemy."

A matter of great concern to officers who read top-secret dispatches were the reports of enemy surface forces in the Celebes area, indicating a possible interception of the amphibious convoys just before A-day. Admiral Wilkinson, taking no chances, sent aircraft searching in that direction from the escort carriers, but they found nothing bigger than praus and sampans.

2. *Clipping the Cat's Whiskers* [9]

As the major amphibious forces moved majestically toward Leyte, smaller units pressed ahead to sweep mines, secure the entrance to the Gulf, explore the beaches and soften up the enemy. Capital ships performed the heavy bombardment, but ahead of them steamed minecraft, large and small, from the handsome H.M.S. *Ariadne* to small motor minesweepers known as "yardbirds," commanded by a reserve ensign or junior grade lieutenant.

[9] Comphibgrp 9 (Rear Adm. Struble) Report of Dinagat Group 11 Nov. 1944; CTG 77.5 (Cdr. Loud) Report of Minesweeping Operations in Surigao Strait and Leyte Gulf 29 Oct. 1944; "History of 6th Ranger Infantry Battalion," an After Action Report at War Department; Comcrudiv 12 (Rear Adm. Hayler) Action Report of Bombardment and Support of Landing on Suluan 2 Nov. 1944. For composition of forces, see Appendix I.

Naval forces assigned to these missions were under Rear Admiral Oldendorf,[10] who commanded all forces in Leyte Gulf until Admiral Kinkaid arrived on the 20th. They comprised the first three groups in the timetable on our previous page. The high command expected these preliminary operations to tip off the enemy as to the target, but in the Pacific it was doctrine to sacrifice tactical surprise in favor of close reconnaissance and a heavy pre-landing bombardment.

Commander Wayne R. Loud's minesweeping and hydrographic group departed Manus 10 October to spearhead the Leyte invasion. A month had not elapsed since these valiant minecraft had successfully completed one of the toughest sweeping jobs in the Pacific war to date, Kossol Passage and the waters around Peleliu and Angaur. On 15 October the sweepers and Rear Admiral Struble's Dinagat Attack Group rendezvoused with three oilers for a last, long drink of fuel. This proved to be a nasty job. The wind was blowing over 30 knots with heavy rain squalls and sea making up, so that the fueling of each small minecraft took about two hours. At 1700, Struble's and Loud's groups resumed course for Leyte. That night, it blew great guns. Heavy seas broke over the bows of the 136-foot motor minesweepers – which were making flank speed in order to maintain station in the cruising disposition – and shattered their topsides. By the evening of the 16th many were straggling, and speed of advance had to be reduced to nine knots.

Dinagat and three smaller islands, Calicoan, Suluan and Homonhon, divided the two entrances to Leyte Gulf from the Philippine Sea. Air reconnaissance showed that the enemy had installations on

[10] Jesse B. Oldendorf, b. Calif. 1887, Annapolis '09. Served in various ships until World War I when he had charge of naval armed guards on various transports. His first command was of *Decatur*, 1922–7. Courses at Naval War College and Army War College; navigator of *New York* 1930–2; instructor in seamanship and navigation, Naval Academy; exec. *West Virginia* 1935–7; C.O. *Houston* 1939–Aug. 1941; staff of War College; Com. Aruba-Curaçao Area and of N.O.B. Trinidad 1942–3. Comcrudiv 4 in Pacific 1944 with flag in *Louisville*. After Battle for Leyte Gulf commanded the battle squadron in Lingayen operation; wounded on board flagship *Pennsylvania* off Okinawa. After the war Com. Eleven, N.O.B. San Diego and Western Sea Frontier. Retired 1948.

them, probably search radar whose electric feelers would signal the approach of the forces of liberation. These "cat's whiskers" must be trimmed, or at least singed.

This job was entrusted to the Dinagat Attack Group, consisting of eight destroyer transports and miscellaneous craft, lifting the 6th Ranger Infantry Battalion U.S. Army, about 500 men, under Lieutenant Colonel H. A. Mucci. Rear Admiral Struble,[11] who had been Admiral Kirk's chief of staff in Normandy, commanded the group; light cruisers *Denver* and *Columbia* and four destroyers, under Rear Admiral Hayler, were in support.

Sweeping the approach channel to Suluan began at 0630 October 17. At 0650, the attack force was sighted by the Japanese lookouts on Suluan; the garrison commander promptly notified Admiral Toyoda, who issued the alert for SHO–1, the Philippine battle plan, at 0809, and promptly ordered Admiral Kurita's First Striking Force to sail from Lingga Roads.[12]

Cruiser *Denver* reached her firing position about 6500 yards off Suluan at 0800 and promptly gave tongue. She had the honor of firing the opening gun for the liberation of Leyte; and the men of Company D, 6th Rangers, who were landed about 0820, could boast that they were the first Americans to "return."

Once ashore on Suluan, the Rangers did not pause to contemplate their historical significance, but walked or ran to the lighthouse,

[11] Arthur D. Struble, b. Portland, Ore. 1894, Annapolis '15. Served in several ships in World War I, helped fit out and became engineer officer of *Stevens;* exec. and C.O. of *Shubrick* and *Meyer*. Instructor in engineering and naval construction at Naval Academy 1921–3; served in *California* to 1927 and in naval communications to 1930; staff duty at sea, gunnery officer of *New York*, communications officer 12th Naval District 1933; 1st Lieutenant *Portland* 1935; various staff duties until 1940 when became exec. *Arizona;* C.O. *Trenton* 1941; in office of C.N.O. 1942–4, when became chief of staff to Admiral Kirk for OVERLORD. After the operations related in this volume he directed several landings in the Philippines as Com Group 9 VII 'Phib; Com. Minecraft Pacific Fleet Sept. 1945; Com Amphibious Forces Pacific Fleet 1946, Deputy C.N.O. 1948. As Com Seventh Fleet commanded the Inchon and Wonsan landings in Sept.–Oct. 1950. Com First Fleet 1951–2; duties on J.C.S. and Military Staff Committee United Nations until retirement as Admiral in 1956.

[12] MacArthur *Historical Report* II 337. Admiral Toyoda got the word at 0749 Oct. 17, Kurita sailed at 0100 Oct. 18, and Toyoda issued the "Execute SHO-GO" at 1110.

whose light had already been smashed by a shot from *Denver*, and whose small garrison had taken to the bush. The troops, royally received by the natives, disposed of 32 Japanese, and suffered only three casualties.

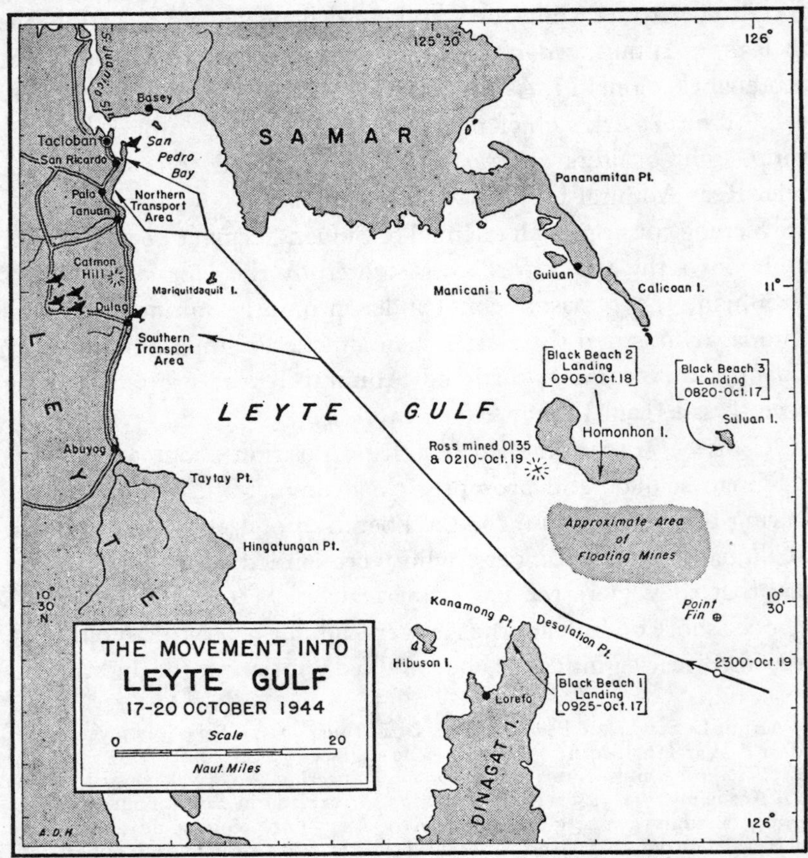

Since the Rangers were wanted at Dinagat, Rear Admiral Hayler instructed APD *Crosby* to reëmbark them and withdraw on the double. That was not easy to execute. By 1130 visibility was reduced to 800 yards with 60-knot wind and incessant rain squalls. The four LCPRs (the original ramped landing craft) in which the troops landed had been broached by the rising sea, and no more were immediately available. Next day, 18 October, the Rangers were taken off in boats from *Sands*. One whisker had been trimmed, but it had already passed the word to the big cat in Formosa.[13]

The Ranger unit for Dinagat Island approached Desolation Point through strong wind and heavy seas. Admiral Struble had selected a 450-yard stretch just south of Kanamong Point on the northwestern coast as the nearest suitable beach. The landing was uneventful. Major Garrett, commanding this Ranger unit, notified Admiral Struble at 1400 that there was "no enemy opposition; evidence of recent evacuation." This evacuation, however, turned out to have been an involuntary departure to another world, compliments of a Filipino guerrilla unit led by a Captain Hemingway of the United States Army Air Force. Good Intelligence material, including Japanese hydrographic charts which were very useful in the Okinawan operation, were obtained by the Rangers on Dinagat and Suluan.

In the meantime the big Bombardment and Fire Support Group under Rear Admiral Oldendorf, and the escort carriers under Rear Admiral Thomas L. Sprague, had been milling about outside the Gulf, with wind and sea making up. Sprague's "rainmaker" made such gloomy predictions of worse weather for two days that he suggested A-day be postponed; but "Oley" had an optimistic staff meteorologist who predicted fair weather. The gale abated during the midwatch October 18 and that day dawned fair and calm, so that the Ranger units designated to land on Homonhon Island did so with ease. No enemy was present; no installations found. The Rangers were disgusted – "Here we are with all these goddam bullets and no Japs!"

[13] The Rangers had to return to Suluan later to rescue their Filipino friends, who sent them, at Homonhon, a message on 19 October to the effect that they were being murdered by the remnants of the Japanese garrison. As no landing craft could be had on A-day or for a week thereafter, the Rangers assembled a flotilla of native sailboats and outrigger canoes in which they attempted to cross the 15-mile passage between the two islands. Their first attempt was frustrated by weather, but a second on 31 October succeeded. The enemy garrison was spotted in the lighthouse, on top of a 300-foot cliff. The Rangers scaled the cliff, surprised the Japanese, killed most of them and disposed of the rest by blowing up the lighthouse.

Thus, the entrances to Leyte Gulf had been secured by noon 18 October. But no large units dared enter the Gulf until channels were swept, which was difficult in the foul weather of the 17th.[14] The first report to reach Admiral Oldendorf from Commander Loud was to the effect that the entrance to Surigao Strait between Homonhon and Dinagat had been completely swept, with negative results. How this erroneous report originated is a mystery; but the Admiral naturally assumed that it was correct and notified Admiral Kinkaid accordingly. At 0637 October 18 he received word from Commander Loud that this critical area was only one-fifth covered, that 26 moored mines had been swept up and that many floaters had been seen in the Gulf. This, too, was erroneous, as it later turned out that there were no mines between Dinagat and Homonhon. Again Oldendorf was forced to decide whether or not to recommend postponement of A-day. He determined to pass through the mine field with some of his fire support ships and to make a personal investigation.[15] With three large minecraft sweeping ahead, "Oley" in *Louisville* boldly led his column, paravanes streaming, into Leyte Gulf at 0900. It took him two hours to traverse the swept channel, passing close aboard Homonhon Island.

Pressed for time and with the necessity of obtaining firsthand beach, surf and hydrographic intelligence for the amphibious forces, Admiral Oldendorf decided to steam into the unswept waters off Dulag and carry out his underwater demolition plan, regardless of possible enemy reaction. By 1247 his force had passed through the waters that would become the Southern Transport Area. *Pennsylvania* with cruisers *Minneapolis* and *Denver* and several destroyers prepared to bombard the southern landing beaches at 1400.

For an hour the Japanese lay quiet and allowed the ships to pound away without reply. Then the underwater demolition teams disembarked from destroyer-transports into landing craft and

[14] Comcrudiv 4 (Rear Adm. Oldendorf, CTG 77.2) Action Report of 16–24 Oct. 1944. Various Intelligence reports indicated that there were 500 to 700 mines in the Gulf.

[15] *War College Analysis* II 152–4; chart of the sweep areas at p. 6.

headed for the Dulag beaches. At 1515 the enemy opened up with machine-gun, mortar and 75-mm fire. *Goldsborough* closed the shore to about 1500 yards and fired her 4-inch guns. Owing to dense foliage overhanging the beach, no accurate estimate could be made of enemy positions; the destroyers and APDs simply tossed shells into the bush in the hope of hitting something. By now several landing craft were under fire, and at 1540 one of them was sunk. Half an hour's shore bombardment left the Japanese still frisky. A 75-mm shell struck the forward stack of *Goldsborough* at 1543, killing two men, but the ship sustained only minor damage. At 1550 her boats returned with the UDTs, which had enjoyed a good look at the landing beaches; they reported that "Chick" Parsons was right — no underwater obstacles or mines, and beaches very suitable for landing. *Chandler* was visited by guerrillas from Samar with important intelligence from their commander, Colonel Causing.

The bombardment ended at 1735; and, owing to the small number of mines encountered by the sweepers, Admiral Oldendorf brought the rest of his fire support ships inside Leyte Gulf for the night.

3. *A-day minus 1, 19 October*

A-day minus 1, 19 October, had hardly opened before Seventh Fleet suffered its first casualty in the Leyte operation. At 0135 destroyer *Ross*, covering the minecraft, struck a mine in the swept channel about eight miles south of Homonhon Island. She lost all power, commenced jettisoning topside weights to prevent capsizing, struck a second mine and developed a 14-degree list. At break of day, fleet tug *Chickasaw* towed her to an anchorage, but she was so badly damaged as to be out of the fight. She lost 23 men killed or missing and 9 injured; yet she hung up a record as the only destroyer in the Pacific war to strike two mines in near succession and survive.

At about 0530, when it began to grow light, Admiral Oldendorf's group moved to assigned positions off the landing beaches. The Southern Unit was divided into two groups which spelled each other all day in an effort to neutralize that area by continuous fire. At the same time Rear Admiral Weyler's Northern Unit, accompanied by underwater demolition teams, headed for Tacloban on San Pedro Bay, the northwestern bight of Leyte Gulf. At 0835 the Southern Unit had Dulag under fire, and 25 minutes later the Northern Unit started giving the enemy at Tacloban a taste of things to come.

One of the underwater demolition teams working off Tacloban was interfered with so much by the enemy that it called for more gunfire support. The extra punch did the trick, and the beach reconnaissance was easily completed, although destroyer *Aulick* received three direct hits from coast defense guns which temporarily jammed her main battery in train. Here as off Dulag no mines or underwater obstacles were found and all beaches were reported on favorably. They were indeed perfect for landing craft, but no place for LSTs.

In a terrain such as that of Leyte, the effectiveness of naval bombardment is difficult to gauge. For want of definite targets revealed by photographic reconnaissance, each ship was assigned an "area of responsibility" within which she was instructed to destroy all known targets, and then to find new ones through the spotters, or by blowing the camouflage off suspected ones. "Some ships," reported Admiral Oldendorf, "took the scarcity of targets to indicate a license to spray their assigned areas with shells" – a procedure that wasted ammunition and incidentally destroyed property belonging to the people we had come to liberate. Not that the Filipinos complained. They were glad to have us there on any terms.

Shortly before sunset 19 October the Bombardment and Fire Support Group – except four destroyers assigned to deliver night harassing fire – retired and steered evasive courses south of the main entrance channel during the night.

Air support for the landing was primarily the responsibility of

Rear Admiral Thomas L. Sprague.[16] While Mitscher's fast carrier forces struck enemy bases, Sprague's escort carriers had the duty to maintain air supremacy over eastern Leyte and the Gulf, keep local airfields neutralized and provide direct support for troops landing and ashore until elements of the Army Air Force had been staged in. Admiral Sprague commanded three groups (usually known by the voice calls of their commanders, as Taffy 1, Taffy 2 and Taffy 3). Each comprised six escort carriers and eight destroyers or destroyer escorts. Prior to 20 October, however, there were only four carriers in each group, since the others were furnishing air cover to convoys making the passage to Leyte. The twelve escort carriers immediately available came up with Admiral Oldendorf.

An important change in Admiral Sprague's plans was caused by Admiral Halsey's movements. Instead of making his scheduled strikes on Luzon and the Visayas on 18–19 October, in the hope of tempting the Japanese Fleet to tangle with Baitdiv 1, Halsey held the bulk of his fast carrier forces northeast of Luzon through the 19th, and warned Admiral Kinkaid that he might not be in a position to deliver the planned strikes to support him on A-day. Thus, for three days, October 18–20, the main responsibility for neutralizing enemy airfields in the Visayas and Mindanao fell upon the escort carriers.

They met perfect flying conditions when moving into their operating areas outside Leyte Gulf on the morning of 18 October. That day and the 19th their planes struck enemy defenses, installations and transport on Leyte itself, destroyed aircraft on the air-

[16] Thomas L. Sprague, b. Ohio 1894, Naval Academy '17. Duty in *Cleveland* to Apr. 1918 when helped fit out destroyer *Montgomery* and became her C.O. 1920. After flight training at Pensacola became a naval aviator and was assigned to various flight and staff duties until 1931, when took command successively of Scoutrons 6 and 10, combined with staff duty with Com Cruisers U.S. Fleet; also served as supt. of the engine lab. at Naval Aircraft Factory, Phila. Air Officer *Saratoga*, navigator *Langley*, supt. aviation training N.A.S. Pensacola 1937–40; exec. *Ranger* to mid-1941. Fitted out and commanded CVE *Charger* to Dec. 1942, chief of staff to Comairlant to June 1943; fitted out and commanded *Intrepid* in Marshall Islands operation and raid on Truk (see Volume VII 321); Comcardiv 22 (CVEs) in Marianas and Morotai operations. Comcardiv 3 (CVs) in 1945; deputy chief of naval personnel 1947–49, Com Air Force Pacific Fleet, retired 1952, as Admiral.

fields of Cebu, Negros, Panay and Northern Mindanao and bombed small shipping. Of the 471 combat sorties flown, about half were directed at Leyte, where slight activity was observed on the rain-sodden airstrips – most of them, in fact, had been abandoned by

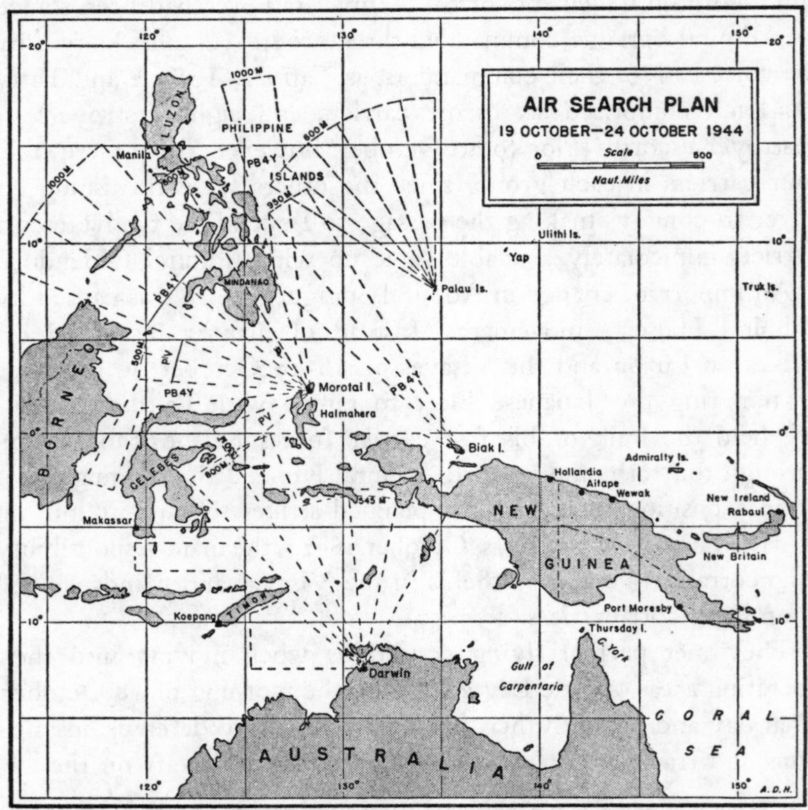

the Japanese. On Cebu, Mactan and Negros, much damage was done to enemy planes on the ground. Japanese airborne opposition hardly appeared before 24 October.[17]

A new air search plan was instituted by Seventh Fleet on 19 October. Privateers (PB4Y), staged in to the newly constructed air

[17] Figures from Comairpac "Air Analysis, Carrier Operations in Support of the Leyte Campaign, 17–31 Oct. 1944," 4 Feb. 1945. Records of *St. Lo* not included as they were lost when she went down 25 Oct.

base on Morotai, permitted routine searches to be extended northwest of Palawan, and, along the outer coast, to lat. 15° north. They failed to discover Kurita or Nishimura, but did make contact on Shima's Second Striking Force north of Palawan at 1220 October 23.

Thus, Admirals Oldendorf, Struble and Sprague had met the situation despite foul weather, carried out their missions and changed plans as required. They were all set for the arrival of the huge amphibious forces due in Leyte Gulf early in the morning of 20 October.

4. *Main Force Enters Leyte Gulf, 20 October*

At 2300 October 19 the "parade," as Admiral Wilkinson called it, was due at Point Fin, 17 miles east of Desolation Point, Dinagat Island. He led the procession since, having loaded for a coral reef landing at Yap, he needed more time to disembark than did Barbey's combat-loaded ships. Wilkinson's assault waves had to be transferred from transports to the LSTs carrying amphtracs (LVT) and dukws, while Admiral Barbey's assault waves were embarked in attack transports and set ashore in davit-borne landing craft. Every effort was made to overcome these differences in time, distance and technique so that the two assault groups could land simultaneously at H-hour, 1000 October 20. A midforenoon landing was planned in order to permit daylight entry of Leyte Gulf by both tractor and transport groups through the swept channel. High water came a few minutes before 1000, but the range of tides along the eastern coast of Leyte is only two and a half feet, and by this time coxswains of the landing craft had been trained to retract from a gradually sloping beach on an ebb tide. Dukws and amphtracs took any tide in their stride.

During the night the men snatched a few hours of restless sleep and then left their sweaty bunks for the fresh air topside. On deck a light breeze was blowing. Homonhon Island could be seen on the starboard hand as a faint blur in the darkness. No one talked much, for there was not much to say, but all hands had plenty to think about. Few episodes in the war were more vivid in the minds of American sailors than the story of heroism and death on Bataan. Yet if any of these men felt like avenging angels or crusaders they kept it very much to themselves. More important to them was the fact that this was a big step along the road to Tokyo and the end of the war. The Japanese may fight for their Emperor, the Germans for conquest and glory, and the British for King and Country, but Americans fight to get done with an unpleasant but necessary duty.

Although our men did not approach Leyte burning with idealism, they were pleased to be the first liberators of the Philippines, because that would give them and their friends something to talk about. This Leyte landing, they guessed, would be "headline stuff," and if young Americans set a low price on glory, they place high value on publicity. Echoes of the fanfare that attended the American invasion of France had reached their ears, and as long as they had to be fighting somewhere, they were glad to be part of another invasion that was certain to be famous. Later in the day, when General MacArthur broadcast his eloquent proclamation to the Filipinos, the reaction of his audience in the Fleet was none too favorable; yet sailors and soldiers alike were hoping that the folks back home were listening in and figuring that Bill and Joe were supporting the General.

As day began to break, it was possible to see the outlines of Samar. The sun rose over heavy clouds on the horizon astern. It was no dawn to inspire a poet, or even an historian. Enough freshness broke through the muggy atmosphere to cool the body and cheer the soul for a moment, but soon the burning sun soaked it up and brought back intense heat and more sweat. By sunrise all hands were looking for the island of which, a month ago, they had never heard. Soon it appeared, rising above the western horizon as a gray, irregular mass. Leyte at last! Admiral Barbey's group was now steaming toward its transport area in San Pedro Bay, and Admiral Wilkinson's for the anchorage off Dulag. A Japanese patrol plane approached to take a look and was shot down. Ashore, Filipinos, and the few Americans who had stayed with them, peered out through the coconut palms at this mighty fleet. Joy filled their hearts, and prayers went up to Heaven; for they knew that the hour of deliverance was at hand.

As President Roosevelt declared in a message to the Philippine people: –

> The suffering, humiliation and mental torture that you have endured since the barbarous, unprovoked and treacherous attack upon the Philippines nearly three long years ago have aroused in the hearts of the American people a righteous anger, a stern determination to punish the guilty and a fixed resolve to restore peace and order and decency to an outraged world. . . .
>
> On this occasion of the return of General MacArthur to Philippine soil with our airmen, our soldiers and our sailors, we renew our pledge. We and our Philippine brothers in arms – with the help of Almighty God – will drive out the invader; we will destroy his power to wage war again, and we will restore a world of dignity and freedom – a world of confidence and honesty and peace.[18]

[18] *New York Times* 21 Oct. 1944.

CHAPTER VIII

The Main Landings

20–29 October 1944

1. *The Northern Landings: A-day at Tacloban* [1]

REAR ADMIRAL BARBEY was responsible for landing Major General Sibert's X Corps on the western shores of San Pedro Bay near Tacloban. That little city, capital of Leyte Province, had docking facilities which would be useful; and directly east of it, on Cataisan Point, was the principal airfield on the island built before the war. Plans called for the prompt development of this as well as airstrips in the Dulag sector to serve Far Eastern Air Forces.

Admiral Barbey's Northern Attack Force was divided into three component parts, two of which, the San Ricardo and the Palo Attack Groups [2] were assigned Beaches White and Red near Tacloban. The third, the Panaon Attack Group, landed on Panaon Island off the southernmost point of Leyte. Rear Admiral Fechteler, commanding the San Ricardo Group, was designated to land 1st Cavalry Division (Major General V. D. Mudge) on Beach

[1] Com VII 'Phib (Rear Adm. D. E. Barbey, CTF 78) Report on Leyte Operation 10 Nov.; Com III 'Phib (Vice Adm. T. S. Wilkinson, CTF 79) Report of Leyte Operation 13 Nov.; Sixth Army Report Leyte Operation 20 Oct.–25 Dec.; Comphibgroup 8 (Rear Adm. W. M. Fechteler, CTG 78.2) Action Report–Leyte 29 Nov. 1944; Com Support Air Seventh Fleet (Capt. R. F. Whitehead) Report of Support Aircraft Operations, Leyte, 2 Nov.; Com Transdiv 6 (Capt. H. D. Baker) Operation Report Assault of Leyte 25 Oct.; British Combined Operations Observers SWPac Report to British Joint Staff mission in Washington 8 Nov.; CTU 78.1.8 (Lt. R. E. Sargent, Com LCI(R) Group 20) "Information Additional to Action Reports" 22 Nov.; Comairpac Analysis of Carrier Operations in Supporting Leyte Campaigns 17–31 Oct. 1944, 4 Feb. 1945.

[2] For composition of these groups see Appendix I.

White, a mile-long sandy stretch extending southward from the base of Cataisan Peninsula. "Uncle Dan" Barbey himself commanded the Palo Attack Group, to land 24th Infantry Division (Major General F. A. Irving) on Beach Red, separated from White by 1500 yards of swampy bush. This lay about eleven miles north of Liberanan Head where the Southern Attack Force beaches began. The selection of these beaches was based entirely on the scheme of maneuver for the land forces.

Northern Attack Force entered Leyte Gulf, escorted by Admiral Berkey's Close Covering Group of four cruisers and seven destroyers, and sandwiched between elements of Southern Attack Force. At 0153 October 20, Admiral Struble's Panaon Attack Group broke off. Toward daybreak, attack transport *Harris* and H.M.A.S. *Shropshire* picked up mines on their paravanes. The sun rose out of a yellow haze over towards Samar, and light spread over the calm green waters of Leyte Gulf. Mist dissolved from the mountains of Leyte, and the palm-fringed beach, behind which lay the enemy, became clearly visible. At 0645, when Admiral Barbey's flagship *Blue Ridge* reached latitude 11° N, he made signal "Deploy." Admiral Fechteler's San Ricardo Group then followed the channel between Mariquitdaquit Island and Samar to its transport area, while Barbey conducted the Palo Group by the channel west of the island with the long name. At 0715 Fechteler's group ran into a traffic jam behind the motor minesweepers, but arrived only half an hour late in the transport area, where there were 12 to 16 fathoms of reef-studded water.

The transports begin moving into their assigned positions, about seven miles from the beach, at 0800. Boats are hoisted out, and then mill around in circles; control craft take positions, signalmen make and execute hoists of colored flags and blink messages with searchlights and light tubes; orders are bellowed through bullhorns, and over all is heard, like the drone of a bagpipe, the whirr of internal-combustion engines in boats and planes. The scene quickly assumes that ordered confusion which characterizes a modern amphibious landing. Only two hours are allowed between the arrival of the transports and placing the first waves ashore; in 1942 at least double that time would have been required.

Throughout this activity, fire support units are delivering pre-landing bombardment. First to arrive, about 0700, are those

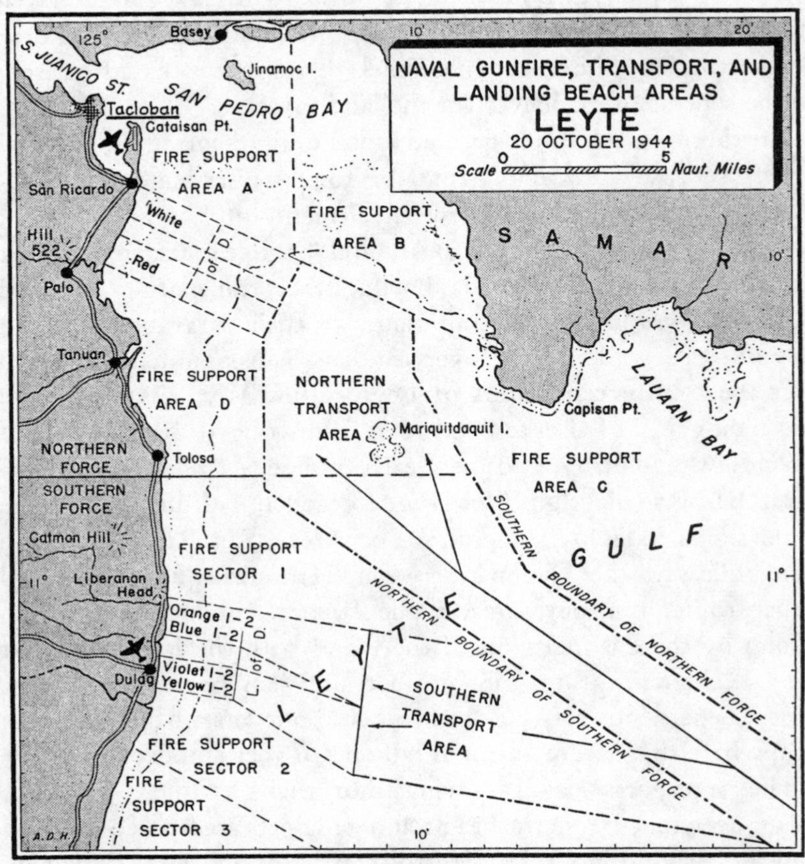

old friends – battleships *Mississippi*, *Maryland*, and *West Virginia*, and three destroyers, under command of Rear Admiral G. L. Weyler. At 0900, when they were supposed to have shot their quota of 30 shells per main battery gun, Rear Admiral Berkey's Close Covering Group relieved them. Eight fire support destroyers were stationed in upper San Pedro Bay.

While these fire support ships were shooting high-capacity explosives onto and behind the beaches, planes from both fleet and escort carriers carried out assigned missions. On the morning of the 20th, McCain's Group 1 and Davison's Group 4 gave air support to the troops and conducted sweeps over airfields in northern Mindanao, Cebu, Negros, Panay and Leyte. Bogan's Group 2 and Sherman's Group 3 stood by east of Leyte to conduct day patrols; *Independence* airmen handled the hazardous night patrols. The escort carriers kept 16 fighters and 6 torpedo-bombers over the Gulf during daylight, and for an hour each side of H-hour provided an additional 8 fighters and 6 torpedo-bombers.

Admiral Barbey, whose air plan was ably administered by Captain Whitehead, Commander Support Aircraft Seventh Fleet in *Wasatch*, departed from standard Pacific procedure in that no bombing or strafing of beaches was allowed for 45 minutes prior to H-hour. Barbey's idea was that gunfire and rockets would be more effective than lifting the bombardment to let planes come in, which needed exact timing in order to avoid an awkward gap. Consequently, from 0915 to 1000, high-angled naval gunfire and rocket barrages only were directed to the beaches. Planes returned to the picture at H-hour, to strike positions on the crest and reverse slopes of Mount Guinhandang, the high hill that overlooks Palo on the left flank off Beach Red.[3]

By 0930, as the bombardment works up to a climax, everything is set for the race to the beach. Even transport *Harris*, late because of her encounter with a mine, has her boats at the line of departure. Boat waves have already formed up; coxswains are jockeying their landing craft, waiting for the signal flag to be two-blocked on control vessel *PC-623* before leaping forward on their 5000-yard course to the shore. At 0943 they are off. The boats are preceded by eleven LCI rocket craft which begin launching 1200 yards from the beach. Within a couple of minutes, 5500 4.5-inch rockets are hurled onto the Red and White beaches, while the cruisers and destroyers lift their fire inland. The Japanese

[3] Called Hill 522 on most of the maps as it is 522 feet high.

have already (at 0940) opened mortar fire from guns concealed in nearby hills, and this fire continues for two hours.

The troops landed on schedule, no boat waves up to the 13th were late, and the 16th and last was only 21 minutes late. Men of the 24th Infantry on Beach Red pushed inland 300 yards in the first seven minutes, with no return fire from the enemy. But at 1016, as the fourth wave was going into the beach, Japanese mortar fire, with the correct range and deflection, was right on its tail. It scored two hits on LCVPs from *Elmore* and sank a boat from *Aquarius*, killing 3 men and injuring 15 more.

This was an easy landing, compared with most amphibious operations in World War II – perfect weather, no surf, no mines or underwater obstacles, slight enemy reaction. British observers on board a control vessel reported that "at first sight, the landing plan appeared complicated, but as regards the landing on Red beaches, the precision with which they were controlled was good to see." They also witnessed the only real foul-up, that of the LSTs which, "owing to the flat beach, were unable to approach near enough to the shore to discharge their vehicles and at the same time were being subjected to reasonably accurate mortar fire." [4]

The LSTs were really in a tough spot. At 1045 they were ordered in to Beach Red and shortly came under mortar fire. Within three minutes, *LST–452*, *–171* and *–181* had been hit. Admiral Barbey immediately ordered two LCIs equipped as fire-fighting ships to assist *LST–181*, which was blazing. They brought the fire under control. In the other two landing ships 26 sailors and soldiers were killed. Total casualties on the northern beaches on A-day were about 50.

Unloading on Beach Red proved to be difficult not only because of the shelving beach, but because Admiral Barbey had not provided his LSTs with pontoon causeway units; not believing

[4] Actually there were suitable berths on Beach Red for only two or three LST. The beach was too shelving and the approaches too shoal for these big beaching craft.

them to be unnecessary, but because there was not time to procure any. Admiral Wilkinson was called on to send some of his up from Dulag, but they did not arrive until after dark. In the meantime Barbey diverted most LSTs destined for Beach Red to the Tacloban airstrip, which thereafter became a supply dump, hampering the work of the airfield construction engineers.[5]

The enemy resumed mortar fire at noon and hit *LST–181* again. Cruisers *Phoenix* and *Boise* hurled 200 rounds of shells at Mount Guinhandang, but that was too late to do the beaching craft any good. She sustained 36 casualties, including 7 killed, lost all power and a large part of her cargo was ruined. An hour later, *LST–458* grounded 400 yards off the Red beach and required a tug to get off. At 1418 word came from Beach White that LSTs could be accommodated there, and this transfer speeded up unloading far better than sending them to Tacloban airstrip. Since all "prime movers" counted on to snake bulk cargoes off Beach Red were loaded in LSTs, their failure to beach on schedule was serious, and most of the cargo landed from the attack freighters had to be manhandled from the water's edge to dumps.

Admiral Fechteler's San Ricardo Group enjoyed all the breaks that day. The landings on Beach White were virtually unopposed, and LSTs were able to beach on the northern half. An enemy battery which fired on incoming craft at 1122 was promptly silenced by *Boise*.[6] By midafternoon 20 October, transports and cargo ships were unloading rapidly, and of all hands present, none could have been better pleased than General Douglas MacArthur.

By the afternoon of 19 October, when the Japanese really decided that the Americans would land on Leyte, Lieutenant General Sosaku Suzuki, commanding Thirty-fifth Army with head-

[5] *Engineers of the Southwest Pacific* VI 290; article by Brig. Gen. S. D. Sturgis USA in *The Military Engineer* Nov. 1947 p. 462; *General Kenney Reports* p. 455. The Engineers claimed that "Uncle Dan" dumping supplies on this airstrip delayed its activation for as much as two days, and on 24 Oct. General Kenney made the drastic threat of bulldozing into the bay everything not removed from the airstrip by daybreak on the 25th!

[6] Force Beachmaster (Naval Beach Parties No. 3 and No. 8) Report of Operations Oct. 13 to Nov. 16, 20 Nov. 1944.

quarters on Cebu, ordered his defense plan executed. This was a compromise between the old concept of "annihilation at the beachhead" and the new one of defense in depth which had been tried with considerable success at Peleliu. No elaborate system of concrete pillboxes and other beach defenses was built up, because, as Suzuki's chief of staff observed after the war, it had been proved at Saipan that no beach defenses could survive the terrific shore bombardment that the United States Navy laid on before every amphibious operation. As a concession, however, to the "annihilation" idea, strongpoints were prepared in Catmon, Guinhandang and other hills that commanded the beaches, and Suzuki organized them as a first line of defense which would be evacuated under pressure. His forces would then retire to a defense line running through Dagami at the foot of the mountain chain. Up to and including A-day plus 2 or 3, the Japanese concept was that of a mere delaying action on Leyte in preparation for the "general decisive battle" for Luzon. And they had but one division, the 16th, on the island.

2. *The General Returns; X Corps Advances*

After luncheon on the afternoon of 20 October, the much-heralded and long-awaited return took place. General MacArthur and a few members of his staff had sailed up from Hollandia in light cruiser *Nashville*. It was the first time he had entered Leyte Gulf since 1903, when he was a Second Lieutenant of Army Engineers. He spent the morning watching the landings from *Nashville's* bridge, and partook of an early luncheon in his cabin. According to one of the press correspondents present at this historic scene: —

> MacArthur appeared on deck in fresh, smooth-pressed suntans, bebraided hat, and sun glasses, and let himself down a ladder into a barge. He took up a position in the stern, directly behind and above Philippines President Osmeña, Resident Commissioner Romulo, Chief of Staff Sutherland, and Air Commander Kenney, looking all the time a pic-

ture of composure and dignified good humor. He smiled broadly and said to Sutherland, "Well, believe it or not, we're here." When the landing barge grounded and the forward end flapped down, MacArthur stepped calmly into knee-deep water and, with Kenney, Sutherland, and other officers around him, waded impressively ashore. The party inspected the beach, walked inland about 200 yards and studied the damage done by the bombardment.

Back on the beach MacArthur delivered his liberation speech. He was genuinely moved; his hands shook and his voice took on the timbre of deep emotion. "People of the Philippines," he said, "*I have returned.* By the grace of Almighty God our forces stand again on Philippine soil. . . . At my side is your President, Sergio Osmeña, worthy successor of that great patriot Manuel Quezon, with members of his Cabinet." His voice became fuller as his rich prose flowed on. "Rally to me. Let the indomitable spirit of Bataan and Corregidor lead on. As the lines of battle roll forward to bring you within the zone of operations, rise and strike! . . . For your homes and hearths, strike! For future generations of your sons and daughters, strike! In the name of your sacred dead, strike! Let no heart be faint. Let every arm be steeled. The guidance of divine God points the way. Follow in His name to the Holy Grail of righteous victory!"

He walked down the beach, sat down under a palm, chatted awhile with President Osmeña. He was introduced to Major General Irving of the 24th Division. Then he went back to the *Nashville*. Douglas MacArthur had returned.[7]

It was MacArthur's day. He was more than a general; he was a symbol.

President Roosevelt remembered the fighting Navy that was responsible for bringing the General to a position whence he could wade ashore. And so, after sending warm congratulations to General MacArthur, he sent this message to Admirals Nimitz and Halsey: –

The country has followed with pride the magnificent sweep of your fleet into enemy waters. In addition to the gallant fighting of your fliers, we appreciate the endurance and super seamanship of your forces.

[7] "Battle for the Philippines" *Fortune* XXXI No. 6 (June 1945) pp. 157–8. This speech was broadcast over the "Voice of Freedom" circuit.

Your fine coöperation with General MacArthur furnishes another example of teamwork and the effective and intelligent use of all weapons.[8]

The General went ashore for three hours on the 21st and again on the 22nd, to see what was going on. On the 23rd, when Tacloban was secured, he and President Osmeña made it an official visit. The General announced the reëstablishment of civil government in the Philippines, and the flags of the United States and of the Philippine Commonwealth were raised simultaneously. Next day Admiral Kinkaid requested General MacArthur to set up headquarters ashore so that *Nashville* could take part in the impending naval battle. The General indicated his desire to remain on board regardless of *Nashville's* employment; but the Admiral, not wishing to risk the life of her distinguished passenger, did not allow the cruiser to take part in the Battle of Surigao Strait. Immediately after that was over, the Admiral sent the General an urgent request to transfer to flagship *Wasatch* "as *Nashville* was badly needed with combatant forces." MacArthur then decided to set up his command post at Tacloban to "release *Nashville* for combatant duty," and that was done at about 1000 October 25. An advance echelon of his Southwest Pacific Area staff was already present, and others came up shortly from Hollandia.

After the war was over an amusing side light on MacArthur's return was contributed by General Yamashita. The "Tiger of Malaya" never believed that the General had landed on Leyte. He thought that the photographs flashed around the world of his wading ashore and addressing the Filipinos were mock-ups done in New Guinea; he never imagined that so important a general would go to the front. Had he known, said Yamashita, he could have thrown the whole strength of the Japanese air forces into one suicide raid on MacArthur's headquarters, and avenged the death of Admiral Yamamoto.[9]

[8] *New York Times* 20 Oct. 1944.

[9] Lt. Cdr. S. S. Stratton USNR "Tiger of Malaya" U.S. Nav. Inst. *Proceedings,* LXXX (Feb. 1954) p. 141.

In the meantime, ground forces were pressing inland. X Corps' main objective was to secure San Juanico Strait between Leyte and Samar, to cut off a possible route of reinforcement. General Tomochika, Suzuki's chief of staff, later revealed that our prompt control and use of this Strait was a great cross to him. By 1530 on A-day 1st Cavalry Division had cleared the Cataisan Peninsula of the enemy.

The 24th Division had a tougher time than did the troopers. Mount Guinhandang just north of Palo was the obstacle, and the primary objective for A-day. Automatic weapons were emplaced in camouflaged caves, emplacements and trenches on the steep slopes. But the enemy made the mistake of evacuating positions on the slope exposed to naval bombardment, and up that slope two companies of the 19th RCT scrambled, just in time to seize the crest and repel an attempt to reoccupy the hill when the bombardment lifted.

Southwest Pacific standard operating procedure was to load assault transports with just enough cargo to be unloaded by daylight the first day, so that they could retire that night and avoid air attack. The build-up at the beachhead was done by successive echelons, as in Normandy, but with fifteen times the distance to cover. Off Tacloban it was the determined purpose of all hands to unload these vulnerable ships and get them out of Leyte Gulf by the night of A-day. Shipping was so barely adequate, owing to the demands of the European Theater, that we could not afford any loss. Every vessel then discharging in Leyte Gulf would be essential for later landings in Luzon, and Pacific Fleet could expect no replacements for APAs or AKAs at the bottom of Leyte Gulf.

Admiral Barbey had four captains commanding his transport divisions in the Northern Attack Force – Brittain, Baker, Carlson and Loomis – who were veterans at this game. They were organizers, drivers and expert seamen; by 1725 on 20 October their ships had completed unloading. Beach Red transports had landed 6750 tons of supplies; and the Beach White transports 4500 tons.[10]

[10] The total figures for A-day unloading, including cargoes of 11 LST on Beach Red and those of 14 LST on Beach White, were 18,150 troops and 13,500 tons

All Barbey's big transports and cargo ships were ready to depart at 1800 A-day; a good day's work by any standard.

Panaon Strait, the narrow boat passage between the rugged southeastern cape of Leyte and Panaon Island, wanted for a motor torpedo boat base, was occupied without opposition by the 21st RCT by 1015 on A-day. Thus all three groups under Admiral Barbey successfully completed their assault missions on 20 October.

3. *The Southern Landings: A-day at Dulag*[11]

The southern landings began about 11 miles south of Palo on the left flank of Admiral Barbey's Beach Red. Their first object was to secure several Japanese-built airstrips behind the beaches. Adding a southern landing to the northern also meant a broader front from which Sixth Army could deploy and receive reinforcements.

Vice Admiral Wilkinson, an amphibious expert second to none, was ably assisted by Rear Admirals Conolly and Royal.[12] His Southern Attack Force landed XXIV Corps (7th and 96th Divisions) on a 5000-yard stretch of excellent sandy beach extending

---

supplies. The LSTs, owing to the bad landing conditions for beaching craft, required about 17 hours more to unload completely, which they had done by 1015 Oct. 21.

[11] Wilkinson Report (see note 1 this chapter); Comphibgroup 3 (Rear Adm. R. L. Conolly) Report of Participation in Amphibious Operations for the Capture of Leyte, 26 Oct.; CTG 79.2 (Rear Adm. F. B. Royal) Report of Leyte Operation 4 Nov. 1944; Operations Report XXIV Corps in Leyte Campaign 20 Oct.–25 Dec. 1944.

[12] For Conolly, see brief biog. in Volume VII 232. He had recently reported from Washington, where he had been Secretary of the J.C.S.

Forrest B. Royal, b. New York 1893, Annapolis '15, served in Atlantic Fleet during World War I, as aide to Admirals Mayo and Andrews; exec. and C.O. of *Harding* 1919, helped fit out *J. D. Edwards* and served as her exec. in Near East and Asiatic Station. Studied ordnance engineering, M.S. from M.I.T. 1924; gunnery officer *Dobbin*, taught ordnance at Annapolis, gunnery officer *Chester* 1930; aide to Admiral Standley, 1932–6; C.O. *Porter*, War College senior course, Chief of U.S. Naval Mission to Brazil 1939–41; C.O. *Milwaukee* during encounter with German runner in 1942 (see Volume I 384); service on J.C.S. and Joint Board; command of amphib. group Pacific Fleet June 1944. A year later, shortly after directing two of the last amphibious assaults of the war in Borneo, he died of a heart attack on board his flagship.

from the Liberanan River to a point about 1000 yards south of Dulag. Once ashore, a part of the troops would thrust north to join X Corps moving south from Tacloban, while the rest pushed south to the Marabang River and moved inland. This would give

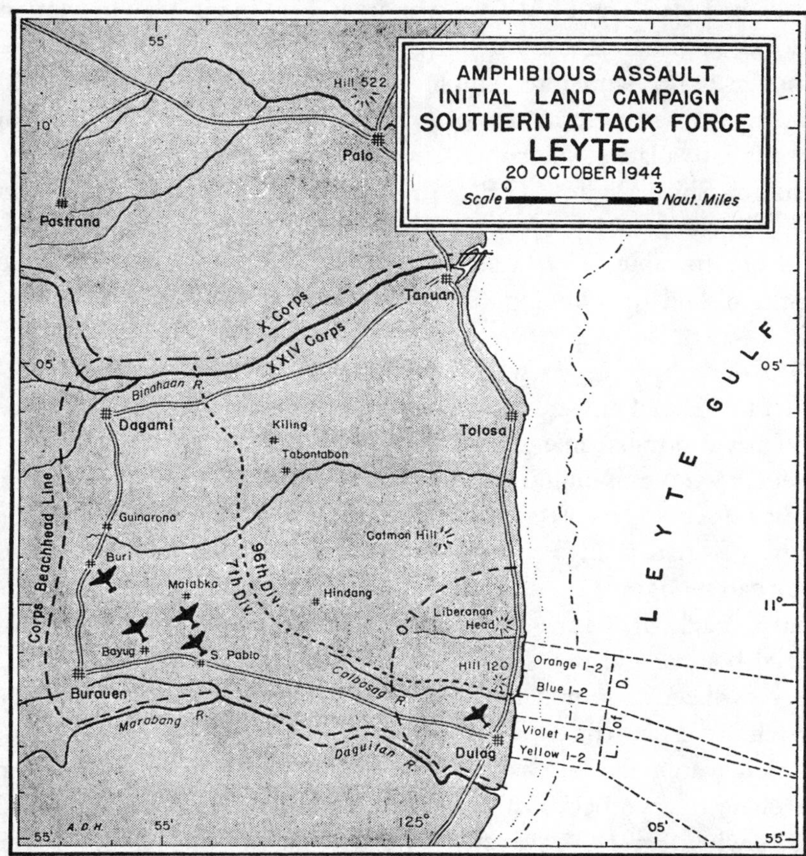

the Corps a beachhead with a coastal front of 13 miles, including the town of Dulag and the seven airstrips. As soon as this beachhead was secured, General Hodge could look to General Krueger for orders to coördinate his efforts with those of General Sibert for the complete reduction of Leyte.

The last of the transports in Admiral Royal's group reached their berths at 0840 off the Orange and Blue beaches, ten minutes after Admiral Conolly's had anchored off the Violet and Yellow beaches, in 40 to 60 fathoms of water. All 51 of the big transport types anchored clear of obstructions. LSTs and other beaching craft were already well along in their unloading schedule, as hundreds of LCVPs and LVTs churning around in circular formation testified. All hands were doing their allotted parts in hoisting out landing craft, launching amphtracs and dukws to be organized into waves, setting up a line of departure and maneuvering control vessels into place. Newcomers in the amphibious set-up were the Landing Ship, Medium (LSM), 203 feet long, 900 tons, which had the vehicle capacity of an LCT but was faster, more seaworthy and comfortable. They had bow ramps like the LSTs, and were distinguished by conning towers resembling the turret of a medieval castle.

At 0915 boat waves were beginning to form at the line of departure, air strikes were coming in from the escort carriers off shore and naval bombardment had reached crescendo. A bombardment preceding an amphibious landing has a stimulating effect upon the attack forces. Just as a seasoned concertgoer can distinguish the notes of brass, strings and woodwinds, so a veteran of amphibious war can recognize the deep boom of the battleship armaments, the sharp crack of 5-inch guns, the rattle of 40-mm, the "bop" of aërial bombs, and the weird whiplike crack of the rockets. When he sees the LCI gunboats forming up to lead amphtracs in to the beach, he listens for their machine-gun, mortar and rocket fire just as you watch the percussion man getting ready to beat his drum or clang his cymbals. Off Dulag the din reached its height around 0930 when the LCIs leaped forward from the line of departure, to be followed two minutes later by the first wave of amphtrac tanks; these in turn were hounded by LVTs, the amphtrac personnel carriers.

The coastal plain in this section of Leyte Gulf is much wider than in the zone of the northern landings; a green, level area covered with rice and cornfields and coconut groves. It is broken only by Catmon Hill, which rises over 1000 feet a short distance inland, and which received special attention from ships and planes. At 0810 the planes bombed it, and at 0915 the LCI mortar boats began to work it over from short range. Their high trajectory was more destructive, especially on the reverse slope, than shells from the larger fire support ships. Half an hour after the mortar boats opened fire, at 0945, the rocket-equipped LCIs which preceded the amphtracs in to the beach, opened up. These little gunboats in a few minutes fired over 5500 4½-inch rockets on each pair of landing beaches.

At 0954 an observation plane dropped flares so bright as to be easily visible in the brilliant morning light, meaning that the first boat wave was almost ready to hit the beach. It did so, almost exactly at H-hour, 1000. All ships now shifted gunfire a mile inland and to the flanks. This scheme of fire was maintained until 1020, when it was lifted another thousand yards inland. Firing on Catmon Hill continued all day. A 75-mm battery on or near it took destroyer *Bennion* under fire between 1010 and 1042, straddling her repeatedly and wounding five men with a near miss. This was the only opposition that the enemy offered during the southern landing, excepting artillery and mortar fire which fell on the Blue beaches as the 96th Division was landing.

Dulag, captured by 7th Division about noon, never had been much of a town according to G.I. standards, and now it was little or nothing. The stone Spanish church, partially destroyed by the bombardment, served as a field hospital; the rest of the town consisted of wooden thatched houses so flimsy as to collapse from a huff and a puff. The narrow streets were littered with papers, clothing and odds and ends, possessions of Filipinos who paid for liberation by the destruction of their property. But few tears were shed, since the Japanese had gone. The very natives whose property was destroyed approached American troops with smiles and gestures of jubilant welcome; and those evacuated to the interior promptly returned to the beaches. Native boats coming out to the ships for food and to "supply enemy information" soon became a nuisance as well as a hazard to navigation.

The 96th Division got off to an easier start than the 7th, despite the fire on Blue beaches. First resistance was encountered about 1025 at the base of Hill 120, so called because someone guessed its height to be 120 feet. It commanded the entire stretch of southern landing beaches. After gun and mortar projectiles had been thrown at the enemy lurking around its base, the hill was taken by the 3rd BLT 382nd Infantry, and the flag raised at 1042.

This flag-raising was never publicized like the one on Iwo Jima four months later, but it was even more significant. Only 42 minutes had elapsed since the first assault troops landed; yet here, floating high and proud, was tangible proof that the Americans had made good their promise to the Filipinos.

By noon 20 October a high percentage of the XXIV Corps assault forces was ashore. Shortly after, Admirals Conolly and Royal ordered LSTs with high priority cargo in to the beaches. Attack transports were moved closer in; causeways and pontoon barges waited to take on cargo from the AKAs. At 1411 the landing of vehicles on Beach Yellow 1 had to be suspended owing to enemy mortar fire. Mortar-equipped LCIs were ordered to counterattack and get the Japanese. Normal activity continued on the other beaches.

By the end of A-day, the Southern Attack Force controlled the coast of Leyte from the north bank of the Liberanan River to the mouth of the Marabang. Gains of the 7th Division were the more spectacular, since the 96th had to contend with a miserable swamp. Both were short of the initial objective line, but XXIV Corps was ready to convert the amphibious phase into a land campaign. Very tough fighting lay ahead for these two divisions before they could call Leyte secured and sail north to take Okinawa.

4. *Naval Support and Casualties*

Japanese aircraft had always attacked amphibious forces at dawn and dusk to take advantage of poor light conditions. Here they did not wait for evening to make their first visitation.

Rear Admiral Walden L. Ainsworth's flagship, light cruiser *Honolulu* (Captain H. Ray Thurber), was one of the happiest and scrappiest ships in the Pacific Fleet. "Blue Goose," as she was called by her crew, had fought through many actions, beginning at Pearl Harbor, but never lost a man, even by illness or accident. Twice torpedoed in the Battle of Kolombangara, she had got off with no more than a damaged bow and a hole in her square stern transom. Throughout the Marianas and Palau campaigns she had been dishing it out yet had taken nothing.

During the afternoon watch on A-day, after completing her bombardment schedule at noon, *Honolulu* was standing by in Leyte Gulf, about five miles off shore, to render call fire. Her engines were turning over, port engine ahead one third, starboard engine astern one third, in order to swing her head to starboard. A warning came over TBS, and a moment later the lookouts shouted, "Torpedo plane port quarter!" Captain Thurber, who had been having his hair cut in his emergency cabin, leaped out on the bridge and saw the Japanese plane as it emerged from the mist overhanging. It approached *Honolulu* on her port beam. A moment later, the splash of a torpedo dropped from the plane was seen, and then the wake.[18] The Captain immediately ordered full speed astern, since, from the angle of the plane's approach, it was evident to his seaman's eye that this maneuver alone offered any chance of escaping a hit. The scant three minutes that elapsed between sighting and impact were not enough to swing *Honolulu* parallel to the torpedo's path, but Thurber's quick thinking saved his ship from a crippling blow in magazine or after engine room. The torpedo hit her on the port side, just forward of the bridge superstructure, tearing a jagged hole 29 by 25 feet, killing 60 officers and men, destroying the ship's plotting room and a marine berthing compartment, and dropping a 40-mm ammunition hoist into the wardroom. A few minutes after 1602, when she received the hit, *Honolulu* was dead in the water and listing about thirteen degrees to port;

[18] *Honolulu* Report of War Damage, 20 Oct. 1944. The writer, who had enjoyed two tours of duty in *Honolulu*, obtained additional details from survivors.

but the power plant had not been injured; the Captain had secured engines at the moment of hitting.[14] Prompt action on the part of the damage control party saved the ship. Captain Thurber said that it was a "matter of everyone doing the right thing at the right time in the first half hour."

At 1615 *Honolulu* got under way and steamed slowly through the transport area toward the shoal water off the landing beaches, pumping fuel oil to correct the list. Ten minutes later, destroyer *Richard P. Leary* came alongside to remove the wounded and furnish power for the submersible pumps. Two fleet tugs subsequently lent a hand, and by 1700 the list had been almost wiped out. But gallant "Blue Goose," already overdue for extensive overhaul, was out of the fighting.

While the soldiers were digging foxholes for their first night's sleep in the Philippines, the sailors were taking measures to protect themselves during a good night's work of unloading.

Southern Attack Force transports were more heavily loaded than the Northern ones, in accordance with Pacific Fleet doctrine. So at 1530 Admiral Wilkinson decided that his transports would not be ready to retire at dusk but must remain anchored in their assigned berths.

Grave concern was felt as to night air attacks, particularly since there was no night fighter protection available. All transport types of the Southern Force, and those of the Northern Force which had not unloaded and retired, remained at anchor. An inner screen of LCI gunboats was stationed near the shore to prevent attack by the

[14] As Lt. D. P. Klain and his assistant, Lt. L. S. Clapper, were busy directing damage control on board the *Honolulu*, Leon Garsian, RM 3/c, was putting in the first of his 16 hours alone, trapped in the radio compartment below decks. He was asleep when the torpedo struck and in no time the compartments above him had 36 inches of water and oil on their decks while the water on his own deck was kept out by watertight doors. The radioman managed to attract attention; communications were established and maintained with him from the second deck by means of an exhaust ventilation duct through which he was receiving air. By using a mattress from which he ripped the padding, Garsian stopped the water and waited patiently for his rescue. To reach him, members of the crew had to cut through 4-inch armor with acetylene torches, which took six hours of hard work; but he was rescued unharmed.

suspected (but nonexistent) enemy torpedo boats, and an outer screen of destroyers was thrown around the entire transport area for antiaircraft gunfire.

The greatest reliance was placed on smoke. The use of smoke is a double-edged sword and, for that reason, the question of its employment had been kicked around the Navy for many months. If used effectively, smoke can lay a blanket over ships. An enemy plane coming in during the half light of early morning or late afternoon sees only a fog mull, and can get no idea of the number or disposition of the ships underneath. Outside the blanketed transport area the screen is stationed; and these ships with their fire control radar are on hand to knock down any enemy plane which penetrates the C.A.P. Several things, however, may go wrong with a smoke screen, making the use of it at times hazardous. With unfavorable wind or a poor smoke plan, transports are only partially covered, and the enemy can attack through holes in the blanket while enjoying smoke protection against antiaircraft gunners. The smoke-making machines provided by the Navy at that time were difficult to start and likely to explode and start bad fires; but, such as they were, all the larger ships were fitted with them and were ordered to use them at dawn and dusk. Small smokepots, fitted into the sterns of LCVPs and other landing craft placed to windward of the transports, helped to augment the pall.

At 1815, a couple of minutes before sunset, the transports started making smoke according to plan. About ten minutes later, "Flash Red" came over the TBS radio circuit and "bogey" kept appearing on radar screens until 2030 when "Flash White" (All Clear signal) was given. Except for one pause of about twenty minutes, smoking was continuous from 1815 until 2042. During this interval the ships in Leyte Gulf showed very poor fire discipline and two of our own ships were hit by indiscriminate antiaircraft fire. Wounded "Blue Goose" was the principal victim. At 1931 an unknown ship fired a 20-mm projectile into one of *Honolulu's* 40-mm mounts, exploding several rounds of ammunition and adding 5 dead and 11 wounded to her casualty list. About the same time *Lindenwald*, an LSD, took a 5-inch burst on her port beam which killed one man and wounded six. Things then quieted down. Smoke was made for the first 20 minutes of every hour for the remainder of the night, to maintain the blanket. About an hour before sunrise, continuous smoking was resumed and continued until fighter planes arrived to maintain C.A.P.

Daylight 21 October revealed the usual untidy spectacle on the invasion beaches. The sand was littered with ration cans, ammunition boxes, cigarette and candy wrappers and parked vehicles. On the beachhead the ground was pitted with foxholes, many of them half filled with water by the night rainfall.

The liberation of the Philippines was off to a good start. It had been a hard twenty-four hours for all hands, but worse lay ahead.

5. *Air Support and Beachhead Consolidation, 21–24 October*

During the four crucial days of beachhead expansion that followed the landings there was a providential lull in the northeast monsoon. There were frequent showers, but the sky was never more than half overcast for any length of time and winds were variable and light – mostly around 5 to 6 knots, never more than 20.

Shortly after first light 21 October, a Japanese plane crashed into the foremast of H.M.A.S. *Australia*, which had covered every amphibious operation in the Southwest Pacific since Arawe. Captain Deschaineux and 19 ratings were killed; Commodore John A. Collins, senior Australian Naval officer present, and 53 others were wounded.[15] *Australia* joined *Honolulu* and, escorted by destroyers *Richard P. Leary* and H.M.A.S. *Warramunga*, retired to Manus.

Enemy air raids on Leyte Gulf were few between 21 and 23 October, and (apart from the sinking of *Sonoma*) only minor damage was inflicted on the amphibious forces. Most of their planes registered on radar screens were merely observing.

[15] This was not an organized Kamikaze attack, of which the first was the one on the escort carrier group 25 Oct.

Two of our escort carrier groups concentrated on the support of troops ashore, while the third directed a part of its effort against enemy airfields on Cebu, Negros, Panay, Bohol and northern Mindanao. The idea was to "get the aircraft at the source before they could take off to attack our landing forces. No attempt was made to bomb runways for there were too many fields and the enemy was too adept at filling in holes" for us to "waste bombs on such temporary damage . . . In the first three days of this 'close support at a distance,' 125 planes were destroyed on the ground." [16] Out of 855 sorties, only 7 of our planes were shot down and all but two of the pilots were recovered.

In the meantime, Imperial General Headquarters completely changed its strategy with respect to Leyte. On 22 or 23 October, after observing the strength of the American landings, it decided to make Leyte instead of Luzon the scene of the "general decisive battle." General Suzuki was told to expect support from the joint air forces on the 24th, a decisive sea battle on the 25th, and on the next day to look for heavy reinforcement of his ground forces on Leyte. Major General Tomochika has recorded that this news cheered up the hitherto overwhelmed Japanese defenders. "We were determined to take offensive after offensive and clean up American forces on Leyte according to original plans. We seriously discussed demanding the surrender of the entire American Army after seizing General MacArthur." [17]

In accordance with this new Japanese plan, the enemy on 24 October began to commit aircraft heavily. So many appeared and at such frequent intervals that missions from the escort carriers had to be canceled or curtailed in order to reinforce C.A.P. over ships in Leyte Gulf. Twelve fighters were continually on station from 0545 until dark and another 16 were kept in readiness for imme-

[16] Comairpac Air Analysis 4 Feb. 1945.

[17] Tomochika "True Facts of the Leyte Operation," written immediately after the war and translated by U.S. Army (reference in Cannon p. 385); summary by Lt. Col. G. W. Dickerson USA "Defeat on Leyte"; *Infantry Journal* LXV (July 1949) pp. 30–33.

diate launching if needed. An estimated 150 to 200 enemy aircraft approached the objective, but only a few actually reached it, and the escort carriers claimed to have shot down 66.[18]

Fast Carrier Forces Pacific Fleet were just around the corner. After supporting the landings on A-day, Admiral McCain's Group 1 and Admiral Davison's Group 4 fueled on the 21st, and headed for Ulithi to provision and rearm on the 22nd. As soon as the first rumblings of trouble became audible on the 23rd, Halsey turned Davison's group back towards Leyte but let McCain keep on until next day, when he, too, was recalled. At that time Davison was already striking enemy surface forces in the Sibuyan Sea. Bogan's Group 2 and Sherman's Group 3, which had stood by on A-day to render support if necessary, hit Visayan airfields on the 21st, stood by again next day, fueled and searched respectively on the 23rd, and played an important part in the Sibuyan Sea battle on the 24th, as did Davison's. This retirement of two task groups for replenishment, at a critical point, led to a further development of the mobile supply system before the next major operation.

General Kenney's Far Eastern Air Force was also helping. During the fourth week in October, out of 2668 sorties flown from various bases in the Southwest Pacific, 465 were directed to the central and southern Philippines in support of the Leyte landings. Beginning 17 October, heavy strikes kept the Mindanao airfields well pounded down. At that time, however, Clark Field, Luzon, was the principal base of the Japanese air forces, which were counted on to scout and attack the approaching enemy. The aggressive attacks of the Far Eastern Air Force against Mindanao, added to those of Task Force 38 over Luzon, forced Japanese naval planes into concealment, and reduced their strength on the critical 24 and 25 October.[19]

Enemy airfields are a primary objective of any amphibious operation, and it is essential that, once secured, they be made operational

[18] Commander Support Aircraft Seventh Fleet (Capt. Whitehead) Report of Support Aircraft Operations, 2 Nov. 1944.

[19] Comairpac Analysis p. 145; Interrogation of Cdr. Yamaguchi of First Air Fleet (*Inter. Jap. Off.* I 178–83).

as quickly as possible. When no airfields exist, they must be built. In an operation like this, carrier-based planes maintain local air control until the Army can relieve them with land-based aircraft. Carrier aircraft endurance dictates this. Their offensive operations are conducted by a limited number of pilots who are subject to exhaustion and cannot be immediately relieved.

The Dulag and Tacloban airfields were both in American hands by 21 October and Army Engineers promptly got to work on them, with the help of Filipino labor. The Dulag field on 25 October was still soft with many rough spots; yet of necessity it became an emergency landing strip for carrier planes.[20] Tacloban field presented a somewhat happier picture, despite the fact that the water table was only 18 inches below the surface – "an airstrip there could at best be a thin slice of coral or metal laid upon a jelly mold." [21] General Krueger visited this airfield and told the Engineers that unless they got the gravel laid they would be digging foxholes for their lives within twenty-four hours; and the General was right. Through intensive efforts, implemented by General Kenney's threat to bulldoze equipment landed by LSTs into the bay, the strip was covered with four to six inches of sand and gravel, sufficiently hard-packed to permit emergency use by about a hundred carrier-based planes on the great day of battle. The surface was still so bad on 25 October that about one quarter of these planes were destroyed in crash landings, nosing over in soft spots, and others were shot down by trigger-happy GIs with anti-aircraft guns; yet Tacloban airfield saved many an American life during the Battle for Leyte Gulf.

Ground troops in the meantime were pushing the enemy farther back from the shores of the Gulf. By 0900 October 21, the 24th Infantry Division had advanced to the top of Mount Guinhandang. Next day, after some tough fighting, it established a protective line along the left bank of the Palo River to protect that flank of the

[20] Between 25 and 28 Oct. some 89 planes from 17 different carriers made emergency landings there.

[21] Lucien Hubbard "Scrub Team at Tacloban" *Reader's Digest* Feb. 1945 p. 8; Cannon *Leyte* p. 187.

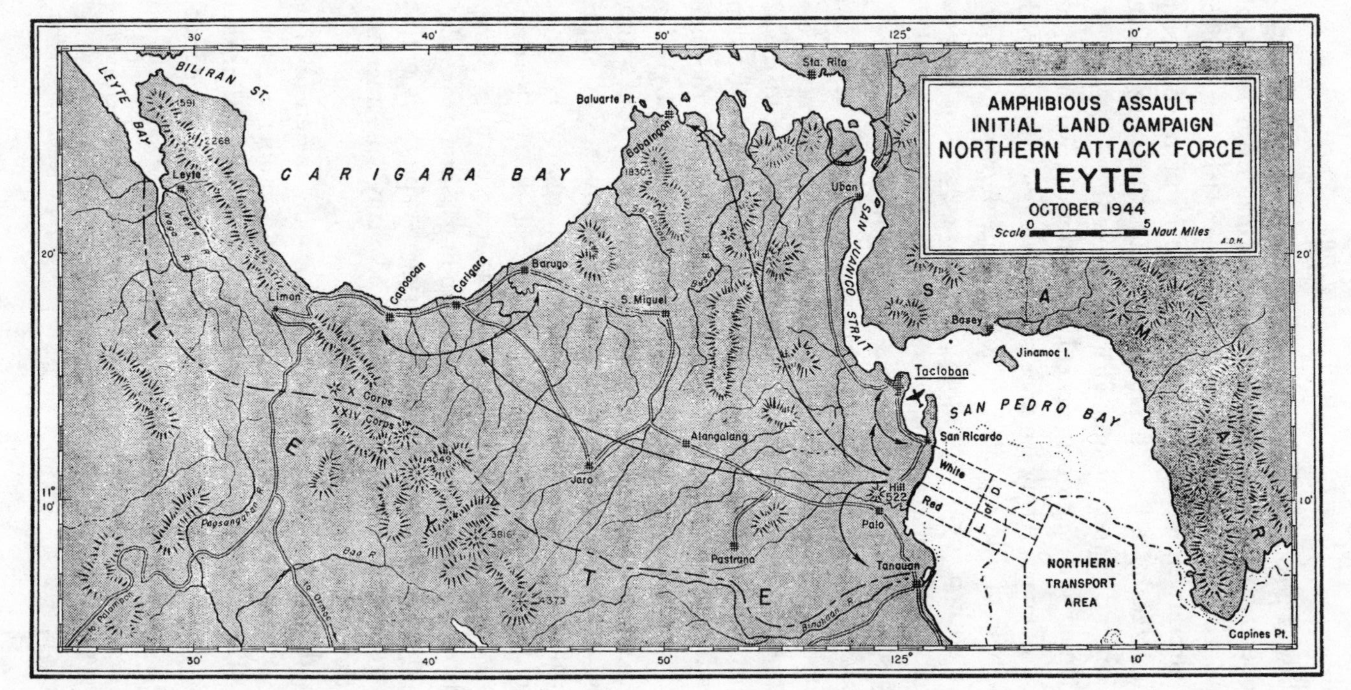
AMPHIBIOUS ASSAULT
INITIAL LAND CAMPAIGN
NORTHERN ATTACK FORCE
LEYTE
OCTOBER 1944
Scale 0 5 Naut. Miles
CARIGARA BAY
SAN PEDRO BAY
SAN JUANICO STRAIT
LEYTE BAY
BILIRAN ST.
NORTHERN TRANSPORT AREA
Tacloban
Sta. Rita
Baluarte Pt.
Babatngon
Uban
Basey
Jinamoc I.
San Ricardo
White
Red
Hill 522
Palo
Tanauan
Pastrana
Atangalang
Jaro
S. Miguel
Barugo
Carigara
Capoocan
Limon
Leyte
Capines Pt.
X Corps
XXIV Corps
L E Y T E
S A M A R
Pagsangahan R.
Binahaan R.
Bao R.
to Ormoc
Naga R.
Leyte R.

Northern Attack Force. Troopers of the 1st Cavalry who rode ashore on Beach White reached their first objective on the 21st and continued to advance against slight opposition, with the support of naval gunfire and air bombardment. During the course of that day enemy antiaircraft guns located in the outskirts of Tacloban, and mortars in Palo and the neighboring hills, were promptly attended to by the Navy; destroyer *Killen* silenced three artillery positions in about 30 minutes. The gunfire support ships provided harassing fire at night and lighted up the area with star shell in order to prevent enemy infiltration and troop movements.

Tacloban, with the only docking facilities on Leyte, and Palo, were captured on 21 October and held against counterattacks. The troopers now fanned out west and north into the Leyte Valley. On the 23rd, as they advanced, they encountered Japanese well dug into strongpoints, which Naval air bombing and gunfire helped to knock out.

That morning, the 1st Cavalry pushed up the Leyte shore of San Juanico Strait to a point about six miles north of Tacloban. One squadron of troopers procured LCM landing craft from the boat pool on Beach Red and sailed clear through the Strait. Another made an unopposed landing at La Paz, Samar, eleven miles north of Tacloban. These, the first of innumerable shore-to-shore amphibious operations conducted by the Army in boats of the Engineer Special Brigades, or in Navy landing craft, secured San Juanico Strait, and put a cork in the one small hole to Leyte Gulf through which the enemy might have lifted troops in barges to make counterlandings, as they had attempted to do at Saipan and Bougainville. But as long as the entire west coast of Leyte lay wide open to reinforcement, the enemy could neglect his former tactics of infiltration.

While these versatile cavalrymen were again wetting their feet, the 24th Division was busy overcoming the enemy on two strongly defended hills west and northwest of Palo town. By 25 October the 24th Division was ready for a major thrust into Leyte Valley.

General Hodges's XXIV Corps was also feeling its way inland.

After capturing Dulag and its airfield on 20 and 21 October, the 7th Infantry Division pushed up the road that paralleled the Marabang River, and on the 24th captured the town of Burauen, about eleven miles inland, which marked the southwest corner of the corps beachhead line, and the edge of the mountains. Isolated centers of fanatically resisting Japanese were encountered and overcome during this advance. Dagami was liberated 30 October after fighting over a cemetery whose tombs had been converted into pillboxes by the enemy.

Catmon Hill, a series of wooded ridges rising to one thousand feet and less than a mile from the beaches, was the most important Japanese strongpoint in a position to embarrass the landing of reinforcements. The Sixth Army bypassed it in order to give plenty of time for naval gunfire and artillery preparation. It was captured in a series of assaults between 26 and 29 October. But the main body of Japanese troops there had previously retired to the Dagami area, and would be heard from again.

While 7th Division was occupying the Dulag-Burauen-Dagami triangle, the 96th Division on the right flank of the Southern Attack Force launched a two-pronged attack. One drove north on the beach road to the town of Tanauan at the mouth of the Binahaan River. The initial objective line of XXIV Corps was completed, and on the 25th contact was made with X Corps north of Tanauan. The second prong drove inland through swamps south of Catmon Hill, meeting little opposition from the enemy until it approached Tabontabon. That town fell on 27 October, after a tough resistance.

By a curious twist of circumstance, the XXIV Corps advance was supported by Marine Corps artillery. During the Saipan operation XXIV Corps artillery had been lent to the Marines, and in Saipan it stayed. So, as a fair exchange, the recently formed V Amphibious Corps artillery, under the command of Brigadier General T. E. Bourke USMC, was attached to XXIV Corps for the Leyte operation.

Land operations were far more difficult than a brief summary can suggest. They were carried out in torrential rains which turned dirt roads into sloughs, open fields into swamps and rice paddies into mud ponds. Success depended on our ability to meet enemy counterattacks by land and sea, which began to develop on 23 October. Leyte was no coral atoll that could be sealed off by superior air and sea power, and so far we had obtained a mere toe-hold.

Fortunately, despite the bad guesses that the Japanese Navy would not fight for Leyte, plans were made on the assumption that it would. With that in mind, it behooved American shipping to unload on the double and clear out. Admiral Barbey loaded his initial assault shipping so lightly that it was able to clear the Gulf after dark A-day; the rest of the gear came up in later echelons, No. 1 arriving from Hollandia 22 October. The two Navy transports, five chartered freighters and 14 LSTs in this echelon unloaded quickly and most of them were able to depart at 1700 same day.[22] Seventeen LSTs and three attack freighters pulled out at the same time; and twenty-four hours later, 20 LSTs and one attack freighter departed. After Tacloban was secured, three LSTs at a time could discharge on the docks in three hours.

Reinforcement Group 2, which arrived on the morning of October 24, comprised 33 LST, 24 Liberty ships, nine service force vessels and one oiler, escorted by four destroyers (*Nicholas* flag) and two frigates. Only a few of these managed to unload and depart the same day; most of them had to sit out the battles of October 25.[23]

By 25 October, 80,900 men and 114,990 tons of supplies and equipment had been landed by the assault echelons of the Northern Attack Force alone; their work was practically completed. During the five days 20–24 October, 37 large ships (AKA, AK, and LSD), together with 90 LST, had unloaded, and all but ten LST, which had special duties at Tacloban, had departed.

[22] See Appendix I for these two echelons.

[23] These 24 merchant ships, in addition to the 5 in Reinforcement Group 1, were not unloaded until 28 October.

These figures are for the Northern Attack Force only. In the Southern Attack Force, frantic efforts were made to unload quickly and withdraw, but Wilkinson's transport types, carried too much cargo to be discharged in twelve hours. Despite inadequate shore parties, the bane of almost every amphibious operation, 18 vessels completed unloading in time to depart by dark 21 October, 11 more departed next day, 7 on the 23rd (Admiral Conolly commanding the convoy) and 8 on the 24th (Admiral Royal commanding), together with 38 LST, 33 LCI and 4 LCM. By the close of that day the entire XXIV Corps of some 51,500 men with about 85,000 tons of cargo, including supplies to meet expected expenditures for 30 days, had been placed ashore.

Thus, by midnight 24–25 October, when the great day of battle opened, only three amphibious force flagships (*Wasatch*, *Blue Ridge* and *Mt. Olympus*), AKA *Auriga*, 23 LST, 2 LSM and 28 Liberty ships, remained in Leyte Gulf, while the fire support battleships, cruisers and destroyers deployed to meet the enemy advancing through Surigao Strait.

At 1600 October 24, when Lieutenant General Krueger set up Sixth Army command post ashore, we may say that the amphibious assault phase of the Leyte operation was over. And the great naval Battle for Leyte Gulf had already begun.

PART III

The Battle for Leyte Gulf[1]

24-25 October 1944

[1]The official name for the series of naval actions on 24–25 October 1944 (Sibuyan Sea, Surigao Strait, Samar, Cape Engaño), whose objective was the defense of Leyte Gulf and Allied forces there against Japanese air and naval attacks. The name "Second Battle of the Philippine Sea," which the newspapers gave it, is a misnomer; for two of the four actions were fought outside that sea. Commo. R. W. Bates's *War College Analysis* carries the story through the Surigao Strait action. Main sources, other than that, are the overall action reports of Admirals Halsey, Kinkaid, Oldendorf, T. L. Sprague, Clifton Sprague and Stump; and, on the Japanese side, those of Admirals Kurita and Ozawa, translated, and the MacArthur *Historical Report* II; the Cincpac Monthly Analysis for Oct. 1944, written by Captain R. C. Parker, is an excellent contemporary account. J. A. Field *The Japanese at Leyte Gulf* (1947) and C. Van Woodward *The Battle for Leyte Gulf* (1947) are good secondary accounts. I have discussed controversial points with Admiral Halsey, Vice Admiral Kinkaid, several members of their staffs, and many other officers who participated.

CHAPTER IX

Moves on the Naval Chessboard

17–24 October 1944

1. *Japanese Forces and Plans*

As the amphibious vessels completed unloading on the shores of Leyte Gulf and Sixth Army extended its beachhead, Japanese naval forces were sallying forth to give battle. The quadripartite Battle for Leyte Gulf which resulted comprised every type of naval warfare invented up to that time – gunfire of heavy and light ships, bombing, suicide-crashing, strafing, rocketing and torpedoing by land-based and carrier-based planes; torpedo attacks by submarines, destroyers and motor torpedo boats. Every naval and air weapon but the mine was employed by both sides. In every part the action was memorable and it resulted in the end of the Japanese Fleet as an effective fighting force. But before victory was attained the situation was puzzling, mistakes were made on both sides, and anything might have happened.

Considering the colossal scale of the operation, the vast number of ships and aircraft, the junction of fleets from distant theaters that had never before operated together, the complicated Japanese strategy, the rapidly changing situation and the vast issues at stake, this Battle for Leyte Gulf must rank with the greatest naval actions of all time.[1] It is to the credit of the United States Navy that so

[1] At the Battle of Jutland, 1 June 1916, 151 British and 99 German ships engaged; in the Battle for Leyte Gulf 216 American, 2 Australian and 64 Japanese ships engaged. This figure includes 39 PTs which took part in Surigao Strait, but no amphibious craft, sweepers, oilers or other auxiliaries. And at Jutland the only aircraft were 4 or 5 seaplanes operating from a tender. Bupers has calculated that the total number of officers and enlisted men in the American and Australian ships

ponderous and intricate a machine worked well, that a gratifying degree of coördination was achieved, that flexibility was shown in dealing with unexpected situations; and that ships faced with almost certain destruction showed the utmost determination and valor.

The general outline of the SHO–1 plan was this. While Ozawa's Northern Force decoyed Halsey's Third Fleet up north out of the way, Kurita's Center Force (our term – see table below) coming through San Bernardino Strait, and the Nishimura-Shima Southern Force, debouching from Surigao Strait, would put a mighty pincer on our amphibious forces and fire support ships in Leyte Gulf, and "annihilate" them. The only feature of this plan already known to United States Naval Intelligence was the gambit tactics of using carriers as a decoy; and that the Fleet refused to believe.[2] Whether the Japanese Navy would engage, and if so by what routes it would approach, was still a matter of conjecture on A-day. Naval Intelligence officers afloat and ashore were busy piecing together sighting reports made by planes, submarines and coast watchers. By 20 October, it was beginning to be assumed that the Japanese Fleet would offer battle; but in what force and how deployed could only be guessed. The initiative, a tremendous advantage in naval warfare, rested with the Japanese. Seventh Fleet was pinned down to protect Sixth Army ashore, and even Third Fleet was not entirely footloose.

The command organization under Admiral Toyoda at the opening of the Battle for Leyte Gulf on 23 October may be represented as follows: —[3]

---

engaged was 143, 668. This was greater than the entire strength of the U.S. Navy and Marine Corps in 1938! Capt. Ohmae estimates that the total number of officers and enlisted men in the Japanese ships engaged was 42,800.

[2] Cincpac-Cincpoa Intelligence translated and circulated to the Fleet, in the summer of 1944, a translation of Japanese manual *Striking Force Tactics* in which they refer explicitly to a decoy group built around *Ise* and *Hyuga* and discuss the gambit strategy; and a Japanese officer, survivor from light cruiser *Natori* sunk 18 Aug. 1944 off Samar by *Hardhead*, confirmed this; his interrogation was published in *Seventh Fleet Intelligence Bulletin* of 13 Oct. 1944.

[3] Chart in *War College Analysis* III, plate xxxvii; postwar interrogations of Admiral Kurita, *Inter. Jap. Off.* I 32–52: Koyanagi, I 147–52; Ozawa, I 219–27;

The highest ranking naval officer under Admiral Toyoda was Vice Admiral Jisaburo Ozawa, commander in chief of the Mobile Force, which included practically all surface combatant ships of the Japanese Navy not engaged in convoy or transport. He retained that command after the major part of his fleet, under Kurita, had been sent to Lingga Roads. In August 1944 he raised his flag in *Amagi*, first of four carriers bigger than our *Essex* class to be completed.[4] *Junyo* and *Ryujo*, 28,000-ton carriers, were also operational at this time; but for lack of carrier-trained pilots, neither they nor *Amagi* could be used before November. Main Body, however, on 20 October was a very small body, including only those carriers that the Japanese intended to use as decoys. Originally these were

and Mori, I 235–44. The Japanese admirals were also known by their former commands, Kurita of Second Fleet, Ozawa of Third Fleet and Shima of Fifth Fleet.

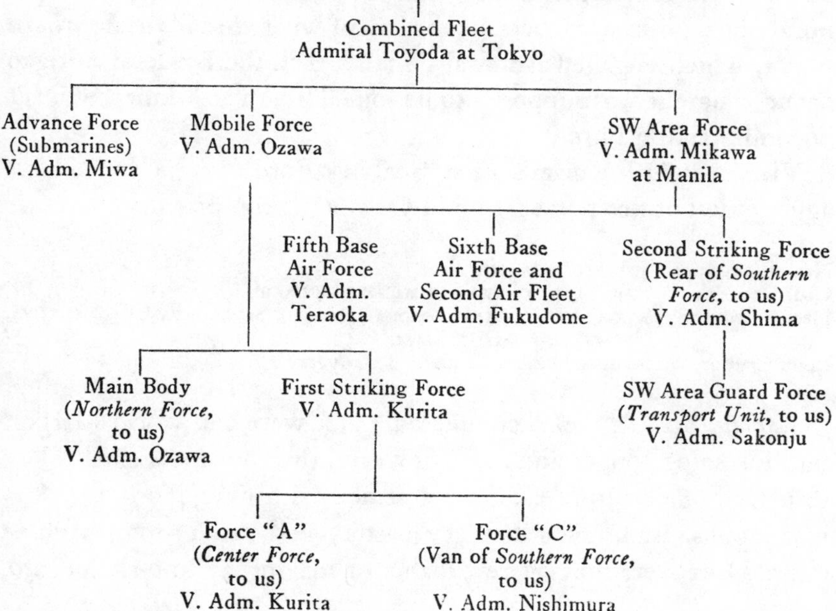

[4] The others were *Shinano* (converted from a *Yamato*-class BB hull and said to displace 69,000 tons) and *Unryu*, sunk by U.S. submarines *Archerfish* and *Redfish* respectively, 29 Nov. and 19 Dec. 1944; and *Katsuragi*, commissioned 15 Oct. 1944.

to be two old battleships half-converted to carriers, *Ise* and *Hyuga;* each retained eight 14-inch guns, but the two after turrets had been removed, which left room for a small flight deck. And, because there were no trained air groups for large carrier *Zuikaku* (veteran of Pearl Harbor) and light carriers *Zuiho*, *Chitose* and *Chiyoda*, these were thrown in to enrich the bait to be dangled before Halsey.

Main Body, which, for sake of clarity, we shall call the *Northern Force*, was screened by light cruisers *Oyodo*, *Tama*, *Isuzu* and eight destroyers.

The most powerful section of the Japanese Fleet, at Lingga Roads, was First Striking Force, under Vice Admiral Takeo Kurita, who had commanded the battle line in the Philippine Sea action. The bulk of it, Force "A," which we shall refer to as the *Center Force*, is the one that engaged our escort carriers in the Battle off Samar. The remainder, Force "C," under command of Vice Admiral Shoji Nishimura, became the van of what we call the *Southern Force*, which engaged Admiral Oldendorf in the Battle of Surigao Strait, where it was supposed to be joined by Vice Admiral Shima's Second Striking Force.

Vice Admiral Kurita's First Striking Force was a formidable aggregation of fire power. In mid-October it comprised: —

New Battleships	YAMATO, MUSASHI
Old Battleships	NAGATO, FUSO, YAMASHIRO, KONGO, HARUNA
Heavy Cruisers	ATAGO, TAKAO, MAYA, CHOKAI, HAGURO, MYOKO, KUMANO, SUZUYA, TONE, CHIKUMA, MOGAMI
Light Cruisers	NOSHIRO, YAHAGI, and 19 destroyers

Yamato and *Musashi*, completed 1942, were the world's largest fighting ships, longer and more powerful than our *Iowa* class. They displaced 68,000 tons each, were armed with nine 460-mm (18.1-inch) guns, an ample secondary battery and 120 25-mm machine guns. Moreover, they were capable of making 27 knots.[5] *Nagato*,

[5] Although *Yamato* had participated in the Battle of Midway, these battleships were "mystery ships" to the world at large; but the Cincpoa and Seventh Fleet Intelligence officers, by piecing together scraps of information, had a good idea of their size early in 1944, which was confirmed by a talkative officer prisoner in September.

completed in 1921, with a 16-inch main battery, was in a class with our *Maryland*, but four or five knots faster. The long-lived, frequently reported sunk *Haruna* and sister ship *Kongo* were older 14-inch-gunned battleships, originally battle cruisers and long objects of derision in the United States Navy for their tall pagoda-like foremasts. These had been somewhat cut down in a reconstruction early in the war, and although both old battlewagons were inferior in gun power to our *Tennessee* and *California* (eight as against twelve 14-inch guns each) they were faster. *Yamashiro* and *Fuso*, younger than the *Kongo* class, had had their speed stepped up to 24 knots, and each mounted twelve 14-inch guns. The heavy cruisers with 8-inch main batteries were superior in everything but fire control to our prewar heavy cruisers of the 10,000-ton treaty class, and were from 5000 to 7000 tons bigger, although supposedly built in accordance with the same treaty. (That is the way naval limitations worked; we respected them, our future enemies did not.) Each battleship mounted, on an average, 120 25-mm machine guns, and each heavy cruiser had 90 units of that useful antiaircraft weapon.

When our "grapevine" learned that this mighty fleet had returned to Lingga Roads after the Battle of the Philippine Sea, it was rightly suspected that the real reason was to be near the source of oil. The Japanese tanker and merchant fleet had been so reduced by United States submarines that it was incapable of supplying a large number of warships anywhere else. Otherwise, the Japanese Navy would have concentrated in the Inland Sea.

Anchored in Lingga Roads, First Striking Force would have made an excellent target for China-based XX Army Air Force of Superfortresses, as it was well within their range. Despite several strongly worded requests from General MacArthur that they should at least reconnoiter the roadstead and report what they saw, the B–29s never flew over Singapore or Lingga until after the Battle for Leyte Gulf was over.[6]

A third but smaller force parallel to Kurita's in the table of or-

[6] Information from Lt. L. F. Ebb; cf. Craven & Cate V 415.

ganization was known as Second Striking Force, commanded by Vice Admiral Kiyohide Shima. Like Ozawa's, it was based on the Inland Sea. It comprised heavy cruisers *Nachi* and *Ashigara*, light cruiser *Abukuma* and about nine destroyers. Shima we have already encountered as he sallied forth from the Inland Sea 15 October to attack Halsey's "remnants" after the air battle off Formosa.[7] He was recalled before coming to grips with them and sent to the Pescadores, inside Formosa. On 22 October Admiral Toyoda ordered Shima to penetrate Leyte Gulf as part of the *Southern Force*, but independently of Admiral Nishimura.

A splinter of Shima's Second Striking Force, split off from it on 23 October to perform transport duty, was called Southwest Area Guard Force by the Japanese, and Transport Unit by us. Commanded by Vice Admiral Naomasa Sakonju, it comprised heavy cruiser *Aoba*, light cruiser *Kinu*, destroyer *Uranami* and five troop carriers like our destroyer-transports. This force had no part in the battle plan, but was ordered to embark troops at Cagayan, Mindanao, and land them on the back side of Leyte.

The Japanese submarine commander, Vice Admiral Shigeyoshi Miwa, had the mission of intercepting the enemy before he reached the invasion target. With only 16 submarines available, four were designated to hold up the fast carrier forces. Upon receiving the alert on 17 October, these four were ordered into the Philippine Sea and seven more were readied to sortie from the Inland Sea. By 24 October these eleven submarines were strung along from San Bernardino Strait to a point about east of Davao in Mindanao. Four more submarines were in the American escort carriers area of operations. This underwater force notably failed to intercept or even embarrass the invasion forces. Their one success was the sinking of destroyer escort *Eversole*.[8]

The Japanese naval high command was not feeling happy about its prospects, as may be seen by a statement issued by Admiral Toyoda's chief of staff about 1 August 1944: –

[7] Above, Chapter VI.

[8] *War College Analysis* III plate xxvi.

The Battle situation has become more serious since the A operation [Battle of Philippine Sea]. However, we are confident that the enemy's operations are growing more difficult because his lines of communication are becoming extended. . . . Because the operational strength of base air forces is insufficient, Mobile Force is expected to exert its utmost strength. . . . It must make a desperate effort to defeat the enemy.[9]

This confession of inadequate air strength provides the key to the SHO-GO plan. Fast carrier air groups had been wiped out in the Battle of the Philippine Sea and land-based air forces were unable to fill the vacuum, although this of course was not anticipated when SHO-GO was drawn up. Commodore Bates estimates that there were fewer than one hundred operational aircraft of all types in the Philippines on 20 October.[10] Even after Admiral Fukudome flew in almost everything he had from Formosa, mostly on 22 October, probably not even 200 planes were operational in the Philippines.[11]

Further reinforcement began the same day. Some 800 planes were ordered into the Archipelago from Japan and China, and about 180 arrived fairly promptly. At the end of October Field Marshal Terauchi sent a staff officer to Tokyo to request 1200 to 1500 replacement planes per month for the Philippines. These, he calculated, would enable him to keep 300 fighter planes operational, an expenditure of 100 per cent per month being anticipated. "In November Tokyo allocated 1000, of which 800 arrived." In December, 800 were allocated and 600 arrived; in January 120

[9] ATIS Special Translation No. 39, Part I pp. 37–8.

[10] *War College Analysis* III 13; cf. I 449–51.

[11] Figures, although checked by Tokyo Historical Section and by Commo. Bates, are still a matter of guess. Admiral Fukudome's are in *Inter. Jap. Off.* II 500. His operations officer, Cdr. M. Yamaguchi (*Inter. Jap. Off.* I, 178), on 26 Oct. 1945, said that First Air Fleet had only 100 operational planes when Second Air Fleet moved in with 300 more, and of these 400, not more than two-thirds were operational at any one time. Commo. Bates believes (III 677) that Fukudome had only 178 on 22 Oct. According to the MacArthur *Historical Report* II 336, 359, Navy had 246 planes and Army 150 in the Philippines on 23 Oct., and 80 more Army planes were due on the 24th.

were allocated and 100 arrived. No more were sent in after 9 January, "because there were no serviceable airfields." [12]

In view of this serious air situation, certain air commanders proposed new and desperate tactics of suicide-crashing enemy ships with their planes. These were the famous Kamikaze tactics. The name, meaning Heavenly Wind, is derived from a well-known episode in Japanese history. In 1570 a Mongol emperor organized a huge amphibious force for the invasion of Japan, and there was little preparation to resist him. But the gods sent a Heavenly Wind in the shape of a typhoon which scattered the Chinese fleet and blew back onto the coast of China all those that were not sunk. Isolated cases of Japanese pilots crashing planes on ships when bombs missed or the plane was very badly damaged, had been observed since 1942, but sacrificial crashing as definite tactics began in the autumn of 1944.[13] The Japanese Navy claims that Rear Admiral Arima "lit the fuse of the ardent wishes of his men" by himself crashing carrier *Franklin* on 15 October; but, as we have already related, he missed her and was shot down by C.A.P. Arima's superior officer, Vice Admiral Onishi of First Air Fleet, was already training a Kamikaze corps, and their first organized attack was the one on escort carriers *Santee* and *Suwannee* on 25 October during the Battle off Samar, which we shall relate shortly.

Admiral Toyoda waited to execute SHO–1 until he had accurate intelligence of the exact American target. That he obtained at daybreak 17 October when Commander Loud's minecraft were sighted from Suluan. At 0809, nine minutes after cruiser *Denver* fired the opening gun in the liberation of the Philippines, all Japanese fleets

[12] Interrogation of Col. Matsumae, USSBS Interrogation 249, 27 Oct. 1945, furnishes these extraordinary figures, covering Army Air Forces only: —

Fourth Air Army had in Philippines, early October:	300 planes
Received reinforcements, 15 Oct–9 Jan. 1945	2300 planes
Evacuated from Philippines, Jan. 1945	30 planes
Lost in Philippines, in three months	2570 planes

[13] Interrogations of Capt. R. Inoguchi, chief of staff of First Air Fleet and of Cdr. M. Yamaguchi (*Inter. Jap. Off.* I 60, 178); also Inoguchi and T. Nakajima "The Kamikaze Attack Corps" Nav. Inst. *Proceedings* LXXIX (Sept. 1953) 933–45.

and squadrons received word from Commander in Chief Combined Fleet: –

SHO–1 OPERATION ALERT [14]

Even then, the high command was not certain that Leyte would be the target. Hence Toyoda did not give the "Execute" to SHO–1 until 1110 October 18. "X-day" – hatchet or execution day for our amphibious forces in Leyte Gulf – was set for the early hours of 25 October.[15] Kurita, Nishimura and Shima would apply the pincer, while Ozawa "will advance into Philippine Sea east of Luzon" and "lure the enemy to the north." [16]

The gambit strategy of this plan was typical of Japanese military thinking. "I expected complete destruction of my Fleet," said Admiral Ozawa when interrogated a year later, "but if Kurita's mission was carried out, that was all I wished." The merit of the scheme was its exploitation of Philippine topography to confuse Allied Intelligence and divide the United States Pacific Fleet. Given the axiom that the Japanese Navy must do something to try to halt the invasion, SHO–1 was as good a plan as could have been devised. It offered a fair chance of inflicting embarrassing losses on the Americans if properly executed; but it required a higher degree of coördination and exact timing than the Combined Fleet was capable of. The great unanswered question is: Supposing SHO–1 worked, and the pincer on our amphibious forces pinched, what would the Japanese Navy do about Halsey's Third Fleet when it swallowed the Ozawa bait and turned south again? There were no land-based air forces capable of handling Halsey. Apparently the Japanese planners never thought of that; or if they did, estimated that the damage they would inflict in Leyte Gulf would ruin the invasion and cause Nimitz to send Third Fleet home. In any event, the Japanese war lords were playing for time. America might yet tire of the war.

[14] *War College Analysis* I 466.

[15] Toyoda first set X-day at 22 Oct., but Kurita protested and pointed out that he could not possibly get there that early. Ozawa War Diary.

[16] MacArthur *Historical Report* II 340; *War College Analysis* III 823.

Now we shall trace the actual movements of the Japanese Combined Fleet. Vice Admiral Kurita's First Striking Force sortied from Lingga Roads at 0100 October 18 and called at Brunei Bay, North Borneo, to fuel and to hold a conference. Admiral Toyoda's battle plan reached Kurita that day, and his battle order arrived on the afternoon of the 20th.[17] That part of First Striking Force which became the Center Force departed at 0800 October 22 and headed for Palawan Passage. Vice Admiral Nishimura's Force "C" sortied at 1500 the same day and, after making a long detour northward to avoid suspected submarines, shot through Balabac Strait into the Sulu Sea, to become the fighting part of the Southern Force in Surigao Strait.

Vice Admiral Shima, whose Second Striking Force was alerted on the 21st, received orders next day to "support and coöperate" with Nishimura; where and how was left to him. Shima made no attempt to rendezvous with Nishimura, or even to catch up with him, but planned to follow him through Surigao Strait at an interval of 30 to 50 miles. The two forces first met when *Nachi* collided with *Mogami* during the Battle of Surigao Strait.

Admiral Ozawa's Main Body, the Northern Force, got under way in two echelons from Kure and Beppu Bay on 20 October, rendezvoused in Bungo Suido, the southwestern channel to the Inland Sea, and sortied that evening, completely undetected. This requires explanation. Between 12 and 18 October a wolfpack of Pacific Fleet submarines, commanded by Commander T. L. Wogan in *Besugo*, had been patrolling Bungo Suido on a reconnaissance mission. They sighted so many fast vessels entering the Inland Sea, as to suggest that the Japanese Navy was seeking security rather than battle. On the evening of 18 October Commander Wogan signaled Admiral Lockwood "consider primary mission of this group is now to attack," and withdrew his wolfpack for the normal employment of sinking enemy merchant shipping. Admiral Lockwood concurred. As a result, Bungo Suido was not covered after 19 October and Admiral Ozawa, who expected to fight his way out

[17] *War College Analysis* II 222, III 190.

to sea through a ring of United States submarines, emerged into the Pacific Ocean completely undetected. He wanted to be seen and reported, though not that early, in order to execute his decoy mission, and thought he had been seen by submarines which were not there.[18]

Kurita's Center Force, after leaving Brunei Bay at 0800 October 22, advanced northeasterly through the Palawan Passage. This lies between the long island of that name and the Dangerous Ground which extends well into the South China Sea. Kurita was soon outside the range of American land-based air, but the lookouts made numerous false sightings of submarine periscopes and the gunners frequently opened fire on bits of flotsam. This apprehension was entirely justified for two Seventh Fleet submarines were tracking the Center Force.[19]

2. *The Fight in Palawan Passage, 23 October* [20]

On 1 October U.S. submarines *Darter* (Commander David H. McClintock) and *Dace* (Commander Bladen D. Claggett) departed Mios Woendi for a patrol of Palawan Passage. They torpedoed and sank two *Marus* out of a convoy on the 12th, but the next ten

[18] *War College Analysis* I 177–82, II 55, 200–02, 315, 321–2, III 203–04.

[19] The movements of Vice Admiral Sakonju's Transport Unit, which I have omitted from the main narrative to avoid confusion, were as follows. It sailed from Manila Bay 23 Oct. Heavy cruiser *Aoba*, which was about to rendezvous with it outside the Bay, was torpedoed by U.S. submarine *Bream* that morning and then towed into Manila by light cruiser *Kinu*, which afterwards rejoined the Transport Unit. Three destroyers which belonged to Shima's Second Striking Force were detached for a separate transport mission. They were hit at 0805 Oct. 24 off Panay by planes from carrier *Franklin*, and *Wakaba* was sunk. The other two returned to Manila.

[20] *Darter* Report of Fourth War Patrol, 5 Nov.; *Dace* Report of Fifth War Patrol, 6 Nov.; endorsements by Comsubron 18 on same, 8 Nov. 1944; Lt. Cdr. R. C. Benitez (exec. of *Dace*) "Battle Stations Submerged" U.S. Nav. Inst. *Proceedings* LXXIV (1948) 25–35. The submarines were operating on Z minus 8 (How) time, one hour earlier than Item time used for the rest of the Philippines Operation; I have therefore corrected their times to Item. The captured War Diaries of DDs *Kishinami* and *Okinami* (translation in C.O. Seventh Fleet Intelligence Center to Opnav, 22 Apr. 1945) and the interrogation of Admiral Kurita in *Inter. Jap. Off.* I 32 yield details from the Japanese end.

days were fruitless. Off the southern entrance to Palawan Passage, at 0116 October 23, *Darter* had a radar contact, distant 30,000 yards. One minute later, McClintock notified Claggett by megaphone, "Let's go!" Both submarines closed at flank speed. They made out eleven heavy ships and six destroyers, steaming in two columns. Actually there were ten heavy cruisers and five battleships in three columns, with two light cruisers and 12 to 14 destroyers screening flanks and center, in a two-section cruising disposition; the second, still invisible to the submarines, being six kilometers astern of the first.[21] This word, which *Darter* got off promptly to Rear Admiral Christie, who relayed it to Admiral Halsey at 0620 October 23, was to prove one of the most significant contact reports in the Pacific war. *Darter* and *Dace* had flushed the Japanese Center Force, whose whereabouts, since it departed Lingga, had been a mystery to Naval Intelligence.

The submarines closed this promising target at best speed, about 19 knots. Kurita was making only 16 knots and he had not stationed picket destroyers ahead of his disposition. Such carelessness is incomprehensible, especially as his radiomen had picked up an Allied submarine transmission. And the weather was clear.

By 0525 October 23 *Darter* was 20,000 yards dead ahead of the enemy's port column of three heavy cruisers. At 0609 *Darter* reversed course, headed toward this column and submerged, planning to attack from the eastward in the half light of dawn, while *Dace* bustled into a position whence she could catch the starboard column. The moment *Darter* waited for came at 0632. At a range of only 980 yards, she began emptying her six bow tubes at heavy cruiser *Atago*, Admiral Kurita's flagship, leading the column. "After firing two fish into him and one spread ahead, target was roaring by so close we couldn't miss, so spread the remainder inside his length," observed Commander McClintock. He then swung hard left to bring his stern tubes to bear on the second cruiser in column, *Takao*. A minute later, four of his bow torpedoes started hitting *Atago*. Immediately he commenced firing his four stern

[21] *War College Analysis* III plate xxxviii.

torpedoes at *Takao*, which had swung 45 degrees left, at a range of 1550 yards. Two of them hit at 0634, blowing off her rudder and two propellers and flooding three boiler rooms. McClintock promptly whipped his periscope back on the first target, to see "the

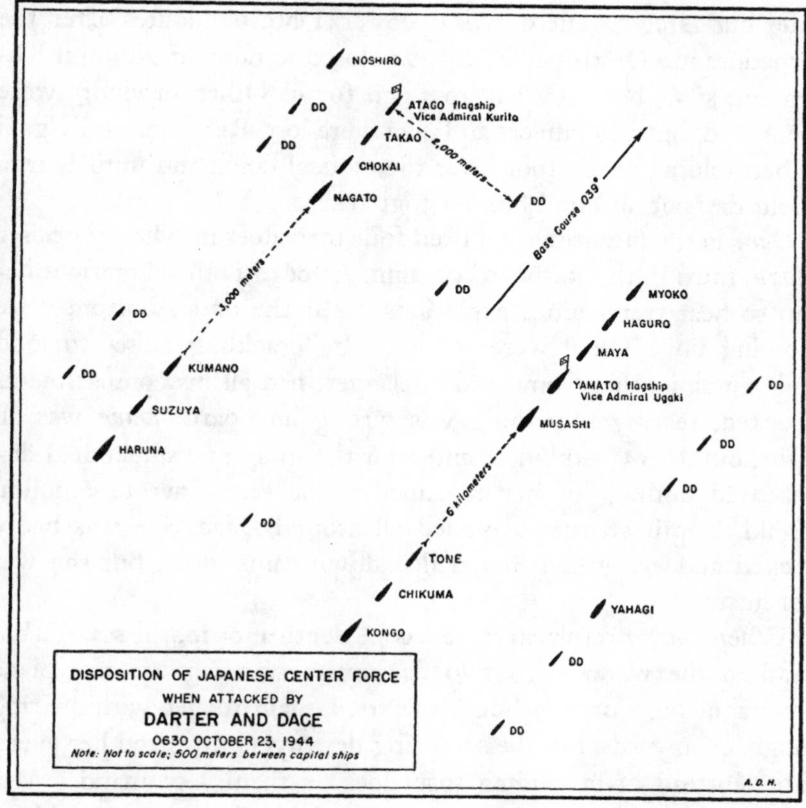

DISPOSITION OF JAPANESE CENTER FORCE WHEN ATTACKED BY DARTER AND DACE 0630 OCTOBER 23, 1944

Note: Not to scale; 500 meters between capital ships

sight of a lifetime." *Atago*, so close that not all of her could be seen at once with periscope in high power, was a mass of billowing black smoke from the forward turret aft, with bursts of bright orange flame shooting through it. She was already going down by the bow.

As *Darter* dove deep to evade, she heard the hits on *Takao* and felt reasonably certain of sinking her, too. But that heavy cruiser stayed afloat, although she had to return to Brunei. Presently four

Japanese destroyers were echo-ranging and milling about over the successful submarine. Their depth charges fell wide of the mark. At 0640 breaking-up noises were heard through *Darter's* hull, and the boat was violently shaken. Japanese heavy cruisers of that class were supposed to have triple hulls and to be virtually unsinkable; but *Atago* went down at 0653, eighteen minutes after the torpedoes hit. Destroyer *Kishinami* closed to take off Admiral Kurita and staff, but they had to swim for it. Other survivors were recovered, but 360 officers and men were lost. Rear Admiral Ugaki in battleship *Yamato* took over the tactical command until Kurita could dry out and pull himself together.

Dace in the meantime had fired four torpedoes into heavy cruiser *Maya*, third in the starboard column. At 0656 both submarines began to hear tremendous explosions "as if the ocean bottom were blowing up." These were followed by crackling noises so loud and gruesome that Commander Claggett had all his compartments checked, fearing something was wrong on board. *Dace* was all right; but *Maya* "exploded, and after the spray and smoke had disappeared nothing of her remained to be seen," wrote Admiral Ugaki. Depth charges exploded all around *Dace*. She was badly rocked and everything not nailed down came loose, but she was not hurt.

When *Darter* returned to periscope depth at 0920, she saw *Takao* dead in the water with two destroyers standing by and plane coverage too. For five hours she tried again to get within firing range, 4000 yards, but the screening destroyers thwarted her every time. Instead of expending torpedoes on them, Commander McClintock decided to trail *Takao* until nightfall to try a combined attack on the crippled cruiser with Commander Claggett. Admiral Ugaki in the meantime had ordered the Japanese disposition to bend on 24 knots and break through.

After dark the two submarines surfaced and their skippers conferred. They planned a surface attack on crippled *Takao*, but abandoned it at 2306 when *Darter's* radar detector picked up a Japanese radar sweep.

The Palawan Passage is difficult in daylight, since the channel between the foul ground that fringes Palawan and the Dangerous Ground of the South China Sea is only 25 miles wide, and various shoals named after unfortunate sailing ships of the past stick out into the fairway like dead men's fingers. *Darter* and *Dace* had been navigating these tricky waters for twenty-four hours on dead reckoning only. Their submerged activities had prevented navigating officers from getting a fix on the mountains of Palawan, and clouds obscured the heavenly bodies. In order to evade the destroyers screening *Takao*, Commander McClintock planned to give a berth of only seven miles to Bombay Shoal, a nasty little coral reef on the China Sea side of the passage that was under water at the then stage of the tide. That proved to be not enough. A mere quarter-knot error in estimating set of current brought *Darter's* course right across the shoal; and at 0105 October 24, when making 17 knots, she ran hard aground with a tremendous crash. The noise registered on the sound gear of one of the enemy destroyers, which immediately closed to 12,000 yards but fortunately could not figure out what had happened, and passed on.

On board *Darter* all hands began burning secret documents, destroying confidential gear, blowing tanks, and giving anchors, ammunition and commissary stores the "deep six." At high water, 0246, they began attempts to pull clear, by sallying ship and other devices, but none succeeded. At 0345 *Dace*, standing by within 50 yards of *Darter's* stern, sent over a line. Twenty minutes later, both submarines broke out their rubber boats and commenced transferring the grounded crew. Demolition charges in *Darter* had been rigged and it was decided to abandon her to permit her destruction before sunrise.

With all hands safely on board *Dace*, a tiny explosion was heard at the planned time, 0555. One or two of the 50-pound charges may have gone off, but not enough to destroy *Darter*. *Dace* attempted to hit her hull with four torpedoes. All struck the reef. She then pumped 21 four-inch shells into *Darter* along the waterline. It was now daylight and she was forced down by a plane before the firing was completed, but the Japanese pilot fortunately elected to bomb *Darter*, not knowing that she had been abandoned. Also a destroyer was seen making a cautious approach. So *Dace* left her running mate hard and fast aground and set a course for Fremantle, Australia, with 81 officers and men on board in addition to her own complement of 74. During the eleven days' passage men slept on empty torpedo skids and the food supply became so depleted that toward the end all hands were subsisting on mushroom soup and peanut butter sandwiches; but the traditional good nature and fellow feeling of submariners "made a pleasant cruise out of what could have been an intolerable situation." [22]

The two submarines had chalked up a good score: two heavy cruisers including the force flagship sunk, and a third knocked out of the war. And by sending in accurate and timely reports, they alerted Third Fleet to give Admiral Kurita a warm reception when he entered the Sibuyan Sea.

3. *Task Force 38 Makes Contact, 24 October* [23]

If anyone still doubted on 23 October what the enemy intended – and many naval officers were cynical on the subject of the Japanese Navy giving battle – all doubt was dissipated that day. The information contained in a number of dispatches, when correlated, proved that two enemy forces were closing in on Leyte Gulf from the rear, and a third from the north and west. Only Ozawa's Northern Force had not been contacted. By the afternoon of the 23rd Admirals Halsey and Kinkaid were preparing for a major fleet action. During a busy night and anxious day, plans were pre-

[22] Interview with Cdr. Claggett in *New York Times*, 9 Nov. 1945; *Dace* Patrol Report.

[23] Com Third Fleet (Admiral Halsey) Action Report and War Diary; Admirals Ozawa, Kurita and Ugaki War Diaries; CTF 38, CTG 38.2, CTG 38.3, CTG 38.4 Action Reports.

pared, the execution of which would decide who was going to own Leyte.

At noon 23 October, Rear Admiral Bogan's Task Group 38.2, Sherman's Group 3 and Davison's Group 4 were operating about 260 miles northeast of Samar. McCain's TG 38.1 was well on its way toward Ulithi to replenish. During the night of 23–24 October all but McCain's were pulled in toward the coast in order to launch dawn searches. Sherman took position east of the Polillo Islands to cover the west coast of Luzon. Bogan moved in close to San Bernardino Strait. Davison operated to the southward near Leyte Gulf.

Tuesday the 24th dawned fair and favorable for strikes and searches. At break of day the three fast carrier groups launched search teams of Hellcats and Helldivers to comb the west coast of Luzon and the Sibuyan, Sulu and Mindanao Seas, for Japanese ships. Admiral Kurita's flagship, battleship *Yamato,* sighted a plane from *Intrepid* at 0812, and the aircraft contact report reached Admiral Halsey ten minutes later. Center Force, still in impressive strength, was then rounding the southern cape of Mindoro and entering Tablas Strait, inferentially bound for San Bernardino Strait. It was impracticable for Third Fleet, or even part of it, to steam through San Bernardino Strait and seek a surface engagement. Those waters were presumably mined, and the channels known only to the enemy. And Admiral Nimitz's orders were to send no ships into the Strait without his express permission.

An air attack by carrier planes was the obvious answer. At 0827 October 24, only five minutes after receiving the contact report, Admiral Halsey acted. He sent orders directly to the task group commanders, bypassing Admiral Mitscher, who throughout 24 October was little more than a passenger in his own task force. Halsey ordered Sherman and Davison to concentrate on Bogan off San Bernardino Strait, recalled McCain's group from its replenishment trip to Ulithi, and arranged a fueling rendezvous for it with Captain Acuff's mobile tankers at lat. 15° N, long. 130° E, early next morning. By noon October 24 three fast carrier groups were deployed on a broad front: Sherman (Group 3) to the northward, Bogan (Group 2) off San Bernardino Strait, Davison (Group 4) about 60 miles off southern Samar. The stage was set for a great air-surface engagement, the Battle of the Sibuyan Sea, first of the four major engagements that constitute the Battle for Leyte Gulf.

CHAPTER X

The Air Battles of 24 October[1]

1. *Loss of* Princeton[2]

BEFORE Admiral Halsey's strike order could be executed, Japanese naval planes based on Luzon fields pulled off the most vigorous and successful air counterattack of the Leyte operation. Fortunately or unfortunately, according to the point of view, they concentrated on Admiral Sherman's Group 3, rather than on Admiral Bogan's Group 2, which was in a position to do Kurita's Center Force the most damage.

Three separate Japanese raids, of 50 to 60 planes each, were met in masterly fashion. First to intercept were seven Hellcats scrambled from *Essex*, led by Commander David McCampbell, her air group commander. At 0833 he encountered a formation of at least 60 fighters, bombers and torpedo-bombers and started to work them over from the top down, with his sections of two and five Hellcats, respectively. The bombers dove through the overcast and escaped, while the fighters, having lost sight of them, commenced orbiting in a tight circle,[3] which left no opening for attack. Commander McCampbell and his wingman, Lieutenant (jg) Rushing USNR, calmly maintained their altitude advantage to await the break-up of the circle; and when it did, enjoyed a field day.

1 *War College Analysis* II, Com Third Fleet (Admiral Halsey) Action Report for 23–31 Oct., General MacArthur *Historical Report* II, the volume compiled by Japanese officers after the war; and all sources mentioned in note 23, p. 174.

2 *Princeton* Action Report 24 Nov.; *Birmingham* Action Report 14 Nov. and War Diary for Oct.; *Irwin* "Report of Rescue and Fire Fighting Operations" 27 Oct.; *Morrison* Action Report for 24–27 Oct.; Capt. T. B. Inglis "The Mighty 'B,'" *Shipmate* June 1945 pp. 51, 124; Capt. W. H. Buracker "Saga of Carrier Princeton" *National Geographic* LXXXVIII (1945) 189–218.

3 Known in World War I as a "Lufbery."

"During the next hour or so," reported the Commander, "we followed the formation of weaving fighters, taking advantage of every opportunity to knock down those who attempted to climb to our altitude, scissored outside, straggled, or became too eager and came to us singly. In all we made 18 to 20 passes, being very careful not to expose ourselves and to conserve ammunition by withholding our fire until within very close range. . . . There were 18 enemy airplanes left in formation when we finally broke off." Commander McCampbell accounted for at least nine, Lieutenant Rushing got six, and the other five pilots at least two each, not counting some not seen to splash. The group stuck together during 95 minutes of combat and, when forced to break off owing to fuel shortage, landed safely on board *Langley*.[4]

Another successful interception was by the Hellcats of *Princeton's* air group. But they missed the one enemy plane that counted. Just as they were returning on board, at 0938, a lone Judy glide bomber, which had hovered above the overcast waiting for his chance, came down through a rift in the clouds and planted a 550-pound bomb with diabolical skill. It struck *Princeton's* flight deck, port side amidships, passed through three decks and exploded in the bakeshop, killing the ship's bakers instantly. The blast entered the hangar deck, which was soon roaring with burning gasoline. The flames greedily licked through open bomb bay doors on six TBFs that had been struck below, enveloping their loaded torpedoes, which exploded one by one, tossing the 25-foot square forward elevator masthead-high – whence it fell back into the pit – and blowing the after elevator onto the flight deck. At 1010 Captain Buracker ordered Salvage Control Phase I, which meant for all but 490 men to abandon ship; ten minutes later he set Phase II, which should have left only fire-fighting parties, amounting to about 240 men, on board.

The sun had come out, a 15- to 20-knot breeze was ruffling the water, and a groundswell running. *Princeton* had almost stopped dead, heading into the wind. Hundreds of men gathered on the

[4] Air Group 15 Action Report.

forward end of the flight deck, farthest spot from the explosions. Admiral Sherman at 0953 ordered destroyers *Gatling*, *Irwin* and *Cassin Young* to stand by, while the rest of his carrier group cleared the area. *Irwin* closed *Princeton's* forecastle but could not come nearer than about 30 feet, owing to the overhang of the carrier's gun sponsons. "Many men jumped or went down lines from the flight deck into the water, and swam the narrow gap to the cargo nets hanging on the destroyer's side. The eccentric wave action between the ships made this, for some, a nightmare of swimming the gap many times only to be thrown back just as fingers clutched for the nets. Equally disconcerting was the sight of five to ten men slopped together in a single wave, catching the net simultaneously, and then the stronger climbing over the weaker. A number drowned in this mess, although most climbed the nets successfully with the help of the destroyer's crew. Others drifted aft of both ships and with the help of machine-gun fire from the destroyer's fantail eluded sharks and were picked up by their boats."

By the time *Irwin* managed to work up to jumping distance from the carrier, "badly burned members of the 'black gang' had felt their way up to the forecastle, and several of us assisted in tossing them across the momentarily narrow gap to waiting hands on the destroyer's bow. This was much more difficult than it sounds, because the two bows were rising and falling at different rates causing a constantly changing vertical gap from minus three feet to plus ten feet. Also the bow of the destroyer at that point was only about three feet wide." [5]

Cruiser *Birmingham*, ordered to join the crippled carrier at 1004, now arrived on the scene and her commanding officer, Captain Thomas B. Inglis, became senior officer present. Having already given thought to the best manner of assisting a burning carrier, he now put his plan into effect. Detailing cruiser *Reno* for antiaircraft protection, and ordering the destroyers to pick up men from the water, he used his own cruiser, which had the best equipment,

[5] Letter of Mr. Richard M. Jackson 22 July 1957. He was the lieutenant in charge of aircraft maintenance on board *Princeton*.

for fire fighting. Accordingly *Birmingham* took the place of *Irwin* and *Cassin Young* on the carrier's weather bow. A line was passed to *Princeton* at 1055. Hoses were run over, and a volunteer fire-fighting party of 38 men under Lieutenant Allen Reed went on board the carrier to aid her own men, who, directed by the First Lieutenant and Air Operations Officers, Lieutenant Commanders H. E. Stebbings USNR and J. M. Large USNR, were making valiant efforts to bring the fires under control.

Destroyer *Morrison*, after picking up some 400 survivors, closed the lee side of *Princeton* to return engineers on board and assist in fighting the fires. In that position she was smothered with smoke and her foremast and stack, wedged between two of the carrier's uptakes, were crushed; heavy debris, including even vehicles, rained down on her decks. Destroyers have had varied experiences in this war, but it was something new to have a jeep and an electric airplane tractor fall on your bridge and bounce off to the main deck. *Irwin* came to her rescue. In several attempts to drag *Morrison* clear all towlines parted, but she managed to shift the bow a few feet so that the damaged destroyer was able to clear under her own power at 1340.

While this was going on another enemy air raid was signaled. *Reno*, after spending an hour alongside *Princeton* and helping with her fire hoses, cast off at 1212 to screen her from the air attack. *Birmingham* was somewhat bruised by helping to fight *Princeton's* fires alongside in a rough sea for two and one half hours, but it looked as if the fires were licked. A sound contact on a submarine was now reported, and Captain Inglis reluctantly cast off at 1330.

This second air counterattack of the day was a complete failure. It came from the carriers of Admiral Ozawa's Northern Force, and was the only air strike that he attempted. One group of "bandits" was broken up by *Lexington's* Hellcats, 45 miles northeast of the main body of Admiral Sherman's group, and another large group was picked up by radar 90 miles to the northeasterly. A few of these got through, and 6 to 8 Judys dove ineffectually on *Lexington*, *Essex* and *Langley*.

The air raid was over, and the sound contact turning out to be no submarine, *Birmingham* returned to *Princeton's* weather side at 1445 and sent her "firemen" on board. During the hour and a half of the cruiser's absence the carrier's fire-fighting parties had made good progress, except on one blaze that seemed impossible to get at. This gave Captain Buracker great concern, as it was approaching the torpedo storage abaft the hangar where some excess bombs had been placed.

The wind had now risen to 20 knots' velocity and the sea was making up. Captain Buracker requested *Reno* to take *Princeton* under tow, but she had no towing gear on board. So Captain Inglis, after conferring with Captain Buracker by TBS, decided to close again to render aid until the fires were out, and then act as tugboat. The cruiser was just closing at 1523 when a tremendous explosion in the carrier's torpedo stowage blew off most of her stern and the entire after section of the flight deck. Steel debris rained down on *Birmingham*, then in the path of greatest destruction, her topside crowded with fire fighters, antiaircraft gunners and sailors preparing to pass lines and rig the tow.

This is what eyewitnesses tell of the effect of the explosion on *Birmingham:* –

The spectacle which greeted the human eye was horrible to behold . . . Dead, dying and wounded, many of them badly and horribly, covered the decks. The communication platform was no better. Blood ran freely down the waterways, and continued to run for some time. Said our Executive Officer, who inspected the ship immediately, "I really have no words at my command that can adequately describe the veritable splendor of the conduct of all hands, wounded and unwounded. Men with legs off, with arms off, with gaping wounds in their sides, with the tops of their heads furrowed by fragments, would insist, 'I'm all right. Take care of Joe over there,' or 'Don't waste morphine on me, Commander; just hit me over the head.' " What went on below decks immediately following the explosion is well depicted by our Chaplain [who was in the wardroom, which became the emergency sickbay]: –

"Within a very few minutes after the explosion, corpsmen and the only medical officer aboard the ship arrived from the sick bay. These in turn were aided by officers and men in giving essential first aid. There was no sign of confusion. The wounded, even though suffering shock, in many cases probably in great pain until the morphine began to take effect, remained quiet and fully co-operative with those attempting to render first aid. Again and again I was urged by those horribly wounded to help others before themselves. There were no outcrys and in cases of those with clean cuts which were not hemorrhaging too badly, when told that those who were bleeding more profusely must be tended first, agreed cheerfully in every case saying: 'O.K. I'm all right, don't worry about me.' By the end of this first hour the care of the wounded was organized to the point at which plasma could be given to the most serious cases. At this point I was ordered by the Commanding Officer to make preparations for the identification and burial of the dead." [6]

Damage to *Birmingham* was slight but the casualties were heavy. After burying the dead she proceeded under her own power to the West Coast, and was repaired in time to take part in the Okinawa operation the following March. She had set a new precedent for fire fighting on the high seas, which was put to good use later on *Bunker Hill* and *Franklin.*

But *Princeton* could not be saved. She was still seaworthy, but no other ship was available to take her in tow and fires ignited by the explosion burned forward toward the gasoline tanks and the main magazines, which had not been properly flooded owing to loss of water pressure. So at 1600 Captain Buracker reluctantly gave orders to damage control party to abandon ship. Destroyer *Gatling* took them off and the Captain went over the side at 1638. In order not to leave her a derelict, Admiral Sherman ordered this gallant light carrier, which had shared his glory and old *Saratoga's* in the memorable 1943 strike on Rabaul, to be destroyed with torpedoes.

Destroyer *Irwin,* cramped and crowded with some 600 survivors, was given the job. Unfortunately her torpedo director had been so pounded alongside *Princeton* as to be useless. She stopped broadside to the carrier one mile away and fired No. 1 torpedo, which curved left and hit the *Princeton's* bow. The second torpedo

[6] *Birmingham* War Diary 24 Oct.

missed astern. Third torpedo porpoised, broached and headed back directly for *Irwin.* The Captain rang up flank speed and hard left rudder, and the "fish" passed about 30 feet away on a parallel course. "Whatever morale was left in the 600 survivors vanished in those few seconds!" Nos. 4 and 5 missed ahead. The track of No. 6, unbelievably, was identical to that of No. 3 and missed *Irwin* by a closer margin. More than one survivor was thinking of taking drastic action on the bridge, when the task group commander relieved *Irwin* of her sinking assignment.[7] Cruiser *Reno,* which had two quadruple torpedo tubes, now went in for the kill. She fired two "fish" simultaneously. Both hit the right spot under the forward gasoline tank, and some 100,000 gallons exploded, blowing *Princeton* to smithereens and creating a mushroom cloud tall enough to have been atomic.

While *Princeton* was struggling for life, the other carriers of Task Force 38 were sending out a series of strikes that seriously damaged Admiral Kurita's Center Force in the Sibuyan Sea.

2. *The Battle of the Sibuyan Sea* [8]

If October 24 was a miserable day for Admiral Sherman, it was still less pleasant for Admiral Kurita.

We left his Center Force early on 24 October, after *Darter* and *Dace* had diminished it by three heavy cruisers. Admiral Kurita's

[7] Letter of Richard M. Jackson, corrected by *Irwin* Report on Fire Fighting and Rescue. *Princeton* sank in a 2700-fathom deep about 83 miles ENE of the Pollilo Islands. Owing to the rescue work by her consorts, casualties were only 7 dead, 101 missing and 190 wounded; less than half those of *Birmingham.* Ninety per cent of her crew survived.

[8] Air Intelligence Group, Opnav, *Carrier Aircraft in Battle for Leyte Gulf* (Air Research Report No. 18), 10 Apr. 1945 p. 53. Sightings tabulated on chart appended to Admiral Kinkaid's Report; dispatches summarized in Cincpac Monthly Analysis Oct. 1944; data from captured logs in Cincpoa *Weekly Intelligence* I No. 43 (7 May 1945) p. 11; details from TF 38 Action Reports and Air Action Reports of Air Groups; Interrogations of Adm. Kurita and Rear Adm. Tomiji Koyanagi, his chief of staff (*Inter. Jap. Off.* I 147). Action Reports of Adm. Kurita, Combatdiv 1 (Rear Adm. Ugaki) and Comcrudiv 7 (Rear Adm. Shiraishi), and of ships involved including *Musashi* and *Yamato.*

flag was now in battleship *Yamato*. A tanker came out from Coron Bay and fueled the destroyers. Submarine *Guitarro*, which had picked up the Center Force shortly after midnight 23–24 October, tracked it halfway through Mindoro Strait, but was not fast enough to close for attack. The force was next sighted by a searching plane from Admiral Bogan's TG 38.2 at 0810 off Semirara Island, just as it was about to turn into Tablas Strait. Bogan got the word at 0820 and the air-surface Battle of the Sibuyan Sea opened before 1030.

The first strike of 21 fighters, 12 dive-bombers and 12 torpedo-bombers, launched by *Intrepid* and *Cabot* at 0910, attacked Center Force at 1026 through intense antiaircraft fire. A second strike of almost equal strength was launched at 1045 and attacked at 1245; a third of 16 VF, 12 VSB and 3 VTB, launched at 1350, attacked at 1550. In the meantime, 8 Hellcats, 5 Helldivers and 11 Avengers from *Lexington* and a smaller number from *Essex* (as she took care of C.A.P.), had been launched at 1050. They reached Center Force at 1330; and before they had finished their attack, 26 Hellcats, 21 Helldivers and 18 Avengers of Admiral Davison's Group 4, launched at 1313 from off Samar, hit the target at 1415.[9] In all, 259 sorties were made against the Japanese Center Force that day. It is not surprising that they were successful, since Kurita had little or no combat air patrol.[10] He put up an impressive but ineffective antiaircraft barrage, battleships even firing main batteries at planes ten miles away.[11] "The small number of enemy planes shot down is regrettable," noted Admiral Ugaki in his diary. Despite the enormous number of antiaircraft guns in the Japanese fleet – 120 in each battleship – only 18 American planes of the hundreds that attacked were splashed.[12]

[9] In addition, Davison's first strike from *Franklin* sank destroyer *Wakaba* of the Japanese Transport Unit off Panay at 0800 and sighted Nishimura's force off Negros at 0905.

[10] Cdr. M. Yamaguchi (*Inter. Jap. Off.* I 178) insists that his naval air fleet kept ten planes over Kurita, but the attacking aviators never sighted more than 4, which they shot down.

[11] *Franklin* Action Report (Enclosure A in that of CTG 38.4).

[12] Also, 2 were lost operationally, 10 more in search, C.A.P. or other sorties that day, and only 3 were saved of the *Princeton's* complement of 34.

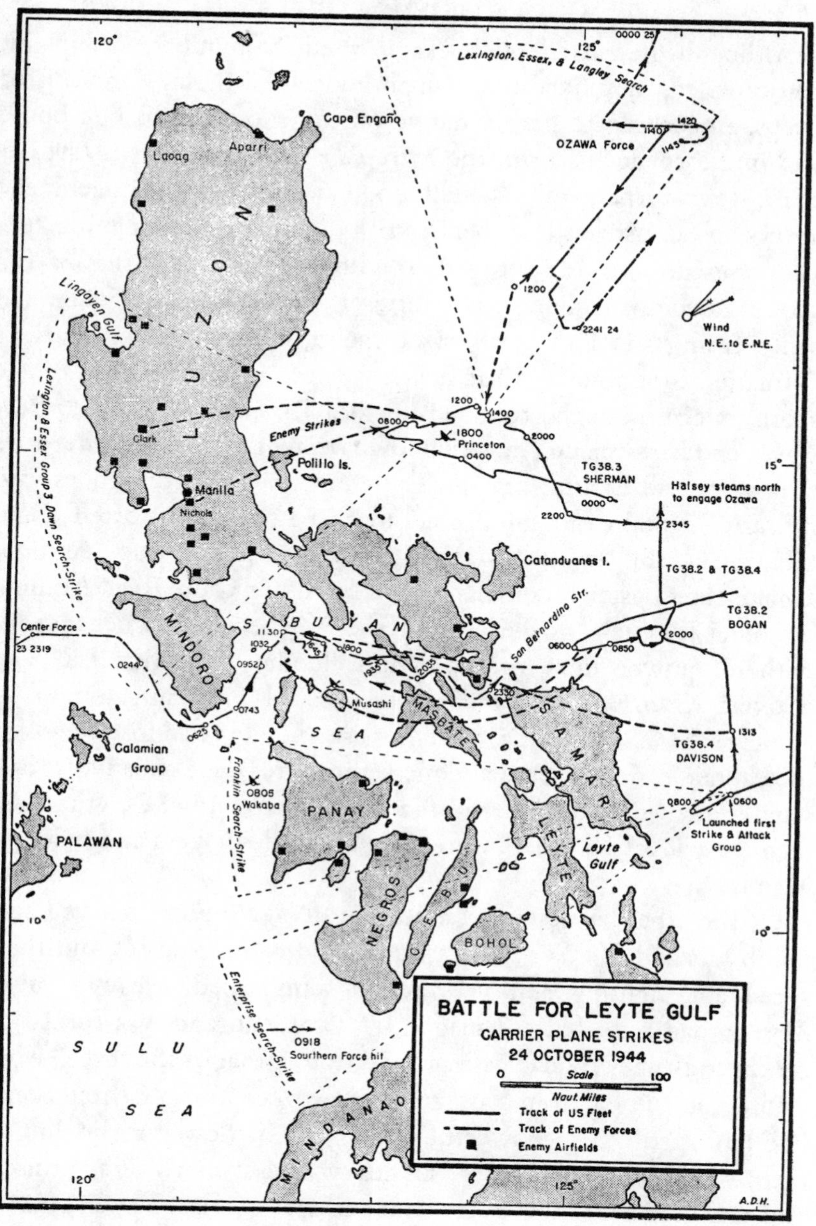
BATTLE FOR LEYTE GULF
CARRIER PLANE STRIKES
24 OCTOBER 1944
Scale
0
100
Naut. Miles
Track of US Fleet
Track of Enemy Forces
Enemy Airfields
120°
125°
15°
10°
Lexington, Essex, & Langley Search
OZAWA Force
Cape Engaño
Aparri
Laoag
LUZON
Lingayen Gulf
Lexington & Essex Group 3 Dawn Search-Strike
Clark
Enemy Strikes
Manila
Nichols
Polillo Is.
1800
Princeton
TG38.3
SHERMAN
Wind
N.E. to E.N.E.
Halsey steams north to engage Ozawa
Catanduanes I.
TG38.2 & TG38.4
TG38.2
BOGAN
San Bernardino Str.
Center Force
MINDORO
SIBUYAN
SEA
Musashi
MASBATE
SAMAR
TG38.4
DAVISON
Calamian Group
Franklin Search-Strike
Wakaba
PANAY
PALAWAN
Launched first Strike & Attack Group
Leyte Gulf
LEYTE
NEGROS
CEBU
BOHOL
Enterprise Search-Strike
0918
Southern Force hit
SULU
SEA
MINDANAO
A.D.H.

Although the carrier pilots exaggerated the number of ships hit and crippled, they fixed the 18-inch gunned battleship *Musashi* for keeps. According to her executive officer, she received one bomb and one torpedo hit from the *Intrepid* and *Cabot* initial strike at 1027, four torpedo hits which flooded some of the machinery spaces and cut steam lines between 1136 and 1217, four more torpedo hits around 1223, together with four bombs. *Musashi* fell astern, accompanied by heavy cruiser *Tone*. By 1330 when the strike from *Essex* and *Lexington* came in, she was trailing Kurita's formation by 20 miles. That strike, apparently, did not add to the score, but at 1520 she received her heaviest attack from *Intrepid*, *Cabot* and *Essex* planes, in which some from *Franklin* and *Enterprise* that were still around joined. They put ten more torpedoes into *Musashi*, a total of 19; and in addition she took 17 assorted bomb hits during the day.[13] *Musashi* was now in a bad way. Admiral Ugaki, the divisional commander, ordered her C.O., Rear Admiral Toshihei Inoguchi, to beach; but she had become unmanageable, with all power lines ruptured and flooding uncontrolled. Destroyers *Kiyoshimo* and *Hamakaze* relieved *Tone* in standing by about 1830. An hour later, when her list had increased to 30 degrees, the captain ordered her abandoned, and at 1935 she rolled over and sank. Thirty-nine of the 112 officers on board and 984 of the 2287 men were lost; the others were rescued by destroyers and taken to Manila.[14]

Of the other battleships, *Yamato* and *Nagato* each received two bomb hits and *Haruna* was damaged by five near-misses, but their speed and fighting ability were not diminished. Heavy cruiser *Myoko* had two shafts damaged by a torpedo and was forced to return to Brunei. These losses, in addition to that of the three heavy cruisers in the Palawan Passage fight, weakened the Center Force but left it still very powerful, with four battlewagons including the 18-inch gunned *Yamato*, six heavy cruisers, two light cruisers and ten or eleven destroyers. But "if we are attacked by planes

[13] *Musashi* Action Report.
[14] Capt. K. Kato, her exec., in *Inter. Jap. Off.* II 362.

as often as this," observed Admiral Ugaki, "we will have expended ourselves before reaching the battle area."

"The most conspicuous lesson learned from this action," wrote Admiral Halsey early in the new year, "is the practical difficulty of crippling by air strikes, alone, a task force of heavy ships at sea and free to maneuver." [15] That is still one lesson of the Sibuyan Sea fight, in spite of the fact that Task Force 38 planes scored one of their most brilliant successes of the war in sinking *Musashi.* On the receiving end, the principal lesson was the folly of taking a fleet of ships within range of fast carrier planes without air protection. Vice Admiral Fukudome, commanding land-based air forces in the Philippines, admitted after the war that Kurita made repeated requests for air support, to which he turned a deaf ear because he believed that he could best help him by flinging planes against the carrier groups outside the strait.[16] His aircraft, however, only attacked two of the fast carrier groups, and the one lucky hit that did in *Princeton* was their only success. There could be no clearer demonstration of the futility of air counterattack as compared with interception.

The approximate position of the Center Force when these strikes were concluded was in the Sibuyan Sea, 20 miles northeast of the north end of Tablas Island. At 1400 our aircraft observed that the ships had reversed course and were steering westerly, as if to retire. Actually they were then simply milling around to support the damaged units, but one hour later Admiral Kurita did set course 290°. At 1600 he reported to Admiral Toyoda that he had been under repeated attack by more than 250 planes; "It is therefore considered advisable to retire temporarily from the zone of enemy air attacks and to resume the advance when the battle results of friendly units permit." [17] What he meant was that he wished to

[15] Com Third Fleet Endorsement 9 Jan. 1945 on CTG 38.4 letter 18 Nov. at end of his Action Report for 22–31 Oct. 1944.

[16] Interrogation of Vice Admiral S. Fukudome (*Inter. Jap. Off.* II 500) 9 Dec. 1945. He sent a few VF to scout for submarines, which were not there.

[17] Commo. Bates's trans. of Batdiv 1 Dispatch file; different wording in MacArthur *Historical Report* II 363; *Kishinami* and *Okinami* War Diaries (Seventh Fleet translation) 22 Apr. 1945.

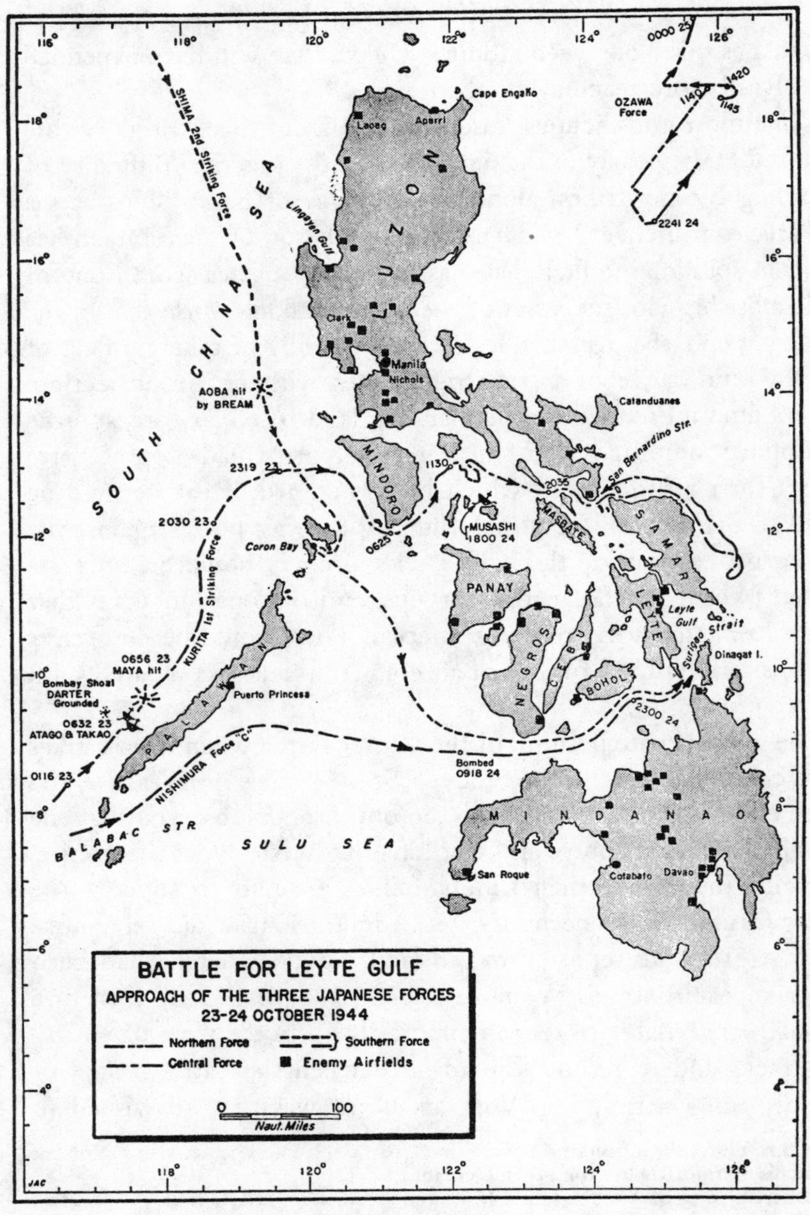
BATTLE FOR LEYTE GULF
APPROACH OF THE THREE JAPANESE FORCES
23-24 OCTOBER 1944
Northern Force
Central Force
Southern Force
Enemy Airfields
0
100
Naut. Miles
SOUTH CHINA SEA
SULU SEA
LUZON
MINDORO
PANAY
NEGROS
CEBU
BOHOL
MASBATE
SAMAR
LEYTE
MINDANAO
PALAWAN
Cape Engaño
Aparri
Laoag
Lingayen Gulf
Clark
Manila
Nichols
Catanduanes
San Bernardino Str.
Coron Bay
Puerto Princesa
Leyte Gulf
Surigao Strait
Dinagat I.
San Roque
Cotabato
Davao
BALABAC STR
SHIMA 2nd Striking Force
KURITA 1st Striking Force
NISHIMURA Force "C"
OZAWA Force
AOBA hit by BREAM
MUSASHI 1800 24
0656 23 MAYA hit
Bombay Shoal DARTER Grounded
0632 23 ATAGO & TAKAO
0116 23
2030 23
2319 23
0625
1130
2035
2300 24
Bombed 0918 24
0000 25
1420
1140
1145
2241 24
JAC

avoid further air attack and give Japanese land-based air time to counterattack before resuming his course to San Bernardino Strait. But Japanese land-based air had shot its bolt, and Kurita's cumulative delay of seven hours [18] upset the SHO-GO plan, which depended on a tight schedule. It was no longer possible for the Center and Southern Forces to rendezvous inside Leyte Gulf at dawn. As it turned out, Kurita had an unexpected encounter with escort carriers, and Nishimura rendezvoused with death in Surigao Strait.

3. *Approach of the Three Japanese Forces*

Kurita at 1714, about an hour before sunset, realizing that he was falling dangerously behind schedule, turned about and headed once more for San Bernardino. One hour later he received a message from Admiral Toyoda: –

> All forces will dash to the attack, trusting in divine guidance.[19]

At 1935 Center Force was spotted by a night-flying pilot from *Independence*, about six miles north of its milling-around position but headed 120°, the course for Ticao or Masbate Passes, the two entrances to San Bernardino Strait.[20] At 1959 Kurita received individual instructions from C. in C. Combined Fleet to proceed according to plan. Kurita replied at 2145, "Main Body First Striking Force will pass through San Bernardino at 0100 October 25, . . . reaching Leyte Gulf at about 1100." From Nishimura, Kurita had received word at 2020 October 24 that he expected to pass through Surigao Strait into Leyte Gulf at 0400 October 25; and Kurita replied, setting a rendezvous with him ten miles northeast of Suluan at 0900 that day. Around 2030 another night flier picked up

[18] Kurita's Action Report states that the originally planned time of sortie from San Bernardino Strait was at sunset on the 24th.

[19] MacArthur II 364.

[20] Contact report sent by plane to *Independence* at 1958 and received by Admiral Halsey at 2006, relayed to Admiral Kinkaid at 2024. "At 1935 enemy Center Force at approximately 12°45′ N, 122°40′ E, speed 12 knots, course 120°." Halsey Action Report Encl. A. This was last contact report received by Kinkaid.

Center Force off the middle of Burias Island;[21] it appeared to be 25 miles nearer the Strait than it had been at 1935. Forming a single column and maintaining a speed of 20 knots, at 2120 it was sighted rounding Aguja Point, Burias Island, headed for Ticao Passage.[22] By 0035 October 25 Center Force was out in the Philippine Sea, every ship at General Quarters, expecting a fight. But nobody was there to give battle. Admiral Halsey's thoughts as well as his forces were streaking northward and the night fliers from *Independence*, which had lost track of Kurita after 2320, had been pulled off to search for Ozawa's Northern Force.[23]

Admiral Kinkaid, on board flagship *Wasatch* in San Pedro Bay, had a good deal to worry about that night. Aircraft attacked the Tacloban airfield near his anchorage and fired a fuel dump. Admiral Oldendorf was about to come to grips with the Japanese Southern Force. But his assumption that Admiral Halsey was covering the Japanese Center Force made his mind easy in that direction.

Vice Admiral Nishimura's Force "C," van of the Southern Force, was first sighted by planes from carriers *Enterprise* and *Franklin* at 0905 October 24 in the Sulu Sea, about 50 miles WSW of Saiton Point, Negros, and 75 miles SE of the Cagayan Islands. Vice Admiral Shima's No. 2 Striking Force, the second and independent part of the Southern Force, was first picked up by a V Army Air Force bomber at 1155 October 24, near the Cagayan Islands. The two forces were thus constituted: —

Force "C," Vice Admiral Nishimura

Battleships	FUSO, YAMASHIRO
Heavy Cruiser	MOGAMI
Destroyer Division 4	MICHISHIO, YAMAGUMO, ASAGUMO, SHIGURE

No. 2 Striking Force, Vice Admiral Shima

Heavy Cruisers	NACHI, ASHIGARA
Light Cruiser	ABUKUMA
Destroyers	SHIRANUHI, KASUMI, USHIO, AKEBONO

[21] The message from *Independence* was received on board *New Jersey* at 2040. Same source.

[22] *Independence* to Halsey, 2320 Oct. 24. Amplified by *Independence* at 0011 Oct. 25 to say that while the enemy's course was NE, they might be intending to proceed through Masbate Pass instead of Ticao Passage.

[23] Halsey to *Independence*, 0025 Oct. 25. Certain charts of tracking reports on Center Force spot positions up to 0230 Oct. 25, but these must have been extrapolations.

General MacArthur, President Roosevelt, Admiral Nimitz and Admiral Leahy

On board U.S.S. *Baltimore*, 26 July 1944, Pearl Harbor

Admiral Thomas C. Kinkaid USN

D-day Landing, Peleliu

LCI gunboats covering advance of boat waves

Official United States Marine Corps Photo

Umurbrogol Ridge, Peleliu

Marine with bazooka

General MacArthur and Captain Coney on bridge of *Nashville*

Rear Admiral Barbey, President Osmeña of the Philippine Republic, and Brigadier General Carlos P. Romulo on bridge of U.S.S. *Blue Ridge* in Leyte Gulf

All Ready to "Return"

Vice Admiral Kurita

Vice Admiral Shima

Commanders First and Second Striking Forces

U.S.S. *Langley* and a destroyer fuel simultaneously from a fleet oiler while another destroyer brings mail

U.S.S. *Pamanset* and *Essex* in a heavy sea

Fueling at Sea

United States Marines Make New Friends on Fais Atoll

The central figure is Lieutenant Colonel George E. Congdon USMCR

Cripdiv 1 off Formosa

U.S.S. *Houston* and *Canberra* under tow

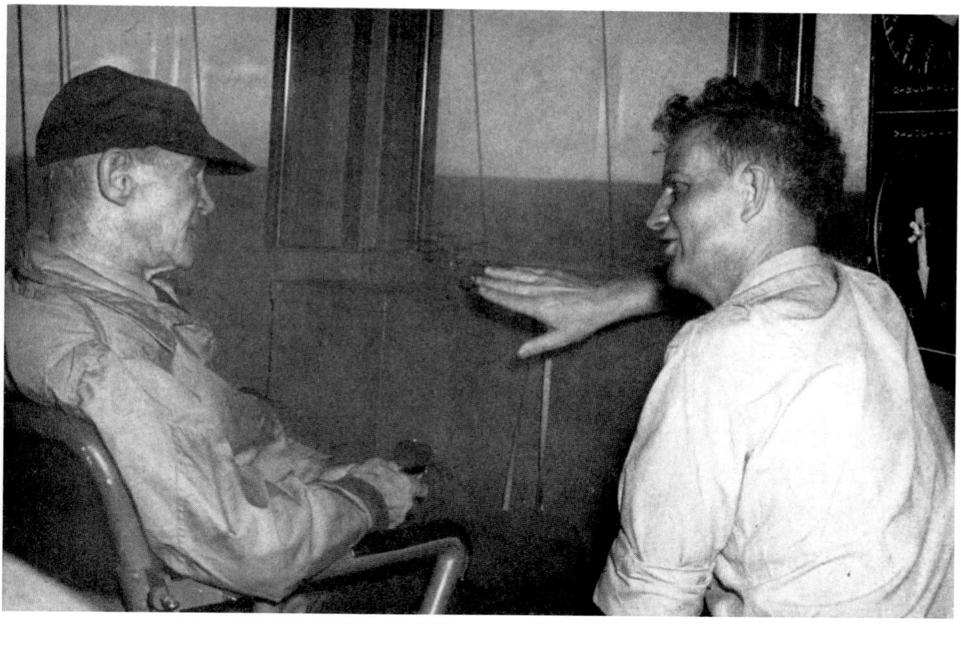

Vice Admiral Marc A. Mitscher USN *and Chief of Staff, Captain Arleigh A. Burke* USN, *on Board U.S.S.* Lexington

Admiral Halsey Adds to the Navy's Treasury of Historic Words

Cartoon by Berryman, 1944

The Invasion Force in Seeadler Harbor,
Admiralties, 6 October

Bird's-eye View of Northern Landings, Leyte, A-day

In foreground: two waves of landing craft approaching beach. *Behind them:* LST Flotilla. *Left center:* LSD has just discharged LCMs, which are circling. LCVPs of Waves 3 and 4 are stationary near Line of Departure, waiting for the word to go. Others are approaching the line snakewise. *In background:* the assault transports (APA) and freighters (AKA)

LSMs of Southern Attack Force Landing Troops near Dulag, A-day

Avenger over the Beachhead

Note wakes of landing craft approaching and retracting from Beaches White and Red; San Ricardo and Cataisan Peninsula at right; Leyte Valley extending to the mountains

After the bomb hit; *Princeton* burning

Going down; survivors on rafts

The Loss of U.S.S. Princeton, *24 October*

Rear Admiral Gerald F. Bogan USN

Rear Admiral Ralph E. Davison USN

Carrier Task Group Flag Officers

Battle of the Sibuyan Sea

Battleship *Yamato* under air attack

Vice Admiral Aubrey W. Fitch Decorates Commander David McCampbell

Vice Admiral John S. McCain looks on

Commanders in Battle of Surigao Strait

Rear Admirals Jesse B. Oldendorf USN and George L. Weyler USN

Captains Jesse B. Coward USN and Richard H. Phillips USN

Captains K. M. McManes USN and Roland N. Smoot USN

Commanders in Battle of Surigao Strait

U.S.S. *McDermut*

Night action, taken from U.S.S. *Pennsylvania*

The nearest line of flashes are gunfire from the U.S. cruisers; the farthest, hits on *Yamashiro* and *Mogami*

The Battle of Surigao Strait

Met ~~enemy~~ force last night according to plan. Enemy [illegible] up Surigao Strait from south in two groups. ~~of large~~ The first group consisted ~~from McGowan~~ as reported by the McGowan of 2 BB, 1 or 2 CA and 1 DD. The second group consisted of 2 large and about 5 smaller craft. All craft were ~~[illegible]~~ sunk or repelled. Number sunk not known but believed to be at least eight of all sizes. Upon arrival this am in lower end Surigao Strait noted eight units burning seven of which [illegible] others had been sunk as we saw them ourselves or picked up ~~[illegible]~~ survivors. No ~~[illegible]~~ opportunity yet for interrogating ships or Japanese survivors. ~~[illegible]~~ Own casualties not known [illegible] — A W Grant

WV T.O.S.

act to CTF 77
Info Com 3rd Flt
78, 79 —

TO - CTF 77 Com 3rd Flt,
Info - All TFC 7, Comind
Cincpac / Supreme
Comdr Sowespac

"Rafe" and "Oley" Send the Word

Original draft of dispatch on Battle of Surigao Strait

In handwriting of Captain Bates with corrections by Rear Admiral Oldendorf

Two Escort Carrier Flag Officers, Victors off Samar

Rear Admiral Thomas L. Sprague USN ("Taffy 1") and
Rear Admiral Felix B. Stump USN ("Taffy 2").

Photographed as Captains

Gambier Bay and destroyer escorts at start of battle

A few minutes later, splashes from enemy salvos

The Battle off Samar, "Taffy 3" Making Smoke

Hit and straddled but still under way

Dead in the water
Note Japanese heavy cruiser on horizon, shooting

Left behind by rest of Taffy 3

Taken from *Kitkun Bay*. These are the only daylight photographs of the Pacific War that show Japanese and U.S. ships on same plate

The Last Fight of Gambier Bay

Destroyer *Heermann* laying smoke during Battle off Samar

Commissioning ceremony of U.S.S. *Johnston* at Seattle
Lieutenant Commander Ernest E. Evans USN in center

Warriors of the Sea

U.S.S. *Fanshaw Bay* seen from flight deck of *Kitkun Bay*

U.S.S. *St. Lo* blowing up after Kamikaze attack

The Battle off Samar, as Seen from Kitkun Bay

U.S.S. *Suwannee* ablaze

Seen from *Santee* after Kamikaze attack

Forward elevator damage

The Battle off Samar

Ise under air attack

Note torpedo track at right

Flight deck of *Zuiho*. Note battleship camouflage

The Battle off Cape Engaño

The Battle off Cape Engaño

Zuikaku under attack
Terutsuki class destroyer in foreground; *Chitose* in background

U.S.S. *Lamson* entering Ormoc Bay

Reno after torpedo hit, 3 November, fantail awash

Operations in November 1944

Commander Richard H. O'Kane USN

U.S.S. *Archerfish*

A Submariner and a Submarine

The planes that sighted Force "C" attacked at 0918, and claimed several hits. According to information obtained from survivors, *Fuso* was hit on her fantail, but sustained little damage other than the destruction of her float planes, and destroyer *Shigure* was hit on No. 1 turret, knocking out a gun crew. The formation maintained speed, but Admiral Nishimura was worried, for he sent Kurita a short message to the effect that his part of the operation was not going successfully.[24] It was never received.

Force "C" was also sighted by a Navy PB4Y out of Morotai and by a V Army Air Force plane, between 0910 and 0950,[25] but not again during daylight October 24. The entire Southern Force escaped air attack during the afternoon and evening because Davison's fast carrier group had to move north in order to launch strikes on the Center Force, and the escort carriers were occupied by their duties in Leyte Gulf. Two of the four "Black Cats" (radar-equipped night-search Catalinas) under Admiral Kinkaid's command were sent into the Mindanao Sea to attack the Southern Force after dark, but failed to locate it. One was shot down by "friendly" PT boats but all hands were rescued. Admiral Kinkaid, however, correctly estimated that the Southern Force intended to break into Leyte Gulf via Surigao Strait, and made such disposition of his forces that only a miracle could have permitted the Japanese to attain their object.

The Northern Force, under command of Admiral Ozawa in carrier *Zuikaku*, sortied 20 October from Hashirashima anchorage near Kure in the Inland Sea of Japan. Altogether, the four flattops of this force had only 116 aircraft, about half their normal complement, on board; and the battleship-carriers *Ise* and *Hyuga* had none.[26] Light cruiser *Oyodo* had two reconnaissance planes. Ozawa shaped a course outside the range of American planes based on Saipan, which might have discovered him earlier than was con-

[24] Kurita interrogation. The P.O.W. intelligence is in Adm. Kinkaid's Memorandum on Losses Inflicted, 10 Jan. 1945.

[25] Adm. Halsey's Message File, received at 0943. The V A.A.F. contact report was not received until 1632.

[26] *War College Analysis* III 196, MacArthur II 354, Ozawa Action Report.

venient. He was eager to be seen at the proper time, and Halsey was especially anxious to locate him; yet neither could figure out where the other was! One of Ozawa's search planes made the first contact, on a Task Force 38 group at 0820 October 24, and a second one at 1145. Ozawa steamed south until he was 210 miles from TG 38.3, launched a 76-plane strike at 1145 on Sherman's group, and steered a box, playing bait, before any American pilot sighted him.

Ozawa's strike launched at 1145 accomplished nothing and the planes did not even attempt to return to their carriers but made for friendly fields in northern Luzon.[27] At 1430, before he knew how this attack had fared, Ozawa detached Group "A" (*Ise*, *Hyuga* and light forces), under command of Rear Admiral Matsuda, with orders to "proceed southward and grasp a favorable opportunity to attack and destroy enemy remnants." Ozawa knew very well that Halsey had something better than "remnants," but he did not wish to reflect even by indirection on the Imperial General Headquarters doctrine of the Formosa air battle.

The afternoon watch was almost spent before an American search plane made first contact on the Northern Force. It was Matsuda's Group "A" that two pilots of Task Group 38.4 sighted at 1540 October 24, in lat. 18°10′ N, long. 125°30′ E. An hour later, at 1640, another carrier pilot had a good look at Ozawa's Main Body in lat. 18°25′ N, long. 125°28′ E, steering west at 16 knots. It then comprised the four carriers, two light cruisers and about five destroyers.

At 1910 Ozawa received Toyoda's "All forces dash to the attack" order; but not until 2000 did he get Kurita's message of 1530 to the effect that he had reversed course in the Sibuyan Sea. At 2110 he received an order from Toyoda to attack as formerly directed. So he turned to a southwesterly course and recalled Matsuda, determined to "carry out diversionary operations at all costs." [28] In that he was only too successful.

[27] Interrogations of Capt. Ohmae and Cdr. Yamaguchi, *Inter. Jap. Off.* I 153, 178.
[28] Ozawa Action Report.

4. *Admiral Halsey's Decision*

Admiral Halsey's reaction to these sightings and to the information already received about the Central and Southern Forces can best be stated in the words of his own dispatch to Admiral Nimitz and General MacArthur at about 2200 October 25, after the battle was over: —

> Searches by my carrier planes revealed the presence of the Northern carrier force on the afternoon of 24 October, which completed the picture of all enemy naval forces. As it seemed childish to me to guard statically San Bernardino Strait, I concentrated TF 38 during the night and steamed north to attack the Northern Force at dawn. I believed that the Center Force had been so heavily damaged in the Sibuyan Sea that it could no longer be considered a serious menace to Seventh Fleet.

Accordingly, at 2022 October 24, Admiral Halsey ordered Bogan's Group 2 and Davison's Group 4 to steam north at 25 knots, join Sherman's Group 3 and attack Ozawa. McCain's Group 1, now returning northwesterly from the direction of Ulithi, was ordered to complete fueling and join the others. By midnight 24–25 October fast carrier groups 2, 3 and 4, including Admiral Lee in *Washington* and Admiral Halsey in *New Jersey* and all their battleships and cruisers, were tearing north, just as the Japanese wanted them to do. In the meantime, Kurita's Center Force, which Halsey had assumed to be no serious menace to Kinkaid, was debouching from San Bernardino Strait unopposed and even undetected.

Admiral Kinkaid assumed in his operation plan, "Any major enemy naval force approaching from the north will be intercepted and attacked by Third Fleet covering force." [29] This was a natural interpretation of Halsey's orders from Nimitz to engage the enemy fleet if and when an opportunity occurred. But now that two major enemy forces were approaching from the north of Leyte Gulf, Halsey ignored the stronger and let it get between him and Seventh Fleet, because he mistakenly assumed that it was the weaker, and

[29] CTF 77 (Adm. Kinkaid) Op Plan 13–44, Appendix 2, Annex E.

"no serious menace." In other words, he made the same mistake that the Japanese higher command did about the air battle over Formosa, accepting aviators' reports of damage as actual damage.[30]

It was not a case of either-or. Halsey had enough gun and air power to handle both Japanese forces. The alternative to rushing everything up north was not, as he said, "to guard statically San Bernardino Strait." Three groups of Task Force 38, even without the gunfire ships of Task Force 34 (Battle Line, of which we shall hear more anon), had more than enough power to take care of Ozawa's 17 ships. Battle Line might have been detached to guard San Bernardino Strait, not statically but actively. But Halsey wished to deal the Northern Force a really crushing blow. In every previous carrier action of the war – Coral Sea, Midway, Eastern Solomons, Santa Cruz and Philippine Sea – the Japanese, although badly mauled, had saved most of their ships. He was determined that this would not happen again. He expected that the Northern Force was planning to shuttle-bomb him by ferrying planes back and forth between carriers and airfields, as they had attempted to do in the Battle of the Philippine Sea. He felt it unwise to leave any considerable surface force to watch San Bernardino Strait without detaching one carrier group for air protection, which would weaken his striking power.[31]

After all, the Northern Force was out in the Philippine Sea, "asking for it." The Center Force might never come out; and Halsey was no man to watch a rathole from which the rat might never emerge. He had just lost *Princeton* to an air attack which he believed, erroneously, to have come from Ozawa. The quickened tempo of enemy air activity on the 24th seemed a presage of worse to come, and it was natural for Halsey to aim at annihilating the

[30] Halsey in his Action Report p. 4 states: "At least four and probably five battleships torpedoed and bombed, one probably sunk; a minimum of three heavy cruisers torpedoed and others bombed; one light cruiser sunk; one destroyer probably sunk and four damaged. . . . Some details of the foregoing information were not available at dusk, but flash reports indicated beyond doubt that the Center Force had been badly mauled with all of its battleships and most of its heavy cruisers tremendously reduced in fighting power and life."

[31] Admiral Lee, however, said after the battle that he would have been only too glad to have been ordered to cover San Bernardino Strait without air cover.

one sure source of Japanese air power, the carriers of the Northern Force. He did know, before ordering Task Force 38 north, that the Japanese Center Force had resumed course toward San Bernardino Strait; but still assumed that it was too "heavily damaged" to be a "serious menace" to Kinkaid.[32]

At least three task force commanders were amazed and disturbed by Halsey's decision. Admiral Bogan even contemplated a protest. After seeing the aircraft reports to the effect that Center Force had resumed an easterly course, he discussed the situation over TBS with Captain Ewen of *Independence*. Ewen not only confirmed the reports but mentioned the ominous fact that all navigation lights in San Bernardino Strait were brightly lit, after a long black-out. Bogan immediately drafted a message to Halsey incorporating this intelligence, then called him personally over TBS and read it. "A rather impatient voice" – of a staff officer, presumably – replied "Yes, yes, we have that information." Bogan was prepared to follow up with another message, recommending that Admiral Lee's Battle Line be formed with his TG 38.2 in support, letting Sherman's and Davison's groups handle Ozawa. But after that brush-off, he said no more.[33]

Lee himself was an officer of alert mind and keen analytical sense, whose advice was often sought on strategy; but not now. Working on the mass of intelligence that reached flag plot, he had figured out that the Northern Force must be a decoy with little or no striking power, and that the earlier turn-around of the Center Force was temporary. Before sunset ended the opportunity for sending visual signals, Admiral Lee in *Washington* sent Admiral Halsey in *New Jersey* a message stating his views. No reply was made other than a perfunctory "Roger." After darkness descended and the *Independence* reports came in, Lee sent Halsey a message by TBS to the effect that he was certain Kurita was coming out. After that he kept silence.[34]

[32] Action Report and Dispatch of 2200 Oct. 25 to Admiral Nimitz, as above.
[33] Letter of Admiral Bogan to writer, 3 July 1957.
[34] Letter of Lt. Cdr. Guilliaem Aertsen USNR, formerly of Admiral Lee's staff, to writer, 6 Mar. 1950.

CTF 38, Vice Admiral Mitscher in *Lexington*, bypassed for days by Admiral Halsey in issuing orders, had become little better than a passenger in his beloved Fast Carrier Forces Pacific Fleet. When, at 2029, he received Commander Third Fleet's order to turn north, he inferred that Halsey intended to assume the tactical command on the following day's battle, and decided to turn in. As he left flag plot his chief of staff, Commodore Arleigh Burke, remarked, "We'd better see where that [Japanese] Fleet is." Mitscher assented. A few minutes later, Burke received the *Independence* aircraft contact on Center Force "still very much afloat and still moving toward San Bernardino"; and at about 2305 a clarifying report came through. No doubt about it! Burke and Commander James Flatley, operations officer, thought it was imperative to detach Battle Line. They woke Mitscher up and urged him to "tell Halsey" to do so. "Does Admiral Halsey have that report?" said the task force commander. "Yes," said Flatley. "If he wants my advice he'll ask for it," said Mitscher. Then he rolled over and went back to sleep.[35]

Thus, three task groups of Third Fleet – 65 ships strong – went steaming north at 16 knots[36] to engage the 17 ships of Ozawa's Northern Force, leaving nothing but empty air and ocean between the Seventh Fleet, in and around Leyte Gulf, and Kurita. His still powerful Center Force completed the transit of San Bernardino Strait at 0035 October 25, amazed to find nobody there to fight, and shaped a course for the rendezvous off Suluan with Nishimura.

Fortunately, this was not the whole picture as 24 October merged into the fateful Wednesday the 25th. Nishimura's Southern Force was already reported by motor torpedo boats to be approaching the southern entrance of Surigao Strait, and Shima's Second

[35] Theodore Taylor *The Magnificent Mitscher* (1954) pp. 261–2, quoting Burke's transcript of voice recordings.

[36] Halsey report. He used this speed in order not to overrun the estimated daylight position circle of Ozawa's Force. Position of Halsey's flagship *New Jersey* at 0000 was lat. 14°31′N, long. 125°34′E. CTF 34 (Vice Adm. W. A. Lee) Action Report 14 Dec. 1944.

Striking Force was catching up. Admiral Oldendorf had formed Battle Line and sent scouting destroyers down the Strait. There and off Samar mighty forces were about to clash in decisive battle, and the issue was far from certain.

CHAPTER XI

The Battle of Surigao Strait[1]

24–25 October 1944

Sunset 24 October at 1815, Moonset 25 October at 0006; Sunrise 25 October at 0630. All at Tacloban.

1. *Plans and Dispositions*

AT fifteen minutes after noon 24 October, Vice Admiral Kinkaid alerted every combatant and merchant ship under his command to prepare for a night engagement. He correctly estimated that Nishimura's Southern Force would try to penetrate Leyte Gulf via Surigao Strait that night. At 1443 he ordered Rear Admiral Oldendorf, commanding the Bombardment and Fire Support Group, to form night patrol disposition across the northern entrance to the Strait, and prepare to meet the enemy.

The 28 Liberty ships in San Pedro Bay were joined by the three amphibious force flagships and cruiser *Nashville* with General MacArthur still embarked. A close inner screen of destroyer escorts and patrol craft was thrown around them. All ship movements in or out of the Gulf were ordered to end at sunset.

At 1513 when Admiral Oldendorf received Kinkaid's order to prepare for night action, his flagship *Louisville* lay alongside ammunition ship *Durham Victory*, replenishing. For two days, watching the Strait, he had been operating under a modified battle plan.

[1] Comcrudiv 4 (Rear Adm. Oldendorf, CTG 77.2) two preliminary Action Reports of Battle of Surigao Strait dated 27 Oct. and 2 Nov. 1944; Action Reports of all unit commanders and ships involved; conversations with Capt. Bates on board *Tennessee* in the Okinawa operation, and at Newport later. He kindly placed the ms. of his *War College Analysis* Vol. V at my disposition, and Capt. Jack C. Titus of his staff, who plotted this battle, has been of great assistance.

His staff, headed by the energetic Captain Richard W. ("Rafe") Bates, now made plans for the actual engagement.

The main groups under Admiral Oldendorf's command, plus Desron 54, were as follows: —[2]

Left Flank
R. Adm. Oldendorf

Heavy Cruisers
LOUISVILLE
PORTLAND
MINNEAPOLIS

Light Cruisers
R. Adm. Hayler
DENVER
COLUMBIA

Sec. 1, Desron 56
Capt. Smoot
NEWCOMB
RICHARD P. LEARY
ALBERT W. GRANT

Sec. 2, Desdiv 112
Capt. Conley
ROBINSON
HALFORD
BRYANT

Sec. 3, Cdr. Boulware
HEYWOOD L. EDWARDS
BENNION
LEUTZE

Battle Line
R. Adm. Weyler

Battleships
MISSISSIPPI
MARYLAND
WEST VIRGINIA
TENNESSEE
CALIFORNIA
PENNSYLVANIA

Desdiv "X-ray"
Cdr. Hubbard
CLAXTON
CONY
THORN
AULICK
SIGOURNEY
WELLES

Right Flank
R. Adm. Berkey

Light Cruisers
PHOENIX
BOISE

Heavy Cruiser
H.M.A.S. SHROPSHIRE

Desron 24, Capt. McManes
HUTCHINS
DALY
BACHE
H.M.A.S. ARUNTA
KILLEN
BEALE

Picket Patrol
Desron 54, Capt. Coward
REMEY
MCGOWAN
MELVIN
MERTZ

Desdiv 108, Cdr. Phillips
MCDERMUT
MONSSEN
MCNAIR

This was more than enough to take care of the Japanese Southern Force, for which Admirals Kinkaid and Oldendorf planned sudden death. Every old Pacific hand retained a grim memory of events centered around a certain little island in the Solomons which Hibuson unpleasantly recalled. As Admiral Oldendorf said, "We didn't want them to pull another Savo Island on us." His dispositions insured that they would not.

Battle Line (Rear Admiral Weyler) would steam east and west between a position about five miles east of Hingatungan Point, and the meridian of the lighthouse on Hibuson Island. Left flank cruisers, which Admiral Oldendorf himself commanded in *Louis-*

[2] For C.O.s of vessels engaged, see Appendix I.

ville, were to steam back and forth over two and a half miles south of Battle Line. Actually, left flank at the time of the engagement was on the wrong (western) side of Battle Line, because Admiral

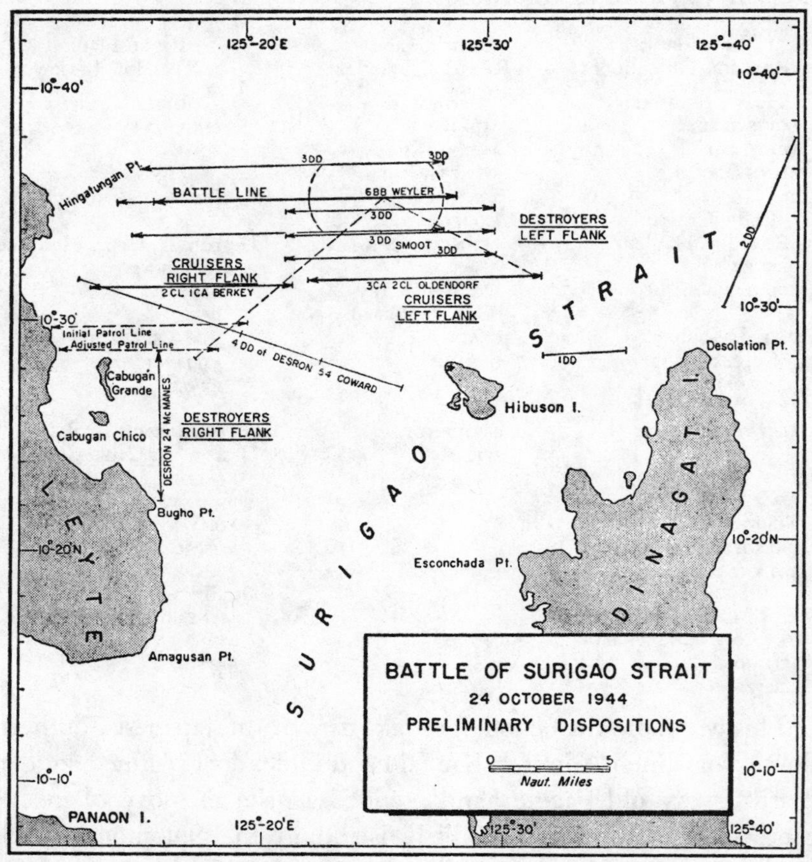

Weyler stepped up his speed from five to ten knots at 0244, after the first destroyer contact with the enemy, and to 15 knots at 0329, in order to be better prepared to comb the tracks of torpedoes. Battleships cannot be maneuvered easily at any less speed than 10 knots.

These dispositions were now strengthened by Rear Admiral Berkey's three cruisers and six destroyers, one of each being Australian, which constituted the right flank. The Strait at this point is barely 12 miles wide, hence "Oley" did not yield any more water to "Count" Berkey than he had to, and directed him to patrol a course parallel to and west of his left flank cruisers.[3] This put Berkey almost on the beach; but the Leyte shore is bold and radar would give ample warning of it. In order to lessen the chance of collision with Captain Coward's four picket destroyers, Berkey directed his own destroyers, under Captain McManes, to patrol on a north–south line off the Cabugan Islands and Bugho Point, Leyte.

As soon as Admiral Oldendorf had formulated his plan, but before it was issued, he summoned Admirals Weyler and Berkey on board *Louisville* in order to discuss it, and to make sure that each task group commander knew what was expected of him. The principal anxiety on the part of these flag officers was shortage of ammunition, especially of 14-inch and 16-inch armor-piercing projectiles for the battleships. Owing to the fact that they had been loaded for bombarding Yap rather than fighting a fleet, the battleships' main battery magazines were initially filled 77.3 per cent with HC (high capacity) bombardment ammunition, and only 22.7 per cent AP (armor-piercing), the only projectile that can penetrate armored decks.[4] Moreover, 58 per cent of their HC had been expended in the shore bombardment at Leyte. The battleships, therefore, placed enough AP in their main turret ammunition hoists for the first five salvos and were prepared to shift to HC if they encountered anything smaller than a battleship. And it was agreed that Battle Line should withhold gunfire until it could shoot at ranges between 20,000 and 17,000 yards, in order to obtain the highest percentage of hits.

The following table, condensed from the one in Chapter XIII,

[3] Berkey's three cruisers patrolled in line of bearing. The flood tide, which was running throughout the action, sets south.

[4] Wilkinson's endorsement to Oldendorf's Action Report. The proportion of 8-inch bullets in the heavy cruisers was 66 per cent HC, 34 per cent AP. Ammunition replenishment ships had been loaded with about 20 per cent AP and 80 per cent HC in anticipation of Yap. Only two of these, *Mazama* and *Durham Victory*, had so far entered Leyte Gulf; the one carried no 16-inch bullets whatever and the other had 48 rounds 16-inch AP and 1000 rounds HC.

is the best estimate I can make from the battleships' logs of the numbers of rounds for main battery each one had on board when the battle opened: –

	AP	*HC*	*Caliber*
MISSISSIPPI	201	543	14-inch
MARYLAND	240	445	16-inch
WEST VIRGINIA	200	175	16-inch
TENNESSEE	396	268	14-inch
CALIFORNIA	240	78	14-inch
PENNSYLVANIA	360	93	14-inch

There were no replacement torpedoes on hand for the destroyers, which were also down to about 20 per cent of their allowance in 5-inch shell.

All available motor torpedo boats were stationed at intervals along the southern entrance to Surigao Strait, and as far west as Camiguin Island in the Mindanao Sea, to report the approaching enemy and if possible to reduce his strength. Next would come classic torpedo attacks, first by the right flank destroyers (Captain McManes), to be followed shortly by those of the left flank (Captain Smoot), while Commander Hubbard's Division "X-ray" screened Battle Line. This plan was augmented through the enterprise of Captain Coward.

The conferences concluded, Admiral Oldendorf at 1725 October 24 notified Admirals Kinkaid and Wilkinson of his intentions by dispatch. He was all set to give the Japanese everything he had. "My theory," he said after the battle, "was that of the old-time gambler: *Never give a sucker a chance*. If my opponent is foolish enough to come at me with an inferior force, I'm certainly not going to give him an even break." [5]

All battleship and cruiser planes that could not be stowed in ships' hangars were put on the beach that afternoon to avoid battle damage and fires, such as had proved disastrous in the Battle of Savo Island. Air power did not participate in the Battle of Surigao Strait until the pursuit phase after break of day.

[5] Conversation with Lt. Salomon at Hollandia, Nov. 1944; similar statement in *New York Times* 28 Oct. 1944 p. 5. Tokyo deeply resented this statement, and Adm. Oldendorf for the time being became the No. 1 target of "Tokyo Rose" and other propagandists.

Destroyer Squadron 54, seven almost new 2100-tonners commanded by Captain J. G. Coward, had been acting as Surigao Strait antisubmarine picket patrol since A-day. On the afternoon of 24 October, four were patrolling the narrows between Leyte and Hibuson Island, a fifth covered the channel between Hibuson and Desolation Point, Dinagat, and two patrolled a north–south line between Desolation Point and Homonhon Island. Admiral Oldendorf did not include Desron 54 in his battle plan because they were under Admiral Wilkinson's command; but that did not faze Captain Coward, a veteran of the Battle of Guadalcanal. At 1950 October 24 he sent "Oley" this message: "In case of surface contact to the southward I plan to make an immediate torpedo attack and then retire to clear you. With your approval I will submit plan shortly." Fifteen minutes later, Oldendorf radioed his approval. At 2008, Captain Coward sent the Admiral his basic plan, details to follow shortly. Coward did not merely volunteer; he announced that he was going in.

The night of 24–25 October was tense for everyone, including the remaining ships of the amphibious forces. Every sailor in San Pedro Bay was conscious of his dependence on Admiral Oldendorf's ships. Although the rest of Seventh Fleet could not support "Oley" directly, they lent him plenty of hope and an assortment of prayers.

2. *The Motor Torpedo Boats' Battle,*[6] *2300 October 24 to 0300 October 25*

Forty-five motor torpedo boats under Commander S. S. Bowling, Commander Motor Torpedo Boat Squadrons Seventh Fleet, made

[6] ComMTBrons Seventh Fleet (Cdr. Bowling) "Report of Action MTBs Surigao Strait, 24–25 Oct." enclosing section and boat action reports; conversations with several participants and reports written by QM Robert W. Stanley and Lt. William E. Garfield USNR; trackings by Capt. Titus of Commo. Bates' staff. Times given in PT reports are unreliable as they kept no deck log and relied on memory after the event.

the 1100-mile run from Mios Woendi to Leyte Gulf via Kossol Roads, accompanied by tenders *Wachapreague*, *Oyster Bay* and *Willoughby*, arriving between 21 and 23 October. Liloan Harbor, on the west side of Panaon Strait, sheltered from all winds but accessible, was selected as base for the first tender and the southernmost patrols, while the northern patrols operated from the other two tenders in San Pedro Bay.

On the afternoon of 24 October, all "Peter Tares" in Leyte Gulf began streaking southward, making so much noise and fuss that everyone's attention was attracted; "Something must be cooking down the Strait" was the current reaction. At noon, Admiral Kinkaid had passed the word to Commander Bowling to collect all available boats and patrol Surigao Strait intensively after dark.

This was just what the PT sailors had been longing to do. Their boats, designed for fast, hit-and-run torpedo attacks on enemy ships, had had little or no torpedo experience since the struggle for Guadalcanal and the action in Blackett Strait on 2 August 1943.[7] In the Southwest Pacific, as in the South Pacific, they had been usefully employed as patrol craft and fast gunboats, but torpedo training had been neglected. The only "fish" that most of them had fired since 1943 was in a practice before departing Mios Woendi.

Lieutenant Commander R. A. Leeson, commanding the battle patrols, disposed his 39 available PTs in 13 sections of three boats each, as follows: —[8]

Section Nos. 1 and 2 patrolled the southernmost line through the Mindanao Sea from Agio Point, Bohol, to Camiguin Island.

Section No. 3 covered the western entrance to Sogod Bay and Limasawa Island.

Section Nos. 5 and 6 extended this line across the eastern entrance of Sogod Bay and around the south end of Panaon Island.

Section Nos. 4, 7 and 8 were the opposite numbers to Section

[7] See Volumes V and VI.

[8] For names of C.O.s and composition of sections, see Appendix I. The other six Pts were not operating, owing to matériel casualties in consequence of their long voyage.

Nos. 5 and 6 on the eastern shore of the Narrows off Sumilon Island and Bilaa and Madilao Points, Mindanao.

Section No. 9 patrolled across the Strait from Kanhatid Point, Dinagat, to the opposite shore on Panaon Island.

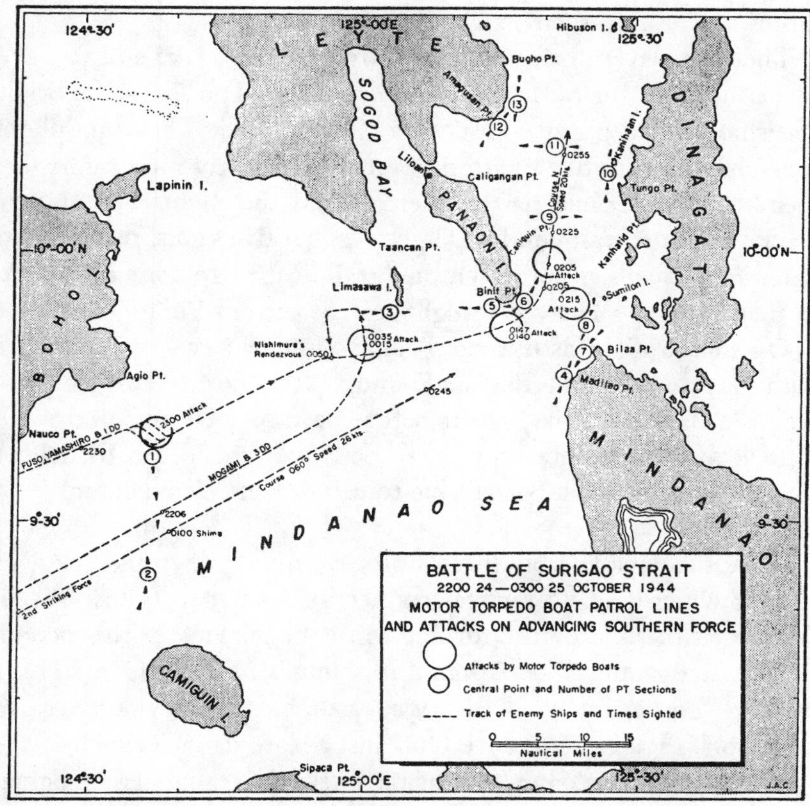

Section No. 11 patrolled cross-strait about three miles north of Section No. 9.

Section No. 10 took care of the Dinagat shore north and south of Kanihaan Island.

Section Nos. 12 and 13 patrolled opposite Section No. 10, around Amagusan Point, Leyte.

All were on station before dark.

For want of night-flying, radar-equipped patrol planes,[9] these PTs were the "eyes of the fleet." Their orders were to report all contacts, surface or air, visual or radar, and attack independently. The four northernmost patrols were instructed to get clear and stay clear "if and when Captain Coward's and Admiral Oldendorf's forces moved into their patrol areas."

The boats lay-to on station, so as to leave no wake and to have best conditions for radar and radio operation. The sea in the Strait was smooth and glassy – just what they wanted. The atmosphere was fairly clear until a quartering moon set shortly after midnight; then the sky became partly overcast and the night went pitch-black. The northeast wind was light – about five knots, rising to ten when rain squalls swept down the Strait. But there were not many of them; it was a fairly dry night for the eastern Philippines.

On such a night as this the Pacific Fleet had swapped punches with the enemy in Iron Bottom Sound, up the Slot, and off Empress Augusta Bay. But it had never before been so well prepared, with a flock of PTs to intercept, three destroyer squadrons to deliver torpedo attacks and a Battle Line to cap the enemy's column.

Since the Japanese Southern Force was really two independent groups which had no tactical connection, we may follow the ill fortune of the first before turning to the better luck of the second.

The first group, Vice Admiral Nishimura's Force "C" of No. 1 Striking Force, included the two battleships. Its mission was to arrive off Tacloban in Leyte Gulf just before dawn (which as the Japanese reckoned dawn was at 0430, the first glimmer of light), at the same time as Kurita's Center Force. This timing was essential to the success of Admiral Toyoda's SHO–1 battle plan, which called for a pincer movement on the American amphibious forces in Leyte Gulf. Whether Nishimura imagined he could get through Surigao Strait without a fight, we do not know; but any hope he may have had of joining Kurita in a merry massacre of am-

[9] *Independence*, the night fighting carrier, had taken her planes north with Halsey, and the escort carriers had no night fighters.

phibious craft and transports, which he believed to be present in great abundance,[10] must have vanished around 1830 October 24 when he received Admiral Kurita's signal of 1600 to the effect that Center Force had been delayed by the air battle of the Sibuyan Sea. Nishimura, nevertheless, maintained course and speed, and felt confirmed in this decision around 1900 by Toyoda's order: "All forces will dash to the attack."

Commander Nishino, skipper of *Shigure* (the only one of Nishimura's ships that escaped destruction), later observed that the Admiral was "the sort of fellow who would prefer to fight a night battle," [11] because the Japanese Navy excelled in night work early in the war. Admiral Nishimura probably reflected that his best chance of penetrating the Gulf lay under cover of darkness, since he had no air support or combat air patrol.

At 2013 he sent off a message to Toyoda and Kurita that he expected "to penetrate to a point off Dulag" at 0400 next morning – a minor change from the Tacloban target at 0430. At about 2200 he received Kurita's message of 2145, to the effect that Center Force was due off Suluan Island at 0600 and would penetrate Leyte Gulf about 1100.[12] This confirmed what he had already learned, that he need expect no help from Kurita within the Gulf. Already Nishimura had sent *Mogami* and three destroyers ahead of the two battleships and *Shigure*, to reconnoiter. The *Mogami* group maintained a NE course, while the flag group stood over toward Bohol.

At 2236 Ensign Peter Gadd's *PT–131* of Section 1, operating off Bohol, picked up the flag group on radar, and the three boats closed to the attack at 24 knots.[13] At 2250 they sighted the enemy,

[10] *Mogami* launched a search plane at 0200 Oct. 24 which reported at 1200 that there were 80 transports off Dulag together with 6 battleships, cruisers and destroyers. *Mogami* Action Report.

[11] *Inter. Jap. Off.* II 346. Nishino's statement (p. 342) that Nishimura was eager to keep ahead of Shima, because if the latter caught up he would, as senior, become O.T.C., and because he had a "personal antipathy" for Shima, I do not believe. There is no sense in ascribing unworthy motives to a decision when there are valid military reasons for it. Nishino's statement, moreover, was based on the supposition that Nishimura speeded up, which is not correct; he merely maintained speed.

[12] *War College Analysis* V 9.

[13] *War College Analysis* V 12.

distant three miles. Two minutes later, destroyer *Shigure* sighted them.

That moment marks the end of peaceful cruising for Nishimura, and the opening of the Battle of Surigao Strait – which neither the Admiral nor any of his ships, except the destroyer that made this sighting, survived.

Admiral Nishimura ordered an emergency turn to starboard, toward the PTs, at 2254. Two minutes later, when the boats were trying to put their contact reports through, they were illuminated, taken under gunfire by *Shigure* and straddled with 4.7-inch shell as they zigzagged violently and made smoke. Deploying, they sought to close range for a torpedo attack, but were unable to do so. *PT–152*, in the beam of *Shigure's* searchlight, received a hit which blew up her 37-mm gun, killed one man and wounded three of her crew of 15. A shell passed right through *PT–130* while she was making smoke to cover *PT–152*. Although it did not explode, the concussion knocked out all her radio apparatus. As soon as the action broke off, *PT–130* made best speed to close the nearby Section 2, in order to get off her contact report. It was relayed from *PT–127* to *Wachapreague* at ten minutes after midnight and reached Admiral Oldendorf at 0026 October 25.

That was the first definite information received by him of the enemy since around 1000 the previous morning. It confirmed the wisdom of his dispositions, and required no change in his battle plan.

In the meantime the *Mogami* group had passed PT Section No. 2, off Camiguin Island, undetected. Both groups kept coming at 18 knots, and at 2330 Nishimura radioed Kurita and Shima: "Advancing as scheduled while destroying enemy torpedo boats." His force was next sighted at 2350, southwest of Limasawa Island, by Lieutenant (jg) Dwight Owen's Section No. 3. *PT–151* and *PT–146* fired one torpedo each at *Mogami* at 0015 but apparently were rattled by her searchlight and missed. All three boats of this section retired, zigzagging and smoking and pursued by shellfire from destroyer *Yamagumo*, but escaped without a hit, despite failure of the port engine of *PT–151* for three minutes. Owing to mechanical failures, and possibly to enemy jamming, no contact report from this section got off until 0330.[14]

It was the same story right up the Strait. Each succeeding motor torpedo boat section along the enemy's course observed gun flashes of the previous fight; made contact itself; attempted to get off its report (and sometimes did); went in for attack; fired torpedoes which missed; became brightly illuminated by enemy searchlights; came under brisk but inaccurate gunfire, and retired under a smoke screen.

Nishimura was well pleased with the way his ships had dealt with these nuisances, At 0100 he advised both Kurita, who was already out of San Bernardino Strait, and Shima, who was then 35 to 40 miles astern, that he would pass Panaon Island at 0130 and "penetrate into Leyte Gulf. Several torpedo boats sighted but enemy situation otherwise unknown."

In the meantime the two halves of Nishimura's Group "C" had reunited. The rendezvous point, set for 0030, about ten miles SW of Limasawa Island, was effected ten minutes later. At 0100 the reunited Force "C" assumed approach formation. Destroyers *Michishio* and *Asagumo* were the van, followed at a distance of four kilometers by *Yamashiro* with *Shigure* and *Yamagumo* on either flank, and at one-kilometer intervals astern of them steamed *Fuso* and *Mogami.*

At the narrows between Panaon and Sumilon Islands, Lieutenant Commander Robert Leeson's motor torpedo boat Section No. 6 closed to attack.[15] His flagship, *PT–134,* fired at Nishimura's force at 0205, just as it was changing to a due north course off Camiguin Point, and was driven off by gunfire. Lieutenant John M. McElfresh's section, already moving south from its patrol sector (No. 9), saw what was going on, closed, and fired four torpedoes at the Japanese destroyers at 0207.[16] None of them hit. In quick succession

[14] *War College Analysis* V 9, 15, 76.

[15] An account of Leeson's part, "Lone PT Attacked Japanese Fleet," is in *New York Times* 14 Nov. 1944 p. 4d.

[16] *War College Analysis* V 115, 124.

came searchlight illumination, gunfire, return fire, launching of two more torpedoes by *PT–490* and a shell hit on the same boat. *PT–493*, whose torpedo hung in the rack, covered the retirement of *PT–490* with smoke and in so doing sustained three 4.7-inch hits which carried away the charthouse, punched a large hole in the bottom, killed two men and wounded five. "All hands in the cockpit were blown aft, but resumed station," reported the skipper, Lieutenant (jg) R. W. Brown USNR. Petty Officer A. W. Brunelle, described by a shipmate as "a slight, sissified-looking boy whom no one expected to be of any use in combat," saved the boat by stuffing his life jacket into the hole; that checked the inflow of water enough to keep the engines running until they could beach her on Panaon Island. Lieutenant Brown and the rest of his crew waded ashore and established their own beachhead; *PT–491* found them there shortly after sunrise, maintaining a perimeter defense with rifles and machine guns. *PT–493* slid off the rocks at high tide and sank in deep water.

Following this brief and somewhat bloody brawl, Lieutenant Commander Tappaan's Sumilon Island patrol (Section No. 8) which had seen the enemy ships silhouetted by their own star shell, attacked from the southeast, firing six torpedoes. The Japanese promptly illuminated and fired on these three boats, which retired without damage, and without making any hits.

PT–327 of Lieutenant C. T. Gleason's cross-strait patrol (Section No. 11) sighted Nishimura's force at 0225, when it was about ten miles away. She reported the contact to Captain Coward, who promptly replied that PTs had better clear out as he was coming down the Strait.

So far as Nishimura was concerned, the motor torpedo boat phase of the Battle of Surigao Strait ended at 0213 October 25, when he drove off the last attack by Tappaan's section. Including later actions in the Strait on 25 October, 30 of the 39 PTs on patrol had got into some sort of fight. Altogether, they fired 34 torpedoes, all but two of which ran "hot, straight and normal," but obtained only the hit on *Abukuma* of Admiral Shima's Second

Striking Force.[17] They neither stopped nor confused the enemy, and were chased away by his gunfire.

Nevertheless, they performed an indispensable service through their contact reports which, in addition to the fireworks that they produced from the enemy, alerted Admiral Oldendorf's forces. Under the battle conditions in which the MTBs operated, their reporting was good; anything approaching it in Guadalcanal days would have saved the Navy several ships and hundreds of lives. The "Peter Tare" boys showed determination in closing for attack, and cool courage in their snakelike retirement under fire. And they proved to be surprisingly tough. Of the 30 boats which came under enemy gunfire, 10 were hit but only one was expended, and the total casualties were 3 killed and 20 wounded.

But Nishimura kept coming, and Shima was not far behind.

3. *Coward's Destroyers Attack,*[18] *0200–0315*

Nishimura seems to have had no inkling of the overwhelming force into whose grip he was advancing. Following the MTB attacks, which ended about 0213 off Sumilon Island, his first serious encounter was with Captain Coward's Destroyer Squadron 54.

When the moon set at 0006 October 25, Captain Coward's seven destroyers were patrolling their stations on the line Hingatungan Point–Hibuson–Desolation Point–Homonhon, anxiously awaiting word from the PT boats. Except when an occasional lightning flash revealed the high shores of the Strait, visibility was not more than two or three miles over open water. The sea was glassy, the temperature about 80°F, and only the wind made by the destroyers' speed brought relief to men topside. Those below decks sweated; for these destroyers, like almost all United States ships at that time,

[17] This will be related in section 7 below.

[18] CTG 79.11 (Capt. Coward) Report of Night Action in Surigao Strait, 12 Nov. 1944. The writer is indebted to Cdrs. W. R. Cox and C. K. Bergin, captains of destroyers *McGowan* and *Monssen* respectively, for their help in gathering material and to Capt. Coward for reading first draft. Details from *War College Analysis* V 23–5, 54, 68, 79–80, 92.

were not air-conditioned. The skippers were worried about their fuel which, owing to their activity during the past few days, was down to 45 per cent capacity.

A few minutes later, at 0026, the first contact report on Nishimura from the PTs reached Admiral Oldendorf, and at 0038 he received a second contact report on Shima and knew that he had to deal with two enemy columns, widely spaced. At 0107 word was received from *PT–523* (relayed from *PT–134*) of star shell seen 10 miles west of Panaon Island – Nishimura's two groups making rendezvous. And at 0200, Oldendorf heard directly from *PT–134* that she had seen a ship proceeding up Surigao Strait with the blunt southern end of Panaon Island abeam. These reports were passed promptly to Captain Coward: the enemy was now about 30 miles south of his patrol line.

Captain Coward planned an "anvil" attack by two groups: the western composed of *McDermut* and *Monssen* [19] with Commander Richard H. Phillips of Desdiv 108 as O.T.C., and the eastern composed of *Remey*, *McGowan* and *Melvin* with himself in command. The remaining two destroyers of his squadron were left on picket patrol between Desolation Point and Homonhon Island, an entrance to the Gulf that had to be covered in case another enemy force attempted to approach that way. The captain announced that attack speed would be 30 knots and that individual target plan with intermediate speed setting would be used in firing torpedoes.[20] After launching the attack, Coward proposed to retire close under the land in order to keep out of the way of friendly forces, with which he was determined not to mix. And he also ordered his squadron to "use 'fish' only." It is the natural inclination to shoot off everything you have when face to face with the enemy, but Cow-

[19] The first *Monssen* commissioned 1940 was a 1630-ton destroyer lost in the Battle of Savo Island. The *Monssen* in this account was a 2050-ton *Fletcher* class commissioned in 1944.

[20] When firing torpedoes, the individual target plan means that each ship launches torpedoes independently of the others and that she aims at her opposite number in the column that shows on her radar screen. Intermediate speed setting, 33½ knots, presupposes the attacking destroyer is nearer the enemy than if a low speed setting is used. The ideal target angle for firing torpedoes was then 40 to 60 degrees, and ideal range 6000 yards.

ard knew that shooting would merely disclose his position and that his 5-inch shell would not stop a battleship. He intended to use his destroyers in the classic manner, to launch an offensive torpedo attack before heavy ships came within gunfire range. The Naval War College in Newport had been preaching this doctrine for years, but it had seldom been practiced in World War II and never quite "clicked."

A deliberate and well-anticipated night attack is far more exacting on the nerves than a surprise engagement. All hands were served coffee and sandwiches after midnight, and all took turns "caulking off." At 0206 Captain Coward ordered his five destroyers to General Quarters. *Remey*, *McGowan* and *Melvin* on the eastern side, *McDermut* and *Monssen* on the western side, formed two columns. *McGowan* and *Melvin* got the word "follow me" from Coward at 0230, and started south at 20 knots. Commander Phillips already had his western group headed south on course 170°. Shortly after they got going, a typical before-the-battle speech was given by the skipper of *Monssen* over the public-address system: "To all hands. This is the Captain. We are going into battle. I know each of you will do his duty. I promise you that I will do my duty to you and for our country. Good luck to you, and may God be with us."

At 0240 *McGowan* reported "Skunk 184°, 18 miles." That was the enemy. By 0245 the "skunk" had resolved itself on the radar screen into a column steering due north, distant 15 miles.[21]

Admiral Nishimura had almost completed a change from approach to battle formation, when his column would be headed by the four destroyers, followed by flagship *Yamashiro* and, at one-kilometer intervals, by *Fuso* and *Mogami*. The last half-hour of his cruise, since chasing off McElfresh's three motor torpedo boats, had been uneventful. There was no sound but the swishing of water alongside and the drafts from the engines within. Perhaps the Admiral and his men hoped to enter the Gulf with no further

[21] *McGowan* Action Report, Enclosure J; *Melvin* picked it up at 0242 at 33,400 yards. Nishimura was actually making 20 knots but there was a 2½ knot current against him.

trouble. If so, they learned better at 0256 when the cat-eyed lookouts in *Shigure* reported three ships (Coward's division) distant 8 kilometers – 4.3 miles.[22] *Yamashiro* snapped open the shutters on her biggest searchlight and swept ahead, but her enemy was then too far away to be caught in the beam.

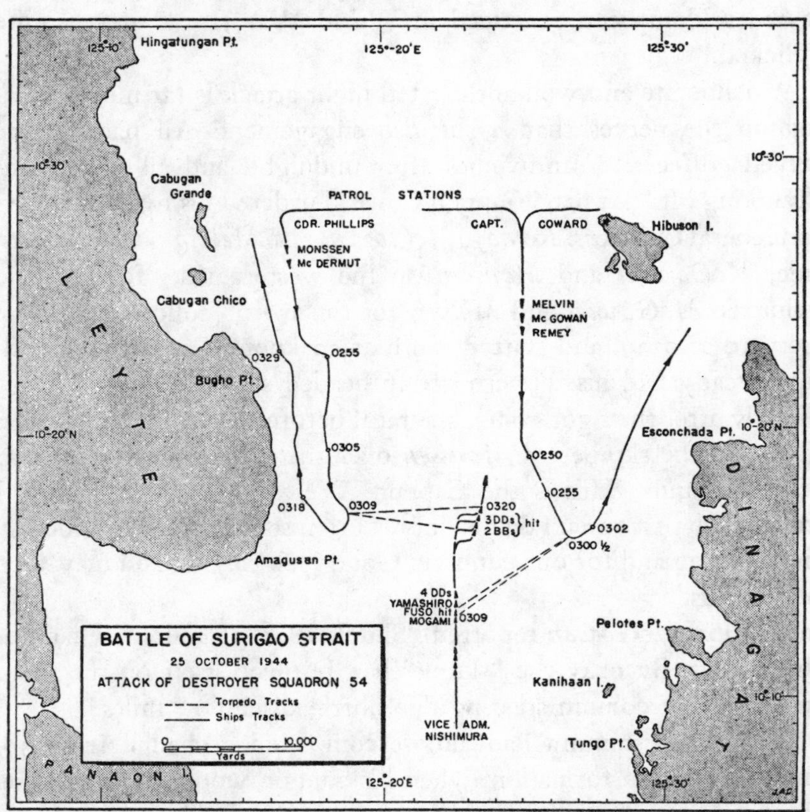

Not for long, however. Coward was closing Nishimura at 45 knots, and at 0250 he began turning his column left to course 150° in order to obtain a good target angle. Commander Phillips in *McDermut* with *Monssen,* steaming close aboard Leyte for protection from radar detection, got the enemy on his screens at 0254. He planned, when the right moment came, to turn his column to-

[22] *War College Analysis* V 126.

wards the enemy and reach a torpedo firing point 50 degrees on his bow, distant 7500 yards. Coward, on the other hand, was steaming in midstrait, almost head-on.[23] The squadron commander planned to turn his column in three successive movements to 120° before firing torpedoes, and at 0257 he so ordered, adding "I will take first target, you and *Melvin* take second; Comdesdiv 108 (Phillips) take small one and also No. 3."

Visibility now slightly improved. Lookouts on *Melvin* at 0258 sighted Nishimura's ships. Range was then 12,800 yards. Coward immediately ordered funnel smoke, turned column left as planned, gave the order "Fire when ready" and bent on 30 knots. At half a minute after three o'clock, *Remey*, *McGowan* and *Melvin* commenced launching torpedoes. Their ranges to the target were then estimated to be from 8200 to 9300 yards. A large, bright searchlight illuminated *Remey*, making her crew feel "like animals in a cage." In about 75 seconds 27 torpedoes left these three destroyers. With eight minutes to wait before the results could be known, Coward swung hard to port and retired on base course 21°, each destroyer making smoke and zigzagging independently. When they were still making the turn, they came under fire by *Yamashiro* and the enemy destroyers. By 0305, salvos of 5-inch shell were falling all around Coward's ships. The searchlight was no longer seen, but enemy star shell was being exploded liberally overhead. With a 35-knot speed, the United States destroyers quickly drew out of gunfire range and sustained not one hit, not even a near-miss.

Admiral Nishimura should have guessed that his enemy had fired torpedoes but he took no evasive action. Between 0308 and 0309, two to five explosions – not gunfire – were seen in the direction of the target from Coward's rapidly retiring destroyers. Shortly thereafter, the largest ship in the enemy van was seen to slow down and sheer out to starboard. This was *Fuso*, hit by a torpedo from *Melvin*. Nishimura did not observe this, and apparently nobody

[23] He accepted the risk of radar detection because he counted on the Japanese following a due north course when entering the Strait, and had to anticipate that, when halfway through, they might turn left in order to cut a corner toward Leyte Gulf.

cared to tell him the unpleasant news, as he continued sending orders to the stricken battleship as if she were still in column.

Now let us shift our attention to Commander Phillips's division, to *McDermut* and *Monssen*. At 0256 they picked up the enemy by radar, distant 29,700 yards. At 0302 they were still steaming due south, about 3500 yards off the Leyte shore, when Phillips received word that Coward's division had fired torpedoes and was retiring. Phillips maintained course, paralleling the enemy's in the opposite direction, until 0308 when he swung 50 degrees towards the target to course 130° in order to bring his destroyers to the planned firing point. At that moment the enemy opened fire on *Monssen*. Six salvos landed short or over in the next three minutes. Commander Bergin promptly brought his ship left, in order to be on *McDermut's* port quarter when firing torpedoes, thus to avoid the possibility of being blanketed or delayed at the firing point. This maneuver also closed range toward the enemy. At 0309 *McDermut* and *Monssen* swung back to course due S, and a minute later Commander Phillips ordered torpedoes to be fired when ready. The word was hardly out of his mouth when *McDermut* began launching, and *Monssen* followed at 0311. This time, Nishimura did take evasive action, two simultaneous right-angle turns, which had the effect of bringing his screen right into the track of Phillips's torpedoes. At 0320 *Monssen* and *McDermut* observed a most welcome sight, the flashes of explosions. After the war it was ascertained that *McDermut* hit no fewer than three destroyers – *Yamagumo*, *Michishio* and *Asagumo* – of which the first immediately blew up and sank, the second was placed in a sinking condition, and the third had her bow blown off, but was able to retire. *Monssen* made a torpedo hit on battleship *Yamashiro* but failed to stop her.

The two destroyers had already swung sharp right (westerly) to retire. *McDermut* now sighted two PTs between herself and the shore and promptly turned north, warning the boats twice not to fire, which they were overheard requesting permission to do. At that moment a bright green light appeared in the direction of Leyte, probably a parachute flare dropped by a plane, whether friendly or enemy we cannot tell; the Japanese, who also observed it, were equally puzzled. A searchlight beam found *Monssen,* and shells began to drop so close aboard her and *McDermut* as to splash water over their after guns. Both destroyers made smoke to the best of their ability, and took a quick zig toward the enemy, masking the green light to the great joy of all hands, and also getting out of the searchlight beam.

Captain Coward was certain that he had scored on at least three ships with the 47 torpedoes fired from his two divisions. Actually he scored on five and sank three, including *Fuso* which went down later. "Brilliantly conceived and well executed," was Admiral Oldendorf's opinion of this torpedo attack.

Admiral Nishimura now knew he was in for it. At 0330, after passing disabled *Michishio* and *Asagumo,* he sent off his last radio message, to Admirals Kurita and Shima: –

> Urgent Battle Report No. 2. Enemy torpedo boats and destroyers present on both sides of northern entrance to Surigao Strait. Two of our destroyers torpedoed and drifting. *Yamashiro* sustained one torpedo hit but no impediment to battle cruising.[24]

4. *Right and Left Flank Destroyers Attack,*[25] *0254–0420*

Only ten minutes after the Japanese absorbed a spread of torpedoes from *Monssen* and *McDermut,* they were subjected to a similar attack from Desron 24, the right flank destroyers under Captain McManes.

At 0254, as Coward and Phillips were getting set to launch torpedoes, Rear Admiral Berkey, commanding the right flank, directed McManes by voice radio: "When released, attack in two groups. . . . Until then, stay close to land." And, at 0302, "Pro-

[24] *War College Analysis* V 206, quoting WDC 161,005.

[25] Capt. McManes Action Report 30 Oct.; Rear Adm. Berkey Action Report 10 Nov. 1944 with good track chart; *War College Analysis* V 156, 208, 268–71.

ceed to attack, follow down west shore line, follow other groups in and return northward, make smoke."

Five of McManes's destroyers were 2100-tonners and *Hutchins*, wearing the Captain's pennant, was the first of her class to have a Combat Information Center below decks. It worked beautifully, providing not only information to the squadron and group commanders, but full gunnery and torpedo information to the ship. McManes directed the battle from C.I.C. instead of, as tradition required, from the bridge; an excellent decision, since thus he was not disconcerted by his own ship's gunfire.

Squadron 24 steamed south in two sections: the first consisting of *Hutchins*, *Daly* and *Bache;* the second of H.M.A.S. *Arunta*,[26] followed by *Killen* and *Beale*. This section, whose O.T.C. was Commander A. E. Buchanan RAN, heard from Captain McManes at 0317; "Boil up! Make smoke! Let me know when you have fired." [27] Two minutes later destroyer *Yamagumo*, hit by a torpedo from *McDermut*, exploded and illuminated the scene beautifully for Commander Buchanan's attack.

At 0323 *Arunta* fired four torpedoes at *Shigure*, leading the enemy column, from a point about three miles northeast of the spot whence Phillips had launched 15 minutes earlier. The range was 6500 yards, but all four missed. *Killen* at 0325 launched five torpedoes at *Yamashiro*, range 8700 yards; one of them hit and slowed her temporarily to 5 knots but did not stop her. A quarter of a minute later *Beale* launched five torpedoes, range 6800 yards. Every one missed.

McManes's own section bent on 25 knots, continued south to a point off Amagusan Point, reversed course to north and fired 15 torpedoes at Nishimura's force between 0329 and 0336, at ranges between 8200 to 10,700 yards. Immediately after launching, two torpedo wakes were seen to cross *Daly's* bows; we do not know which Japanese ship was responsible. *Bache* also opened with gun-

[26] H.M.A.S. *Arunta* was of the Tribal class, built at Sydney 1940; she displaced 1870 tons and was armed with six 4.7-inch 50 cal.; *Hutchins* and the others displaced 2050 tons and were armed with five 5-inch 38 cal.

[27] *War College Analysis* V 156.

fire on the enemy, who replied with inaccurate salvos. After steaming in a complete loop, McManes at 0344 commenced a wide turn to the east and north in order to close range. In Nishimura's column *Yamashiro* had now built up speed to 15 knots and was steering

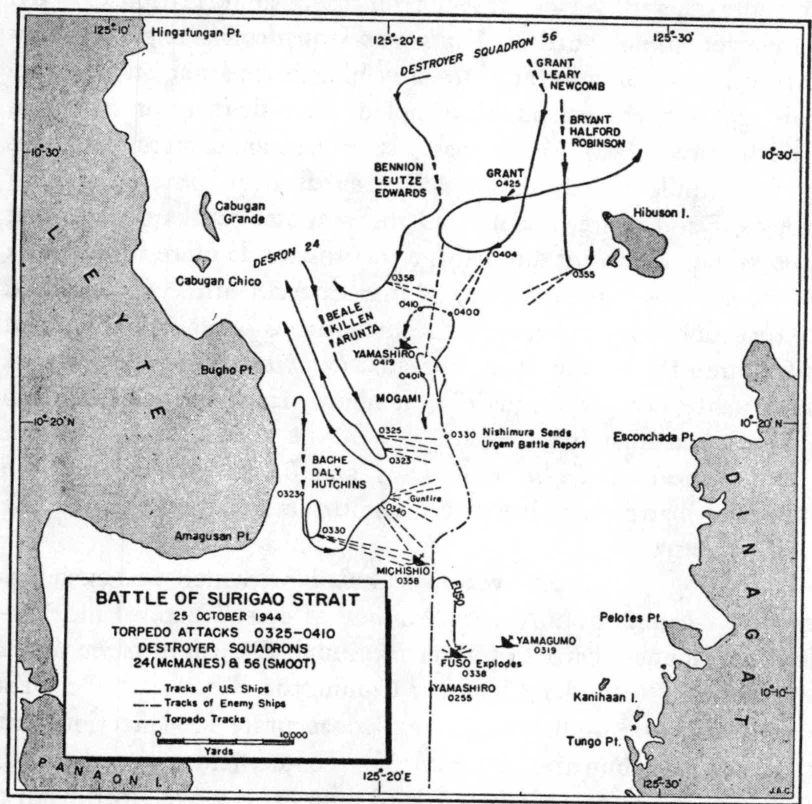

340°, about N by W; *Mogami* was making 20 knots due north, and *Shigure*, 26 knots. All three of McManes's destroyers opened gunfire at 0340 on two damaged Japanese destroyers, presumably *Michishio* and *Asagumo*, which were trying to retire.

In a brisk destroyer action, the time it takes for torpedoes to make their run seems interminable. *Hutchins*, *Daly* and *Bache*, since launching theirs, had been under fire for twelve minutes, had executed one 180-degree turn and were about to make another when, at 0344, three large explosions were heard and round balls of orange flame were seen. These may have been the result of *Fuso* blowing up,[28] but were probably flashes from *Yamashiro's* guns.

The picture of the enemy on McManes's radarscopes was now decidedly ragged, very different from the neat formation Coward had viewed an hour earlier. *Yamashiro* was pressing imperturbably northward but *Shigure* and *Mogami* had sheered out on her starboard quarter; the others, all crippled, were drifting or trying to retire southward. McManes was just preparing to press his attack on the cripples when Admiral Berkey at 0349 ordered him to knock off and retire, lest he foul the range of the battleships and cruisers; but *Hutchins* did manage to launch five more torpedoes a minute later at *Asagumo*. She had just started a turn, which caused the torpedoes to miss her well ahead; but meanwhile *Michishio* had drifted into the course of the spread. *Hutchins's* torpedoes hit that unfortunate destroyer squarely, at about 0358, and she blew up and sank immediately.

In the meantime, *Hutchins, Daly* and *Bache* were firing with their main batteries at heavy cruiser *Mogami*, which was turning south to retire.

In retiring, McManes overtook *Yamashiro*, which was exchanging major-caliber gunfire with Admiral Weyler's Battle Line. The doomed Japanese battleship took *Hutchins, Daly* and *Bache* under fire with her secondary battery. Commander Visser of *Daly* reported that one of her salvos was so accurate in deflection that its tracer gave him the sensation of a center fielder on a baseball diamond waiting for a fly ball to land right in his glove. Fortunately, the salvo was an over – and Visser did not jump for the ball. *Hutchins*, too, was near-missed. She ceased fire at 0400, observing that the light cruisers' fire on her targets was "more than adequate." *Daly* carried on until 0405½. Rear Admiral Berkey, who had followed McManes's movement with "gratification and comfort," was now taking over the fight on the American right flank.

[28] *Fuso* blew into two halves, which drifted slowly southward; the bow part sank around 0420 and the stern within an hour.

Admiral Oldendorf still had another destroyer squadron to throw at Nishimura before opening gunfire. This was Captain Smoot's Destroyer Squadron 56, which had the duty of screening the left flank cruisers. At 0335, before McManes's final torpedo attack, Smoot got the word: "Launch attack – get the big boys!" [29]

The squadron deployed, Captain Smoot's Section 1 (*Albert W. Grant, Richard P. Leary* and *Newcomb*) and Captain Conley's Section 2 (*Bryant, Halford, Robinson*) passing east, and Commander Boulware's Section 3 (*Bennion, Leutze, Heywood L. Edwards*) west of the left flank cruisers. The exact areas from which each section should attack had been predetermined. They steamed southward, speed 25 knots, approaching the enemy column on both bows. At 0345 Captain Conley, having reached his allotted firing area and observing a glow on the southern horizon which he believed to be enemy gun flashes, signaled: "This has to be quick. Stand by your fish." The Japanese observed him and opened fire at 0351, but the splashes fell so short and wide that counterfire was withheld lest gun flashes give away his position. Conley's three destroyers fired five torpedoes each between 0354 and 0359, ranges 8380 to 9000 yards. All missed. The section then retired close to Hibuson Island.

Commander Boulware's Section 3 fired torpedoes between 0357 and 0359 – range 7800 to 8000 yards – at *Shigure* and *Yamashiro*. The former escaped by a radical turn from 010° to 185°. She possibly, and the battleship certainly, took *Edwards, Bennion* and *Leutze* under gunfire at the moment of launching torpedoes and the shell splashes chased them as they turned toward Leyte and retired under smoke. No hits were scored by either side.

Captain Smoot's own Section 1 ran into trouble. His plan was to attack the enemy from dead ahead, right in the center of the Strait. At 0400, as he was evaluating the target on his radar screen and making sure it was not Coward, *Yamashiro* slowed down and turned from a northerly to a westerly course. Smoot's destroyers

[29] Capt. Smoot and Capt. Conley Action Reports 29 and 31 Oct.; *War College Analysis* V 240, 351–2.

turned right to parallel the battleship, and at 0404 commenced launching torpedoes (*Leary* three, *Newcomb* and *Grant* five each) from a range of 6200 yards. Of *Newcomb's* torpedoes, it is believed that at least one scored. Two large explosions were observed on *Yamashiro* at 0411½, the exact moment when her "fish" should have found their mark; and a Japanese warrant officer who survived reported that the battleship took four torpedo hits, of which we have accounted for only two in the earlier destroyer attacks.

Since the main gunfire action had now been going on for almost fifteen minutes, an assortment of projectiles arched over *Newcomb*, *Leary* and *Grant* from both contending forces. Captain Smoot was not too busy to observe the gorgeous pyrotechnic display. As the enemy gave him considerable attention, he ordered retirement northward immediately after firing torpedoes. *Newcomb* and *Leary* made their getaway successfully, shells from both sides falling all around them; but the rear destroyer, *Albert W. Grant*, was hit at 0407, just as she started to turn. Realizing that she was to be the goat, she launched all remaining torpedoes toward the enemy and made best possible speed. But she absorbed 18 more hits – eleven of them 6-inch from a "friendly" light cruiser and the others 4.7-inch from the enemy – and by 0420 lay dead in the water. Thirty-four officers and enlisted men were killed or missing and 94 were wounded, the skipper (Commander Nisewaner) himself going below to pull wounded men from the oil-soaked, burning engine-room.

Captain Smoot ordered *Newcomb* to lash herself alongside *Grant* and haul her clear. She was saved, and repaired in time to take part in the Okinawa operation.

The torpedo attacks in this battle were some of the best of the entire Pacific war, and that of Phillips's division may well be considered the most successful. It would be difficult to make a comparison of these destroyer commanders with Arleigh Burke and Moosbrugger; but they were certainly in the same class. Coward and McManes have been criticized for launching torpedoes at long range with poor target angles, instead of closing to the most effective firing points. But in so narrow a strait they had to be careful to avoid running aground or firing on friendly forces, and their collective efforts accounted for about 75 per cent of the fire power in Nishimura's force. Not one of their ships sustained a casualty, or even a scratch. Captain Smoot pressed his attack admirably close, which is the main reason why his squadron was the only one to suffer.

5. *The Major Gunfire Phase,*[30] *0351–0410 October 25*

While these torpedo attacks were being delivered, Battle Line and the two cruiser groups were waiting for the enemy to come within range. Shortly after 0230 General Quarters was sounded. Flares from torpedo hits were visible from 0320 on.

At 0330 all three task groups were near the western side of the Strait, steaming east. Nearest Leyte was the right flank, Admiral Berkey's two light cruisers and H.M.A.S. *Shropshire.* About six miles east of his formation were the three heavy and two light cruisers of Admiral Oldendorf's left flank. *West Virginia,* leading Battle Line, lay about four miles north of *Louisville* and five miles or more northeast of *Phoenix.*

This situation was an answer to the prayers of a War College strategist or a gunnery tactician. The enemy column, now reduced to one battleship, one heavy cruiser and one destroyer, was steaming into a trap. It was a very short vertical to a very broad T, but Oldendorf was about to cap it, as Togo had done to Rozhdestvensky in 1905 at the Battle of Tsushima Strait, and as thousands of naval officers had since hoped to accomplish.

At 0323, radar screens registered the enemy disposition. Ten minutes later – the range then being 33,000 yards – Admiral Weyler made signal to Battle Line to open fire at 26,000 yards, believing that if he waited longer his ships would lose their initial advantage

[30] *War College Analysis* V 293–7, 321, 330–5, 372; Capt. S. H. Hurt "Battle for Leyte Gulf, Staff Presentation to ANSCOL" (Naval War College, 27 Aug. 1945); conversations with Rear Adm. Oldendorf, Capt. R. W. Bates, Capt. Hurt of *Louisville,* Capt. J. B. Heffernan of *Tennessee,* in 1944–6.

of having five salvos of armor-piercing ammunition immediately available. Admiral Oldendorf ordered all cruisers to open fire at 0351 when *Louisville's* range to the nearest target was 15,600 yards. They promptly complied, and at 0353 Battle Line joined in, range 22,800 yards. Five of these six battleships had been hit or sunk in the Pearl Harbor attack of 7 December 1941. They had been getting their revenge only by installments – this was *Tennessee's* eleventh operation since Pearl – but the payoff was only a few minutes away.

Yamashiro slowed to 12 knots at 0352 but continued on course 20° for seven minutes, firing at visible targets, for she had no fire control radar. Nishimura was steaming boldly into a terrific concentration of gunfire, supported only by heavy cruiser *Mogami* astern and destroyer *Shigure* on his starboard quarter. His last message was to *Fuso* at 0352, asking her to make top speed. There was no reply from that sinking battleship, and as "all hell broke loose" just then, Nishimura never informed Shima what was happening; Commander Second Striking Force had to find that out for himself.

West Virginia, *Tennessee* and *California*, equipped with the newest Mark-8 fire control radar, had a firing solution in main battery plot and were ready to shoot long before the enemy came within range. These three were responsible for most of the battle line action. *West Virginia* opened fire at 0353, and got off 93 rounds of 16-inch AP before checking. *Tennessee* and *California*, starting at 0355, shot 69 and 63 rounds of 14-inch AP respectively, fired in six-gun salvos so as to conserve their limited supply. The other three battleships, equipped with Mark-3 fire control radar, had difficulty finding a target. *Maryland* picked it up by ranging on *West Virginia's* splashes and got off 48 rounds of 16-inch in six salvos, starting at one minute before 0400. *Mississippi* fired a single salvo and *Pennsylvania* never managed to locate a target and took no part in the action.[31]

[31] *Pennsylvania* was censured for failing to fire by the division commander, Rear Adm. T. E. Chandler, who was particularly well pleased with the work of *Tennes-*

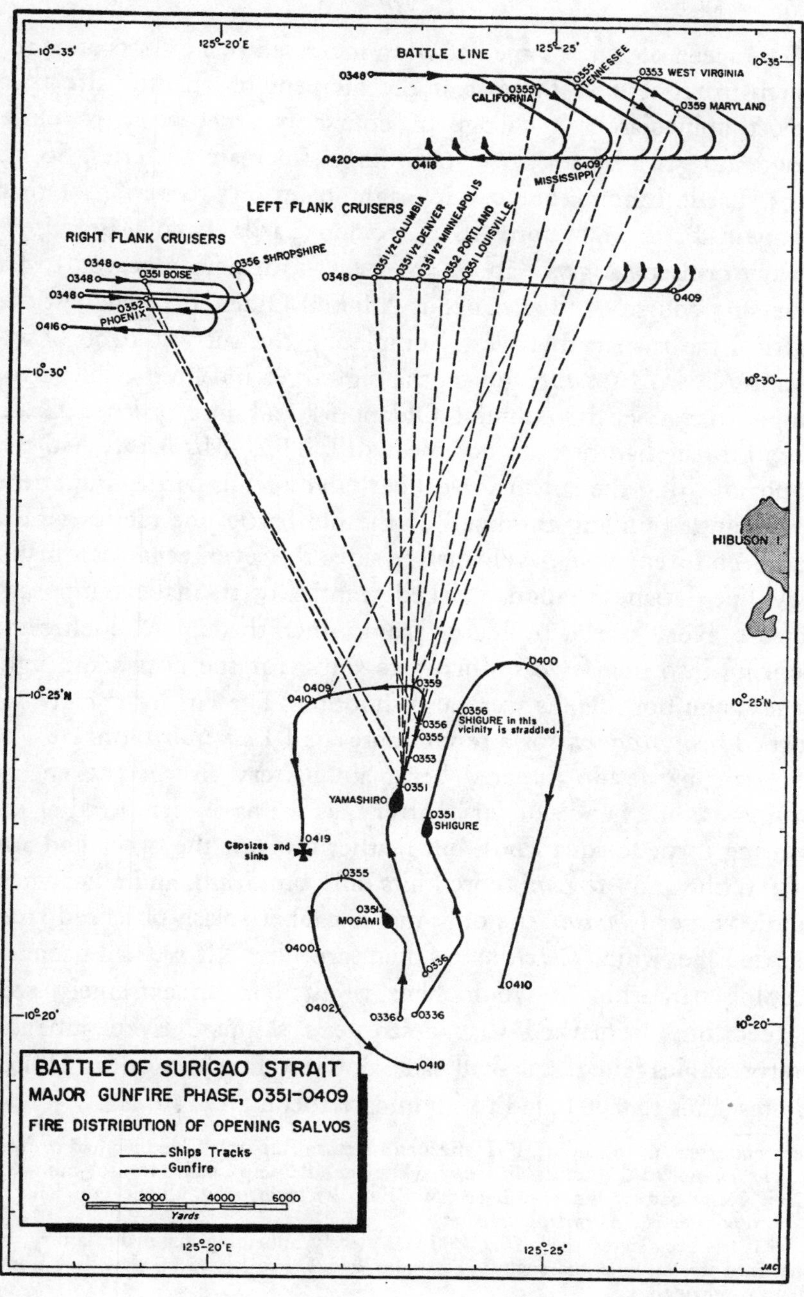

10°-35'
125°-20'E
125°-25'
BATTLE LINE
0348
0355
CALIFORNIA
0355 TENNESSEE
0353 WEST VIRGINIA
0359 MARYLAND
0420
0418
0409
MISSISSIPPI
LEFT FLANK CRUISERS
0351 1/2 COLUMBIA
0351 1/2 DENVER
0351 1/2 MINNEAPOLIS
0352 PORTLAND
0351 LOUISVILLE
0348
0409
RIGHT FLANK CRUISERS
0348
0356 SHROPSHIRE
0348
0351 BOISE
0348
0352
PHOENIX
0416
10°-30'
HIBUSON I.
10°-25'N
0409
0410
0359
0356
0355
0353
0351
0400
0356
SHIGURE in this vicinity is straddled.
YAMASHIRO
0351
SHIGURE
0419
Capsizes and sinks
0355
0351
MOGAMI
0400
0336
0402
0336
0336
0410
10°-20'
0410
BATTLE OF SURIGAO STRAIT
MAJOR GUNFIRE PHASE, 0351-0409
FIRE DISTRIBUTION OF OPENING SALVOS
Ships Tracks
Gunfire
0
2000
4000
6000
Yards
125°-20'E
125°-25'
JAC

The speed of Battle Line had been increased to 15 knots at 0329, which brought it so far east at the moment of opening fire that almost immediately a change of course was necessary to close range and get a better turret train angle for main batteries. So, at 0355, Battle Line executed ships right from 90° to 120°. At that moment *Yamashiro* bore 192°, 20,990 yards from *Mississippi.* Heavy cruiser *Mogami,* about 3000 yards further, appeared to be reversing course. And at 0402, at Admiral Oldendorf's suggestion, Battle Line turned due west, completing the turn at 0406. Two minutes later *Mississippi* got on the big target and fired a full salvo, range 19,790 yards. Admiral Oldendorf had just ordered Cease Fire, but she had not yet got the word. Thus, *Mississippi* had the honor of firing the last major-caliber salvo of this battle; and at the same time, sounding the knell of the old battle line tactics which had been foremost in naval warfare since the seventeenth century.[32]

While Japanese sailors worked frantically to make temporary repairs, every size of projectile from 6-inch through 16-inch came pouring into their two unfortunate ships; for the heavy and light cruisers on both flanks were also shooting. The enemy gamely returned fire, *Mogami* for a few minutes and *Yamashiro* longer. The Japanese battleship directed her main battery fire at the enemy cruisers, while her secondary battery, as we have seen, fired at the retiring torpedo squadrons; but neither one nor the other had any effect. She and *Mogami* scored hits only on *Grant,* and a near-miss on destroyer *Claxton,* the only major-caliber splash observed from Battle Line, which *Claxton* was then screening. "If we had been the leading battleship, it would have resulted in an extremely well placed hit," remarked that destroyer's skipper. Even Japanese pyrotechnics failed; star shell came down so far short of the United States ships that it failed to illuminate them.

---

see (endorsement to Capt. J. B. Heffernan's Action Report). Chandler had ordered *Tennessee* not to fire until *Mississippi* (Weyler's flagship) had done so; but when Capt. Heffernan's gunnery officer saw *West Virginia* open up, he conveniently "mistook" her for *Mississippi* and let fly.

[32] It has been stated that *Mississippi* was merely unloading her main battery, but she fired this salvo at the enemy. The gunners were so keyed up that they immediately reloaded.

On the left flank, *Denver* commenced firing at 0351 at a range of 15,800 yards; within a minute *Minneapolis*, *Columbia* and *Portland* followed. These cruisers contributed materially to the weight of gunfire on *Yamashiro*. At 0358 *Portland* shifted fire to *Mogami*, then trying to retire, and *Denver* attempted to stop the lively and elusive destroyer *Shigure*, but probably hit friendly *Albert W. Grant* instead. *Louisville* also tossed salvos at the unfortunate *Grant*, and fortunately missed. In return, these cruisers received most of such attention as the enemy was in a position to give. *Denver*, *Columbia* and *Minneapolis* were straddled by 8-inch or larger splashes. The left flank cruisers, after shooting the fantastic total of 3100 rounds,[33] obeyed Oldendorf's order to check fire at 0409, reversed course to port, and commenced a westerly run.

In the meantime "Count" Berkey's two right flank light cruisers, *Phoenix* and *Boise*, were adding to the assortment of hardware falling on hapless *Yamashiro*, their opening range being 16,600 yards. *Phoenix* fired 15-gun salvos at quarter-minute intervals; *Boise* went to continuous rapid fire at 0353, but was ordered by Berkey to "fire slow and deliberate" to save bullets. Flashless powder was used, and the easterly night breeze on the cruisers' bows was just strong enough to clear smoke between salvos and render optical spotting and visual observation possible. Large, bright flashes of explosions were seen on *Yamashiro's* decks and the cruisers believed that they were responsible. Their Australian companion, *Shropshire*, was having trouble with fire control radar and did not commence firing her 8-inch guns until 0356, and then did so slowly and deliberately. One minute later the two United States cruisers checked fire when the formation turned right to begin a westerly run. *Shropshire* continued shooting during the turn, and, as enemy salvos fell near her, commenced rapid fire; the other two resumed firing at 0400.[34]

[33] *Columbia* alone fired 1147 rounds in 18 minutes, which meant the equivalent of a full 12-gun salvo every 12 seconds.

[34] The three right flank cruisers shot off 1077 rounds AP and 104 rounds HC in this action, before they ceased fire at 0408 on intercepting a message from Capt. Smoot that he was being fired upon.

At that moment, when eight bells marked the end of the eventful midwatch and the beginning of the morning watch, several things happened. *Yamashiro,* which had been zigzagging in a northerly direction during the last ten minutes, firing doggedly and, absorbing numerous hits, straightened out on a W by S course.[35] She was burning so brightly that even her 5-inch mounts stood out against flames which seemed to arise from her entire length. Heavy cruiser *Mogami* had already turned south to retire; Nishimura's only surviving destroyer, *Shigure*, which had sheered out eastward, turned at 0356 when she was within sight of Hibuson Island. She received but one hit, an 8-inch AP which failed to explode, but a multitude of near-misses knocked out her gyrocompass and radio. For want of radar she was unable to locate her enemy and missed a golden opportunity to launch torpedoes.

Battle Line, as we have seen, changed course from 120° to 270° at 0402 by simultaneous turns, and continued to fire as it steered west.[36] Right flank cruisers followed suit; left flank kept on westward. Since this maneuver closed the battleships' range, the volume of fire became even greater and more accurate.

"The devastating accuracy of this gunfire," reported Captain Smoot, who was in a good position to observe, "was the most beautiful sight I have ever witnessed. The arched line of tracers in the darkness looked like a continual stream of lighted railroad cars going over a hill. No target could be observed at first; then shortly there would be fires and explosions, and another ship would be accounted for."

This show did not long continue. At 0409 Admiral Oldendorf, on receiving word that *Grant* and her sisters were being hit by "friendlies," ordered all ships to cease fire, in order to give the destroyers time to retire. Admiral Nishimura and the officers and

[35] Track in *Monssen* Action Report; *War College Analysis* V 294–5.

[36] *California* misinterpreted the signal, although it was not coded. Commander Battle Line telephoned, "Turn One Five," which is the usual manner of saying, "Turn 150°", but this was reported to *California's* skipper as a "change course 15°." Combatdiv 2 (R. Adm. Chandler) Action Report, p. 11. *California* naturally went astray at the turn and fouled *Tennessee's* line of fire for about five minutes. A collision was avoided only by *Tennessee* backing all engines full speed.

crew of *Yamashiro* must have regarded this cease-fire as God's gift to the Emperor. In spite of the punishment their battleship had been taking, she increased speed to 15 knots, turned 90 degrees left, and began to retire southward. But she had less than ten minutes to live. At 0419 she capsized and sank, taking down Admiral Nishimura and all but a few members of the crew, who when recovered were too dazed or defiant to contribute any details about the end of their gallant ship.[37]

Heavy cruiser *Mogami*, whose capacity for absorbing punishment exceeded even that of *Yamashiro*, turned left at 0353 when the shooting began, launched torpedoes at 0401, and at the same time was taken under gunfire from Captain McManes's destroyers to the southwestward. She caught fire at 0356, turned south to retire, increased speed and made smoke, but received many more hits. At 0402 a salvo, probably from cruiser *Portland*, exploded on the bridge, killing the C.O., the exec., and all other officers present; other hits were scored in engine and firerooms and she slowed almost to a stop.[38]

At 0413, during the unearthly silence that followed the check-fire, destroyer *Richard P. Leary* reported torpedoes overtaking and passing her close aboard. These had been fired by *Mogami* just before she retired. As *Leary* was then headed north and only 11,000 yards from Battle Line, whose experience counseled a healthy respect for Japanese "fish," Admiral Weyler ordered *Mississippi*, *Maryland* and *West Virginia* to turn due north, away from the enemy, at 0418. Admiral Chandler conducted the other battleships westward. The northward turn took half of Battle Line out of the fight, for when Admiral Oldendorf ordered all ships to resume fire at 0419, no target was left on their radar screens; *Mogami* was too far distant and *Yamashiro* had gone down. Nor were the cruisers able to find targets. The ten minutes' grace accorded by the American check-fire allowed *Shigure* and *Mogami* to escape.

Even so, by twenty minutes after four on 25 October, with only

[37] Position lat. 10°22.3′ N, long. 125°21.3′ E.
[38] *War College Analysis* V 297.

another twenty minutes to go before the first glimmerings of dawn appeared over Dinagat Island, Nishimura's force, which had counted on being off Dulag by that time, was done for. Of the two battleships only the burning stern of *Fuso* was still afloat, three destroyers were sunk or stopped by torpedoes in mid-strait, a badly damaged heavy cruiser and a damaged destroyer were retiring. And there was no consolation for the vanquished in having damaged the victors; for of Admiral Oldendorf's force only destroyer *Grant* had been hit, and that mostly by her own side.

Admiral Shima's Second Striking Force had not yet been heard from.

6. *Shima Fires and Falls Back, 0353–0455*[39]

In the last chapter we left Vice Admiral Shima's Second Striking Force in the Mindanao Sea, making 22 knots to enter Leyte Gulf behind Vice Admiral Nishimura's Force "C." He had two heavy cruisers, *Nachi* and *Ashigara*, each carrying ten 8-inch guns and eight torpedo tubes, and each capable of making 36 knots. He had *Abukuma*, a three-piper light cruiser completed in 1925, flagship of Destroyer Squadron 1. She had the "Indian sign" on her as one of the ships that took part in the attack on Pearl Harbor; both she and *Nachi* had been in Admiral Hosogaya's force which "Soc" McMorris had defeated in the Battle of the Komandorskis.

At midnight Shima received a message from Nishimura that he was being attacked by motor torpedo boats. At that time Second Striking Force was west of Camiguin Island and about 40 miles astern of Nishimura.[40] Two destroyers abreast – two kilometers apart – led the column, consisting of the three cruisers and two other destroyers. At 0100 they observed gunfire flashes ahead, and

[39] *Mogami* Action Report; log of heavy cruiser *Nachi*, Admiral Shima's flagship, recovered from her wreck in Manila Bay (C.O. Seventh Fleet Intel. Center, Cdr. Henri deB. Claiborne, to Cominch 29 Apr. 1945); interrogation of Cdr. K. Mori of Shima's staff (*Inter. Jap. Off.* I 235); *War College Analysis* V 221, 303.

[40] See chart of MTB Patrol Lines, this Chapter, for this part of Shima's track.

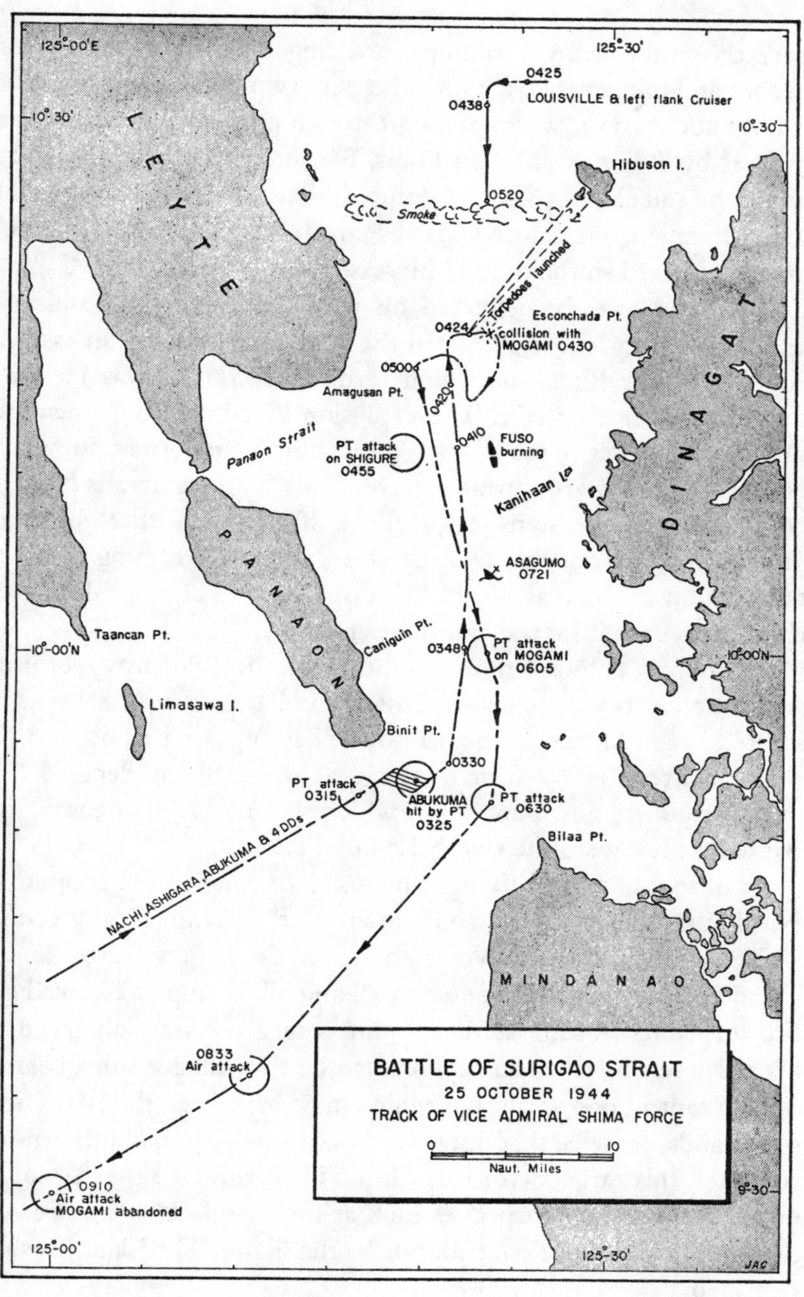
125°-00'E
125°-30'
10°-30'
10°-30'
0425
0438
LOUISVILLE & left flank Cruiser
L E Y T E
Hibuson I.
0520
Smoke
Torpedoes launched
Esconchada Pt.
0424
collision with MOGAMI 0430
0500
Amagusan Pt.
0420
D I N A G A T
Panaon Strait
0410
PT attack on SHIGURE 0455
FUSO burning
Kanihaan I.
P A N A O N
ASAGUMO 0721
Taancan Pt.
10°-00'N
Caniguin Pt.
0348
PT attack on MOGAMI 0605
10°-00'N
Limasawa I.
Binit Pt.
0330
PT attack 0315
ABUKUMA hit by PT 0325
PT attack 0630
Bilaa Pt.
NACHI, ASHIGARA, ABUKUMA & 4 DDs
M I N D A N A O
0833 Air attack
BATTLE OF SURIGAO STRAIT
25 OCTOBER 1944
TRACK OF VICE ADMIRAL SHIMA FORCE
0
10
Naut. Miles
0910 Air attack MOGAMI abandoned
9°-30'
125°-00'
125°-30'
JAC

over the radio heard Nishimura ordering his ships to avoid torpedoes and take evasive action. The next two hours were uneventful. At about 0315, when passing through a rain squall, they were fired at by *PT–134* off Binit Point, Panaon, and missed. By 0320, when the squall had passed, Admiral Shima, observing that his left wing destroyer was close aboard Panaon Island, ordered a simultaneous turn to starboard and increased speed to 26 knots. Captain Coward had already delivered his torpedo attack on Nishimura and was retiring. At 0325, when the disposition was on an easterly course to clear Binit Point, light cruiser *Abukuma* was hit by a torpedo on her port side. The explosion killed about 30 men and slowed the cruiser to ten knots. She fell out of the formation, which continued northward, turning to course 20° at 0330. It was *PT–137* commanded by Lieutenant (jg) I. M. Kovar USNR that got *Abukuma*. He was actually shooting at a destroyer steaming south to take station at the rear of Shima's disposition. The torpedo missed the destroyer, but hit the light cruiser.

As Shima's column, now consisting of the two heavy cruisers and four destroyers, came due north and turned up 28 knots, it sighted broad on the starboard bow what appeared to be two big ships on fire. Passing west of them, at 0410, Shima decided that they were *Fuso* and *Yamashiro*, which was not very encouraging. Actually they were the two halves of *Fuso*.

At 0420, Shima still thought he was hastening to the support of Nishimura, who had just gone down with his ship. Heavy cruiser *Ashigara* was astern of *Nachi;* the four destroyers were ranging ahead northwesterly on course 330°, and all six ships were ready to fire torpedoes as soon as they found a target. Shima observed on his radar screen what he supposed to be two enemy ships bearing 25°, distant 13,000 yards, but which must have been the two Hibuson Islands, at twice that distance. At 0424 he ordered both cruisers to attack this target with torpedoes. They turned right to course 90° and fired eight torpedoes each at the island. This was Second Striking Force's only contribution to the battle. The island was not damaged.

Shima now made a quick estimate of the situation. He did not know what had happened to Nishimura, but guessed the worst, and the heavy smoke made by American destroyers curtained his view northward. He decided to retire "temporarily" and await development of events. His four destroyers, which had now penetrated farther north than the cruisers without seeing anything to shoot at, were recalled about 0425. At the same time he sent a radio dispatch to Vice Admiral Mikawa and to all SHO forces, "This force has concluded its attack and is retiring from the battle area to plan subsequent action." Shima had unusual discretion for a Japanese admiral.

Presently burning *Mogami* was encountered. Believing her to be dead in the water, Captain Kanooka of *Nachi* turned to course 110° to clear, but *Mogami* was actually moving slowly south and the two heavy cruisers collided at 0430. *Nachi's* stern was badly damaged, there was some flooding and her speed was reduced to 18 knots. *Mogami*, miraculously, managed to turn up enough speed to fall in with Shima's column, now heading south at *Nachi's* best speed. And Shima ordered *Shigure* to join. She had some difficulty in so doing as her steering engine was out of order. She ran afoul of Lieutenant Gleason's MTB section at 0455, attacked, and made one slight hit on *PT-321*.

Thus, by five in the morning on 25 October, with an hour and a half to go before sunrise, the Japanese Southern Force was broken up and in retreat. Battleships *Fuso* and *Yamashiro* had been sunk in the middle of the Strait; destroyers *Yamagumo* and *Michishio* had gone the same way, and of Nishimura's force only lucky *Mogami*, swift *Shigure* and crippled *Asagumo* had so far escaped.

But Shima's two heavy cruisers and four destroyers, which had not been brought under American gunfire or torpedo attack, retired safely.

There were plenty of pickings left for the pursuit phase of the battle.

7. *Pursuit and Mop-up, 0430 October 25–November 5*

This pursuit phase of the battle commenced at 0433 when Admiral Hayler reported to Admiral Oldendorf that his radar screen showed three enemy ships (*Nachi, Ashigara, Mogami*) retiring southward, distance 14 miles, and Oldendorf ordered Destroyer Division X-ray to attack with torpedoes. "Oley" had already headed down the middle of the Strait in *Louisville*, followed in column by the other left flank cruisers and screened by Captain Smoot's destroyers.[41] He ordered right flank cruisers to start south along the Leyte shore, and at 0440 sent a message to Admiral Kinkaid: "Enemy cruisers and destroyers are retiring. Strongly recommend an air attack."

Division X-ray had been formed in order to screen Battle Line; it was under the tactical command of *Claxton's* skipper, Commander M. H. Hubbard. Admiral Oldendorf took no risk in stripping Battle Line of its screen, because no Japanese submarines had ever penetrated Leyte Gulf; but it is too bad that he did not give the order earlier. It took the X-ray boys, for one reason or another, almost half an hour to form up and get going. Hubbard then bent on 25 knots but never got within range of the escaping ships. At 0535, when he caught up with the left flank cruisers, he was ordered to join their screen.

Twenty minutes later, *Claxton* in midchannel off Bugho Point sighted about 150 Japanese in the water and was ordered by Admiral Oldendorf to recover a few. The motor whaleboat was lowered but recovery was difficult without coöperation from the swimmers; there appeared to be an officer afloat who ordered them to stay clear. Finally three were picked up and, from one of these, a warrant officer who spoke English, was obtained the welcome information that his own ship, *Yamashiro*, had gone down.[42]

[41] Less *A. W. Grant* and *Newcomb* standing by her.

[42] *Claxton* Action Report 5 Nov. 1944. Next day, 26 Oct., *Claxton* sighted three more Japanese in the water and again initiated rescue operations. One came on

Oldendorf's left flank cruisers began pursuit at 0432 at the moderate speed of 15 knots, screen ahead by Smoot's destroyers. Again, this slow start was regrettable. A few minutes before 0500, *Louisville* picked up on her radar screen four or five enemy ships in mid-strait east of Amagusan Point. This was Second Striking Force, Shima having taken it into his head, unaccountably, to turn north again. A minute or two later Shima thought better of this and resumed retirement.

Day was now breaking. In the gray half-light one could just see the high, verdure-clad shores of Dinagat and Leyte. Visayan patriots had been gazing seaward all night, wondering what the flashes meant, but trusting they were ships of the hated "Hapon" Navy going down. Small groups of Japanese survivors began swimming ashore, to find a reception committee ready with sharp knives and bolos. On board the United States ships, everyone who could be spared topside came up for a breath of cool morning air, a look-around, and a discussion as to whether any of "them bastards" were still afloat. It was good that morning in Surigao Strait to be alive and with a deck under your feet. Up in San Pedro Bay, thousands of sailors in the amphibious forces had been up all night, watching the gun flashes reflected on the clouds, but too far off to hear even the distant mutter of gunfire. Now they began to receive a few reassuring words over the radio. Although it was not yet certain that the Southern Force was disposed of, the news from that quarter sounded well, and as all hands were piped to breakfast they mentally belayed the Southern Force.

By 0520 Admiral Oldendorf's left flank cruisers had reached a point in the Strait about eight miles west of Esconchada Point, where *Nachi* and *Mogami* had collided an hour earlier. To the southward one could see two Japanese ships on fire and a third that showed no sign of damage. Oldendorf ordered his column to turn right, to course 250°. Then – having checked and ascertained that

---

board "without much urging," a second attempted to swim away and eluded a chief machinist's mate, who rigged a lasso and tried to rope him from the bow of the whaleboat. "But the survivor was brought aboard by a firm hand on the seat of his breeches."

the force to the southward was enemy – *Louisville, Portland* and *Denver* engaged *Mogami.* She received several direct hits.[43] Although from *Louisville* she appeared to be "burning like a city block," the last of her nine lives was not yet expended. Left flank cruisers at 0537 turned north, probably because "Oley" was unwilling to place them in Japanese torpedo water.

At about 0600 *PT–491* of Lieutenant McElfresh's cross-strait patrol sighted a heavy cruiser accompanied by several small vessels, four miles off Panaon Island, steaming south at six knots. She was identified as *Mogami.* The PT, commanded by Lieutenant (jg) H. A. Thronson USNR, trailed her while trying to make his contact report over a jammed circuit. While so engaged he came under 8-inch fire from the cruiser for as much as 20 minutes, shells exploding as little as 25 yards away, drenching the boat and causing her to "leap right into the air." When *Mogami* was about three miles off Caniguin Point, *PT–491* fired two torpedoes at her and retired under heavy fire. Both missed.[44]

Admiral Shima's force was retiring so fast as to keep out of radar range of Oldendorf and Berkey, and Berkey was pulled out of the chase at 0540 to screen Battle Line. But Shima ran afoul of other motor torpedo boats. Lieutenant Mislicky's patrol No. 5 picked him up southwest of Binit Point, Panaon Island, at about 0620. *PT–150* fired a torpedo at *Nachi* which she dodged, and gunfire was exchanged. *PT–194* received a hit which seriously wounded the section commander and two other men.[45] A column of "six large ships," which must have been Shima's, was encountered by *PT–190* at 0630. Two enemy destroyers peeled off and opened fire on the boat – which retired under smoke toward Sogod Bay. The enemy column stood toward the Mindanao shore at cruising speed of 16 knots in order to avoid more motor torpedo boats, and appar-

[43] Lt. Fukushi, survivor of *Mogami,* report on Army Hist. Div. Microfilm HS–39A; *Mogami* Action Report.

[44] A few days later, Lt. Thronson visited an Army outfit on Panaon Island where there were some Japanese prisoners. One of them drew a picture of the action and gave the time as 0600.

[45] Time from Capt. Titus's plot; the PT reports say 0503, which is over an hour too early.

ently was successful. It would have made good its escape but for air attacks later that morning.

At 0645, *PT–137* of Section 6, patrolling about one mile southwest of Binit Point, sighted *Mogami* burning aft and heading south at twelve to fourteen knots. The heavy cruiser, still full of fight, opened up with secondary batteries, and a screening destroyer chased the PT away. Lieutenant Preston's Section 10 sighted *Mogami* "proceeding SSW at high speed" around 0650. She was certainly hard to stop.

It was now 20 minutes after sunrise. At 0643 Oldendorf, who turned south again at 0617, directed Rear Admiral Bob Hayler [46] to take his two light cruisers and three destroyers southward a second time "to polish off enemy cripples." All five opened fire at 0707 on destroyer *Asagumo,* whose bow had been knocked off in Captain Coward's attack two hours earlier. She was still swapping shots with destroyers *Cony* and *Sigourney* of Division X-ray when *Denver* and *Columbia* showed up and opened gunfire. This gallant Japanese destroyer returned fire from her after turret when her forward part was awash, and her last salvo was fired as the stern went under. *Asagumo* sank at 0721, about midway between Tungo Point, Dinagat, and Caligangan Point, Panaon.[47]

Two minutes later, Admiral Oldendorf recalled Hayler's light forces, and at 0732 he received the electrifying report that battle had been joined off Samar between Kurita's Center Force and Sprague's escort carriers. So, before any staff officer had a chance to sleep off the fatigue of a night action, he had to be drafting plans for a second battle.

At 1018 October 25, Commander Nishino, skipper of the lucky destroyer *Shigure,* sent this radio dispatch to his Commander in

[46] Robert W. Hayler, b. Ohio 1891, Annapolis '14. "Plank owner" of *Oklahoma,* in which he served through World War I. C.O. of three destroyers 1921–3; three tours of duty at Newport torpedo station; gunnery officer Desron 9, of *Omaha,* and on staff of Com Scouting Force, 1933–4, Comdesdiv 28, officer in charge of naval torpedo schools and torpedo stations. C.O. *Honolulu* 1942; Comcrudiv 12 Mar. 1944; General Board Mar. 1945; retired 1951.

[47] Rear Adm. Hayler Action Report; letter from his flag lieutenant Frank T. Howard in 1950.

Chief, Admiral Toyoda, and to Vice Admiral Kurita: "All ships except *Shigure* went down under gunfire and torpedo attack."

Admiral Kurita received this message while he was debating whether or not to press on into Leyte Gulf, after being worked over by Seventh Fleet escort carrier planes off Samar. It was one of the factors that determined his retirement.

Captain Whitehead, Commander Support Aircraft Seventh Fleet, attempted on the morning of 25 October to direct bombers of V Army Air Force to the fleeing enemy ships. He was unable to raise them or their base, and no Army planes participated in the battle on 25 October. It was Naval Air that took over from Oldendorf's ships after daylight, pursuing relentlessly and effectively. Rear Admiral Thomas L. Sprague's escort carriers launched a strike of torpedo-bombers and fighters for the chase at 0545. Three hours later 17 of the Avengers found Shima's force, with injured *Mogami* tagging along, in the Mindanao Sea, west of the Surigao Peninsula. They attacked *Mogami* shortly after 0910 and left her dead in the water. Destroyer *Akebono* took off the crew and at 1230 dispatched that fighting cruiser with a torpedo. The attacking planes had to come down for gas at Tacloban, where they learned what a tough spot their escort carrier units were in, refueled, and dashed off to get into the Battle off Samar.

Abukuma, hit by a motor torpedo boat in the early morning, was still able to steam at 9 knots, not enough to keep up. Shima sent Rear Admiral Kimura's flagship, destroyer *Kasumi*, to escort her to safety. They put in at Dapitan, a harbor protected by the northwest point of Mindanao, sortied on the morning of the 27th, and at 1006 were attacked by 44 B–24s and B–25s of V and XIII Army Air Forces based on Noemfoor and Biak. The bombers made several direct hits and started fires which reached the torpedo room. The consequent explosion blew a large hole in *Abukuma* and she went down southwest of Negros, at 1242.[48] Thus, belatedly

[48] Mori interrogation; conversation with Capt. Itaya, who was on Adm. Kimura's staff, in 1957; Cdr. E. C. Holtzworth's Target Report Summary of Japanese Warship Losses; Craven & Cate V 367.

but successfully, the Army Air Force got into the pursuit phase of the battle.

Shima's Second Striking Force, now consisting of two undamaged heavy cruisers and three destroyers, underwent another attack by carrier planes at 1500 October 26 in the Mindanao Sea, but escaped with only light damage to destroyer *Shiranuhi. Ashigara* made good her escape to Bacuit Bay, Palawan, where she was sighted from the air on 4 November. *Nachi* proceeded to Manila Bay, where she was sunk by Helldivers and Avengers from *Lexington* on 5 November 1944. Her hull, well searched by divers from U.S.S. *Chanticleer* and evaluated by Naval Intelligence after the liberation of Manila, yielded valuable documents on this and earlier battles.

Vice Admiral Sakonju's Transport Unit, light cruisers *Kinu* and *Kitagami*, destroyer *Uranami*, and four destroyer-transports, never engaged United States ships. Some 2000 troops that they embarked at Cagayan in Mindanao were landed at Ormoc on the back side of Leyte early on 26 October. That morning, Admiral T. L. Sprague's escort carriers, despite the struggle they had been through the day before, furnished 29 fighters and 23 bombers to continue the chase. One group happened upon the Transport Unit and tracked it into the Visayan Sea, where *Kinu* and *Uranami* were sunk after repeated bombing and strafing, around noon 26 October. On their return flight the carrier aircraft saw a ship which they supposed to be *Mogami*, not knowing that she had already been sunk, and worked over her until it was time to leave. Captain Whitehead put this contact report on the general warning net at 1246; Admiral Mitscher picked it up and ordered some of his planes to get on the scent. They caught up with the ship, which turned out to be seaplane tender *Akitsushima*, unescorted; they bombed her and saw her go down.

Destroyer *Shigure*, sole survivor of Nishimura's Force "C," made Brunei Bay safely on 27 October.[49] Shima's four destroyers got through with no great damage. Thus, by 5 November, of the

[49] Cdr. Nishino Action Report, and interrogation (*Inter. Jap. Off.* II 341).

Southern Force that had entered Surigao Strait only heavy cruiser *Ashigara* and five destroyers were afloat.

In no battle of the entire war did the United States Navy make so nearly a complete sweep as in that of Surigao Strait, at so little cost; but in no other battle except the one off Cape Engaño that same day did it enjoy such overwhelming strength, both on the surface at night and in the air next morning. Other than this, the immediate factors that made for victory were the tactical dispositions and battle plan worked out by Admiral Oldendorf and his staff, the early contact reports sent in by the motor torpedo boats, and the skillful torpedo attacks by destroyer squadrons, which left little for the gunfire ships to do. Japanese casualties in the night battle, never computed, must have run into the thousands. The American casualties were very few – 39 men killed and 114 wounded, most of them in *Albert W. Grant*, and possibly a few pursuing aviators.[50]

It is difficult to see what consolation the enemy could have derived from this battle. His torpedo technique fell short of 1943 standards, his gunfire was ineffective; even his seamanship, as judged by the collision of *Nachi* with *Mogami*, was faulty. The most intelligent act of any Japanese commander in the entire battle was Admiral Shima's retirement.

The Battle of Surigao Strait marks the end of an era in naval warfare. It was the last naval battle in which air power played no part, except in the pursuit. It was the last engagement of a battle line. Here an old sailor may indulge in a little sentiment.

Battle Line, as a tactical device for naval combat, dates from the reign of James I – when Sir Walter Raleigh ordered the Royal Navy to abandon attempts to board, as the main objective, in favor of "the whole fleet" following "the admiral, vice-admiral, or other leading ship within musket shot of the enemy. Which you shall

[50] Aviation casualties in this battle are impossible to disentangle from the total casualties of the air groups.

either batter in pieces, or . . . drive them foul one of another to their utter confusion."[51]

Battle Line was first successfully employed in 1655 by James, Duke of York, against the Dutch Admiral Opdum in the Battle of Lowestoft. Standard tactics throughout the days of sail, it was used in all great sea battles, such as Beachy Head, Ushant, the Capes of the Chesapeake, the Battle of the Saints, Cape St. Vincent and Trafalgar. With ever-increasing range, it served equally well in the era of steam and high-powered ordnance, because it enabled ships of a battle line (whence "battleship" is derived) to render mutual support; and, if properly deployed against an irresolute enemy, or one with an imperfect line, to defeat him piecemeal. Dewey's victory at Manila Bay, Sampson's off Santiago, Togo's at Tsushima and the Battle of Jutland were classic line-of-battle actions in the nineteenth and twentieth centuries. The knell of the battle line was sounded by the development of air power, which made it impossible to maintain line under air attack; and besides the night actions off Guadalcanal and Empress Augusta Bay, and that of Surigao Strait, there was only one line action in the Pacific War in which air power played no part – Rear Admiral McMorris's Komandorski fight on 26 March 1943. Vice Admiral Willis A. Lee should have been the one to fire the last broadside, but he was denied the opportunity. Thus, when *Mississippi* discharged her twelve 14-inch guns at *Yamashiro*, at a range of 19,790 yards, at 0408 October 25, 1944, she was not only giving that battleship the *coup de grâce*, but firing a funeral salute to a finished era of naval warfare. One can imagine the ghosts of all great admirals from Raleigh to Jellicoe standing at attention as Battle Line went into oblivion, along with the Greek phalanx, the Spanish wall of pikemen, the English longbow and the row-galley tactics of Salamis and Lepanto.

[51] Raleigh's Orders to the Fleet of 1617, in J. S. Corbett ed. *Fighting Instructions 1530–1816* (Navy Records Society 1905) p. 34.

CHAPTER XII

The Battle off Samar— The Main Action[1]

25 October 1944

1. *The Three "Taffies"*

AS Admiral Halsey was hurrying north to intercept the enemy carrier force, Rear Admiral T. L. Sprague's sixteen escort carriers were steaming back and forth in their night operating areas off Leyte Gulf.

"Baby flattops" or "jeep" carriers, as they were often condescendingly called, were regarded by many an old sailor as interlopers in the Navy – something like reservists, to be tolerated during the war but not taken too seriously. Escort carriers were first

[1] CTG 77.4 (Rear Adm. T. L. Sprague) Action Report 15 Nov. and "Brief Preliminary Summary of Damage and Losses" 7 Nov.; CTU 77.4.3 (Rear Adm. C. A. F. Sprague) Action Report Leyte Operation, 6 Nov., Special Report of Action off Samar, 29 Oct., and Supplementary Comment on same 14 Nov.; CTU 77.4.34 and .32 (Rear Adm. R. A. Ofstie) Action Report 12 Oct.–1 Nov., and Special Report Action off Samar, 28 Oct.; CTU 77.4.2 (Rear Adm. Felix Stump) "Reoccupation of Leyte Island 18–29 Oct." 2 Nov., and Addenda to same, 8 Nov.; Action Reports of individual ships. Some good articles by participants have also appeared: Rear Adm. C. A. F. Sprague "The Japs Had Us on the Ropes" and Cdr. A. T. Hathaway "The Battle as I Saw It" *American Magazine* Apr. 1945; Lt. R. C. Hagen "We Asked for the Jap Fleet and Got It," *Sat. Eve. Post* 26 May 1945.

On the Japanese side, MacArthur *Historical Report* Vol. II and translated Action Reports of the following: Com First Striking Force (Kurita) in WDC 161, 641; Combatdiv 1 (Ugaki) and Comcrudiv 7 in WDC 161,005; personal diary of Vice Adm. Matome Ugaki, translated from *Sansoroku* (Tokyo, 1953); Rear Adm. T. Koyanagi "Battle of Leyte Gulf, a Retrospection" (1952), trans. by Capt. Ohmae from his book on Kurita's Fleet; an abstract "With Kurita in the Battle for Leyte Gulf," is in U.S. Nav. Inst. *Proceedings* lxxix (Feb. 1953), 119–33; postwar Interrogations of Adm. Kurita, his chief of staff, Rear Adm. Koyanagi, and his operations officer, Cdr. Otani.

employed by the United States Navy in the Atlantic in 1942, in order to bring air power to bear on the coast of Morocco. In 1943 other uses were found for them, providing air cover for amphibious landings and for convoys in waters remote from land-based air range. As such, they paid their cost many times over.

Owing to the stringent security on antisubmarine warfare, the public never knew the vital work done by CVEs in the Atlantic. And in the Pacific, the big flattops of the fast carrier groups won the glory. There, ever increasing numbers of CVEs performed monotonous routine tasks of providing air cover for convoys and amphibious operations. They did this under conditions more rigorous than those on board the fast carriers, and in temperatures of 93° to 98° F. in berthing spaces and on the hangar deck. *Marcus Island* had a temperature above 100° in the pilots' ready-room during the Battle off Samar. Seldom did the sailors in these useful and gallant ships enjoy a liberty ashore.

Task Group 77.4, under the overall command of Rear Admiral Thomas L. Sprague,[2] was divided into three task units called Taffy 1, Taffy 2 and Taffy 3 – from the voice radio call sign used by each unit commander. Their regular operating areas were 30 to 50 miles apart; that of Taffy 1 to the southward, off northern Mindanao; that of Taffy 2 (Rear Admiral Stump[3]) in the center, off the entrance to Leyte Gulf; and that of Taffy 3 (Rear Admiral Clifton Sprague[4]) to the northward, off Samar. On 25 October they were organized as follows: –

[2] For brief biography see above, Chapter VII.

[3] Felix B. Stump, b. West Va. 1894, Naval Academy '17. Navigator *Cincinnati* in World War I; flight training at Pensacola and studied aeronautical engineering at M.I.T. Various aviation duties, C.O. Scoron 2 in *Saratoga*, navigator *Lexington* 1936–37; and exec. *Enterprise*, 1940–41; C.O. *Langley*, 1941; C.O. new *Lexington* 1943–44, in Gilberts and Marshalls operations (see Vol. VII 94, 196); Comcardiv 24 at Leyte; chief of air technical command 1945; Comairpac 1948 and Cincpac 1953. Retired 1958.

[4] For brief biography see Preface to this Volume.

Escort Carrier Group (TG 77.4), Rear Admiral Thomas L. Sprague [5]
(*As of 25 October 1944*)

Taffy 1 (77.4.1)	Taffy 2 (77.4.2)	Taffy 3 (77.4.3)
R. Adm. T. L. Sprague	R. Adm. F. B. Stump	R. Adm. C. A. F. Sprague
CVE SANGAMON	CVE NATONA BAY	CVE FANSHAW BAY
SUWANNEE	MANILA BAY	ST. LO (ex-MIDWAY)
SANTEE		WHITE PLAINS
PETROF BAY	Cardiv 27	KALININ BAY
	R. Adm. W. D. Sample [6]	
	MARCUS ISLAND	Cardiv 26
	KADASHAN BAY	R. Adm. R. A. Ofstie
	SAVO ISLAND	KITKUN BAY
	OMMANEY BAY	GAMBIER BAY
Screen	Screen	Screen
DD MCCORD	DD HAGGARD	DD HOEL
TRATHEN	FRANKS	HEERMANN
HAZELWOOD	HAILEY	JOHNSTON
DE RICHARD S. BULL	DE R. W. SUESENS	DE DENNIS
RICHARD M. ROWELL	ABERCROMBIE	J. C. BUTLER
EVERSOLE	LE RAY WILSON	RAYMOND
COOLBAUGH	W. C. WANN	S. B. ROBERTS

The first three ships of Taffy 1, which attracted the first Kamikaze attack, were of the converted-tanker class which had been blooded off Casablanca in November 1942; all others were Kaiser-built on the West Coast in 1943–1944. Each carried 12 to 18 Wildcats and 11 or 12 Avengers. Operating in assigned areas east of Leyte Gulf, their primary task was to provide air support for the amphibious forces, such as pounding enemy airfields in the Visayas (which most of them had been doing since 17 October) and intercepting enemy strikes on the beachhead. In addition, they had routine missions such as maintaining combat air patrol over the am-

[5] For C.O.s and plan complements, see Appendix I.

[6] William D. Sample, b. Buffalo 1898, Naval Academy '19. Served in destroyers in World War I; Asiatic Fleet 1921; flight training and subsequently instructor at Pensacola, Scoutron 1, 1923, service with aviation units *Raleigh* and *Richmond;* aviation with *Arizona*, *New York* and *Saratoga* 1928–31; aide to Com Aircraft Battle Force and C.O. VF 5 in *Lexington* 1932; Buaer duty 1935; navigator *Ranger* 1938; Air ops. officer *Yorktown* 1939; supt. aviation training Pensacola 1940; C.O. *Santee* 1942; C.O. *Intrepid*, *Hornet* and Comcardiv 24, 1944; Comcardiv 22 1945; and went missing Oct. 1945 when plane in which he was flying failed to return from a flight over Japan.

phibious forces, antisubmarine patrol for the whole Leyte area. And, owing to the absence of Army air forces at Leyte, they were assigned special tasks such as attacking Japanese truck convoys, bombing fuel concentrations and dropping supplies for the Army ashore.

2. *Double Surprise, 0645* [7]

While Admiral Oldendorf was tangling with the enemy in Surigao Strait, the escort carriers were passing a tranquil midwatch off shore. At 0155 Admiral Kinkaid had ordered Admiral Thomas Sprague to launch three daybreak searches, one of them to cover the northward sector between 340° and 30°, 135 miles out from Suluan Island. Admiral Sprague at 0330 directed Taffy 2 to fly these searches. Admiral Stump received the order at 0430 and, after checking the "spot" on each of six carriers, decided that *Ommaney Bay* was best prepared to do it, and sent her the order at 0509. A re-spot of planes on an escort carrier's flight deck is at best a time-consuming task, as there is so little room to work in; and this re-spot had to be done in complete darkness on slippery, rain-lashed decks. Moreover, escort carrier pilots were not supposed to be trained in night take-off and recovery.[8] Thus, it is not surprising that *Ommaney Bay* did not complete launching her ten-plane search until 0658, which was too late.

All innocent of impending disaster, the three groups pulled shoreward from their night operating areas and before break of day began heading into the northeasterly wind to catapult or launch planes. Tom Sprague's Taffy 1, the southermost in location, began at 0545 to launch a strike for the pursuit of Japanese ships fleeing from Surigao Strait. Taffy 2, the next northward, and Taffy 3, then

[7] CTG 77.4 and CTU 77.4.2 Action Reports; Seventh Fleet Message File; *Ommaney Bay* Action Report; Letter from Admiral Stump 14 Jan. 1958 clearing up some of the discrepancies in the reports.

[8] In the same letter Admiral Stump states that it was contrary to Comairpac's orders to train CVE pilots for night work, but he and other flag officers had disregarded this and trained most of the newly assigned pilots at Manus and Ulithi for pre-dawn take-offs and dusk landings.

about 60 miles due east of Paninihian Point, Samar,[9] were the groups that performed routine air missions which, for the most part, had been ordered by Captain Whitehead the evening before. By 0530 Taffy 3 had launched combat air patrol of twelve fighters to cover the ships in Leyte Gulf, and by 0607 it had airborne an additional support group of four torpedo planes and two fighters for gulf antisubmarine patrol, as well as the usual C.A.P. and A/S patrol for its own disposition. Between 0614 and 0627, three minutes before sunrise, the carriers of Taffy 3 secured from general quarters and set Condition Three. Deck crews settled down to breakfast and the usual morning routine was resumed.

At 0645 strange things began to happen. Lookouts observed antiaircraft fire to the northwestward. What could that be? Our own vessels shooting at friendly planes? At 0646 *Fanshaw Bay* made an "unidentified surface contact" on her SG radar screen and her radio watch heard what sounded like "Japs gabbling" on the interfighter direction net. Surely there could be no Japs around; somebody joking? At 0647 Ensign Jensen, pilot of an antisubmarine patrol plane from *Kadashan Bay*, encountered what he described as four Japanese battleships, eight cruisers, and a number of destroyers, 20 miles from Taffy 3; he made a glide-bombing attack on a cruiser, and reported that he was being fired upon.[10] Admiral Sprague yelled "Check indentification!" at Air Plot, his unspoken thought being that the pilot had sighted part of Task Force 38. He got verification all right, and from his own lookouts: the unmistakable pagodalike masts of Japanese battleships and cruisers pricking up over the northern horizon. At 0658, when the Japanese ships were still hull-down, their guns opened fire. At 0659 colored splashes from their shells began rising astern of Taffy 3.

Many sailors could not believe their eyes or ears. Kurita's Center

[9] *Ommaney Bay* Action Report p. 13.

[10] CTG, 77.3 Action Report. *Kadashan Bay* Action Report gives sighting as 0645, but contact report was not logged on board *Fanshaw Bay* until 0648. Radioman D. G. Lehman ARM 3c of Jensen's plane noted blips on his radar screen 20 miles away, and the pilot investigated, although they were in a sector outside his responsibility. Ensign Hans L. Jensen USNR was later killed.

Force, in Admiral Halsey's estimation an aggregation of cripples, had covered 125 to 150 miles in the last seven hours, completely undetected. One might have been in the age of Drake. Lord Nelson would have left a frigate to watch San Bernardino Strait and give

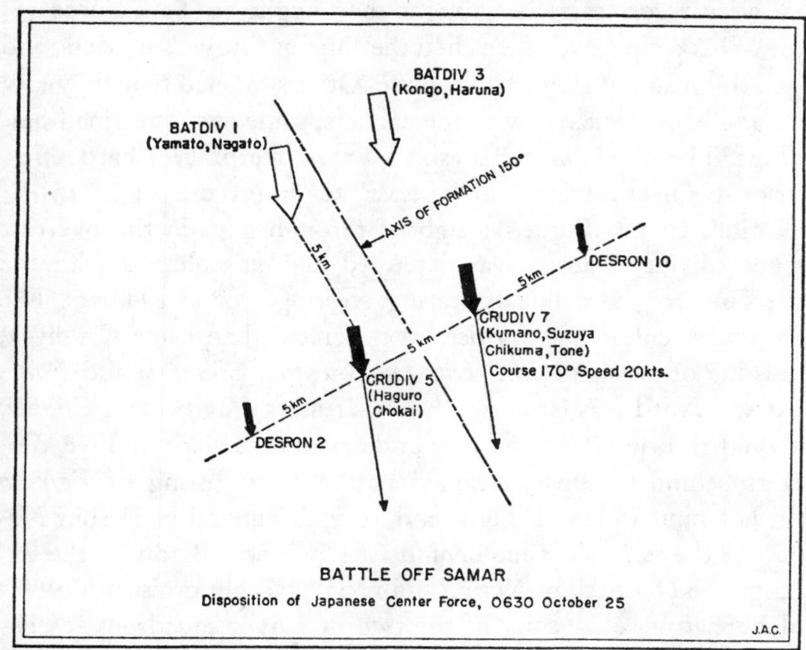

BATTLE OFF SAMAR
Disposition of Japanese Center Force, 0630 October 25

him advance notice of the approach of an enemy fleet. How could such a thing happen in broad daylight, in the age of air power and electricity? And to top it all, as if the god of battles wished to test the Americans, he shielded Kurita's fleet from the probing invisible fingers of radar almost until the lookouts sighted it with their own eyes.

But both sides were equally surprised, and the effect of it on Kurita's vastly superior force was far more devastating than on his inferior enemy. He should have welcomed it as a golden opportunity for the fleet action against carriers that he preferred over the SHO–1 plan of shooting up amphibious shipping.[11] A lookout in the

[11] According to his chief of staff Rear Adm. T. Koyanagi "Battle of Leyte Gulf, a Retrospection."

crow's nest of *Yamato* made the first sighting, at 0644. The Admiral noticed Ensign Jensen's plane dropping depth charges, "and then I saw the masts and I then was able to see the shape of aircraft carriers to the southeast." [12] He could not tell, from that distance, that they were escort carriers, thought they might be Task Force 38; some of his people even identified the ships as Ozawa's carriers, and urged the Admiral to withhold fire.[13] Others fancied that they saw light and heavy cruisers with the carriers; some even imagined battleships. The chief of staff's estimate was one or two battleships, four or five fleet carriers and "at least" ten heavy cruisers!

Kurita's Center Force, as sighted through gaps in the overcast by one of our aviators, was deployed in four columns with the leaders in a 60°–240° line of bearing, steering 170° at 20 knots. The easternmost column was a destroyer screen, then came Crudiv 7, consisting of heavy cruisers *Kumano*, *Suzuya*, *Chikuma* and *Tone*. Next westward was Crudiv 5, heavy cruisers *Haguro* and *Chokai;* and on their other flank was a second destroyer squadron. Five kilometers behind Crudiv 5 steamed Batdiv 1, consisting of *Yamato* with her nine 18.1-inch guns, and 16-inch-gunned battleship *Nagato*. At the same distance behind Crudiv 7 was Batdiv 3, the 14-inch-gunned battleships *Kongo* and *Haruna*. Light cruisers *Noshiro* and *Yahagi* were flagships of the two destroyer squadrons screening the van; the battleships had no screen of their own.[14] All hands below the flag officers are said to have been elated over their unopposed sail along the coast of Samar, anticipating easy pickings in Leyte Gulf.

But Kurita was uneasy; the events of the last two days had not given him confidence in his antiaircraft gunners, and it was with sinking heart that he encountered enemy carriers. It would not have mattered greatly if he had known that they were only escort

[12] Interrogations of Kurita and Koyanagi (*Inter. Jap. Off.* I 39, 147).

[13] "We found ourselves perplexed by your carriers," said his operations officer, Cdr. T. Otani, "because they did not correspond to their photographs." (*Inter. Jap. Off.* I 171.) He hadn't the right photographs for Kaiser class!

[14] Comairgrp 26 (Cdr. R. L. Fowler) "Observations and Comments of Action with Enemy Surface Fleet 25 Oct. 1944" (in *Kitkun Bay* Action Report), checked from diagrams in Crudiv 7 and *Tone* Action Reports.

carriers mounting but one 5-inch gun apiece; they had aircraft, and he had only a few float planes on his battleships which were of no use in combat.

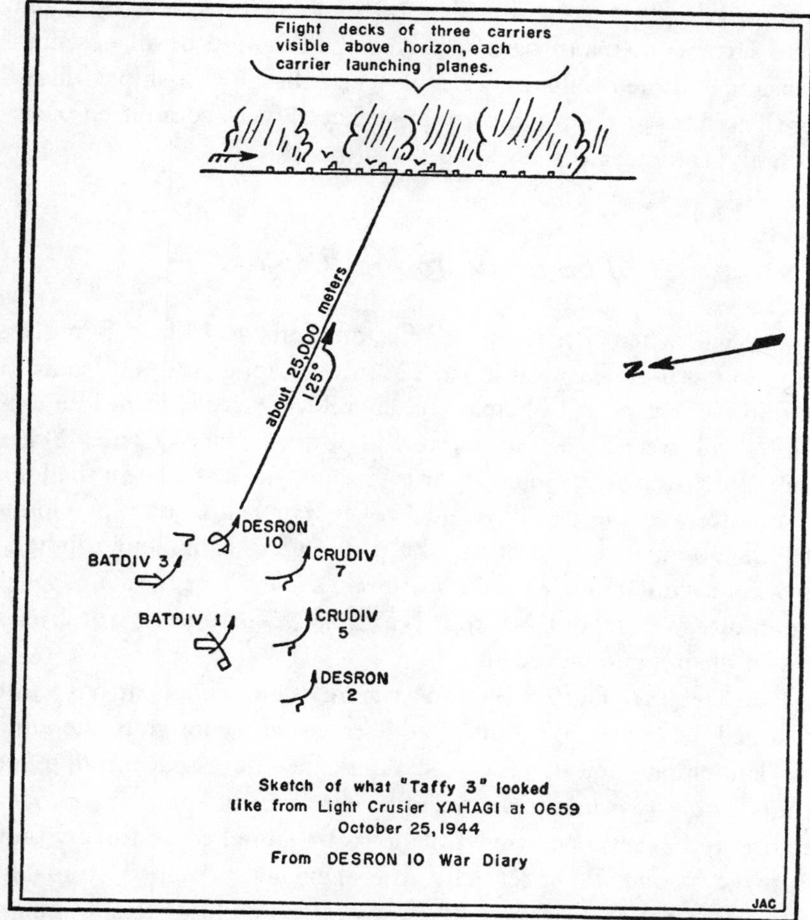

Sketch of what "Taffy 3" looked like from Light Crusier YAHAGI at 0659 October 25, 1944
From DESRON 10 War Diary

At the very moment of sight contact, 0644, Kurita was about to deploy his force from columnar cruising formation on course 170° to circular antiaircraft formation on course 110°. The order was given; but before it could be completely executed, Kurita ordered "General Attack," and that threw the Japanese Fleet into confusion; "No heed was taken of order or coördination," said his chief of staff. That was the fatal error. Kurita should have formed battle line with his four battleships and six heavy cruisers, which would have allowed his superior fire power to count, and he should have committed light forces immediately for torpedo attack. But complete surprise seems to have deprived the Admiral of all power of decision, and the result was a helter-skelter battle. His ships, following the whims of their commanding officers, were committed piecemeal and so defeated.

3. *The Battle Joined, 0658–0713*

At 0658, when Kurita opened fire on Taffy 3, Clifton Sprague's flagship *Fanshaw Bay* was in lat. 11°46.5′ N, long. 126°11′ E, about 40 miles off the coast of Samar and 80 miles NE by E from Homonhon Island, steering a southwesterly course. Kurita's Center Force bore northwesterly, 30,000 yards distant. It was almost half an hour after sunrise; the day had broken fair with cumulus clouds shading about one third of the sky, the sea was calm, and a light 6- to 8-knot wind, rising to 15 knots in rain squalls, was blowing, varying in direction from ENE to NNE. Smoke, fortunately for us, lay low in the hot and humid air.

Rear Admiral Clifton Sprague began issuing orders at 0657. He changed the course of his unit to due east – near enough to the wind for launching, but opening the range; he increased speed to 16 knots, and a few minutes later upped it to flank speed, 17½ knots; he ordered every operational plane to be launched and every ship to make smoke. Providentially, the enemy approached from leeward so that the carriers could launch planes without closing range. At 0701 the Admiral broadcast an urgent contact report in plain language, giving his position and that of the enemy, and asking all who could to send assistance.

Further course changes were initiated from time to time, aimed to edge around the rim of a wide circle to the southwest. Sprague's purpose was to avoid encirclement by the enemy and to meet

Oldendorf, whom he hoped to see coming out to help. The Battle off Samar was a running fight around the edge of a partly opened fishhook, whose curve was 20 miles in diameter.

At the moment of attack, Admiral Tom Sprague's Taffy 1 lay about 130 miles S by E, and Admiral Stump's Taffy 2 between them, but much nearer to Taffy 3. The escort carrier group commander acted quickly. At 0702, within four minutes of Admiral Clifton Sprague's urgent plea for assistance, he had requested and received permission from Admiral Kinkaid to launch all available planes to strike the enemy fleet, and passed the word to Stump. Captain Whitehead, in flagship *Wasatch*, in San Pedro Bay, pulled planes away from other missions to assist. Thus, within ten minutes of the time the enemy opened fire, every available aircraft was flying to help, and the rest were in process of launching. But would they arrive in time? There was plenty of frantic worrying on board the ships in San Pedro Bay, not only about the escort carriers but about themselves, in case Kurita broke through.

Kurita's heavy ships now became strung out without any coördination in consequence of his order "General Attack." Batdiv 1 (*Yamato* and *Nagato*) kept in column, but the two other battleships (*Kongo* and *Haruna*) operated as individuals. The six heavy cruisers operated more or less in three columns of two each, which became widely separated; and the light forces – the two light cruisers and 12 destroyers – were in the rear, in accordance (says Admiral Ugaki) with an order from Kurita. This left the heavy ships without a screen, and precluded the Admiral from ordering a destroyer counterattack until the battle had gone on for almost an hour.[15] Even so, it was not long before Clifton Sprague's escort carriers found two cruiser columns on their port quarter, one of them, of four ships, pulling up to a position abeam, while the four battleships were right on their fantails. "A perfect setup to polish off this unit," as Captain D. J. Sullivan, commanding officer of

[15] Kurita's order to his destroyer squadron to "follow in rear" was sent out at 0708 (*Naguro* Action Report), but they were already in the rear. Apparently this was Japanese battle doctrine, contrary to American and British battle tactics.

White Plains, wrote. "We could only go in the direction the Japs wanted to go themselves, to Leyte Gulf." Sprague's only hope of escape was to slow down his superior enemy by repeated air bombings and destroyer torpedo attacks; and that is what he did.

All hands on board carriers and screen knew they had been caught cold, but they met the situation with the gay cynicism behind which the modern bluejacket hides indomitable courage. As the enemy started firing, one of the signalmen on *White Plains* remarked, "I can't read their signals but they certainly send a lot of dashes." "Yeah," retorted another, "and they are likely to be periods by the time they get here!" [16] Anxious as the officers on the flag bridge were, they could spare a smile for the voice of Admiral Stump over TBS, trying to reassure his friend Clifton Sprague, whose nickname was "Ziggy." "Don't be alarmed, Ziggy – remember, we're back of you – don't get excited – don't do anything rash!" And as he conjured Ziggy to keep calm his voice rose in crescendo. He was indeed backing up Taffy 3, and in the finest way, with planes. The Sprague unit took the rap as far as ships were concerned, but Taffy 2 made the larger contribution of aircraft to the battle.

Ziggy Sprague was mighty glad to know that Felix Stump's planes were coming in from just over the horizon, but he never lost his presence of mind. He made the right decisions promptly. His first orders, as we have seen, were to steer east, turn up maximum speed, make smoke and launch all planes. The resulting disposition was simple and effective: – the six carriers formed a rough circle 2500 yards in diameter, while their destroyer screen patrolled sectors of an outer circle 6000 yards from the center. At 0659 enemy salvos began falling astern the CVEs.[17] Six minutes passed, with the escort carriers slicing planes off their flight decks faster than they had ever done before, and Japanese salvos coming nearer, though not yet hitting. Flagship *Fanshaw Bay* and *White Plains* on the exposed flank were the first to come under fire. The flagship,

[16] *White Plains* Action Report 27 Oct. 1944.

[17] Admiral Kurita later said he thought his opening range was 32,000 to 33,000 meters; *Fanshaw Bay* estimated the range as 29,000 yards.

even before 0700, launched her remaining fighter planes and eleven torpedo-bombers. *White Plains* got a double dose of near-misses; three 14-inch straddles in the first four minutes after six bells. The last salvo twisted the vessel violently, throwing men from their feet, tossing gear about and opening the generator circuit breakers so that steering control was momentarily lost. "Wicked salvos straddled *White Plains*, and their colored geysers began to sprout among all the other carriers from projectiles loaded with dye . . . yellow and purple, the splashes had a kind of horrid beauty." [18] Cried a seaman in *White Plains:* "They're shooting at us in technicolor!" Two minutes later, this carrier completed launching her fighter planes and started arming her Avengers with bombs and hoisting them up from the hangar deck.[19]

At that moment, 0706, remarked Admiral Sprague, "the enemy was closing with disconcerting rapidity and the volume and accuracy of fire was increasing. At this point it did not appear that any of our ships could survive another five minutes of the heavy-caliber fire being received." His task unit being surrounded by "the ultimate in desperate circumstances," the Admiral saw that counteraction was urgently and immediately required. He ordered all escorts to attack the enemy with torpedoes. We shall relate this attack presently.

Kitkun Bay and *Gambier Bay*, although part of Taffy 3, were a separate carrier division under Rear Admiral Ralph Ofstie. He was one of the most expert aviator flag officers in the Navy, as later appeared when he commanded the fast carriers in the Korean War.[20]

[18] Clifton Sprague's article in *American Magazine* Apr. 1945 p. 41.

[19] It was too late to arm them with torpedoes, because before these could have been loaded the carriers had changed course and were headed downwind, and an Avenger armed with torpedoes was too heavy to launch downwind. Fortunately, many Avengers in the three Taffies were already armed with torpedoes, as ordered by Captain Whitehead the previous evening, for pursuing ships down Surigao Strait. For it took time to prepare aërial torpedoes. They had to be removed from racks on hangar deck; moved on dollies, with care, as the CVEs were very tiddly; air pressure, alcohol, rudder throws and depth mechanism had to be checked, and then they were loaded on the planes.

[20] Ralph A. Ofstie, b. Wisconsin 1897, Naval Academy '19. Destroyers in World War I and to 1922, when took flight training duty with VF–1 to 1924, and while attached to Buaer made three speed records at Naval Air Meet Oct. 1924 (178.25

His flagship launched eleven Wildcats and six Avengers shortly after 0700, and the skipper of his air group, Commander R. L. Fowler, did the most valuable work of any aviator in this battle, staying aloft for eight hours to direct air strikes on the enemy ships. Aircraft from all carriers of Taffy 3 attacked the enemy in "deuces and treys" at once; but it was not possible to collect and organize enough of them for a properly coördinated air attack before 0830.

A compassionate providence sent a rain squall, which the carriers entered between 0706 and 0715 and which, in conjunction with the smoke that they and the escorts were making, covered them for about fifteen minutes. Under this cover Clifton Sprague did some quick thinking and decided to bear around to the south and southwest, in order to bring his disposition nearer to the hoped-for help from Leyte Gulf. A hard decision, since it offered the enemy a chance to take the inside track; but it proved to be correct, even though no help appeared. Kurita was so obsessed with keeping the weather gauge that instead of cutting corners he maintained 110° as axis until he was due north of the carriers, and then bore down. Actually most of his ships steered a mean course almost due east between 0706 and 0750, owing to repeated dodging of air and torpedo attacks.

As Sprague's first change of course from 90° to 119°, and Kurita's maintaining course, opened the range, enemy fire slackened and fell off in accuracy. Kurita ordered his force to commence radar rangefinding; but his search radar, the only kind he had, was ineffective, and his shooting, never good, went completely wild when the carriers were concealed by rain and smoke cover. There was something the matter, too, with Kurita, for at 0725 he informed his

m.p.h in a seaplane). With Scoutron 5 and aviation officer *Detroit* 1927; flight test div. N.A.S. Anacostia 1929; C.O. of VF–6 in *Saratoga* 1933, asst. naval attaché Tokyo 1935, helped commission *Enterprise* and served as her navigator 1938, staff duty in *Saratoga* and *Yorktown*, 1941; asst. naval attaché London, aviation officer on Cincpac staff 1942; C.O. *Essex* in Gilberts, Marshalls and Marianas ops.; Comcardiv 26 Aug. 1944; Comcardiv 23 Jan. 1945; chief of staff to Comairlant Aug. 1945, and head of naval analysis div. Navy Dept., naval member military liaison to Atomic Energy Commission 1946; Comcardiv 5 in Korean War 1950; chief of staff to Com Naval Forces Far East 1951, and on the Korean armistice commission; Com First Fleet 1952; deputy C.N.O. (Air) 1953; Com Sixth Fleet 1955; died 1956.

force from flagship *Yamato*, "I have sunk one heavy cruiser!" He later admitted that he was bothered by Sprague's smoke screen,[21] and by the air attacks, the evasion of which caused his ships to break formation and lose distance. And, on top of that, came the surface torpedo attacks.

4. *Destroyers Counterattack, 0716–0830*

This battle, so beautifully and bravely fought against overwhelming odds, was filled with gallant and memorable episodes; none more so than the torpedo and gunfire attacks by the screen. Admiral Clifton Sprague ordered his three destroyers to make the first counterattack on the Japanese heavy ships at 0716, just after his escort carriers had entered the rain squall. And one, at least, of the destroyers was already in the fight. The most admirable thing about this battle was the way everything we had afloat or airborne went baldheaded for the enemy. Kurita was bewildered by this superaggressiveness, and readily concluded that we had more there than met the eye.

The three destroyers of Taffy 3's screen were *Hoel*, flying the pennant of Commander W. D. Thomas, *Heermann* and *Johnston* — all 2100-tonners of the *Fletcher* class. *Johnston*, two days less than a year old, was known to her crew as "GQ Johnny" as she seemed to be at general quarters most of the time — off Kwajalein and Guam, Bougainville, Peleliu and Ulithi. Her skipper, Commander Ernest E. Evans, was a fighting Cherokee Indian of the same kind as "Jocko" Clark — short, barrel-chested, loud of voice, a born leader. As soon as the Japanese were sighted he ordered all boilers to be lighted off, called all hands to general quarters, and passed the word "prepare to attack major portion of Japanese Fleet." As *Johnston* sheered out to lay a smoke screen — her patrol sector was the nearest to the enemy — she commenced firing at

[21] Kurita interrogation p. 12. Our method of smoke, he said, "was very serious trouble. . . . It was exceedingly well used tactically."

0710, when her range to the nearest Japanese heavy cruiser was 18,000 yards. This, it will be observed, was in the opening phase of the battle – before the carriers found a few minutes' grace in the rain squall, and before four heavy cruisers pulled out ahead. At that time, the carrier planes were making their first strike on the Japanese ships, two or three of which, as soon as the strike was over, opened fire on *Johnston*.[22]

As *Johnston* bore in to a flanking position, she delivered rapid salvo fire from her main battery, aiming at *Kumano*, which was leading a heavy cruiser column. Over two hundred rounds were fired and numerous hits were observed. Since the angle of her approach brought all Japanese heavy ships in echelon, so that their forward guns could fire at her without fouling each other's range, many of them did; and splashes of four or five different colors began rising about *Johnston* in her mad, brave course.

At this moment Commander Evans passed the word which he had already received from Sprague, to deliver torpedo attack in conjunction with *Hoel* and *Heermann*. Nearest to the enemy, *Johnston* was the first to comply. Closing at 25 knots to within 10,000 yards of the heavy cruiser, she fired her ten torpedoes. They were observed to run "hot, straight and normal." Having expended her entire supply, *Johnston* whipped around and retired behind her own heavy smoke. What happened next can best be told in the words of her senior surviving officer: –

> Two and possibly three heavy underwater explosions were heard by two officers . . . at the time our torpedoes were scheduled to hit. Upon emerging a minute later from the smoke screen, the leading enemy cruiser was observed to be burning furiously astern.

Admiral Kurita later admitted only one hit from a destroyer torpedo on his force, and that was *Johnston's* on heavy cruiser *Kumano*, flagship of Crudiv 7, at 0727. The flag officer, Vice Admiral

[22] *Johnston* Action Report 14 Nov. 1944. This report was written, with the help of the other survivors, by Lt. R. C. Hagen, Gunnery Officer in *Johnston* and senior surviving officer. Lt. Hagen's article, "We Asked for the Jap Fleet – and Got It," *Sat. Eve. Post*, 26 May 1945, is one of the best stories of the war.

Shiraishi, shifted to *Suzuya*, which had already been air-bombed and her speed reduced to 20 knots. Both heavy cruisers then dropped astern and out of the fight:

The senior officer of *Johnston* continues: —

> At this time, about 0730, this ship got it. Three 14-inch shells from a battleship, followed thirty seconds later by three 6-inch shells from a light cruiser, hit us. It was like a puppy being smacked by a truck. These hits knocked out the after fire room and engine room, lost all power to the steering engine, all power to the after three 5-inch guns and rendered the gyro compass useless.[23]

The destroyer's speed was now reduced to 17 knots. The "whirling bedspring" SC radar, snapped clean off the mast, came tumbling down by the bridge, where three officers were killed. Great holes were blasted in the deck. Many men were killed below. Commander Evans's clothes above the waist were blown off, together with two fingers of his left hand. But all gun stations answered "Aye!" to control testing. Steering was shifted to manual aft, orders being received from the bridge via JV phones. The stable element and FD radar conked out for about five minutes. The same rain squall that saved the carriers passed over *Johnston* to leeward, giving her a valuable ten minutes' respite to estimate extent of damage. Enough power was restored to Nos. 3 and 5 guns for partial fire control — their crews would match pointers, shift to telescope control, and set in, by hand, the sight angle and sight deflection received from plot. No. 4 fired in complete local control.

At this stage of the battle confusion reigned supreme. Smoke and showers rendered the location of escorts a matter of by guess and by God. And, as *Johnston's* log went down with the ship, it is impossible to reconstruct an accurate track for her course; her survivors' memory of what happened is fragmentary.

Hoel was the screen flagship. Her skipper, Commander L. S. Kintberger, reported she commenced an approach on the nearest battleship, *Kongo*, which was then about 7½ miles NE of the spot

[23] Lt. Hagen's *Sat. Eve. Post* article.

where *Kumano* was torpedoed. The range was then 18,000 yards. She opened gunfire at 14,000 yards, and so did the enemy. At 0725 she received a hit on the bridge which destroyed all voice radio communication. Two minutes later, at a range of 9000 yards, she launched a half-salvo of torpedoes at *Kongo,* then steering an evasive course of 140° at 20 knots. The results were unobserved, but *Kongo's* Action Report states that she avoided four torpedoes by turning sharp left at 0733. Before the "fish" had run their course, *Hoel* received hits on her after fireroom and after turbine, knocking out three guns and the port engine and jamming the rudder hard right. Before steering control could be shifted aft, *Hoel* found herself headed straight for the battleship that she was engaging. "Guns Nos. 1 and 2 continued to fire on the targets of opportunity." Seldom has a destroyer encountered so many opportunities.[24]

Hoel may have been Kurita's imaginary "cruiser observed blowing up and sinking at 0725," but she wasn't sunk yet. The one idea of her skipper, as of Commander W. D. Thomas (Comdesdiv 93) on board, was to inflict maximum damage on the enemy while she floated, in the hope of diverting major-caliber fire from the escort carriers and giving them a few minutes' grace. So, undismayed by the loss of one engine, of her Mark-37 fire control director, of FD radar, of bridge steering control and of three out of five 5-inch guns (all shot out by *Kongo*), *Hoel* returned to the fray in the hope of getting the rest of her torpedoes into *Haguro,* which was leading the Japanese heavy cruiser column. At about 0750,[25] "using manual train and selective aim with the torpedo officer on No. 2 mount due to the loss of communications with the torpedo mounts," a half-salvo of torpedoes was launched at the leading cruiser at a range of about 6000 yards, target angle 50 degrees. All torpedoes ran "hot, straight and normal" and "large columns of water were observed to rise from the cruiser at about the time scheduled for the

[24] *Hoel* Combined Action Report and Report of Loss 15 Nov., enclosed with that of CTU 77.4.3.

[25] Cdr. Kintberger's Action Report says, "at about 0735," but *Heermann* observed her to fire torpedoes at 0753; and as *Hoel* with all her records went down an hour later it is assumed that *Heermann's* estimate was more nearly correct.

torpedo run." Japanese records indicate that these torpedoes missed, which is difficult to accept, as there were no bombers about at the time to create the geyser effect with their near-misses.

Heermann, engaged in screening a disengaged angle of the escort carrier disposition, did not get the word to join the torpedo attack until just after *Hoel* launched her first spread. By that time Admiral Sprague had ordered a second torpedo attack (0742, "execute" at 0750). *Heermann* got into that one, having steamed right through the carrier formation to form column on screen flagship *Hoel*. Visibility, reported her skipper, Commander Amos T. Hathaway, was an open-and-shut affair, varying from 100 to 25,000 yards owing to rain and smoke. She narrowly avoided collision with destroyer escort *Roberts* in the screen, then bent on knots to close *Hoel*, and and at 0749 had to back emergency full to avoid colliding with her.[26] Straightening out in column, at 0754 she commenced launching seven torpedoes at *Haguro*. The cruiser then bore due north, distant 9000 yards, and was steaming at 25 knots on Kurita's base course 120°, leading a column of four. *Haguro* evaded the torpedoes and replied with 15 gunfire salvos, which missed *Heermann*.

Just as the torpedoes were leaping out of *Heermann's* tubes, she spied another column of heavy enemy ships to the northward (350°), and at the same distance – 4½ miles – from the cruiser columns already under fire. When about half her "fish" were swimming and the rest about to be launched, the gunnery officer, Lieutenant W. W. Meadors USNR, sighted, on the port bow, battleship *Kongo*, and splashes from 14-inch shells began plowing up the water round about. *Haruna* next appeared astern of *Kongo;* and behind them in the dim distance were *Yamato* and *Nagato*. But four battlewagons did not faze Commander Hathaway. Climbing to the exposed fire-control platform to help the conn, he changed course to 270° to get in position to fire the rest of his torpedoes at the leader, and shifted 5-inch gunfire to her superstructure, one of those pagodalike affairs favored by the British designers of the older

[26] *Heermann* Action Report, 1 Nov. 1944.

Japanese battleships. He was not allowed to do this unopposed. Big yellow splashes began walking up on *Heermann* – this time accurately, since the Japanese gunnery officer could easily figure out the destroyer's course and speed. *Heermann*, fortunately, was too nimble for him; and, still unhit by anything bigger than shell fragments, she commenced, at 0800, firing her remaining three torpedoes at *Haruna*, distant only 4400 yards, bearing 350° and tracked as steaming 100° at 20 knots. *Heermann* then whipped around and retired to the carrier formation, believing that one of her torpedoes hit the battleship right under No. 4 turret.[27]

This duel between the destroyer and the battlewagon lasted from 0755 to 0803. *Heermann* changed course to meet *Haruna;* opened fire with her 5-inch guns, launched three torpedoes, and broke off – all in eight minutes. On retiring, she fired at targets of opportunity astern, resumed laying smoke, and proceeded to the starboard quarter of the carrier formation, pursued by salvos which in turn were chased by her. "Chasing" salvos – or, more properly, chasing the splashes – means that when one's ship is missed by an enemy salvo one alters course and heads right for the splash, anticipating that the enemy ship will correct his last solution so that he will not hit the same spot twice.

Mighty *Yamato*, when firing at one of our destroyers at 0754, spotted torpedo tracks bearing 100° starboard. As ordered by Admiral Kurita, who flew his flag on board, she turned to port, first to 60° and then almost due north, to evade. Vice Admiral Ugaki, Batdiv 1 commander, who was also on board, called this maneuver "highly unfortunate,"[28] because it caught the battleship between two torpedo spreads, four to starboard and two to port, chasing her from astern.[29] She dared not reverse course, but continued in a northerly direction for almost ten minutes before the torpedoes ran

[27] *Heermann* Action Report and article by Cdr. A. T. Hathaway in *American Magazine* Apr. 1945 p. 41.

[28] *Sensoroku*, Personal Diary of Vice Adm. Ugaki.

[29] It is difficult to say what ship fired these torpedoes. Probably they were from *Hoel* and had missed *Haguro*.

their course and their tracks disappeared. This effectively took *Yamato* out of the battle and made her "tail-end Charlie" of the ragged Japanese disposition.

Hoel, minus one engine and three of her 5-inch guns, was not so lucky. She attempted to retire southwesterly, but could not get out of the box into which her commander's courage had led her. *Kongo* lay 8000 yards on her port beam and the heavy cruisers were 7000 yards on her starboard quarter. Her one engine turned up just enough speed to "string along" with the enemy, but not enough to pull clear. Every Japanese ship within range took a crack at her, but by fishtailing and chasing salvos she was able to keep afloat for an hour and five minutes after her first hit, and her two bow guns barked continuously at whatever enemy seemed the most menacing, expending some 500 rounds of 5-inch 38 between them. She took over 40 hits: 5-inch, 8-inch and even 16-inch. All those of major caliber were armor-piercing and went right through without exploding, but they were punching her full of holes below the waterline. The Japanese heavy ships passed so close that *Hoel's* crew observed their "pitiful" antiaircraft fire, which they said resembled the "zone-barrage" system that the United States Navy had abandoned in 1942. *Hoel's* crew got a closer look at *Yamato* than did any other American bluejackets.

Finally at 0830 an 8-inch shell put the remaining engine and generator out of commission and *Hoel* went dead in the water. All engineering spaces were flooded, No. 1 magazine was afire, the ship listed heavily to port and settled by the stern, and at 0835 the word passed: "Prepare to abandon ship." The firemen and water tenders went about their task preparing the engineering plant so that no explosions would occur, and *Hoel* was left to her fate. The Japanese continued to pump shells into her, and at 0855 she rolled over and sank in about 4000 fathoms.[30]

[30] The position of *Hoel's* sinking is given in her Action Report as lat. 11°46′N, long. 126°33′E, but judging from her survivors' accounts it must have been farther to the westward in the track of the battle.

Commander Thomas, the screen commander, was severely wounded, but recovered; Commander Kintberger, who also survived, wrote a seaman's epitaph to this memorable action: —

FULLY COGNIZANT OF THE INEVITABLE RESULT OF ENGAGING SUCH VASTLY SUPERIOR FORCES, THESE MEN PERFORMED THEIR ASSIGNED DUTIES COOLLY AND EFFICIENTLY UNTIL THEIR SHIP WAS SHOT FROM UNDER THEM.

5. *"Little Wolves" Counterattack, 0750–0918*

Hoel and *Heermann* were not alone in this second torpedo attack, nor was *Hoel* the only loss. When Admiral Clifton Sprague ordered the second torpedo attack at 0742 he used his code word for the destroyers, "Wolves make torpedo attack." The destroyer escorts were known as the "Little Wolves," and Lieutenant R. W. Copeland USNR of *Samuel B. Roberts* was so eager to get into it that he signaled Commander Thomas, the screen commander: "Do you want Little Wolves to go in with Wolves?" Thomas replied "Negative," but quickly followed that discouraging word with "Little Wolves form up for second attack." [31] That did not help matters much, as the DEs never had been taught to "form up" and had never delivered a torpedo attack. They were in somewhat the same situation as the motor torpedo boats, mounting torpedoes but with no chance to use them, as their employment in the Pacific had been almost entirely in antisubmarine work. But they flinched not; and *Roberts*, despite the clear intimation that she was not wanted in the destroyer column, tagged along 3000 yards behind *Hoel* and *Heermann* rather than seek out her fellows on the other flank of the carrier formation.

At 0750, when Admiral Sprague gave the "Execute" to the second torpedo attack, "GQ Johnny" was coming out of the rain

[31] *Samuel B. Roberts* and *John C. Butler* Action Reports; conversation with Lt. Cdr. Pace, C.O. of *Butler*, at Manus in Dec. 1944.

squall to leeward and heading back to station. As *Hoel, Heermann* and *Roberts* passed him, Commander Evans of *Johnston* roared out: "We'll go in with the destroyers and provide fire support!" "Aye, aye, Sir!" said his executive officer, and GQ Johnny fell in, making a fourth in the column, although she had no torpedoes left.

Owing in part to *Yamato's* taking herself out of the way, but mostly to a judicious laying of smoke by herself and the two destroyers, *Roberts* was able to approach the heavy cruiser column to within 4000 yards undetected. She launched her three torpedoes after *Hoel* and *Heermann* had fired theirs. They ran hot, straight and normal, but were evaded.[32] The little fellow then retired, firing her 5-inch battery from 0805 on, at an enemy cruiser with range decreasing from 7500 to 5300 yards, and miraculously was not once hit.

Now let us follow the other Little Wolves. While *Roberts* joined *Hoel* and *Heermann, J. C. Butler* was frantically seeking the whereabouts of *Dennis,* the senior destroyer escort, while *Raymond* attacked individually. When her skipper, Commander A. F. Beyer, received the word for the torpedo attack at 0743, he decided that it meant him, too, and turned his little vessel due north to close range on the leading enemy cruiser, *Haguro,* which promptly trained her 8-inch turrets and at 0755 put a salvo into the water 200 yards astern of him. This was one of 15 salvos that the cruiser fired at *Raymond.* She was making 25 knots and the destroyer escort 24; something was bound to happen soon.

Eight or nine destroyers approaching on the "inside track" were observed by *Johnston* and *Raymond,* then on the carriers' starboard quarter; and *Raymond* states that torpedo wakes passed her; but there is no mention of a torpedo attack at this time in the Japanese records.

At 0756 *Raymond* launched a spread of three torpedoes at the cruiser, then distant only 6000 yards. *Haguro* at that moment was

[32] *Roberts* Action Report states that one hit on an "*Aoba* class" cruiser was observed. She probably meant *Chokai,* which was not hit just then.

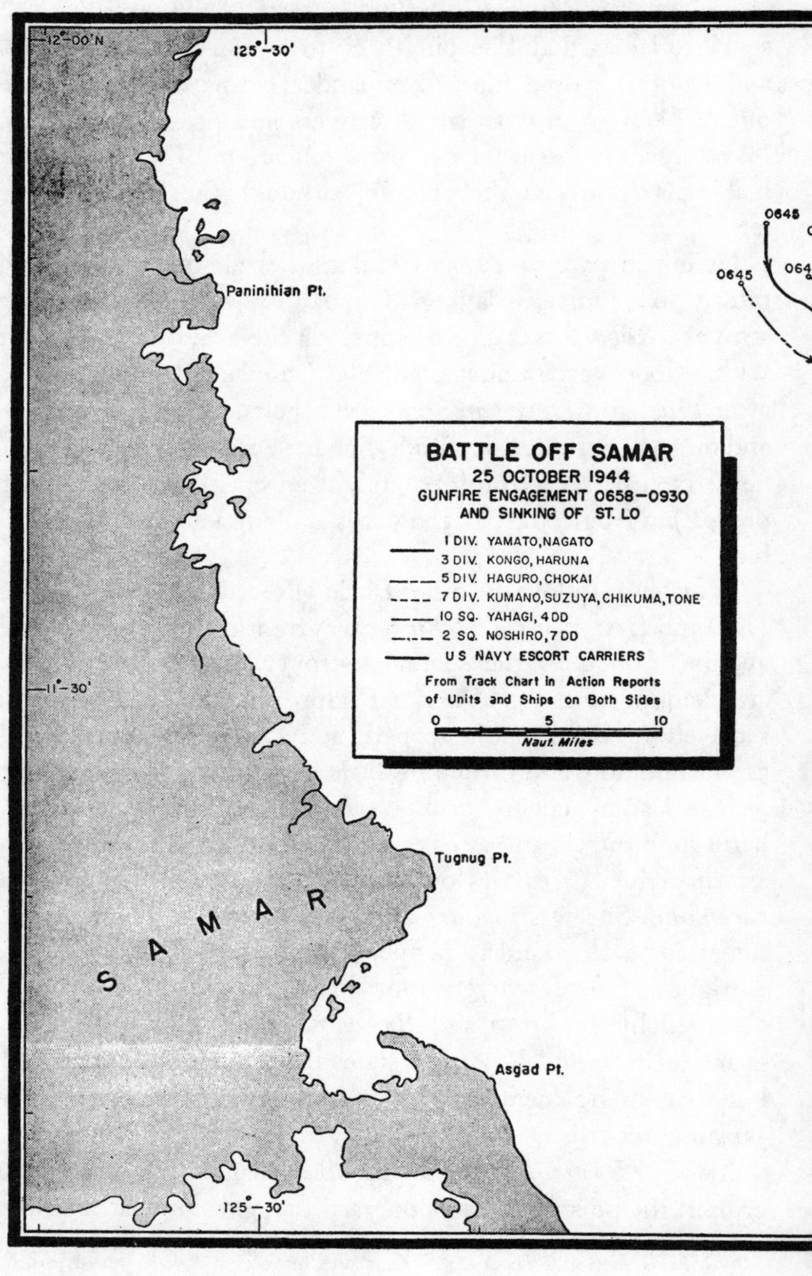

12°-00'N
125°-30'
0645
0645
0645
Paninihian Pt.
BATTLE OFF SAMAR
25 OCTOBER 1944
GUNFIRE ENGAGEMENT 0658–0930
AND SINKING OF ST. LO
1 DIV. YAMATO, NAGATO
3 DIV. KONGO, HARUNA
5 DIV. HAGURO, CHOKAI
7 DIV. KUMANO, SUZUYA, CHIKUMA, TONE
10 SQ. YAHAGI, 4 DD
2 SQ. NOSHIRO, 7 DD
U S NAVY ESCORT CARRIERS
From Track Chart in Action Reports
of Units and Ships on Both Sides
0
5
10
Naut. Miles
11°-30'
Tugnug Pt.
S A M A R
Asgad Pt.
125°-30'

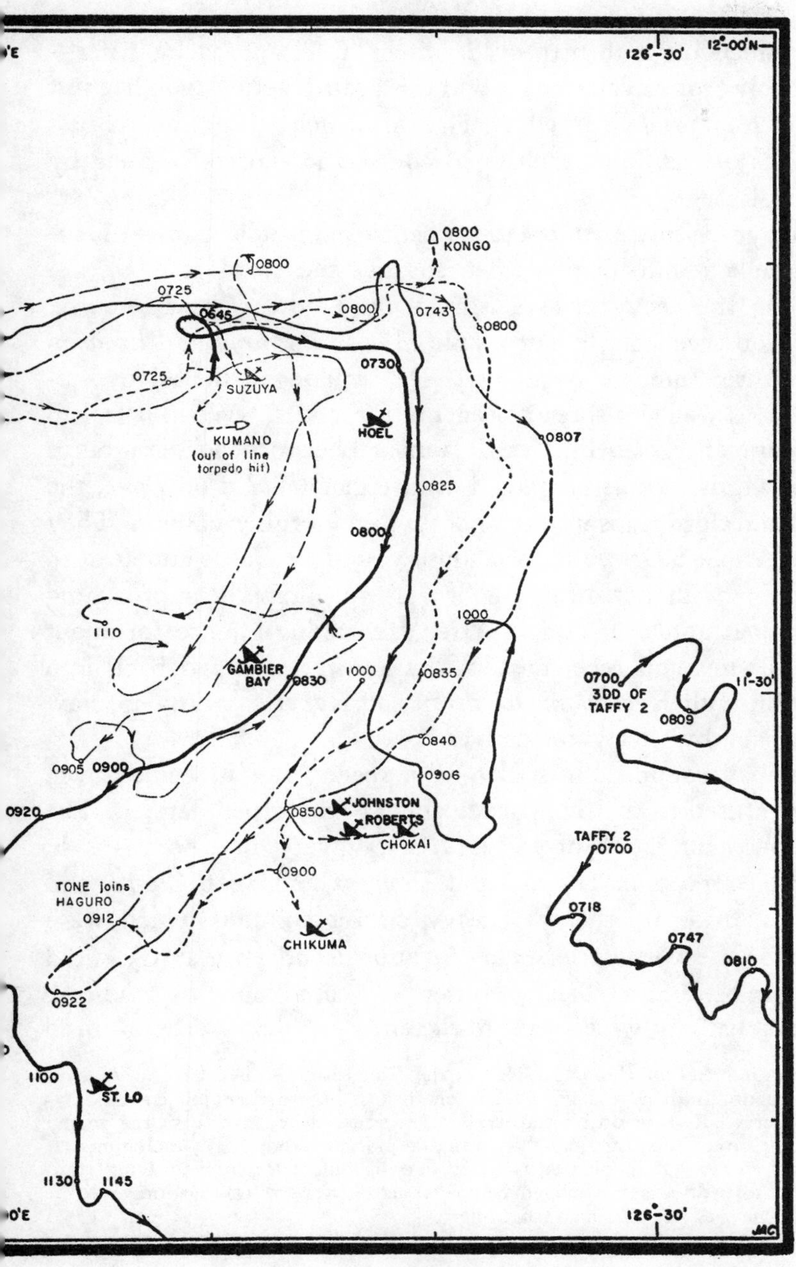

126°-30'
12°-00'N
0800
KONGO
0800
0725
0645
0800
0743
0800
0725
SUZUYA
0730
HOEL
0807
KUMANO
(out of line
torpedo hit)
0825
0800
1000
1110
GAMBIER
BAY
0830
1000
0835
0700
3DD OF
TAFFY 2
11°-30'
0809
0840
0905
0900
0906
0920
0850
JOHNSTON
ROBERTS
CHOKAI
TAFFY 2
0700
0900
TONE joins
HAGURO
0718
0912
CHIKUMA
0747
0810
0922
1100
ST. LO
1130
1145
126°-30'
JMC

just commencing a turn to evade other "fish" approaching her – presumably from an airplane – and this evasive action took her just clear of *Raymond's* torpedoes, two of which were seen to pass astern. *Raymond* quickly changed course and retired, pursued by 8-inch splashes.[33]

Destroyer escort *Dennis* (Lieutenant Commander Samuel Hansen) attacked individually when she got the word at 0750, approaching the heavy cruiser column on a northwesterly course. *Haguro* observed her, about a mile SE of *Raymond* and fired on her for three minutes, 0752–0755. *Dennis* dodged the salvos successfully, as well as a spread of enemy torpedoes.[34] When it lacked one minute of eight bells, *Dennis* launched her torpedoes at a range of 8000 yards; not at *Haguro*, but at either *Chokai* or *Tone*, the second and third ships in the Japanese heavy cruiser column. They missed. At 0802 *Dennis* turned southwesterly (240°), and at 0810 opened up with her after 5-inch gun on a rapidly approaching cruiser then under air attack. After exchanging gunfire for about seven minutes and receiving no hits, *Dennis* whipped back into formation with *Heermann*, *Johnston* and *Roberts*, who were now steering southwesterly themselves.[35]

This may sound confused to you, reader, but it seemed even more confused to the five participants in this torpedo attack. The only consistent story of it – and that a very brief one – is in the action reports of *Haguro* and *Tone*, which, with *Chokai* and *Chikuma*, made up the two heavy cruiser columns which were closest to the escort carriers. *Haguro* at 0746 and *Tone* at 0758 fired with main batteries at "heavy cruiser" – a compliment to *Johnston;* all ducks that day were swans to the enemy. "Heavy cruiser" fired

[33] *Raymond* Action Report, 2 Nov. 1944, Enclosures A and C; and *Haguro* Action Report. Both have a good track chart. Just before changing course *Raymond* observed *Roberts* on his starboard beam under heavy fire from the enemy and taking direct hits, but gamely spitting rapid fire from her 5-inch guns. A curtain of flashes and splashes surrounded her; but when *Raymond*, having completed her torpedo attack, changed course to retire, *Roberts* was no longer to be seen; but she was still afloat and fighting.

[34] Where they came from, we cannot make out – probably from one of the heavy cruisers.

[35] *Dennis* Action Report, 5 Nov. 1944.

back at 0750, and a "destroyer" (one of the DEs), laying smoke at 0752, fired on *Haguro*, which in turn shot 15 salvos at a destroyer (probably *Raymond*) closing her. Same "destroyer" fired two torpedoes, which were evaded, and at 0800 *Haguro* took an aviation bomb hit on No. 2 turret, which knocked it out. She continued pursuit, firing with other turrets on the carriers. That is all we have on the receiving end, since *Chokai* and *Chikuma* were sunk later in the action and their records were not saved.

The time was now 0820. As soon as they had delivered their torpedo attacks, all ships of the screen made best speed to close the escort carriers and made smoke, firing on the pursuing enemy as they retired. Visibility was still open and shut; for a moment the sun would shine forth and one could see every escort carrier and the enemy's entire formation; then rain or smoke would blot out parts of the picture. It is amazing that no collisions occurred, for the carriers themselves were maneuvering violently to evade salvos. *Heermann's* log reads: "0835 – Back emergency full to avoid collision with *Fanshaw Bay*, which crossed our bow from port to starboard." (*Fanshaw Bay* simply noted "Destroyer crossed our stern.") Five minutes later, *Heermann* "backed emergency full to avoid collision with *Johnston* who crossed our bow from port to starboard. *Johnston* was apparently having steering difficulty."[36] She certainly was. As the two destroyers missed each other by inches, a spontaneous cheer arose from all hands on the topsides of both vessels. *Johnston*, after taking a long breath, observed battleship *Kongo*, which had just crossed the stern of *Haruna* and taken station on her consort's starboard quarter, to be 7000 yards distant on her port beam. Having expended all torpedoes, Commander Evans used gunfire, radar ranging, at a battleship sighted at around 0750. In forty seconds he got off thirty rounds, and believed that he made at least fifteen hits. "As far as accomplishing anything decisive, it was like bouncing paper wads off a steel helmet; but we did kill some Japs and knock out a few small guns. Then we ran

[36] *Heermann* Action Report p. 10. *Johnston* Action Report p. 3 notes this near collision at 0810, but her action report was compiled from memory.

back into our smoke. The battleship belched a few 14-inchers at us, but, thank God, registered only clean misses."[37]

At 0826 Admiral Sprague ordered the destroyer escorts on the starboard quarter of his flagship to interpose between the carrier disposition and a heavy cruiser coming in on his port quarter. This was probably *Tone*, which with *Chikuma* was trying to head the carriers off from the seaward side; *Haguro* and *Chokai* were following some distance astern.[38] At that moment the ominous message was received on board the carriers, "Screen reports all torpedoes expended." A humorous radioman in *White Plains* approached the signal officer and remarked, "The situation is getting a little tense, isn't it? "

When Sprague gave the order at 0826, the only destroyer escorts on the starboard hand of his flagship were *John C. Butler* and *Dennis;* but *Raymond*, on the port hand, took it upon herself to join the party. She had, in fact, been firing on the same cruiser for 14 minutes.[39] *Roberts*, *Johnston* and *Heermann*, as we have seen, had also been trying to divert the heavy cruisers from the carriers.

John C. Butler did have three torpedoes left, but it was questionable whether she could manage to reach a firing position. As soon as she and *Dennis* received Admiral Sprague's order, they steamed through the carrier formation to its left flank, laying smoke en route, and avoiding the near collision of *Heermann*, *Fanshaw Bay* and *Johnston* which we have already noted. The leading Japanese heavy cruiser, *Chikuma* or possibly *Tone*, was making better speed than *Butler*, which could not close to effective torpedo range unless the enemy changed course toward the carriers.[40]

[37] Hagen in *Sat. Eve. Post* 28 May 1945 p. 74. Action Report gives time as 0820 but it cannot have been earlier than 0840. *Kongo* Action Report does not mention this encounter.

[38] *John C. Butler* Action Report, 9 Nov. 1944. *Haguro* Action Report at 0849 indicates that *Tone* was ahead of her, and her course was about 250°.

[39] *Raymond* Action Report. Her bearing at 0814 was 058°, initial range 11,000. This must have been *Tone* or *Chikuma*. He says it was *Nachi* class.

[40] At 0847, when salvos were falling close aboard, *Dennis* received the report that eight enemy destroyers were closing the starboard quarter of the carriers, directly opposite to the flank where she and *Butler* were.

He was not so obliging and *Butler* lost her opportunity to launch torpedoes. Both she and *Dennis* exchanged gunfire with the cruiser at ranges from 17,000 down to 14,000 yards. *Raymond*, out ahead of them, converged so closely with the enemy that the range came down to 5900 yards. *Tone* for a brief time shifted fire to her from *Gambier Bay*, but never hit her.

Chikuma, probably to avoid air attack, made a complete circle at 0842. *Tone* then took the lead and kept parallel to the carriers on their port beam, taking them as well as *Butler*, *Dennis* and *Roberts* under fire. The destroyer escorts picked her up and followed, firing briskly. *Dennis* at 0850 received a direct hit which passed through her deck and punctured the starboard side three feet above the waterline without exploding. At 0900 she received a second and more serious hit on her after 40-mm gun director, and a third on top of her No. 1 five-inch gun shield. Enough of the crew were knocked out to render this gun inoperative, as already was No. 2, owing to a broken breech operating spring. So at 0902 *Dennis* changed course to 220° and retired behind *Butler's* smoke screen, leaving *Raymond* to deliver gunfire on the enemy.

Four salvos landed close aboard *Butler* and she performed a rapid right-and-left zigzag. Apparently scorning such small fry, *Tone* at 0905 shifted fire to one of the escort carriers. Although *Butler's* smoke screen covered this carrier, five or six salvos landed very close to her port bow. Ten minutes later, the cruiser shifted fire to flagship *Fanshaw Bay*, then on *Butler's* starboard bow. At 0918 the DE had to cease fire as she was low in ammunition; Admiral Sprague promptly ordered her to move forward on the port bow of his disposition to afford it better smoke coverage. The enemy's Main Body by this time had a clear line of vision to the bow of the leading carrier, *St. Lo;* Admiral Sprague, alert to make the best use of his small means, saw that she might be concealed by sending *Butler* ahead and letting her smoke drift back.

Roberts took her first hit, which holed her below the waterline and knocked out No. 1 fireroom, around 0850, and after that received hits in rapid succession. At about 0900, according to Lieutenant Commander R. W. Copeland USNR, "a tremendous explosion took place" which he believed to have been caused by two or three 14-inch HC shells.[41] These tore a great, jagged hole 30 to 40 feet long and 7 to 10 feet high on the port side of *Roberts* right at the waterline, wiped out No. 2 engine room, ruptured the after fuel oil tanks, and started fires on the fantail. All power was lost, and the ship abaft the stack became "an inert mass of battered metal."

After all power, air, and communications had been lost, and before the word to abandon ship was passed, the crew of No. 2 gun, who as a crew distinguished themselves throughout the entire action, loaded, rammed and fired six charges entirely by hand, and with the certain knowledge of the hazards involved due to the failure of the gas ejection system caused by the air supply having been entirely lost. While attempting to get off the seventh charge in this manner, there was an internal explosion in the gun, killing all but three members of the gun crew, two of whom subsequently died on rafts.

Abandon Ship was ordered at 0910 but not completed until 0935, because the skipper insisted that the wounded be given first aid and placed on rafts. *Roberts* lay over to about 80 degrees, then gave a twist and slowly sank by the stern at 1005.[42] Of her crew of 8 officers and about 170 men, 3 officers and 86 men were killed, missing or died of wounds, or in rafts during their long wait for rescue.

Lieutenant Commander Copeland thus concluded his report: —

To witness the conduct of the average enlisted man on board this vessel, newly inducted, married, unaccustomed to Navy ways and with an average of less than one year's service, would make any man proud to be an average American. The crew were informed over the loudspeaker system at the beginning of the action of the Commanding Officer's estimate of the situation; that is, a fight against overwhelming odds from which survival could not be expected, during which time we would do what damage we could.

[41] They must have been from *Kongo*, which at 0912 claims to have sunk a "Kuramben" (*Craven*) class destroyer.

[42] Cdr. Copeland does not give position of sinking, which is entered on our chart in the position *Heermann* last sighted her, at about 0910.

IN THE FACE OF THIS KNOWLEDGE THE MEN ZEALOUSLY MANNED THEIR STATIONS WHEREVER THEY MIGHT BE, AND FOUGHT AND WORKED WITH SUCH CALMNESS, COURAGE, AND EFFICIENCY THAT NO HIGHER HONOR COULD BE CONCEIVED THAN TO COMMAND SUCH A GROUP OF MEN.

6. *Enemy Torpedo Attack; Last of* Johnston, *0902–0945*

Heermann's last exchange of gunfire with *Chikuma* almost ended her brave career. She took a series of 8-inch hits. One of them struck near her waterline well forward, flooding the forward magazines and tearing through a big storage locker packed with Navy beans. In a jiffy it reduced these to hot paste which the uptake sucked up and (with poetic justice) spurted over the supply officer who was standing by the stack. Seas rushed in through the hole in the waterline flooding the forward part of the ship and pulling her down by the head so that her anchors were dragging in the bow wave; yet four of her five guns continued firing and the power plant was not affected. Commander Hathaway (remembering what happened to destroyers who slowed down in that maëlstrom) kept the engines turning up full speed at imminent danger of running her under. If he had not taken on board extra shoring timbers at her last port he could never have kept her afloat.[43]

Chikuma, under heavy air attack at 0902, suddenly turned away and did not long remain afloat; but her place, as far as *Heermann* was concerned, was filled by *Tone*, which came roaring along. The destroyer fired on her for three minutes (0907–0910) at ranges of 14,000 yards opening to 17,500, then resumed laying smoke for the carriers. *Tone* now came under a severe air attack from the escort carrier planes of Admiral Stump's Taffy 2. She fell in astern of *Haguro*, reversed course in her company at 0920, and retired from the battle.

[43] Cdr. A. T. Hathaway article in *American Magazine* Apr. 1945 p. 116; oral testimony from members of crew.

Before *Johnston* checked fire on one of the cruisers that sank *Gambier Bay*, she observed light cruiser *Yahagi* and four Japanese destroyers [44] rapidly closing the carriers. This was the one organized torpedo attack by Admiral Kurita's destroyers. So far as the records show it was not even ordered by him, but undertaken by the squadron commander on his own initiative at 0845.

By that time *Hoel* had been abandoned well to the rear, *Roberts* was burning furiously, and the rest of the screen was engaging the heavy cruiser column. *Johnston* signed her own death warrant by taking on the five. In the words of the Japanese squadron commander, Rear Admiral Kimura: "0850 – Enemy destroyer plunged out of smoke screen on our port bow and opened gunfire and torpedo attack on us. *Yahagi* executed right rudder, making wide evasive turn, at same time ordering destroyers to attack."

Lieutenant Hagen of *Johnston* says that the Japanese destroyers were sighted at a range of about 10,000 yards and fire was immediately opened on *Yahagi*. The range gradually closed to about 7000 yards. *Johnston* was hit several times during this encounter by 5-inch projectiles. About twelve hits were made on *Yahagi* when "a most amazing thing happened. She turned 90 degrees right and broke off action." *Johnston* immediately shifted gunfire to the first destroyer and hits were observed at a range of around 8000 yards. "During firing on this second destroyer the Captain attempted to cross the T on the Jap column. However, before this was accomplished, amazingly enough, all remaining Japanese destroyers turned 90 degrees right and the range began to open rapidly." [45]

Admiral Kimura provides additional details. His sharp right turn in *Yahagi* was simply doctrine, to allow his destroyers to launch torpedoes. Before they did so, *Yahagi* was hit by *Johnston* and strafed by one of the escort carrier planes, killing one officer and wounding several. The light cruiser fired seven torpedoes at 0905, and at 0915 the Japanese destroyers began firing theirs. Kimura

[44] *Urakaze, Isokaze, Yukikaze, Nowaki.* Desron 10 Action Report.
[45] *Johnston* Action Report p. 4.

stated in his Action Report that these torpedoes reached their targets, when "three enemy carriers and one cruiser were enveloped in black smoke and observed to sink one after another."

Sad for us if true; but it was not true. Commander Evans had bluffed Admiral Kimura into a premature torpedo attack. His ships were 10,500 yards astern of *Kalinin Bay*, the nearest carrier, and that was too far, considering that the CVEs were doing $17\frac{1}{2}$ to 18 knots. By the time the torpedoes approached the carriers they had slowed down. An Avenger plane from *St. Lo*, piloted by Lieutenant Leonard E. Waldrop USNR, performed the extraordinary feat of exploding one of these torpedoes by strafing as it was porpoising toward the end of its run, and a second was deflected from its collision course by an accurate shot from *St. Lo's* 5-inch 38.[46] One of the most threatening episodes in the entire action proved a complete fiasco.

Thus, one damaged destroyer, which had expended all her torpedoes and lost one engine, managed to delay, badger and disconcert a Japanese destroyer squadron. Commander Evans "was so elated that he could hardly talk. He strutted across his bridge and chortled, 'Now I've seen everything!' " But, adds Lieutenant Hagen, "We had more fighting to do, and GQ Johnny's number was about up." [47]

For the Japanese destroyer squadron, as soon as it had fired torpedoes, concentrated on *Johnston*. She was observed from *Heermann*, her mast shot away and hanging over the superstructure deck, and on fire amidships. She was almost done for. Lieutenant Hagen thus records her end: —

We checked fire as the Japanese destroyers retired, turned left and closed range on the Japanese cruisers. For the next half hour this ship engaged first the cruisers on our port hand and then the destroyers on our starboard hand, alternating between the two groups in a somewhat desperate attempt to keep all of them from closing the carrier formation. The ship was getting hit with disconcerting frequency throughout this period.

[46] *Kalinin Bay* and *St. Lo* Action Reports.
[47] Lt. Hagen's *Sat. Eve. Post* article.

At 0910 we had taken a hit which knocked out one forward gun and damaged the other. Fires had broken out. One of our 40-mm ready-lockers was hit and the exploding shells were causing as much damage as the Japs. The bridge was rendered untenable by the fires and explosions, and Commander Evans had been forced at 0920 to shift his command to the fantail, where he yelled his steering orders through an open hatch at the men who were turning the rudder by hand. . . .

We were now in a position where all the gallantry and guts in the world couldn't save us. There were two cruisers on our port, another dead ahead of us, and several destroyers on our starboard side; the battleships, well astern of us, fortunately had turned coy.[48] We desperately traded shots first with one group and then the other.[49]

Shortly after this an avalanche of shells knocked out her one remaining engine room and fireroom. Director and plot lost power. All communications were lost throughout the ship. All guns were out of operation with the exception of the No. 4 5-inch, which was still shooting by local control. All depth charges were scuttled. At 0945, five minutes after the ship went dead in the water, the captain gave the order Abandon Ship.

The Japanese destroyer squadron, whose torpedo attack *Johnston* had thwarted, now made a running circle around her, shooting at her "like Indians attacking a prairie schooner." At 1010 she rolled over and began to sink. One destroyer closed to give her the *coup de grâce*. One of her swimming survivors saw the Japanese skipper on the destroyer's bridge salute as *Johnston* went down.[50]

From her complement of 327, only 141 were saved. Of the 186 lost, about 50 were killed by enemy action while the destroyer was still afloat; 45 died on the rafts from injuries received in action; and 92, including Commander Evans, were alive in the water after the ship sank, but were never heard from again.

[48] The enemy Main Body had reversed course and was retiring.

[49] Hagen in *Sat. Eve. Post* 26 May 1945 p. 74. His times, not unnaturally, are wrong – the attack on the *Yahagi* group given as about 20 minutes behind what the time really was. On the other hand, Rear Adm. Kimura states he saw men abandoning ship at 0930. *Noshiro* Action Report notes enemy ships going down at 0922 and 1018.

[50] Position not stated in Action Report; that on our chart is conjectural.

Strange things happened in the water. As the gunnery officer was afloat his torpedoman, Jim O'Gorek, swam over and remarked brightly, as if meeting on a street corner, "Mr. Hagen, we got off all ten of them torpedoes and they ran hot, straight and normal!" One man was killed by a shark; but a veteran gunner's mate was actually bitten twice by a shark which then let go, evidently not relishing his salty flavor – leaving this ancient mariner with a row of shark-tooth imprints on his right thigh to exhibit to the incredulous.[51]

Admiral Kurita declared, after the war was over, that of the 20 to 30 torpedoes fired at his force before 0880, all but one missed. That was *Johnston's* on *Kumano*. But it is likely that some torpedo hits were made on *Chokai* and *Chikuma*, of which Kurita had no report because those ships went down. In any case, it is clear that the major damage inflicted on the Japanese ships came from air bombs and aërial torpedoes. The great contribution of the surface torpedo and gunfire attacks was to force enemy ships into evasive action. That not only seriously impeded Kurita's speed of advance, but made confusion worse confounded, so that he lost tactical control of his force and had to break off, turn north and regroup. Kurita admitted this himself: "Major units were separating farther all the time because of the destroyer torpedo attack." And his chief of staff wrote, "The enemy destroyers coördinated perfectly to cover the inferior speed of the escort carriers. They bravely launched torpedoes to intercept us, and they embarrassed us by putting up a dense smoke screen." [52]

In no engagement of its entire history has the United States Navy shown more gallantry, guts and gumption than in those two morning hours between 0730 and 0930 off Samar. Yet we have not told the half of it. We must turn back to the early stages of the battle, and tell what the escort carriers had been doing to defend themselves.

[51] Lt. R. C. Hagen in *Sat. Eve. Post* 26 May 1945 pp. 74, 76.
[52] Rear Adm. T. Koyanagi "Battle of Leyte Gulf, a Retrospection."

7. *The Carriers' Running Fight, 0723–0907*

During the destroyer and destroyer escort gunfire and torpedo attacks – in fact continuously from 0658 to 0924 – the escort carriers were under gunfire of assorted calibers from 14-inch down to 4.7-inch. *Yamato*, thanks to our destroyers, was out of range. And our own planes were counterattacking lustily.

At 0723, *Fanshaw Bay*, *St. Lo*, *White Plains*, *Kalinin Bay*, *Kitkun Bay* and *Gambier Bay* were making top speed, 17½ knots, on course 110°. They had emerged, or were emerging, from the rain squall to see the worst menace yet. A column of four heavy cruisers, *Chikuma*, *Tone*, *Haguro* and *Chokai*, had pulled out ahead of the enemy formation and begun to overhaul Taffy 3 on the port quarter, obviously to encircle and cut off its retreat. We have already seen how the destroyers and DEs dealt with them. "Ziggy" Sprague, observing this at 0729 just as he was emerging from the rain squall, changed course to 200° (SSW) then back to 170° (S b. E) at 0732, to due South at 0746, and by 0800 was around to SW again. His purpose was to keep the inside track toward Leyte Gulf, hoping to meet assistance en route. But he really had no choice, as he was boxed in, with heavy cruisers to port, more heavy cruisers and battleships astern, and destroyers coming in on his starboard quarter. His carriers now had to launch planes in a following wind.

Sprague ordered all airborne planes to concentrate on the four intrusive heavy cruisers. As his carriers were making best speed and dodging salvos, he gave them the humorous order: "Open fire with the pea-shooters when range is clear." Already some of their lone 5-inch 38s were snapping back at *Chikuma* and *Tone*. "As he watched the one on *St. Lo* plug doggedly away over the stern, one old chief petty officer was heard to mutter, 'They oughtta fire that thing under water – we could use a little jet propulsion right now!' "[53]

[53] Sprague article in *American Magazine* Apr. 1945 p. 114.

Kalinin Bay received her first direct hit at 0750 as she was launching the last of her fighter planes. Ten minutes later, when one of the heavy cruisers on her port quarter closed the range to 18,100 yards, this game flattop opened up with her single gun. The cruisers

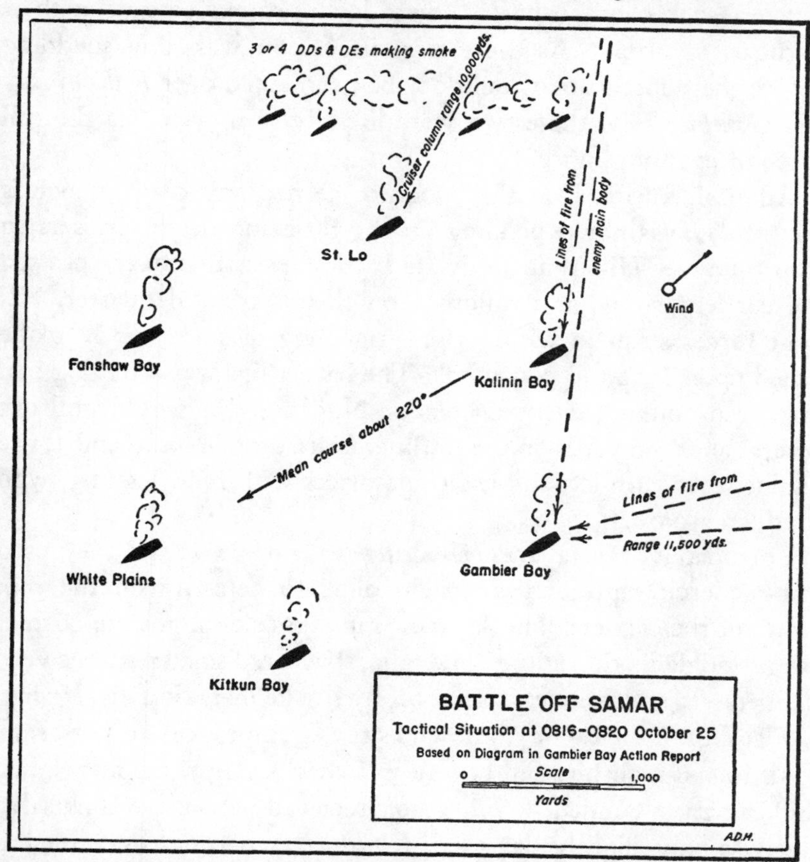

then intensified their fire; one 8-inch shell exploded on the aviation lube-oil tank, after disabling the evaporator en route; but at 0825 *Kalinin Bay* had the great satisfaction to score a direct hit at 10,000 yards' range on the No. 2 turret of one of the heavy cruisers.

The tactical situation at about 0816–0820 may be grasped from the above diagram. Owing to the several simultaneous turns made by the carriers, *White Plains* was now in the van on a southwest course, with *Fanshaw Bay* and *St. Lo* on her starboard quarter; *Kitkun Bay* and *Gambier Bay* on her port quarter and *Kalinin Bay* astern. They were making all the funnel and chemical smoke of which they were capable, and *Heermann* with two or three destroyer escorts, and *Johnston*, were laying smoke screen on their starboard quarter.[54] As the entire disposition was now scudding before the wind, smoke could not be maintained over *Kalinin Bay* and *Gambier Bay;* these two were literally "bare-arse" to the full force of enemy gunfire.

Admiral Kurita, if at this juncture he had any plan (which is doubtful), was not depending on the thrusting heavy cruisers to stop Sprague. His Main Body of battleships and cruisers crossed the carriers' sterns and followed on their starboard quarter. His light forces steamed within visual signaling distance, ready to be called upon for a torpedo attack. The battleships were steering in a staggered column, changing places. Nos. 2 and 4 would pull out several hundred yards on the starboard quarter of Nos. 1 and 3, fire a salvo, then turn left and exchange places with Nos. 1 and 3, who fired; and so on.[55]

Fortunately, the Japanese shooting was not good, and they used armor-piercing projectiles which failed to detonate on the thin plates of the carriers. The Japanese gunners seldom got the correct range and deflection at the same time; they fired small patterns very deliberately and were easily put off by smoke or radical zigzagging.

Flagship *Fanshaw Bay*, known as the "Fannie Bee" to her crew, took four 8-inch hits and two near-misses, losing three men killed and twenty wounded; *White Plains* received part of a 6-inch salvo but was only slightly damaged; *Kitkun Bay* was not once hit but had several casualties from near-miss shell fragments. *Kalinin Bay* appears to have been the only carrier that got under a battleship's shell,[56] and she also took 13 eight-inch hits. Only the heroic efforts

[54] This was before they steamed through the disposition and almost collided with *Fanshaw Bay*.

[55] Cdr. Fowler's observations, in *Kitkun Bay* Action Report.

[56] One 14-inch or 16-inch hit according to Sprague's Action Report, but not mentioned in the carrier's Action Report.

of her people kept her in formation. Boatswains' crews worked in as much as five feet of water to plug holes below the waterline; engineers and firemen risked death by scalding steam, working knee-deep in oil, choked by the stench of burning rubber, to repair ruptures in the power plant. Main steering control was knocked out and quartermasters steered the ship by hand from far down in her bowels, like helmsmen on the ancient Spanish galleons.

An Olympian scorekeeper, watching this battle from a height of 10,000 to 20,000 feet, might have plotted it, shot by shot; but even then the story would be so confusing as to be unretentive by the human brain. Your historian has tried to describe separately various phases and subordinate actions, even though they overlapped in time. We have told how the carriers fired back with their 5-inch guns; how Admiral Sprague sent in his entire screen to make torpedo attacks; how bravely the destroyers and DEs closed to short gunfire range when they ran out of torpedoes. But as yet we have barely mentioned the air counterattack, which seems to have been the principal factor in causing Kurita to break off action.

All escort carriers of Taffy 3 commenced launching planes as soon as they were fired upon, and Taffy 2 followed suit, as we shall presently relate. They continued launching under the rain squall, and by 0730 almost every operational plane was airborne. Most of these flew in immediately and made individual attacks; one of them drew first blood for the airmen in hitting and slowing down *Suzuya*.

At the same time, Captain Whitehead, Support Aircraft Commander in *Wasatch*, ordered all aircraft around Leyte Gulf not actually engaged on strikes to attack the Japanese Center Force. Six torpedo-bombers and 20 fighter planes were thus collected to help, and at 0830 these, with planes just launched from the CVEs, went in for their first coördinated attack.[57] But it was very difficult even for Commander Fowler to organize a coördinated attack. The planes had been too hurriedly armed and launched; the mêlée

[57] Commander Support Aircraft Seventh Fleet Report 2 Nov. 1944 p. 12.

and confusion were too great. Avengers were armed with torpedoes as long as torpedoes lasted and when these gave out they went in with bombs – even the little 100-pounders which were meant for hitting shore targets. When the bombs gave out, they made "dry" runs to divert the Japanese gunners.

> For two hours, with not so much as a machine-gun bullet to fight with, Lieutenant Commander Edward J. Huxtable (Air Group Commander *Gambier Bay*), glided his Avenger through the flak to make dry runs on enemy capital ships, once flying down a line of cruisers to divert them from their course and throw off their gunfire for a few precious minutes. . . .
>
> The Wildcat pilots were given a free hand to strafe, with the hope that their strafing would kill personnel on the Japanese warships, silence automatic weapons, and, most important, draw attention from the struggling escort carriers. Sometimes two, or four Wildcats would join up for a strafing run. Again, a Wildcat would join up and run interference for an Avenger. Then, likely as not, it would turn out that the Avenger had no torpedo or bomb and was simply making a dummy run. When their ammunition gave out, the fighters also made dry runs to turn the pursuers. Lieutenant Paul B. Garrison USNR made 20 strifing runs, 10 of them dry.[58]

These attacks, said Commander Otani after the war, were "almost incessant," although the number of aircraft engaged at any one instant was small. "The bombers and torpedo planes were very aggressive and skillful and the coördination was impressive; even in comparison with the many experiences of American attacks we had already had, this was the most skillful work of your planes." [59] It was in consequence of these, as well as of the torpedo attacks, that Kurita at 0925 decided to close up and re-form his disposition before pushing through to Leyte Gulf.

As Admiral Sprague was forced to turn southwesterly to avoid

[58] Clifton Sprague in *American Magazine* Apr. 1945 pp. 114, 116.

[59] *Inter. Jap. Off.* I 174; Kurita in same pp. 32–44. He added that our torpedoes were "very slow" and easy to evade by turning away, which further separated his formation.

the jaws of the enemy pincers, his carriers from 0730 were steering downwind, and, with the Japanese in hot pursuit, could not afford to head up into the wind and recover planes. Hence, when Taffy 3 aircraft ran out of bombs or fuel, or their carrier was sunk, they had to make a temporary landing on Tacloban Field or on a carrier of Taffy 2. This did not please the aviators; they had the same feeling that any Navy man has when his ship is attacked. *Kitkun Bay's* eleven Wildcats, which had been launched for a routine patrol shortly after 0700, refueled at Tacloban (about 100 miles away) and picked up some 500-pound S.A.P. bombs. At 0833 they sent word to Admiral Ofstie that they were on their way out to attack. The Tacloban field was fortunately made operational by Army Engineers in the nick of time; a naval lieutenant who happened to be there organized an operating force with volunteer personnel, and scores of planes were handled successfully.[60]

Commander R. L. Fowler with five planes from *Kitkun Bay* orbited for 20 minutes looking for a hole in the clouds through which to dive on the enemy ships. From 8000 feet he watched a group of fighters and torpedo-bombers attacking the battleships. "The attacks were well executed," said Commander Fowler, "but in many cases lacked sufficient numbers and different loadings to effect a smooth, coördinated attack." [61]

After this attack, Fowler's group stayed close to *Haruna* and *Kongo*, just out of antiaircraft range. At that time, the two battleships appeared to be steaming at 27 knots right for Admiral Stump's Taffy 2, 30 miles to the southeastward. Fowler called Stump at 0910 and gave him this interesting news. It was soon confirmed by 14-inch splashes falling astern of Stump's destroyers.

St. Lo at 0816, on course 205°, could see a heavy cruiser column dead astern, firing full broadsides; range had closed to only 10,000

[60] Lucien Hubbard "They Kept 'Em Flying at Tacloban" *Liberty* 27 Jan. 1945 p. 18.

[61] *Kitkun Bay* Action Report, Enclosure H p. 4. In Enclosure I he gives the credit for the hits to Lt. (jg) Raymond Globokar USNR and Lt.(jg) Jack D. Turner USNR.

yards. But their salvos fell short; *St. Lo's* smoke clung close to the water and she was not hit. *Kalinin Bay*, in dodging salvos, crossed *St. Lo's* stern and then returned to station. *Gambier Bay* (as we shall see shortly) dropped out. A new threat developed around 0845, when light cruiser *Yahagi* and several destroyers closed to 6900 yards on the starboard quarter; this was the light force that *Johnston* took on and whose torpedo attack she helped to spoil.

Gambier Bay on the exposed flank of the carrier disposition was the unlucky one. She began replying with her single gun at 0741 when the range was over 17,000 yards and closing. The Japanese fired four-gun salvos in very small patterns (Captain Vieweg says only 25 yards in diameter) and over a minute elapsed between salvos. The enemy fire-director would step them up about 100 yards each time, so regularly that when it appeared that the next salvo would land right on her, *Gambier Bay* changed course about two points and had the satisfaction of seeing it hit the water where she would have been, had she maintained speed and course. Then the Japanese would start plotting all over again. This snake dance on the carrier's part continued for 25 minutes, at the end of which the range had closed to 10,000 yards. At 0810 she received her first hit, on the after end of her flight deck, and fires were started on flight deck and in hangar. Thereafter she was hit incessantly. Her forward port engine room was holed below the waterline, within five minutes these spaces flooded to burner level, the boilers had to be secured and the engine room abandoned. The ship slowed to eleven knots, and dropped astern of her fighting formation.

At 0830, when *Gambier Bay* was listing heavily and being fired on continuously by *Chikuma*, Commander Evans of destroyer *Johnston* gave this courageous order to his gunnery officer: "Commence firing on the cruiser, Hagen. Draw her fire away from the *Gambier Bay*." Hagen continues the story: –

We closed to 6000 yards and scored five hits. Reacting with monumental stupidity, the Japanese commander ignored us completely and concentrated on sinking the *Gambier Bay*. He could have sunk us both. By permitting us to escape, he made it possible for us to interfere a few minutes later with a destroyer attack that might have annihilated our little carrier force.[62]

This happened before *Johnston* thwarted the enemy torpedo attack, as related in our last section.

Heermann, as yet undamaged, closed the disengaged side of *Gambier Bay*, now burning amidships and listing 20 degrees, and at 0841 commenced firing at 12,000 yards' range on *Chikuma,* then throwing full salvos into *Gambier Bay*. The heavy cruiser turned in a tight circle and shifted a part of her gunfire to *Heermann*. In the meantime the main body of the enemy was rapidly closing this desperate little group, left behind as the other five carriers steamed on. Two more heavy cruisers (probably *Haguro* and as yet active *Chokai*), light cruiser *Noshiro,* and a big destroyer took *Gambier Bay* and both American destroyers under fire. In the words of *Heermann's* skipper: —

At least four vessels concentrated on *Heermann* during the next few minutes, as red, yellow, green, and no-color splashes were observed. At 0845 action . . . was still continuing and we suffered a shell hit in the pilothouse which killed three men and fatally wounded a fourth. . . . During this period water from near-misses drenched the director and director platform deck from which station the commanding officer was conning, making him wish he had a periscope with which to see over the wall of water. Everything looked rosy, but only because the splashes were colored red by the dye loads. This ship was between the port enemy cruiser column and our own carrier formation during this phase of the battle. At 0902 the *Tone* class cruiser turned sharply to her port, and retired to the eastward. At this time a large fire was observed on her fantail.

Despite the heroic efforts of two destroyers to help her, *Gambier Bay's* number was up. Concentrated short-range gunfire knocked out steering controls and power by 0837, all radars by 0840; then her after engine room was hit, water poured into it rapidly, and by 0845 she was dead in the water and sinking. All classified publica-

[62] Hagen's *Sat. Eve. Post* article 26 May 1945 p. 74. Confirmed by *Tone* Action Report, which says that *Chikuma* was shooting at a "*Baltimore* class cruiser" between 0818 and 0833, and shifted to a "*Ranger* class carrier" at 0844.

tions were destroyed, and at 0850 Captain Vieweg gave the order Abandon Ship. Soon the navigator, Lieutenant Commander George Gellhorn USNR, who had done an outstanding job zigzagging, was alone on the open bridge with the Captain. About 750 of the total complement of 854 went over the side, and as they did so, they could see *Chikuma* and another heavy cruiser firing at their ship from what seemed to be very short range; men in the water were killed by shell fragments. At 0907 *Gambier Bay* capsized and sank.

Survivors assembled into seven or eight groups, lashing floater nets, life rafts and sections of deck planking together; but they had to wait two days and nights for rescue. Lieutenant William H. Buderus USNR saved the lives of many men by directing them from the ship's side to a raft, and ordering them to kick it beyond the suction from the sinking. Refusing to take a seat in the raft, he hung onto the side, imparting his own courage to the wounded, until early the next morning, when he was torn to pieces by a shark.[63]

By 0905, when Asgad Point, Samar, was sighted bearing 240° and distant about 30 miles,[64] "enemy ships extended from starboard quarter aft to the port quarter" of *White Plains*, and two heavy cruisers had closed to 11,700 yards. Salvos were falling close aboard, but by making frequent course changes this flattop escaped a hit. As each enemy ship closed below 18,000 yards she was taken under fire by the ship's 5-inch 38 gun on the fantail. "At least six hits were observed on a heavy cruiser, one of which appeared to decommission a forward turret." [65] This was *Chokai*, hit repeatedly by shellfire at 0851 according to Japanese sources, and her engines put out of commission. "Hold on a little longer, boys," sang out Chief Gunner Jenkins of an automatic quad. "We're sucking them into

[63] *Gambier Bay* Action Report; total complement does not include aviators airborne or absent at the time; position of sinking, lat. 11°31′ N, long. 126°12′ E. Details from Robert Moore S 1c, a survivor, in 1957. He was in Lt. Buderus's group. After the lieutenant's death a chief photographer's mate, W. H. Sparrow, who had had the presence of mind to take some medical equipment over the side with him, took charge of that group and gave morphine injections to the wounded.

[64] Rear Adm. Ofstie's Action Report (Enclosure G, p. 2) says 40 miles, but *Fanshaw Bay's* track chart indicates that 30 miles is nearly correct.

[65] *White Plains* Action Report p. 10 (Enclosure A, p. 3).

40-mm range!" All values were being reversed; for an escort carrier to knock out a heavy cruiser was like "man bites dog." But it was Fowler's planes that really did her in. To quote his report: —

> We circled the heavy cruisers for three turns to gain a cirrus cloud cover and attacked from out of the sun and through this cloud at about 0905. We caught the second heavy cruiser (*Mogami* class) in column completely by surprise as we received absolutely no antiaircraft fire. At this time we had only four torpedo-bombers as the twelve fighters and other torpedo-bombers had fallen out of formation in the thick weather. We completed all dives in about 35 seconds, scoring five hits amidships on the stack, one hit and two near-misses on the stern and three hits on the bow. The third plane hitting the stern sent the heavy cruiser into a sharp right turn. After pulling out of the dive, I observed the heavy cruiser to go about 500 yards, blow up and sink within five minutes.[66]

Haguro's track chart traces *Chokai's* slow retirement to 0930, when she disappears below the waves.

8. *The Contribution of Taffy 2, 0658–0935* [67]

When action opened, Rear Admiral Stump's Taffy 2 was steaming westward to its day operating area, about 20 miles SSE of Taffy 3 and another 15 miles from Kurita's Center Force.

Although not alerted for the battle that they actually fought, all escort carriers had been ordered by Admiral Kinkaid the evening before to be prepared to load torpedoes at short notice, in order to get into the fight in Surigao Strait. Ground crews were up all night rigging for torpedoes the Avengers which had earlier been used for bombing. This was most fortunate, as it expedited the launching of torpedo missions; and when Admiral Stump at 0657 ordered all available TBMs to be de-bombed and loaded with torpedoes, no time was lost.[68]

[66] *Kitkun Bay* Action Report, Enclosure H.

[67] CTU 77.4.2 (Rear Adm. Stump) Action Report, 2 Nov. 1944.

[68] *Ommaney Bay* Action Report, 3 Nov. 1944; *Kadashan Bay* Action Report, 31 Oct. 1944.

These Taffy 2 escort carriers, which did not engage ship-to-ship, gave everything they had in the way of aircraft, but were delayed in lending a hand by the fact that so many planes had already departed on routine missions. Those that Captain Whitehead succeeded in recalling were not armed for striking capital ships and had to return on board to pick up torpedoes or 500-pound bombs. *Marcus Island*, for instance, had launched at 0545 a flight of ten TBMs loaded with 880 gallons of water and 1200 K rations for 96th Division troops isolated on Leyte.[69] This left her with only two Avengers capable of taking part in the torpedo-plane counterattack. Planes belonging to Taffy 3 carriers landed on *Marcus Island* and borrowed her torpedoes, so that when the "ration run" returned on board, there were none left – only bombs.

Even so, Admiral Stump's Taffy 2 launched three strikes totaling 36 fighters and 43 torpedo-bombers within an hour and a half. In any air attack on a heavy ship like those of the Japanese, torpedoes are the most effective weapon. Taffy 2 dropped 49 torpedoes on them during the day and claimed between five and eleven hits, all but one on battleships and heavy cruisers. Its 65 fighter planes that got into the fight expended 133 S.A.P. 500-pound bombs, hundreds of 100-pound GP bombs, and 276 rockets. These, and similar weapons from Taffy 3 planes, probably did the greater part of the damage to enemy ships, which were "liberally strafed, bombed and rocketed." [70]

The details of the participation by Taffy 2 are interesting. Admiral Stump ordered his pilots not to concentrate on one or two ships (as Task Force 38 had done in the Sibuyan Sea) but to cripple as many as possible.[71] He headed NNE to launch, then turned his group ESE to open distance on the enemy and held that course except at 0805 when he turned into the wind again to launch

[69] *Marcus Island* Action Report, 1 Nov. 1944 and CTU 77.4.22 (Rear Adm. W. D. Sample) Action Report, 3 Nov. 1944. "This order," observes Adm. Sample, "would appear to have been cleared without cognizance of naval commanders who had a plainer concept of the naval situation existing at the time, and this is not hindsight."

[70] CTU 77.4.2 (Rear Adm. Stump) Action Report, 8 Nov. 1944.

[71] *Kadashan Bay* Action Report, p. 7.

C.A.P., both local and Gulf. Stump had already sent his screen commander, Captain L. K. Reynolds, with destroyers *Haggard, Hailey* and *Franks* astern of his formation. They were sighted by *Gambier Bay* at 0750, creating a momentary hope that they were coming to help; but their duty was to cover Stump's rear against a possible attack by Japanese light forces. Again, at 0833, Taffy 2 turned to windward to launch a strike of eight fighters and 16 torpedo-bombers, and to recover six Avengers which were lost from Taffy 3. By this time the enemy was about 17 miles astern; and 14-inch shells began at 0841 to straddle the three rear-guard destroyers. The masts of the Japanese battleships became visible from Admiral Stump's carriers for a short time at 0924, and shell splashes were seen walking up toward them. After the destroyers had been under fire for half an hour, Admiral Stump recalled them.[72]

As soon as Taffy 3 had completed another air attack, at 0855, Taffy 2 sent in two strikes, its third and fourth, on the heavy cruisers and on a battleship astern of them. The Avengers, supported by the Wildcats, struck persistently, displaying the highest degree of enterprise and valor. Stump claimed torpedo hits on two cruisers; one of these may have been *Chikuma*, which, according to *Tone's* Action Report, was observed being knocked out by a torpedo attack at 0853.[73] At 0935 Taffy 2 launched a fifth strike consisting of eleven Avengers equipped with four 500-pound S.A.P. bombs each, and one with torpedoes, as well as eight Wildcats, with the wind 6½ points on the port bow. At around 1000 this strike added a few 500-pound S.A.P. bomb hits to those already scored on the heavy cruisers.

Stump's torpedo-plane attacks, like Sprague's, were highly successful. And it must be remembered that the Avenger pilots on escort carriers were not well trained to attack ships. They were specialists in routine C.A.P. and antisubmarine patrol, as well as special missions such as knocking out Japanese lookout posts in trees and firing ammunition dumps. When delivering torpedo at-

[72] Comdesdiv 94 and CTU 77.4.2 Action Reports.
[73] *Inter. Jap. Off.* I 43; Crudiv 7 Action Report gives the time and details.

tacks, the pilots followed standard doctrine, using plenty of altitude (10,000 feet and upward), a high-speed approach, steep dive, and low, fast, jinking recovery. The ring-tail, one-ton torpedoes that they carried were well adapted for these tactics, since they could be dropped at 800 feet altitude and at speeds up to 290 knots.[74] And although the Japanese ships put up heavy antiaircraft fire it was so inaccurate that only 12 Avengers and 11 Wildcats were shot down from Taffy 2.[75] The plane losses of Taffy 3, never recorded, were probably greater.

Returning now to Clifton Sprague's Taffy 3: *Haguro* and *Tone*, two of the four heavy cruisers that endeavored to close the port flank, broke off at 0905 and 0920 respectively; the other two, *Chokai* and *Chikuma*, were sunk by a combination of air and surface attacks. Admiral Kurita's final offensive thrust was the destroyer attack which went home at 0915 and was thwarted by *Johnston*. In Admiral Sprague's own words: –

> At 0925 my mind was occupied with dodging torpedoes when near the bridge I heard one of the signalmen yell, "Goddamit, boys, they're getting away!" I could not believe my eyes, but it looked as if the whole Japanese Fleet was indeed retiring. However, it took a whole series of reports from circling planes to convince me. And still I could not get the fact to soak into my battle-numbed brain. At best, I had expected to be swimming by this time." [76]

The main action was over.

[74] *Savo Island* Action Report pp. 6–13; *Kadashan Bay* Action Report p. 40.
[75] CTU 77.4.2 Action Report, 8 Nov. p. 25.
[76] Article in *American Magazine* Apr. 1945 p. 116. The torpedoes he refers to were those of Desron 10.

CHAPTER XIII

The Battle off Samar—Break-off and Pursuit[1]

25–29 October 1944

1. *Responsibility and Reaction*

BEFORE taking up the final phases of the Battle off Samar, it will be convenient to go into the hotly debated question of who was responsible for the complete surprise of the escort carriers at 0645 October 25, and to see what Commanders Third and Seventh Fleet attempted to do about it.

Admiral Halsey's erroneous estimate that the Japanese Center Force had been too badly damaged to be a "serious menace" was the primary event in a chain of wrong assumptions. Admiral King after the war "inquired into Kinkaid's air searches," and "regretfully concluded that the Seventh Fleet – notwithstanding its excellent performance in other respects – had failed to take the reasonable precaution that would have discovered the approach of the Japanese Central Force." He attributed the surprise "not only to Halsey's absence in the north but also to Kinkaid's failure to use his own air squadrons for search at the crucial moment." [2]

Let us examine this statement. Admiral Kinkaid ordered two separate searches to the north: the first by escort carrier planes, which (as we have seen in the previous chapter) was launched too late; and the second by PBY–5s, the "Black Cat" Catalina equipped for night flying. Kinkaid ordered this search to be made by five

[1] Same authorities as in Chapter XII footnote 1.

[2] King & Whitehill *Fleet Admiral King* p. 580.

planes, starting from their tender then anchored in Hunanagan Bay, Leyte, having just arrived from Mios Woendi. But only three actually took off, and only one of them could conceivably have encountered Kurita. Piloted by Lieutenant (jg) C. B. Sillers USNR, this PBY–5 flew around Samar. As Lieutenant Sillers described his flight, over twelve years later, he took off after dark 24 October, and after climbing to 10,000 feet to avoid "friendly" antiaircraft fire, came down to 800 feet beyond Homonhon Island, followed the Samar coastline very close – only about 500 yards away – and reached the entrance to San Bernardino Strait some time between 2200 and 2230.[3] He flew through the Strait before Kurita entered it, then into the Samar Sea, and returned outside Samar, after daybreak on the 25th. Kurita had sortied from the Strait at 0035 and Sillers never caught up with him.

A feeling of confidence that "Halsey would take care of the northern sector" seems to have pervaded Seventh Fleet forces in and around Leyte Gulf. A number of individuals, including Admiral Wilkinson, feared that Kurita might be coming south, but did not consider it their place to communicate their thoughts to Commander Seventh Fleet, who was entitled to assume that the northern sector was being taken care of. Task Force 38 was in a position to do it, and one could fairly infer from the operation plan that Halsey would do it. Moreover, Kinkaid intercepted dispatches which convinced him that Halsey actually was watching the Strait with his gunfire forces. The texts and times of these dispatches are important.

Commander Third Fleet, 1512 October 24 to all task force and group commanders Third Fleet, and to Cominch and Cincpac for information, was intercepted by Kinkaid, not an addressee. This dispatch, headed "Battle Plan," named battleships and other heavy units which "will be formed as Task Force 34" under Vice Admiral

[3] Cdr. Sillers to Commo. R. W. Bates 13 Apr. 1957. He explains that he hugged the coast according to "his instructions to observe shipping visually as a ship would be lost in the 'land return' on radarscope." It is obvious that Sillers was operating under instructions to report barge and sampan traffic; no high seas fleet could have been reported from a position so far inshore, at night.

Willis A. Lee, who had already been designated Commander Battle Line Third Fleet. It states that TF 34 "will engage decisively at long ranges" and that Rear Admirals Davison and Bogan will keep their two carrier groups clear of surface fighting.[4]

Should a naval officer have assumed from this dispatch that Task Force 34 actually *had* been formed and *would* be left to watch San Bernardino Strait? A battle plan is a very different thing from a battle or operation order. Admiral Wilkinson understood the correct meaning of the dispatch, as a plan for future battle, but Admiral Kinkaid and his communications officer, Commander Leland G. Shaefer, thought it meant what they wanted it to mean — that TF 34 had been formed and detached from TF 38 in order to watch San Bernardino Strait. They took the "will" in "will be formed" to be present imperative rather than future indicative. Other members of Kinkaid's staff disagreed; but Admiral Nimitz at Pearl Harbor and Rear Admiral C. M. ("Savvy") Cooke, Deputy C.N.O. in Washington, put exactly the same interpretation on it that Admiral Kinkaid did, which certainly absolves him of blame.

The next bit of information Kinkaid had to go on was Halsey's "Secret, Urgent" of 2022 October 24 to all task group commanders in his own fleet, ordering Bogan's and Davison's groups to rendezvous with Sherman's at midnight, when Mitscher in *Lexington* would take charge and "attack Japanese Northern Force."[5] Now, every ship mentioned in the 1512 dispatch as part of TF 34 also belonged to one or another of these three carrier groups, and steamed north with them; but Admiral Kinkaid, having assumed that TF34 had already been formed and pulled out of TF 38, made the further assumption that the heavy ships had been left behind to watch the Strait.

Certain Seventh Fleet staff officers who disagreed with the Ad-

[4] CTF 79 dispatch file; checked from Third Fleet Message File (Enclosure A in Halsey Action Report), paraphrased. That Halsey, when drafting this 1512 battle plan, envisaged TF 34 engaging Kurita, not Ozawa, is proved by (1) a TBS message sent out by him at 1710 to CTG 38.4 (Davison) which includes the words "If enemy sorties, TG 34 will be formed when directed by me," and (2) the fact that Halsey's first contact on Ozawa came at 1540.

[5] Halsey Message File, paraphrased.

miral's interpretation of these dispatches finally persuaded him to seek information from Third Fleet. At 0412 October 25, when sending Halsey news of the victory in Surigao Strait, Kinkaid added a query as to whether Task Force 34 was guarding San Bernardino Strait. Halsey did not receive this message until 0648, and at 0705 he sent the discouraging reply that TF 34 was with the fast carriers going north.

Six minutes earlier, the escort carriers had received a much more emphatic answer in the same sense from the muzzles of Kurita's guns. That startling news was received by Captain Whitehead at 0700, and was referred immediately to Admiral Kinkaid,[6] who says in his report: —

> The first news of this enemy force was received on board the flagship about 0724 [*sic*] when CTU 77.4.3 [Clifton Sprague] reported he was under gunfire attack by four battleships, eight heavy cruisers and many destroyers, at a range of 30,000 yards. This was the first indication that the enemy's Central Force had succeeded in passing through San Bernardino Strait. Up to this time, from information available to Commander Seventh Fleet, it was assumed that Third Fleet forces were guarding the San Bernardino Strait position to intercept and destroy any enemy forces attempting to come through.[7]

Back in Pearl Harbor, Admiral Nimitz was as surprised as anyone at the Japanese attack on the escort carriers. Apparently, he too wanted to know the answer, for at 1000 October 25 Admiral Halsey received a message from him inquiring the whereabouts of Task Force 34.[8]

Was the escort carrier command in any way to blame for the

[6] Commander Support Air Seventh Fleet Report 2 Nov. 1944 p. 12. Kinkaid's statement in following quotation that he did not receive the report until 0724 must be a misprint for 0704, for his plain-language message passing the word to Halsey was originated at 0707 Oct. 25. — Halsey Message File.

[7] Vice Adm. Kinkaid "Preliminary Action Report of Engagements in Leyte Gulf and off Samar Island on 25 Oct. 1944."

[8] Halsey Dispatch File p. 34. The query was followed (not preceded as quoted in *Admiral Halsey's Story* p. 220) by what communicators call padding, in the form of a quotation suggested by Tennyson's "Charge of the Light Brigade," but so phrased that Halsey took it to be an integral part of the message, and that Cincpac was reproaching him in a somewhat insulting manner.

surprise? Apparently not; for the dawn search northward that Kinkaid had ordered several hours earlier, and that T. L. Sprague had relayed to Stump, was countermanded when already in the air. None of the escort carrier commanders were on guard against Kurita. Their eyes and thoughts were all turned south and west, toward pursuing Japanese cripples beyond Surigao Strait, and on routine missions. Rear Admiral Clifton Sprague wrote with deep feeling on the failure of Admiral Halsey to guard the Strait; and his statement represents the reaction of most sailors in and around Leyte Gulf on 25 October: "In the absence of any information that this exit was no longer blocked, it was logical to assume that our northern flank could not be exposed without ample warning." [9]

Too much confidence was placed by Seventh Fleet flag officers in what Halsey would do, and Halsey placed too much confidence in the preliminary assessments of his carrier pilots' flash reports of the Sibuyan Sea action on the 24th. Even the stationing of one destroyer off San Bernardino Strait to give warning would have helped the escort carriers; for if the Spragues had expected Kurita they would have tracked his force and stationed their units beyond his gunfire range.

In conclusion, the reason why Kurita was able to sortie from San Bernardino Strait and steam toward Leyte Gulf for about seven hours, completely undetected, was a series of faulty assumptions on the part of his enemies.

Now let us see what Commanders Seventh and Third Fleets did to relieve this critical situation. Captain Whitehead's diversion of planes from routine and other missions to attack the Center Force brought much-needed aid to Taffy 3 before it was too late. Admiral Kinkaid lost no time in getting in touch with Halsey. A plain-language dispatch sent at 0707 and received at 0822 told him that enemy battleships and cruisers were firing on Clifton Sprague's CVE unit. This was followed by a dispatch originated at 0725, in which he said that Oldendorf's battleships were low on ammunition; this reached Halsey only at 0922. At 0727 Kinkaid radioed in

[9] CTU 77.4.3 "Special Report" 29 Oct. 1944.

plain English, and Halsey received the message at 0900: "Request Lee proceed top speed to cover Leyte; request immediate strike by fast carriers." Clifton Sprague, too, let Halsey know at 0735 that he was under attack by battleships and heavy cruisers. More particulars and repeated requests from Kinkaid to Halsey followed at 0739 ("Help needed from heavy ships immediately"), 0829 ("Situation critical, battleships and fast carrier strike wanted to prevent enemy penetrating Leyte Gulf"). Halsey replied at 0927 that he was himself engaged with Ozawa's Northern Force, but had (at 0848) ordered Admiral McCain's carrier group to assist Seventh Fleet immediately.[10] McCain was then fueling hundreds of miles to the eastward (lat. 15° N, long. 130° E). He was unable to get *Hancock*, *Hornet* and *Wasp* to a new launching position 335 miles northeast of the Center Force until 1030; and another hour and a half were required for planes to reach the target. There was some hope of Halsey's turning back Task Force 34, Admiral Lee's Battle Line, to engage Kurita; and that is what Halsey finally did, too late, after repeated needling by Kinkaid and even Nimitz.

Why was not Admiral Oldendorf's Battle Line sent out to help the "Taffies," after it had disposed of the Japanese Southern Force? The word spread around that these ships were left very short of armor-piercing ammunition (AP) after the Battle of Surigao Strait. That was in some measure true. The light cruisers had been pouring it out so liberally (as light cruisers were wont to do) that they only had 50 to 80 rounds apiece of AP, but an ample supply of HC, which in that caliber can (in the opinion of some cruiser commanders) be profitably employed against ships. They went at once in search of replenishment, but found that the two ammunition ships in Leyte Gulf were difficult to locate and had no 6-inch AP to offer.

The following table tells the story of the battleships' main battery ammunition, which would have been crucial had they engaged Kurita: –

[10] Various message files in Commo. Bates's office. That of 0727 is the one quoted in *Admiral Halsey's Story* p. 120 as "Where is Lee – send Lee."

BATTLESHIPS' EXPENDITURE MAIN BATTERY AMMUNITION, *18–25 Oct. 1944*[11]

	AP			HC		
	On Board 17 Oct.	*Expended, 25 Oct.*	*Left 25 Oct.*	*On Board 17 Oct.*	*Expended Bomb'dt.*	*Left 25 Oct.*
16-inch (8 guns)						
WEST VIRGINIA	200	93	107	616	440	172
MARYLAND	240	48	192	856	411	445
14-inch (12 guns)						
TENNESSEE	396	69	327	960	692	262
CALIFORNIA	240	63	177	960	882	78
MISSISSIPPI	201	12	189	1200	657	543
PENNSYLVANIA	360	0	360	960	946	14

It will be observed that *Maryland, Tennessee* and *Pennsylvania* had 24 rounds or better of AP per gun; *Mississippi,* 15¾ rounds; *West Virginia* and *California* a trifle over 13 rounds per gun. Every gunnery officer wants his magazines full, but the shortage here was nothing to be alarmed about.

What help Oldendorf could have afforded the escort carriers is doubtful, for at 0800 he was a good 65 miles (over three hours' steaming) from gunfire range of the position where the Japanese Center Force turned away at 0925. "Oley" was eager to do his best to help; but his chief of staff insisted that the proper strategy was to keep his ships together inside Leyte Gulf and let the enemy seek battle where we, not he, chose. "Rafe" Bates, as usual, was right. If Kurita had pressed inside the Gulf, "Oley" might have pulled another "crossing of the T" with his Battle Line. He had enough ammunition for that kind of battle, but not for a running fight.

Nevertheless, at 0850 Oldendorf received an order from Kinkaid to proceed with his entire force to a point a few miles north of Hibuson Island and stand by. His destroyer screen was augmented at that point.[12] At 0953 he received a second order from Kinkaid to take about half his force north to assist the escort carrier group.

[11] Expenditures from action reports. Amounts on board initially from individual ships' records. "Left 25 Oct." means left after the battle.

[12] By 5 DDs of Desron 21 (*Nicholas,* flag) and 4 of Desron 49 (*Haraden,* flag). In addition, at about 1015 Admiral Kinkaid ordered the remaining destroyers of Desron 49 (Capt. E. R. McLean in *Picking*), which were escorting unloaded transports home, to peel off, proceed to Leyte Gulf and "attack enemy encountered en route." These destroyers arrived on the scene several hours after the battle was over.

Scarcely had "Oley" issued the order to his ships than he received word from Kinkaid to belay it, because Kurita had broken off action. The orders were renewed at 1127 when the Japanese seemed to be coming back. One hour and a half later, when Oldendorf's force was already outside the eastern entrance to Leyte Gulf and looking for a fight, his mission was finally canceled.[13]

Kinkaid's primary and overriding responsibility was to protect the beachhead, the amphibious forces, and the Army ashore. He had to keep a part, at least, of Oldendorf's force available against a possible return of Admiral Shima's still intact Second Striking Force.[14] If, after the lapse of time, his calls to Halsey for assistance seem out of scale with the situation, we must be mindful of his responsibility for MacArthur's Army and remember that he did not know that Kurita would lose heart and turn back.

The American-born Japanese propagandist known as "Tokyo Rose," putting her best face on the situation after the battle, commented, "Kinkaid hallooing for help in plain English showed his great anxiety."

"She didn't know how true that was!" said the Admiral when it was all over.

2. *Kurita Breaks Off and Circles, 0915–1236*

In a running fight lasting almost two hours and a half, six escort carriers and their screen of three destroyers and four destroyer escorts, aided by planes from Stump's escort carrier unit, had stopped Kurita's powerful Center Force, and inflicted a greater loss than they suffered. And Admiral Kurita allowed five out of the six escort carriers that his force brought under gunfire, to get away. There is no better summary than that of Rear Admiral Clifton

[13] Comcrudiv 4 War Diary.

[14] Until the end of the day, Admiral Kinkaid had no reliable information of the damage done to the Japanese Southern Force. He suspected that a part of that force had not engaged and would take advantage of the withdrawal of our heavy units to thrust up through the Strait again. As he remarked to the writer, two Japanese heavies loose in Leyte Gulf could have upset the whole amphibious force.

Sprague, whose quick thinking and sound tactics extricated his group from an apparently hopeless situation: —

"The failure of the enemy main body and encircling light forces to completely wipe out all vessels of this task unit can be attributed to our successful smoke screen, our torpedo counterattack, continuous harassment of enemy by bomb, torpedo and strafing air attacks, timely maneuvers, and the definite partiality of Almighty God."

It was at 0911 that Kurita issued his order to break off action: "Rendezvous, my course north, speed 20." [15] His intention at that time was merely to close up and re-form his fleet, which had become widely dispersed, owing to his original order and frequent evasive action. He proposed to ascertain damage, and, if it seemed best, resume his march to Leyte Gulf in more orderly fashion. But the longer he postponed the decision the less he liked the thought of Leyte.

For the next three hours he maneuvered the Center Force as follows: —

Due north until 1055, then west and southwest, west again at 1147, heading straight for Leyte Gulf. After half an hour on that course — which caused Admiral Kinkaid to think that he was really pressing on in — he set a southwesterly course (240°) at 1215, and gradually worked around at 1236 to due north again. At 1310 Center Force passed only a few miles on the Samar side of the spot where the battle had begun. And from that point it definitely retired toward San Bernardino Strait.

There was nothing to prevent him from charging through or past Taffy 3 into Leyte Gulf. Three heavy cruisers had been done for, but *Yamato* was practically unscathed (she received some bomb damage on the 24th and she took three 5-inch hits on the 25th which did not hurt her much), as well as three more battleships. Some of his destroyers were running low in fuel, but not desperately so; and he had plenty of AP ammunition. His appearance in

[15] *Yamato* Action Report. Comcrudiv 7 got it at 0914 in the form "All ships reassemble," and *Haguro* at 0916, "Gradually reassemble."

Leyte Gulf would have been extremely embarrassing to Admirals Kinkaid and Oldendorf. So, why did he not press on?

His explanation, coupled with that of his chief of staff, Rear Admiral Koyanagi, is interesting; and, I believe, sincere. In the first place he broke off chasing Taffy 3 because he believed the escort carriers were making 30 knots! ("I knew you were scared, Ziggy," said another admiral to Clifton Sprague after reading this; "but I didn't know you were that scared!") The absolute top speed of the CVEs was 18 knots, and Kurita's ships could make 24 or 25 knots, but not all of it in pursuit; they were slowed up by taking evasive action every time they sighted a plane or a torpedo. Apparently the remarkable smoke-making powers of Taffy 3 prevented the Japanese optical rangefinders from tracking the escort carriers, and they had no radar capable of doing it. Kurita also had very poor communications within his force; his chief of staff, when interrogated a year later, said it was news to him that two or three of the heavy cruisers, when recalled, had closed to within 10,000 yards of the carriers.

The apparently aimless maneuvering betwen 0911 and 1236 which we have described was owing to Kurita's efforts to avoid air attack while making up his mind. And that mind was initially uncertain. Kurita had had to swim for his life on the 23rd, and taken a beating from Third Fleet on the 24th. Before daybreak on the 25th he received Admiral Shima's message sent off at 0425 that he was retiring from Surigao Strait; and a message from *Shigure* received a little later indicated that she was the sole survivor of Nishimura's force. And now, what was this obstinate force that barred his passage? His staff evaluated it as a part of Halsey's Third Fleet – Sprague's CVEs were either *Independence* class CVLs or *Ranger* class CVs; the *Fletcher* class destroyers were all *Baltimore* class heavy cruisers (their profiles are somewhat alike); a *Pennsylvania* class battlewagon was reported to be lurking among the carriers; and when Taffy 2 was sighted from *Yamato's* lofty masthead it was reported as another fast carrier group.

Other factors as well caused Kurita to retire. Two planes from

Yamato that he sent to reconnoiter Leyte Gulf failed to return. He had no word from Ozawa as to what was going on up north, but at 0945 he received a mysterious report to the effect that an enemy task force lay only 113 miles north of Suluan Island; and he thought that might be Halsey.[16] Several of Kinkaid's plain-language calls for help were intercepted by the Japanese communications center at Takao, Formosa, and relayed to Kurita, and these were not conducive to his peace of mind. Off Manus Fox circuit he picked up Kinkaid's 0940 "Being attacked by four battleships, light cruisers and other ships. Request dispatch of fast battleships and a fast carrier air strike." Kurita received that at 1144. An hour earlier he got Kinkaid's 1000 "We are still being attacked." At around 1120 the communications center at Owada, Honshu, gave him a plain-language from Kinkaid ordering certain ships to "proceed to a point 300 miles southeast of entrance to Leyte Gulf and await orders." [17] In the year 1947 Kurita told a *Life* correspondent "that he had been definitely influenced in deciding to withdraw by hearing this plain-language transmission, which led him to believe that powerful aid was on the way for the forces he was attacking." [18] Having intercepted a message from Commander Whitehead inviting all carrier planes to make emergency landings at Tacloban airfield, Kurita now imagined that field to be crowded with aircraft that would attack Center Force as soon as it entered the Gulf, resulting in another Sibuyan Sea debacle. A *Nagato* plane reported at 1235 that there were 35 transports in Leyte Gulf, but Kurita figured that if he pressed on, most of these would have escaped, preventing him from accomplishing anything important for the Emperor.[19]

[16] Adm. Kurita Action Report p. 33; not in *Yamato's* message file. A probable explanation suggested by Rear Adm. Anderson is a Second Air Fleet message logged in Adm. Ozawa's Action Report at 0635 Oct. 25 giving positions, mostly wrong, of five enemy forces, the southernmost 50 miles bearing 45° from San Bernardino Strait.

[17] *Yamato* Action Report pp. 31–2. The last was a mistranslation of Kinkaid's orders to Desron 49 to peel off from a convoy and come to a point 30 miles southeast of the Gulf.

[18] Gilbert Cant in *Life* Magazine 24 Nov. 1947 p. 85.

[19] Confirmed by his then chief of staff, Rear Admiral Koyanagi, in "Battle of Leyte Gulf, a Retrospection." He feared to find himself in an empty gulf, a target for land- and carrier-based aircraft.

Thus, partly from what he knew, but still more from what he imagined, Kurita reached the conclusion that his prospects in Leyte Gulf were both thin and grim, and that he had better save the rest of his fleet, possibly to fight another day.

So it is not surprising that, just as he was about to receive another air attack from the planes of Taffy 2, Admiral Kurita decided to make no further attempt to break through to the Gulf. At 1236 he sent this message to C. in C. Combined Fleet at Tokyo: –

> First Striking Force has abandoned penetration of Leyte anchorage. Is proceeding north searching for enemy task force. [He meant the phantom force reported at 0945.] Will engage decisively, then pass through San Bernardino Strait.[20]

3. *Enter Kamikaze, 0740–1130 October 25*

Even after Kurita retired the battle was not over for the escort carriers. Other hostile forces had been released which had to be dealt with; some of them were already being fought during the main phase of the battle. Rear Admiral T. L. Sprague's Taffy 1, comprising three *Sangamon* class and one Kaiser class escort carrier, with a screen of three destroyers and five DEs, was having a tough fight to the southward. This group had the honor of receiving the first deliberate Kamikaze suicide plane attack of the war.

Taffy 1, in its regular day operating area about 40 miles off Siargao Island, and some 130 miles to the southward of Taffy 3, had launched a strike of 11 Avengers and 17 Hellcats to join the chase down Surigao Strait, an hour before the battle opened off Samar. As soon as word came through of the attack on Taffy 3, "Tommy" Sprague prepared to send assistance to his friend "Ziggy," and did. His carriers were in the process of recovering and rearming planes returning from other missions at 0740 when they were jumped by six Japanese planes from Davao.

Santee had just finished launching five TBMs and eight FM-2s

[20] Combatdiv 1 (Ugaki) Report p. 48.

when a Japanese plane dove onto her out of a cloud, and so near that no guns could be brought to bear. It came in strafing, crashed the flight deck on the port side forward and continued on through the hangar deck. The explosion blew a hole 15 by 30 feet, and started fires in the immediate vicinity of eight 1000-pound bombs.[21] Failure of these bombs to detonate is probably the most fortunate event in *Santee's* long and active career. The fire was brought under control by 0751, but the carrier sustained 43 casualties, 16 of them fatal.

Half a minute after this suicide crash another Kamikaze circled *Suwannee* astern, and, when hit by her antiaircraft fire, spiraled down and rolled over into a dive, heading for *Sangamon.* One 5-inch shell fired by *Suwannee* hit the plane when it was about 500 feet from her sister flattop, causing it to swerve and splash at a safe distance. At the same time *Petrof Bay* was closely missed by a third Kamikaze which was knocked down by antiaircraft fire.

Five minutes after the fire had been extinguished on *Santee,* she was hit on the starboard side between frames 58 and 60 by a torpedo, launched by Japanese submarine *I–56.*[22] The explosion caused a certain amount of damage, but no casualties. *I–56* had picked the wrong ship, for the large converted tankers of this class safely absorbed hits that would have been lethal to the Kaiser class. *Santee,* with a slight list from flooding, was making 16½ knots before eight bells struck.

Suwannee, after shooting down two Zekes, spotted a third off her stern, circling in the clouds at 8000 feet. Her antiaircraft gunners were on it in a jiffy. It rolled over, smoking, toward the carrier's starboard side and then plummeted, hitting *Suwannee* about 40 feet forward of the after elevator, making a 10-foot hole in the flight deck. Its bomb exploded between the flight and hangar decks, tearing a 25-foot hole in the latter, injuring the main deck and causing numerous casualties. The fire on the hangar deck was promptly quenched but the after plane elevator remained inopera-

[21] *Santee* Action Report 5 Nov. 1944 p. 14.
[22] M. Hasimoto *Sunk* (London 1954) p. 113.

tive. Within two hours the flight deck damage had been temporarily repaired so that landings could be made, and at 1009 air operations were resumed.

Five aircraft from Malabacat, Luzon, jumped Taffy 3 at 1050, just as Clifton Sprague's carriers, respited from enemy gunfire, were trying to recover their own aircraft. These Kamikazes never showed on the radar screen; they approached from very low altitude, climbed rapidly inside SK radar range, and started dives from 5000 to 6000 feet. So sharp and sudden was their onslaught that C.A.P. was unable to intercept.

Kitkun Bay, Admiral Ofstie's flagship, caught the first attack. A Zeke, crossing her bow from port to starboard, climbed rapidly, rolled and dove directly at the bridge, strafing. It missed the bridge, passed over the island, crashed the port catwalk and bounced into the sea, but the bomb that it carried exploded, causing considerable damage. Two planes went for *Fanshaw Bay*, but both were shot down. The other two dove toward *White Plains*. At an altitude of 500 feet they pulled out of their dive, both under fire by 40-mm guns. One that was already smoking turned and dove onto *St. Lo*.

Captain McKenna had secured from General Quarters and set Condition II to give the men a chance to rest and drink coffee. *St. Lo* sighted these planes at 1051 and opened fire at once, but the Zeke which had her number crashed through the flight deck and burst into flames below. Quickly there followed seven explosions of torpedoes and bombs on the hangar deck. Great sections of the flight deck and elevator and entire planes were hurled hundreds of feet into the air. The ship blazed from stem to stern, and at 1125 the unluckily renamed *St. Lo* foundered under a cloud of dense smoke.[23]

The second member of this pair partly circled the formation, turned, and started a run on *White Plains*, which maneuvered to evade with hard left rudder. The plane came in weaving under fire

[23] *Kitkun Bay* Action Report 28 Oct. The position was lat. 11°10′ N, long. 126°05′ E. *St. Lo* had been commissioned as *Midway*, but when that name was wanted for the new class of big carriers it was taken from her – which as all old sailors know brings bad luck.

of all after guns; a torrent of blazing tracers could be seen entering its fuselage and wing roots. When only a few yards astern, it rolled over and dove, missing the port catwalk by inches and exploding between that level and the water. The flight deck was showered with debris and fragments of the pilot, and eleven men were injured.

As *Kitkun Bay* was steaming on course 200° at 1110, she sighted 15 Judys approaching the formation from astern, distant about five miles. She launched two Wildcats by catapult for combat air patrol, but not in time. She and the three remaining carriers, *Fanshaw Bay*, *White Plains* and *Kalinin Bay* were without a screen, owing to rescue work. One of three Kamikazes got through the C.A.P. and dove at *Kitkun Bay* from astern. Its wings were shot off as it neared the ship, and just in time, for the bomb struck the water 25 yards on the starboard bow and parts of the plane hit the forecastle. *Kalinin Bay* received a crash dive on her flight deck which damaged it badly, but the fires then started were quenched in less than five minutes. A second plane crashed her after stack and two others dove but missed. Admiral Sprague's flagship, the lucky "Fannie Bee," alone sustained no damage in this assault.

Thus the Navy was confronted with a new problem of air defense. Nobody realized that this was the beginning of new and desperate tactics on the part of the Japanese, but the prospects were distinctly unpleasant. As a steward's mate of *Wichita* said, when that cruiser had to deal with Kamikazes a few days later: "We don't mind them planes which drops things but we don't like them what *lights* on you!"

4. *Exeunt Taffies, Fighting, 2000 October 25–0643 October 29*

The air attack on Taffy 3 was over by 1130. All four surviving vessels of the screen searched for *St. Lo* survivors until 1534. This left Taffy 3 with no screen for eight hours, a "desperate expedient," as Admiral Clifton Sprague admitted, necessitated by "absence of any rescue effort from other sources." His four remaining carriers retired southward at reduced speed, steering various courses to evade submarines and also to continue flight operations. During the afternoon, strike groups from Admiral McCain's carriers *Hornet* and *Wasp*, which had missed Kurita's force, were intercepted by radio and vectored to their objective.

After *Heermann*, *Butler*, *Dennis* and *Raymond* had combed for four hours the waters where *St. Lo* went down, recovering 754 men, they headed south to rejoin Taffy 3. Their speed was limited to 15 knots by the fact that both *Heermann* and *Dennis* had flooded compartments forward. At 1625 Commander Hathaway ordered *Raymond* and *Butler* to push ahead and try to reach Taffy 3 before dark. Having done so, these two were sent into Leyte Gulf to fuel and to land badly wounded survivors. *Heermann* and *Dennis* proceeded to Kossol Passage, the nearest friendly haven where damaged ships might consult the doctors of Service Squadron 10.

Clifton Sprague could afford to dispense with the services of these ships, because at 2000 destroyers *Sproston*, *Hale* and *Picking*, detached by Admiral Kinkaid from escorting transports to Manus, reported to his screen. Taffy 3 arrived Mios Woendi early in the morning of 29 October and next day departed for Manus, where it was joined by the other two Taffies for much-needed upkeep.

Around noon on 25 October, and again at 1220, three or four enemy fighter planes carrying bombs attacked Taffy 1 and were driven off by ships' gunfire. Taffy 1 then steamed in a northeasterly direction to join Taffy 3, and at 1700 launched all remaining planes to attack Kurita's Center Force, which by that time was well out of range. Many planes of this group landed on Tacloban Field; others made night landings on *Santee* and *Petrof Bay* around 1945. At 2237, before rendezvous with Taffy 3 was effected, destroyer escort *Coolbaugh* (Lieutenant Commander S. T. Hotchkiss USNR) of the screen sighted a submarine periscope in the darkness. Admiral Sprague immediately ordered a 90-degree emergency turn. Just as it was completed, a torpedo passed along each side of

Petrof Bay. *Coolbaugh* promptly attacked the submarine with hedgehog, unsuccessfully.[24] Taffy 1, after sighting Taffy 3 and exchanging signals, turned southward again. Next morning, 26 October, destroyer escort *Richard M. Rowell* of the screen made a sound contact on a submarine. Within half an hour she had sighted the periscope and made a series of hedgehog and depth-charge attacks; but that I-boat, too, got away.[25]

Shortly after noon 26 October, the Kamikazes pulled off another attack on Taffy 1, then at lat. 09°37′ N, long. 126°53′ E. Her own combat air patrol saved *Santee* from twelve Judys. *Sangamon* and *Petrof Bay* were narrowly missed. A Zeke that chose *Suwannee* as the place to die crashed a torpedo-bomber which had just been recovered and was sitting on the forward elevator. Both planes exploded, both pilots and two crewmen were killed, nine more planes spotted on the flight deck forward were ignited and exploded, lighting a fire that was only subdued after several hours of hard work. Despite this and her earlier mishap, *Suwannee's* luck held; the plane's depth charges burned but did not explode. But the carrier lost 85 killed, 58 missing and 102 wounded, some of whom subsequently died.

The story of an unknown hero of *Suwannee* is told by Commander S. Van Mater, her executive officer. A number of men in the forecastle were cut off from the rest of the ship by flames.

After several calls to have medical supplies brought to the forecastle for those seriously injured were unproductive of results, an enlisted man informed Chief Aviation Electrician's Mate C. N. Barr that he would try to get through the flames to get medical supplies because he could no longer stand the sufferings of the wounded. Despite Barr's efforts to stop him, the man climbed to the 20-mm mounts just forward of the flight deck. A second later a torpedo-bomber directly in his path exploded and the man was seen holding on the starboard side of the flight deck with one leg blown off. A moment later he fell into the

[24] Rear Adm. T. L. Sprague Report p. 31. "We saw it explode," said Lt. David Acheson USNR of *Coolbaugh* to the writer, "but only got an E assessment." *German, Japanese and Italian Submarine Losses* indicate that this submarine did not sink. It was probably *I-362*. Position was lat. 09°52′ N, long. 127°30′ E.

[25] Enclosure D to *Rowell* Action Report 30 Oct. 1944.

water and was not seen again. Every effort to ascertain his name has proved unavailing.[26]

So it is in any battle. The efforts of many an unknown sailor save hundreds of his shipmates' lives and turn possible disaster into victory. Others, like the unknown hero of *Suwannee*, fail gloriously in the attempt, but their example is not lost. As Pindar wrote 2500 years ago: –

> Across the fruitful earth and o'er the sea
> Shoots a bright beam of noble deeds, unquenchable . . .

After 26 October the Kamikazes transferred their attention to shipping in Leyte Gulf and let the embattled escort carriers alone. But Japanese submarines were not yet through with them.

Destroyer escorts *Eversole* and *Richard S. Bull* of Taffy 1 screen were sent by Rear Admiral T. L. Sprague at 1700 October 25 to search for survivors of *St. Lo* and *Gambier Bay*. After a fruitless search of 24 hours they were recalled and then sent to San Pedro Bay carrying wounded from *Santee*, and seeking fuel, which they needed badly. Arriving at 0600 October 28, they found the oilers too busy fueling Admiral Oldendorf's force to attend to them. *Eversole* borrowed hose couplings from a Navy tanker and fueled from a Liberty ship. *Bull* went begging from ship to ship until Captain Granum of *Wasatch* invited her alongside. An air alert forced her to cast off at 1710 before completion and she got under way well astern of *Eversole*, hoping to clear Leyte Gulf and rendezvous with Taffy 1 off shore at daylight.

It was a dark and rainy night. *Eversole* (Lieutenant Commander G. E. Marix) at 0228 October 29 had reached a point about 60 miles off Dinagat Island, when her sonar operator got a contact, distant 2800 yards. Even before the skipper could reach the bridge from C.I.C., his ship was hit by two torpedoes whose explosions fairly tore her apart. He ordered Abandon Ship at 0240, himself lowered a sailor with a broken leg into the water and towed the man to a

[26] *Suwannee* Action Report. Following quotation is from *Isthmian Ode* iv. 43.

floater net. He then ordered all nets lashed together and told surviving officers to swim around to pick up other survivors.

After the men had been in the water about an hour, and *Eversole* had sunk, a tremendous underwater explosion occurred which killed about 30 survivors, wounded everyone in the water and ruptured most of the pneumatic life preservers. Unconscious men began drifting away from the floater nets but Marix and other officers, aided by some of the slightly injured, pulled them back and dragged them on board.[27]

Fortunately, *Bull* was on the same course as *Eversole* and about an hour's steaming astern. At 0325 her officer of the deck reported a "faint light on the horizon," and in a moment she was in the midst of *Eversole* survivors using their flashlights. Lieutenant Commander A. W. Gardes, the C.O., promptly lowered his motor whaleboat to recover survivors. An oiler unit commanded by Captain Jefferson Davis Beard, which happened to be crossing the destroyer escorts' track about twelve miles distant, was raised by radio, warned of the presence of a submarine and requested to send help. The skipper with the historic name obliged by detaching from his screen destroyer escort *Whitehurst*, which not only covered *Bull's* rescue operations, but got a submarine. About 50 miles from the scene of *Eversole's* sinking, *Whitehurst* obtained a sound contact and made four successive hedgehog attacks. At 0643 October 29, after completing her fourth run, five or more violent underwater explosions were heard and felt. This was submarine *I-45* breaking up; presumably she is the one which had torpedoed *Eversole*.[28]

By 0630 *Bull* had 139 survivors on board and under treatment. She transferred them to hospital ship *Bountiful* at Kossol Passage and rejoined Taffy 1 at Manus.

[27] *Eversole* Action Report 7 Nov. 1944.

[28] *Bull*, *Eversole* and *Whitehurst* Action Reports. A humorous relief to the loss of *Eversole* was this: Lt. Cdr. Marix came up to *Bull's* bridge still dripping water and fuel oil, sank into the skipper's deck chair and put his hand over the telephone receiver. The result was that "Skeet" Gardes skidded on fuel every time he walked the bridge, was plastered with it when he sat down, and got it into his mouth when he tried to telephone.

5. *Air Chase of Kurita, 1100 October 25–October 27*

After Commander Fowler of *Kitkun Bay's* air group had directed from the air the attacks on Kurita's force that we described in the last chapter, he landed on *Manila Bay* of Taffy 2, rearmed all planes with four 500-pound S.A.P. bombs each, and relaunched at 1100. About 16 Avengers and 16 fighters from various ships rendezvoused with him, and a few others joined Lieutenant Commander John R. Dale USNR, C.O. of *Kadashan Bay* air group. In all 35 Avengers and the same number of Wildcats were soon streaking north toward Kurita, then steering his great circle of indecision. They sighted heavy cruiser *Suzuya,* badly bombed early in the battle, with main deck awash and destroyer *Okinami* standing by. In accordance with orders from Admiral Tom Sprague to concentrate on damaging many ships rather than sinking a few, Fowler wasted no ammunition on *Suzuya.* She sank at 1322, third of Kurita's heavies to go down that day.[29]

At 1220 Commander Fowler sighted Center Force some 15 miles off the middle of Samar. He made a full contact report and shadowed the disposition until it turned north; his appearance, apparently, was the "last straw" on Kurita's back which decided him to quit. Fowler ordered Dale's group to attack from the starboard hand while he took the port, diving at 1245 out of a big cumulus cloud, Wildcats strafing ahead of the Avengers. The Japanese ships at once started hard left turns, which actually made the attack easier to execute. One of the Avengers dropped a bomb on battleship *Nagato* which went through her bows and exploded in the water. *Tone,* Admiral Shiraishi's third flagship of the day, took a bomb hit aft that put her steering gear temporarily out of commission. According to Admiral Kurita, this attack inflicted no serious damage, but one gets a different story from the ships' reports. Anti-

[29] Identification and times from *Okinami* War Diary.

aircraft fire was severe; Fowler's plane had over 30 holes shot in her.[30]

Center Force was now definitely retiring. At 1236 Admiral Kurita sent out the message to that effect which we have already quoted. The Fowler-Dale strike came immediately after. And within an hour Kurita was subjected to the long-planned attack by Vice Admiral McCain's Fast Carrier Group 1.

That task group, which included fleet carriers *Wasp*, *Hornet* and *Hancock* and light carriers *Monterey* and *Cowpens*, had been ordered by Admiral Halsey at 0848 to go to the aid of the escort carriers. It knocked off fueling, formed up at 0940, and five minutes later was steaming course 245° at 30 knots to reach a practicable launching position. Admiral McCain at 0950 delegated the search to *Hornet*. Between 1030 and 1040 she launched six Hellcats to search, and at the same time her share of the first strike — 48 Hellcats, 33 Helldivers and 19 Avengers. On the completion of this launching at 1045, Kurita's reported position bore 229°, distant 335 miles. It was to be one of the longest carrier strikes of the war. Urgent requests for help kept coming in from Captain Whitehead, but no information could be obtained as to whether the planes could or could not land at Tacloban. Consequently, in order to insure their return to the carriers, they had to be rigged with wing tanks and loaded with bombs instead of the heavier torpedoes.[31]

The first strike found the Center Force easily, since Kurita had circled back almost to his starting position; it went in at 1316 and made only one hit on *Tone*, which was a dud. A second and smaller strike, launched from *Hornet* and *Hancock* at 1255 had 320 miles to fly, and attacked at 1500. In all, 147 sorties were flown

[30] *Kitkun Bay* Action Report, Cdr. Fowler's Report Encl. 1; *Kadashan Bay* Action Report, Report of Compron 20 (Lt. Cdr. Dale). Dale was reported missing, but with several other pilots landed successfully on *Kitkun Bay*. His squadron had a fight with nine Zekes on the way back.

[31] CTG 38.1 (Vice Adm. McCain) Report on Operations 2–29 Oct., 15 Dec. 1944; *Hornet* Action Report 28 Oct. 1944.

against the Center Force by McCain's task group.[32] Many hits were claimed, but none were admitted by Kurita and certainly no serious damage was inflicted. These strikes were very expensive, however, for TG 38.1. Ten planes were lost in combat and four operationally, with five pilots and seven crewmen. A few planes damaged or out of gas made Tacloban safely or found temporary harbors on the flattops of Taffy 2; the rest made the long flight back to their own carriers and were recovered between 1545 and 1845.

Rear Admiral Stump's Taffy 2 was not yet through with the Center Force. At 1508 its sixth and last strike of the day, consisting of 26 Avengers, some armed with torpedoes, and 24 Wildcats, was launched from *Kitkun Bay, Savo Island* and other carriers, with instructions to find and attack the enemy. It was easy enough to locate Center Force, then 135 miles to the north, since several ships were trailing oil. The results of this strike were nil. Kurita's antiaircraft gunners seem to have improved with practice, of which they certainly had plenty.

Kurita was now fast approaching his route to safety, San Bernardino Strait. A plane from carrier *Independence* observed him entering it at 2140, in single column. All surviving ships except destroyer *Nowaki*, which had been standing by *Chikuma* and was unable to catch up, got through that night.

In the meantime McCain's TG 38.1 was steaming westward at high speed in order to be at a good launching position at dawn, and Bogan's TG 38.2 was ordered by Halsey to join in the air chase of Kurita. Admiral McCain had a plan ready for the day's strike. He warned his carrier pilots to look for the enemy force near Mindoro, and passed the word "listen for contacts from searchers and kick the hell out of those ships." Bogan rendezvoused with McCain at 0500 and their first strikes were launched at 0600.

Kurita's weakened Center Force was reported in Tablas Strait approaching Semirara Island at 0810 October 26. McCain at once

[32] Whitehead Report p. 13; Air Research Report No. 18 (see footnote 1 next chapter).

sliced off his second strike and sent a third away at 1245. In all, 174 planes from McCain's group and 83 from Bogan's reached the Center Force, only two less than had hit it on the 24th in the Sibuyan Sea.[33] Kurita continued southward and endeavored to escape by Cuyo East Pass. And all his ships except two did escape. Light cruiser *Noshiro*, hit at 0910 near Batbatan Island, sank at 1137. Heavy cruiser *Kumano* at about 0850 October 26 was hit by a bomb that left her with but one boiler. In the Battle off Samar she had taken a destroyer torpedo hit which blew off her bow; but she managed to make five knots, entered Coron Bay, and proceeded to Manila escorted by destroyer *Hamanami*. After temporary repairs *Kumano* started for Japan. On 6 November she was attacked by four American submarines and again hit but not sunk. She then took refuge in Dasol Bay near Lingayen Gulf, where planes from *Ticonderoga* sank her on 25 November.[34] This relentless hunting down of individual ships was typical of the last phase of the Pacific War.

During the morning of 26 October, 47 Morotai-based Liberators of the Far Eastern Air Force, each armed with three half-ton bombs or their equivalent, attacked the Center Force west of Panay, and near the Cuyo Islands.[35] They claimed eight direct hits on *Nagato*, *Kongo* and a light cruiser, out of some 150 bombs dropped; [36] but according to her own records *Nagato* was undamaged, and she survived the war.

Destroyer *Hayashimo* ran out of fuel in the Sibuyan Sea and had to borrow from *Okinami* to reach Coron Bay, where a tanker was waiting. On the 27th she was hit by a bomb from a Task Force 38 plane and beached at Semirara Island south of Mindoro, providing American aircraft with excellent bombing practice for the

[33] Total sorties from Air Research Report No. 18 (see footnote 1 next chapter) p. 53; those of TG 38.1 from McCain's Report.

[34] Information from Lt. W. T. Longstreth, USNR, Air Intelligence Officer on Vice Adm. McCain's staff, confirmed by JANAC.

[35] Position given as lat. 11°10′ N, long. 121°10′ E and time 1144 on Seventh Fleet Chart of Sightings Reported and Damage Inflicted 26–29 October.

[36] Airpac Analysis for Oct. 1944, p. 15; in *Intelligence Summary* A.A.F., S.W.P.A. Nov. 1944; *Nagato* Action Report.

next six weeks. The same day *Shiranuhi*, a survivor of Admiral Shima's Second Striking Force, was sunk by carrier aircraft off Mindoro. Five other destroyers entered Coron Bay to fuel on 26 October, while the rest of the Center Force continued on Kurita's chosen course to Brunei Bay, Borneo, whence all four battleships and some of the cruisers later proceeded to Kure in the Inland Sea of Japan for repairs.[37]

Admiral Kurita broke off action and retired from the Samar field of battle just in time to save a "fleet in being" which was incapable of offensive action but a cause of worry to the planning and operations officers of Seventh Fleet. None of his capital ships are known to have been in action again before 6 April 1945, when mighty *Yamato* sortied from home waters to certain death at the hands of fast carrier planes.

Successful retirement was small consolation for the complete failure of Kurita's mission, to break up amphibious shipping in Leyte Gulf. His defeat was due, in the last analysis, to the indomitable spirit of the Spragues' escort carriers, with their screen and aircraft. It was they that stopped the most powerful surface fleet which Japan had sent to sea since the Battle of Midway.

6. *Rescue Operations, 25–27 October*

Rescue operations in the Battle for Leyte Gulf were, in general, well done. For instance, Lieutenant Commander Fred E. Bakutis, skipper of the *Enterprise* fighter squadron, was shot down while conducting a search-strike mission on Nishimura's Southern Force in the Sulu Sea at 0905 October 24. As he was observed to climb onto his life raft, his shipmates estimated rate of drift and sent the information to every fleet headquarters, to Army Air Force at Tacloban and to Submarines Pacific Fleet and Southwest Pacific.

[37] War Diaries *Kishinami* and *Okinami*, Seventh Fleet Intelligence Center 22 Apr. 1945.

Six days later submarine *Hardhead*, directed to the estimated spot, picked up Bakutis, none the worse for his ride.[38]

Surface survivors of the Battle off Samar were picked up in less time, but many who were already wounded before making a raft died before rescue appeared. Rear Admiral Clifton Sprague, as we have seen, stripped his battered escort carriers of their screen to pick up *St. Lo* survivors immediately after that ship went down. This left him without any screen whatsoever, a great risk in submarine-infested waters. So he had to depend on others to pick up survivors of *Gambier Bay*, *Hoel*, *Johnston* and *Samuel B. Roberts*. He informed Seventh Fleet headquarters promptly of the sinking of these ships, and requested that rescue measures be started forthwith.

Although Seventh Fleet had a well organized air-surface search plan, it was not put into effect here. Swimmers from *Gambier Bay* and the destroyers reported that planes "buzzed" them at intervals for two days, but dropped not so much as a rubber raft or a biscuit; and if they made contact reports, nobody acted upon them. The explanation is that the Leyte beachhead and San Pedro anchorage were under intermittent Kamikaze attack during most of the day of battle. Catalinas, attached to tender *San Carlos* anchored in San Pedro Bay, were too busy rescuing the victims of plane crashes to go looking for survivors from ships. One of them picked up a plane's crew from *Kalinin Bay*.

In the surface search, the initial error stemmed from a plane report received on board Admiral Stump's flagship at 1230 October 25. It stated that several hundred survivors were floating in the vicinity of lat. 11°12′ N, long. 126°30′ E. This position, 20 to 40 miles south of where the ships actually went down, was at once passed to Seventh Fleet. The error was not great enough to have frustrated an air search. Admiral Stump heard shortly after 1800 that air search had started from Leyte, and assumed that it had, but none did; and the error in the reported position of survivors

[38] *Hardhead* Report of 2nd War Patrol, 5 Dec. 1944; letter of Mr. R. L. Poor, former air officer of *Enterprise*, 1957.

sent ships searching so far distant from the actual sinkings that almost two whole days passed before any survivors were recovered.[39]

After Seventh Fleet headquarters received Admiral Stump's report of the erroneous position, several hours passed before anything was done. At 1531 October 25 Admiral Kinkaid ordered Admiral Tom Sprague to send all his available escorts out for survivor search starting at lat. 11°15′N, long. 126°30′E, which was very near the earlier erroneous position.[40] As we have already seen, destroyer escorts *Richard S. Bull* and *Eversole* were given this mission. Half an hour before midnight they reached the inaccurately reported position and commenced a systematic search. After they had been steaming for hours in the wrong direction they received a second and equally inaccurate location of the sinkings and tore off on another wild goose chase. Not one survivor was sighted that night or on 26 October; and at 1725, after being gone 24 hours, they were recalled to reinforce the depleted screen of Taffy 1.

In the meantime, Admiral Kinkaid himself had initiated the surface search that succeeded. Rear Admiral Barbey, the amphibious force commander, set it up, and issued a plan at 1711 October 25. He ordered Lieutenant Commander J. A. Baxter USNR of *PC–623* to close flagship *Blue Ridge* and take command of a rescue mission, composed of *PC–1119* and six LCI gunboats.[41] A staff surgeon and a pharmacist's mate were borrowed from the amphibious force flagship, together with a small box of medical supplies; but there was no time to procure extra blankets or clothing.

39 Another group that might have made a rescue next morning was the destroyers of Admiral Badger's Task Group 34.5, which were scouring the waters off Samar for crippled Japanese ships. They picked up nine men from splashed planes of the escort carriers, but encountered no floating survivors of the sunken ships. As Third Fleet destroyers had heard nothing definite of the Battle off Samar, and Seventh Fleet had no knowledge of Third Fleet movements, the destroyers made no survivor search.

40 Seventh Fleet Message File. Why he added 03′ to the latitude does not appear.

41 Designated TG 78.12; only the two PCs and five LCIs actually went. Lt. Cdr. Baxter's Report is in his *PC–623* War Diary; additional information is in *PC–1119* (Lt. J. E. Martin) and *LCI(G)–340* (Lt.(jg) J. O. Luby USNR) War Diaries.

This rescue mission departed San Pedro Bay about 1835 October 25, made best speed (9½ knots) that the state of the sea allowed, and at about 0830 October 26 arrived at the position where floating survivors had been incorrectly reported. This was a good 30 miles south of where *Gambier Bay* went down. Commander Baxter, correctly predicting that the tradewind and set of current would carry the survivors westward, formed line abreast of his seven little ships, a mile apart, and began north–south sweeps on 25-mile legs, working westerly toward Samar. At noon they were about 18 miles northeast of the spot where *Gambier Bay* actually went down; at sundown they were about the same distance southwest of it; and all day long they sighted no living thing except a Japanese aviator sitting on a floating box. No aircraft were sent out to locate survivors and guide the ships. Finally, at 2229 October 26, Very lights sent up by survivors on life rafts, 18 to 20 miles west of Baxter's ships, attracted their attention. *PC–623* made best speed in their direction, and at midnight was among the main group of *Gambier Bay* survivors.[42] In 39 hours the rafts had drifted westerly some 30 miles.

During the midwatch 27 October the two PCs began their rescue work by visiting each group of rafts and removing the seriously wounded. *PC–1119* was immediately sent back to San Pedro Bay with these wounded and other survivors, 183 in all, to transfer them promptly to hospitals and to seek further assistance. The poor fellows were shivering with cold and suffering from thirst, hunger and fatigue. Every bunk on board and a large part of the deck space was turned over to them. Owing to the devotion and skill of Pharmacist's Mate H. Otis Miller USNR, not one of the wounded died.

In the meantime *PC–623* and the five LCIs worked over the area until by 0335 October 27 they had rescued over 700 survivors of *Gambier Bay*, who had drifted to a position only a few miles off

[42] Lt. Cdr. Baxter in letter to writer estimates position of survivors when found to be lat. 11°25′ N, long. 125°41′ E. This is about 30 miles from the spot where *Gambier Bay* foundered and 50 miles from the erroneously reported position.

Tugnug Point, Samar. The search continued; at 0745 rafts from *Samuel B. Roberts* were sighted at a position about 12 miles northeasterly from those of the carrier's survivors.[43] An hour later more rafts from *Roberts* and *Hoel* were sighted, and at 0930 fifteen men from *Johnston* who had been on their one raft for 48 hours. At 1000, after taking on board his seven small vessels some 1150 survivors, Lieutenant Commander Baxter decided that he had recovered all who were alive, and headed for San Pedro Bay. The group came to an anchor at 0113 October 28 and completed the transfer of survivors to hospital ships and transports before daylight.

This rescue was effected in a good seamanlike fashion. The staff medicos, Lieutenant D. B. Lucas (M. C.) and Pharmacist's Mates William Wattengel and James E. Cupero, did a splendid job, and the LCI crews gave the survivors everything they had. But, owing to the initial mistake about the position and failure to correct it by air search, at least 116 men from *Johnston, Hoel* and *Roberts* who had been seen alive and floating after their ships went down died before rescue. Lieutenant Hagen, senior surviving officer of *Johnston,* observed that if another day had passed without help there would have been no survivors whatever from his ship.[44]

[43] *Johnston, Hoel* and *S. B. Roberts* Action Reports; story of *Gambier Bay* survivors in *New York Times* 21 Nov. 1944.

[44] AMERICAN CASUALTIES, BATTLE OFF SAMAR:

	Killed & Missing	*Wounded*
Taffy 1 Ships' Crews	283	136
Taffy 3 Ships' Crews	792	768
Aviators, escort carriers	43	9
Aviators, TG 38.1	12	0
TOTAL	1130	913

CHAPTER XIV

The Battle off Cape Engaño[1]

25–26 October 1944

1. *Deployment and Maneuver*

WE have already seen that Admiral Halsey, rejecting what he considered a static watch on San Bernardino Strait, led three of the fast carrier groups north in search of Ozawa's Northern Force. He began making up his mind around 1700 October 24, when the first contact reports on Ozawa's force off Cape Engaño came in. When, at 2022, Third Fleet changed course to North, the die was cast. *Independence* had to recall her planes, which had been shadowing Kurita's Center Force. San Bernardino Strait was now unwatched, unguarded by even a patrol destroyer; every pair of eyes, every search radar, every search plane, every thinking mind and fighting heart in Task Force 38 was turned northward toward Ozawa – exactly as the Japanese intended. That hard-boiled

[1] Adm. Halsey's Action Reports for 23–26 Oct. and for 27 Oct.–30 Nov.; CTF 38 (Vice Adm. Mitscher) Action Report, Summary of Operations 29 Aug.–30 Oct., 3 Nov. 1944; CTG 38.2 (Rear Adm. Bogan) Action Report, 8 Nov.; CTG 38.3 (Rear Adm. Sherman) Action Report, 2 Dec. (a particularly well written and detailed one); CTG 38.4 (Rear Adm. Davison) Action Report, 18 Nov. 1944. All available aircraft Action Reports of air groups and squadrons involved have been consulted. Some are fragmentary; I have found none for the sixth strike; most of them contradict each other and estimates of damage to the enemy are exaggerated, as is inevitable in air warfare. I have done my best to interpret these conflicting data. The Air Intelligence Group Division of Naval Intelligence's Analytical Report *Carrier Aircraft in Battle for Leyte Gulf* (Air Research Report No. 18) 10 Apr. 1945, which I have used for statistics, is based on the same data and subject to similar reservations. Adm. Ozawa's Mobile Force Action Report (WDC No. 161,005) and the interrogations of his chief of staff Capt. Ohmae, of Cdr. Yamaguchi and of himself (*Inter. Jap. Off.* I 153, 158, 178, 219), are best for the Japanese side.

old salt was out for one purpose only, to suck Third Fleet out of Kurita's way. "My chief concern was to lure your forces farther north," he said a year later. "We expected complete destruction." [2] All his movements were planned for that object, in the light of the slender information he had.

Referring to Appendix I for a detailed list of the ships, captains and air groups of TF 38, we may refresh the reader's memory at this point with a succinct task organization, such as it was on 25 October, omitting Vice Admiral McCain's Task Group 38.1 because it took no part in the Battle off Cape Engaño. Ships designated "34" or "34.5" were included in Vice Admiral Lee's Task Force 34, formed at 0240 October 25; those designated "34.5" belonged to Rear Admiral Badger's Task Group. Ships preceded by an asterisk belonged to the cruiser-destroyer group commanded by Rear Admiral DuBose which took part in the pursuit of Ozawa's force.

Task Force 38, Vice Admiral M. A. Mitscher in LEXINGTON
(On 25 October, 1944)

Task Group 38.2 Rear Admiral G. F. Bogan	Task Group 38.3 Rear Admiral F. C. Sherman	Task Group 38.4 Rear Admiral R. E. Davison
	Fleet Carriers	
INTREPID	ESSEX LEXINGTON	ENTERPRISE FRANKLIN
	Light Carriers	
CABOT INDEPENDENCE	LANGLEY	SAN JACINTO BELLEAU WOOD
	Battleships	
34.5 IOWA 34.5 NEW JERSEY	34 MASSACHUSETTS 34 SOUTH DAKOTA	34 WASHINGTON 34 ALABAMA
	Light Cruisers	Heavy Cruisers
34.5 BILOXI 34.5 VINCENNES 34.5 MIAMI	*34 SANTA FE *34 MOBILE RENO	*34 NEW ORLEANS *34 WICHITA

[2] The same, in other words, appears in his Action Report pp. 6, 7 and 16.

Destroyers

34.5 OWEN
34.5 MILLER
34.5 THE SULLIVANS
34.5 TINGEY
34.5 HICKOX
34.5 HUNT
34.5 LEWIS HANCOCK
34.5 MARSHALL
CUSHING
COLAHAN
HALSEY POWELL
UHLMANN
YARNALL
TWINING
STOCKHAM
WEDDERBURN

* PORTERFIELD
*34 C. K. BRONSON
*34 COTTEN
*34 DORTCH
34 HEALY
*34 COGSWELL
*34 CAPERTON
*34 INGERSOLL
*34 KNAPP
CALLAGHAN
CASSIN YOUNG
PRESTON
LAWS
LONGSHAW

MAURY
GRIDLEY
HELM
MCCALL
MUGFORD
RALPH TALBOT
*34 PATTERSON
*34 BAGLEY
WILKES
NICHOLSON
SWANSON

Opposed to them was the inferior Northern Force of Admiral Ozawa – inferior not only in the number of combatant ships (17 against Mitscher's 64) but in the small number of aircraft on board.

Mobile Force, Vice Admiral J. Ozawa

Cardiv 3 Fleet Carrier ZUIKAKU
Light Carriers ZUIHO, CHITOSE, CHIYODA
Cardiv 4 (Rear Admiral C. Matsuda) Converted battleships ISE, HYUGA
Screen: 4 DDs of Terutsuki class
Escort Squadron 31 (Rear Admiral H. Edo) Light cruiser ISUZU and 4 DDs
Light cruisers OYODO and TAMA, 1 DD, 2 tankers, 6 escort vessels

Cardiv 4 carried no planes. The combat air strength of Cardiv 3 at the time of sortie was 52 Zeke fighters, 28 bomb-equipped Zekes, 25 Jill torpedo-bombers, 7 Judy torpedo-bombers, 4 Kate high-level or torpedo-bombers, total 166. By midnight 24–25 October there were only 19, 5, 4, 1 and 0 respectively of these types, a pitiful total of 29.[3]

Admiral Halsey's first problem was one of deployment. When he decided to attack Ozawa, his four fast carrier groups were widely separated. McCain's Group 1 was returning from the direction of Ulithi, Bogan's Group 2 (which included Third Fleet flagship *New Jersey*) was off San Bernardino Strait with Davison's Group 4 closing from the southward, and Sherman's Group 3 was off Central

[3] Ozawa Action Report p. 22.

Luzon, east of the Polillo Islands and steering southeasterly. Shortly after 2000 October 24, Halsey issued his orders. McCain to proceed at best speed toward lat. 15°00′ N, long. 130°00′ E to fuel from Captain Acuff's tankers, and then join Mitscher; Bogan and Davison, who joined at 2000, to steam north to a rendezvous point with Sherman at lat. 14°28′ N, long. 125°50′ E, at midnight. At that time Admiral Mitscher in *Lexington*, with Sherman's group, would take charge of all three and "attack enemy carrier force." That is all there was to it; the rest was up to that able veteran of carrier warfare, Vice Admiral Marc A. Mitscher.

Rendezvous was duly made around 2345, between Groups 2, 3 and 4. In all there were now 4 *Essex* class carriers and the old *Enterprise*, 5 light carriers, 6 battleships, 2 heavy cruisers, 6 light cruisers and 41 destroyers. *Independence* and two destroyers rode on the weather flank of the formation in order to launch and recover planes for night search. At 0100 October 25, just as Kurita was well clear of San Bernardino Strait, and as Nishimura was approaching Surigao Strait, *Independence* sliced off five radar-equipped night flyers to search the sectors from 320° to 10° northward for 350 miles.

At 0430 Mitscher ordered all carriers to arm their first deckloads immediately and be prepared to launch both C.A.P. and No. 1 strike at earliest dawn.[4] All through the morning watch, deck crews were arming and spotting planes and aviators were either taking a last nap or eating early breakfast. Not since the Battle of the Philippine Sea in June had these air groups gone after enemy carriers, and even in that battle few men had seen a Japanese flattop. This was what they had been looking and praying for during those weary months of striking airfields and intercepting bogies. And the new battleships were longing for some good floating targets to test the power and accuracy of their main batteries.

Although we have already followed the enemy's approach (in Chapter X), we may briefly recapitulate here. On the morning of 24 October Ozawa steamed south to launch a strike on Task Force

[4] Adm. Sherman's Report pp. 7–8.

38. This was one that came in on Sherman's Group 3 in the afternoon as they were standing by burning *Princeton.* Many Japanese carrier planes were shot down, a number[5] made emergency landings on Luzon and only 29 returned to their ships with a tall tale that Sherman's group (which they supposed to be the whole of TF 38) was now reduced to one carrier and two battleships.

By noon of the 24th Ozawa was feeling rather desperate about the situation. He had hung out an attractive bait, but the fish either did not smell it or would not bite. In his Action Report he noted that so far he had been "ineffective," and that it was "imperative" to divert the enemy "in support of the First Striking Force" (Kurita). So, at 1430, he organized Force "A" under Rear Admiral Matsuda as an Advance Guard, consisting of *Ise*, *Hyuga,* light cruiser *Tama* and four destroyers, to press south and "divert the enemy effectively." One hour later Force "A," and two hours later, Main Body, were sighted by Halsey's search planes. Ozawa's communications staff picked up the radio message of the second one to Halsey giving his position, and even got the "Roger." Commander Mobile Force was delighted. He sent off a dispatch at 1650 to all friendly forces that he was in contact with enemy carrier aircraft at lat. 17° 10′ N, long. 124° 50′ E.[6] Next, at 2000, the Northern Force commander intercepted Kurita's message announcing his reversal of course in the Sibuyan Sea. This, for the moment, shattered his hopes. Assuming that Operation SHO-GO had failed, he turned north.

Another hour passed, and at 2110 Ozawa received an order from Admiral Toyoda to attack as he had formerly been directed. So he made another radical turn, headed 240° (about SW b. W), and recalled Matsuda to his Main Body. "Soon after 10 P.M," remembered Matsuda, "I received orders from Admiral Ozawa to terminate the surface operation and turn northward."[7]

[5] Cdr. Yamaguchi's estimate (*Inter. Jap. Off.* I 178) is probably the most accurate, since, as operations officer on the staff of Vice Adm. Fukudome, it was his business to know. He says 15 to 20.

[6] According to Ozawa's track chart it was really lat. 18°25′ N, long. 125°15′ E.

[7] *Inter. Jap. Off.* I 277. His Action Report shows that he did so at 2230, changing course from 90° to 30°, which he maintained until 0600 Oct. 25.

Ozawa had no news of Task Force 38's whereabouts during the night of 24–25 October, but he guessed what Halsey would do upon learning where he was. And Ozawa did everything necessary to bait the fast carriers into a position where they could do Kurita's Center Force no harm, and his Northern Force no good.

2. *The Air Strikes, 0800–1800 October 25*

From shortly before midnight 24–25 October, when Admiral Halsey returned command to him, Admiral Mitscher was Officer in Tactical Command of Task Force 38. The Battle off Cape Engaño was Mitscher's battle.

October 25 dawned bright and clear in these northern latitudes, with only a few clouds on the horizon and a brisk (13- to 16-knot) NE tradewind. Subsequent to the 1635 October 24 contact that so delighted Ozawa, Halsey lost the Northern Force for nine hours. The next contacts by his carrier planes were at 0205 and 0235 October 25 when they saw first the "A" group and then the Main Body of the Japanese Northern Force. Ozawa's four carriers and screen were steaming on course 150°, about 205 miles E by N of Cape Engaño, Luzon.[8] That, however, is not what the search planes reported, probably because of an error in transmission. Mitscher thought that the enemy was about 120 miles nearer to him than the 210 miles that the two forces were actually apart.

These contacts, bad as they were, gave at least the right direction, and were the last that Mitscher had until daylight. He ordered dawn searches to be flown from *Lexington,* with planes to relay communication stationed at intervals from the launching point. In the hope that the enemy would continue his course, which would bring contact by 0430, six battleships, seven cruisers and 17 destroyers, under Vice Admiral Lee, were formed as Task Force 34 at 0240 and given station ten miles north of *Lexington,* the fleet

[8] Track chart in Ozawa Action Report.

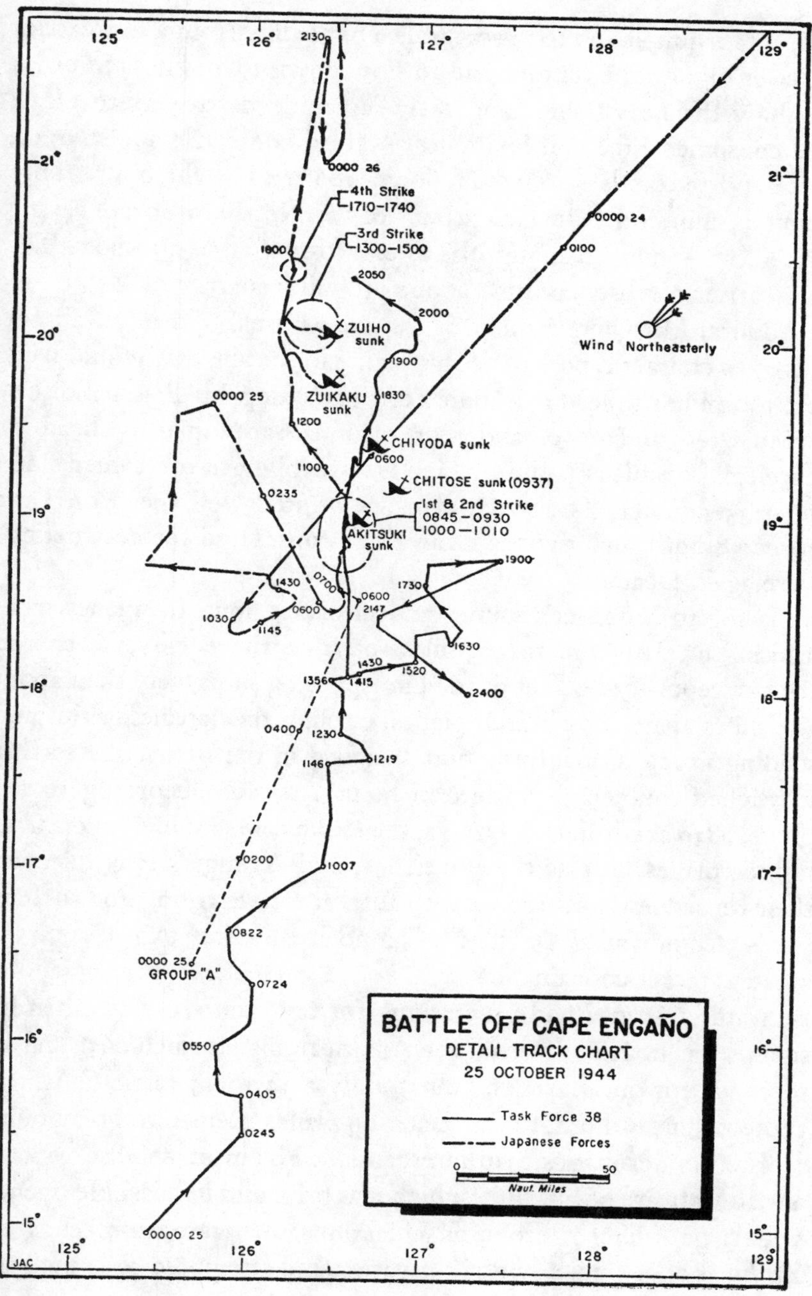

BATTLE OFF CAPE ENGAÑO
DETAIL TRACK CHART
25 OCTOBER 1944
Task Force 38
Japanese Forces
0
50
Naut. Miles
ZUIHO sunk
ZUIKAKU sunk
CHIYODA sunk
CHITOSE sunk (0937)
AKITSUKI sunk
4th Strike 1710-1740
3rd Strike 1300-1500
1st & 2nd Strike 0845-0930 1000-1010
Wind Northeasterly
GROUP "A"
0000 24
0000 25
0000 26
JAC

guide. It is quite a job to unscramble a battle line from a fast carrier force at night. The flattops had to slow down to 10 knots in order to allow the heavy ships and their screening destroyers to clear; this consumed time and lost miles. A third contact, made at 0710, was reported at lat. 18°37′ N, long. 126°45′ E, which was only about 15 miles off. The two groups of the Northern Force, having united, were now steaming NE as one formation at 20 knots. The two carrier forces were now about 150 miles apart.

Admiral Mitscher, cannily aggressive as usual, did not wait for this 0710 contact report to get his planes in the air; that would have lost too much time. He commenced launching his first strike between 0540 and 0600, and sent reconnaissance planes ahead to search all possible areas into which Ozawa might have steamed since his 0235 contact. The striking planes orbited well ahead of Task Force 38 until such time as Ozawa's flattops, fated for destruction, were again located.

Owing to Mitscher's sound tactical dispositions, his planes were orbiting at points 70 to 90 miles south of the enemy, when the contact report came in at 0710. The opposing ships were then about 145 miles apart. The search planes, circling the Japanese ships and sending in loads of information, coached in the first strike so that it reached the enemy within an hour. At 0800 according to the pilots, 0830 according to Ozawa, the strike came in. Helldivers first, fighter planes next as they overshot, and Avengers last, releasing their torpedoes from 700 to 1000 feet, at ranges from 1400 to 1600 yards. Commander David McCampbell of *Essex* Air Group 15 acted as target coördinator.

Admiral Ozawa had been asking for this, and was not taken by surprise, as he had observed the American planes since 0653. As he too had sent out searches, he had only a 12 to 15 plane C.A.P. to protect him; and this, to the attacking planes, seemed to be more interested in acrobatics than interception. His main defense was the antiaircraft fire of his ships, which was brisk and intense. He opened with large-caliber phosphorus when the planes were ten miles away. *Zuiho* at once pulled out of formation and attempted to launch the few planes spotted on her flight deck. The torpedo-bombers from *Essex* and *Lexington* missed her, and although she received one bomb hit from an *Intrepid* plane she was not slowed down. Her sister ship, *Chitose*, received a number of bomb hits, including three below the waterline, which did her in; she sank at 0937. The big carrier *Zuikaku* took one torpedo hit either from a *San Jacinto* or an *Intrepid* plane which knocked out her communications and gave her a six-degree list. Steering became so difficult that at 1100 Admiral Ozawa shifted his flag to *Oyodo*. Destroyer *Akitsuki* was sunk instantaneously, and at least nine Japanese planes were shot down, leaving Ozawa with not more than six. A good beginning indeed.

One hour before planes of this initial strike returned to their carriers, those of the second strike were in the air. About 16 torpedo planes, six bombers and 14 fighters took off around 0835 from Sherman's and Davison's task groups and went in between 0945 and 1000.

While these planes were on their way north, a group of 20 to 25 bogeys was detected closing Davison's group at 0957. These probably belonged to Fukudome's land-based air force. Combat air patrol, vectored out to meet them, apparently caused the inexperienced Japanese pilots to turn and flee.[9]

On account of Ozawa's lack of air cover after the first strike came in, Mitscher was able to keep a target coördinator over the Northern Force all day to track and report,[10] and pilots returning from Strike No. 1 gave advice over the air to oncoming pilots of Strike No. 2. Upon the arrival of Strike 2 at the target, around 0945, "the enemy force presented a picture of wild confusion," maneuvering every which way. *Lexington's* planes, and *Franklin's* also, made bomb hits on *Chiyoda*. That carrier was "set heavily afire, causing flooding and a sharp list." Her engines were disabled by a bomb hit at 1018. *Hyuga* attempted to take her in tow, but was frustrated by Strike No. 3. Matsuda ordered *Isuzu* and destroyer

[9] CTG 38.4 Action Report, Enclosure D (*San Jacinto*).
[10] CTG 38.3 Action Report pp. 8–9.

Maki to close her and take off the crew; but they could not even do that, and *Chiyoda* with her people was abandoned. She stayed afloat until 1630 when sunk by DuBose's cruisers.

Other planes from *Franklin* and *Langley* concentrated on a group of stragglers consisting of one destroyer, light cruiser *Tama* and *Hyuga*, which appeared to be protecting *Chiyoda*. Planes from *San Jacinto* and *Belleau Wood* concentrated on a couple of light cruisers, and apparently hit *Tama*.[11]

As the fighter squadron from *Belleau Wood* still had plenty of fuel, Lieutenant C. O. Roberts USNR kept it over Ozawa for purposes of tracking. He reported that it took the Northern Force about 45 minutes after this attack to straighten out. Around 1100–1200 the picture (which Roberts conveyed to planes of Strike No. 3 about to be launched) was as follows. A *Terutsuki* class destroyer was leading *Zuikaku* and *Zuiho*, steaming at 22 to 25 knots on course 345°, with three destroyers protecting their flanks and *Ise* their rear (*Zuikaku's* own report indicates that her speed was down to 18 knots at 1145). Twenty miles behind *Ise* was light cruiser *Tama* making 10 to 12 knots and trailing oil. Five or six miles south of her, the other converted battleship, *Hyuga*, and one damaged destroyer were circling *Chiyoda*, dead in the water. Ten miles more to the rear, one light cruiser was circling, apparently undamaged, and a third was trailing oil; ten miles to the rear of them one destroyer lay dead in the water.[12] Thus, 14 ships of the Northern Force were still afloat and, if Mitscher had flown no more strikes, these would probably have got away.

In view of the information received from Lieutenant Roberts, Strike No. 3 was ordered to concentrate on Ozawa's main body to the northward, bearing 351°, distant 102 miles from *Lexington*, with the intention of creating more cripples that could be disposed of at leisure. Strike No. 3, launched between 1145 and 1200 and

[11] *Belleau Wood* Action Report; Report of Air Group 21. Ozawa's chief of staff later said that the heaviest damage was received in the second strike; but he probably meant the third, and was considering the first and second as one.

[12] Same reference, with ship identifications corrected.

over the target for about an hour from 1310, was the largest of the day. It comprised over 200 aircraft, three quarters of which had participated in Strike No. 1. Commander T. Hugh Winters from *Lexington* relieved Lieutenant Roberts as target coördinator and directed the attack.[13]

Lexington planes concentrated on *Zuikaku*, those from *Essex* on *Zuiho; Langley's* divided their attention between the two. Immediately after the attack, in which three torpedoes were seen to hit *Zuikaku* simultaneously, both carriers started to burn and the big one to settle; but *Zuiho* got her fires under control and steamed off at high speed. The planes from Admiral Sherman's Group 3 now started home, while Commander Winters remained, coaching in planes from Davison's TG 38.4 to finish *Zuiho*, which was hard to sink; about 40 planes attacked her at 1310, more at 1330, and she was severely damaged. In the meantime Winters made a "sight-seeing tour" of the cripples, returning to the main group just in time to see *Zuikaku* roll over and go down at 1414. Some neat bombing was done in Strike No. 3 and no casualties to planes or pilots were suffered. One young Helldiver pilot was so excited when landing that he immediately ran up the ladder of *Lexington's* island to Admiral Mitscher, shouting, "I gotta hit on a carrier! I gotta hit on a carrier!"

The crippled group, which was given some attention by *Franklin's* planes, was observed to break up at 1410, leaving *Chiyoda* to her fate.

Strike No. 4, with about the same number of planes as No. 2, took off around 1315 and reached the Northern Force at 1445. It concentrated on Main Body, now some 30 miles ahead of the rest. *Lexington* and *Langley* planes claimed several bomb and torpedo hits on *Ise*, but this converted battleship was rugged; she put up an "exceedingly intense antiaircraft fire" and received only four near-

[13] Cdr. Winters's interesting account is with the Air Action Report of CAG–19, *Lexington's* Air Group. Later reliefs were Cdr. R. L. Kibbe of *Franklin* and Cdr. M. T. Wordell.

misses.[14] Some 27 planes concentrated on crippled *Zuiho* and did her in. She went down at 1526.

The fifth attack of the day – third for most of the participating planes – took its departure from the carriers at 1610, and reached the target in an hour. Strike No. 5, consisting of full deckloads from all five carriers, concentrated on *Ise* but got only 34 near-misses and failed to sink that tough old "hermaphrodite." Reference to our illustration of her under air attack will suggest the reason. She threw up a heavy antiaircraft fire and her commanding officer, Rear Admiral Nakase, was an expert at evasive maneuvering.

A sketch made by one of *Franklin's* pilots at 1700 shows a very depleted and scattered Northern Force. *Hyuga* and a light cruiser, followed at a distance of 20 miles by a second light cruiser and a destroyer, were making best speed northward, 18 knots. *Hyuga* had seven near-misses in this attack, the nearest thing to a hit she got all day. About 20 miles on her port beam a damaged light cruiser, probably *Tama*, was steaming slowly, trailing oil. *Ise*, another light cruiser and three destroyers were recovering *Zuiho* survivors from the water. Far to the southward, at least 60 miles astern of *Hyuga*, *Chiyoda* was being shelled by Admiral DuBose's cruisers.[15] About 12 of Ozawa's 17 ships were still afloat.

A sixth and final attack of 36 planes from Admiral Davison's group took off at 1710 and claimed a few hits, but sank nothing. Admiral Ozawa said a year later that the strikes after No. 3 were not nearly so damaging to his force as the earlier ones; and his chief of staff remarked, "I saw all this bombing and thought the American pilot is not so good."

He was pretty good to have sunk four carriers and a destroyer with a total of 527 plane sorties – 201 of them fighter planes.[16] But, blow for blow, the escort carrier planes of Taffy 2 and Taffy 3 inflicted more damage than did the aircraft of two fast carrier groups. And neither had any air opposition worth mentioning.

[14] Rear Adm. Matsuda, whose flag was in *Ise*, said (*Inter. Jap. Off.* I 277), "No damage to *Hyuga*, very little to *Ise*."

[15] *Franklin* Action Report, Enclosure A to that of CTG 38.4, Sketch B.

[16] *Carrier Aircraft in Battle for Leyte Gulf* p. 53.

3. *Surface Maneuvers, 1115 October 25 to 0300 October 26*

While Strike No. 2 was coming in at 0822, Admiral Halsey received Admiral Kinkaid's plain-language message about the surprise off Samar. A succession of urgent pleas for any kind of assistance, air or surface, that Halsey could spare, began to flow in on his flag plot in *New Jersey*. As early as 0848 Halsey instructed McCain "to proceed at best possible speed" to strike Kurita's Center Force, but he did not detach TF 34, Lee's Battle Line, to block Kurita's escape, until it was too late.

At 1000 Halsey received Nimitz's query as to the whereabouts of TF 34. Halsey wished to keep these heavy gunfire ships with TF 38 to sink Ozawa's cripples and catch up with *Ise* and *Hyuga*. But the pressure on him to help Seventh Fleet became so great that after another hour's cogitation he yielded. At 1055 he ordered Bogan's TG 38.2, together with the major part of Lee's Battle Line, to reverse course and steam south to help Kinkaid. When this order was executed at 1115, the battleships had reached lat. 18° N, long. 126° E.[17] Even by making best speed they could not expect to reach San Bernardino Strait before 0100 next day.

It almost broke Halsey's heart to pull out Task Force 34 just as the battleships were on the point of reaching good gunfire targets. He afterwards told the writer that it was the only move in the Battle for Leyte Gulf that he regretted; that the query from Nimitz, which he knew meant that Cincpac was alarmed for the safety of the Seventh Fleet, was the final factor that influenced his decision.

Admiral Lee with the six battleships steamed south at only 20 knots, slowing down to about 12 at 1345 in order to fuel destroyers

[17] CTF 34 (Vice Adm. Lee) Action Report 14 Dec. 1944. The way Adm. Halsey states it in his Report is as follows: "Although TF 34 was within 42 miles of the crippled Northern Force, Commander Third Fleet at 1115 turned back Group 38.2 [plus 4BBs] south and dispatched TG 34.5, Rear Admiral Badger, ahead at high speed to the assistance of the Seventh Fleet Forces." Reference to the composition of TF 38 earlier in this chapter indicates that what then went south was the whole of TG 38.2 excepting 8 DDs, and 4BBs of TGs 38.3 and 38.4.

that particularly needed it. At 1622, when fueling was completed, TG 34.5 was formed, under Rear Admiral Badger's command, and at 1701 Halsey ordered it to push on to San Bernardino Strait. This he did at 28 knots. TG 34.5 included Badger's flagship *Iowa*, Halsey's flagship *New Jersey*, three light cruisers and eight destroyers. Admiral Bogan's carriers operated to the eastward of them in order to render air support if required.[18]

Badger's orders were to arrive off the Strait by 0100 October 26, sweep the approaches, and continue along the coast of Samar to Leyte Gulf, destroying all enemy ships encountered. This was over three hours too late to catch Kurita before he reëntered San Bernardino Strait. The only ship of Kurita's force that he encountered was destroyer *Nowaki*, which had been unable to catch up. She was sunk by gunfire at 0110 October 26. Badger's group then made a southerly sweep, but picked up nothing except six survivors from heavy cruiser *Suzuya*. Unfortunately it missed the floating survivors from Clifton Sprague's escort carrier unit.

If TF 34 had been detached a few hours earlier, after Kinkaid's first urgent request for help, and had left the destroyers behind, since their fueling caused a delay of over two hours and a half, a powerful battle line of six modern battleships under the command of Admiral Lee, the most experienced battle squadron commander in the Navy, would have arrived off San Bernardino Strait in time to have clashed with Kurita's Center Force. We may well speculate what might then have happened. Apart from the accidents common in naval warfare, there is every reason to believe that Lee would have crossed Kurita's T and completed the destruction of Center Force. As it was, Badger's TG 34.5, consisting of only two battleships, three light cruisers and eight destroyers, was both too late and too weak for the work in hand. Supported by Bogan's carrier group it would doubtless have put up a good fight, but it would have been seriously outgunned by Kurita's four battleships. Halsey

[18] Vice Adm. Lee's Action Report. See table of ships designated TG 34.5, at head of this Chapter.

should have sent all TF 34 or nothing, and done it earlier. It is clear that his heart was with the carriers up north, although he himself gallantly sought action down south in *New Jersey*.

When Halsey sent the major part of Task Force 34 south at 1115, he detached cruisers *Santa Fe*, *Mobile*, *Wichita*, *New Orleans* and nine destroyers to continue northward with the carriers.[19] As gunfire is the proper method of disposing of damaged ships, Mitscher at 1415 ordered this cruiser group, under command of Rear Admiral Laurance T. DuBose, to pursue the limping units of Ozawa's fleet. Commander Winters, the air coördinator, when returning to his ship, happened to fly over *Chiyoda* dead in the water; and as he then sighted DuBose's cruisers on the horizon, he gave them the bearing and spotted fall of shot for them. They commenced firing at *Chiyoda* around 1625. Thirty minutes later she turned turtle and sank.

Admiral DuBose continued pursuit northward. The cruisers, coached in by two night-fighter planes from *Essex*, encountered *Hatsuzuki* and two smaller destroyers at 1840, almost at the end of evening twilight. *Mobile* opened fire from a range of nearly 14 miles at 1853. *Hatsuzuki* returned fire and worked up speed to escape. The cruisers pursued, but the big destroyer twice placed herself (as the radar screen showed) in a position to deliver a torpedo attack, upon which DuBose, schooled by experience, caused his cruisers to execute radical evasive maneuvers to keep out of torpedo water. Resuming stern chase at 28 knots, DuBose gradually overhauled this group, and at 1915 sent destroyers *Clarence L. Bronson*, *Cotten* and *Patterson* ahead to make a torpedo attack. This was successful in slowing up *Hatsuzuki*. The cruisers then closed to 6000 yards, illuminated with star shell, slowly and deliberately brought the destroyer under gunfire, and saw her explode and sink at 2059.[20]

[19] CTG 38.3 Action Report, Enclosure E., 30 Oct. 1944.
[20] Position: lat. 20°24′ N, long. 126°20′ E.

A destroyer which had been about to finish her off with a torpedo signaled: "He has gone down, we were cheated!" to which Admiral DuBose replied, "It breaks our hearts!"

DuBose almost had a little more than he bargained for when engaging this tough destroyer. Admiral Ozawa, when he heard she needed help at 2041, collected *Ise, Hyuga* and one destroyer, and with his flag in light cruiser *Oyodo,* headed for the scene of battle. Before he reached it, *Hatsuzuki* and her tormentors had vanished; but Ozawa continued southward until 2330, hoping to find some other American ships to engage with gunfire. He then resumed his northward retirement. Two *Independence* night fighters sighted his ships steaming north at 22 knots. They were then abreast of Bashi Channel, the northern entrance to Luzon Strait, and a simple calculation showed that even if DuBose pursued at 30 knots he could not overhaul Ozawa before daylight, when he would be within striking distance of enemy land-based air on Formosa and the Sakashima Gunto.

DuBose assumed a circular disposition at 2130 and retired. Not one hit was received by his ships during these engagements, although *Santa Fe* was several times straddled by *Hatsuzuki.* That Japanese destroyer received a good deal of posthumous admiration for the long, tough fight she put up and the number of hits she absorbed before going down. One of the American destroyer captains insisted that she must have been a heavy cruiser – the same compliment that Kurita's officers accorded to Admiral Sprague's destroyers.

4. *Submarine Attacks, 1845 October 25 to 0900 October 26* [21]

During the afternoon Admiral Mitscher sent Vice Admiral Lockwood, Commander Submarines Pacific, a radio warning that the

[21] Conversations with Vice Adm. Lockwood; Capt. R. G. Voge, his operations officer; and Cdr. B. A. Clarey, in Jan. 1946; patrol reports of the submarines mentioned.

Admiral expected to be fighting the enemy until about 2000 as far north as 20°30′ N and between 126° and 127° E. Six of his pilots had splashed around 19°45′ N, 126°35′ E and he hoped that they might be picked up. He described the composition of the Northern Force and, thinking of the pleasure submarine sailors would have in knocking them off, added "We hope to get them, but if not you won't let them get back to Japan."

By the time Admiral Lockwood received this, some ten hours later, his submarines had done their best. But most of the Japanese ships did get home.

On 24 October two wolf-packs of three submarines each – *Haddock*, *Tuna* and *Halibut* under Commander J. P. Roach, and *Pintado*, *Jallao* and *Atule* under Commander B. A. Clarey – were proceeding from Tanapag Harbor, Saipan, in order to relieve the "Convoy College Patrol"[22] in Luzon Strait. At 0815 October 25 both groups got the word from Vice Admiral Lockwood to make best speed and set up scouting lines along lat. 20°30′ N between long. 125°30′ and 129° E, "to knock off possible cripples or Japanese forces retiring from an expected battle off the coast of Luzon" – said battle being already well under way. By 1830 October 25 they were in position: "Clarey's Crushers" on an east–west scouting line with 20 miles between boats; "Roach's Raiders" to the westward on the same latitude, with 15 miles between boats. The latter were near enough to the fleeing Northern Force at 1700 to hear distant explosions and pick up on their high-frequency radio the interplane chatter of aircraft pilots going in for the last strike.[23] At 1742, about half an hour before sunset, the pagodalike superstructure of *Ise* came into *Halibut's* vision at 31,000 yards, and the range closed fast. The submarine dove to periscope depth and then sighted light cruiser *Oyodo*, now Admiral Ozawa's flagship, and a destroyer. *Halibut* made a good approach, and at 1844 fired her six forward torpedoes at what she supposed to be *Ise*.

[22] So-called in the submariners' own code; it was divided into three sectors called the Bachelors, the Masters and the Doctors.

[23] "Yippee! I gotta battleship!" one pilot was heard to say – but he didn't get her; this was the apparently unhittable *Ise*.

Five explosions were heard, followed by breaking-up noises; and when the submarine surfaced an hour later, an object resembling the hull of a capsizing ship was sighted in the moonlight. Who was the victim? It is still a mystery. Looks like a whale to me.[24]

Haddock pursued *Ise* and *Hyuga*, which escaped under cover of darkness. "Disappointment was a foot thick on this ship," said Commander Roach.

At about 2300 *Halibut* sighted and pursued five more ships – probably *Hyuga* and four destroyers – but "by successive zigs away to keep us astern" they succeeded in opening the range. She continued the chase all night. At 0600 October 26, having reached lat. 23° N, long. 126°30′ E, east of central Formosa, she returned to her patrol station.

Another submarine to get into action was *Jallao* of "Clarey's Crushers." This Wisconsin-built boat, so new that she had not been three months in salt water, at 2004 October 25 made a radar contact at 27,000 yards on the bomb-damaged light cruiser *Tama*, then making 16 knots. *Pintado*, operating 20 miles to the westward, also picked up *Tama* and closed *Jallao* before the attack, which the latter delivered submerged between 2301 and 2305 with seven torpedoes from both bow and stern tubes. In the misty moonlight and surface refraction, the little three-piper cruiser looked "as big as the Pentagon Building," and when the three stern torpedoes hit, Commander Clarey, who was watching from *Pintado*, saw her break up and go down.

Tama was the last ship of Northern Force to be sunk; the Battle off Cape Engaño was over. "Clarey's Crushers" continued up to lat. 24° N without making another contact, and at 1110 October 26 reversed course and returned to their patrol line.

The rest of the Northern Force – *Ise*, *Hyuga*, *Oyodo* and five destroyers – made best speed in order to enter the protected waters of the East China Sea. They successfully ran the gantlet of another

[24] *Akitsuki* is credited to *Halibut* by JANAC, but *Imp. Jap. Navy W. W. II* (1952) pp. 211, 248, states that *Akitsuki* was a victim of air attack, and Ozawa's track chart shows that she was the first ship sunk in the 25 Oct. carrier attacks.

United States submarine wolf-pack commanded by Commander F. J. Harlfinger in *Trigger*. That boat picked up *Ise* and *Hyuga* around 0900 Actober 26 at lat. 24°07′N, long. 125°41′E, but was unable to overtake them. The hermaphrodites put into Amami O Shima on 27 October, and after two days' rest proceeded to Kure on the Inland Sea. Repairs were effected there in two weeks' time. After carrying ammunition to the Paracels for transshipment to Manila,[25] *Ise* and *Hyuga* rendezvoused with Vice Admiral Shima's survivors of the Battle of Surigao Strait and proceeded to Lingga Roads in the hope of affording protection to the dwindling Japanese merchant marine. Their last employment was to carry a load of drummed gasoline from Singapore to Kure in February, 1945.

The action off Cape Engaño left Third Fleet with mixed feelings of disappointment at having missed an opportunity to smash Kurita off San Bernardino Strait, and elation at its tactical victory over the Northern Force. Task Force 38 had rubbed out half the enemy's available carriers by sinking *Zuikaku*, *Zuiho*, *Chitose* and *Chiyoda*, and destroyer *Akitsuki*. The cruisers and submarines added destroyers *Hatsuzuki* and *Nowaki* and light cruiser *Tama* to the score; but Halsey's firm bid at complete annihilation had to be withdrawn when he tardily heeded Kinkaid's calls for help. Thus the overwhelming fire power of the six new battleships in Task Force 34 was never brought to bear on the enemy.

The sinking of *Zuikaku* gave particular satisfaction to the Pacific Fleet, for she was the last afloat of the six carriers that pulled off the sneak attack on Pearl Harbor almost three years before. Four of them had been sunk in the Battle of Midway; United States submarine *Cavalla* had disposed of *Shokaku* in the Battle of the Philippine Sea; and now mighty *Zuikaku* joined her sisters at the bottom of the Pacific, with a good three thousand fathoms of salt water over her remains.

Admiral Ozawa is entitled to claim a strategic success in the

[25] Matsuda interrogation (*Inter. Jap. Off.* I 282). The munitions were transshipped in small cargo ships, in order to avoid exposing the battleships to air attack.

Battle off Cape Engaño. He performed his mission of drawing off the major portion of the Pacific Fleet then in Philippine waters, and saved Kurita, as well as his own force, from annihilation. Nevertheless, the battle was a "bitter experience," as he said in his Report. For him, protagonist of carrier warfare in the Japanese Navy, to be defeated twice in five months, and to be forced to expend his beloved flattops as bait, was bitter indeed. But he faced the situation without flinching, and it may be some satisfaction to him in his honorable retirement that his former enemies, now friends, consider him the ablest of the Japanese admirals after Yamamoto.

The temptation is strong to devote final comments on the Battle for Leyte Gulf to a eulogy of the superb skill, heroism and aggressiveness displayed by both sides, by all forces and groups, and by the individual seamen.[26] Volumes could be written, and yet fail to do justice to even a small part of what took place. Yet we should not cater to complacency; nor would it be honest to brush off errors on the ground that they were canceled out by what was done supremely well.

Although the total carrier-based air strength of the Third and Seventh Fleets was exploited to the limit, and accomplished things commensurate with its superiority over Japanese air forces, the same cannot be said of American strength in gun power. The mighty gunfire of the Third Fleet's Battle Line, greater than that of the whole Japanese Navy, was never brought into action except to finish off one or two crippled light ships. That of the Seventh Fleet, although more fully utilized, engaged for only half an hour a minor part of the Japanese Fleet, of about one fifth its strength, and after that force had been crippled by two well-delivered torpedo attacks.

Despite this vast preponderance of power on the American side, the Japanese Center Force, comprising more than half the enemy's naval gunfire, and therefore a prize of first importance, steamed

[26] This conclusion in part is paraphrased from Capt. R. C. Parker's original draft of Cincpac Monthly Analysis for Oct. 1944, which he did not use.

undetected into gun range, caught Seventh Fleet by surprise and inflicted losses which fell short of a major catastrophe only by the resolute application of air power, aided by the self-sacrificing courage of a few destroyers and destroyer escorts.

The Japanese sailors fought bravely as usual, but their operation plan, not flexible enough to meet an unexpected tactical situation, was too complicated to succeed except under optimum conditions that are seldom encountered outside war colleges. The Japanese timing was bad, their torpedo technique timid and ineffective, their gunnery inferior and their communications terrible. Their battle efficiency had suffered from infrequent action. Nishimura's force, steaming straight into the trap set for it in Surigao Strait, was a useless sacrifice. The Center Force, after outwitting Halsey, made no use of its wonderful opportunity. Almost any admiral in Kurita's place, when sighting a group of six escort carriers, would have formed battle line and with superior speed gone roaring past the enemy formation at advantageous range, sinking the carriers one at a time, while destroyers engaged the screen. But Kurita imagined his enemy to be manyfold the strength that it was, ordered General Attack, lost tactical control of his force and broke off after doing relatively slight damage.

Was the Battle for Leyte Gulf a decisive battle? "Decisive" is a relative term in warfare. Leyte was not as decisive as Midway, but it did decide that the United States and her Allies would rule the Pacific until the end of the war, and by so doing hasten the war's end. One need only think of what would have happened had Operation SHO-GO worked. General MacArthur's Army would have been cut off, like that of Athens at Syracuse in 413 B.C. Third Fleet alone could not have maintained its communications.

Historians, however, are not supposed to deal with what might have been but with things as they were. In naval warfare, according to that old Navy handbook *Sound Military Decision*, "mistakes are normal, errors are usual; information is seldom complete, often inaccurate and frequently misleading." In this series of night and day actions, the mistakes made by the Japanese sea lords were so much more numerous and serious than ours, that they added up to a costly defeat. Was not, indeed, the decision to seek battle at this juncture in itself a mistake? Would not Japan have been well advised to have saved her Navy for the invasion of Luzon, where it might have inflicted greater damage? The sacrifice of the Japanese Navy in the Battle for Leyte Gulf enabled the United States Navy to transport troops and base longe-range bomber planes in positions so close to Japan that victory was a matter of months, even had there been no atomic bomb.

"Our defeat at Leyte," said the Japanese Navy Minister, Admiral Yonai, after the war was over, "was tantamount to the loss of the Philippines. When you took the Philippines, that was the end of our resources."

However you look at it, the Battle for Leyte Gulf should be an imperishable part of our national heritage. The night action in Surigao Strait will always be an inspiring example of perfect timing, coördination and almost faultless execution. And the Battle off Samar had no compeer in this war. The story of that action, with its dramatic surprise, the quick thinking and resolute decisions of Clifton Sprague; the little screening vessels feeling for each other through the rain and smoke and, courting annihilation, making individual attacks on battleships and heavy cruisers; naval aviators making dry runs on enemy ships to divert gunfire from their own; the defiant humor and indomitable courage of bluejackets caught in the "ultimate of desperate circumstances," will make the fight of the "Taffies" with Kurita forever memorable, forever glorious.

CHAPTER XV

Naval Operations around Leyte[1]

26 October–25 November 1944

1. *Movements of Task Force 38, October 26–31*

AT the height of the Battle off Cape Engaño, Admiral Halsey had to consider the future employment and deployment of Third Fleet. Most of his ships were low on fuel, yet had to be ready for any eventuality. At noon October 25, he ordered Admiral Mitscher upon conclusion of the battle to set a fueling rendezvous at lat. 16° 10′ N, long. 129°30′ E (where nine oilers were waiting) for Sherman's TG 38.3 and Davison's TG 38.4, which at that moment were doing most of the fighting. And a second fueling rendezvous, at lat. 14° N, long. 125° E, was appointed for McCain's TG 38.1, Bogan's 38.2 and Badger's 34.5.

After the second rendezvous, Vice Admiral McCain took charge of Groups 1 and 2 and directed air sweeps into the Sibuyan Sea and Tablas Strait which inflicted the final losses on Kurita's retreating Center Force. These we have already related, as the pursuit phase of the Battle off Samar; but it was Halsey's fight, ordered by him and directed by his senior group commander.

Early on 26 October, the day following the great battles, Admiral Kinkaid requested Admiral Halsey to provide combat air patrol over Leyte Gulf. The Tacloban airstrip was still in emergency status and the first 34 P–38s only arrived on the 27th. Their

[1] Com Third Fleet (Admiral Halsey) Report on Operations 27 Oct.–30 Nov., 9 Dec. 1944, and War Diary for Oct.–Nov.; Comairpac (Rear Adm. George D. Murray) Analysis of Pacific Air Operations, "Carrier Support of Leyte Campaign"; Cincpac Monthly Analyses for Oct. and Nov., Vol. II.

operational strength was down to 20 planes on the 30th, but on that date and the last day of October, 80 more P–38s and 12 P–61s came in.[2]

Nobody could accuse Halsey of playing a lone hand. He could not immediately comply with Kinkaid's request to fill the gap,

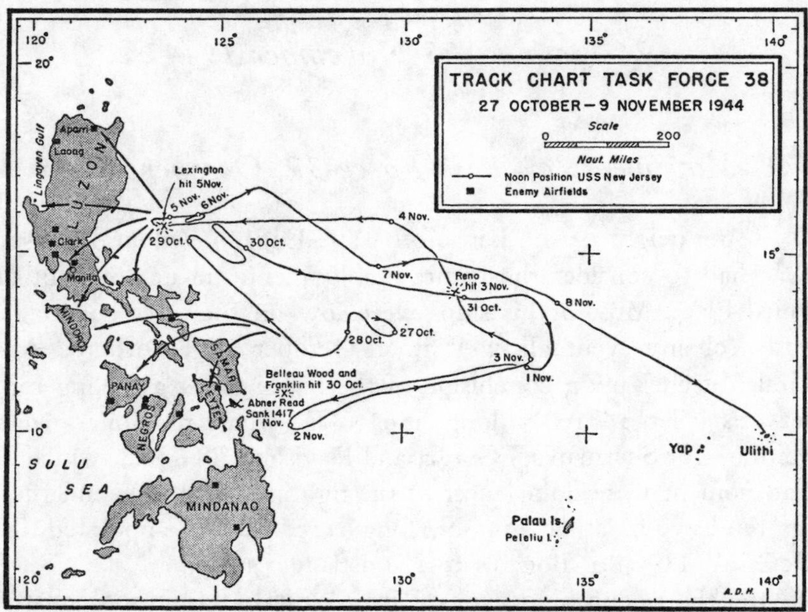

owing to the distance of his fast carrier groups from Leyte Gulf, but he ordered Mitscher, with Sherman's Group 3 and Davison's Group 4, as soon as they had finished fueling on 26 October, to be "prepared to make strikes or furnish fighter cover over Leyte Area if later directed." Not understanding the "real estate problem" which prevented Army Air from taking over promptly, Halsey at 2135 October 26 sent a dispatch whose correct military language conveyed a certain impatience:

> For General MacArthur. After 17 days of battle my fast carriers are unable to provide extended support for Leyte but 2 groups are available 27 October. The pilots are exhausted, and the carriers are low in

[2] Craven & Cate V 369.

provisions, bombs and torpedoes. When will land-based air take over at Leyte?

The General was unable to say when Army Air could take charge, and Third Fleet stood by for another three days, which were as eventful as any that were not counted as days of battle. On 27 October Admiral Sherman's group, in addition to sharing C.A.P. over Leyte Gulf, sent fighter sweeps over the Visayas and southern Luzon. A dawn sweep from *Essex* found a small troop convoy north of the Calamian Islands and scored bomb and rocket hits, sinking destroyers *Fujinami* and *Shiranuhi*. On 28 October Bogan's Group 2, after refueling, joined Davison's Group 4 in giving close support to ground forces on Leyte and striking enemy airfields and shipping, while McCain's Group 1 was given the long-promised maintenance period that had been postponed by the Battle for Leyte Gulf. Sherman's Group 3 joined McCain's at Ulithi on the 30th but remained for two days only. "Scrappy" Kessing's haven of refuge looked pretty good to carrier bluejackets and aviators who had been fighting three days out of every four since their last sortie on 6 October.[3]

Admiral Davison's Group 4, including carriers *Franklin*, *Enterprise*, *San Jacinto* and *Belleau Wood*, carried the burden of air action off Leyte on 28 October. It was a busy day for all hands. A fighter sweep was flown against shipping off Cebu. About 44 enemy planes attacked the group and 13 were shot down by C.A.P., from which four aircraft and three pilots were lost. One interception was carried out at dusk near the shore, which forced some of the carrier planes to land on Dulag airfield, still inactivated and also under attack, and that resulted in several being wrecked. Foul weather caused other operational losses. And around noon, when most of its planes were airborne, Group 4 was under attack by submarines.

Destroyer *Helm* at 1228 made a sound contact on a submarine

[3] Task Group 38.4 had been 64 days at sea on 30 October, except for 3½ days in Ulithi or other advanced bases. Over half of *Franklin's* crew were suffering from heat rash.

only 600 yards away. While the task group cleared that area at high speed, destroyer *Gridley* assisted *Helm* in developing the contact. Three patterns of depth charges were dropped within an hour; *Gridley* dropped a deep ten-charge pattern whence air bubbles arose at 1342 and *Helm* made a fourth and very deep drop at 1411. Splintered deck planking and human remains shot to the surface, and a tremendous explosion occurred. The attack was only assessed as a "probable," but after the war it was ascertained that the two destroyers sank *I-54*. That boat and *I-45*, which was sunk by *Whitehurst* the same day about 50 miles distant, were part of a group of four that were operating east of Mindanao in the hope of sinking Allied shipping en route to Leyte.[4]

In order to destroy enemy aircraft being staged in from the north, Admiral Bogan's Group 2 on 29 October struck airfields around Manila. He claimed 71 planes shot down in the air and 13 destroyed on the ground, at the cost of 11 with 9 pilots and 4 crewmen. And one of his carriers, *Intrepid*, was hit by a Kamikaze, with a loss of 10 men killed and 6 wounded. Next day, 30 October, Bogan stood by off Samar while Davison's TG 38.4 took over the Leyte patrol. Carrier *Franklin*, favorite target for Japanese planes, caught it again. Five Kamikazes managed to elude C.A.P. and screen by approaching at the height of about 18,000 feet. The radarscopes picked them up and three were shot down, but one crashed *Franklin's* flight deck, making a 40-foot hole, putting her No. 3 elevator out of commission, destroying 33 planes, killing 56 men and seriously injuring 14. A second crashed *Belleau Wood*. Her flight deck was punctured, she lost 12 planes and 92 of her crew besides 54 seriously injured, and she was badly damaged by fire. Both carriers retired to Ulithi under escort.

It now became urgent to rearm and replenish the fast carrier task groups, and to remedy critical shortages incurred by the "unprecedented length of the period of active operations."[5] As Third

[4] *Helm* Report A/S Action 28 Oct., 4 Nov. 1944; "Analysis of A/S Action by *Helm* and *Gridley*," Incident No. 7214 prepared by Rear Admiral F. S. Low, Enclosure (A) to Cominch Letter 20 Dec. 1944; *War College Analysis* III 206-7.

[5] Halsey's Report for period 27 Oct.-30 Nov., 9 Dec. 1944.

Fleet retired to Ulithi, on 30 October, General MacArthur sent Admiral Halsey a gracious message which effectually disposes of the rumors of bad blood between them after the great battle:

> I send my deepest thanks and appreciation to your magnificent forces on the splendid support and assistance you and they have rendered in the Leyte operation. We have coöperated with you so long that we are accustomed and expect your brilliant successes and you have more than sustained our fullest anticipation. Everyone here has a feeling of complete confidence and inspiration when you go into action in our support.

Task Force 38 now took a breather and received a new commander. Vice Admiral Marc A. Mitscher was relieved 30 October by Vice Admiral John S. McCain, and TG 38.1 was taken over by Rear Admiral A. E. Montgomery, Commander Carrier Division 3.[6] But Admiral Halsey remained in command of Third Fleet.

2. *Rough Days in Leyte Gulf, 1–2 November*[7]

Admiral Kinkaid reorganized Seventh Fleet at Leyte on 29 October, sending all the ships that could be spared to Ulithi, leaving Rear Admiral Weyler as S.O.P.A. Leyte Gulf. Of his battle line, Weyler retained *Mississippi*, *California* and *Pennsylvania;* of the cruisers, H.M.A.S. *Shropshire*, *Phoenix*, *Nashville* and *Boise*, with 13 destroyers. Weyler's mission was to protect Leyte Gulf, in case the Japanese organized a striking force from Kurita's and Shima's ships which had escaped destruction. But the enemy was too much battered to try another surface action; and Admiral Weyler, instead of the surface action he was looking forward to, found an air battle on his hands.

From the Allied point of view, the air situation deteriorated at

[6] Biog. in Vol. VIII 237*n*.

[7] Combatdiv 3 (CTG 77.1, Rear Adm. Weyler) Action Report, Engagement with Japanese Air Forces in Leyte Gulf 1 Nov., 7 Nov. 1944. Action Report of destroyers attached.

the end of October. The enemy was able to stage in fresh planes to his Philippine fields from Formosa and Kyushu, but our carrier-based air power diminished, and the Army Air Force was not yet ready to take over, because Tacloban Field, the one serviceable airstrip on Leyte, could not yet accommodate more than a few land-based planes.

On 1 November the Japanese accented their relative aërial recovery by penetrating the C.A.P. over Leyte Gulf, and doing much damage. Several low-flying torpedo planes, sighted at 0950, attacked through intense antiaircraft fire. One, driven off from H.M.A.S. *Shropshire*, climbed into a cloud and then dove on destroyer *Claxton*, damaging her severely. At 0952 a twin-engine Fran, already hit and flaming, crashed *Ammen's* midship superstructure at bridge level. Fortunately it bounced off into the water; and although the destroyer sustained considerable damage and suffered 5 men killed and 21 wounded, she promptly shot down another plane on her port quarter. *Killen*, attacked by seven aircraft within four minutes, shot down four, but was hit by a bomb which killed 15 men outright, started fires and flooded forward compartments. *Bush*, acting as antisubmarine picket in Surigao Strait, was attacked eight times between 0940 and 1110 with bombs, torpedoes and strafing, but she escaped a hit by expert maneuvering.

At 1126 four destroyers which had just arrived, *Flusser*, *Mahan*, *Smith* and *Lamson*, reported to Admiral Weyler. *Claxton* and *Killen* were sent into San Pedro Bay and *Richard P. Leary*, *Bennion* and H.M.A.S. *Arunta* were recalled from antisubmarine duty to augment the screen around the battleships and cruisers. About two hours later a pair of Vals were sighted from destroyer *Abner Read* (Commander A. M. Purdy) through a break in the clouds. As the leading plane nosed into a dive, prompt gunfire action shot away its port wing, but the fuselage crashed the deck and started a fire which exploded the destroyer's magazines, let in a flood of water and gave her a list of 25 degrees. Abandon Ship was ordered at 1358 and, 17 minutes later, *Abner Read* rolled over and sank stern first.[8] Destroyers *Claxton* and *Leary* recovered survivors with such speed and efficiency that only 22 men were lost. There were intermittent air attacks until nightfall, and in one of them destroyer *Anderson* was hit with a small bomb on her main deck under the bridge and lost a number of men.

Rough as this day was in Leyte Gulf, it was but a foretaste of many worse days off Leyte, Lingayen and Okinawa that the Kamikazes would provide. This time the destroyers took the rap; soon it would be the turn of larger ships. Not since the Guadalcanal operation had the Navy experienced anything like this in the Pacific.

The tactical situation at Leyte on 1 November 1944 was serious. The Japanese had virtually recovered control of the air and reports of their ships being on the way back to fight kept coming in. Admiral Halsey received word from V Army Air Force and Radio Manus that a large enemy task force had been sighted in the western part of the Mindanao Sea. The Admiral "evaluated the contact as of doubtful value," and it later turned out to be a Japanese trick to get Weyler's force into Surigao Strait where it could be worked over by the Kamikazes. But one could not ignore such reports. Halsey decided "to place his forces in position to intercept any offensive move that might be made." Since three task groups of TF 38 had retired to Ulithi, he formed a new TG 34.5 out of Bogan's group at 1800 November 1, and sent it to augment Weyler's force. TG 34.5, comprising battleships *New Jersey* (flying Admiral Halsey's flag) and *Iowa*, light cruisers *Biloxi*, *Vincennes* and *Miami* and six destroyers, commenced a high-speed run westward in order to arrive at a point 80 miles east of Leyte at dawn 2 November, and Bogan's depleted TG 38.2 was directed to provide combat air patrol for it from a point 100 miles to the eastward. In the meantime Admiral Sherman's Group 3 was turned back from

[8] *Abner Read* Action Report and Report of Loss 1 Nov., 13 Nov. 1944. Before abandoning ship, Cdr. Purdy jettisoned torpedoes. They headed for Weyler's battleships, which had to maneuver sharply to avoid.

its passage to Ulithi and routed to a supporting position east of Leyte; while Admiral Montgomery's Group 1, already at Ulithi, was ordered to make best speed to another position in support. Admiral Davison's Group 4 was allowed to remain at Ulithi because it included the two badly damaged carriers, *Franklin* and *Belleau Wood*.

Before midnight 1 November, Admiral Halsey received a copy of Admiral Kinkaid's dispatch in which he informed General MacArthur that one destroyer had been sunk and five damaged that day, and urged him to request further assistance from TF 38 if Army Air could not provide more fighter cover. He considered the situation in Leyte Gulf to be critical. Halsey, after receiving this message, notified Nimitz that if more carrier operations were immediately required, they should be done by at least three carrier groups, both to do a thorough job and to minimize the loss from Japanese suicide attacks.

Next day, 2 November, Admiral Bogan sent out a search mission for the reported Japanese task force, with negative results. It was now obvious that the report of heavy enemy forces in the Mindanao Sea had been "phony." But there was nothing phony about the Japanese reinforcements being landed at Ormoc Bay on the western shore of Leyte, or the planes being staged in to enemy-held airfields. Halsey's remedy was a series of strikes on Luzon airfields by three carrier groups, which he estimated would be ready by 5 November. This, he hoped, would stop the Japanese air reinforcement program and achieve lasting results.

3. *Working over Luzon, 3–6 November*

On 2 November Admiral Nimitz gave Admiral Halsey the green light for a 5 November strike on Luzon, requesting General MacArthur "to release the forces of the Third Fleet as soon as the situation permitted." At the moment this release seemed to be a long way off. As long as Army Air Forces could not support MacArthur, the Navy must.

On the morning of 3 November, TG 34.5 rendezvoused with and was dissolved into TG 38.2. Bogan's group, now its old self again, set forth to join Groups 1 and 3 which were steaming up from Ulithi. Halsey was getting set to hit Luzon in an effort to deprive the enemy of his air superiority over Leyte. But as he poised to strike, the enemy pulled a surprise.

Half an hour before midnight, 3 November, in a calm sea under a bright moon, the three fast carrier groups, having refueled, were making passage north. They were well off San Bernardino Strait and zigzagging when suddenly, without warning from radar or sound gear, light cruiser *Reno* (Captain Ralph C. Alexander) in Sherman's Group 3 was struck by a torpedo from *I–41*, an "Advanced Force SHO" submarine that was awaiting just such an opportunity.[9]

Violent explosions occurred on *Reno's* port quarter, a huge geyser of oil rose from the fuel tanks, the ship immediately listed to port and her after engine room and firerooms flooded, power and lighting circuits were disrupted, steering control was temporarily lost. The casualties, however, were mercifully few: 2 dead, 4 injured.

Admiral Sherman ordered four destroyers to stand by the cruiser, form antisubmarine screen, and escort her back to Ulithi, whence fleet tug *Zuni* (Lieutenant R. E. Chance) was summoned to take her in tow. She was over nine feet down by the stern, and two feet by the bow. Small fires broke out, but were successfully controlled. Her difficulties under tow were enhanced by high winds and heavy seas from a nearby typhoon. Through the skillful seamanship of Captain Alexander and Lieutenant Chance, and unremitting efforts of the crew of 242 left on board, *Reno* made Ulithi

[9] Cincpac Monthly Analysis, Nov. 1944. This was the first time in almost two years that a Japanese submarine successfully attacked a ship operating with fast carriers. *I–41* was later awarded a citation by the Emperor for sinking an "*Essex* class carrier in close quarter combat 3 Nov., east of the Philippines." Cincpac *Weekly Intelligence* II No. 4 (6 Aug. 1945) p. 27.

on 10 November. During the passage of over 700 miles, 1250 tons of water had been pumped from her flooded compartments.[10]

In accordance with the operation plan which Admiral Halsey drew up for the strikes on Luzon, TF 38 arrived off the Polillo Islands at 0615 November 5. A specific target area was assigned to each task group, as follows: –

TG 38.1 Northern Luzon including Clark Field, Aparri and shipping in Lingayen Gulf.

TG 38.2 Luzon south of lat. 14° N, Verde Island Passage, Mindoro airfields and North Sibuyan Sea.

TG 38.3 Area between 14° N and 15° N, including shipping in Manila Bay.

The tactics adopted were a dawn fighter sweep, followed by successive deckloads of bombers, fighter escorted.

Owing to the Kamikaze threat, Admiral McCain strengthened C.A.P. and kept his carriers at least 80 miles offshore. This made it difficult to furnish a proper fighter escort for the bombers, diminished the number of planes available for strikes, and reduced their net time over the target. But the enemy was caught napping. Although Luzon was swarming with recently staged in Japanese aircraft, only light airborne opposition was met, except on the first day over Clark and Mabalacat fields. There, a fighter sweep from Admiral Montgomery's Group 1 claimed to have shot down 58 interceptors. Grounded planes were widely dispersed, well camouflaged, concealed under trees and mingled with dummy planes to divert attack. Total claims of aircraft destroyed in the two-day strike amounted to 439. The dive- and torpedo-bombers that went after enemy shipping in Manila Bay, Santa Cruz, Silanguin Bay and Mariveles found plenty of targets. The principal sinking was that of heavy cruiser *Nachi*, Vice Admiral Shima's flagship in the Battle of Surigao Strait.

[10] *Reno* Report of Torpedoing Nov. 3 and Subsequent Passage to Ulithi, 18 Nov. 1944. In his endorsement on the above report, Vice Adm. C. H. McMorris, chief of staff to Admiral Nimitz, called it a "classic example" of remedial measures to extensive flooding, and recommended its distribution to all damage control schools.

The cost of this impressive bag was 25 aircraft lost in combat, 11 operational, 18 pilots and crewmen missing, in addition to casualties inflicted by one Kamikaze on *Lexington*. Four Zekes eluded C.A.P. and attacked this big carrier, Admiral McCain's flagship, at 1330 November 5. Three were shot down by antiaircraft fire; the fourth crashed *Lexington* on the starboard side of her island structure aft, demolishing secondary control and inflicting heavy casualties – 50 killed and missing and 132 injured, many very seriously. Damage control had the fires out within 20 minutes; the carrier maintained speed, and doggedly continued flight operations.[11]

After recovering all planes on the evening of 6 November, the task force retired to a fueling position well off shore, about 450 miles east of Manila. Admiral Bogan's Group 2 returned to Ulithi with *Lexington*. *Wasp*, now flying Admiral McCain's flag, proceeded to Guam to embark a new air group.[12] During his absence until 13 November, Groups 2, 3, and 4 (the last having left Ulithi before Group 2 entered) were under the tactical command of Rear Admiral Frederick C. Sherman in *Essex*.

The immediate effect of this two-day strike on Luzon was a sharp reduction in Japanese air opposition at the Leyte beachhead. Once more TF 38 had successfully carried the air war to the enemy.

4. *Air Power and the Ormoc Convoys, 1–11 November*

The reasons for our slow air base development on Leyte were simply foul weather and the nature of the ground. "It was a real estate problem, and the real estate agents failed badly," said an officer who knew the facts. Tacloban turned out well, but the old

[11] *Lexington* Action Report, 22 Nov. 1944.

[12] The composition of this Air Group 81 (Cdr. F. J. Brush), indicates how greatly the proportion of fighters to bombers on *Essex* class carriers had been increased in recent months. VF–81, Lt. Cdr. F. K. Upham, had no fewer than 54 F6F Hellcats of 5 different types, VB–81, Lt. Cdr. H. P. Lanham, had 24 SB2C–3; and VT–81, Lt. Cdr. G. D. M. Cunha, had 15 Avengers.

Japanese mud-and-grass strips at Bayug, Buri, Dulag and San Pablo long defied the efforts of the Army Engineers. The first two were made operational for fighter planes on 3 and 5 November in dry weather; but when rain fell, as it did to the tune of 35 inches in the next 40 days, these strips became seas of mud and had to be abandoned. So was the San Pablo field on 23 November after the labor of one Navy Seabee and three Army Engineer battalions had been expended on making it fit to use. Dulag strip was in fairly good shape by 19 November. Engineer units released by the abandonment of the three strips concentrated on building an entirely new one on the Leyte shore of San Pablo Bay at Tanauan, which was readily drained and had a good sandy surface. This became operational 16 December. The Navy, in the meantime, after equally costly and futile attempts to construct a strip on the Samar shore of San Pablo Bay, settled on Guiuan on the southeast promontory of Samar. The 93rd Seabees had that ready for the first plane landing on 18 December, and the Army as well as Navy planes began using it around Christmas time. Thus, almost two months were wasted in trying to improve strips that were unimprovable and to construct new ones on unsuitable subsoil.[13]

The carriers simply could not take up all this slack, but they returned to the fight, in a big way, on 11 November.

A destroyer commander in Leyte Gulf well remarked, "The Japanese had air supremacy over Leyte Gulf after sundown. Within 60 seconds of the time that the last of the Army combat air patrol settled down on Tacloban field for the night, bogeys appeared on the radar screen." [14] These intruders seldom did any damage, but they made night hideous with Red alerts and antiaircraft fire.

The monsoon season was raising the devil for all hands, and it was an unusual monsoon, with about double the normal amount of rainfall. Foul weather, which spoiled the development of airstrips, also

[13] Sixth Army Report; History of Naval Air Base, Samar, 23 Dec. 1944–1 July 1945.

[14] Cdr. Mell Peterson, C.O. of *Cooper,* statement to writer. Confirmed by his squadron commander, Capt. W. L. Freseman.

made land operations more difficult than any that General Krueger had experienced since Cape Gloucester. It was impossible to keep schedule. But foul weather did not prevent the Japanese from reinforcing their Leyte garrison by sea. In this TA Operation, as they called their reinforcement program, they landed an estimated 45,000 troops and 10,000 tons of supplies on the west coast of the island by 12 November. On A-day, 20 October, there were probably only 21,700 enemy troops on Leyte; a 200 per cent reinforcement was serious. They were outnumbered by the 101,635 American troops who were ashore by 1 November, and the Japanese had some 365,000 troops elsewhere in the Philippines who were doing nothing,[15] but the situation bore a distressing resemblance to that on Guadalcanal two years earlier. We had won a great naval battle and secured our sea communications; but without round-the-clock air supremacy it was impossible to prevent the running in of reinforcements by "Tokyo Express." Admiral Halsey, observing the situation, suggested to General MacArthur on 2 November that the Marine Corps air squadrons then stationed in the Solomons be brought up to Leyte as soon as a field could be found for them, in order to concentrate on striking enemy shipping, for which they had been specially trained.

Japanese reinforcement convoys discharged troops at Ormoc with no trouble on 23 and 25 October, and daily thereafter until the 30th. The next one ran into opposition. It consisted of six destroyers, four other escorts and four merchant ships, embarking 1st Infantry Division and elements of the 26th Division at Manila. One or more air attacks were made on it en route by P–38s from Tacloban and B–24s from Morotai, but no serious damage was done. Lieutenant Commander Noriteru Yatsui described after the war what happened after the convoy arrived in Ormoc Bay around sunset 1 November: —

> We anchored near and to west of Ormoc Pier . . . On 2 November, shortly after dawn, P–38s commenced attacking and continued all day, both strafing and dive-bombing. No serious damage but quite a num-

[15] Cannon pp. 93, 102.

ber of casualties to men on deck and material damage to guns and equipment on deck were sustained. At about 1400, three groups of 8 each of B–24s bombed from high level concentrating on *Noto Maru* which was sunk at anchor. Ninety percent of her cargo had been unloaded. No other ship was hit. All cargo was unloaded from other ships. . . . The three remaining ships of the convoy and escort sailed from Ormoc at sunset 2 November and returned to Manila without further incident.[16]

A whole division from Manchuria and a regiment of another division, adding up to about 11,000 troops and 9000 tons of supplies, were landed by this convoy at Ormoc.[17] Japanese transport No. 9 now set up a shuttle service to bring troops over from Cebu, and during the following week, reinforcements were brought in by barge from other islands of the Visayan group. On November 5, 7 and 8 these were bombed and strafed by Army B–25s from Morotai and fighter planes from Tacloban. Three or four barges were sunk and all landing craft left on the beach were destroyed.

Another large resupply convoy, using some of the same ships, lifted 2000 troops of the 26th Infantry Division and 6600 tons of supplies from Manila on 8 November and approached Ormoc the following evening. Just as it was rounding into Ormoc Bay, it was jumped by 20 to 30 B–25s, escorted by 15 P–38s. Nevertheless most of the troops were landed that night. At dawn 10 November the fighter planes returned, followed by 30 B–25s and later by 32 more P–38s. These aircraft inflicted heavy damage on the convoy as it got under way and attempted to escape beyond air range. Two transports were set afire by bomb hits and sunk during the day, together with a small minesweeper, and a third transport when returning to Manila was attacked by aircraft and sunk.[18]

This damaged convoy on its return trip was passed during the night of 10–11 November by a fresh one from Manila consisting

[16] *Inter. Jap. Off.* I 161, 26 Oct. 1945. Dates have been corrected in light of other information. Not more than 80 P–38s were then operational at Tacloban and two thirds of them had just arrived 31 Oct., so it is unlikely that they attacked all day long.

[17] Cannon p. 99; MacArthur *Historical Report* II 380.

[18] Same references and *Imp. Jap. Navy W. W. II;* Craven & Cate V 374, 377–8. Some of the B–25s probably belonged to XIII A.A.F., which moved into Morotai 29 Oct.

of five or six transports escorted by four destroyers, a minesweeper and a subchaser. Three destroyers from the homebound convoy joined to strengthen its screen.[19] Of the about 10,000 troops embarked in this convoy, all save a few who swam ashore were drowned, thanks to Task Force 38. A search plane reported the convoy to Admiral Halsey as it sortied from Manila Bay. Task Groups 38.1, 38.3 and 38.4 were then operating about 400 miles west of the Marianas, approaching a fueling rendezvous nearer to Saipan than to Luzon. Acting upon General MacArthur's request, Admiral Halsey directed Rear Admiral Frederick Sherman, in temporary command of Task Force 38, to cancel fueling, reverse course and proceed at best speed westward to attack the transports. By 0600 November 11, the carriers were 200 miles off San Bernardino Strait and launching a search mission which found the Japanese ships in the Camotes Sea, approaching Ormoc Bay.

Within 45 minutes of this sighting, the carriers had launched 347 planes for the attack. The target coördinator arrived ahead of the first strike and directed that the *Marus* be attacked first. And, about a mile off the Ormoc beach, every one was sunk by bombing.[20] The next wave of carrier planes, although intercepted by 25 to 30 enemy aircraft (of which 16 were shot down), bombed and sank four destroyers, *Hamanami*, *Naganami*, *Shimakaze* and *Wakatsuki*. And when the remnant returned to Manila, destroyers *Akebono* and *Akishimo* were sunk by carrier-based aircraft in the Bay. American losses were nine planes only.

Japan could ill afford to lose these ships. Their destruction materially shortened the Leyte campaign, and over two weeks elapsed before General Yamashita could collect enough vessels for another try.

Shortly before this strike, on 9–10 November, Field Marshal Terauchi, Japanese Southern Army commander, held staff conferences at his Manila headquarters with Yamashita and other

[19] Interrogation of Rear. Adm. Matsuyama (*Inter. Jap. Off.* I 230) 31 Oct. 1945.

[20] The number is given as 3 by *Imp. Jap. Navy W. W. II*, but 5 by MacArthur *Historical Report* II 387.

generals. The "Tiger of Malaya" proposed that Leyte be written off. He pointed out that there was slight chance of shoving more reinforcements into Leyte, that it would be better to withdraw and concentrate on Luzon. But the Field Marshal overruled him, and ordered that the reinforcement program continue and that the battle for Leyte be "brought to a successful conclusion." So, thousands of more lives were expended on an operation that was doomed to failure.

5. *Fast Carrier Operations, 12–25 November*

It was high time for Task Force 38 to break off supporting the Leyte operation, if Admiral Halsey were to strike the Japanese home islands, as he longed to do, before the close of 1944. This had once been postponed in order to continue support to Sixth Army. Must it again be put off? The question was discussed at General MacArthur's Tacloban headquarters around 10 November with General Kenney and Rear Admiral Forrest Sherman, who represented Admiral Nimitz. The conferees estimated correctly that the Japanese, despite loss of the naval battle and the devastating strikes on the last Ormoc convoy, would bitterly defend Leyte. The dismal prospect of another long-drawn-out Guadalcanal campaign had to be envisaged. General MacArthur could not approve releasing TF 38 for the three or four weeks that would be necessary to give Japan a proper pounding. On 11 November, Admiral Halsey, then at Ulithi, regretfully recommended to Admiral Nimitz "that the planned strikes against Japan be indefinitely postponed and that the fast carrier forces concentrate upon the continued support of the Philippine campaign with adequate rehabilitation and improvement of material condition for future amphibious operations." [21] Nimitz consulted MacArthur, who on 13

[21] Account of Tacloban conference, obtained orally from Rear Adm. Forrest Sherman early in 1945. The rest is in Halsey's War Diary for Nov. 1944. He suggested that the next strike be on Brunei Bay, North Borneo, where Kurita had assembled most of his ships still afloat after the Battle for Leyte Gulf. Nimitz

November declared that until airfield construction permitted the A.A.F. on Leyte to be built up to the required strength, "he considered the support of fast carriers essential." [22] So that was that. No wings over Tokyo until next year.

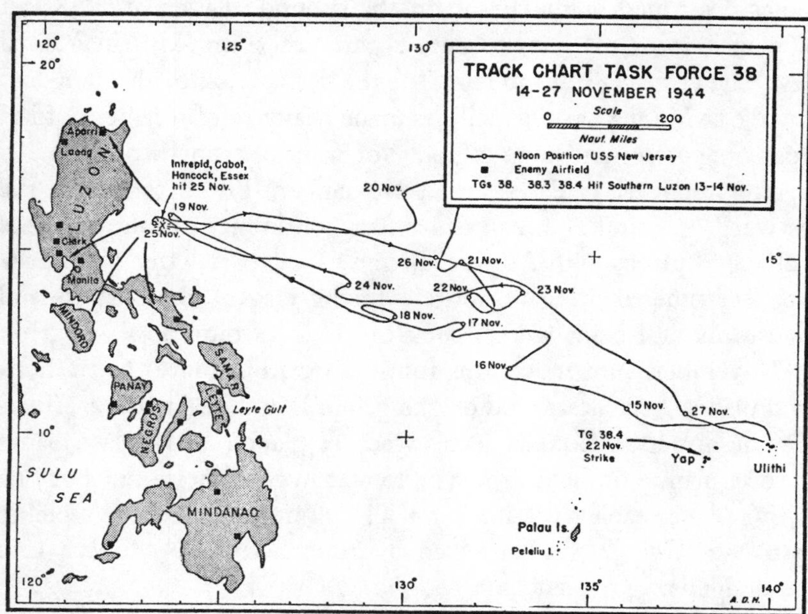

Admiral Halsey accepted this decision, a bitter disappointment to him, with good grace. The three fast carrier groups (1, 3 and 4), after fueling in the morning of 12 November, closed in again toward central Luzon. They were snooped that night approaching the launching area, but the Japanese failed to take advantage of the tactically weak condition of carriers at dawn, and the few small raids that developed during the next two days were easily struck down.

The air strikes on Luzon of 13–14 November were aimed at ship-

referred this to MacArthur who preferred that the carrier planes concentrate on Luzon. The General was right, as it proved, because these ships were in no condition to offer any serious threat.

[22] Vice Adm. C. H. McMorris (Cincpac chief of staff) endorsement to radio message from MacArthur to Nimitz 16 Nov.

ping which might be used to reinforce Leyte rather than at the airfields. The carrier planes made an impressive bag – light cruiser *Kiso*, five destroyers (*Akebono*, *Akishimo*, *Okinami*, *Kiyoshimo* and *Hatsuharu*) and seven *Marus* sunk;[28] an estimated 84 enemy planes destroyed in the air or on the ground. Task Force 38 lost 25 planes, most of them to antiaircraft fire from ships in Manila Bay. The cost was not too high, for the destruction of shipping and damage to Manila harbor facilities made heavy reinforcement of the Japanese garrison in Leyte difficult for want of troop lift.

After recovering planes on 14 November, TF 38 retired to the eastward, Admiral Sherman's Group 3 continuing to Ulithi, where it changed places with Admiral Bogan's Group 2. After giving the Japanese time to bring up more shipping targets, the harbors and roadsteads of Luzon were struck by Task Groups 1, 2 and 4 on 19 November. Not much was found afloat, but more than a hundred planes were destroyed on the ground, despite Japanese efforts at wide dispersal. Combat losses were 13 planes. As the last planes were returning on board their carriers, eleven separate raids of one to five planes each were made on TF 38, unsuccessfully. A picket destroyer, *Collett*, was attacked by four Bettys, shot down two and dodged two torpedoes.

As diminishing returns did not justify further strikes on the 20th, the fast carriers withdrew to a fueling rendezvous. Admiral Davison's Group 4 was detached to give bypassed Yap a working over, as Admiral McCain had been about to do on 25 October when diverted to a better target. Accordingly, 96 fighter planes carrying rockets and napalm bombs struck Yap on 22 November. Results were disappointing because more than half the napalm bombs refused to ignite. Rear Admiral Ofstie had already expressed the opinion that this "secret weapon," which was supposed to spread and ignite a penetrating incendiary jelly, was a washout; that if napalm could not be made to ignite more frequently the planes might as well drop empty beer bottles. But the bombs were soon

[28] *Imp. Jap. Navy W. W. II.* Destroyer *Ushio* and oiler *Ondo* were damaged and a patrol craft sunk.

improved and used with good effect on Okinawa and in the Korean War.

The Yap strike concluded, Group 4 joined Group 3 at Ulithi to reprovision, rearm, and receive other much needed services. This meant that only two groups comprising four *Essex* class and three light carriers were immediately available for further attacks on Luzon.

During the night of 24–25 November, Admirals Bogan and Sherman made the usual high speed approach to a launching point about 165 miles east of Manila to strike Luzon on the 25th. Heavy cruiser *Kumano*, already damaged in the Battle off Samar and by United States submarine *Guitarro*, was a primary target. Planes from *Ticonderoga* found her in Dasol Bay, on the other side of the Bolinao Peninsula from Lingayen Gulf, and sank her in shoal water. A small coastal convoy was located about 15 miles southwest of Dasol Bay and from it, frigate *Yasoshima* and three LSV (the Japanese equivalent of LST) were sunk. Other carrier planes found a convoy about 30 miles north of Lingayen Gulf and nicked it of two small *Marus*.[24]

A significant feature of the 25 November raid was the large number of enemy planes encountered airborne. Over Luzon, 26 of these were shot down in addition to 29 destroyed on the ground. Obviously, the Japanese air forces had come to life. And several submarines were out looking for Task Force 38.[25] The fast carriers had carried water to the well once too often and too regularly. The enemy had learned to look for them every six or seven days, and must have observed that they always launched from about the same ocean area. Now that TF 38 was limited to two groups, C.A.P. available for interception was much reduced. And the carriers were effectively snooped.

At noon 25 November Admiral Bogan's Group 2 was operating

[24] *Imp. Jap. Navy W. W. II* p. 214; JANAC p. 76 calls her *Yasojimo*.

[25] Submarine *RO-50* was awarded a citation for having "engaged in close quarter combat with an enemy task force" in waters east of the Philippines 25 Nov., and having sunk "one large carrier and one destroyer." Cincpac-Cincpoa *Weekly Intelligence* II No. 4 (6 Aug. 1945) p. 27. TF 38 is ignorant of this exploit.

about 60 miles off Dijohan Point on the San Ildefonso Peninsula of Luzon, with Group 3 about 35 miles away. Each had the usual airborne protection. Preparations were being made for launching the third strike of the day while planes from the second were coming in. Enemy aircraft approached from the direction of southern Luzon, an area only lightly covered by the fighter sweep in the morning. *Hancock*, *Cabot* and *Intrepid* commenced launching at 1226, when bogeys were reported 25 to 30 miles out, approaching so rapidly and in such numbers that it was virtually impossible to plot them. At 1229 Admiral Bogan ordered speed increased to 24 knots. C.A.P. attacked six Zekes, but shot down only two and damaged a third. The others dived low to escape, and at 1234 one of them went for *Hancock*. It was exploded by antiaircraft fire about 300 feet above the ship, but a piece of the wing fell on the carrier's flight deck, starting a small fire and knocking out a 20-mm gun. It might well have been worse, and soon it did become worse.

The radar screens were still full of bogeys. At 1248 a raid consisting of 10 to 12 planes which had eluded C.A.P. was picked up about 15 miles away, flying at 1000 feet. The ships soon opened fire, but at 1253 a plane dove on *Intrepid*, crashed a 20-mm gun that was served to the last moment by six steward's mates, and plunged through her flight deck. Its bomb exploded in the gallery deck, forcing the flight deck upwards and starting serious fires. A second Kamikaze struck *Cabot* on the port side of her flight deck forward and on the catwalk. Two minutes later a third narrowly missed *Cabot*. As a result of the hit and the near-miss, that light carrier had two six-foot holes in her flight deck, a similar hole in the hull, severe damage to the catapult, and lost 36 men killed and 16 seriously injured. Despite this damage she was able to recover her own planes an hour later.

Admiral Sherman's Group 3 was also catching it. Two Kamikazes came in on *Essex* at 1255, before launching was completed; one was shot down in time, but the other, although hit, crashed the port side of the flight deck forward. The damage was not serious and did not impair the battle efficiency of *Essex*, but she lost 15 of her crew.

Before two bells struck Group 2 was in for it again. *Intrepid*, already damaged, opened fire on an enemy plane approaching from astern at an altitude of 160 feet. It dove onto her flight deck at a shallow angle and the bomb went through and exploded in the hangar deck. The plane disintegrated into small burning pieces which spread all over, but "the engine and pilot continued on to the forward end of the flight deck." [26] Resulting fires were under control by 1309 but smoke was very dense throughout the ship and other fires were kindled by the intense heat of those on the hangar deck. The damaged flight deck and arresting gear made further flight operations impossible, and *Intrepid* had 75 planes airborne. These landed on *Hancock*, *Essex* and *Ticonderoga*, re-gassed, and (as there was no room for them on board) flew off to Tacloban Field, Leyte, where they arrived safely and even participated in a strike from that base next day.

By 1447 all fires on board *Intrepid* were out. During this time she never lost propulsion or left station in the task group. Her casualties were heavy: 69 dead and missing, 35 seriously injured. During the attacks on the carriers 19 enemy planes were shot down over them and 13 more were destroyed by antiaircraft fire or by suicide.

Damage suffered by the carriers forced a planned strike on shipping in the Visayas for 26 November to be canceled. Task Force 38 withdrew temporarily from the Philippine Sea, covered by night air patrols launched from *Independence*. Group 2 was ordered to Ulithi, leaving only Group 3 at sea.

This action of 25 November concluded the fast carrier support of the Leyte operation which had begun on 6 October. For reasons that we have already related, this support had been prolonged for four weeks after the originally planned date of its termination.

[26] CTG 38.2 (Rear Adm. Bogan) Action Report 13 Dec. 1944.

And, as TF 38 had been out against the Philippines since early September, it is reckoned that by the end of November, it had been at sea almost continuously for 84 days. The resulting strain on all hands was severe. No ship had been lost since *Princeton* went down; but *Cabot* and *Intrepid* as well as *Lexington, Franklin* and *Belleau Wood* needed extensive repairs. Under these conditions, wrote Admiral Halsey, "further casual strikes did not appear profitable; only strikes in great force for valuable stakes or at vital times would justify exposure of the fast carriers to suicidal attacks – at least until better defensive techniques were perfected." November operations again proved the ability of American warships, sailors and naval aviators to carry on for long periods with almost no letup.

The net result of this pinch-hitting activity, as we may fairly call these support strikes of TF 38 in November, was to make a further drain on Japanese air forces, and to destroy so much shipping that the enemy could not effectively reinforce his hard-pressed positions in Leyte. His garrisons throughout the Archipelago were now almost isolated, so that General MacArthur, if properly supported, could effect their destruction in detail. But there was plenty of detail to be surmounted and work to be done before the Philippines could be considered liberated.

CHAPTER XVI

Leyte Secured[1]

16 November 1944–10 May 1945

1. *Progress Ashore in November*

EVEN after the defeat at sea, Imperial General Headquarters decided to make the defense of Leyte the "general decisive battle." Lieutenant General Sasaku Suzuki, commanding general 35th Army (which was roughly equivalent to a U.S. Army Corps) was charged with the defense. At A-day his command was spread throughout the Visayas and Mindanao, but he pulled these forces into Leyte as quickly as possible. He sent an advanced headquarters party into Ormoc, led by his chief of staff General Tomochika, on 30 October, and himself followed a few days later. Suzuki's plan was a modified defense in depth. There was no effort, as we have seen, to "annihilate the enemy at the beachhead," but the Japanese put up a tough fight against American penetration inland. Taking advantage of their interior lines and command of the mountains, and for a time of the air, they imposed a slow and painful advance on the American forces.

It may be wondered why General MacArthur did not establish a perimeter around the airfields and southern Leyte Valley, and simply contain the enemy in the mountains. That strategy had been adopted successfully by Major General Oscar W. Griswold at Bougainville, but it was not practical on Leyte because, so long as

[1] Maj. Gen. J. R. Hodge USA Operation Report XXIV Corps, Leyte, 20 Oct.–25 Dec. 1944; Sixth Army *Report of Leyte Operation;* MacArthur *Historical Report* I 223–39, II 374–80; R. J. Bulkley ms. "PT History"; Action Reports of ships and units concerned.

the west side of the island was not under our control, the enemy could run in reinforcements at will. Moreover, the General felt that he owed it to the loyal Filipinos, who were being treated abominably by the Japanese, to liberate all populated sections of the island. He could, and did, neglect the southern part of the island – the Winged Victory's hips and legs below the Abuyog–Baybay waistline – as no significant enemy forces were there, or could get there.

General Krueger's Sixth Army continued to push ahead on Leyte despite the handicap of having to operate without benefit of close air support. In General Sibert's X Corps territory, a part of the 1st Cavalry Division moved into the northern Leyte Valley, after a difficult march across the mountains, while others pushed southwest from Babatugon on San Juanico Strait by land and water, concentrating at Barugo on Carigara Bay on 29 October. That day two troops of cavalrymen were driven out of Carigara town by 450 Japanese who had infiltrated during the night.[2]

The enemy obviously intended to defend Carigara, a road junction and key both to northern Leyte Valley and to the approach to Ormoc Valley. General Sibert therefore directed that no offensive action be taken against Carigara until the 1st Cavalry and 24th Infantry were in position to launch a coördinated attack with artillery support. When the two divisions launched this attack on 2 November, there were no longer any Japanese in Carigara. By clever deception the enemy had gained time for a withdrawal and completed a successful delaying action.

After securing Carigara, X Corps moved west along the Bay and by 4 November had captured the towns of Capoocan and Pinamopoan. The Corps now headed south along highway No. 2 to drive through the Ormoc Valley to Ormoc town. Directly south of Pinamopoan, and between it and Limon, is a watershed known as Breakneck Ridge. The Japanese made a determined stand here, the northern anchor of their defense line, and some of the toughest and bitterest fights in the Leyte campaign ensued.

[2] See map in Chapter IV, above.

While X Corps was engaged in the north, XXIV Corps was pushing west from its rectangular beachhead, encountering no important opposition except in the foothills west of Dagami. By 7 November this opposition was virtually eliminated.

As soon as it became evident that the enemy would take his stand on X Corps front, General Krueger deployed his forces in order to continue hammering from the direction of Pinamopoan. At the same time he pushed small parties all along both corps fronts through the central mountain range, especially across the narrow neck of Leyte between Abuyog and Baybay. At the Camotes Sea terminus of that mountain road he planned to start a northward drive toward Ormoc, supported if possible by an amphibious landing. This job was done by the 7th Infantry Division. On 11 November at Damulaan, about twelve miles south of Ormoc, it made contact with elements of the 96th Division which had come across the mountains from Burauen.

Thus, less than three weeks after the initial landings, the enemy was on the point of being contained in a narrow sector north of Ormoc. Encompassed on three sides by American troops, General Suzuki was forced to revise his plans. A captured Japanese operation order of 6 November stated that two divisions would advance east from Ormoc across Mount Mamban, by the trail running from Dolores to Daro, and outflank the Americans. To meet this threat, General Krueger placed additional troops in the area west of Palo. Reinforcements were already on their way to assist the tired soldiers of X and XXIV Corps.

Throughout this campaign the weather, always foul, grew worse. Tropical storms almost brought operations on Leyte to a standstill. Small streams became rushing torrents, washing out bridges and flooding roads and trails vital to the movement of supplies and matériel from beachhead to interior. Pressure was continuously applied to the enemy, especially around Limon, where the 32nd Infantry Division relieved the 24th on 16 November. After confused and bitter fighting, the 32nd and 1st Cavalry captured that anchor of the enemy's defense line during the last week of November, virtually destroying the Japanese 1st Division. By 4 December elements of X and XXIV Corps made contact with each other south of Limon, which resulted in giving General Krueger a solid front in northern Leyte.

Not since the Guadalcanal, Buna-Gona, or Bougainville campaigns had fighting been as arduous as on Leyte. An observing correspondent wrote: —

> It took three and one half days from beachhead for supplies to reach the front lines of the 12th Cavalry. . . . It took thirty-four tons of food and ammunition daily to supply a single regiment of our foot soldiery under the peculiar conditions of this campaign. Buffaloes [amphtracs, LVTs] designed to carry four tons at sea and two tons on land carried four tons here. We tried airplane dropping wherever possible, but most days were so rainy in the forest that air drops were impossible. Food and ammunition sometimes ran short, but the war continued.[3]

All this sort of thing is anticlimax after the great naval battle, but it must be told. In spite of the victories of 25 October, soldiers, sailors and aviators were dying daily for the liberation of Leyte.

There is a bit of glamour, however, in the bold bid by the Japanese to grasp the initiative. Beginning 27 November, and extending for two weeks, they attempted, bravely but fumblingly, a desperate plan to recapture the Dulag and Tacloban groups of airfields. General Yamashita informed General Suzuki that he must have them to prevent General Kenney's Southwest Pacific Air Forces from severing the Japanese air route to the Netherlands East Indies. Suzuki then worked out an ingenious plan to crash the two main fields with big transport planes carrying demolitioners, who were to coöperate with a parachute drop, while troops infiltrated through the mountains and captured the airstrips near Burauen — Buri, Bayag and San Pablo. It was an air counterpart to the SHO-GO plan of naval battle, and worked no better.

First phase began in the early hours of 27 November. One Japanese transport plane crashed Buri airfield and all its occupants were

[3] Allen Raymond "The Japs Had Allies on Leyte" *Sat. Eve. Post* 3 Feb. 1945.

killed; a second crashed on the beach, and most of its occupants escaped; a third landed in the surf right off the headquarters of the United States 728th Amphibious Tractor Battalion, between Rizal and Tarragona. A sentry, assuming the plane to be friendly, swam out and climbed on a wing to offer assistance; but the passengers ungratefully tossed hand grenades at Helpful Harry. This awakened his buddies and a brisk hand-to-hand fight ensued, in which some of the Japanese were killed and others escaped to the "boondocks."

A second and more serious attempt on the Buri strip was made on the night of 5–6 December. About 150 Japanese infantrymen who had sneaked down from the mountains broke into the bivouac area and jumped the surprised GIs. They were driven off after daylight. Through a mistake in coördination a big parachute drop – 39 or 40 planes, carrying 15 to 20 men each – was pulled off 20 hours later. The planes destined for Tacloban were destroyed or driven off by antiaircraft fire and the Dulag section crash-landed, killing all hands. But the drop from 35 different aircraft on the Burauen fields created pandemonium for two days and three nights. Finally the Japanese paratroops were eliminated by Air Force ground personnel. Ironically, the United States Army Air Force had already abandoned operation of the Burauen strips as hopelessly soggy, leaving only headquarters, hospital and service forces in the area.

By December 1 Sixth Army controlled most of Leyte except the San Isidro Peninsula west of Carigara Bay, and a semicircular sector with a 12-mile radius from Ormoc. The Japanese still had about 35,000 men to defend this area, but Sixth Army effective strength had risen from 101,635 on 12 November to 183,242 on 2 December. Losses up to that time were 2260 killed and missing[4] and several thousand laid up from wounds, dysentery, "immersion foot," skin diseases, and other ills incident to campaigning in tropical mud. Over 24,000 enemy dead had been counted. It was time to finish.

[4] Sixth Army *Report*.

2. *Kamikazes in Leyte Gulf, 16–29 November*

Rear Admiral Weyler was relieved by Rear Admiral T. D. Ruddock as commander of Allied naval forces operating in defense of Leyte Gulf on 16 November. After a number of changes Task Group 77.2 on 25 November was composed of battleships *Maryland*, *West Virginia*, *Colorado* and *New Mexico*, heavy cruiser *Minneapolis*, light cruisers *Columbia*, *Denver*, *Montpelier* and *St. Louis*, and 16 destroyers.

There were no longer any fire support duties for these ships. The only reason for keeping them in Leyte Gulf was to protect reinforcement convoys from air attack with their antiaircraft fire. Frequent harassing night attacks were made by Japanese planes, mostly singly. Attack transport *Alpine* was hit on 17 November, and *James O'Hara* on the 23rd.

On the morning of 27 November members of Admiral Ruddock's task group were standing by to fuel. Combat air patrol had been grounded, because of "closing weather," yet the ships were attacked at about 1125, by 25 to 30 enemy planes. Two crashed *St. Louis* well aft, destroying her catapult and float planes and knocking out the after turrets. Two headed for *Colorado*, one struck the port side amidships and the other splashed close aboard. Four picked on *Montpelier*, three passing over and the fourth inflicting minor damage by ricocheting from the water into her topsides. Following this Kamikaze attack, torpedo planes approached the task group from the southeast. Although two or three were shot down prior to reaching their dropping point, one succeeded in directing a torpedo at *Maryland*. She dodged it, and the plane was splashed. At noon, when the fight was practically over, Army P–38s flew out from their Leyte bases and shot down one enemy plane.[5]

[5] CTG 77.2 (Rear Adm. Ruddock) Report of Operations, Leyte Gulf, 16 Nov.–2 Dec., 20 Dec. 1944. Cruiser *Portland* and destroyers *Ingraham* and *Conner* joined TG 77.2 on 28 Nov. Next day *Colorado*, *St. Louis*, *Taylor* and *Mustin* departed for Manus while Desron 60 (*Barton*, flag) joined Adm. Ruddock.

At sunset 29 November, *Maryland* was acting as guide in the center of the Task Group 77.2 formation, which was steaming on a northerly course in Leyte Gulf. *Colorado* and *St. Louis* with four destroyers were four or five miles to the eastward, beginning the first leg of their trip back to Manus. The sky that evening was overcast with passing rain squalls and a few breaks in the clouds. It was almost a theatrical setting for a suicide attack. *Maryland* was the first victim. A suicider hit her deck between the two forward turrets, causing extensive damage to the ship's structure and heavy casualties; 31 killed and 30 injured.[6] While she was still under attack, two more Kamikazes went after picket destroyers *Saufley* and *Aulick* at the eastern entrance to Leyte Gulf. *Saufley* sustained only minor damage, but the crash on *Aulick* was horribly successful; in addition to a smashed bridge, she lost two 5-inch guns and one third of her crew – 32 dead or missing and 64 wounded.

Later experience of the Kamikazes at Lingayen Gulf and Okinawa would make the suicide technique of this period seem amateurish in comparison; but already it was no laughing matter. The Japanese had perfected a new and effective type of aërial warfare that was hard for the Western mind to comprehend, and difficult to counteract. Nothing could be done about it except to step up antiaircraft defense all around; one thing could be done right away: get planes up to Leyte that could and would intercept enemy flights. General MacArthur became so concerned over the failure of the A.A.F. night fighters on Leyte to catch the fast Japanese "Oscars" that were making nightly attacks on Tacloban that he suggested to Admiral Nimitz on 26 November that these P–61s be exchanged for Squadron VMF (N)–541 of Marine Corps night-fighter Hellcats then on Peleliu.[7] Cincpac was agreeable, and on 3 December the 12 Hellcats flew up to Tacloban. Already, on 30 November, General Kenney had sent word to Major General

[6] *Maryland* Action Report of Suicide Plane Attack, 7 Dec. 1944.

[7] Maj. C. W. Boggs USMC *Marine Aviators in the Philippines* (1951) p. 29. Robert Sherrod *History of the Marine Corps Aviation World War II* (1852) chap. xix. Admiral Halsey's War Diary indicates that he had suggested using Marine Corps planes for support on 2 Nov.

Ralph J. Mitchell USMC, commanding Marine aircraft in the Solomons, that he wanted four fighter squadrons at Leyte. Mitchell was delighted; his Marine aviators had been fretting for months in a rear area with nothing to do but bomb Japanese hideouts in the jungle. Consequently, on 3 December, 85 Corsairs (F4U) of Colonel William A. Willis's Marine Air Group 12, and 12 PBJ (Navy B–25) of Air Group 61 arrived at Tacloban. These planes went into action promptly and the air situation over Leyte quickly improved.

3. *Sweep and Countersweep in Ormoc Bay, 27 November–5 December*

As long as the Japanese held Ormoc and the San Isidro Peninsula, it was fairly certain that they would attempt to run in reinforcements. Their most recent attempt to do so, on 11 November, had been thwarted by fast carrier planes; but Task Force 38 had too many duties to perform to keep a cork in the Camotes Sea bottleneck. Army Air Forces on Leyte had more than they could handle giving air support to troops, and the Army bombers based at Morotai and Biak were not much good at bombing small fast ships, especially at night. The only way to slam shut this back door to Leyte was by destroyer sweeps in the Camotes Sea. When one remembers the exploits of Arleigh Burke, Frederick Moosbrugger and other squadron commanders up the Slot in 1943, one naturally asks why this method was not tried earlier.

One reason was fear of mines. The only possible approach to the Camotes Sea and Ormoc from Leyte Gulf [8] is through the Canigao Channels, two narrow passages between the southwestern "leg" of Leyte and the long line of reefs that juts eastward from Bohol. Canigao East Channel was swept by *Pursuit* (Lieutenant Commander R. F. Good USNR) and *Revenge* (Lieutenant Commander

[8] San Juanico Strait is too narrow and shoal for anything bigger than small craft; even the PTs found it difficult to navigate.

J. L. Jackson USNR) on 27 November, and on 4 December *Pursuit* and *Requisite* (Lieutenant Commander H. R. Peirce USNR) swept Canigao West Passage, giving a second entrance through the reefs.[9]

Captain Robert H. Smith, Comdesron 22, was given tactical command of the first Camotes Sea foray, comprising destroyers *Waller*, *Saufley*, *Renshaw* and *Pringle*. During the evening of 27 November they stood down Surigao Strait at 30 knots. Their mission was to bombard enemy installations in Ormoc Bay and sweep through the Camotes Sea to destroy enemy shipping. A Black Cat flying boat on regular night search was expected to keep Captain Smith informed of enemy shipping approaching.

At a few minutes before midnight the destroyers commenced firing at the first target sighted, southeast of the town of Ormoc. Bombardment completed at 0100 November 28, Captain Smith led his division north of Ponson Island. Shortly after, a message was received from the patrolling Black Cat that an enemy submarine (*I–46*) was approaching Ormoc Bay. *Waller* picked it up on her radar at 0127 and, within three minutes, all three destroyers opened fire. The submarine attempted to "fishtail" on the surface; under star shell illumination, the destroyers closed and opened fire with their 40-mm guns, which was returned for a few minutes. *Waller* prepared to ram at 0144, but it was not necessary; *I–46* sank stern first. Captain Smith, being behind schedule, did not tarry in the faint hope of recovering survivors, but retired to Leyte Gulf.[10]

Two escorts of the reinforcement convoy that Captain Smith had hoped to encounter were sunk by PT boats the following night, 28–29 November. Motor torpedo boat crews who had taken part in the Battle of Surigao Strait had been kept busy ever since with odd jobs, but like the Marine aviators they were chafing for lack of combat. PTs *127*, *331*, *128* and *191*, under squadron commander Lieutenant Roger H. ("Woof") Hallowell USNR, were given the pioneer mission for Ormoc. At midnight they separated

[9] CTU 87.3.6 Action Report 8 Dec. 1944.

[10] Comdesron 22 (Capt. R. H. Smith) Action Report 2 Dec., *Saufley* Report of Shore Bombardment in Ormoc Bay and A/S Action 27 Nov., 10 Dec. 1944.

into deuces. In bright moonlight the first pair sighted what looked like a large patrol craft anchored in Ormoc Bay. She opened fire at 800 yards' range, the two PTs fired eight torpedoes and a flight of rockets, and saw a large explosion. Retiring under fire, they intercepted *PT–128* and *PT–191*, which had been patrolling the Camotes Islands. Lieutenant Hallowell boarded the former and returned to Ormoc Bay, where the four boats were unable to find the shot-at patrol craft. Under heavy fire from the shore, the boats that still had torpedoes launched them at a freighter tied to a dock at the bay's head. Japanese sources indicate that they sank *SC–53* and *PC–105*; the latter was found ten days later, when the PTs made Ormoc their advanced base, resting on the bottom.[11]

On the night of 29–30 November it was the destroyers' turn. Captain Smith led *Waller*, *Renshaw*, *Cony* and *Conner* to Ormoc Bay. But the hunting was not good that night. Ormoc Bay was empty, so the destroyers swept up the coast of the San Isidro Peninsula. They found a barge convoy close to shore but were unable to chase it owing to shoal water. And they retired too early to encounter a Japanese reinforcement convoy which unloaded at Ipil on the 30th.

The next sweep was made by destroyers *Conway*, *Cony*, *Eaton* and *Sigourney* during the night of 1–2 December. Since no shipping was discovered in Ormoc Bay, course was again set along the San Isidro Peninsula. At about 0200 *PT–491*, which had come around through San Juanico Strait to the northwest cape of Leyte, reported an escorted enemy freighter and asked for assistance. By 0224 the four destroyers had made contact with a vessel which they assumed to be the freighter, opened fire, and 20 minutes later it was at the bottom of the Camotes Sea.[12] On their return passage to Leyte Gulf the destroyers bombarded shore installations at Palompon and enemy positions on the north shore of Ormoc Bay.

[11] Bulkley "PT History" pp. 518–19; letter from Mr. Hallowell, 1958. Presumably this is the fight described in MacArthur *Historical Report* II 396 as taking place on night of 27–28 November.

[12] No mention of this sinking (which is vividly described in *Conway* Action Report), in JANAC or *Imp. Jap. Navy W. W. II*. Possibly it was a barge too small for these works to notice.

Aircraft sightings on 2 December indicated that a "Tokyo Express" run might be heading for Ormoc Bay the following night. Commander J. C. Zahm, junior divisional commander of Captain W. L. Freseman's Desron 60, was given the duty. In *Allen M. Sumner*, accompanied by *Moale* and *Cooper*, he departed Leyte Gulf at 1829 December 2 to intercept.[13] It was a beautiful night with a six-knot northerly breeze blowing, a calm sea and a rising moon to aid visibility.

The three destroyers had hardly stuck their noses inside Ormoc Bay when enemy aircraft were after them. From 2308 until they retired at 0145 December 3, the ships were under almost continuous air attack, partly in bright moonlight, which made the enemy planes easy to see. The best they could do was a few near-misses on *Sumner*, which caused slight damage, and nine or ten were shot down.

Shortly after midnight, before this phase of the battle was over, but after the moon had set, radar contact was made on two enemy ships. Gunfire action began at once. *Sumner* and *Cooper* took care of *Kuwa*, a 1000-ton destroyer with two gun mounts forward and large numbers of men topside. Eight minutes after they opened fire, "the enemy ship was in flames, thoroughly wrecked and sinking." Shore batteries joined [14] and the fracas became very lively – an artist's conception of a naval battle in a popular picture magazine, said *Cooper's* skipper – tracers shooting back and forth; balls of fire as shells detonated.

Sumner and *Cooper* now transferred their fire to target No. 2, destroyer *Take*, at which *Moale* was already firing; but it was too late. *Take* made a torpedo hit on *Cooper* amidships, which broke her in two in less than thirty seconds. Men tumbled into the sea off the decks, popped up from hatches, slid out of the hot-case scuttles of the 5-inch turrets. Petty Officer Earl M. Auspach, the only man

[13] Comdesdiv 120 (Cdr. Zahm) Action Report 6 Dec. 1944.

[14] Information later received through guerrilla sources indicated that there may have been two camouflaged Japanese destroyer escorts moored against the western shore of Ormoc Bay. This would account for the "shore battery." Cdr. Zahm's Action Report.

left alive in the forward fireroom, took time to shut off all water and oil lines and to vent steam through the stack before he escaped. The exec., Lieutenant W. P. Hodnett, was lost; the skipper, Commander Mell A. Peterson, stepped off his bridge into the water and organized survivors, in the deathly silence that descended over the bay after the ship went down.[15]

The explosion was so shattering and the sinking so nearly instantaneous that less than half the ship's company were left alive in the water, and they had to shift for themselves, since the division commander decided that any attempt at rescue, under heavy air opposition and fire from shore batteries, would only lose more ships. There were not rafts for even half the men. Gunner's Mate A. A. Masulis USNR, with a back injury that almost paralyzed him, managed to paddle a raft with his bare hands toward helpless survivors; Torpedoman's Mate W. F. Wiedemann USNR, whose fourth sinking this was, "did a beautiful job keeping up men's spirits," and Lieutenant (jg) W. J. Steed USNR dove in after men who tried to swim ashore and pulled them back to the raft. Incidents such as this happen whenever a United States ship goes down. *Cooper's* men had no monopoly of fortitude; but they had one experience shared by no others: after daybreak a group of survivors from *Kuwa* drifted so near that a conversation with them was actually carried on, in English.[16] A number of *Cooper's* survivors did swim ashore and were secreted by loyal Filipinos in the jungle; almost all the others were picked up by Catalinas near Ponson Island the following afternoon. One PBY rescued 56 survivors and another 48, both loads breaking all previous records. But 10 officers and 181 men were lost.

After the conclusion of this destroyer sweep, an amphibious landing by the 77th Infantry Division at Ormoc Bay was planned. But other important business came first.

Heavy rains had so damaged the dirt roads of Leyte that Sixth

[15] Article by Frank Kelley, after interviewing survivors, in *N.Y. Herald-Tribune*, 31 Dec. 1944.

[16] Told to the writer by Cdr. Peterson.

Army found it very difficult to transport men and matériel from the gulf beachhead to the west coast. In order to alleviate this situation, and to strengthen the American position south of Ormoc Bay prior to an amphibious assault in that sector, Captain W. M. Cole, Comdesron 5, was given the assignment of transporting troops, vehicles and ammunition from Leyte Gulf to a beach in friendly territory one mile north of Baybay on the west coast of Leyte. His task unit consisted of destroyers *Flusser*, *Drayton*, *Lamson* and *Shaw*, eight LSM and three LCI.[17] Landing Ships Medium were chosen for this operation rather than LSTs because their superior speed would enable them to make the greater part of the round trip, as well as unload, under cover of darkness.

Captain Cole's unit, destined for a rough trip, departed Leyte Gulf 4 December and arrived off the designated beach at 2248. Unloading began within the hour and was successfully accomplished, except that *LSM–22* was unable to beach because of too heavy a load and had to return to Leyte Gulf with her cargo. Two Japanese planes intruded but did no damage. By 0315 December 5 the amphibious craft had retracted and were stealing close to the shore at 12 knots. About 0534, as the task unit was approaching Canigao Island which marks the eastern channel of that name, *Drayton* was strafed by a plane that made a gliding attack.

The task unit threaded the channel, rounded the southwest cape of Leyte at 0600 and stood eastward in the growing light. Four Marine Corps night fighters arrived as C.A.P. and shot down a hovering enemy plane. At 1100 December 5, when the convoy was threading Surigao Strait, and a C.A.P. of four Army P–38s had relieved the Marines, about eight enemy planes appeared overhead. Ships' radar was of little use, because of the nearby high shores of the Strait. About four miles to the northward Comdesdiv 12 (Captain K. F. Poehlmann) in *Mugford*, who with *LaVallette* was conducting an antisubmarine and radar picket patrol, caught on to

[17] Comdesron 5 (Capt. Cole) Action Report of TU 78.3.10 – Amphibious Movement from Leyte Gulf to Baybay, 11 Dec. 1944; the LSMs were Nos. *18–23*, *34* and *318*; the LCIs were Nos. *1014*, *1017*, *1018*. Details from *Drayton* and *Mugford* Action Reports.

what was happening and rushed over to help at flank speed, just as the enemy planes began making suicide dives. Action was rapid and lively. The P–38s sent two planes into the waters of Surigao Strait, a third was shot down by *LaVallette,* a fourth by *Flusser* and a fifth was splashed by a combination of fire. But three more left their mark. One crashed squarely amidships on *LSM–20,* killing eight men, wounding nine, and sinking the ship; one crashed alongside *LSM–23* and ricocheted into her, causing extensive damage; the eighth and last dove on *Drayton* from her starboard quarter.

All batteries opened fire. Commander R. S. Craighill ordered left full rudder and the plane passed down her starboard side at about 350 knots with its wing tip just missing the bridge. When the Japanese pilot saw that he was in danger of missing, he stood the plane up on its left wing and struck near the forward 5-inch gun. Most of its wreckage passed clear, but part of the wing and landing gear killed six men and wounded twelve. By prompt and efficient action the fires that it started were quickly extinguished. *Drayton's* "entire performance was observed with thrill and admiration," according to Captain Cole.[18]

More P–38s arrived to join C.A.P. and Captain Poehlmann turned over *Mugford* and *LaVallette* to Captain Cole in *Flusser,* who then directed them to escort the damaged LSM while *Shaw* and *Drayton* proceeded to San Pedro Bay with the four undamaged LSMs at best speed. After the survivors from *LSM–20* had been picked up, and *LSM–23* taken in tow, the rest of the task unit steamed north under escort of *Mugford, Flusser* and *Lamson,* while *LaVallette* returned to patrol Surigao Strait.

The enemy was not yet through with Captain Cole's task unit. About 1710, when it had passed the Cabugan Islands and was approaching Hingatungan Point, a Val attacked *Mugford* and dropped a bomb about 200 yards on her starboard beam. It retired, shortly reappeared and attacked at low altitude, weaving violently. Although hit by machine-gun fire, it crashed into the port side about three feet above the main deck. A second plane was shot

[18] Endorsement to *Drayton* Action Report, 29 Dec. 1944.

down by two P–38s of the combat air patrol. *Mugford* lost two men killed outright, and six died from burns. Fires were brought under control promptly, but the ship was seriously damaged in No. 2 fireroom. At 1818 she was taken under tow by *LSM–34*. Other destroyers in the Gulf came to the rescue, but by this time *Mugford* was able to cast off the towline and work up a speed of 12 knots.

Thus another tough twenty-four hours for the Navy in Leyte waters came to an end. In the light of Captain Cole's round trip to Baybay, the prospects for Admiral Struble's assault landing at Ormoc Bay, scheduled for two days thence, did not look very bright.

4. *Landings at Ormoc and Air Battle of 7 December*

Amphibious operations roll on at an even tempo, provided the island or land mass is fairly large. After the initial *élan* is over there is a tremendous struggle for air and sea supremacy, both sides pour in reinforcements, land operations seem to bog down; but finally everything is set to go in for the kill. So it had been on Bataan, Guadalcanal and Saipan; so on Leyte. With the enemy closed in on three sides, it was evident that a successful landing by us at Ormoc Bay would slam the back door. It would give the Navy a new advanced base in Philippine inland waters and at the same time afford Sixth Army a jumping-off place for severing the southern sector of the enemy's main line of defense. During the first week of December three divisions – 1st Cavalry, 24th and 32nd Infantry – were pressing the Japanese on Leyte from the north and east, while two divisions – the 7th and 96th Infantry – were pushing from the south and east. Land the 77th Infantry at Ormoc, between these two reinforced Army corps, and you would have a third front in Leyte. After that, the end could not be far off.

The Ormoc landing was decided upon 30 November after much argument. General MacArthur was eager to keep his target date for an amphibious landing on the island of Mindoro, a good 250 miles NW of Leyte and almost next door to Manila, on 5 December. Admiral Kinkaid strongly opposed. He argued that until the balance of air power tipped in our favor any such move deep into enemy-held territory would be unduly risky and might end in disaster. General Kenney backed him up and General MacArthur consented to postpone the Mindoro operation ten days. That gave an interval for the landing at Ormoc, greatly to the delight of the Army corps commanders still battling for Leyte. General Krueger, too, was all for it.

Admiral Barbey designated Rear Admiral Struble, Commander Amphibious Group 9, to transport the 77th Division to Ormoc Bay and land it there. He broke off planning the Mindoro operation to assume this new responsibility. The postponement of the Mindoro landings made available enough amphibious shipping and naval support to lift a division to Ormoc, but the operation was considered very hazardous in view of continued Japanese enterprise in the air, and the risk of incurring losses which would cut into the task force destined for Mindoro.

The 77th Infantry Division, Major General A. D. Bruce USA, which had fought in the Marianas, was a part of Sixth Army reserve, from which it was released on 29 October against General Krueger's wishes, to garrison Guadalcanal. About 7 November, when Rear Admiral Forrest Sherman of Admiral Nimitz's staff was visiting General MacArthur at Tacloban, the General said he would give a great deal for another infantry division to throw into Leyte. "Why don't you take the 77th?" said Admiral Sherman. It was already en route to Guadalcanal, but the transports were turned around, and the 77th arrived at Tacloban on 23 November, "inadequately equipped and with only a limited supply of rations," says the Sixth Army *Report.* Military supplies on Leyte being critically low at this time, the arrival of another division made a difficult supply situation worse.

Admiral Struble issued his attack order promptly. The mission of his Task Group 78.3 was to "embark at Leyte, transport, escort, protect and land the landing force together with its supplies and equipment in the Ormoc Bay Area and support the landing by naval gunfire, in order to assist the Army in destroying Japanese forces opposing our advance on Leyte Island."

The composition of the Ormoc Attack Group resembled that of the shore-to-shore amphibious operations that had taken place in the Southwest Pacific. There was no combatant ship larger than a destroyer, no troop-lift larger than a destroyer transport. It was organized as follows: —[19]

TG 78.3. Ormoc Attack Group, Rear Admiral A. D. Struble in HUGHES

Fast Transport Unit	8 APD	Comdr. W. S. Parsons
Light Transport Unit	27 LCI, 12 LSM	Comdr. W. V. Deutermann
Heavy Transport Unit	4 LST	Comdr. J. C. Schivley
Escort	12 DDs (6 of the old *Mahan* class, 6 new 2200-tonners)	Capt. W. L. Freseman in BARTON[20]
Minesweeping Unit	9 AM, 1 APD	Comdr. E. D. McEathron
Control and Inshore Support	2 SC, 4 LCI(R), 1 ATR	Lt. Cdr. P. C. Holt USNR

Air Support to be furnished by the Army Air Force, including the Marine Air Group.

Four destroyers, *Nicholas*, *O'Bannon*, *Fletcher* and *LaVallette*, were assigned the preliminary task of sweeping the Camotes Sea on the night of 6–7 December, to intercept and destroy enemy shipping and submarines in the vicinity of Ormoc Bay. Their arrival off the village of Deposito was set for 0130, subsequent to the departure of motor torpedo boat patrols, which were to retire before midnight. This mission was executed with relative ease but disappointing results. No shipping was found and three small fires were the only visible results of a shore bombardment. The destroyers were shadowed by one or more planes until an hour before dawn, and undoubtedly reported.[21]

In support of this operation, the 7th Infantry Division on 5 December launched an attack northward from Damulaan, about seven

[19] Comphibgroup 9 Attack Order No. 5–44, 1 Dec. 1944.

[20] Maj. Gen. S. J. Chamberlain, General MacArthur's assistant chief of staff for operations, was embarked in destroyer *Barton* as observer.

[21] Comdesron 21, "Report on Camotes Sea Sweep and Bombardment Vicinity Ormoc," 13 Dec. 1944.

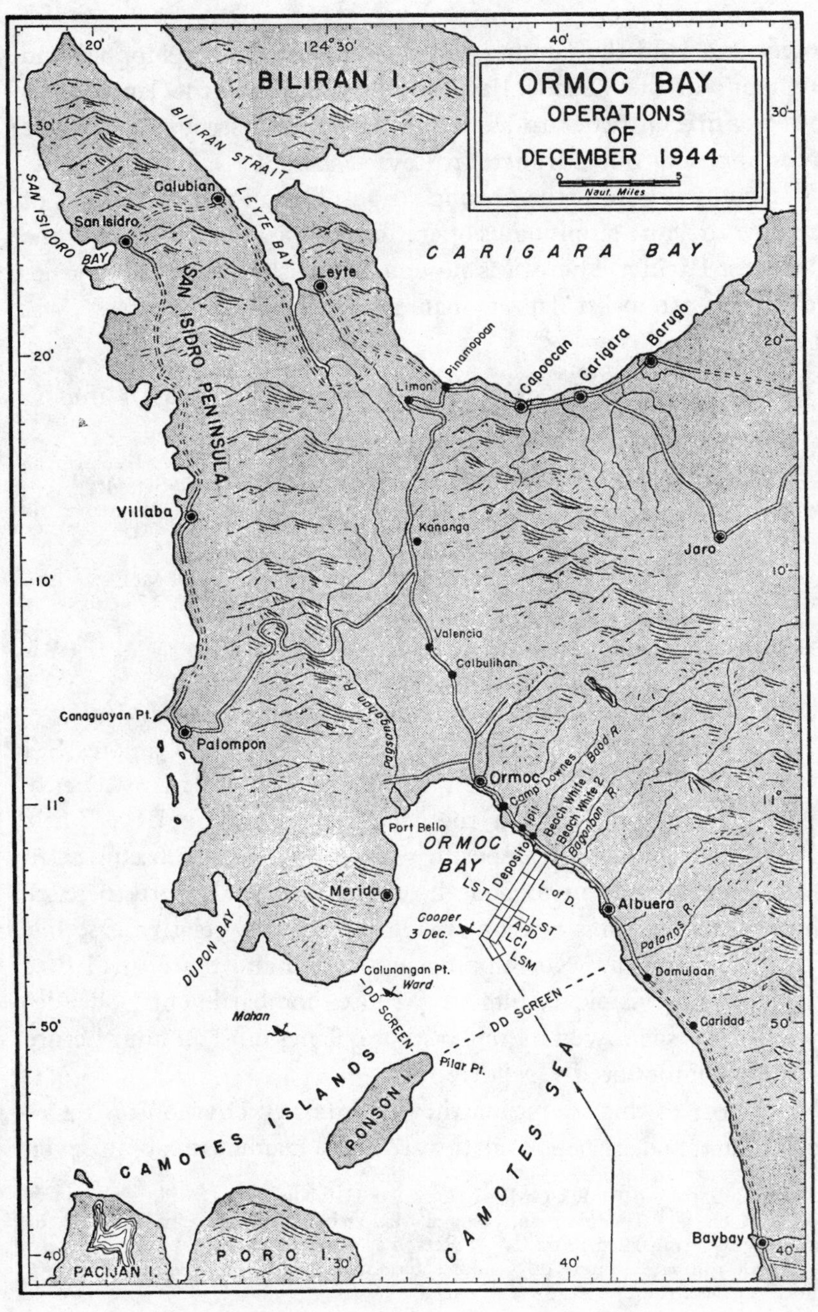
ORMOC BAY
OPERATIONS
OF
DECEMBER 1944
Naut. Miles
BILIRAN I.
BILIRAN STRAIT
LEYTE BAY
SAN ISIDORO BAY
SAN ISIDRO PENINSULA
CARIGARA BAY
Calubian
San Isidro
Leyte
Pinamopoan
Limon
Capoocan
Carigara
Barugo
Villaba
Kananga
Jaro
Valencia
Colbulihan
Canaguayan Pt.
Palompon
Pagsangahan R.
Ormoc
Camp Downes
Ipil
Beach White 1
Beach White 2
Baod R.
Bagonbon R.
Port Bello
ORMOC BAY
Deposito
L. of D.
LST
APD
LCI
LSM
Cooper 3 Dec.
Merida
Albuera
Palanas R.
DUPON BAY
Calunangan Pt.
Ward
Damulaan
DD SCREEN
Mahan
Caridad
Pilar Pt.
PONSON I.
CAMOTES ISLANDS
CAMOTES SEA
PACIJAN I.
PORO I.
Baybay
124°30'
20'
30'
40'
10'
11°
50'

miles south of the landing beaches; and the 11th Airborne Division (Major General J. M. Swing USA), which had recently arrived at Leyte, attacked westward through the mountains to cut off the Japanese 26th Division and deliver its fate to the landing force. Both attacks were progressing satisfactorily when the amphibious operation was launched.

Admiral Struble's Ormoc Attack Group embarked the 77th Division at the Dulag beaches on Leyte Gulf and departed at 1330 December 6. The passage through Surigao Strait and Canigao Channel was uneventful. Destroyers *Barton*, *Laffey* and *O'Brien* were straddled by two or three salvos from a 3-inch shore battery as they maneuvered into their fire support positions in Ormoc Bay, but the battery was quickly silenced. Day broke warm, with a light breeze and a calm sea. At 0642 December 7 all destroyers began scheduled bombardment of the beach area. Five minutes later, landing craft shoved off from the destroyer transports. The two beaches selected, White 1 and 2, were three and four miles respectively southeast of Ormoc, and adjacent to Deposito. After a 25-minute bombardment by destroyers and LCI rocket craft, the first wave of 16 landing craft hit the beach at the scheduled hour, 0707, and the troops came ashore standing up. The second wave, of the same strength, followed shortly; the third and fourth waves were composed of 12 and 14 LCI respectively, and the fifth wave of 12 LSM brought in supplies and vehicles. The beaches proved to be excellent, all landing craft retracted promptly to fetch more troops from the APDs; and by 0900 all beaching craft were unloaded, with the exception of an LSM and an LCI stuck on a reef. At 0930 General Bruce assumed command of his troops ashore, two full regimental combat teams of the 77th Division.

Tactical surprise was achieved. Although a few of the caves and ravines in the low cliffs behind the coastal road were occupied by the enemy, he had concentrated most of his forces farther down the coast to oppose the 7th Division, driving north. Two small rivers in the beachhead area proved no obstacle. The troops crossed the Baod River by a bridge which the Japanese had mined but failed to demolish, and, supported by naval and artillery fire, reached Ipil and occupied the ruined village. By nightfall they held a beachhead extending more than two miles along the coast and over a mile inland.

At 0815 Admiral Struble received word of a Japanese convoy approaching through the Visayan Sea 60 to 70 miles to the northwest. Time and distance factors decided him against detaching destroyers to attack, but he requested the Army Air Force to intercept. Twenty-one Corsairs from Marine Fighter Squadrons 313,211 and 218 took off from Tacloban, located the convoy entering San Isidro Bay some 18 miles north of Ormoc, and delivered an attack. With all the planes' guns firing, 1000-pound bombs were released from masthead height onto three destroyers, two other small escorts and four medium freighters. One LSV and all four *Marus* were sunk, but unfortunately they had already landed 4000 fresh troops. This was the eighth "Tokyo Express" run, and not the last.[22]

Everything looked rosy at 0930 December 7. Assault troops were safely ashore and fanning out, the San Isidro convoy had been bombed. Then, at 0934, bogeys 12 miles away appeared on the radar screen of destroyer *Lamson.* Six minutes later, 4 P-38s intercepted about 12 Japanese bombers and four fighters approaching the picket destroyers.

Destroyer *Mahan* (Commander E. G. Campbell), destroyer transport *Ward* and minesweepers *Saunter* and *Scout* were then patrolling an antisubmarine picket line between Calunangan Point, Leyte, and Pilar Point, Ponson Island. At 0948 there opened one of the most unusual and devastating air assaults of 1944. A multiple attack, in which the Japanese planes used torpedo tactics but switched to Kamikaze after they had been hit, was delivered against *Mahan* and *Ward* simultaneously.

Mahan opened gunfire on the enemy planes at 3000 yards, but checked when the P-38s attacked, and they knocked three fighters out of the formation and hit two bombers. These two, followed

[22] Cincpac Monthly Analysis, Nov. 1944; JANAC.

by other bombers, began diving at the ships, at intervals of about 1500 yards. No. 1 burst into flames and splashed about 50 yards short of *Mahan*, knocked down by her machine guns. No. 2 passed right over the ship. Nos. 3 and 4 bombers were shot down at a safe distance. No. 5 hit *Mahan* just abaft the bridge. No. 6 hit her at the waterline; and almost simultaneously No. 2, which had turned back, hit her between waterline and forecastle deck. No. 7 contented itself with a thorough strafing, in the course of which it was splashed by the ship's gunfire. No. 8, already in flames from its conflict with the P–38s, tried to crash but splashed instead. No. 9 passed over the ship and disappeared. All this within four minutes.

Commander Campbell now steadied his ship on course 90°, still making her top speed of 34 knots, in an effort to reach other vessels of the picket line, while damage control parties worked on the fires that had been started. It soon became evident that the high speed was fanning the fires out of control, and *Mahan's* way was stopped. The fires had spread to the flooding controls so they could not be reached, consequently the forward magazines could not be flooded. The skipper had all rafts and floatable material jettisoned and ordered Abandon Ship at 1001.

There, indeed, was a great fight. The heroic efforts of the outnumbered P–38 pilots inspired sailors who are not easily impressed, and the ship's company did everything humanly possible against overwhelming odds.

Before 1100, destroyers *Walke* and *Lamson* were picking up *Mahan's* survivors. Despite the multiple Kamikaze attack, casualties were amazingly low – 10 killed or missing in action and 32 wounded. At 1150 this gallant eight-year-old destroyer, bearing the name of the greatest naval historian, was sunk by gun and torpedo fire from *Walke*, in accordance with Admiral Struble's orders.

In closing [Commander Campbell wrote in his Action Report], it is desired to emphasize the reluctance with which both officers and men abandoned the *Mahan*. A great many members of the crew had been on board since the beginning of the war and had helped bring the ship through many exciting moments such as the Battle of Santa Cruz; the landings at Woodlark and Trobriand Islands, Salamaua, Lae, and Finschhafen; the torpedo plane attack on Finschhafen 22 September 1943; the six-hour night attack off Finschhafen the early part of November, 1943; the bombardment of Madang and Sio; and the landings at Arawe, Cape Gloucester, Saidor and the Admiralty Islands. It was like leaving behind an old friend who had seen you through a great deal of trouble, and now that he was in trouble you were powerless to save him. After the word had been given for the damage control personnel to leave the ship, it was decided to make another attempt to flood the forward magazines. Even at that time, with the ship rocking back and forth from the force of the explosions, two men volunteered to go forward. The explosions then became so intense it was decided not to make the try but the willingness to do so was a grand gesture on the part of a fine crew for a wonderful ship.

Destroyer transport *Ward* (Lieutenant R. E. Farwell USNR) also received a death blow from the Kamikazes. Three broke formation at 0945 after being attacked by P–38s and dove in her direction. *Ward* commenced firing both her 3-inch 50s and 20-mm batteries. The skipper ordered full left rudder but it was of no avail. The leading plane leveled off from a 45-degree dive and struck *Ward* just above the waterline on the port side, entering the forward part of the boiler room. A heavy explosion followed, a huge sheet of flame enveloped her amidships and broke into the troop space. An instant later a second plane passed low over the forecastle, strafing, and splashed about 200 yards off *Ward's* starboard bow; the third splashed about 600 yards astern. *Ward* ceased firing at 0947 and concentrated on fighting fires. Within three minutes she lay dead in the water. With all power lost, the fires could not be brought under control and orders were given to abandon ship because of the danger from unflooded magazines. Destroyer *O'Brien*, destroyer transport *Crosby* and two minesweepers stood over to help; but by this time the fires were completely out of control and even the diesel oil tanks were ablaze. *Ward* was abandoned shortly after 0948 and, on orders from Admiral Struble, she was sunk by *O'Brien's* gunfire. A few men were badly burned, but there was no loss of life. By a strange coincidence the skipper of *O'Brien*, Commander Outerbridge, had been commanding officer of *Ward* three years earlier when she fired the first shot of the war with Japan and sank a midget submarine outside Pearl Harbor.[23] Another beloved little ship that had fought all through the war was expended.

For the next hour, no enemy planes bothered the Ormoc Attack Force. Admiral Struble was then concerned with retracting three LSMs which had stuck on the beach. When, at 1112, planes started diving on destroyer *Smith* (they missed), the Admiral decided it was time to retire, ordered cruising disposition, and got his ships under way promptly for Leyte Gulf. A flock of Zekes pursued. One dove on destroyer *Hughes* but splashed about 50 yards off her port bow. A second dove on destroyer transport *Cofer*, but was exploded in the air by gunfire from her and *Liddle;* a third that went for *Liddle* in a low, fast attack, was exploded in midair by her gunfire only 30 feet from her port side. She had just coped with the resulting shower of plane fragments. Then, at 1120, a fourth Kamikaze attacked her from dead ahead. She opened fire with all forward guns, but this Zeke crashed *Liddle's* flying bridge and exploded, demolishing the combat information center, radio room and captain's sea cabin, killing her skipper, Lieutenant Commander L. C. Brogger USNR, and wounding two other officers. Lieutenant R. K. Hawes USNR assumed command, sent to *Hughes* and *Cofer* for medical assistance, and shortly after noon got his destroyer transport under way to rejoin Admiral Struble's convoy. She had lost 36 killed and missing and had 22 on board seriously wounded.

Two hours later, just as destroyer *Edwards* closed *Liddle* and was passing lines to take off the wounded, another air attack developed. Both ships cast off and made flank speed and radical maneuvers, endeavoring to join the convoy. The first indication of this attack was a report from *Lamson* that a "Dinah" (a twin-engined Army reconnaissance plane), was overhead, altitude 10,000 feet. *Lamson*, as fighter-director destroyer, was then controlling

[23] CTG 78.3 (Rear Admiral Struble) Action Report; *Ward* Action Report, 16 Jan. 1945; see Vol. III 96 for the Pearl Harbor action.

12 P–38s. She vectored four of them up to Dinah, which immediately dove on her. When 50 yards off the water, the plane leveled off and dropped a bomb described by those who saw it as being at least six feet long. It missed *Lamson's* port quarter by 30 yards and Dinah was splashed by her gunfire.

The convoy by this time had passed Baybay. Three enemy planes, coming in over Himuquitan Island, made a low, fast torpedo attack on destroyer *Edwards*. Two were shot down and the third skimmed the top of *Edwards's* mast. At the same time a Kamikaze approached from behind the island. *Lamson* managed to train her main battery onto it at a range of about 1000 yards, but the plane came in weaving and strafing about 30 feet off the water, crossed *Lamson* amidships as she was turning hard-a-port, hit her No. 2 stack with its right wing, spun around, crashed into a corner of the transmitter shack, and dropped until its propeller was embedded in the port side of a bulkhead. Flames flashed more than masthead high and enveloped the ship up to No. 1 gun. Part of the crew gathered on the forecastle, while all survivors aft of No. 2 stack, together with after fireroom and engine room crew, quietly gathered on the fantail. Twenty-one men were killed and 50 wounded, most of the dead being burned to death in No. 1 fireroom, whose hatches were jammed by the explosion of the plane's bomb. Rescue tug *ATR–31* closed *Lamson* to fight fires and remove wounded. When her skipper reported the fires to be uncontrollable and approaching the magazines, Captain Cole, who was standing by in *Flusser*, decided to sink *Lamson*. Later, convinced that she could be saved, he directed *ATR–31* to take her in tow; and saved she was. *Flusser*, escorting the wounded ship, came under heavy air attack but escaped unscathed, despite the fact that she had expended all her ammunition. That very unusual circumstance proves what a tough fight the Ormoc Attack Group had sustained.[24] Destroyer

[24] Ammunition expended by all 12 DDs of the escort unit during this operation was approximately as follows: 4320 rounds of 5-inch 38 AA common; 6809 rounds of 40-mm; 6224 rounds of 20-mm, 700 rounds of .50 cal.

Reid relieved *Flusser* because of this predicament, and she returned to San Pedro Bay independently.

In the same air attack that damaged *Lamson,* destroyer *Barton,* Captain W. L. Freseman's new 2200-ton flagship, was very nearly hit by a Kamikaze at 1526. The 20-mm machine-gunners on the fantail continued firing although a 5-inch gun was shooting right over their heads. Between them they shot the plane down, so close to the ship that gasoline fumes got into her ventilating system. Next morning, 8 December, cruisers *Portland* and *Nashville* and destroyers *Hall* and *Paul Hamilton* joined up and covered *ATR–31, Lamson* and *Reid* until they reached San Pedro Bay.

As Admiral Struble's reduced attack group continued toward Leyte Gulf, his flag destroyer *Hughes,* together with *Smith, Edwards* and *Barton,* came under air attack. All were as fortunate as *Flusser.*[25]

By dusk, TG 78.3 was rounding the southern cape of Leyte and no more air attacks developed. A quiet evening followed a hard day, and since the night was very dark and stormy, the convoy was unmolested.

These little ships of the Ormoc Attack Group had been under air attack almost constantly for ten hours. The group had suffered severe losses – *Mahan* and *Ward* sunk, *Liddle* and *Lamson* severely damaged, *LSM–318* abandoned – but with the aid of the Marine air squadron and Army P–38s it had performed its mission. As General Krueger later commented: "The landing of the 77th Division near Ormoc, serving to split the enemy forces and to separate them from their supply base, proved to be the decisive action of the Leyte Operation."

[25] The landing and beaching craft left on the beach were also attacked. During the day, suicide divers hit *LSM–318,* which had to be abandoned and *LST–737,* which was able to return.

5. *Ormoc Resupply Convoys, 8–12 December* [26]

The Navy now had the duty of keeping the 77th Division properly supplied. Men and matériel could be moved more quickly by water than by land; if suicide planes were bad, the mud was worse. Hitherto, military operations on the west coast of Leyte had been supported almost exclusively by truck hauls over the narrow, one-way mountain road between Abuyog and Baybay.

The difficulty in collecting enough shipping to supply the 77th was complicated by the fact that General MacArthur was planning two more amphibious operations in the immediate future. Target dates for landing on Mindoro and Luzon, originally 5 and 20 December respectively, were now postponed to 15 December and 9 January 1945; but these dates were not far off and preparations for them were being actively pursued. American soldiers, sailors and aviators were on the move all over the world, fighting or being transported to places where they would fight, or lifting supplies to those who were fighting. Ormoc Bay resupply made very small demands in relation to the entire World War, but in a highly integrated war one must often look far afield for the cause of a local shortage. Our British Allies were (and still are) fond of blaming Admiral King's supposedly exclusive love of the Pacific for their not getting as many beaching craft as they wanted. It would have done them good to hear some of the remarks passed on Leyte about the "Limies and the Atlantic Fleet getting everything."

The persistent and stubborn Japanese were still intent on reinforcing their Leyte garrison, although by all military doctrine and logic their situation was hopeless.

One such attempt was carried out on the very night of 7 December, after the 77th Division had been landed at Ormoc. General

[26] *Fletcher* "Action Report – Destroyer Sweep of Ormoc Bay," 20 Dec. 1944; ComLCI(L) Flot 8 (Cdr. F. B. C. Martin) Report of First, Second, and Third Resupply Echelons to Ormoc Bay, Leyte Island, Philippine Islands, 25 Dec. 1944.

Yamashita, "in order to ease the difficult Leyte Island Operation," sent from Luzon a reinforced infantry regiment, an artillery battalion and one of the special naval landing forces that we called Japanese Marines, to land at or north of Ormoc and oppose the advance of the 77th Division. The convoy carrying these forces was severely bombed by the U.S. Army Air Force when unloading at Ormoc, two destroyers were damaged and *LSV–11* sunk; only the 400 naval landing troops reached their destination. The rest of the ships turned north and landed a regiment and a battalion at Palompon on the San Isidro Peninsula, where they were isolated from the rest of the Leyte garrison.

Admiral Struble, suspecting that Japanese reinforcements were under way, ordered destroyers *Nicholas*, *O'Bannon*, *Fletcher* and *LaVallette* to break off on the night of 7 December from his retiring TG 78.3 to arrive in Ormoc Bay about 0130 December 8 and conduct an antishipping sweep. Owing to the successful activity of the P–38s, there was a lack of targets other than native canoes; so they circled the Camotes Islands, and retired through Canigao Channel at 0500.

December 8 and 9 were the quietest days since the Philippine campaign began. That was a lucky break for United States forces, since the first resupply echelon from Leyte Gulf to Ormoc Bay was then run. Admiral Struble designated Commander F. B. C. Martin of LCI Flotilla 8 to handle the resupply unit, which comprised 12 LSM and 4 LCI, escorted by Captain R. N. Smoot's Destroyer Squadron 56. The entire run to Ormoc Bay and return was uneventful.

The 7th and 26th Divisions U.S. Army, which had crossed to the west coast by the Abuyog–Baybay road, had been fighting a tough battle – the "Battle of the Ridges" – since late November. It resembled the campaign along the north coast of Sicily in 1943. The enemy, taking advantage of heavily forested mountain ridges, divided by torrential streams that came almost down to the sea, made advance difficult and expensive. The two U.S. divisions had almost reached Deposito when the 77th landed there on 7 December, and soon closed the gap between the two forces; and on 10 December the 77th captured Ormoc town.

December 10 brought renewed enemy air activity. The Japanese, seeking the source of their trouble, hit Leyte Gulf again. Eight Bettys attacked Allied warships and other vessels. Destroyer *Hughes* was on picket duty that day in Surigao Strait. One Betty suicide-dived into her midship section, flooding her engine and fire-rooms, and inflicting 23 casualties. Liberty ship *William S. Ladd* was crashed, causing such serious fires that she had to be abandoned and later sunk. Two other planes crash-dived *PT-323* in Surigao Strait, rendering that motor torpedo boat a total loss. *LCT-1075* was also sunk during this same attack.

Next day, 11 December, was one of the wildest yet. Both sides, in trying to reinforce their Leyte units, threw in all the air power they could muster. An enemy convoy, the last "Tokyo Express," consisting of three transports and two destroyer transports with troops embarked, escorted by five destroyers or destroyer escorts with a cover of some 30 fighter planes, was sighted late in the afternoon of 10 December northwest of Leyte by a Catalina search plane. At 0840 December 11, Corsairs from the same Marine squadrons which had hit the enemy resupply convoy on 7 December, set forth to bomb this convoy in the Visayan Sea as it approached the west coast of Leyte. The Marines delivered a dive-bombing attack in the face of intense antiaircraft fire. Eight planes were assigned to the biggest enemy transport (*Tasmania Maru*) and each released a 1000-pound bomb on her from 2000 feet. When the planes left the scene, the transport was burning and a hole some 25 by 35 feet had been made in her port side. She and two other *Marus* were sunk and an entire battalion of troops was lost.[27] Two Corsairs were damaged by antiaircraft fire, and as they retired they were attacked by several enemy planes, two of which they shot down.

A few hours later, at 1530, a composite flight of 42 planes, Marine Corps and Army, took off from Tacloban to make a second attack on this convoy and intercepted it 30 miles off Leyte's west coast. A

[27] MacArthur *Historical Report* II 401; JANAC.

medium freighter was set afire and sunk; and two others on fire were seen to beach themselves on a small island west of Palompon. Pilots of the Corsairs described the flak as "terrifically intense" and four planes were damaged. Despite these air attacks, a part of this convoy succeeded in discharging troops and supplies on the west coast of Leyte on 11 December.[28]

The second American resupply echelon, to be known as the "Terrible Second," departed Leyte Gulf at 0930 December 11, under the command of Captain J. D. Murphy. Owing to the assembly of forces for Mindoro, only eight LSM and four LCI were available. Commander Martin went along as convoy commodore, and Captain J. F. Newman of Desron 4 (*Caldwell*, flag) commanded the escort of six destroyers. Four Corsairs provided fighter cover as this echelon headed south through Surigao Strait. The C.O. of destroyer *Smith*, the fighter-director ship, complained that this was not enough, but he could get no more.

At about 1700, as the convoy was steaming at 12 knots on course 307°, a group of about ten Jills attacked. Four of them concentrated on destroyer *Reid*, Commander Samuel A. McCornock. The first crashed close on her starboard bow, starting a fire and causing underwater damage; the second after being hit by gunfire exploded in midair about 500 yards on her starboard beam, a third dropped a bomb or torpedo which missed and then passed on, and the fourth came in low from astern and crashed the ship between guns No. 3 and 4, on the port quarter. *Reid* heeled over, circled at high speed, listed until she lay on her beams' ends and within two minutes sank in 600 fathoms of water in lat. 09°05′ N, long. 124°55′ E. Shortly after, a terrific underwater explosion occurred which even damaged gyro and magnetic compasses in nearby beaching craft. As survivors were being strafed, the Corsairs, which had already shot down two or three of the attacking planes, drove them away from the unfortunate victims struggling in the water. Two LSM and two LCI, screened by *Coghlan*, were told off to recover survivors, but despite their best efforts only 152 men, about half *Reid's* comple-

[28] Cincpac Monthly Analysis for Dec. 1944; MacArthur *Historical Report* II 401.

ment, were rescued. Another fine vessel whose fighting career had begun at Pearl Harbor was gone. During the last three years she had participated in 13 landings, 18 shore bombardments, shot down 12 planes, sank one submarine, and expended nearly 10,000 rounds of 5-inch projectiles.[29]

Destroyer *Caldwell* (Commander D. R. Robinson USNR) also received attention from Japanese aviators. Shortly after she opened fire, one was splashed. A moment later another plane came over and was taken under fire by *Caldwell's* main battery while her port machine guns fired on a third passing down her port side. A Marine Corsair pilot, observing the danger she was in, disregarded the danger of the ship's gunfire, and crossed her at masthead height to get the enemy plane. Fortunately the one 20-mm gun that shot at him did not hit. The Japanese, banking steeply, crossed *Caldwell's* stern and crashed 20 feet on her starboard beam, drenching the bridge with gasoline and debris. "Everyone was pretty much shaken up," [30] admitted Commander Robinson. That is exactly how everyone felt after a Kamikaze attack — but the writers of Action Reports seldom felt called upon to admit it.

Still another enemy plane dropped a bomb in the vicinity of the LSM leading the right column, but it went wide and did no damage. By 1709 this action was over and the convoy was not again molested on the friendly side of Ormoc Bay.

At 2300 December 11, *LSM-38* and *LSM-39* were detached from the convoy and, in company with destroyer *Conyngham*, unloaded at Caridad, 15 miles south of Ormoc, as planned. The rest of the convoy proceeded to Ipil, whereupon occurred one of the strangest mêlées of the Leyte campaign. Two Japanese ships and a barge attempted to land troops at the same time and almost the same place, near Ipil, that the United States forces had chosen! [31] At about 0155 December 12 destroyer *Coghlan* (Commander B. B. Cheatham) encountered, by radar, the two ships, distant seven

[29] *Reid* Action Report, 14 Dec. 1944.

[30] *Caldwell* Action Report, 15 Dec. 1944.

[31] MacArthur *Historical Report* I 232, II 401. The same night, the Japanese landed the Ito Naval Unit at Palompon.

miles, and kept them under fire as they tried to steal away along the west side of Ormoc Bay. At 0213 a large column of flame arose and the pip disappeared from the radar screen. This may have been destroyer *Uzuki*. But she is also said to have been sunk that night off Palompon, where another small convoy was unloading, by *PT–492* and *PT–490*, led by Lieutenant Melvin W. Haines USNR. Anyway, she went down. *Coghlan* now concentrated gunfire on the other ship, which made off at high speed. This was probably destroyer *Yuzuki* which, according to Japanese records, was sunk by aircraft the same night off San Isidro. The barge, apparently, escaped.

During the midwatch 12 December, while the United States beaching craft were unloading, destroyers of the screen were intermittently harassed by enemy planes. *Caldwell*, *Coghlan* and *Smith* were each strafed once and the last-named was twice unsuccessfully bombed. At about 0024 *Caldwell* was illuminated by a 36-inch searchlight on Biasong Point on the west coast of Ormoc Bay, still in enemy hands. Heavy machine-gun fire and light artillery opened up on the destroyer. She returned the fire, knocked out the searchlight and received no hits, although frequently straddled. After this experience, the screen headed south into waters where it would have sufficient room to maneuver.

The convoy departed for Leyte Gulf at the scheduled hour, 0400 December 12. Fate decreed no peace for American sailors that night. After a delay of two hours for the convoy to pull stranded LSMs off the beach, enemy planes began to appear. At 0613 a bomb exploded about 100 feet from *Conyngham*. This was followed by two strafing attacks on the destroyer, but both planes were driven off by her gunfire. A C.A.P. of seven Marine fighters arrived over the convoy at 0700.

Caldwell caught it again on the return passage. Between Himuquitan Island and Amogotada Point, at 0800, she opened fire at a flight of enemy planes on her starboard bow. Three Zekes peeled off and made a perfectly planned and executed attack on her. Two, attempting to dive-bomb, were kept under fire by the destroyer's main battery. The third roared down her port side under continuous machine-gun fire and crossed her stern. The pilot then went into a vertical bank and at 0807, just as he was turning over on his back, crashed. One wing hit the bridge and the fuselage landed in main radio. Simultaneously with this suicide crash, *Caldwell* was straddled by several bombs, one striking and landing in No. 2 handling room. A bomb from the Kamikaze glanced off No. 2 gun and exploded just to starboard of No. 1 gun. The damage was serious and the casualties many: 33 killed and missing, 40 wounded. Fires were out an hour later and *Caldwell* rejoined the formation.[32] *Conyngham* was attacked at 0807 by a suicider who missed and splashed just clear of her port propeller guard. *Smith*, *Edwards* and *Coghlan* were all subjected to bombing, fortunately unsuccessfully. In the meantime the Marine Corps C.A.P. shot down eleven enemy planes without suffering any damage or loss, and several more were disposed of by ships' gunfire.

Samar never posed the nasty problem that Leyte presented to the armed forces, and there was no need for naval assistance on that island. Elements of the 1st Cavalry Division landed on Samar on 24 October, pushed slowly northward and overcame heavy resistance, captured Wright on the west coast on 8 December. There they established contact with guerrillas who had fought westward from Taft on the east coast. When the troopers occupied Catbalogan, the provincial capital, on 19 December, Samar could be considered completely liberated from Japanese control.

6. *Liberation of Leyte Completed, 15 December 1944–10 February 1945*[33]

No later resupply convoy from Leyte Gulf to Ormoc Bay suffered as did the "Terrible Second," and most of them passed unmolested. The reason is clear. On December 12 the Mindoro opera-

[32] Comdesron 14 (Capt. Newman) Action Report 18 Dec. 1944.

[33] Sixth Army and XXIV Corps Reports, *O.N.I. Weekly* III No. 52, 27 Dec. 1944, Cannon *Leyte* chap. xvii.

tion got under way from Leyte Gulf, and the Mindoro landings on the 15th were followed at a three weeks' interval by the huge amphibious operation in Lingayen Gulf.[34] Convoys to Mindoro and Lingayen offered the Japanese air forces so many attractive targets that they laid off the little ones that were supplying the 77th Division at Ormoc.

For the same reason, the Leyte–Ormoc resupply convoys were stripped down to only 23 LSM and 13 LCI. This was not enough to support the Division in its coming drive northward. General Krueger, accordingly, on 15 December requested Admiral Kinkaid to make more amphibious vessels available. He did so, promptly. A strong resupply convoy reached Ormoc 22 December with enough supplies and equipment, including medium tanks, to end the critical situation.

Even before this convoy arrived the long-planned liberation of Ormoc Valley was effected. The 1st Cavalry Division, advancing south along No. 2 highway from Carigara Bay, and the 77th Infantry Division, advancing north along the same highway from Ormoc Bay, met near the village of Konanga on 21 December. The 77th then turned west across the San Isidro Peninsula to the port of Palompon, the only harbor of any importance that remained in Japanese hands. This movement was supported by a shore-to-shore amphibious operation from Ormoc to a beach a mile north of Palompon. Word was passed to civilians and guerrillas to evacuate the town, which was blasted by V A.A.F. on the 23rd and by 155-mm guns from San José, 12½ miles distant in the Valley; and on Christmas Eve the 1st BLT 77th Division with many attached units, in LCMs and Army-manned LVT amphtracs, embarked at Ormoc. During the ten-hour passage three LVTs filled and sank, but nobody was lost. There was no opposition to the landing, and by noon Christmas Day the troops were in possession of Palompon. General Bruce signaled XXIV Corps: "The 77th's Christmas contribution is the capture of Palompon, the last main port of the enemy. We are all grateful to the Almighty on this birthday of the

[34] These operations will be covered in Volume XIII of this series.

Son and on the Season of the Feast of Lights." Prayers were appropriately answered by an air drop of turkey for the troops.

General MacArthur, in congratulating General Krueger on the capture of Palompon, said: "This closes a campaign that has had few counterparts in the utter destruction of the enemy's forces with a maximum conservation of our own. It has been a magnificent performance on the part of all concerned." Next day, in an official communiqué, the General declared "the Leyte-Samar campaign can now be regarded as closed except for minor mopping-up operations." With the gaining of a day owing to the international date line, this news reached the American public observing their fourth and last wartime Christmas.

Like other announcements during the war of the "end of organized resistance," this one was a bit premature, and Japanese unorganized resistance can be very tough. It was nearer the truth, however, than the Imperial General Headquarters communiqué of the same date, claiming that they still held the Burauen and San Pablo airfields, where the remnants of the paratroops had been mopped up two weeks earlier, and were "fighting fiercely on the eastern mountain slopes near Ormoc and Albuera." On Christmas Day General Yamashita, from his headquarters at Manila, notified General Suzuki that he had written off Leyte as a loss, and that except for units that could be transferred to other Philippine islands, the 35th Army on Leyte must be self-supporting. He followed this unpleasant message by another to explain that the high command had decided to concentrate on the defense of Luzon, and that he was shedding "tears of remorse" for the tens of thousands of his countrymen who must fight to the death on Leyte.

On the American side, mopping-up operations were conducted under Commanding General Eighth Army, Lieutenant General Robert L. Eichelberger, the veteran of the Papuan campaign. General Hodge's XXIV Corps remained to finish the job. All Naval supporting forces were withdrawn for the Mindoro and Lingayen operations; the Engineer Special Brigade craft did whatever convoy work was required.

Over a full division of Japanese troops was still left on Leyte, but they were divided into several units which showed no indication of control or organized effort. The terrain, much of which was inaccurately mapped, offered great defensive advantages. Some of the units exploited their opportunity to make trouble, whilst others concentrated on finding or building boats to escape to Cebu, 20 to 25 miles across the Camotes Sea. Three motor launches carrying 70 men each made four round trips between 13 and 20 January, but these craft were spotted from the air and not only bombed but shelled by motor torpedo boats, which had established a small advanced base at Ormoc on 28 December. Close liaison with guerrilla leaders in Cebu and with Marine Air Group 12, the Corsairs based at Tacloban, enabled the PTs to root out and destroy many Japanese small craft during this period.

The Camotes Islands between Leyte and Cebu were still occupied by the enemy, who was reported to be torturing the natives in retaliation for their ill-concealed joy at the American return. General Hodge, deciding to put a stop to this, sent a BLT in amphtracs and LCMs, with four PTs under Lieutenant Weston C. Pullen USNR as fire support, to occupy Ponson Island on 15 January 1945. Finding that island evacuated by the enemy, they moved on to Poro, Lieutenant Commander Leeson commanding the PT screen, and there encountered plenty of resistance. By the end of the month the defense of the islands was turned over to the Filipinos.

The 77th Division destroyed a pocket of resistance in the mountains southeast of Villaba during the week of 27 January–3 February 1945, but there were still several thousand troops in that region, hoping to be evacuated. No vessels came for them until 17 March 1945 when two Japanese ships appeared off the coast. General Suzuki and part of his staff left in them. Significant of the almost complete control that the Allies had then established in Philippine waters, these craft cruised from island to island for a month, vainly looking for a friendly port, until on 16 April they were bombed by American aircraft off Negros and General Suzuki was killed.

Support by the motor torpedo boats was indispensable to the American mopping-up operations. As General Hodge recorded, "wholehearted coöperation by the PT boats provided invaluable support to elements of the XXIV Corps. Operating primarily at night, boats of the PT squadrons located at Ormoc sortied continuously to the east coast of Cebu and north along the western coast of Leyte. Many Japanese barges, at least two sizable freighters and several schooners, many of which were loaded with Japanese troops or equipment, were sunk by PT boats." During these attacks the boat crews were often fired upon by shore batteries of light caliber or by weapons mounted in the Japanese vessels. The eagerness of the PTs "to close with the enemy and furnish aid to our ground operations was outstanding throughout their support of the XXIV Corps." [35]

This support continued to the end. The PTs stayed in Leyte until May 1945, and until the end of the war they operated all through the Visayas, and off Borneo and the Celebes.

The liberation of Leyte was reasonably complete on St. Patrick's Day, when General Suzuki decamped; but the last mopping-up operation was not concluded until 5 May 1945. As on other islands captured from the Japanese, many no-surrender units attempted to hold out indefinitely in the hills. But the Filipino population was so hostile to them, and the guerrillas so thirsty for Japanese blood, that these men were all hunted down and killed by the end of the war.

This was a costly operation. In addition to the heavy losses in the Battle off Samar,[36] the Navy and Marine Corps lost several hundred men on and around the island before it was secured. The Army, not including the A.A.F., had 15,584 battle casualties, including 3508 killed, about equally distributed between X and XXIV Corps. This out of a peak strength of 257,766 officers and men in January.[37] Estimates of the number of Japanese sacrificed in this hopeless defense vary greatly. Sixth and Eighth Armies to-

[35] Report of XXIV Corps.
[36] See end of Chapter XIII, above.
[37] Cannon p. 367.

gether reported 80,557 dead actually counted, almost one third of them in the mop-up period, and 828 prisoners; but Japanese authorities claim that they never had more than 70,000 troops on the island, of which 48,790 had been killed and over 13,000 were still alive when General Suzuki got out. No battle casualties for the Imperial Navy, in the various actions that we have covered in this volume, have ever been compiled.

The Leyte campaign offered another convincing demonstration of the immense striking power of a coördinated Army–Navy team, with its air components. Despite the handicap of the vast distances over which American men and supplies had to be transported, as compared with the same problem for Japan – despite the pouring in of Japanese ships, troops and planes from China and other parts of her conquered empire – failure, complete and absolute, was the result of the "general decisive battle" of Leyte.

General Yamashita admitted as much after the war when he said that after the loss of Leyte he "realized that decisive battle" – meaning, a decisive victory for Japan – "was impossible." The Battle for Leyte Gulf destroyed the Imperial Japanese Navy as an offensive force; the land battle caused such attrition in Japanese army and air force strength that failure in the campaign for Luzon became inevitable.

Thus, General MacArthur's terse expression of his wishes to President Roosevelt, in July 1944, was fulfilled before the end of the year: –

"Where do we go from here?"
"Leyte, Mr. President, and then Luzon."

CHAPTER XVII

Submarine Patrols[1]

September–November 1944

1. *September Patrols*

SUBMARINES of the United States Navy were exceedingly busy and very successful during the crucial three months in which Morotai, the Palaus and Leyte were invaded. Their operations, which were coördinated with those of the Seventh and Third Fleets, have been described in the chapters covering the Battle for Leyte Gulf. Other submarine patrols, which brought victory nearer by sinking 158 Japanese naval auxiliaries and merchant ships, and 37 warships of the Imperial Navy, to a total of over 900,000 tons, will be described here. During the war these underwater operations were supersecret, in order to keep the enemy smugly confident that he was sinking a submarine every time he attacked one.

As in the earlier years of the war,[2] American submarines operating in the Pacific were divided between Submarines Pacific Fleet under Vice Admiral Charles A. Lockwood, and Submarines Southwest Pacific, Rear Admiral Ralph W. Christie. The "Subpac" boats, as we may call Lockwood's for short, operated from Pearl Harbor and advanced bases at Eniwetok, Majuro and Guam. Organized in wolf-packs, they covered the waters off Japan and down to the

[1] Office of Naval History ms. "Submarine Operational History World War II"; *U.S. Submarine Losses in World War II* compiled by Comsubpac; JANAC; *Imp. Jap. Navy W. W. II* (1952); USSBS publication *The War Against Japanese Transportation;* War Patrols of boats mentioned; Theodore Roscoe *U.S. Submarine Operations in World War II* (1949); Vice Adm. C. A. Lockwood *Sink 'Em All* (1951). See Appendix I for names of boats and their C.O.'s.

[2] For earlier operations of U.S. submarines see Volumes IV chaps. x-xi; VI chap. vi; VII chap. xii; and VIII chap. ii.

South China Sea, which for hunting purposes were divided into areas bearing picturesque names such as "Hit Parade," "Marus' Morgue" and "Convoy College." The "Sowespac" boats, as we may call Christie's, were based at Fremantle, Western Australia, and at Brisbane, Queensland. They patrolled the South China Sea and waters of the Netherlands East Indies, and the Brisbane group made the supply runs to the Philippines.

The first day of September found Subpac boats vigorously and successfully combing waters around Formosa. Captain E. R. Swinburne's wolf-pack, *Barb*, *Tunny* and *Queenfish*, was enjoying a profitable term in Convoy College, whose campus extended from Pratas Reef south of Swatow through Luzon Strait to long. 130° E. On 16 September Swinburne received word that another pack (Commander Oakley's, to be mentioned shortly) had sunk a Japanese transport carrying Allied prisoners of war, and was ordered to send *Barb* and *Queenfish* to assist the rescue operation. En route that evening they picked up a five-ship convoy screened by torpedo boats and a large ship that looked like an escort carrier. *Queenfish* made the first attack, then *Barb* (Lieutenant Commander E. B. Fluckey) took over. Making a surface approach she maneuvered to bring a tanker and the big target in line for a double shot. An escort sighted and started for her full speed, but Fluckey coolly waited until she was less than a thousand yards away, fired his bow tubes at the overlapping targets and swung around to bring stern tubes to bear. He had to dive before getting set for a second shot, but while he was going down five hits and breaking-up noises were heard. *Barb* had sunk 10,000-ton tanker *Azusa Maru* and escort carrier *Unyo* with her single spread.

Operating in Convoy College at the same time as Swinburne was Commander G. R. Donaho's pack consisting of *Picuda*, *Redfish* and *Spadefish*. They had already accounted for two merchant ships and a destroyer when, on 8 September, while east of Formosa, *Spadefish* sank three or four merchant ships out of a single convoy. By the time Donaho had concluded his patrol, on 21 September, he had eliminated 64,456 tons of enemy shipping, the highest wolf-pack score so far; *Spadefish* (Commander G. W. Underwood), then on her first war patrol, alone accounted for 26,812 tons.

The third wolf-pack in this scholarly area during September was Commander T. B. Oakley's: *Growler*, *Pampanito* and *Sealion II*. First blood for them was a 1345-ton minelayer sunk by the last-named on 31 August. During the night of 11–12 September they picked up a Singapore-Japan convoy of nine ships with seven escorts, about halfway between Hainan and Cape Bojeador, Luzon. After *Growler* had blown up frigate *Hirado*, *Sealion* at 0524 torpedoed three ships, one of which, *Rakuyo Maru*, had on board 1350 English and Australian prisoners of war. She and one of the others sank later in the day. In the meantime *Growler* at 0653 sank destroyer *Shikinami*, after which the convoy turned and fled towards Hong Kong. But *Pampanito* hung on all day 12 September and at 2240 sank a tanker and 10,509-ton *Kachidoki Maru*, in which were 750 prisoners. The Japanese escorts picked up their own survivors next day but left the prisoners struggling in the water. Many managed to survive by clinging to wreckage.

The presence of prisoners was unknown to Commander Oakley's submarines until 15 September when *Pampanito*, passing through the waters where she had made her attack, discovered a crude raft loaded with men. Her C.O., Commander P. E. Summers, sized up the situation at once and called on *Sealion* for help, *Growler* having already left the area; and as soon as Admiral Lockwood got the word he ordered Captain Swinburne's pack, as we have seen, to assist. By 2000 *Sealion* had 50 and *Pampanito* 71 oil-covered and emaciated men on board, all they could carry. "It was heartbreaking to leave so many dying men behind," reported Commander E. T. Reich of *Sealion*. *Barb* and *Queenfish* arrived in the area on the 17th and combed it until a 60-knot wind forced them to quit, but they rescued 30 more British and Australians. Seven of these unfortunates died before the rescuing submarines reached port.[3]

Other Allied prisoners were evacuated by the Japanese from

[3] Capt. D. N. C. Tufnell RN (British Liaison Officer at Cincpac-Cincpoa HQ) Report of Rescue of Allied P.O.W.s, 30 Oct. 1944.

Mindanao. They were herded into the hold of rusty old tramp steamer *Shiniyo Maru* and placed under a much-hated prison guard commander. This sadistic character told the prisoners that if the ship was attacked by an Allied plane or submarine his guards had orders to man the hatch coamings and shoot them down in the hold. The five-ship convoy in which this vessel sailed north was caught by *Paddle* (Lieutenant Commander B. H. Nowell) on 7 September off Lanboyan Point on the Zamboanga Peninsula of Mindanao, and *Shiniyo Maru* was sunk. True to their promise the Japanese guards opened fire with tommy guns on the prisoners below. Many of them, nevertheless, fought their way out of the hold with fists, clubs and improvised weapons and jumped over the side to swim to the nearby land. About 15 or 20 of the swimmers were picked up by boats rescuing Japanese survivors and taken on board another ship where they were lined up against the rail with hands tied behind their backs, and, as a punishment for attempting to escape, shot down one by one. One man managed to cut his bonds on a frayed steel cable behind his back, jumped overboard a second time, and made his way ashore. The few survivors of this brave struggle for life were cared for by natives until they were picked up by *Narwhal*.[4]

2. Tang *off Turnabout, 23–25 October*

In early October, a bold raid into the Formosa Channel was performed by Commander Richard H. O'Kane in U.S.S. *Tang*.[5] This was her fifth war patrol. O'Kane obtained permission to make it as a lone wolf, well knowing the risk but hoping to encounter an abundance of targets in these protected waters; and he was not disappointed.

After safely weathering the typhoon on 6 October, *Tang*

[4] *Paddle's* Report of Fifth War Patrol; details from Capt. J. C. Titus, former C.O. of *Narwhal*, in June 1957.

[5] *Tang* Action Report 25 Sept. 1945, written after O'Kane's return from captivity; recording of experiences by Lt. Cdr. Lawrence Savadkin USNR, her engineer officer, and conversations with Cdr. Savadkin in 1946 and 1957.

threaded an enemy minefield between Formosa and the Sakashina Gunto on the 10th, and passed close aboard Huki Kaku at the northern extremity of Formosa. At 0400 October 11, she finished off her first victim, a small, heavily loaded diesel freighter. That night, close to the shore, another small freighter was sunk; the enemy replying with 40-mm fire from the beach at hypothetical planes overhead. "We were clicking!" noted Commander O'Kane. No United States submarine had penetrated Formosa Strait during the war, and Japanese vessels were sailing unescorted, believing themselves as safe as in the Inland Sea.

Observing with pleasure the fires on Formosan airfields kindled by Task Force 38 planes, *Tang* passed through the tide rips into midchannel. Finding nothing there, she returned to prowl off Kiirun Harbor; but no ship steamed into her sights and small enemy patrol craft badgered her. So, off she went to the China coast to intercept a reported task force heading north. In midchannel she encountered a light cruiser and two destroyers, but they were zigzagging so violently that with 19 knots' speed and a Mark-18 electric torpedo it was no use trying an "up-the-kilt" shot; besides, the Formosan banks were not far away. So north she went to Turnabout Island off Haitan. That provided the payoff, as its name promised; for Turnabout was the landmark where, for thousands of years, shipping northbound through Formosa Strait had changed course for Foochow.

Shortly after midnight 23–24 October the submariner's dream came true. A reinforcement convoy for the Philippines composed of four deeply laden freighters carrying planes on deck, a transport with crated planes piled high forward and aft, a destroyer and several small escort vessels, headed right for *Tang*. Commander O'Kane turned over the conn to his exec., Lieutenant Commander Frank H. Springer USNR; and as "Frank's" one idea of sinking *Marus* was to work in so close that it was impossible to miss, he maneuvered the boat inside the screen to a firing position whence the ships seemed to overlap, bow and stern, on both sides of her.

With *Tang* pointing at both columns of the enemy like the bar of an H, the skipper made a quick setup, and fired torpedoes from both ends. In a few minutes three freighters were floating torches. The unhit freighter and the transport promptly converged on *Tang* with intent to ram. They were too close to be evaded by diving, and the blazing freighters barred her escape in the other direction; so *Tang*, under a shower of small-arms fire, slipped between the converging stems of the two ships that were trying to ram her, and had the humorous satisfaction of seeing them collide after she had escaped. O'Kane fired four torpedoes from his stern tubes into this pair of ships at 400 yards' range and made a hit, but did not sink them. *Tang* circled to avoid a destroyer, returning within ten minutes to find the bow of one freighter disappearing after a violent explosion, and the escort indulging in an orgy of wild gunfire at anything or nothing. "It looked like a good place to be away from, so we cleared the area at full power," reported the skipper.

Tang headed north for deeper waters to relax for a few hours, surfaced before dawn 24 October, and then turned in again toward Turnabout.

After dark, the boat's radar picked up the biggest convoy anyone on board had ever seen – "a solid line of pips across the screen." It was tracked close to the jagged coast of Fukien; and, as *Tang* closed, the Japanese escort commander obligingly illuminated his charges with a large searchlight, revealing two three-decker transports and several tankers. These last O'Kane selected as preferred targets, and sank one. *Tang* then turned to fire three stern torpedoes at another transport and a tanker astern of the first victim at ranges of 600–700 yards. "Things were anything but calm and peaceful now," he remembered; "for the escorts were directing good salvos at us and at the blotches of smoke we left behind on going to full power to pull clear of the mêlée. Just after firing at the transport, a full-fledged destroyer charged under her stern and headed for us." Exactly what took place in the following seconds will never be determined; but the tanker was hit nicely and blew up, scattering burning gasoline over the Formosa Channel.[6] One torpedo appeared to hit the transport, and an instant later the destroyer looked as if she were exploding; but that was but one of the delusions of night combat – Japan lost no destroyer that night. *Tang* herself was untouched.

After putting five miles between himself and the milling escorts, O'Kane slowed down to make a careful check of his two remaining torpedoes. Everything appeared to be in order. *Tang* now cautiously closed a transport that appeared to be dead in the water. The 23rd torpedo to be launched on this patrol seemed to be a hit; but the 24th and last, fired at about 0200 October 25, broached and porpoised, circled quickly back, and only 20 seconds after its launching struck the submarine abreast her after torpedo room, and exploded. "*Tang* sank by the stern much as you would drop a pendulum suspended in a horizontal position" and hit the bottom 30 fathoms down.

The sailors in the control room succeeded in closing the conning tower hatch, leveled off the boat by flooding tanks, destroyed secret publications by burning and smashed the radar. Thirty officers and men reached an escape position in the forward torpedo room, where smoke from the burning documents as well as lack of oxygen knocked half of them out. Enemy escorts were depth-charging all about but failed to discover the motionless sunken boat. At 0600 October 25 thirteen men, the only ones still strong enough to make the attempt, started leaving the escape trunk. Eight reached the surface through 160 feet of water, and five clung to the buoy until picked up; these five, together with O'Kane and two sailors who floated off topside when she sank, and Lieutenant Savadkin who escaped from the conning tower, were the sole survivors. Frank Springer, six other officers and 71 enlisted men were lost.

Thus, after scoring hits with a majority of her torpedoes and sinking some 22,000 tons of merchant shipping within two weeks, *Tang* fell victim to one erratic torpedo.

[6] The two tankers sunk were *Kogen Maru*, 6600 tons, and *Matsumoto Maru*, 7024 tons.

The nine submariners still afloat were picked up at about 1000 October 25 by a Japanese destroyer escort which had been recovering survivors of the convoy. The Americans were shocked by seeing the horrible burns resulting from a torpedo explosion; and they too suffered, since able-bodied Japanese survivors made a point of taking it out on them as they lay trussed-up on the vessel's deck. "When we realized," wrote O'Kane, "that our clubbings and kickings were being administered by the burned and mutilated survivors of our own handiwork, we found we could take it with less prejudice." They were landed at Takao and transferred to the naval interrogation center at Ofuna, where they were questioned by Japanese graduates of American universities, who were very decent fellows, hinting that any sort of yarn would be acceptable, so long as they had something on paper to show the commanding officer.

Tang's nine survivors were given fairly good treatment, according to Japanese standards. They suffered badly from malnutrition, but recovered when liberated at the close of the war.

3. *October and November Patrols*

October 1944 was a peak month in the war of United States submarines on Japanese shipping; 322,265 tons were sunk, and almost one third of that total was tankers. In late September, as plans for the Leyte landings were being drafted, Admiral Lockwood set up a new patrol covering the Ryukyus, with the appropriate name "Maru Morgue." The main purpose of this patrol was to persuade ships bound from Japan to the Philippines to go through Formosa Strait and enter Convoy College; if they passed that examination fully they would encounter Sowespac submarines in the South China Sea.

It seemed to work. One of Admiral Christie's wolf-packs under Commander V. B. McCrea in *Hoe*, with *Aspro* and *Cabrilla*, operating southwest of Lingayen Gulf, accounted for some 38,000 tons of shipping in the first week of October. *Whale* and *Snook* were almost equally successful off northwest Luzon. One of Admiral Lockwood's packs known as "Blakely's Behemoths," composed of *Shark II* (Commander E. N. Blakely), *Seadragon* and *Blackfish*, operated in Convoy College, along lat. 20° N, about midway between Hainan and Bashi Channel. On 24 October *Shark* informed *Seadragon* that she was about to attack a lone freighter. This ship, carrying 1800 American prisoners of war, was not hit; but the Japanese escorts sank *Shark* in their depth-charge attacks. She was the second U.S. submarine to be lost that day, the other being *Darter* on Bombay Shoal.

Icefish and *Drum* together sank 26,901 tons of enemy shipping in Convoy College in October. During that month Captain E. H. Bryant in *Hawkbill*, with *Flasher* and *Becuna*, worked over the Japanese Sea traffic with success. Off southwest Luzon and north of Palawan *Lapon*, *Angler* and *Raton* added to the bag. On 18 October *Bluegill* (Commander E. L. Barr) sank three *Marus* from one convoy for a total score of 19,631 tons. *Hammerhead* (Commander J. C. Martin) sank three ships off Borneo on 1 October and two more on the 20th for a total of 25,178 tons, and on the 27th *Bergall* got a 10,500-ton tanker off Borneo.

Guitarro had an unusual experience off the west coast of Luzon on the last day of October. Sighting a convoy early in the morning, she worked her way inside the screen and into a good torpedoing position. At 0853 her skipper, Commander E. D. Haskins, reported: "Number two torpedo hit same target as number one – a timed hit with 2300-yard torpedo run, followed by a tremendous explosion. This ship was carrying ammunition and must have gone in the air almost as far as Manila." His boat, 1900 yards distant at periscope depth, was driven down 50 feet by the blast, which sprang her vents, spraying fuel oil over her interior and causing other damage. "The Commanding Officer never wishes to hit an ammunition ship any closer than that one," concluded Commander Haskins.

Bold tactics saved *Salmon* of Commander Harlfinger's pack from becoming a victim of enemy escorts off the southern cape of Kyushu in the night of 30 October. After she had sent two torpedoes into a tanker (damaged earlier by *Trigger*), four screening frigates went for her and sent her down fast. At 2013 an accurate pattern of depth charges jolted *Salmon*, damaged her hull, and sent clocks, gauges and other detachable objects hurtling about her compartments. By maintaining an uptrim of 20 degrees her skipper, Commander H. K. Nauman, checked her dive at an estimated 500 feet, then worked her up to 150 feet; but down she again plummeted when Nauman tried to level off. He decided that his only chance was to fight it out with gunfire. Surfacing at 2030, *Salmon* found herself 7000 yards up-moon from the escorts who either did not see her or decided to delay their attack. This precious respite gave the skipper and crew time to correct a 15-degree list, plug holes, pump bilges and get the engines capable of turning up 16 knots. Around 2200 one Japanese frigate began jabbing at *Salmon*, like a dog attacking a bear, closing repeatedly to bark and retire. After this had happened several times, and the other frigates began to show signs of closing, Commander Nauman felt ready to take the offensive. *Salmon* attacked the frigate that had been dogging her, passing parallel on opposite course only 50 yards distant, raking topsides clear, knocking all the fight out of the Japanese and scaring away the other escorts. She then ducked into a rain squall, repaired battle damage, and called her sister boats. Joined the next night by *Trigger*, *Silverside* and *Sterlet*, as an informal screen, and subsequently supported by air cover as well, she made Saipan safely.

This brilliant gunfire action by one of the "fightin'est" submarines of the Pacific Fleet, fought within a hundred miles of the Japanese mainland, was characterized by Admiral Lockwood as "an epic in submarine history." [7]

Submarine activity against enemy shipping was maintained at a high level in November, but earlier successes had so reduced the Japanese merchant fleet that targets were fewer. And the sub-

[7] *Salmon* Report of 11th War Patrol 10 Nov. 1944. The damage was found to be so extensive that *Salmon* retired from the active list and Cdr. Nauman and crew were transferred to newly constructed *Stickleback*.

marines now had to share the game with Admiral McCain's carrier planes of Task Force 38. The enemy, too, had become more wary. Singapore convoys no longer followed the west coast of Luzon but hugged the western shore of the South China Sea closer and closer, even steaming a mile or two off land.[8] And it was some time before American airmen and submarines caught onto this change. Of the Subpac boats, Commander Clarey's *Pintado*, *Jallao* and *Atule*, after participating in the Battle off Cape Engaño on 25 October, operated in Convoy College where *Atule* sank 16,975-ton transport *Asama Maru* and a 7266-ton freighter in November. *Peto* got three freighters southwest of Kyushu in the midmonth. *Scabbardfish* (Commander F. A. Gunn), on lifeguard duty southeast of Tokyo Bay, at 0615 November 29 sighted a target, later identified as a submarine, was forced down by an enemy plane, surfaced again at 0935, fired two torpedoes and shortly afterward heard an explosion followed by breaking-up noises. Surfacing again, she picked up a Japanese survivor who informed Commander Gunn that he had sunk submarine *I-365*, returning from a patrol off Guam.

Early in November Commander W. C. ("Moon") Chapple's pack consisting of *Bream*, *Guitarro* and *Raton*, with *Ray* nearby, was patrolling off western Luzon. All four boats took a crack at heavy cruiser *Kumano* on 6 November. Damaged in the Battle off Samar and patched up in Manila, she was en route to Japan in a convoy. *Guitarro* had the first chance at her, firing nine torpedoes from which three hits were observed, but failed to stop the cruiser. Next, *Bream* fired four and counted two timed hits; but when the convoy crossed *Raton's* sights the cruiser was still with it. Six more torpedoes, three of which hit, still failed to stop *Kumano*, but some of *Raton's* "fish" swam right over *Ray* as she was making an approach for an attack. *Ray* fired four torpedoes and then dove deep. Surfacing an hour later, she saw *Kumano* dead in the water with her bow blown off. Determined to finish her off, Commander W. T. Kinsella of *Ray* started another approach but grounded, and before he could get clear, *Kumano* was taken in tow to a beach on Luzon,

[8] *Inter. Jap. Off.* I 195.

where on 25 November, aircraft from carrier *Ticonderoga* finished her off.

The fate of a big Japanese convoy carrying the 23rd Infantry Division from Manchuria to Luzon is a good measure of the enemy's loss of sea control. The convoy consisted of seven transports and an oiler, escorted by six destroyers and escort carrier *Jinyo*. On 15 November it was attacked in the East China Sea by *Queenfish* of Commander Charles E. Loughlin's wolf-pack, and one transport was sunk, eliminating two battalions and the divisional artillery. The wolf-pack pursued, and at 1808 on the 17th, in the Yellow Sea, *Picuda* sank a second troop-filled transport and damaged the tanker. In the meantime *Spadefish*, flag of a wolf-pack under Commander G. O. Underwood, had sighted the smoke of this convoy. With only an hour and a half to go before sunset, Underwood decided to let it pass directly over him and make a night surface attack. At 1754 he came to periscope depth and made out five large *Marus* and an escort carrier, screened by destroyers and subchasers. Eighteen minutes later he observed the results of *Picuda's* attack.[9] After working up to a firing position at 2303, Commander Underwood aimed six "fish" from his bow tubes at the carrier and four more from his stern tubes at a tanker. Four of the former hit, the carrier burst into flames, settled by the stern, and planes could be seen sliding overboard. When last seen her blazing bow was pointing skyward. She was the 21,000-ton *Jinyo*, fourth Japanese escort carrier to become a submarine victim.

Shortly after midnight *Spadefish* bore in for another attack on the convoy. She was picked up by two subchaser escorts which closed to 1000 yards and opened fire. Owing to the helmsman mistaking his skipper's orders, the boat remained on the surface under battery propulsion. To escape from his dangerous position, Underwood fired four torpedoes at the nearest target, and three explosions were heard. "By this time," reported Commander Underwood, "we were getting considerably more than rated horsepower

[9] He saw smoke coming from a merchant ship and heard 17 depth charges, meant for *Picuda*, explode.

out of our ten-cylinder engines." *Spadefish* escaped but added nothing more to her Yellow Sea bag.

Very early on 21 November *Sealion II* (Commander E. T. Reich) was patrolling on the surface about 40 miles north of Formosa when she picked up a distant target by radar. It developed into two battleships, two cruisers and three destroyers making 16 knots and not zigzagging. The skipper made a surface approach and at 0256 fired six bow torpedoes at the second ship in column and the nearest battleship; then, swinging ship, let fly four torpodoes at the second battleship from his stern tubes. Three hits were heard on the first target – it was destroyer *Urakaze*, which sank – and one hit was seen on the battleship. Commander Reich steered *Sealion* westward as the escorts chased phantoms in the other direction. When he had opened distance to four miles he came around parallel to the convoy and chased it at maximum speed. At 0450 the convoy divided, two destroyers with the battleship dropping astern. Twenty minutes later *Sealion* was about to attack when a tremendous explosion lighted up the waters around her and her intended target disappeared. It proved to be battleship *Kongo*, which had survived many battles of the war, including the recent one off Samar; *Sealion's* one hit had done for her.

Even bigger game was bagged by *Archerfish* (Commander J. F. Enright) on lifeguard patrol for B–29s off Inamba Shima, 100 miles south of Tokyo Bay. Enright received word on 28 November that there would be no bomber raids that day, so he was free to prowl. Nothing happened until 2048 when *Archerfish* made a distant radar contact, identified an hour later as an escorted aircraft carrier making 20 knots and zigzagging. Commander Enright decided on a surface attack as the target was too fast for him to gain a firing position submerged. He could barely hold his own by steering the target's base course, but a lucky break came at 0300 November 29 when the carrier made a radical zig toward him. *Archerfish* submerged as the range closed. The carrier conveniently zagged into a perfect position for the submarine to fire six torpedoes at 1400 yards' range. Enright observed two hits and then went deep for the expected depth-charge attack. Four more hits and breaking-up noises were heard and 14 depth charges exploded about 300 yards away. At 0614 Enright cautiously raised his periscope for a look, but there was nothing to be seen. He modestly claimed only an escort carrier, but his victim was the 59,000-ton supercarrier *Shinano*. Converted from a battleship hull of the *Yamato* class, she had been commissioned only ten days before, and was sunk on her trial run with yard workmen still on board.

On 25 November *Cavalla* (Commander H. J. Kossler), which had sunk carrier *Shokaku* in the Battle of the Philippine Sea, made contact on a single ship near Great Natoena Island, west of Borneo. Kossler attacked on the surface at 0346, observed two torpedo hits followed by heavy explosions and blazing fires; the target sank within a few minutes. All hands thought that they had got a heavy cruiser, but postwar assessment identified the victim as the 2300-ton destroyer *Shimotsuki*.

All these successes cost the submarine fleet dear. The loss of *Shark*, *Darter* and *Tang* in October have already been mentioned. *Albacore* (Lieutenant Commander H. R. Rimmer), assigned to cover the approaches to Hakodate (Hokkaido), was never heard from after departing Midway 28 October. It is probable that she was the submarine reported by the Japanese as hitting a mine off Hokkaido on 7 November and going down with all hands. *Growler* (Commander T. B. Oakley) was last heard of on the 8th when attacking a convoy southwest of Luzon. Her pack mates *Hardhead* and *Hake* heard distant explosions and both were later subjected to intense depth-charge attacks. Postwar search of Japanese records sheds no light on *Growler's* loss. *Scamp* (Commander J. C. Hollingsworth), assigned to an area off the Bonins, was never heard from after 9 November. She was probably the submarine which, following a Japanese plane's sighting of an oil slick, was depth-charged by a coast defense vessel south of Tokyo Bay on 11 November.

4. *Conclusion*

After the war General Tojo observed to General MacArthur that in his opinion the three main causes of the defeat of Japan were (1) the Navy's "leapfrogging" strategy of bypassing important centers of Japanese military power like Rabaul, Wewak and Mindanao; (2) the far-ranging activities of Fast Carrier Forces Pacific Fleet; and (3) the destruction of merchant shipping by United States submarines. A glance at the table indicates how immense this destruction was during the three crucial months of 1944. And comparison with the tables in our earlier Volumes of Allied losses to German U-boats is instructive.[10] It will be seen that while the highest monthly tonnage score by the U-boats of 106 ships and 636,907 tons sunk in November 1942, was never attained by United States submarines, the German scores for three-months' periods were inferior to ours after March 1943, and at the corresponding period in 1944 amounted to only 72,960 tons. The Germans at times had over a hundred U-boats operating daily, on a monthly average, whilst the two United States submarine commands never had more than 50 operating daily in the Pacific, and of those, 22 would be en route to or departing from patrol areas.[11] Moreover, the Western Allies were in a better position than Japan to accept heavy losses of merchant shipping. The curve of new construction in the Allied countries passed that of tonnage lost in December 1942, and the two curves continued to diverge to Germany's loss and Allied gain. Japan had a fair capacity for shipbuilding but her facilities were not wisely used; for instance, the materials and labor that went into the construction of 59,000-ton carrier *Shinano* would have been much better employed in building smaller types.

[10] Volumes I and X, Appendix I in each.

[11] Comsubpac Operational History IV 1426. This was monthly average for 1945, which was the highest.

JAPANESE TONNAGE SUNK BY UNITED STATES SUBMARINES
September–November 1944[12]

	WARSHIPS		MARUS			
1944	*Number*	*Tons*	*Number*	*Tons*	*Total Ships*	*Total Tons*
Sept.	7	26,905	48[13]	152,505	55	179,410
Oct.	9[14]	27,662	66[15]	320,906	75	348,568
Nov.	18	125,877	56	214,506	74	340,383
Total	34	180,444	170	687,917	204	868,361

Merchant tonnage owned by Japan declined from about 6,000,000 tons at the beginning of the war to about 2,450,000 tons on 1 December 1944, despite the conquest of some 800,000 tons in the early months of the war, and the addition of 3,293,814 tons' new construction. At the end of the war she had only 1,800,000 tons left in her merchant marine, mostly small wooden vessels in the Inland Sea.[16] United States forces were responsible for the sinking of 2117 Japanese merchant vessels of 7,913,858 tons during the war. Submarines caused 60 per cent, aircraft (mostly Navy) 30 per cent of this tonnage destruction; the rest was done by mines, surface craft and other agents. Other Allied forces, mainly British and Dutch, sent another 73 ships of 211,664 tons to the bottom. And United States submarines accounted for 201 of the 686 Japanese warships sunk during the war.[17]

A factor in the success of American submarines was the poor quality of Japanese escort-of-convoy, antisubmarine tactics and antisubmarine weapons. The Imperial Navy, enjoying the natural advantage of routing convoys largely in protected coastal waters, instead of over broad reaches of open ocean, and having no expectation, until the end of 1943, that an enemy would ever threaten these routes, neglected shipping protection. At the close of 1943 a Combined Escort Fleet was organized and retired officers were

[12] Data from JANAC and *Imp. Jap. Navy in W. W. II.*
[13] Includes one ship of 5061 tons shared with carrier-based aircraft.
[14] Includes 5100-ton light cruiser *Tama*, shared with carrier-based aircraft.
[15] Includes one ship of 2407 tons shared with carrier-based aircraft.
[16] USSBS "War Against Japanese Transportation" pp. 3, 54, 58.
[17] JANAC *Japanese Naval and Merchant Ship Losses* (Feb. 1947) pp. vi, vii.

recalled to act as convoy commodores. But the Japanese ended the war with about the same antisubmarine equipment that they had at the beginning – depth charges which were not very accurate or capable of going deep enough, small-caliber gunfire and aircraft bombs. And they were not experts in employing the equipment they had. Having located an American submarine after a torpedo attack, "they failed miserably in the solution of the mathematical problem of where to drop their depth charges. Their attacks were characterized by a consistent lack of persistence. They were prone to accept the most nebulous evidence as proof of a sinking, and, being sure of a kill, to let the submarine surface and thank God for the Japanese superiority complex." [18] During the war they sank between 41 and 44 United States submarines,[19] but at the same time lost 128 of their own to Allied attacks. Germany lost 781 U-boats in the same war.

If the prospects of a Japanese victory after the loss of Saipan were hopeless, as many leaders realized, they had declined to zero by December 1944, when the great Battle for Leyte Gulf had been lost, Leyte itself overrun, and the Japanese merchant navy reduced to a mere skeleton. But Japan, by virtue of her traditions, her victorious past, her no-surrender psychology, and other factors in the national make-up, was unable as yet to make a conciliatory move. Some of her leading militarists still entertained the vain hope that the Western Allies would lose heart over the great expenditure of life necessary to carry the war into the home islands of Japan, and be the first to cry, "Let us have peace!"

[18] *U.S. Submarine Losses World War II* p. 4.

[19] Same p. 1. Four others, including *Darter*, were lost by stranding; *Dorado* and *R-12* were lost in the Atlantic, and two operationally. This represents 18 per cent of the American submarines that saw combat duty.

APPENDIX I

Task Organization for the Invasion of Leyte[1]

17–25 October 1944

SUPREME COMMANDER, ALLIED FORCES, SOUTH-WEST PACIFIC AREA

General Douglas MacArthur USA

SEVENTH FLEET and CENTRAL PHILIPPINES ATTACK FORCE

Vice Admiral Thomas C. Kinkaid in WASATCH

Chief of Staff, Commodore Valentine H. Schaeffer

Also embarking Commander Expeditionary Troops and Sixth Army, Lieutenant General Walter Krueger USA.

Deputy Commander, Vice Admiral T. S. Wilkinson in MOUNT OLYMPUS

TG 77.1 Fleet Flagship Group, Vice Admiral Kinkaid, with Commander Air Support Seventh Fleet, Capt. R. F. Whitehead.

Amphibious Command Ship WASATCH, Captain A. M. Granum

Light cruiser NASHVILLE Capt. C. E. Coney; destroyers AMMEN Cdr. J. H. Brown, MULLANY Cdr. A. O. Momm, ABNER READ Cdr. A. M. Purdy, BUSH Cdr. R. E. Westholm.

TF 78 NORTHERN ATTACK FORCE

Rear Admiral Daniel E. Barbey

Chief of Staff, Commodore Albert G. Noble

Embarking X Army Corps, Major General F. C. Sibert USA.

Amphibious Command Ship BLUE RIDGE, Commander L. R. McDowell

1 The ships that participated in the Battle for Leyte Gulf are listed at the beginning of Chapters XI, XII and XIV, excepting the submarines. The first ship mentioned in a group is the flagship unless otherwise stated.

TG 78.1 PALO ATTACK GROUP, Rear Admiral Barbey

Embarking 24th Infantry Division, Major General F. A. Irving.

Transport Unit, Captain T. B. Brittain

Transdiv 24, Capt. Brittain: Attack transports DU PAGE Capt. G. M. Wauchope USNR, FULLER Capt. N. M. Pigman, ELMORE Capt. D. Harrison, WAYNE Capt. T. V. Cooper; attack cargo AQUARIUS Cdr. I. E. Eskridge USCG; transport JOHN LAND Cdr. F. A. Graf; LSD GUNSTON HALL Cdr. D. E. Collins USNR.

Transdiv 6, Capt. H. D. Baker: Attack transports FAYETTE Capt. J. C. Lester, ORMSBY Capt. L. Frisco USNR, LEEDSTOWN Capt. H. Bye; attack cargo ship TITANIA Cdr. M. W. Callahan; cargo HERCULES Cdr. W. H. Turnquist USNR; LSDs EPPING FOREST Cdr. L. Martin USNR, CARTER HALL Lt. Cdr. C. E. Blount.

Destroyer Screen, Captain Henry Crommelin (Desron 25)

JOHN RODGERS Cdr. J. G. Franklin, MURRAY Cdr. P. R. Anderson, HARRISON Cdr. W. V. Combs, MCKEE Cdr. R. B. Allen.

Control Vessels, Capt. N. D. Brantly: 3 PC, 1 SC.

Close Support Vessels: 2 LCI(G), 5 LCI(R), 9 LCI.

Army Headquarters Unit: 3 PCE, 1 FP, 3 LSM.

Fleet tugs APACHE Lt. C. S. Horner, QUAPAW Lt. Cdr. N. H. Castle USNR.

12 LST of LST Group 20 (Flot. 7), Lieutenant Commander D. M. Baker USNR

TG 78.2 SAN RICARDO ATTACK GROUP, Rear Admiral W. M. Fechteler in FREMONT Capt. C. V. Conlan

Embarking 1st Cavalry Division, Major General Verne D. Mudge.

Transport Unit, Captain M. O. Carlson

Transdiv 32, Capt. Carlson: Attack transports HARRIS Capt. M. E. Murphy, BARNSTABLE Capt. H. T. Walsh; transport HERALD OF THE MORNING Cdr. H. A. Dunn; attack cargo ARNEB Capt. H. R. Shaw; LSD WHITE MARSH Cdr. G. H. Eppleman USNR.

Transdiv 20, Capt. D. W. Loomis: Attack transports LEONARD WOOD Capt. H. C. Perkins USCG, PIERCE Capt. F. M. Adams, JAMES O'HARA Capt. E. W. Irish; transport LA SALLE Cdr. F. C. Fluegel USNR; attack cargo ELECTRA Lt. Cdr. D. S. Holler USNR; LSD OAK HILL Cdr. C. A. Peterson; 9 LSM.

Destroyer Screen, Captain A. E. Jarrell

FLETCHER Cdr. J. L. Foster, LAVALLETTE Cdr. W. Thompson, JENKINS Cdr. P. D. Gallery, ANDERSON Lt. Cdr. R. H. Benson; Control vessels, 4 PC, 1 SC; Close Support vessels, 2 LCI(G), 6 LCI(R); Fleet tug * SONOMA Lt. W. R. Zursler USNR.

14 LST of Flotilla 7, Capt. R. M. Scruggs

FIRE SUPPORT UNIT NORTH, Rear Admiral G. L. Weyler

Battleships MISSISSIPPI Capt. H. J. Redfield, MARYLAND Capt. H. J. Ray, WEST VIRGINIA Capt. H. V. Wiley; destroyers CONY Cdr. A. W. Moore, AULICK Cdr. J. D. Andrew, SIGOURNEY Lt. Cdr. F. Hale. Also, 3 DDs were borrowed from Fire Support Unit South.

TG 78.3 PANAON ATTACK GROUP, Rear Admiral A. D. Struble in HUGHES

Embarking 21st RCT 24th Division, Lt. Col. F. R. Weber.

Destroyer HUGHES Cdr. E. B. Rittenhouse; Landing Ships Infantry H.M.A.S. KANIMBLA Cdr. A. V. Bunyan RANR, H.M.A.S. MANOORA Cdr. A. P. Cousins RANR,

* Lost in this operation.

H.M.A.S. WESTRALIA Cdr. A. V. Knight RANR; minelayer H.M.S. ARIADNE Capt. the Lord Ashbourne RN. Escorts, Capt. H. O. Parish: destroyers SCHROEDER Cdr. R. W. McElrath, SIGSBEE Cdr. G. P. Chung-Hoon, RINGGOLD Cdr. W. B. Christie, DASHIELL Cdr. D. L. L. Cordiner.

Control and Support Unit, Captain C. D. Murphey

2 PC, 2 LCI(G), 2 LCI(R), 1 LCI(D).

TG 78.4 DINAGAT ATTACK GROUP, Rear Admiral Struble in HUGHES

Embarking 6th Ranger Battalion, Lt. Col. H. A. Mucci and Co. B 21st Infantry.

Destroyer transports KILTY Lt. L. G. Benson USNR, SCHLEY Lt. Cdr. E. T. Farley USNR, WARD Lt. R. E. Farwell USNR, HERBERT Lt. G. S. Hewitt USNR, CROSBY Lt. G. G. Moffatt USNR; fleet tug CHICKASAW Lt. L. C. Olsen USNR.

Escorts: destroyers LANG Cdr. H. Payson, STACK Cdr. R. E. Wheeler; frigates [2] GALLUP Lt. Cdr. C. M. Opp, BISBEE Cdr. J. P. German.

Bombardment Group, Rear Admiral R. W. Hayler

Light cruisers DENVER, COLUMBIA and Desdiv 112 (see Fire Support Unit South, below).

TG 78.6 REINFORCEMENT GROUP ONE, Captain S. P. Jenkins
(Arrived 22 October)

Attack transports CRESCENT CITY Capt. L. L. Rowe, WARREN Capt. W. A. McHale USNR, WINDSOR Capt. D. C. Woodward USNR, CALLAWAY Capt. D. C. McNeil USCG, LEON CAPT. B. B. Adell, SUMTER, Cdr. J. T. O'Pry USNR; transport STORM KING Cdr. H. J. Hansen; cargo ship JUPITER Cdr. J. M. Bristol; repair ship ACHILLES Lt. C. O. Smith USNR; 4 merchant ships.

32 LST from Flotilla 8, Capt. O. R. Swigart; 12 LCI.

Escort, Captain E. A. Solomons (Comdesron 2)

Destroyers MORRIS Lt. Cdr. R. V. Wheeler, HOWORTH Cdr. E. S. Burns, STEVENS Cdr. W. M. Rakow, MUSTIN Lt. Cdr. J. G. Hughes; frigates CARSON CITY Cdr. H. B. Roberts USCG; BURLINGTON Cdr. E. V. Carlson USCG.

TG 78.7 REINFORCEMENT GROUP TWO, Captain J. K. B. Ginder
(Arrived 24 October)

33 LST of Flotilla 14, Capt. E. A. Seay; 24 Liberty and other merchant marine freighters; 12 units of Service Force Seventh Fleet, mentioned below.

Escort, Captain Ginder (Comdesron 21)

Destroyers NICHOLAS Cdr. R. T. S. Keith, O'BANNON Cdr. R. W. Smith, HOPEWELL Cdr. W. S. Rodimon, TAYLOR Cdr. N. J. Frank; frigates MUSKOGEE Cdr. R. E. Mroczkowski USCG, SAN PEDRO Lt. H. L. Sutherland USCGR.

TG 78.8 REINFORCEMENT GROUP THREE Cdr. J. L. Steinmetz USCG
(Arrived 29 October)

6 LST, 19 Liberty and Victory ships; units of Service Force Seventh Fleet.

Escort, Captain W. M. Cole (Comdesron 5)

Destroyers FLUSSER Cdr. T. R. Vogeley, MAHAN Cdr. E. G. Campbell, DRAYTON Cdr. R. S. Craighill, SMITH Cdr. F. V. List, LAMSON Cdr. J. V. Noel; frigates

[2] These frigates became Harbor Control Group in San Pedro Bay under Capt. F. W. Benson, together with 4 LCI.

EUGENE Cdr. C. R. MacLean USCG, EL PASO Cdr. R. J. Barromey USCG, VAN BUREN Cdr. C. B. Arrington USCG, ORANGE Cdr. J. A. Dirks USCG.

TF 79 SOUTHERN ATTACK FORCE
Vice Admiral T. S. Wilkinson

Chief of Staff, Commodore Paulus P. Powell

Embarking XXIV Army Corps, Major General J. R. Hodge.

Amphibious Command Ship MOUNT OLYMPUS, Capt. J. H. Shultz

TG 79.1 ATTACK GROUP "ABLE," Rear Admiral R. L. Conolly
Embarking 7th Infantry Division, Major General A. V. Arnold.

Amphibious Command Ship APPALACHIAN, Captain C. R. Jeffs

TG 79.3 Transport Group "ABLE," Captain C. G. Richardson

Transdiv 7, Capt. Richardson: Attack transports CAVALIER Capt. A. G. Hall USCG, J. FRANKLIN BELL Capt. O. H. Ritchie USNR, FELAND Cdr. G. F. Prestwich; transport GOLDEN CITY Cdr. C. M. Furlow USNR; attack cargo THUBAN Cdr. J. C. Campbell USNR; LSD LINDENWALD Capt. W. H. Weaver USNR.

Transdiv 30, Capt. C. A. Misson: Attack transports KNOX Capt. J. H. Brady, CALVERT Cdr. J. F. Warris, CUSTER Capt. W. Terry, RIXEY Capt. P. H. Jenkins;[8] attack cargo CHARA Cdr. J. P. Clark USNR; LSD ASHLAND Lt. Cdr. W. A. Caughey USNR.

Transdiv 38, Capt. Charles Allen: Attack transports LAMAR Capt. B. K. Culver, ALPINE Cdr. G. K. G. Reilly, HEYWOOD Cdr. G. M. Jones USNR; transports STARLIGHT Cdr. W. O. Britton, MONITOR Cdr. K. J. Olsen; attack cargo ALSHAIN Capt. R. E. Krause.

Transdiv "X-Ray," Capt. J. A. Snackenberg: Attack transports GEORGE CLYMER Capt. Snackenberg, PRESIDENT HAYES Capt. H. E. Schieke; cargo MERCURY Lt. Cdr. N. D. Salmon USNR.

Destroyer Screen, Captain W. J. Marshall (Comdesron 48)

ERBEN Lt. Cdr. Morgan Slayton, WALKER Cdr. H. E. Townsend, HALE Lt. Cdr. D. W. Wilson, ABBOT Cdr. F. W. Ingling, BLACK Cdr. E. R. King (with Comdesdiv 96, Cdr. T. H. Kobey, embarked), CHAUNCEY Cdr. L. C. Conwell, BRAINE Cdr. W. W. Fitts, GANSEVOORT Lt. Cdr. J. M. Steinbeck.

TG 79.5 LST Flotilla 16, Captain R. C. Webb: 31 LST

TG 79.11 Destroyer Screen for LST and LCI, both "ABLE" and "BAKER," Captain J. G. Coward (Comdesron 54)

Destroyers REMEY Cdr. R. P. Fiala, MERTZ Cdr. W. S. Estabrook, MONSSEN Cdr. C. K. Bergin, MCDERMUT Cdr. C. B. Jennings (with Comdesdiv 108, Cdr. R. H. Phillips, embarked), MCGOWAN Cdr. W. R. Cox, MCNAIR Cdr. M. L. McCullough, MELVIN Cdr. B. K. Atkins

3 PCE(R) and small craft assigned from Control Units.

Control Vessels, Cdr. V. K. Busck: destroyer STEMBEL Cdr. W. L. Tagg; 3 PC; 3 PC(S); 3 SC.

LCI Gunboat Unit: 18 LCI(G).
Salvage and Fire-fighting Unit: 2 LCI(L).
LCT Unit, Lt. M. Wassell USNR: 12 LCT.

[8] Fitted for evacuation of wounded.

TG 79.2 ATTACK GROUP "BAKER," Rear Admiral F. B. Royal
Embarking 96th Infantry Division, Major General J. L. Bradley.

Amphibious Force Flagship ROCKY MOUNT, Captain S. F. Patten

TG 79.4 Transport Group "BAKER," Captain H. B. Knowles

Transdiv 10, Capt. G. D. Morrison: Attack transports CLAY Capt. N. B. Van Bergen, ARTHUR MIDDLETON Capt. S. A. Olsen USCG, BAXTER Capt. V. R. Sinclair, WILLIAM P. BIDDLE Capt. R. W. Berry; transport GEORGE F. ELLIOTT Cdr. W. F. Weidner; attack cargo CAPRICORNUS Lt. Cdr. B. F. McGuckin USNR; Landing Ship Vehicle CATSKILL Capt. R. W. Chambers USNR.

Transdiv 18, Capt. Knowles: Attack transports CAMBRIA Capt. C. W. Dean USCG, MONROVIA Capt. J. D. Kelsey, FREDERICK FUNSTON Cdr. C. C. Anderson; transport WAR HAWK Cdr. S. H. Thompson USNR; attack cargo ALCYONE Cdr. H. P. Knickerbocker; LSDs CASA GRANDE Lt. Cdr. F. E. Strumm USNR, RUSHMORE Cdr. E. A. Jansen USNR.

Transdiv 28, Capt. H. C. Flanagan: Attack transports BOLIVAR Capt. W. L. Field, SHERIDAN Capt. P. H. Wiedorn, DOYEN Cdr. J. G. McClaughry; transport COMET Lt. Cdr. T. C. Fonda USNR; attack cargo ALMAACK Lt. Cdr. C. O. Hicks USNR; cargo AURIGA Cdr. J. G. Hart USNR; LSD BELLE GROVE Cdr. M. Seavy USNR.

Destroyer Screen, Captain E. R. McLean (Comdesron 49)

PICKING Cdr. B. J. Semmes, SPROSTON Cdr. M. J. Luosey, WICKES Lt. Cdr. J. B. Cresap, ISHERWOOD Cdr. L. E. Schmidt (with Comdesdiv 98, Capt. W. G. Cooper, embarked), CHARLES J. BADGER Cdr. J. H. Cotten, HALLIGAN Cdr. C. E. Cortner, HARADEN Cdr. H. C. Allan, TWIGGS Cdr. George Philip, MACDONOUGH Lt. Cdr. B. H. Shupper.

LST Flotilla 3, Cdr. A. A. Ageton in destroyer LUCE (Cdr. H. A. Owens): 24 LST

Control Unit, Lieutenant Commander W. K. Rummel USNR

3 PC, 4 SC, 3 YMS.[4]

LCI Flotilla 14, Capt. T. W. Rimer: 4 LCI(M) Lt. Cdr. G. W. Hannett USNR; 4 LCI(E), 9 LCI(G), Lt. F. R. Giliberty USNR; 2 LCI(L), for salvage and fire-fighting.

LSM Unit, Lt. Cdr. J. G. Blanche: 6 LSM.

LCT Unit, Lt. G. P. Franklin USNR: 11 LCT.

FIRE SUPPORT UNIT SOUTH, Rear Admiral J. B. Oldendorf in LOUISVILLE

Chief of Staff, Captain Richard W. Bates

Batdiv 2, Rear Admiral T. E. Chandler: TENNESSEE Capt. J. B. Heffernan, CALIFORNIA Capt. H. P. Burnett, PENNSYLVANIA Capt. C. F. Martin.

Crudiv 4, Rear Admiral Oldendorf: Heavy cruisers LOUISVILLE Capt. S. H. Hurt, PORTLAND Capt. T. G. W. Settle, MINNEAPOLIS Capt. H. B. Slocum.

Crudiv 9, Rear Admiral W. L. Ainsworth: Light cruiser HONOLULU Capt. H. R. Thurber.

Crudiv 12, Rear Admiral R. W. Hayler: Light cruisers DENVER Capt. A. M. Bledsoe, COLUMBIA Capt. M. E. Curts.

Destroyer Screen, Captain R. N. Smoot (Comdesron 56)

LEUTZE Cdr. B. A. Robbins, NEWCOMB Cdr. L. B. Cook, BENNION Cdr. J. W. Cooper, HEYWOOD L. EDWARDS Cdr. J. W. Boulware, RICHARD P. LEARY Cdr. F. S. Habecker.

Desdiv 112, Capt. T. F. Conley: ROBINSON Cdr. E. B. Grantham, ROSS Cdr. Benjamin Coe, ALBERT W. GRANT Cdr. T. A. Nisewaner, BRYANT Cdr. P. L. High,

[4] Beachmaster Unit "Baker," Lt. Cdr. H. E. Le Barron USNR in *YMS–176*.

HALFORD Cdr. R. J. Hardy, CLAXTON Cdr. M. H. Hubbard, THORN Lt. Cdr. F. H. Schneider, WELLES Lt. Cdr. J. S. Slaughter.

Salvage Group, Commander H. O. Foss

Salvage vessel PRESERVER Lt. L. B. Frank; fleet tugs MENOMINEE Lt. J. A. Young, POTAWATOMI Lt. C. H. Stedman, CHOWANOC Lt. R. F. Snipes; repair ship EGERIA Lt. A. H. Wilson USNR.

TG 77.4 ESCORT CARRIER GROUP
Rear Admiral Thomas L. Sprague

"TAFFY 1," Rear Admiral Sprague

SANGAMON, Capt. M. E. Browder, with Air Group 37, Lt. Cdr. S. E. Hindman: 12 F6F-3 (Hellcat), 5 F6F-5, Lt. Cdr. Hindman; 9 TBM-1C (GM Avenger), Lt. Cdr. P. G. Farley USNR.

SUWANNEE, Capt. W. D. Johnson, with Air Group 60, Lt. Cdr. H. O. Feilbach USNR: 22 F6F-3; 9 TBM-1C, Lt. W. C. Vincent USNR.

CHENANGO,[5] Capt. George Van Deurs, with Air Group 35, Lt. Cdr. F. T. Moore: 22 F6F-3; 9 TBM-1C, Lt. C. F. Morgan USNR.

SANTEE, Capt. R. E. Blick, with Air Group 26, Lt. Cdr. H. N. Funk: 24 FM-2 (GM Wildcat); 6 TBF-1C (Grumman Avenger), 3 TBM-1C, Lt. Cdr. T. M. Bennett.

Cardiv 28, Rear Admiral G. R. Henderson

SAGINAW BAY, Capt. F. C. Sutton, with Composite Squadron 78, Lt. Cdr. J. L. Hyde USNR: 15 FM-2, 12 TBM-1C.

PETROF BAY, Capt. J. L. Kane, with Composite Squadron 76, Cdr. J. W. McCauley: 16 FM-2, 10 TBM-1C.

Screen, Captain I. H. Nunn

Destroyers MC CORD Cdr. F. D. Michael, TRATHEN Cdr. J. R. Millett, HAZELWOOD Cdr. V. P. Douw; destroyer escorts EDMONDS Lt. Cdr. J. S. Burrows USNR, RICHARD S. BULL Lt. Cdr. A. W. Gardes, RICHARD M. ROWELL Cdr. H. A. Barnard, * EVERSOLE Lt. Cdr. G. E. Marix, COOLBAUGH Lt. Cdr. S. T. Hotchkiss USNR.

"TAFFY 2," Rear Admiral Felix B. Stump

NATOMA BAY, Capt. A. K. Morehouse, with Composite Squadron 81, Lt. Cdr. R. C. Barnes: 16 FM-2, 12 TBM-1C.

MANILA BAY, Capt. Fitzhugh Lee, with Composite Squadron 80, Lt. Cdr. H. K. Stubbs USNR: 16 FM-2, 12 TBM-1C.

Cardiv 27, Rear Admiral W. D. Sample

MARCUS ISLAND, Capt. C. F. Greber, with Composite Squadron 21, Lt. Cdr. T. O. Murray USNR: 12 FM-2, 11 TBM-1C.

KADASHAN BAY, Capt. R. N. Hunter, with Composite Squadron 20, Lt. Cdr. J. R. Dale USNR: 15 FM-2, 11 TBM-1C.

SAVO ISLAND, Capt. C. E. Ekstrom, with Composite Squadron 27, Lt. Cdr. P.W. Jackson: 16 FM-2, 12 TBM-1C.

* Lost or killed in this operation.

[5] *Chenango, Saginaw Bay, Edmonds* and *Oberrender,* under command of Rear Admiral Henderson, departed for Morotai at 1645 Oct. 24.

OMMANEY BAY, Capt. H. L. Young, with Composite Squadron 75, Lt. A. W. Smith USNR: 16 FM–2, 11 TBM–1C.

Screen, Captain L. K. Reynolds

Destroyers HAGGARD Cdr. D. A. Harris, FRANKS Cdr. D. R. Stephan, HAILEY Cdr. P. H. Brady; destroyer escorts RICHARD W. SUESENS Lt. Cdr. R. W. Graham USNR (with Comcortdiv 69, Cdr. T. C. Pifer, embarked), ABERCROMBIE Lt. Cdr. B. H. Katschinski USNR, OBERRENDER Lt. Cdr. S. Spencer USNR, LERAY WILSON Lt. Cdr. M. V. Carson USNR, WALTER C. WANN Lt. Cdr. J. W. Stedman USNR.

"TAFFY 3," Rear Admiral Clifton A. F. Sprague

FANSHAW BAY, Capt. D. P. Johnson, with Composite Squadron 68, Lt. Cdr. R. S. Rogers: 16 FM–2, 12 TBM–1C.

* ST. LO, Capt. F. J. McKenna, with Composite Squadron 65, Lt. Cdr. R. M. Jones USNR: 17 FM–2, 12 TBM–1C.

WHITE PLAINS, Capt. D. J. Sullivan, with Composite Squadron 4, Lt. E. R. Fickenscher: 16 FM–2, 12 TBM–1C.

KALININ BAY, Capt. T. B. Williamson, with Composite Squadron 3, Lt. Cdr. W. H. Keighley USNR: 16 FM–2, 1 TBF–1C, 11 TBM–1C.

Cardiv 26, Rear Admiral R. A. Ofstie

KITKUN BAY, Capt. J. P. Whitney, with Composite Squadron 5, Cdr. R. L. Fowler: 14 FM–2, 12 TBM–1C.

* GAMBIER BAY, Capt. W. V. R. Vieweg, with Composite Squadron 10, Lt. Cdr. E. J. Huxtable: 18 FM–2, 12 TBM–1C.

Screen, Commander W. D. Thomas

Destroyers * HOEL Cdr. L. S. Kintberger, HEERMANN Cdr. A. T. Hathaway, * JOHNSTON * Cdr. E. E. Evans; destroyer escorts DENNIS Lt. Cdr. S. Hansen USNR, JOHN C. BUTLER Lt. Cdr. J. E. Pace, RAYMOND Lt. Cdr. A. F. Beyer USNR, * SAMUEL B. ROBERTS Lt. Cdr. R. W. Copeland USNR.

TG 77.3 CLOSE COVERING GROUP, Rear Admiral R. S. Berkey

Light cruisers PHOENIX Capt. J. H. Duncan, BOISE Capt. J. S. Roberts; heavy cruisers H.M.A.S. AUSTRALIA * Capt. E. F. V. Dechaineux RAN (with Commo. J. A. Collins RAN embarked), H.M.A.S. SHROPSHIRE Capt. H. A. Showers RAN.

Destroyer Screen, Captain K. M. McManes (Comdesron 24)

HUTCHINS Cdr. C. B. Laning, BACHE Cdr. R. C. Morton, BEALE Cdr. D. M. Coffee, DALY Cdr. R. G. Visser, KILLEN Cdr. H. G. Corey, H.M.A.S. ARUNTA Cdr. A. E. Buchanan RAN, H.M.A.S. WARRAMUNGA Cdr. N. A. MacKinnan RAN.

TG 77.5 MINESWEEPING AND HYDROGRAPHIC GROUP

Commander W. R. Loud

High speed minesweeper HOVEY Lt. A. A. Clark; minelayers PREBLE Lt. Cdr. E. F. Baldridge, BREESE Lt. Cdr. D. B. Cohen; destroyer transport SANDS Lt. J. M. Samuels USNR; minesweepers TOKEN Lt. W. T. Hunt USNR, TUMULT Lt. W. K. McDuffie USNR, VELOCITY Lt. G. J. Buyse USNR, ZEAL Lt. Cdr. E. W. Woodhouse USNR, REQUISITE Lt. Cdr. H. R. Peirce USNR, PURSUIT Lt. Cdr. R. F. Good USNR, REVENGE Lt. Cdr. J. L. Jackson USNR, SAGE Lt. Cdr. F. K. Zinn USNR, SALUTE Lt. J. R. Hodges USNR, SAUNTER Lt. Cdr. J. R. Keefer USNR, SCOUT Lt. E. G. Ander-

* Lost or killed in this operation.

son USNR, SCRIMMAGE Lt. Robert Van Winkle USNR, SENTRY Lt. Cdr. T. R. Fonick USNR; high speed minesweepers SOUTHARD Lt. J. E. Brennan USNR, CHANDLER Lt. F. M. Murphy USNR, LONG Lt. S. Caplan USNR, HAMILTON Lt. Cdr. J. Cleague USNR, HOWARD Lt. Cdr. O. F. Salvia, PALMER Lt. W. E. McGuirk USNR; 26 YMS; frigate H.M.A.S. GASCOYNE; H.M.A.S. HDML–1074.

TG 77.6 BEACH DEMOLITION GROUP
Lieutenant Commander C. C. Morgan USNR

Embarking UDT 3, UDT 4 Lt. W. G. Carberry USNR, UDT 5 Lt. J. K. De Bold USNR, UDT 6 Lt. D. M. Logsdon USNR, UDT 8 Lt. Cdr. D. E. Young USNR, UDT 9 Lt. Cdr. James B. Eaton USNR UDT 10 Lt. A. O. Shoate USNR.

Destroyer transports TALBOT Lt. Cdr. Morgan, MANLEY Lt. R. T. Newell USNR, GOLDSBOROUGH Lt. W. J. Meehan USNR, KANE Lt. F. M. Christiansen USNR, BROOKS Lt. S. C. Rassmussen USNR, BELKNAP Lt. R. Childs USNR, OVERTON Lt. Cdr. D. K. O'Connor USNR, HUMPHREYS Lt. Cdr. O. B. Murphy USNR, RATHBURNE Lt. Cdr. R. L. Welch USNR, GEORGE E. BADGER Lt. Cdr. E. M. Higgins USNR, CLEMSON Lt. W. F. Moran USNR.

TG 73.7 SEAPLANE TENDERS, SAN PEDRO BAY

SAN CARLOS Lt. Cdr. DeL. Mills, HALF MOON Cdr. Jack I. Brandy.
Tending Patron 34, Lt. Cdr. V. V. Utgoff: 12 PBY–5.

TG 70.1 MOTOR TORPEDO BOAT SQUADRONS SEVENTH FLEET
Commander S. S. Bowling

Tenders OYSTER BAY Lt. Cdr. W. W. Holroyd USNR, WACHAPREAGUE Lt. Cdr. H. A. Stewart, WILLOUGHBY Lt. Cdr. A. J. Church USNR.

Surigao Strait Patrols, Lieutenant Commander Robert Leeson USNR

Section 1, Lt. W. C. Pullen USNR: PT–152 Lt. (jg) J. A. Eddins USNR, *PT–130* Lt. (jg) I. D. Malcolm USNR, *PT–131* Ens. P. R. Gadd USNR.

Section 2, Lt. (jg) J. A. Cady USNR: *PT–127* Ens. D. J. Johnson USNR, *PT–128* Ens. G. J. Azarigian USNR, *PT–129* Ens. A. D. Leeson USNR.

Section 3, Lt. (jg) D. H. Owen USNR: *PT–151* Ens. J. M. Ladd USNR, *PT–146* Ens. B. M. Grosscup USNR, *PT–190* Ens. E. S. Haughen USNR.

Section 4, Lt. Cdr. T. R. Stansbury USNR: *PT–192* Lt. (jg) K. W. Denman USNR, *PT–191* Lt. (jg) Nelson Davis USNR, *PT–195* Ens. W. S. Diver USNR.

Section 5, Lt. R. G. Mislicky: *PT–196* Lt. (jg) J. R. Beck USNR, *PT–194* Lt. (jg) T. C. Hall USNR, *PT–150* Lt. (jg) W. J. West USNR.

Section 6, Lt. Cdr. Robert Leeson: *PT–134* Lt. (jg) E. F. Wakelin USNR, *PT–132* Ens. P. H. Jones USNR, *PT–137* Lt. (jg) I. M. Kovar USNR.

Section 7, Lt. J. H. Moran II USNR: *PT–494* Lt. Moran, *PT–497* Lt. (jg) J. C. Beckman USNR, *PT–324* Ens. H. F. Dumas USNR.

Section 8, Lt. Cdr. F. D. Tappaan USNR: *PT–523* Lt. R. W. Orrell, *PT–524* Lt. (jg) J. P. Wolf USNR, *PT–526* Lt. D. Hamilton USNR.

Section 9, Lt. (jg) J. M. McElfresh USNR: *PT–490* Lt. McElfresh, *PT–491* Lt. (jg) H. A. Thronson USNR, * *PT–493* Lt. (jg) R. W. Brown USNR.

Section 10, Lt. A. M. Preston USNR: *PT–495* Lt. F. H. Olton USNR, *PT–489* Ens. H. A. Gregg USNR, *PT–492* Lt. M. W. Haines USNR.

Section 11, Lt. C. T. Gleason: *PT–327* Ens. K. B. Sharpe USNR, *PT–321* Ens. L. E. Thomas USNR, *PT–326* Ens. H. L. Terry USNR.

* Lost in this operation.

Section 12, Lt. G. W. Hogan USNR: *PT-320* Lt. Hogan, *PT-330* Lt. (jg) E. H. Reeks USNR, *PT-331* Ens. W. P. West USNR.

Section 13, Lt. H. G. Young USNR: *PT-328* Lt. Young, *PT-323* Lt. (jg) H. Stadler USNR, *PT-329* Lt. (jg) J. L. Mee USNR.

TG 77.7 SERVICE FORCE SEVENTH FLEET UNITS PARTICIPATING

Rear Admiral R. O. Glover

Fueling at Sea Unit, Captain J. D. Beard

Oilers SARANAC Cdr. H. R. Parker, ASHTABULA Lt. Cdr. M. K. Reece USNR, SALAMONIE Cdr. L. J. Johns, SUAMICO Cdr. A. S. Johnson, KISHWAUKEE Lt. F. M. Hillman USNR, SCHUYLKILL Capt. F. A. Hardesty, TALLULAH Lt. Cdr. W. F. Huckaby USNR.

Amunition ships MAZAMA Cdr. P. V. R. Harris USNR, DURHAM VICTORY, IRAN V., BLUEFIELD V., CANADA V.

Escort Unit, Cdr. F. W. Howers: Destroyer escorts WHITEHURST Lt. J. C. Horton USNR, WITTER Lt. G. Herrmann USNR, BOWERS Lt. Cdr. C. F. Highland USNR.

Kossol Roads Unit, Lt. Cdr. H. K. Wallace USNR: oiler CHEPACHET Lt. Cdr. Wallace; 2 merchant tankers; destroyer escort WILLMARTH Lt. Cdr. J. G. Thorburn USNR.

Leyte Gulf Unit, Captain E. P. Hylant (Coördinator Service Force Seventh Fleet)

Tankers ARETHUSA Lt. R. L. Barrington USNR, CARIBOU Lt. J. B. Humphrey USNR, MINK Lt. W. J. Meagher USNR, PANDA Lt. W. Polk USNR, PORCUPINE Lt. D. N. Paul USNR, H.M.A.S. BISHOPDALE; water tanker SEVERN Lt. Cdr. O. Rees; net tenders INDUS Lt. Cdr. A. S. Einmo USNR, TEAK Lt. B. P. Hollett USNR, SILVERBELL Lt. H. N. Berg USNR, SATINLEAF Lt. A. B. Church USNR; repair and salvage vessels ACHILLES Lt. C. O. Smith USNR, CABLE Lt. Cdr. H. Pond USNR, MIDAS Lt. R. A. Young USNR; floating drydock *ARD-19;* ammunition ships MURZIM Lt. Cdr. D. S. Walton USCGR, H.M.A.S. POYANG Lt. J. W. Edwards RANVR, H.M.A.S YUNNAN Lt. D. Morrison RANR(S); provision ships AREQUIPA, CALAMARIES Lt. Cdr. D. R. Phoebus USNR, MIZAR Cdr. C. H. Christenson USNR, OCTANS Cdr. O. J. Stein USNR, CRUX, GANYMEDE Lt. Cdr. G. H. Melichar USNR, TRIANGULUM Lt. Cdr. C. B. S. Latus USNR, POLLUX Cdr. H. L. Bixby, ACUBENS, H.M.A.S. MERKUR.

THIRD FLEET [6]

Admiral William F. Halsey in NEW JERSEY

Chief of Staff, Rear Admiral Robert B. Carney

TF 38 FAST CARRIER FORCE

Vice Admiral Marc A. Mitscher in LEXINGTON

Chief of Staff, Commodore Arleigh A. Burke

TG 38.1 TASK GROUP ONE, Vice Admiral John S. McCain

Carrier	WASP	Captain O. A. Weller
	Air Group 14: 1 F6F-3 (Hellcat)	Commander W. C. Wingard
VF-14	29 F6F-3, 3 F6F-3N, 2 F6F-3P, 7 F6F-5, 1 F6F-5N	Lt. Cdr. R. Gray
VB-14	3 F6F-3, 7 F6F-5, 25 SB2C-3 (Helldiver)	Lt. Cdr. J. D. Blitch
VT-14	5 TBF-1C (Avenger), 1 TBF-1D, 11 TBM-1C, 1 TBM-1D	Lt. Cdr. H. S. Roberts USNR
Carrier	HORNET	Captain A. K. Doyle
	Air Group 11: Commander F. R. Schrader	
VF-11	11 F6F-3, 2 F6F-3N, 1 F6F-3P, 21 F6F-5, 2 F6F-5N, 3 F6F-5P	Lt. Cdr. E. G. Fairfax
VB-11	25 SB2C-3	Lt. Cdr. L. A. Smith
VT-11	1 TBF-1C, 17 TBM-1C	Lt. Cdr. R. Denniston
Light carrier	MONTEREY	Captain S. H. Ingersoll
	Air Group 28: Lieutenant Commander R. W. Mehle	
VF-28	21 F6F-5, 2 F6F-5P	Lt. Cdr. Mehle
VT-28	9 TBM-1C	Lt. R. P. Gift USNR
Light carrier	COWPENS	Captain H. W. Taylor
	Air Group 22: Lieutenant Commander T. H. Jenkins USNR	
VF-22	25 F6F-5, 1 F6F-5P	Lt. L. L. Johnson USNR
VT-22	9 TBM-1C	Lt. Cdr. Jenkins

Crudiv 6, Rear Admiral C. Turner Joy: Heavy cruiser WICHITA [7] Capt. D. A. Spencer.

Crudiv 10, Rear Admiral L. J. Wiltse: Heavy cruisers BOSTON Capt. E. E. Herrmann, CANBERRA [8] Capt. A. R. Early; light cruiser HOUSTON [8] Capt. W. W. Behrens.

[6] As of 6–31 Oct. 1944. There was much shifting of ships from one carrier group to another, especially of destroyers.

[7] Transferred to TG 38.4 Oct. 21.

[8] Detached 15 Oct. owing to battle damage.

Screen, Captain C. F. Espe (Comdesron 46)

Destroyers IZARD Cdr. M. T. Dayton, CHARRETTE Lt. Cdr. G. P. Joyce, CONNER Cdr. W. E. Kaitner, BELL Cdr. J. S. C. Gabbert, BURNS Cdr. J. T. Bullen.

Comdesdiv 100, Capt. W. J. Miller: COGSWELL Cdr. R. E. Lockwood, CAPERTON Cdr. G. K. Carmichael, INGERSOLL Cdr. A. C. Veasey, KNAPP Lt. Cdr. W. B. Brown.

Comdesdiv 92, Capt. W. M. Sweetser: BOYD Cdr. U. S. G. Sharp, COWELL Cdr. C. W. Parker.

Comdesron 12, Capt. W. P. Buford: MCCALLA Lt. Cdr. E. Vinock, GRAYSON Cdr. W. V. Pratt, BROWN Cdr. T. H. Copeman, WOODWORTH Cdr. C. R. Stephan.

TG 30.2, Rear Admiral Allan E. Smith

Formed 6 Oct. 1944; joined TG 38.1 Oct. 16.

Heavy cruisers CHESTER Capt. Henry Hartley, PENSACOLA Capt. A. P. Mullinnix, SALT LAKE CITY Capt. L. W. Busbey.

Comdesron 4, Capt. Harold P. Smith: DUNLAP Lt. Cdr. C. R. Welte, FANNING Cdr. J. C. Bentley, CASE Lt. Cdr. R. S. Willey, CUMMINGS Lt. Cdr. W. J. Collum, CASSIN Cdr. V. J. Meola, DOWNES Cdr. R. S. Fahle.

TG 30.3, "Cripdiv" or "Baitdiv 1," Rear Admiral Du Bose [9]
in SANTA FE with MOBILE

Formed 15 Oct. to tow CANBERRA and HOUSTON to Ulithi; formed mostly from TG 38.1.

CVLs COWPENS and CABOT; cruiser BOSTON; all Desron 46 except IZARD; all Desdivs 100 and 92; GRAYSON; 3 DDs from TG 38.2 (see below). (The DDs gradually were returned to their respective task groups.)

TG 38.2 TASK GROUP TWO, Rear Admiral Gerald F. Bogan

Carrier INTREPID Captain J. F. Bolger

Air Group 18: 1 F6F-5, Commander W. E. Ellis

VF-18	5 F6F-3N, 35 F6F-5, 3 F6F-5P	Lt. E. J. Murphy
VB-18	28 SB2C-3	Lt. Cdr. M. Eslick
VT-18	18 TBM-1C	Lt. Cdr. L. W. VanAntwerp USNR

Carrier HANCOCK [10] Captain F. C. Dickey

Air Group 7: Commander J. D. Lamade

VF-7	37 F6F-5, 4 F6F-5N	Lt. Cdr. L. J. Check
VB-7	30 SB2C-3, 12 SB2C-3E	Lt. Cdr. J. L. Erickson
VT-7	18 TBM-1C	Lt. C. B. Marshall USNR

Carrier BUNKER HILL [11] Captain M. R. Greer

Air Group 8: 1 F6F-5, Lieutenant Commander R. L. Shifley

VF-8	27 F6F-3, 13 F6F-5, 4 F6F-3N, 4 F6F-5N	Cdr. W. M. Collins
VB-8	17 SB2C-1C, 3 SBF-1 (Helldiver), 4 SBW-1 (Helldiver)	Lt. Cdr. J. D. Arbes
VT-8	17 TBM-1C, 2 TBM-1D	Lt. Cdr. K. F. Musick

[9] Relieved by Rear Adm. Joy 16 Oct. and he by Rear Adm. Wiltse 19 Oct.
[10] To TG 38.1 Oct. 22–26.
[11] Detached 23 Oct.

Light carrier		CABOT[12]	Captain S. J. Michael
	Air Group 29: Lieutenant Commander W. E. Eder		
VF–29	3 F6F–3, 18 F6F–5		Lt. Cdr. Eder
VT–29	1 TBF–1C, 8 TBM–1C		Lt. J. H. McPherson
Light carrier		INDEPENDENCE	Captain E. C. Ewen
	Night Air Group 41: Commander T. F. Caldwell		
VFN–41	3 F6F–3, 2 F6F–5, 14 F6F–5N		Cdr. Caldwell
VTN–41	8 TBM–1D		Lt. W. R. Taylor USNR

Batdiv 7, Rear Admiral Oscar C. Badger: IOWA Capt. A. R. McCann, NEW JERSEY Capt. C. F. Holden.

Crudiv 14, Rear Admiral F. E. M. Whiting: light cruisers VINCENNES Capt. A. D. Brown, MIAMI Capt. J. G. Crawford, SAN DIEGO[13] Capt. W. E. Mullan, OAKLAND[13] Capt. K. S. Reed.

Screen, Captain J. P. Womble (Comdesron 52)

Destroyers OWEN Cdr. C. B. Jones, MILLER[14] Lt. Cdr. D. L. Johnson, THE SULLIVANS[14] Cdr. R. J. Baum, STEPHEN POTTER[14] Cdr. L. W. Pancoast, TINGEY Cdr. J. O. Miner.

Desdiv 104, Capt. W. T. Kenny: HICKOX Lt. Cdr. J. H. Wesson, HUNT Cdr. H. A. Knoertzer, LEWIS HANCOCK Cdr. W. M. Searles, MARSHALL Cdr. J. D. McKinney.

Desron 50, Capt. H. B. Jarrett: HALSEY POWELL Cdr. S. D. B. Merrill, CUSHING Cdr. L. F. Volk, COLAHAN Cdr. D. T. Wilber, UHLMANN Cdr. S. G. Hooper, BENHAM Cdr. F. S. Keeler.

Desdiv 106, Capt. B. E. Tompkins: STOCKHAM Cdr. E. P. Holmes, WEIDERBURN Cdr. C. H. Kendall, TWINING Cdr. E. K. Wakefield, YARNALL Cdr. J. H. Hogg.

TG 38.3 TASK GROUP THREE, Rear Admiral Frederick C. Sherman

Carrier		ESSEX	Captain C. W. Weiber
	Air Group 15: 1 F6F–5, Commander David McCampbell		
VF–15	22 F6F–3, 3 F6F–3N, 2 F6F–3P, 22 F6F–5, 1 F6F–5N		Lt. Cdr. J. F. Rigg
VB–15	25 SB2C–3		Lt. Cdr. J. H. Mini
VT–15	15 TBF–1C, 5 TBM–1C		Lt. Cdr. V. G. Lambert
Carrier		LEXINGTON	Captain E. W. Litch
	Air Group 19: 1 F6F–5, Commander T. H. Winters		
VF–19	14 F6F–3, 2 F6F–3N, 1 F6F–3P, 21 F6F–5, 2 F6F–5N, 1 F6F–5P		Lt. Cdr. F. E. Cook
VB–19	30 SB2C–3		Lt. Cdr. Richard McGowan
VT–19	18 TBM–1C		Lt. Cdr. F. C. Perry
Light carrier		* PRINCETON	Captain W. H. Buracker

* Lost in this operation.

[12] To TG 38.1 Oct. 14–20.
[13] To TG 38.1 Oct. 15.
[14] Detached 14 Oct. as part of "Cripdiv 1." Returned 20 Oct.

Air Group 27: Lieutenant Commander F. A. Bardshar

VF–27	18 F6F–3, 7 F6F–5	Lt. Cdr. Bardshar
VT–27	9 TBM–1C	Lt. Cdr. S. M. Haley USNR

Light carrier LANGLEY Captain J. F. Wegforth

Air Group 44: Commander M. T. Wordell

VF–44	19 F6F–3, 6 F6F–5	Cdr. Wordell
VT–44	9 TBM–1C	Lt. Cdr. E. F. Craig

Com Battleships Pacific Fleet, Vice Admiral Willis A. Lee in WASHINGTON,[15] Captain T. R. Cooley

Batdiv 8, Rear Admiral Glenn B. Davis: MASSACHUSETTS Capt. W. W. Warlick.

Batdiv 9, Rear Admiral Edward W. Hanson: SOUTH DAKOTA [16] Capt. C. B. Momsen, ALABAMA [15] Capt. V. R. Murphy.

Crudiv 13, Rear Admiral Laurance T. DuBose.[17] Light cruisers SANTA FE [18] Capt. Jerauld Wright, MOBILE [18] Capt. C. C. Miller, BIRMINGHAM [19] Capt. T. B. Inglis, RENO Capt. R. C. Alexander.

Screen, Captain C. R. Todd

Desron 50, Capt. E. R. Wilkinson: destroyers CLARENCE K. BRONSON Cdr. Gifford Scull, COTTEN Cdr. P. W. Winston, DORTCH Cdr. R. E. Myers, GATLING,[20] Cdr. A. F. Richardson, HEALY Cdr. J. C. Atkeson.

Desron 55, Capt. A. E. Jarrell: PORTERFIELD Lt. Cdr. D. W. Wulzen, CALLAGHAN Cdr. C. M. Bertholf, CASSIN YOUNG Cdr. E. T. Schrieber, IRWIN [21] Cdr. D. B. Miller, PRESTON Cdr. G. S. Patrick.

Desdiv 110, Cdr. M. Van Metre: [22] LAWS Cdr. L. O. Wood, LONGSHAW Cdr. R. H. Speck, MORRISON Cdr. W. H. Price, PRITCHETT Cdr. C. T. Caulfield.

TG 38.4 TASK GROUP FOUR, Rear Admiral Ralph E. Davison

Carrier FRANKLIN Captain J. M. Shoemaker

Air Group 13: 1 F6F–5, Commander R. L. Kibbe

VF–13	1 F6F–3, 3 F6F–3N, 29 F6F–5, 1 F6F–5N, 4 F6F–5P	Cdr. W. M. Coleman
VB–13	31 SB2C–3	Lt. C. A. Skinner USNR
VT–13	18 TBM–1C	Lt. Cdr. L. C. French

Carrier ENTERPRISE Captain Cato D. Glover

Air Group 20: 1 F6F–5, Commander Dan F. Smith

VF–20	4 F6F–3N, 35 F6F–5	Lt. Cdr. F. E. Bakutis
VB–20	34 SB2C–3	Cdr. R. E. Riera
VT–20	19 TBM–1C	Lt. Cdr. S. L. Prickett

Light Carrier SAN JACINTO Captain M. H. Kernodle

[15] To TG 38.4 Oct. 23.
[16] To TG 38.4 Oct. 28.
[17] Relieved by Rear Adm. Morton L. Deyo 1 Nov. 1944.
[18] Detached 13 Oct. as part of "Cripdiv 1," returned 18 Oct.
[19] Detached 24 Oct. owing to battle damage.
[20] Detached 24 Oct.
[21] Transferred to TG 38.4 Oct. 23.
[22] Transferred to TG 38.4 Oct. 23.

Air Group 51: Commander C. L. Moore

VF-51	14 F6F-3, 5 F6F-5	Cdr. Moore
VT-51	7 TBM-1C	Lt. Cdr. D. J. Melvin USNR

Light Carrier BELLEAU WOOD Captain John Perry

Air Group 21: Lieutenant Commander V. F. Casey

VT-21	24 F6F-5, 1 F6F-5P	Lt. Cdr. Casey
VF-21	9 TBM-1C	Lt. Cdr. R. A. Kennard USNR

Heavy cruiser NEW ORLEAN: Capt. J. E. Hurff; light cruiser BILOXI [23] Capt. P. R. Heineman.

Screen, Captain. V. D. Long (Comdesron 6)

Destroyers MAURY Cdr. J. W. Koenig, GRIDLEY Cdr. P. D. Quirk, HELM Cdr. S. K. Santmyers, MCCALL Lt. Cdr. J. B. Carroll. Desdiv 12, Capt. K. F. Poehlman: MUGFORD Cdr. M. A. Shellabarger, BAGLEY Cdr. W. H. Shea, PATTERSON Lt. Cdr. W. A. Hering, RALPH TALBOT Lt. Cdr. W. S. Brown USNR. Desdiv 24, Capt. A. J. Greenacre: WILKES Lt. Cdr. F. E. McEntire, NICHOLSON Cdr. W. C. Bennett, SWANSON Lt. Cdr. W. K. Ratliff.

TG 30.8 AT SEA LOGISTICS GROUP THIRD FLEET, Captain J. T. Acuff [24]

Oilers: ATASCOSA Cdr. H. L. DeRivera, AUCILLA Lt. Cdr. C. L. Cover USNR, CACHE Lt. Cdr. C. R. Cosgrove USNR, CALIENTE Lt. Cdr. A. E. Stiff USNR, CHICOPEE Cdr. C. O. Peak USNR, CHIKASKIA Lt. Cdr. G. Zimmerman USNR, CIMARRON Lt. Cdr. H. G. Schnaars USNR, ESCAMBIA Lt. Cdr. R. Goorigian USNR, GUADALUPE Cdr. H. A. Anderson, KANKAKEE Lt. Cdr. W. G. Frundt USNR, KASKASKIA Lt. Cdr. W. F. Patten USNR, KENNEBAGO Lt. Cdr. C. W. Brockway USNR, LACKAWANNA Cdr. A. J. Homann, MANATEE Lt. Cdr. J. B. Smyth USNR, MARIAS Cdr. J. G. Olsen USNR, MASCOMA MERRIMACK Capt. Vaughn Bailey, MILLICOMA Cdr. G. E. Ely USNR, * MISSISSINEWA Cdr. P. G. Beck USNR, TAPPAHANNOCK Cdr. C. A. Swafford, NANTAHALA Capt. P. M. Gunnell, NECHES Cdr. H. G. Hansen USNR, NEOSHO Lt. Cdr. F. P. Parkinson USNR, NIOBRARA Cdr. R. C. Spalding USNR, PAMANSET Cdr. D. J. Houle USNR, PATUXENT Lt. Cdr. F. P. Ferrell USNR, PECOS Lt. Cdr. G. W. Renegar USNR, PLATTE Cdr. F. J. Gibson USNR, SABINE Lt. Cdr. H. C. Von Weien USNR, SAUGATUCK Lt. Cdr. J. F. Ardagh USNR, SEBEC Lt. Cdr. H. M. Elder USNR, TALUGA Cdr. H. M. Mikkelsen USNR, MONONGAHELA Cdr. F. J. Ilsemann, TOMAHAWK Capt. B. W. Cloud.

Escort carriers with replacement planes: [25] ALTHAMAHA Capt. A. C. Olney, BARNES Capt. D. N. Logan, SITKOH BAY Capt. R. G. Lockhart, CAPE ESPERANCE Capt. R. W. Bockius, NASSAU Capt. N. W. Ellis, KWAJALEIN Capt. R. C. Warrack, SHIPLEY BAY Capt. E. T. Neale, STEAMER BAY Capt. S. Teller, NEHENTA BAY Capt. H. B. Butterfield, SARGENT BAY Capt. W. T. Rassieur, RUDYARD BAY Capt. C. S. Smiley.

Screen: AYLWIN Lt. Cdr. W. K. Rogers, CAPPS (Desdiv 102, Capt. B. V. Russell) Cdr. B. E. S. Trippensee, DALE Lt. Cdr. S. M. Zimmy, DAVID W. TAYLOR Cdr.

* Lost in this operation.

23 Transferred to TG 38.2 Oct. 22.

24 Capt. Acuff's successive flagships were destroyers *J. D. Henley, Aylwin* and *Welles.* Ships listed here under TG 30.8 are those which qualified for Philippine Liberation Ribbon. Data from Servron 8 office, Servpac.

25 No division commanders accompanied CVEs on this duty. Because screens were frequently reformed to accompany oiler and CVE groups going to and fro, there was no overall screen commander, and both squadrons and divisions were being constantly broken up.

W. H. Johnson. Desron 1, Capt. P. V. Mercer: DEWEY Lt. Cdr. C. R. Calhoun, DYSON Cdr. L. E. Ruff, EVANS Cdr. F. C. Camp, FARRAGUT Lt. Cdr. C. C. Hartigan, HAILEY Cdr. P. H. Brady. Desron 51, Capt. H. J. Martin: HALL Cdr. L. C. Baldauf, HOBBY (Desdiv 38, Cdr. J. B. Cochran) Cdr. G. W. Pressey, HULL Lt. Cdr. J. A. Marks, JOHN D. HENLEY Cdr. C. W. Smith, MONAGHAN Cdr. W. F. Wendt, PAUL HAMILTON Cdr. L. G. May, THATCHER Cdr. W. A. Cockell, THORN Lt. Cdr. F. H. Schneider, WELLES Lt. Cdr. J. S. Slaughter.

The following destroyer escorts were also assigned to screen duty with TG 30.8: DEs ACREE, BANGUST, CROWLEY, DONALDSON, ELDEN, HALLORAN, HILBERT, KYNE, LAKE, LAMONS, LEVY, LYMAN, MCCONNELL, MITCHELL, O'NEILL, OSTERHAUS, PARKS, RALL, REYNOLDS, RIDDLE, SAMUEL S. MILES, STERN, SWEARER, WATERMAN, WEAVER, WESSON.

Fleet Tugs: HITCHITI Lt. H. A. Guthrie, JICARILLA Lt. Cdr. W. B. Coats, MATACO Lt. C. O. Hall, MENOMINEE Lt. J. A. Young, MOLALA Lt. R. L. Ward, MUNSEE Lt. Cdr. J. F. Pingley, PAWNEE Lt. H. C. Cramer USNR, SIOUX Lt. L. M. Jahnsen, TEKESTA Lt. (jg) P. D. Petrich USNR, ZUNI Lt. R. E. Chance.

Ammunition ships: * MOUNT HOOD [26] Cdr. M. Toal, SANGAY Lt. Cdr. H. C. Taylor USNR, MAUNA LOA, Cdr. G. D. Martin, AUSTRALIAN VICTORY Master C. N. Oslen, SHASTA Cdr. W. L. Ware, LASSEN Cdr. J. E. Wade USNR. December Echelon: PROVO V. Lt. J. W. Carpenter USNR, ELMIRA V. Master Chris Trandsen, BOULDER V. Lt. Cdr. F. E. Church, RAINIER Cdr. F. S. Conner, MOUNT BAKER Cdr. F. P. Hamblin USNR, NITRO Cdr. F. Trimble USNR, ALAMOSA Lt. Cdr. K. C. Ingraham.

TF 17 SUPPORTING SUBMARINES PACIFIC FLEET

Vice Admiral Charles A. Lockwood

"Clarey's Crushers": PINTADO Cdr. B. A. Clarey, JALLAO Cdr. J. B. Icenhower, ATULE Cdr. J. H. Maurer.

"Roach's Raiders": HADDOCK Cdr. J. P. Roach, HALIBUT Cdr. I. J. Galantin, TUNA Cdr. E. F. Steffanides USNR.

"Banister's Beagles": SAWFISH Cdr. A. B. Banister, DRUM Lt. Cdr. M. H. Rindskopf, ICEFISH Cdr. R. W. Peterson.

"Blakely's Behemoths": * SHARK * Cdr. E. N. Blakely, BLACKFISH Cdr. R. F. Sellars, SEADRAGON Cdr. J. H. Ashley.

"Coye's Coyotes": SILVERSIDES Cdr. J. S. Coye, SALMON Cdr. H. K. Nauman, TRIGGER Cdr. F. J. Harlfinger.

"Wogan's Wolves": BESUGO Cdr. T. L. Wogan, RONQUIL Cdr. H. S. Monroe, GABILAN Cdr. K. R. Wheland.

* TANG Cdr. R. H. O'Kane, STERLET Cdr. O. C. Robbins, BARBEL Cdr. R. A. Keating, SNOOK Cdr. G. H. Browne.

TG 71.1 SUPPORTING SUBMARINES SEVENTH FLEET

Rear Admiral Ralph W. Christie

* DARTER Cdr. D. H. McClintock, DACE Cdr. B. D. Claggett, ANGLER Cdr. F. G. Hess, BLUEGILL Cdr. E. L. Barr, BREAM Cdr. W. G. Chapple, RATON Cdr. M. W. Shea, GUITARRO Cdr. E. D. Haskins.

* Lost or killed in this operation.

[26] Blew up, cause unknown, Seeadler Harbor 10 Nov. 1944, with loss of all hands.

APPENDIX II

Japanese Forces in the Battle for Leyte Gulf[1]

COMBINED FLEET

Admiral Soemu Toyoda, at Tokyo from 20 October

MOBILE FORCE

Vice Admiral Jisaburo Ozawa

MAIN BODY (NORTHERN FORCE), Vice Admiral Ozawa

Cardiv 3, Vice Admiral Ozawa: Carrier * ZUIKAKU * Rear Admiral T. Kaizuka; light carriers * ZUIHO * Capt. K. Sigiura, * CHITOSE * Capt. Y. Kishi, * CHIYODA * Capt. E. Zyo. Their combined air groups were 80 Zekes, 25 Jills, 4 Kates, 7 Judys.

Cardiv 4, Rear Admiral Chiaki Matsuda: Converted battleship-carriers HYUGA Rear Admiral T. Nomura, ISE Rear Admiral N. Nakase.

Desdiv 61, * Capt. S. Amano: * HATSUZUKI, * AKITSUKI, WAKATSUKI, plus * SHIMOTSUKI of Desdiv 41, * Capt. K. Wakita.

Escort Squadron 31, Rear Admiral Heitaro Edo: Light cruiser ISUZU Capt. G. Matsuda; part of Desdiv 43, MAKI, KIRI, KUWA, SUGI.

Light cruisers: OYODO Capt. K. Mudaguchi and * TAMA * Capt. I. Yamamoto.

Supply Unit: Destroyer AKIKAZE; escort vessels 22, 29, 31, 33, 43, 132; oilers * JINEI MARU, TAKANE M.

FIRST STRIKING FORCE, Vice Admiral Takeo Kurita

FORCE "A" (CENTER FORCE), Vice Admiral Kurita

FIRST SECTION, Vice Admiral Kurita

Batdiv 1, Vice Admiral Matome Ugaki: YAMATO Rear Admiral N. Morishita, * MUSASHI * Rear Admiral T. Inoguchi, NAGATO Rear Admiral Y. Kobe.

Crudiv 4, Vice Admiral Kurita: * ATAGO Capt. D. Araki, TAKAO Capt. S. Onoda, * CHOKAI * Capt. K. Ariga, * MAYA * Capt. R. Ooe.

* Sunk or lost in this operation.

1 As of 22 Oct. 1944. Other units of Combined Fleet did not sortie. Capt. Ohmae has checked this organization.

Crudiv 5, Vice Admiral Shintaro Hashimoto: MYOKO Capt. H. Ishiwara, HAGURO Capt. K. Suguira.

Desron 2, Rear Admiral Mikio Hayakawa: Light cruiser * NOSHIRO * Capt. S. Kajiwara; destroyer SHIMAKAZE; Desdiv 2, * Capt. N. Shiraishi, * HAYASHIMO, AKISHIMO; Desdiv 31, Capt. T. Fukuoka, KISHINAMI, OKINAMI, NAGANAMI, ASASHIMO; Desdiv 32, Cdr. K. Aoki, HAMANAMI, * FUJINAMI.

SECOND SECTION, Vice Admiral Yoshio Suzuki

Batdiv 3, Vice Admiral Suzuki: KONGO Rear Admiral T. Shimazaki, HARUNA Rear Admiral K. Shigenaga.

Crudiv 7, Vice Admiral Kazutaka Shiraishi: Heavy cruisers KUMANO Capt. S. Hitomi, * SUZUYA * Capt. W. Takahashi, * CHIKUMA * Capt. S. Norimitsu, TONE Capt. H. Mayuzumi.

Desron 10, Rear Admiral Susumu Kimura: Light cruiser YAHAGI Capt. M. Yoshimura; destroyers * NOWAKI, KIYOSHIMO; Desdiv 17, Capt. T. Tanii: URAKAZE, YUKIKAZE, HAMAKAZE, ISOKAZE.

FORCE "C" (Van of SOUTHERN FORCE)

* Vice Admiral Shoji Nishimura

Batdiv 2, Vice Admiral Nishimura: * YAMISHIRO * Rear Admiral T. Shinoda, * FUSO * Rear Admiral M. Ban; heavy cruiser * MOGAMI * Capt. R. Tooma, from Crudiv 5.

Desdiv 4, * Capt. K. Takahashi: * MICHISHIO, * ASAGUMO, * YAMAGUMO, plus SHIGURE from Desron 2.

SOUTHWEST AREA FORCE

Vice Admiral Guinichi Mikawa, at Manila

SECOND STRIKING FORCE (Rear of SOUTHERN FORCE)

Vice Admiral Kiyohide Shima

Crudiv 21, Vice Admiral Shima: Heavy cruisers NACHI Capt. E. Kanooka, ASHIGARA Capt. H. Miura.

Desron 1, Rear Admiral Masatomi Kimura: Light cruiser * ABUKUMA * Capt. T. Hanada; Desdiv 7, Cdr. J. Iwagami: AKEBONO, USHIO; Desdiv 18, Capt. Yoshio Inoue, KASUMI, * SHIRANUHI; Desdiv 21, * Cdr. Hisashi Ishii, * WAKABA, HATSUSHIMO, HATSUHARU.

TROOP TRANSPORT UNIT, Vice Admiral Naomasa Sakonju

Crudiv 16, Vice Admiral Sakonju: Heavy cruiser AOBA Capt. C. Yamazumi, light cruiser * KINU Capt. H. Kawasaki; destroyer * URANAMI.

Destroyer transports Nos. 6, 101, * 102, 131.

* Sunk or lost in this operation.

THIRD BASE and PHILIPPINE AIR FORCES, Vice Admiral Mikawa, at Manila

FIFTH BASE AIR FORCE and FIRST AIR FLEET, Vice Admiral Takijiro Onishi,[2] at Clark Field

SIXTH BASE AIR FORCE and SECOND AIR FLEET, Vice Admiral Shigeru Fukudome, at Takao (at Clark Field 23 October)

ADVANCE EXPEDITIONARY FORCE (SIXTH FLEET), Vice Admiral Shigeyoshi Miwa, at Kure in tender TSUKUSHI MARU

First Submarine Force, Vice Admiral Miwa

"A" Division, * *I-26*, * *I-45*, *I-53*, * *I-54*, *I-56*.
"B" Division, *I-38*, *I-41*, *I-44*, *I-46*, *RO-41*, *RO-43*, *RO-46*.
"C" Division, *RO-109*, *RO-112*.
Ulithi Attack Group of 20 Nov., *I-36*, * *I-37*, *I-47*.

* Sunk or lost in this operation.

2 Relieved Vice Adm. Teraoka 20 Oct. 1944.

Index

Names of Combatant Ships in SMALL CAPITALS
Names of Lettered Combatant Ships, like LSTs and RO-boats, of Merchant Ships and of all *Marus*, in *Italics*

In the Task Organizations (T.O.), only main headings are indexed.

D

E

T

Y

Z